London

Pat Yale

London

1st edition

Published by

Lonely Planet Publications

Head Office: PO Box 617, Hawthorn, Vic 3122, Australia
Branches: 155 Filbert St, Suite 251, Oakland, CA 94607, USA
10a Spring Place, London NW5 3BH, UK
71 bis rue du Cardinal Lemoine, 75005 Paris, France

Printed by

Colorcraft Ltd, Hong Kong

Photographs by

Rachel Black
Charlotte Hindle
Mark Honan
Doug McKinlay
Judi Schiff
Tom Smallman
Paul Steel
Tony Wheeler
Pat Yale

Front cover: London bus & taxi, Romilly Lockyer (The Image Bank)

Published

March 1998

Although the authors and publisher have tried to make the information as accurate as possible, they accept no responsibility for any loss, injury or inconvenience sustained by any person using this book.

National Library of Australia Cataloguing in Publication Data

Yale, Pat, 1954-.
London.

Includes index.
ISBN 0 86442 495 7.

1. London (England) - Guidebooks. I. Title. (Series: Lonely Planet city guide).

914.2104

Pat Yale

Pat was born and brought up in Ealing, west London. As a student she supplemented her grant through stints of photographing students for ID cards at Southall College, issuing rail tickets to MPs in the House of Commons travel office, numbering pieces of old clay pipe at Gunnersbury Park Museum and weeding out the files at the Council for Places of Worship in All Hallows, London Wall. Later she sold holidays for Thomas Cook, High St Kensington, and then told other people how to sell holidays for American Express, Haymarket, commuting home in the evenings to Putney, south London. These days she's retreated to Bristol and has worked on Lonely Planet's *Britain*, *Ireland*, *Dublin* and *Turkey*, in between bouts of globetrotting.

From the Author

Any number of people have helped in the preparation of this guide, particularly when it came to recommending places to eat and drink! First and foremost I would like to thank my mother Eileen for providing me with a wonderful home from home while I did my research, and Lesley Levene, who let me crash in her Crouch End house when she was off travelling. Warm thanks are also due to Charlotte Hindle in the London office of Lonely Planet, without whom all sorts of stones might have escaped unturned; to Vicky Wayland who cast her experienced clubbers' eye over the nightlife section; and to Simon Calder for last minute checking.

I'm also indebted to Barney Andrews, Lucy DaSouza, Terri Doyle, Sam & Emma Farmer, Stewart Foulkes, Jamie Gidlow-Jackson, Clare McElwee, Brian Roberts, Maggie Stapleton and Neil Taylor for their help and/or company while I was working on the book.

Thanks, too, to Louise Wood and Alex Brennan of the London Tourist Board. Finally, Bill Scanlon made sure that my cat was fed and my Bristol home went unburgled while I was away, services for which a medal should surely be struck!

This Book

Parts of this book were based on Lonely Planet's *Britain* guide, written by Bryn Thomas, Sean Sheehan, Pat Yale, Richard Everist and Tony Wheeler.

From the Publisher

This 1st edition of this city guide was edited in Lonely Planet's Melbourne office by Paul Harding, with help from Anne Mulvaney, while Liz Filleul and Miriam Cannell added some red ink at the proofing stage.

Jacqui Saunders was the maestro behind the design and mapping, assisted by Piotr Czajkowski. Rachel Black, Jane Fitzpatrick and Michelle Lewis handled the final checking. Adam McCrow and Simon Bracken designed the cover and Jacqui Saunders and Tamsin Wilson added some illustrations. Thanks also to Richard Everist and the staff at Lonely Planet's London office for their help with updates and checks.

Thanks

Thanks to Dave Allen of DJA Design Ltd in London, who organised the livery and licensing of the LP taxi with such speed; to Lawrence Sheffer, our driver, who drove around Trafalgar Square 11 times and crossed Tower Bridge nine times!; to the taxi photographer, Doug McKinlay; and to Joanna Clifton and Charlotte Hindle of Lonely Planet's London office who managed the project. Finally, thanks to the London Transport Museum for providing us with the London Underground map.

Warning & Request

Things change – prices go up, schedules change, good places go bad and bad places go bankrupt – nothing stays the same. So, if you find things better or worse, recently opened or long since closed, please tell us and help make the next edition even more accurate and useful.

We value all of the feedback we receive from travellers. Julie Young coordinates a small team who read and acknowledge every letter, postcard and email, and ensure that every morsel of information finds its way to the appropriate authors, editors and publishers. Everyone who writes to us will find their name in the next edition of the appropriate guide and will also receive a free subscription to our quarterly newsletter, *Planet Talk*. The very best contributions will be rewarded with a free Lonely Planet guide.

Excerpts from your correspondence may appear in new editions of this guide; in our newsletter, *Planet Talk*; or in updates on our Web site – so please let us know if you don't want your letter published or your name acknowledged.

Contents

Introduction

Of all the world's great cities, London must be right up there at the top of the list. Not only is it home to landmarks like Big Ben, Trafalgar Square, the Statue of Eros and the Tower of London so famous that they're the stuff of clichés, but it also boasts some of the greatest museums and art galleries, crammed full of booty from the days when the British Empire turned half the world map pink.

London is Europe's largest city, indeed one of the largest in the world, a sprawling metropolis accommodating between seven and 12 million people, depending on where you stop counting. Amid this already seething mass of humanity another 26 million tourists a year struggle to make space for themselves. Not surprisingly all this can come as quite a shock if you've just landed from somewhere small and quiet.

Whatever kind of a roll the capital may be on right now, there's a very real sense in which its heyday was way back before WWI. Much of the Underground was created then and it shows in a creaking old system struggling to keep up with demand. If you've arrived from somewhere with a shiny new metro, this too will come as a nasty surprise.

But these shocks out of the way, you'll find yourself in a buzzy, bustling, vibrant city where every street, even every street name, seems to come with a history attached to it. Sure, you should see all those great monuments but there are hours of pleasure to be had just poking down backstreets and finding your own favourite corners.

Despite the densely packed streets London is also one of the world's greener cities, with more open spaces than you might expect – some of them neatly kept, tame city-centre parks, others wild expanses of heath and woodland where you can roam for hours and leave the city hassle behind you.

Of course there's always a downside, and on the sort of cold, grey day England specialises in London can seem dirty and depressing, the many beggars on the street an affront to a city which could so clearly afford to do better by all its citizens.

Thirty years ago *Time* magazine turned the spotlight on Swinging London, the London of the hippies and free love, of Carnaby St and King's Rd, of miniskirts and the Beatles. Now things have come full circle. After the gloom of the early 90s, London is on the up and up. The restaurants are full, the shops are heaving with buyers, the nightlife has never been glitzier. Wherever you look you'll see cranes and scaffolding as a splurge of Lottery-funded renovation work readies the capital for the Millennium.

Rock stars like the Gallaghers, chefs like Marco Pierre White, restaurateurs like Sir Terence Conran, architects like Richard Rogers, artists like Damien Hirst and Rachel Whiteread, everyone seems agreed that London's the place to be right now. *Newsweek* let the cat out of the bag when it dubbed London the coolest city in the world – but then any Londoner could have told them that!

Facts about London

HISTORY

The site of modern London has been almost continuously inhabited since Roman times. This has made life difficult for archaeologists, who must glean what information they can when redevelopment makes sites available for excavation. The building boom of the 1980s brought a commensurate boom in finds, especially in the City of London. Many of these are on display at the Tower Hill Pageant.

For an easily accessible run through London's history your best bet is a visit to the Museum of London (see The City in Things to See & Do).

The Celts & Romans

While there's no evidence that what later became the City of London was settled before the Romans arrived, there's plenty to prove that surrounding areas were already occupied by the Iron Age. Caesar's Camp, an earthwork fort on Wimbledon Common, was probably constructed during the 3rd century BC, and the beautiful Celtic shield dredged from the Thames near Battersea Bridge dates from a similar period. The horned helmet found near Waterloo Bridge dates from a period when a Celtic community is believed to have settled round a ford on the River Thames and traded with the Romans, especially after Caesar's visit of 55 BC. Both of these finds can be seen in the British Museum.

However, London never developed into a major tribal centre like Colchester or St Albans and even the Romans hung about for almost a century after their arrival in Britain before founding Londinium, the first real settlement at London, around 50 AD. They then constructed a wooden bridge across the Thames near what is now London Bridge and this became the focus for a network of roads fanning out around the province.

This first settlement was promptly destroyed in 61 AD by Queen Boudicca (aka Boadicea), queen of the East Anglian Iceni tribe, but the Romans re-established a port at Londinium by around 100 AD, wrapping a defensive wall round it by around 200. Towers were then added to the landward side to strengthen it. Excavations in the City have revealed that Londinium was an imposing city whose massive public buildings included an amphitheatre, forum, basilica and fort.

Roman London was almost as multicultural as modern London, with temples celebrating many different cults. Few traces of Londinium survive outside museums, although you can see the relocated Temple of Mithras in Victoria St. Stretches of the Roman wall also survive, notably outside Tower Hill station where there's also a modern statue of the Roman emperor Trajan.

In 312 AD Christianity became London's official religion and in 314 AD a Bishop of London attended the Council of Athens.

The Saxons & Danes

From around 410 AD the Romans abandoned Britain, and London was reduced to a barely-populated ruin. Scant evidence from this period survives although we know that the Saxons eventually arrived to fill the gap left by the Romans. The first church at St Paul's was built in 604 and the focus of the town moved westwards, towards what is now Aldwych. However, recent excavations along the foreshore at Chelsea have uncovered a dyke seemingly built to protect a palace constructed here for King Offa in the 8th century. This new settlement, named Lundenwic, seems to have traded with France and the Rhineland but as it grew in importance it attracted the attention of the marauding Danes who attacked in 841 and again in 851. Under King Alfred the Saxon population fought back and in 886 he resettled the old Roman city further east, renaming it Lundenburg and developing a trading wharf at Billingsgate.

Saxon London grew into a prosperous and well-organised city divided into 20 wards, each with its own alderman, but the Danes still had their eyes on it and eventually managed to force one of their own, the famous King Canute (Cnut), onto the throne. During his reign London finally took over from Winchester as the English capital, but Canute had no heir and on his death the throne passed to the Saxon Edward the Confessor who went on to found the abbey and palace at Westminster. When he moved his court to Westminster he started the process whereby the City became the trading centre of London while Westminster was its seat of government.

The Normans & Plantagenets

Following the Battle of Hastings in 1066, London at first held out against William the Conqueror, who reacted by burning Southwark and bypassing the city. When it became obvious that all of south-east England had caved in, London too surrendered and William returned to be crowned king at Westminster Abbey on Christmas Day, 1066. He found a city that was by far the largest and richest in the kingdom. It was William who built the White Tower (heart of the Tower of London) to the east of London and Baynard's Castle to the west (later destroyed during the Great Fire), but he also confirmed the city's independence and right to self-government.

In 1154 King Stephen died and the throne passed to the first Plantagenet king, Henry II. Shortly afterwards the monk William FitzStephen provided one of the earliest written accounts of London, describing a 'flourishing city a prey to frequent fires' (in 1087 fire had consumed the original St Paul's).

Always short of a penny or two, the 12th century kings were happy to allow the City to keep its independence so long as its merchants continued to finance their schemes. When King Richard needed money to go crusading, he recognised the City as a self-governing commune in return for cash. In 1215 King John was forced to cede some say in government to the powerful barons he had alienated. Among those pressing him to sign the Magna Carta at Runnymede was the powerful mayor of the City of London.

Old London Bridge was built towards the end of the 12th century and Old St Paul's in 1314. The descendants of the Runnymede barons built themselves sturdy houses with riverside gardens along what is now the Strand linking Westminster to the City. The area flourished on trading wine, fur, cloth and other goods with Europe. Many City street names (Poultry, Cornhill, Milk St) still commemorate the goods that were traded in their markets.

By 1300 the population of London stood at around 100,000, but then rats brought plague to the overcrowded, unsanitary streets of the capital; the Black Death of 1348-9 is believed to have killed one-third of the population.

In 1381 Wat Tyler and Jack Straw led the Peasants' Revolt against an iniquitous flat-rate poll tax, and many London buildings, including John of Gaunt's grand Savoy Palace, were burnt down. Tyler himself was stabbed to death by the Lord Mayor.

By then the Palace of Westminster was firmly established as the centre of royal power. In 1295 a model parliament with representatives of the barons, the clergy and the knights and burgesses met for the first time in Westminster Hall but by the 14th century the embryonic House of Lords was meeting in the Palace of Westminster, and the House of Commons in the Westminster Abbey Chapter House. To raise more money the king levied taxes on the City merchants and foreign money-lenders; after the Jews were expelled in 1290, the burden of this taxation fell on the Lombard bankers who had set up base in the City.

In 1483 12-year-old Edward V reigned for only two months before vanishing, with his younger brother, into the Tower of London, never to be seen again. Whether or not Richard III, their uncle and the next king, had them killed has been the subject of much conjecture, but few tears were shed when he

Kings & Queens of England

Royalty has played perhaps the most memorable part in English history and London has long been the seat of royal power.

The following table traces the royal lineage from its beginnings to the present.

Saxons & Danes
Alfred the Great 871-99
Edward the Martyr 975-79
Ethelred II (the Unready) 979-1016
Canute 1016-35
Edward the Confessor 1042-66
Harold II 1066

Normans
William I (the Conqueror) 1066-87
William II (Rufus) 1087-1100
Henry I 1100-35
Stephen 1135-54

Plantagenet (Angevin)
Henry II 1154-89
Richard I (Lionheart) 1189-99
John 1199-1216
Henry III 1216-72
Edward I 1272-1307
Edward II 1307-27
Edward III 1327-77
Richard II 1377-99

Lancaster
Henry IV (Bolingbroke) 1399-1413
Henry V 1413-22
Henry VI 1422-61 & 1470-71

York
Edward IV 1461-70 & 1471-83
Edward V 1483
Richard III 1483-85

Tudor
Henry VII (Tudor) 1485-1509
Henry VIII 1509-47
Edward VI 1547-53
Mary I 1553-58
Elizabeth I 1558-1603

Stuart
James I 1603-25
Charles I 1625-49

Commonwealth & Protectorate
Oliver Cromwell 1649-58
Richard Cromwell 1658-59

Stuart Restoration
Charles II 1660-85
James II 1685-88
William III (of Orange) 1689-1702
& Mary II 1689-94
Anne 1702-14

Hanover
George I 1714-27
George II 1727-60
George III 1760-1820
George IV 1820-30
William IV 1830-37
Victoria 1837-1901

Saxe-Coburg-Gotha
Edward VII 1901-10

Windsor
George V 1910-36
Edward VIII 1936
George VI 1936-52
Elizabeth II 1953-

was tumbled from the throne by Henry Tudor, first of the Tudor dynasty, in 1485.

Tudor London

When Henry Tudor became king, London was far and away the largest and wealthiest town in England. During his reign commerce continued to flourish (the trade in wool was a mainstay) and the population started to rise again. Most manufacturing industry was concentrated in Southwark and Bermondsey where the noise and smells couldn't reach the nobs in their Westminster mansions.

Between 1536 and 1540 his son Henry VIII dissolved the many monasteries and priories during the course of his quarrel with the Pope over his right to divorce first wife Catherine of Aragon and marry Anne Boleyn. Fifty London churches were closed, some becoming hospitals or private houses. Church plate was given to the king and most of it melted down and refashioned. Much church land was requisitioned to become royal hunting ground.

Henry VIII divided his time between Richmond, Whitehall, Greenwich and Nonsuch palaces. When the chancellor Thomas Wolsey was foolish enough to build himself a palace at Hampton Court grand enough to catch the greedy king's eye, he was forced to make a gift of it to Henry...which didn't prevent the king from charging Wolsey with high treason (luckily for him he died before the trial could commence). Keen on public display Henry brought skilled craftsmen from the continent to decorate his palaces. When the Holy Roman Emperor Charles V came visiting in 1553 he arranged for the new Bridewell Palace to be built specially to accommodate him.

Because of his readiness to settle all quarrels with the axe (two of his six wives and an earlier chancellor, Sir Thomas More, all found their way to the scaffold), Henry VIII gets a pretty bad press. However, he was responsible for establishing the docks at Woolwich (1512) and Deptford (1513), and for founding the Royal Navy.

The reign of Henry VIII's daughter by Catherine of Aragon, Mary, led to a short-lived attempt to return England to the Catholic fold. London seems to have been particularly unsympathetic to renewed Catholicism and more than 300 martyrs were burned to death at Smithfield. Ever afterwards the queen was known as 'Bloody Mary'.

When Elizabeth, Henry's daughter by Anne Boleyn, ascended the throne, the Catholic cause was effectively lost. London began to expand rapidly – in the 40 years to 1603 the population doubled from 100,000 to 200,000. The first recorded map of London was published in 1558 and John Stow produced his history of the city in 1598. Many landmark buildings were erected during Elizabeth's reign, among them the Royal Exchange (1570) and the Rose (1587) and Globe (1599) theatres, the latter built in Southwark which was notorious for its brothels, bear-baiting and cockpits.

Early Stuart London

When Elizabeth died without heir in 1603 she was succeeded by her second cousin, James VI of Scotland, who became James I of England. James was the son of the Catholic Mary Queen of Scots, but when he showed no sign of improving conditions for England's Catholics, Guy Fawkes concocted his preposterous plot to blow up the Houses of Parliament on 5 November 1605. For his pains he was hanged, drawn and quartered.

Later it was to be the turn of a monarch to come to a sticky end when Charles I was beheaded outside the Banqueting Hall in Whitehall after the Protestant Puritans and the expanding merchant class of London and the towns of the south-east threw their support behind Oliver Cromwell and the Parliamentarians (aka the Puritans or Roundheads) to win the Civil War. A statue of Cromwell stands outside the House of Commons, one of Charles at the Trafalgar Square end of Whitehall.

After Charles' death there was a brief period of Commonwealth (1649-60), during which the Puritans had the theatres closed down and rampaged through the churches, destroying stained glass and anything they regarded as idolatrous. As Lord Protector, Cromwell took up residence in Whitehall but his popularity was short-lived. When he died in 1658 his son, 'Tumbledown Dick', only managed to cling to power for five months before Parliament invited Charles I's son to return as king. Cromwell's body was dug up and hanged at Tyburn, and Charles II was reinstated at the Royal Exchange.

The Great Plague & the Great Fire

These were still the days when the shout 'garde-loo' would go up to alert passers-by to the fact that a chamberpot was about to be emptied into the street from the upper storey of a cantilevered wooden house. Crowded, filthy London had suffered from recurrent outbreaks of bubonic plague since the Black Death emerged in the 14th century, but nothing had matched the Great Plague of 1664-5 which is thought to have carried off around 110,000 people in eight months.

The Plague was only brought to an end by another disaster which proved a watershed in the development of London. On 2 September a fire broke out at a baker's shop in Pudding Lane in the City. It raged out of control for four days, watched by Samuel Pepys who provided a wonderful eyewitness account of the catastrophe in his diary.

By the time the fire was finally brought under control on 6 September, four-fifths of London had been burnt down and 89 churches, among them Old St Paul's, destroyed. Amazingly only eight people are recorded as having died in the fire, which did at least cleanse the city of plague.

Almost all traces of medieval, Tudor and Jacobean London fell victim to the fire, but it did give Sir Christopher Wren, in particular, the chance to redesign a modern city. Wren had his plans for a new London ready within a week of the fire, but with no powers of compulsory purchase it proved impossible to force reluctant landowners to give him a free hand. A special Fire Court was set up in Clifford's Inn to settle disputes over property and by 1673 most of the houses had been rebuilt, this time of stone and brick instead of combustible wood. Wider streets were given pavements for the first time and new squares ensured it would be harder for any future fire to get such a grip. The fire also accelerated the movement of the wealthy away from the City and into homes in what is now the West End. In 1711 the new St Paul's Cathedral opened as the culmination of the restoration work.

Late Stuart & Georgian London

With the trauma of the fire out of the way, many Londoners continued to make their living out of trade. In 1685, after King Henry IV of France revoked the Edict of Nantes granting freedom of worship to Protestants, 1500 Huguenot refugees arrived in London, most of them quickly turning their hand to the manufacture of luxury goods: watches, jewels and, most of all, silk, stockings and ribbons.

In 1688 the Glorious (ie bloodless) Revolution brought William of Orange to the throne with his wife Mary, daughter of the same James II they had deposed. When William's asthma was badly affected by the proximity of Whitehall Palace to the Thames, they moved into a house in Kensington Gardens and had it converted into a new palace. In 1694 William's need to raise loans to wage war with France led to the creation of the Bank of England.

By 1700 London was the largest city in Europe with more than 500,000 residents. Increasingly it was becoming a financial rather than a commercial centre. Sure enough it soon experienced its first major financial disaster, an incident known as the South Sea Bubble, when an orgy of speculation in a company set up to trade with South America ended with its collapse and the ruin of thousands.

William and Mary had no heirs and were succeeded by Mary's sister Anne. Although she had 17 pregnancies only one of her children survived and then not to adulthood. Since the 1701 Act of Settlement forbade a Catholic to ascend the throne, the hunt was on for any Protestant relative. Eventually it came up with George of Hanover, who arrived in London speaking no English and was supposedly mugged in the gardens of Kensington Palace by someone who mistook him for a German tourist.

During George I's reign Sir Robert Walpole became the first effective prime minister and took up residence at 10 Downing St. The city was becoming ever more segregated. This was the artist Hogarth's world in which the wealthy built fine new houses in attractive squares while the poor huddled together in appalling slums, downing cheap gin to deaden their misery. In 1751 the Bow Street Runners came into existence as the capital's first effective police force.

Until Westminster Bridge was built in

The Romance of the Century

The ill-fated marriage of Prince Charles and the late Diana Spencer may have brought dynastic matches into disrepute but not all such arranged royal partnerships have proved so rocky.

In 1840 Queen Victoria married her first cousin, Albert of Saxe-Coburg-Gotha, whom she had known as a child but met only once as an adult before their wedding.

It was a match made in heaven. While the British never took to Albert, the queen fell wildly in love with the man who introduced the Christmas tree to England. They went on to have four sons and five daughters.

In 1861 Albert died of typhoid and the queen was prostrate with grief. All railings in the capital were painted black and Victoria wore mourning clothes for the rest of her life. A memorial to Prince Albert (right) stands in South Kensington, an area of London he had helped develop.

That's as far as the story went until recently when a new film, Mrs Brown, starring Judi Dench and Billy Connolly, shone a spotlight on the Widow of Windsor's later friendship with her Scottish manservant, John Brown. The precise nature of their relationship can never be certain but what is known is that his photograph went with her to the grave. ■

Albert Memorial

1750, the horse ferry between Lambeth and Millbank was the only crossing place on the Thames apart from London Bridge. But as the population grew, so did the pressure to make it easier to move around. The remaining shops and houses that look so charming on pictures of old London Bridge were torn down, as were much of the medieval city wall and the gates that led into it; these days they survive only in place names like Aldgate.

In 1780 Parliament proposed to lift the law which prevented Catholics from owning property but one MP, Lord George Gordon, led a demonstration in protest which got out of hand and turned into the so-called Gordon Riots, when a furious crowd of 50,000 burnt the Newgate and Clink Prisons and several of the courts. Roughly 300 people died during the riot. You can see a model of the unsuccessful attack on the Bank of England in the museum there.

Around the turn of the century Londoners were diverted by the antics of the monarchy. George III had descended into dementia (see the film *The Madness of King George*) and his son, the Prince Regent, set up an alternative, and considerably more fashionable, court at Carlton House in Pall Mall. When the king died in 1820, his son attempted to divorce his wife Caroline, only to have her attempt to force her way into his coronation at Westminster Abbey. The public generally sided with the queen, but she died shortly afterwards.

The 18th century was a period of great creativity. In 1717 Handel wrote his *Water Music* while living in London and in 1755 Dr Johnson produced the first English dictionary. Many of London's most elegant streets and squares were laid out at this time.

Victorian London

In 1837 Queen Victoria ascended the throne, ready to preside over the years when London became the capital of the biggest empire the world had ever known, covering a quarter of the globe and encompassing 500 million people. New docks were built to take advantage of booming trade with the Empire and, as congestion in the capital worsened, the 1840s saw the first railways fanning out from London to the Home Counties. The world's first underground railway, from Paddington to Farringdon Rd, opened in 1863 and was such a success that other lines followed in quick succession. The full story of how closely the development of London was linked to the development of its transport systems is related in the excellent London Transport Museum in Covent Garden.

In 1851 Victoria's husband, Prince Albert, organised a huge celebration of new technology in Hyde Park. The Great Exhibition was displayed in an iron and glass Crystal Palace designed by the gardener Joseph Paxton. Six million people flocked from all corners of the country to see it and so great was the success that Albert arranged for the profits to be ploughed into building two permanent exhibitions which eventually became the Science Museum, and the Victoria & Albert Museum. The Crystal Palace itself was moved to Sydenham where it burnt down (a recurrent theme in London's history) in 1936.

The development of London landmarks continued apace. Big Ben first boomed out in 1859. The Albert Hall was built in 1871 and Tower Bridge first graced the skyline in 1894.

As a result of the Industrial Revolution and rapidly expanding commerce, the population jumped from around 1 million in 1800 to 4.5 million by 1900. The result was the steady growth of miles of inner-city slums and of leafy suburbs where the more comfortably-off could take refuge. The greatest chronicler of 19th century London was Charles Dickens, whose *Oliver Twist* first appeared in 1837 and whose works took as their themes the poverty, hopelessness and squalor of so many lives. Similar conditions inspired Friedrich Engels and Karl Marx, working from the British Museum Reading Room, to develop the theory of Communism. Others took more practical steps to alleviate the problems, among them Lord Ashley, the Earl of Shaftesbury, who championed social and industrial reform and is commemorated by the statue of Eros in Piccadilly Circus.

In 1854 Florence Nightingale (1820-1910) led a team of nurses to Scutari (Turkey) during the Crimean War, where she worked to improve conditions for the soldiers before returning to set up a training school for nurses in London. The museum in her name, which is attached to St Thomas' Hospital, has the details.

His name may not trip off many tongues but Londoners owe more than they usually realise to the engineer Sir Joseph Bazalgette (1819-91) who supervised the creation of a 1300-mile network of tunnels and pumps to deal with the sewage outflow responsible for recurrent outbreaks of cholera. Bazalgette also oversaw the reclamation of 37 acres of foreshore mud and the construction of 3½ miles of the Victoria, Albert and Chelsea embankments to protect the capital's streets from flooding. In his spare time this frantic overachiever also managed to find time to draw up the plans for the Albert, Battersea and Hammersmith bridges.

Around this time Charles Darwin (1809-82) published his *Origin of Species* in which he used his experiences during a voyage to South America and the Galapagos Islands to develop the theory of evolution which is still capable of stirring up passions, at least across the Atlantic. Down House, Darwin's home in Orpington, Kent, has recently been restored and opened to the public.

During the course of Victoria's long reign many great-name prime ministers served in Parliament, most famously Gladstone (1809-98) and Disraeli (1804-81), whose monuments can be seen in Westminster Abbey.

Queen Victoria lived to celebrate her Jubilee in 1897, but died four years later, aged 81. Admiralty Arch, off Trafalgar Square, was erected to commemorate what was, in retrospect, the climax of British world supremacy.

Edwardian London, WWI & its Aftermath

Just as Prince Charles looks fated to wait until old age before he becomes king, so Queen Victoria's son Edward was nearly 60 before he became Edward VII in the brief lull before the war. By now change was happening at an ever-increasing pace; the first motor bus only went into service in 1904 but by 1911 all the horse-drawn versions had vanished.

The Great War broke out in 1914 and the

first Zeppelin bomb fell near the Guildhall in 1915. Planes were soon dropping bombs on the capital, but only around 300 people were killed, a drop in the ocean compared with the carnage of the Blitz (see following section).

Once the war ended in 1918, London's population started to rise again, reaching nearly nine million in 1939. The London County Council started work to clear the slums and create new housing estates, while the suburbs spread ever further into the countryside. But unemployment was rising steadily, and 1926 saw the nine-day General Strike when so many people downed tools that the army had to be called in to keep London running.

The 1930s were the heyday of the Bloomsbury Set, among them the brilliant economist John Maynard Keynes and the writer Virginia Woolf. The first television programme was broadcast from Alexandra Park in 1936 and this was the great age of the cinema and the radio.

But political tension was bubbling beneath the glitzy surface. In 1936 Sir Oswald Mosley attempted to lead the British Union of Fascists on an anti-Jewish march through the East End. In Cable St he was repulsed by a mob of up to half a million. By 1938 the threat from Germany looked sufficiently alarming for children to be evacuated from London.

Winston Churchill led the WWII campaign from the Cabinet War Rooms in Whitehall

WWII & the Blitz

In 1939 WWII broke out and this time London suffered far more harshly. The first year was one of anxious waiting, when although more than 500,000 women and children had been evacuated from London and some of Clerkenwell's Italian community found themselves interned as aliens, no bombs fell to disturb the blackout. But in September 1940 the 'Phoney War' came to an end when the Blitz began with hundreds of bombs dropped on the East End and more than 2000 people killed.

For the next 57 nights bombs fell on London and the Underground was turned into a giant bomb shelter. For the following six months the bombs continued to rain down, if less frequently. Westminster Abbey, Buckingham Palace, St Paul's Cathedral, Guildhall, Broadcasting House and innumerable City churches were all hit. The air raids finally stopped in May 1941, only to start up again in 1944 when pilotless doodlebugs began to fly overhead, slyly dropping their bombs when their humming engines stopped. Finally London became the target of 500-odd V2 ground-to-ground missiles.

When the war finally ended in 1945, up to a third of the East End and the City lay in ruins. In all 18,800 tons of bombs had dropped on the capital and 29,890 Londoners had been killed. It was during these appalling months that Queen Elizabeth (now the Queen Mother) ventured out to inspect the ravaged streets of the East End, earning the enduring admiration which makes her one of the most popular of the royals even today.

In 1940 Sir Winston Churchill had succeeded Neville Chamberlain as prime minister. He orchestrated much of Britain's war strategy from the Cabinet War Rooms deep beneath Whitehall, which are now open to the public. It was from here that he made many of his stirring wartime speeches. The story of the war is told in more detail in the Imperial War Museum, while the Britain at War exhibition in Southwark focuses on the everyday lives of Londoners during the Blitz.

Post-War London

After the war, ugly housing and low-cost developments were thrown up on many of the bomb sites and the character of London began to change as immigrants from the West Indies and the Indian subcontinent arrived to stay. Notting Hill, Ladbroke Grove and Brixton acquired an increasingly Caribbean feel, Southall became markedly Punjabi and the old Jewish East End vanished as the Jews moved north to Golders Green, to be replaced by a lively Bengali presence.

The Festival of Britain took place in London in 1951 and left as a legacy the ugly concrete buildings of the South Bank. The first civil flight left Heathrow airport in 1946 and the first red Routemaster bus appeared on the streets in 1956. During the 1960s 'Swinging London' was very much the place to be, with hippies flocking to Carnaby St and the King's Rd, bringing colour and vitality to the streets. Even during the harsher 1970s and early 80s London was spared much of the distress of northern England and Scotland, although the docks never recovered from the loss of empire and the changing needs of modern container ships. Shipping moved east to Tilbury, and the Docklands declined to the point of dereliction, only to be rediscovered by developers in the 1980s. Although development faltered with the recession of the early 1990s, this is now one of the most vital parts of London, perhaps the only place where you can feel some of the forward-looking vibe of the Far East.

The 1970s was a nondescript decade squeezed in between the rampant optimism of the 60s and the disastrous recession of the early 1980s. In 1973 a bomb went off at the Old Bailey, signalling the arrival on English soil of the IRA's campaign for a united Ireland. In 1979 the IRA succeeded in blowing up the Tory MP Airey Neave in the grounds of the House of Commons. But the mid-70s were at least brightened up by the spike-haired punks, pogoing their way to fame at clubs like the Marquee (now a run-of-the-mill pub).

The Thatcher Years

In 1979 Margaret Thatcher became Britain's first female prime minister. Her monetarist policy soon sent unemployment rocketing up, and when riots broke out in Brixton in 1981 this was seen as significant spark; afterwards the Scarman inquiry found that 55% of men under 19 in Brixton were unemployed. Riots flared in Tottenham in 1985 and again unemployment and heavy-handed policing took the rap as contributing factors.

Thatcher didn't have it all her own way. The Greater London Council, under the leadership of Ken Livingstone (now MP for Brent East), fought a spirited campaign to bring down the price of travelling round London. Thatcher responded by abolishing the GLC in 1986. If Londoners vote for a new mayor and assembly in the referendum of 1998, London will have its first citywide council for more than a decade.

But if poorer people suffered under Thatcher's assault on socialism, for the business community things had rarely looked better. Riding on a wave of confidence partly engendered by deregulation of the stock exchange in 1986 (the 'Big Bang'), London

Margaret Thatcher's tumultuous tenure as prime minister saw her abolish the Greater London Council in 1986, after it had campaigned to bring down the cost of city transport

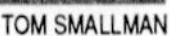

TOM SMALLMAN

JUDI SCHIFF

PAT YALE

Left: Sculpture outside the British Museum
Right: President Roosevelt and Prime Minister Churchill statues, New Bond Street
Bottom: Carnaby St mural

PAT YALE

RACHEL BLACK

PAT YALE

PAT YALE

JUDI SCHIFF

A	B
C	D
E	

A: Heron on the Serpentine, Hyde Park
B: John Keats' Garden, Hampstead
C: The pelicans have been at St James's Park since the 17th century
D: The Sunken Garden, Kensington Gardens
E: Flower bed, Canary Wharf

underwent explosive growth in the late 1980s. The new property developers proved to be only marginally more discriminating than the Luftwaffe, although some outstanding modern buildings, including the new Lloyd's Building, went up amid the dross.

Like previous booms, that of the late 1980s proved unsustainable. As unemployment started to rise again and people found themselves living in houses worth much less than they had paid for them, Thatcher had the bright idea of introducing a flat-rate poll tax. Protests all round the country culminated in a march on Trafalgar Square which ended in a riot. Shortly afterwards Canary Wharf, the flagship of the Docklands redevelopment, went into receivership and John Major replaced Thatcher as prime minister.

The 1990s

In 1992 the British elected the Conservatives for a fourth successive term in government. Shortly afterwards the economy went into a tailspin and Britain was forced to withdraw from the European Exchange Rate Mechanism (ERM), a humiliation from which it was impossible for the government to recover. To add to their troubles, the IRA exploded two huge bombs, the first at the Baltic Exchange (1992), which did millions of pounds worth of damage and forced the police to introduce a 'ring of steel' (armed police stopping cars to check their details) around the City, the second in Docklands (1996).

Over the last few years the economy has pulled back from disaster as the exchange rate moved in favour of British exporters, and the atmosphere in London is much headier now than it has been since the 1960s. Ambitious plans will see parts of the much-derided South Bank rebuilt with proceeds from the National Lottery, and Greenwich is undergoing a facelift which should leave it much more accessible now that it has been chosen as Britain's official site for ushering in the third millennium.

When the general election of May 1997 returned a Labour government to power for the first time in nearly 19 years, it was just the icing on the cake, and the sight of new prime minister Tony Blair gladhanding it in Downing St was enough to lift the spirits of more than just Islington residents.

But London, and indeed the world, was stunned on August 31, 1997, by the tragic death of Princess Diana. The depth of public emotion for the 'people's princess' was overwhelming and all sorts of protocols were broken for her funeral at Westminster Abbey a week later, which saw over two million people line the streets of London to pay their respects.

GEOGRAPHY

The 625-odd square miles of Greater London that are enclosed by the M25 ring road lie in the south-east of England, on the River Thames which extends west through Windsor, Maidenhead and Oxford to the Cotswolds. The Thames is a clay and gravel-lined tidal river with its estuary facing east.

London is divided into widely differing boroughs run by local governments with significant autonomy. Two traditional 'cities', Westminster and the City of London, each with their own cathedral, technically make up London. The 'one square mile' of the City of London that lies at the heart of the conurbation is known simply as 'the City'.

Boroughs are further subdivided into districts, which generally tally with the first group of letters and numbers of the postal code. The letter(s) correspond to compass directions from London's principal post office near St Paul's Cathedral: EC means East Central, WC means West Central, W means West, NW means North West, and so on. The numbering system after the letters is less helpful: 1 is the centre of the zone, but other numbers relate to the alphabetical order of the postal district names, which are not always in common use. (See the Postcodes map in the Facts for the Visitor chapter.)

Districts and postal codes often appear on street signs, which is obviously vital when names are duplicated (there are 47 Station Rds), or cross through a number of districts. To further confuse visitors, many streets change name (Holland Park Ave becomes

Notting Hill Gate, which becomes Bayswater Rd, which becomes Oxford St...), or duck and weave like the country lanes they once were. Street numbering can also bewilder: in big streets the numbers on opposite sides can be way out of kilter (315 might be opposite 520) or, for variation, go up one side and down the other.

To add to the confusion, some London suburbs well within the M25 don't even give London as a part of their addresses, and don't use London postal codes. Instead they're considered part of a county; perhaps Surrey which does, at least, still exist, or Middlesex which doesn't!

CLIMATE

London has one of England's mildest climates...which is not to say you'd be well advised to leave the woollies and brollies back home. In fact, it's wise to expect cloudy weather and rain even in high summer.

In July and August temperatures occasionally soar to 30°C or more and you'll wish they hadn't as the tube turns into a Black Hole and the heat concentrates the traffic fumes horribly. Most years you'll be lucky if they reach the lower 20s. In spring and autumn temperatures slither to around 11 to 15°C; in winter they slump to around 6°C.

Fortunately many of the capital's attractions are safely undercover with heating systems geared to keeping the cold at bay.

ECOLOGY & ENVIRONMENT

London's worst environmental problems will be obvious even to a visitor on the shortest of stays. Traffic congestion is now so bad that fire engines may have to be despatched from two depots to ensure that one at least will manage to fight its way through the jams. Speed of vehicle movement is almost as slow as it was in 1945 – around 11 miles an hour.

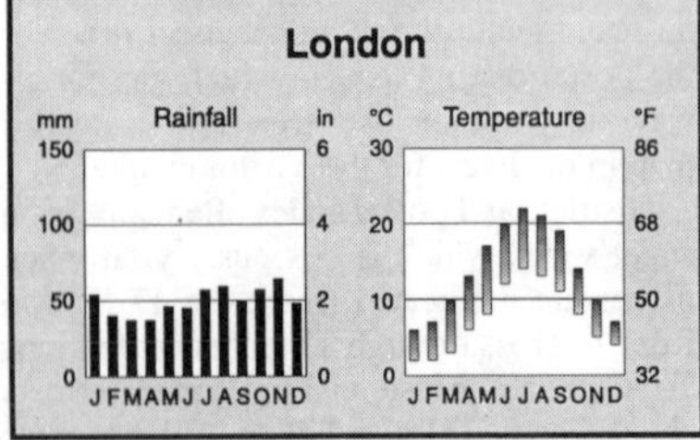

The traffic congestion is also largely responsible for the other obvious problem, which is the poor air quality. Many cyclists wear masks to protect themselves from breathing in the poisonous traffic fumes. Dickensian fogs may be a thing of the past due to the Clean Air Act, but these days anyone with asthma or other respiratory problems would be well advised to pay attention to the air quality forecasts attached to weather forecasts. The worst problems occur on the hottest days when you don't need anyone to tell you that the thick, putrid air isn't doing you any good.

That said, that other notorious air pollutant, the cigarette, is on its way out in public places. All theatres and almost all cinemas have banned smoking, and only the most obdurate restaurateurs refuse to provide no-smoking areas. Pubs remain one of the last strongholds of the smoker and even then the Wetherspoon chain now sets aside corners for non-smokers.

To look at the murky waters of the Thames you'd assume it was another pollution blackspot, but in fact things are improving on that front – they could hardly get worse than they were in 1858 when the Great Stench was so bad that MPs were forced to vacate Parliament! By 1962 the combined impact of untreated sewage and industrial pollution had killed off every sign of life in the river. But since 1974 a clean-up has brought fish – including salmon for whom special ladders over the weirs are being built – back to the water, and with them the herons and cormorants who feast on them. Much of the murkiness is now said to be sediment from the riverbed. Even so it would be a singularly reckless individual who went swimming in the river, let alone swigged a drink from it.

FLORA & FAUNA

Given the capital's size and built-up nature,

it would seem an unlikely mecca for plant or animal lovers. However, London boasts more parks and open spaces than most comparable cities. These range from the neatly manicured (Holland Park, St James's Park) to the semi-wild (Richmond Park, Bushy Park) and between them they provide suitable habitats for a wide range of animals and birds. The growing network of city farms have also reintroduced cattle and sheep to the capital.

Flora

Plant-lovers should hop straight on a bus or train to Kew Gardens in west London, where staff at the Royal Botanic Gardens have been collecting and studying plants since the 18th century. Here you can see all sorts of trees and flowers from around the world, some displayed in historic glasshouses.

If you're more interested in Britain's indigenous plants, then London's many parks boast a wide range of trees, shrubs and flowers. Many Londoners also take pride in gardens which range from pocket-handkerchief-sized backyards to sprawling mini estates. If you'd like to see some of them it's worth knowing that many of the best gardens open for a few days each year through the National Gardens Schemc. Normally they charge £1 or £2 which goes to charity. Most gardens open in June and July but it's only in November, December and January that none are open. For a list of dates contact the National Gardens Scheme, Hatchlands Park, East Clandon, Guildford GU4 7RT (☎ 01483-211535).

Fauna

The mammal you're most likely to spot in London is the grey squirrel which has colonised every big park and is often so tame that it'll tug at your trouser leg to be fed. Foxes have also moved into town in a big way, although their nocturnal habits mean that casual visitors are unlikely to spot them unless they come scavenging in the back garden of your B&B. The same goes for the hedgehog which hangs out in some gardens but only emerges after dark, and the badger which lurks amid the bracken of Richmond Park.

Richmond and Bushy Parks also boast visible herds of red and fallow deer. Although the deer are culled annually to keep numbers down, in general they're allowed to live a normal life and depending on when you visit you might be able to catch courtship rituals or see the deer with their young (watch from a safe distance though – deer can be dangerous at these times).

To see domestic sheep, pigs, cows and goats you can visit one of the city farms that have sprung up over the last 10 years. These are more popular with Londoners than overseas visitors so they also offer a way of escaping the beaten track. Some of the more accessible city farms include:

Coram's Fields, 93 Guildford St, WC1 (☎ 837 6138; tube: Russell Square)
Freightliners Farm, Sheringham Rd, N7 (☎ 609 0467; tube: Holloway Road)
Hackney City Farm, 1A Goldsmith's Row, E2 (☎ 729 6381; tube: Bethnal Green)
Kentish Town City Farm, 1 Cressfield Close, Grafton Rd, NW5 (☎ 916 5421; tube: Kentish Town)
Mudchute Park Farm, Pier St, E14 (☎ 515 5901; tube: Mudchute DLR)
Stepping Stones Farm, Stepney Way, E1 (☎ 790 8204; tube: Stepney Green)
Surrey Docks Farm, Rotherhithe St, SE16 (☎ 231 1010; tube: Rotherhithe)

Birdwatchers can have a field day in London, especially if they're keen on waterfowl. Many of the ducks and swans in St James's Park have their wings clipped to prevent them from flying away, but some are there because they're attracted by the lake and the guarantee of easy pickings from the visitors. Hyde Park's Serpentine Lake is also well-stocked with ducks and you may also see pairs of beautiful, chestnut-headed great crested grebes diving for fish. Herons can often be seen both here and along the Thames which also attracts cormorants, especially as you head east into Docklands.

Garden birds, like blue and great tits, robins and blackbirds, can be seen in all the parks, but some parks attract more interesting migrants. In spring in Holland Park, for example, you might be lucky enough to glimpse flocks of tiny goldcrests. Kestrels also nest around the Tower of London. Other birds can be seen at the reservoirs, particularly at Staines Reservoir in Stanwell Moor Road, out west of the centre but accessible via Hampton station. The wide open stretches of Wimbledon and Barnes Commons also harbour a rich assortment of birds and mammals.

London has several nature reserves which offer the chance to see a range of birds and occasional small mammals while also appreciating the natural plants and trees. Battersea Park Nature Reserve has several organised nature trails for visitors, while the Trent Country Park (tube: Cockfosters) even boasts a braille trail through the woodlands. Parts of Hampstead Heath have been designated a Site of Special Scientific Interest for their wealth of natural history.

For more information on nature reserves and wildlife habitats call the London Wildlife Trust on ☎ 278 6612.

GOVERNMENT & POLITICS

As the capital city, London is home to almost all the main offices of state, and will continue to be so until the planned Scottish Parliament and Welsh Assembly come into being.

As yet, Britain doesn't have a written constitution but operates under a mixture of Parliamentary statutes, common law (a body of legal principles based on precedents dating back to Anglo-Saxon customs) and convention.

The monarch is the head of state, but real power has been whittled away so that the current Queen is just a figurehead who acts entirely on the advice of 'her' ministers and parliament.

Parliament has three separate elements – the Queen, the House of Commons and the House of Lords. In practice, the supreme body is the House of Commons, which is directly elected every five years. Earlier elections can be called at the request of the governing party, or if it loses a vote of confidence.

Voting is not compulsory and, under the existing 'first past the post' system, candidates are elected if they win a simple majority in their constituencies. There are 650 constituencies (seats) – 523 for England, 38 for Wales, 72 for Scotland and 17 for Northern Ireland.

The House of Lords consists of the Lords Spiritual (26 senior bishops of the Church of England) and more than 1100 Lords Temporal (all hereditary and life peers), plus the Lords of Appeal (or 'law lords'). None are elected by the general populace. If the Lords refuse to pass a bill, but it's passed twice by the Commons, it's sent to the Queen for her automatic assent. In addition, any 'money' bill (bills which involve the raising of revenue) automatically becomes law one month after the Commons passes it on to the Lords, regardless of whether or not the Lords have given it the OK.

The prime minister is the leader of the majority party in the House of Commons and is technically appointed by the Queen. All other ministers are appointed on the recommendation of the prime minister, most of them coming from the House of Commons. Ministers are responsible for government departments. The senior 20 or so ministers make up the Cabinet, which, although answerable to Parliament, meets confidentially and in effect manages the government and its policies.

For the last 150 years a predominantly two-party system has operated. Since 1945 either the Conservative ('Tory') Party or the Labour Party has held power, the Conservatives drawing their support mainly from suburbia and the countryside, Labour from urban industrialised areas, and Scotland and Wales.

Put crudely, Labour is left-wing in the social-democratic tradition while the Conservatives are right-wing, free-enterprise supporters. In recent years, however, the Labour Party has shed most of its socialist credo, and the Conservatives have softened their hard-right approach so the differences are less striking. In the 1997 election Tony Blair led Labour to a landslide victory, ending 19 years of Tory rule. It's still early days but there's reason to hope his government will prove more radical than left-wingers initially feared.

Local Government

Until 1986 London had its own local government, the Greater London Council (GLC), which had its 'parliament' at County Hall on the South Bank, a stone's throw from the Palace of Westminster. However, in the early 1980s a notably left-wing GLC led by Ken Livingstone (now MP for Brent East) clashed head-on with Mrs Thatcher. Figures for the rising number of jobless were strung on a banner across the front of County Hall facing Westminster. The 'fares fair' campaign to reduce the cost of public transport and get more people off the roads was popular with Londoners but sounded the death knell for the GLC. The Council was abolished and since then London has had no overall coordinating local government.

In May 1998 a referendum will be held to decide whether the capital should once again have an elected mayor who would preside over an assembly of 25 to 30 members. They would have a say on transport; economic development; strategic planning; the environment; the police, fire brigade and civil defence; and cultural matters. Should the outcome be favourable (and even the Tories no longer oppose the idea), it's expected that the first new mayor could be in office in time for the Millennium.

Rather like the Vatican City, the City of London has its own government in the form of the Corporation of London which is headed by the Lord Mayor and an assortment of picturesquely named (and often dressed) aldermen, beadles and sheriffs. These men – and they're usually men – are elected by the freemen and liverymen (see boxed aside entitled The Livery Companies in the Things to See & Do chapter) of the City who owe this privilege to their ancestors' negotiations with kings and queens from William the Conqueror onwards. It's easy to say this doesn't matter, that the Lord Mayor's post is purely honorary and will fade into insignificance once an elected mayor returns, but the Corporation of London still owns roughly a third of the supremely wealthy square mile. It has a good record for patronage of the City arts but remains an extraordinary, and little-commented, anachronism.

Different areas of London also have democratically-elected local councils like the rest of Britain. These generally deal with education and other less absorbing minutiae like road sweeping. That they have a will of their own was illustrated recently when Westminster Council refused to allow David Cronenberg's film *Crash* to be shown in Westminster although it had been passed for general release by the British Board of Film Censors.

Thrice Mayor of London

If, as is expected, London soon has its own mayor again, he or she will have their work cut out to achieve the same fame as Dick Whittington who became mayor of London three times in the 15th century.

Whittington was a country lad from Gloucestershire who came to the city to seek his fortune. He was about to turn back disillusioned when he heard the bells of St Mary-le-Bow ringing out the message 'turn again, Whittington, thrice mayor of London'. Taking heed of them, he retraced his footsteps and went on to find fame and fortune.

A milestone on Highgate Hill, at the point where he is said to have heard the bells ringing, has a bronze cat sitting on top of it in memory of Whittington's equally famous pet. ■

ECONOMY

London and the south-east continue to be the driving force behind the British economy, but you'll see few signs of heavy industry. Instead London is one of the world's major financial centres, with a flourishing service sector in which tourism is one of the three most successful industries. In 1996 the London economy was estimated to be worth £122 billion, or 15% of the entire GDP of Britain. Overall levels of unemployment are low and falling, which is not to say that life is any easier for those who don't have jobs.

During the Thatcher years (1979-90) the British economy suffered two recessions. The first of these more or less passed London by, as it stripped out the manufacturing industries of the north. Second time round things were rather different and the south-east felt the impact just as harshly. The 'Big Bang' of 1988 had seen the financial market deregulated and an explosion of new activity in the City and the developing Docklands office sites. In the early 1990s the same businesses found life much tougher. High-profile business collapses even saw Canary Wharf, the flagship Docklands development, fall into the hands of receivers and the City wine bars fell quiet as the braying brokers saw their 'bonuses' vanish.

By 1992 the situation was so bad that the government was forced to withdraw Britain from the ERM. Although politically this was a disaster, economically it marked a turning point; exchange rates came down and exporters found business looking up again in the face of a devalued pound.

By the late 1990s, the recession was well and truly over and the British economy looked in better shape than that of many of its European neighbours. Docklands took off again, empty City office spaces filled up and the dealers started throwing their money around again, forcing up property prices in areas close to the City like Clerkenwell and Spitalfields.

The demon of inflation is low and seems to be staying steady, although interest rates are rising and the pound is overvalued, making life tough for exporters. Some would see ominous signs that London and the south-east are heading back to the fateful days of the late 1980s when a consumer boom fuelled by unrealistic house prices undermined the economy and helped precipitate the recession. Optimists would prefer to point to the changed circumstances of the 1990s, with even the Labour government accepting that capitalism is king.

POPULATION & PEOPLE

Roughly 12 million people live in the 625 square miles of Greater London, 6.8 million of them in central London alone. When you bear in mind that roughly 26 million people a year also visit London, it's quickly apparent why there are always crowds and queues and why the transport system is under such strain.

Although most Londoners are still white Anglo-Saxon Protestants, the capital becomes more multicultural by the year. Ever since the Industrial Revolution, it has been sucking in people from all round Britain and Ireland. In the 18th, 19th and 20th centuries there have also been significant influxes of refugees: Huguenots (French Protestants) arrived in the 18th century, Jews in the 19th and first half of the 20th century, African Asians in the 1960s and 70s, and an assortment of Kurds, Somalis, Bosnians and other victims of conflict in the 1980s and 90s.

Since the 1950s there has also been significant immigration from many of the former colonies, especially the West Indies, Pakistan and India. These different groups of immigrants and refugees have tended to settle in areas close to each other rather than spreading out around the city, so depending on where you are in London you may find yourself surrounded by people from distinct ethnic minorities: Irish in Kilburn and Stoke Newington, Sikhs in Southall, Bengalis in Brick Lane, Chinese in Soho, West Indians in Brixton, and Jews in Golders Green and Finchley.

Roughly 15% of Londoners are from ethnic minorities. According to the most recent census (1991) there were 278,000 people from South Asia in London, 256,000 from Ireland, 183,000 from Africa, 150,000 from the Caribbean, 106,000 from South East Asia, 50,000 from Cyprus, 30,000 from Italy and 21,000 from Poland. Almost 200 different languages can be heard around the capital.

ARTS

London has a flourishing cultural life which has contributed in no small part to its present popularity. It doesn't matter whether you're talking about the culture of the past as exemplified by the National Gallery, the Tate, the Victoria & Albert Museum and the British Museum, or present-day culture as typified by the likes of Damien Hirst, Tracey Emin and Rachel Whiteread, London still manages to cream off the best, to the chagrin of other British cities. It's hardly a fluke that the largest award yet made by the National Lottery went to help restore the Royal Opera House in Covent Garden.

Architecture

London's architectural heritage stretches back to the Roman period, although little is left to show for the earliest period, bar the bottom of some walls and a few foundation stones. Complete Norman buildings are also rare. Perhaps the finest survivor from this period is the sturdy White Tower, the Norman keep at the heart of the Tower of London, although the church of St Bartholomew-the-Great at Smithfield also has solid Norman columns marching down the nave.

Although the Great Fire of London obliterated many of the city's medieval churches, Westminster Abbey is a splendid reminder of what the medieval master masons were capable of. The much smaller church hidden away in the Temple courtyard reveals the architectural transition between the round-arched, clumpy Romanesque Norman style and the pointed-arched, more delicate Gothic Early English style. But most surviving medieval churches in London reflect centuries of rebuilding and additions; what you now see is a hotch-potch of different Gothic styles from Early English through to Perpendicular. Perhaps the finest surviving medieval church in the City of London was St Ethelburga in Bishopsgate which had stood more or less intact for 500 years, only to fall victim to the powerful IRA bombs of 1992 and 1993. Now you'll have to make do with St Olave in Hart St or St Etheldreda's in Ely Place.

Of the medieval city's secular buildings, traces are even scarcer, although the Jewel Tower opposite the House of Commons dates from 1365. Most of the Tower of London also dates back to the Middle Ages. Staple Inn in Holborn dates back to 1378 but the half-timbered facade you see now is mostly Elizabethan.

Perhaps the finest London architect of the first half of the 17th century was Inigo Jones (1573-c.1652) whose masterwork is the Banqueting Hall in Whitehall. Often overlooked is the much plainer church of St Paul's which he designed to go with the new piazza in Covent Garden, describing it as 'the handsomest barn in England.'

But the greatest architect ever to leave his mark on London was Sir Christopher Wren (1632-1723) who was responsible not just for St Paul's Cathedral but also for many of central London's finest churches (including St Bride's in Fleet St and St Stephen's, Walbrook), and for the Royal Hospital in Chelsea and the Royal Naval College at Greenwich. His neoclassical buildings are taller, lighter and generally more graceful than their medieval predecessors – as anyone who has visited Westminster Abbey and then St Paul's will recognise.

Nicholas Hawksmoor (1661-1736) was a pupil of Wren's who worked with him on several of his churches before moving on to design his own masterpieces: Christ Church Spitalfields; St George's Bloomsbury; St Anne's at Limehouse; St George-in-the-East at Wapping; and St Mary Woolnoth.

As well as the churches, a few pre-18th century buildings still survive, among them the half-timbered Prince's Room in Fleet Street and several old pubs in Fleet St and the Strand. But the Great Fire effectively wiped out most of the old cityscape and many more secular buildings survive from the 18th century when some of London's finest squares were laid out.

The Georgian period saw the revival of severe Greek classicism, with Sir Robert Smirke's design for the British Museum one of its finest expressions. John Nash (1752-1835) was responsible for the layout of Regent's Park and the surrounding elegant crescents. He also planned Trafalgar Square and Regent St, although his facades there have long since been replaced. Nash's hand is also visible in some of the more attractive rooms of Buckingham Palace.

Other 18th century architects who made their mark on the city were Robert Adam (1728-92) whose work can be seen at Syon and Osterley Houses; George Dance (1741-1825) who designed the Mansion House; James Gibb (1682-1754) who designed St Mary-le-Strand; William Kent (1695-1748) who worked on Kensington Palace and Chiswick House; and Sir William Chambers (1723-96) whose works include the Pagoda in Kew Gardens and Somerset House.

A century later a reaction set in as the highly decorative Gothic Revival got into its stride. Champions of this style were Sir George Gilbert Scott (1811-78), Augustus Pugin (1812-52), Alfred Waterhouse (1830-1905) and Sir Charles Barry (1795-1860). Scott was responsible for the elaborate Albert Memorial, Waterhouse designed the flamboyant Natural History Museum, and Pugin and Barry worked together on the House of Commons.

Immediately after WWII some unfortunate rebuilding took place, partly in the push to make good the damage as quickly and cheaply as possible. But one person's carbuncle is often another person's jewel; the Royal Festival Hall, designed for the Festival of Britain in 1951 by Sir Robert Mathew and Sir Leslie Martin, attracts as many accolades as brickbats, although hardly anyone seems to have a good word for the Royal National Theatre, a stone's throw away. The 1960s saw the ascendancy of the workaday glass and concrete high-rises exemplified by the dreary King's College building in the Strand which can't hold a candle to buildings erected less than 50 years earlier on the opposite side of the road.

Fortunately, while there are still glaring examples of callous disregard for setting, the 1980s and 1990s have also witnessed the erection of some outstanding new buildings. London is home to several wonderful Modernist and post-Modernist buildings and you only have to take the Docklands Light Railway east to see a multitude of different shapes and forms that steer well clear of the pastiche favoured in developments like Terry Quinlan's waterside development by Richmond Bridge.

The Wren and Hawksmoor of modern London are probably Richard Rogers and Norman Foster, whose multifarious buildings dot the capital. Foster designed Stansted airport, while Rogers was responsible for the Lloyd's Building. He is also the brains behind the Millennium Dome, now shaping up in Greenwich.

Other recent additions to the London scene which have won more praise than criticism include the London Ark by Ralph Erskine, and the Waterloo International train terminal and *Financial Times* Print Works by Nicholas Grimshaw. Whatever you may think of its straight up and down design, the Canary Wharf Tower is another unmissable addition to the skyline, visible from the heart of London.

Given the increasing interest in hanging on to every reminder of the past, it's perhaps not surprising to find that some of the most interesting architectural developments of recent years have not been new buildings so much as adaptations of existing buildings for new uses. Fine examples are the old Michelin factory in Fulham Rd that now houses the Bibendum restaurant; the Oxo Tower on the South Bank, converted into a mixture of flats and eateries; the old Bankside power station which is being turned into the new Tate Bankside; and the power station at Battersea, the latest plans for which envisage a vast multiplex cinema rising up between its four towers.

But the prize for the most unlikely award-winning development must go to the cantilevered public lavatory at Westbourne Grove where it joins Colville Rd, designed by the same architects who gave us the Cascades in Docklands and China Wharf in Bermondsey.

Literature

The history of English literature is peppered with writers for whom London has provided the greatest inspiration. That situation continues today, with a metropolitan literary mafia often accused of scooping all the attention and reviews while the efforts of their 'provincial' counterparts go unnoticed. Literally thousands of books take London as their setting. This section can only highlight the most important.

The first reference to London in literature comes in Chaucer's *Canterbury Tales* (c. 1387) where the pilgrims gather for their trip to Canterbury at the Tabard Inn in Southwark.

Fast-forwarding a couple of centuries, William Shakespeare lived part of his life in London and acted in several Southwark theatres, most famously in the Globe; the new Globe Theatre near the site of the original was partly reconstructed from references in his plays. His great tragedies, *Hamlet*, *Othello*, *Macbeth* and *King Lear*, were probably written to be performed at the original Globe.

The most vivid insight into 17th century London life comes courtesy of Samuel Pepys' *Diary*. Written in shorthand from 1660 to 1669 and containing enough references to women other than his wife to confirm that London was swinging long before the 1960s, the diary is one of our most important sources of information for both the Great Plague and the Great Fire of London. If you don't think you could cope with the whole unabridged version, Penguin Classics publishes *The Shorter Pepys* which should see you through.

Two 18th century poets found inspiration in London. Keats wrote his *Ode to a Nightingale* while living near Hampstead Heath, and his *Ode on a Grecian Urn* after inspecting the Portland Vase in the British Museum. Wordsworth visited London in 1802, a trip which inspired *On Westminster Bridge* (see boxed aside entitled Bridging the Thames).

The novelist Charles Dickens (1812-70) is equally closely associated with London, so closely in fact that there are benighted students in remote corners of the globe who still imagine London swathed in the peasouper fogs he found so atmospheric. Although Dickens had been born into a middle-class family, his father eventually wound up in the Marshalsea, the debtors' prison in Southwark; only Charles and one of his sisters managed to avoid joining the rest of the family there. His novels most closely associated with London are *Oliver Twist*, with its story of a gang of boy thieves organised by Fagin; *Little Dorrit*, whose heroine was born in the Marshalsea and married in nearby St George the Martyr; and *The Old Curiosity Shop*. An Old Curiosity Shop still exists just off Lincoln's Inn Fields but it has nothing to do with Dickens; these days the only curiosity is the price of the shoes and clothes it sells.

Forever associated with 221b Baker St is Sir Arthur Conan Doyle's great detective Sherlock Holmes and sidekick Dr Watson – around 20 letters a week still arrive here addressed to Holmes! Like Dickens' novels, Conan Doyle's started life in serialised magazine form and went on to become bestsellers. Their settings may roam far from London but the connection is nonetheless so close that a new 221b has been created further along the road just to provide a suitable shrine.

Towards the end of the 19th century Jerome K Jerome inserted a memorably witty description of visiting Hampton Court maze into his *Three Men in a Boat*, an account of three men and a dog messing about on the Thames.

At the turn of the 20th century Joseph Conrad chose Soho as the setting for *The Secret Agent*, a novel which explores a murky world of espionage in London.

Colin MacInnes described the bohemian, multicultural world of 1950s Notting Hill in *City of Spades* and *Absolute Beginners*, the latter made into a film starring Patsy Kensit.

More recently Doris Lessing painted a picture of 1960s London in *The Four Gated City*, a part of her 'Children of Violence' series.

Some of the funniest and most vicious portrayals of 1990s Britain come in Martin Amis' *London Observed*, a collection of stories set in the capital; his *London Fields* also has the capital as a backdrop but is pretty heavy going. In *Metroland*, Amis' sometime friend Julian Barnes wrote of growing up in the suburbs connected to London by the Metropolitan line. Most recently, Nick Hornby immortalised the London football club Arsenal in the virtually unreadable (to non-football fans) *Fever Pitch*, now a film starring Colin Firth. Hornby's *High Fidelity*, about an almost equally fanatical indie music lover, is much easier on the brain.

Other modern writers look at London from the perspective of its ethnic minorities. Hanif Kureishi writes about the lives of London's young Pakistanis in *The Black Album*, while Caryl Phillips describes the Caribbean immigrants' experience in *The Final Passage*.

To get to grips with London's complicated history in novel form, look out for the simply named *London* by *Old Sarum* author, Edward Rutherford (Century, £16.99); until it's out in paperback, it'll double as a handy stool while you wait at bus stops.

It's also worth looking out for novels by Peter Ackroyd, many of which focus on aspects of London history. *Hawksmoor*, his fictionalised biography of the great 17th century architect, would be a good one to start with.

London Wins the Lottery

After years in which a shortage of cash saw leaky museum roofs going unrepaired and old buildings standing neglected, the National Lottery has brought a complete turnabout, raining down cash for repairs, redevelopment and new buildings. Despite rumblings of irritation from other parts of Britain, there's no doubt that the lion's share of this bounty has flowed to London. The following are just the most prominent grants awarded to London recipients in the last three years:

Greenwich Dome	£200 million
South Bank Centre	£113 million
Royal Opera House	£55 million
Tate Bankside	£50 million
Royal National Theatre	£31.5 million
British Museum	£30 million
Tate Gallery Millbank	£18.7 million
Imax Cinema for National Film Theatre	£15 million
Globe Theatre	£12.4 million
Hungerford Bridge	£8.1 million
Millennium Bridge	£5 million

Another £217 million has been divided between the Royal Court Theatre, Sadler's Wells, the Imperial War Museum, the Royal Academy of Dramatic Arts, Somerset House, the National Portrait Gallery, the National Maritime Museum and the Science Museum. And that's without all the smaller grants to beneficiaries like Christ Church, Spitalfields. ■

Theatre

The history of London theatre begins and, with the coming of the new Globe, almost ends with Shakespeare, but that's not to say other playwrights haven't got a word in too.

Little is known about drama before the 16th century when rowdy theatres were exiled to the south bank of the Thames around Southwark. The Globe was just one of a cluster of theatres, including the Swan, the Hope and the Rose; recently remains of the Rose, where *Titus Andronicus* and *Henry VI* were first performed, were excavated. Other playwrights working here included Beaumont and Fletcher, Thomas Middleton, Ben Jonson and Christopher Marlowe, who was killed in a tavern brawl in Deptford in 1593. Jonson wrote *Eastward Hoe* and *Bartholomew Fair*; Marlowe wrote *Dr Faustus* and *Edward II*.

The Puritans closed the theatres as dens of iniquity, but with the return of the monarchy came a revival with a spate of so-called Restoration comedies. Among the new writers were William Congreve (1670-1729), whose *The Way of the World* still gets occasional outings, John Dryden (1631-1700) and Sir John Vanbrugh (1664-1726), author of *The Provok'd Wife*.

By the 18th century the theatre was well established and largely respectable. These were the years when John Gay wrote his *Beggar's Opera*, a sort of *Les Misérables* of the 1720s set in Newgate Prison. In 1773 Oliver Goldsmith's *She Stoops to Conquer* was first staged, followed in 1775 by Richard Sheridan's *The Rivals* and, in 1777, *The School for Scandal*.

The 19th century saw the great comedies

of Oscar Wilde (1854-1900), *The Importance of Being Earnest* and *Lady Windermere's Fan*, hit the stage, although his precarious popularity was soon eclipsed by scandal, persecution and a jail sentence. George Bernard Shaw (1856-1950) produced such masterpieces as *Pygmalion*, *Major Barbara*, *Androcles and the Lion* and *Saint Joan*. Shaw and Wilde were both Irish by origin but moved to London for much of their working lives, as had Oliver Goldsmith before them.

Of the playwrights working in the first half of the 20th century who have continuing relevance, Noel Coward (1899-1973) was author of *Hay Fever*, *Blithe Spirit* and *Brief Encounter*, all given regular airings in the capital. Of JB Priestley's oeuvre, *An Inspector Calls* is rarely off the stage for long.

Despite the tendency to err on the side of conservatism and guaranteed box-office success, London's theatres (especially the subsidised theatres) still stage a wide range of plays by modern authors. Harold Pinter is known for his obscure language and storylines; *The Caretaker* and *The Homecoming*, the latter set in north London, are two of his best-known plays. Plays by David Hare and Simon Gray are likely to be more accessible to non-theatre addicts; check National Theatre listings to see if they're playing.

Alan Ayckbourn and Michael Frayn continue to turn out genuinely entertaining farces; *Absurd Person Singular* and *The Norman Conquests* are two of Ayckbourn's finest, *Noises Off* and *Donkey's Years* are two of Frayn's best.

If you don't think you could cope with Shakespeare the full monty, then note that the Reduced Shakespeare Company at the Criterion has been whipping through his plays in just 97 minutes for the last nine years.

Musicals The signs were already there in the 1960s when *Hair* and then *Jesus Christ Superstar* were phenomenal successes. Then, during the cash-strapped 1980s, London stages started to fill up with blockbusting musicals, proven favourites with audiences and therefore a safe bet for covering the bills. It sometimes seems as if they're all by Sir Andrew Lloyd-Webber *(Cats, Starlight Express, The Phantom of the Opera* and, of course, *JCS* itself) but probe more carefully and you'll find musicals by Lionel Bart *(Oliver)*, Boublil and Schonberg *(Miss Saigon, Martin Guerre* and *Les Misérables)*, Willy Russell *(Blood Brothers)* and even Cole Porter revivals.

Film

Like New York and San Francisco, London is one of those cities everyone knows before they get here because of the frequency of its film appearances.

The first sighting of Trafalgar Square on film dates back to 1889 but was hardly the widescreen, stereo offering your modern cinema-goer expects. A few pre-talkie films of the 1920s were set in London, but a London of film sets rather than location. For films using real London locations you have to jump a few decades and even then there can be deceptions, as in the 1964 film of *My Fair Lady*, shot in a mock-up of Covent Garden in California.

Alfred Hitchcock set several of his movies in London, including *The Lodger, Sabotage, The Man Who Knew Too Much, Stagefright* and the much later *Frenzy*. The villain in his *Blackmail*, the first British talking picture, came crashing through the massive glass dome of the British Museum Reading Room in the movie's climax.

Colin MacInnes' *Absolute Beginners* (1986) was set in the Notting Hill of the 1950s, but more films have celebrated the Swinging London of the 1960s. Foremost among these is Nicholas Roeg's *Performance* (1969) starring Mick Jagger and James Fox, but Antonioni's *Blow-Up* (1966), starring David Hemmings as a photographer, is usually seen as pretty essential. *Alfie* with Michael Caine and *Georgy Girl* with Lynn Redgrave (both 1966) homed in on the social changes that were taking place on a more workaday level.

Many film-makers have used London as a backdrop for crime stories, true or otherwise.

One of the earliest was *Ladykillers* (1955), starring Alec Guinness, which focused on a rather less dodgy-looking King's Cross than *Mona Lisa*, filmed there in 1986 and starring Cathy Tyson as a high-class callgirl who runs rings around Bob Hoskins. In *Dance with a Stranger* (1984), Miranda Richardson played Ruth Ellis, the last woman to be hanged in Britain, and Rupert Everett her faithless lover whom she finally killed. A nasty little film, *The Krays* (1990) was occasionally as violent as the twin East End gangsters it portrayed, but still somehow had audiences sympathising with them.

Other film-makers have looked at London life behind the front doors. *The Pumpkin Eater* (1964), with Anne Bancroft, homed in on the St John's Wood area, while Mike Leigh (*Life is Sweet*, *Naked* and *Secrets and Lies*) has preferred to concentrate on the more down-at-heel corners. A more unexpected romance was the one portrayed in Stephen Frear's *My Beautiful Laundrette* (1985), in which an ex-member of the National Front (played by Daniel Day-Lewis) teams up with a young Asian man somewhere in south London.

Docklands has provided a setting for all sorts of recent movies, including *The Long Good Friday* with Bob Hoskins, which preceded the redevelopment, *A Fish Called Wanda* and the quirky *Elephant Man*, about a deformed man who was exhibited as a fairground freak in Victorian London; some of this was filmed in Shad Thames before Terence Conran got his hands on it. In 1969 warehouses in St Katherine's Dock were actually set on fire for their part in *Battle of Britain*, which involved a reconstruction of the Blitz. More unexpectedly, parts of Stanley Kubrick's Vietnam epic *Full Metal Jacket* (1987) were also filmed in the derelict Royal Docks with a few palms dropped in for authenticity.

Royalty, especially Tudor and Stuart royalty, crop up time and again in films which showcase the best-known London landmarks. Some such films are *A Man for All Seasons*, the story of Sir Thomas More; *Lady Jane* (1985) in which Dover Castle stood in for the Tower of London, and *Cromwell* (1970), in which Alec Guinness played Charles I. More recently, scenes at Kew crop up in *The Madness of King George* with Nigel Hawthorne in the lead role.

Not surprisingly several Dickens stories have wound up on celluloid; the lengthy version of *Little Dorrit*, filmed in 1987, is regarded as the best of the genre, although *Great Expectations* (1946) is an interesting period piece. Shakespeare, too, has found his way onto film, although not always in the way one might expect; in *Richard III* (1995) the action has shifted to pre-war Britain, with sets including St Pancras station.

Some films incorporate scenes of London now lost forever. The old police epic *The Blue Lamp* (1949), for example, preserves footage of the area around Paddington Green which was levelled to make space for the Westway. Others present a futuristic look at the city as in Stanley Kubrick's notoriously violent *Clockwork Orange* (1971) which is no longer shown in England.

Some children's films with London settings include *Mary Poppins* (1964) in which our heroine floats across the city, and the original *One Hundred and One Dalmatians* (1961) with scenes of Scotland Yard.

Should you get a chance to see it, Patrick Keiller's art-house semi-documentary *London* (1994) is set around events in 1992. It's a wonderful one-off, full of details you'd never otherwise notice and with Paul Schofield as the smooth-voiced narrator.

For more details, see Colin Sorensen's *London on Film* (£14.95) produced by the Museum of London and on sale at the Museum of the Moving Image (MOMI).

Classical Music

London could lay fair claim to being the classical music capital of Europe, with five symphony orchestras, various smaller outfits, a brilliant array of venues, reasonable prices and high standards of performance. Despite this, Britain is not known for its great classical composers. Handel moved to London in 1710 and became a naturalised citizen in 1727, dying here in 1753; many of his

Italian operas and oratorios were written in London. JS Bach's youngest son, Johann Christian, also worked in London, which earned him the tag the 'English Bach'. Haydn, too, worked in London from 1791-2 and 1794-5, composing all his last 12 symphonies here; *No. 104 in D* is actually nicknamed the London Symphony.

But when it comes to composers actually born here you're mainly looking at Purcell (1659-95), Arne (1710-78), Elgar (1857-1934) and Vaughan Williams (1872-1958), composer of another London symphony. Virtuosos from this century include Benjamin Britten, author of the opera *Peter Grimes* and the orchestral work *Young Person's Guide to the Orchestra*, and William Walton, who wrote for the ballet and opera as well. Edward Elgar composed *Land of Hope and Glory*, Britain's unofficial national anthem and the tune which brings the Last Night of the Proms to its rowdy close.

Gilbert & Sullivan They're neither classical nor pop but the comic operas produced by WS Gilbert and Arthur Sullivan between 1875 and 1896 deserve a mention since their authors were Londoners; from 1882 onwards all their works were produced at the Savoy Theatre. The *Yeoman of the Guard*, written in 1888, is so far the only musical to be set inside the Tower of London. If you get a chance to see it, leave your prejudices at home – the songs are very whistleable.

Popular Music

Over the years, English musicians have had an enormous impact on popular music – much greater, strangely, than their influence on 'serious' music.

After Cliff Richard, England's pale imitation of Elvis Presley, Britain quickly snatched the musical lead from the United States. The swinging 60s produced The Beatles, the Rolling Stones, The Who and the Kinks. The late 60s and the glam years of the early 70s brought stardust-speckled heroes like David Bowie, Marc Bolan and Bryan Ferry, and bands like Fleetwood Mac, Pink Floyd, Deep Purple, Led Zeppelin and Genesis. Then came punk and its best known spokesmen, the Sex Pistols, The Clash and The Jam.

The turbulent, ever-changing music scene of the 80s invented the New Romantics and left-wing 'agit-pop', and also developed a chaotic club and rave scene featuring house and techno music. New bands that made it big included the Police, Eurythmics, Wham!, Duran Duran, Dire Straits, UB40 and The Smiths.

The Americans snatched back the cutting edge with Seattle grunge but recent years have seen the renaissance of the quintessentially English indie pop band with the likes of Suede, Pulp, Blur, Elastica and, above all, Oasis.

As in all things, London grabs the best for its own. By no means were all members of the aforementioned groups Londoners, but once the big-time beckoned most of them became honorary citizens of the capital. The Gallagher brothers may be Manchester lads but Supernova Heights is in Belsize Park, not Burnage.

Visual Arts

Although London is home to some astounding collections of art, English artists have never dominated an historical epoch in the way that Italian, French and Dutch artists have.

Although there are a few medieval gems like the Wilton Diptych to look out for, British art only really got into its stride with the Tudors. From the 1530s the Swiss artist Hans Holbein (1497-1543) lived in London and painted Henry VIII's court; one of his finest works, *The Ambassadors*, can be seen in the National Gallery. The English miniaturist Nicholas Hilliard (1547-1619) had similar access to the court of Queen Elizabeth I.

The 17th century saw a batch of great portrait artists working at the royal court. Best known is probably Sir Anthony van Dyck (1599-1641), a Belgian artist who spent the last nine years of his life in London and painted some hauntingly beautiful portraits of Charles I. Charles I was himself a great art lover; it was during his reign that many great paintings, including the *Raphael Cartoons* now in the National Gallery, came to England. Van Dyck was succeeded as court artist by Sir Peter Lely (1618-80), a German who moved to London in 1647 and a prolific producer of portraits, many of them on display in Hampton Court. He was succeeded as court artist by Sir Godfrey Kneller (1646-1723), another German resident in London from 1674, many of whose works can be seen in the National Portrait Gallery.

The 18th century saw art diversifying away from the obsession with court portraits. British-born artists also started to get into their stride. Thomas Gainsborough (1727-88) still went for portraits in a big way but at least some are of the gentry rather than the real aristocrats. In contrast, William Hogarth (1697-1764) is famous for his serial prints of London lowlife, most famously *The Rake's Progress* and *The Harlot's Progress*; look for his work at the Sir John Soane Museum and in his house in Chiswick. Thomas Rowlandson (1756-1827) went for gentler cartooning which nonetheless packed a punch; some are on display in the Courtauld.

Perhaps the quality of English light helps, but Britain has a fine tradition of watercolourists, beginning with the mystic poet-engraver William Blake (1757-1827) whose lovely pictures hang in the Tate. In sharp contrast Turner and Constable concentrated on painting sea scenes (Turner) and the English countryside (Constable); their works are scattered between the National Gallery and the Tate, with most of the Turner's in the Tate.

The pre-Raphaelite artists, Holman Hunt, Millais, Rossetti and Burne-Jones, threw aside such pastel-coloured rusticity, going instead for big, bright, detailed invocations of medieval legends which are of a piece with the gilded Gothic Revival architecture of men like Pugin.

Post-WWII names include Francis Bacon and Lucien Freud, both of whom concentrated on painting human figures, if in a distorted, grotesque way the pre-Raphaelites would never have recognised. David Hockney lightened things up with his pop-art realism and sketches of his dachshunds.

Recently, however, all the attention has been focused on artists like Damien Hirst and the late Helen Chadwick who sometimes seem as interested in shocking – half-cows preserved in formaldehyde (Hirst) and flowers sculpted from urine streams (Chadwick) – as in pleasing. Other names to watch for include Rachel Whiteread who famously turned a whole East End house into a sculpture only to see it knocked down, and Tracey Emin who erected a tent with the names of everyone she'd ever slept with sewn into it.

The same is as true of art as of pop – London patronage sucks in the talent from the provinces until in the end it's hard to remember that it originally came from elsewhere. Is Damien Hirst a Londoner? Who knows, but now that he's in fruitful partnership to revolutionise the London restaurant scene with that other immigrant to the capital, chef Marco Pierre White, it hardly seems worth asking.

SOCIETY & CONDUCT

Traditional Culture

The most common preconception of Londoners is of a reserved, inhibited and stiflingly polite bunch, although the public reaction to the death of Princess Diana suggested that this is a long outmoded stereotype. Still, tourists are often amazed at the silence on London tube trains, where the general approach is to get in, grab a seat, then open a newspaper or book and read it, studiously avoiding catching anyone's eye, let alone engaging in conversation. But London is one of the planet's most crowded cities and such behaviour is partly a protective veneer, essential for coping with the constant crush of people.

In general, Londoners are a pretty tolerant bunch, unfazed by outrageous dress or even outrageous behaviour. Indeed, the British pride themselves on ignoring anyone who's trying to draw attention to themselves – it just ain't cool to show an interest.

On the whole, this tolerance means low levels of racism, sexism or any other -ism.

The annual Gay Pride Festival is a vast celebration of homosexual culture which passes off without incident, and London has a long history of absorbing wave upon wave of new immigrants and refugees. But of course the picture can never be completely rosy. There are pockets of bigotry all over the capital, and the south-east, in particular, has been the scene of vicious, unprovoked racist attacks, even murders. Nor is the police force always as colour blind as people would like to believe.

Many visitors arrive in London expecting to find it populated by people conversing in cockney rhyming slang. Historically the cockneys were people born within the sound of the church bells of St Mary-le-Bow in the City. Since few people live in the City, this meant most cockneys were actually East Enders.

The cockney language is thought to have been developed by London's costermongers or street traders as a code to communicate without the police being able to understand them. Although the term cockney is often used to describe anyone speaking what is also called estuarine English (in which 't's and 'h's rarely put in an appearance), true cockney is also known as rhyming slang because it replaced common nouns and verbs with rhyming phrases. So 'going up the apples and pears' meant going up the stairs, the 'trouble and strife' was the wife, and 'would you Adam and Eve it?' meant would you believe it? Over time the second of the two words tended to be dropped so the rhyme vanished. But never fear – you are not about to be assailed by people speaking double Dutch. Few – if any – people still use pure cockney. You're more likely to come across it in residual phrases like 'use your loaf' ('loaf of bread' for head) or 'ooh, me plates of meat' (feet).

Closely linked with the cockneys are the Pearly Kings and Queens. Impoverished costermongers used to appoint their own 'kings' to represent them in brushes with the law. In the 19th century an orphan road-sweeper, Henry Croft, dreamt of creating a charity army to help the poor and sewed pearl buttons onto his clothes to attract attention. The coster kings were duly impressed and soon they too were decking themselves out in pearls to go fund-raising.

London's streets are no more packed with people in pearly suits than they are with folks speaking cockney, but you can see the massed ranks of Pearly Kings and Queens at their annual harvest festival in St Martin-in-the-Fields in early October. Each suit is made of something like 30,000 buttons sewn into mystic symbols like the sun, moon and stars; the most elaborate one ever had a grand 90,000 buttons.

Dos & Don'ts

London being the reasonably tolerant place it is, it's not particularly easy to cause offence without meaning to. That said, it's as well to be aware that most Londoners would no more speak to a stranger in the street than fly to the moon. If you're obviously a tourist battling with directions, there's no problem – but try starting a general conversation at the bus stop and you'll find people reacting as if you're mad.

Queuing The British are notoriously addicted to queuing, and many comedy sketches depend on the audience accepting that people might actually join a queue without knowing what it's for. The order of the queue is sacrosanct – few things are more calculated to spark an outburst of tutting than an attempt to 'push in' to a queue.

The Tube Given the vital role it plays, it's hardly surprising that the Underground has its own rigid, if unwritten, etiquette that starts as soon as you enter the station. Where there's an escalator you're expected to stand on the right so that people in a hurry or keen to get in some exercise can rush up or down on the left. Once on the platform you should move along, away from the entrance (this is vital for safety...bunched bodies blocking doorways could cause someone to fall on to the rails). When the train pulls in you're supposed to stand aside until everybody inside has got off.

Once inside, it's fine to rush for a seat. In theory you're supposed to give it up again to anyone in greater need (the elderly, disabled, pregnant women etc) but as the years go by Londoners get steadily worse at doing this. Putting your feet (or your bags) on the seats is not on. And if you see an unattended parcel or bag you should wait until you're in a station and then pull the communication cord to alert the guard.

Clothes In some countries what you wear or don't wear in churches can get you into trouble. In general, London is as free and easy about this as it is about how you dress in the streets. Bear in mind, however, that if you go into any of the city's mosques or temples you may be expected to take off your shoes and cover your arms, legs and/or head.

Some classy restaurants and many clubs operate strict dress codes. In restaurants that usually means a jacket and tie for men and no trainers for anyone; in clubs it means whatever the management and their bouncers choose it to mean and can vary from night to night. If in doubt, phone ahead to save embarrassment.

RELIGION

The Church of England, a Christian church that became independent of Rome in the 16th century (see Tudor London in History earlier in this chapter), is the largest, wealthiest and most influential in the land. It's an 'established' church, meaning it's the official national church, and it has a close relationship with the state: the queen or king appoints archbishops and bishops on the prime minister's advice.

It's difficult to generalise about the form of worship which varies from High church – full of pomp and ceremony, and close in many ways to Roman Catholicism – to Low church, which is less traditional and has been more influenced by Protestantism. In 1994, the first women were ordained as priests after many years of debate. Now the spotlight is on whether to accept practising homosexuals as priests.

Other significant Protestant churches include the Methodists, Baptists, the United Reformed Church and Salvation Army, all of which have had women priests for some years. Evangelical and charismatic churches are the only Christian movements which still seem to be gaining converts.

At various times since the 16th century Roman Catholics have been terribly persecuted; one modern legacy is the intractable problem of Northern Ireland. They didn't gain political rights until 1829 or a formal structure until 1850, but today about one in 10 Britons calls themselves Catholic.

But church attendances are falling steadily. Recent estimates suggest there are now well over one million Muslims, as well as significant congregations of Sikhs and Hindus. Nowadays more non-Christians visit their places of worship than do Christians.

LANGUAGE

The English language is perhaps England's most significant contribution to the modern world, but these days you'll hear a veritable Babel of languages being spoken in London. Indeed there are pockets of the capital where more people will be speaking languages other than English than are speaking it. You're unlikely to bump into many residents who can't understand English although behind closed doors there are many women in particular who speak only their mother tongue and depend on their children as translators.

TOM SMALLMAN

TOM SMALLMAN

PAT YALE

PAT YALE

MARK HONAN

PAT YALE

A	B	C
D	E	F

A: Clock at Selfridge's, Oxford St
B: Stroller with a bowler, Buckingham Palace
C: Street lamp, Chelsea
D: Statue of Dr Johnson behind St Clement Danes, Strand
E: London Marathon
F: Lady Jane Grey, Fleet St shop

PAT YALE

CHARLOTTE HINDLE

PAT YALE

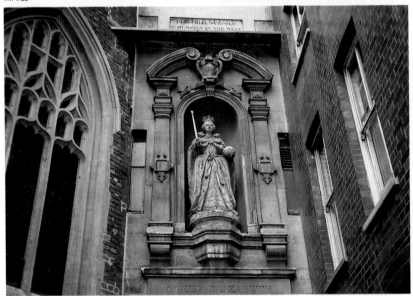

Left: Modern statue of Emperor Trajan in front of surviving stretch of the original Roman Wall near Tower of London
Right: Detail on Houses of Parliament
Bottom: Statue of Queen Elizabeth I outside St Dunstan-in-the-West, Fleet Street

Facts for the Visitor

WHEN TO GO

Unlike most of Britain, London is a year-round tourist centre, with few of its attractions closing or significantly reducing their opening hours in winter. While it's probably true to say that your best chance of good weather to appreciate the parks is in July and August, there's no cast-iron guarantee of sun even in those months. On the other hand, those are the months when you can expect the worst crowds and highest prices.

If you can pick a time to travel it's probably better to opt for April/May or September/October when there's still a better than average chance of some good weather but the queues for popular attractions are shorter. Opting for these off-peak times should also reduce the cost of getting to London and may mean slightly cheaper room rates in some hotels. Of course, if you don't mind braving the winter winds, the cheapest air fares and hotel rates are likely to be obtainable from November through to March. At those times even real favourites like Madame Tussaud's and the British Museum are not too unmanageably crowded ... although be warned that noisy school groups often take up the tourist slack!

ORIENTATION

London's main geographical feature is the Thames, a tidal river that enabled an easily defended port to be established far from the dangers of the English Channel. Flowing around wide bends from west to east, it divides the city into northern and southern halves.

London sprawls over an enormous area. Fortunately, the Underground system (the 'tube') makes most of it easily accessible, and the ubiquitous (though geographically misleading) Underground map is easy to use. Any train heading from left to right on the map is designated as eastbound, any train heading from top to bottom is southbound. Each line has its own colour.

Most important sights, theatres, restaurants and even some cheap places to stay lie within a reasonably compact rectangle formed by the tube's Circle line, just to the north of the river. All the international airports lie some distance from the city centre but transport is easy. See the Getting Around section later for details on airport transport.

London blankets mostly imperceptible hills, but there are good views from Primrose Hill (adjoining Regent's Park), Hampstead Heath (north of Camden), and Greenwich Park (downriver east of central London).

Throughout this chapter, the nearest tube station has been given with addresses; the Central London map shows the location of tube stations and the areas covered by the detailed district maps. The London Postal Areas map in this chapter will also be helpful, especially for locating outlying suburbs.

> **Phone Codes**
> All phone numbers in this chapter should be prefixed with the code ☎ 0171 unless the text says otherwise.
> If calling from within central London, it is not necessary to use the 0171 code. ■

The City & the East

The City refers to the area that was once the Roman and medieval walled city, before the inexorable colonisation of the surrounding towns and villages began. Although it lies in the south-eastern corner of the Circle line, the City is regarded as the centre of London. As you may have guessed, the West End (much more the tourist centre) lies to the west of the City.

The City is one of the world's most important financial centres; full of bankers and dealers during the working week, deserted outside work hours. The same is not true of its most famous sights: the Tower of London, St Paul's Cathedral and Petticoat Lane market.

To the east, beyond the Circle line, is the East End, once the exclusive habitat of the cockney, now a cultural melting pot. The East End incorporates districts like Shoreditch and Bethnal Green, with some lively corners and relatively cheap rents. In general though it's blighted by traffic and urban decay. Much of the East End was flattened during WWII and it still shows.

Further east again lie the Docklands. Once part of the busiest port in the world, these thousands of acres of prime real estate fell into disuse after WWII, mirroring the decline of the empire. In the early 1980s, a light railway was built and the property developers moved in.

The West

West of the City, but before the West End proper, are Holborn and Bloomsbury. Holborn (pronounced hoeburn) is Britain's sedate legal heartland, the home of Rumpole and common law. Bloomsbury is still synonymous with the literary and publishing worlds. Besides dozens of specialist shops, this is where you'll find the incomparable British Museum, stuffed to the hilt with loot from every corner of the globe.

The West End proper lies west of Tottenham Court Rd and Covent Garden, which is tourist-ridden but fun, and south of Oxford St, an endless succession of department stores. It includes such magnets as Trafalgar Square, the restaurants and clubs of predominantly gay Soho, the famous West End cinemas and theatres around Piccadilly Circus and Leicester Square, and the elegant shops of Regent and Bond Sts – not forgetting Mayfair, the most valuable property on the Monopoly board.

St James's and Westminster lie to the south-west. This is where you'll find Whitehall, No 10 Downing St, the Houses of Parliament, Big Ben, Westminster Abbey and Buckingham Palace.

To the south of Victoria station lies Pimlico, not a particularly attractive district but with a good supply of cheapish, decentish hotels to top up the lure of the Tate Gallery.

Earl's Court, South Kensington and Chelsea are in the south-west corner formed by the Circle line. Earl's Court, once infamous as Kangaroo Valley and home to countless expatriate Australians, now feels more Middle Eastern but still boasts the drawcards of some cheap hotels, several backpackers' hostels and a couple of Australian pubs, plus cheap restaurants and travel agents. It's still a good enough place to start your visit.

South Kensington is much more chic and trendy, with a clutch of world-famous museums (the Victoria & Albert, Science and Natural History). Chelsea is no longer so much bohemian as expensively chic. King's Rd has bid farewell to the punks but remains an interesting place to hunt out youthful fashion.

Further west you come to some very comfortable residential districts like Richmond and Chiswick. Sites worth trekking out west for include Hampton Court Palace, Kew Gardens and Syon House.

The North

Notting Hill is a lively, interesting district, with a large West Indian population. It gets trendier by the day, but the Portobello Rd market is still fun and there are pubs, lively bars and interesting shops.

North of Kensington Gardens and Hyde Park, Bayswater and Paddington are virtual tourist ghettos, but there are plenty of hostels, cheap and mid-range hotels, good pubs and interesting restaurants (particularly along Queensway and Westbourne Grove).

From west to east, the band of suburbs to the north of the Central Line include Kilburn, Hampstead, Camden Town, Highgate, Highbury and Islington. Kilburn is London's Irish capital amid bedsit land. Hampstead, with its great views and the marvellous heath, is quiet, civilised and extremely expensive, while Camden Town, although well on its way to gentrification, still nurtures a gaggle of over-populated but enjoyable weekend markets.

In the mid-1990s Islington shot to fame as the home of the Blairs, where some of the strategies which won Labour the election of 1997 were worked out. In Upper St it also boasts one of London's most densely packed array of eating places.

The South

Cross the Thames from central London and you could be excused for thinking you've arrived in a different country. This is working-class London and it seems a long way from the elegant, antiseptic streets of Westminster. Much of south London, especially to the east, is still distressingly poor and run-down.

Even short-term visitors are likely to want to take in cultural oases like the South Bank Centre (a venue for interesting exhibitions and concerts) and Wimbledon with its tennis courts. Beautiful Greenwich is also home to the *Cutty Sark*, and contains superb architecture, open space and the Prime Meridian – and that's before it takes delivery of the Dome which is to play the starring role in the forthcoming Millennium Experience!

If you stay for any length of time, however, there's a fair chance you'll end up living in suburbs like Clapham, Brixton or Camberwell, although westerly suburbs like Putney and Wimbledon are more inviting.

Notorious for racial problems in the early 1980s, Brixton is definitely no Harlem, even though unemployment is high and the crumbling buildings and piles of rubbish may look the part. You'll enjoy its tatty market and arcades whatever your skin colour. Most of the district is as safe as anywhere else, but don't wander too far off the main streets until someone locates the 'front line' for you – an area around Railton Rd which is best left to the locals.

MAPS

A decent map is vital. Preferably get a single-sheet map so you can see all of central London at a glance; the British Tourist Authority (BTA) produces a good one.

If you're only staying for a few days that may be all you need. For a longer stay you might want to invest in either the *A-Z Map of London* or the *A-Z Visitor's Atlas & Guide* (both £2.25). The foldout map has the advantage that the place you want is never on the join between two pages. However, the map books are sometimes easier to consult and are less likely to label you a tourist. A bit longer in the capital and it becomes worth investing in a *Mini A-Z* for £3.45. Finally, if you're in for the long-haul you'll need to buy the fully-fledged *A-Z London* atlas which shows the city down to its smallest side street and without which social life in the capital would come to a halt.

Two other maps are vital for getting around London. The first is the map of the Underground network reproduced in this book; it's a design classic which shows not just where the stations are in relation to each other but which zone they lie in, something you need to know to buy the right ticket.

To identify all London's bus routes you'd need to cart around 36 separate map sheets. Luckily the whole of central London is covered on sheet No 1 which should see you through. If you do need a local bus map phone ☎ 371 0247 or write to London Transport Buses (CDL), Freepost Lon7503, London SE16 4BR, stating which route you're interested in.

TOURIST OFFICES

London is a major travel centre, so aside from information on London it also houses offices that deal with England, Scotland, Wales, Ireland and most countries worldwide.

Local Tourist Offices

British Travel Centre The British Travel Centre, 12 Regent St, Piccadilly Circus SW1Y 4PQ (Map 3) is two minutes walk from Piccadilly Circus tube. This chaotic and comprehensive information and booking centre offers information on tours, theatre tickets, train, air and car travel, and accommodation. It also houses a *bureau de change*, a map and guidebook shop, and the Welsh and Irish tourist boards. It's very busy but open every day: Monday to Friday from 9 am to 6.30 pm, Saturday and Sunday from 10 am to 4 pm (Saturday from 9 am to 5 pm between May and September). For general inquiries phone ☎ 0181-846 9000.

Tourist Information Centres There are Tourist Information Centres (TICs) at Heathrow Terminal 3 and the Heathrow Terminals 1 to 3 Underground station concourse, and at Gatwick, Luton and Stansted airports. As well as providing information, the main centre on the Victoria train station forecourt handles accommodation bookings, and has a book and map shop. It's open daily from 8 am to 7 pm, and can be extremely busy. There's also a TIC at the Arrivals Hall in Waterloo International Terminal and one in the Liverpool St Underground station which is open Monday to Saturday from 8 am to 6 pm and from 8.30 am to 5 pm on Sunday.

The City of London Corporation also maintains an information centre (☎ 332 1456) in St Paul's Churchyard, opposite St Paul's Cathedral. From April to September it's open daily from 9.30 am to 5 pm, closing Saturday afternoons and Sundays for the rest of the year. It doesn't handle accommodation queries.

Other, possibly less overstretched, TICs can be contacted at:

Bexley
: Central Library, Townley Rd, Bexleyheath DA5 1PQ (☎ 0181-303 9052)

Croydon
: Katherine St, Croydon CR9 1ET (☎ 0181-253 1009)

Greenwich
: 46 Greenwich Church St SE10 (☎ 0181-858 6376)

Hackney
: Central Hall, Mare St E8 (☎ 0181-985 9055)

Harrow
: Civic Centre, Station Rd, Harrow HA1 2UJ (☎ 0181-424 1103)

Hillingdon
: Central Library, 14 High St, Uxbridge UB8 1HD (☎ 01895-250706)

Hounslow
: Library Centre, Treaty Centre, Hounslow High St, Hounslow (☎ 0181-572 8279)

Islington
: 11 Duncan St N1 (☎ 278 8787)

Kingston-upon-Thames
: Market House, Market Place, Kingston-upon-Thames, Surrey KT1 2PS (☎ 0181-547 5592)

Lewisham
: Lewisham Library, Lewisham High St SE13 (☎ 0181-297 8317)

Richmond
: Old Town Hall, Whittaker Ave, Richmond, Surrey (☎ 0181-940 9125)

Southwark
: Hay's Galleria, Tooley St SE1 (☎ 403 8299)

Tower Hamlets
: 107A Commercial St E1 (☎ 375 2549)

Twickenham
: The Atrium, Civic Centre, York St, Twickenham, Middlesex (☎ 0181-891 7272)

Written inquiries should be sent to 26 Grosvenor Gardens SW1W 0DU (☎ 730 3488).

Given how busy the tourist offices are you may prefer to make use of their Visitor Call system. You simply dial ☎ 0839-123 and then add another three digits depending on the information you're after. Bear in mind that these are premium-rated calls costing 49p a minute plus any surcharge your hotel may make for using the phone. These numbers can only be dialled within the UK:

What's on this week	400
What's on for the next three months	401
What to do on Sunday	407
Summer in the Parks	406
Christmas & Easter Events	418
Changing the Guard	411
Current Exhibitions	403
Rock & Pop Concerts	422
State Opening of Parliament & Trooping the Colour	413
Getting Around London	430
River Trips/Booking a Boat	432
Guided Tours & Walks	431
Booking a Guide/Bespoke Guided Tours	420
Getting to the Airports	433
Shopping News	486
Street Markets	428
Dining Out	485
What's on for Children	404
Places to Visit with Children	424
Popular West End Shows	416
Beyond the West End	434

Tourist Offices Abroad

The British Tourist Authority (BTA) stocks masses of information, much of it free. Contact the BTA before you leave home because some discounts are only available to people who book before arriving in Britain. Travellers with special needs (be it disability, diet etc) should also contact the nearest BTA office.

Addresses of some overseas offices are as follows:

Australia
: Level 16, The Gateway, 1 Macquarie Place, Circular Quay, Sydney, NSW 2000 (☎ 02-9377 4400; fax 02-9377 4499)

Canada
: Suite 450, 111 Avenue Rd, Toronto, Ontario M5R 3JD (☎ 416-925 6326; fax 416-961 2175)

Denmark
: Montergade 3, 1116 Copenhagen K (☎ 33 33 91 88)

France
: Tourisme de Grand-Bretagne, Maison de la Grande Bretagne, 19 Rue des Mathurins, 75009 Paris (entrance in les Rues Tronchet et Auber) (☎ 01 44 51 56 20)

Germany
: Taunusstrasse 52-60, 60329 Frankfurt (☎ 069-238 0711)

Ireland
: 18-19 College Green, Dublin 2 (☎ 01-670 8000)

Italy
: Corso V, Emanuele 337, 00186 Rome (☎ 06-6880 6464)

Netherlands
: Stadhouderskade 2 (5e), 1054 ES Amsterdam (☎ 020-685 50 51)

New Zealand
: 3rd floor, Dilworth Building, corner Queen & Customs Sts, Auckland 1 (☎ 09-303 1446); fax 09-776 965)

Norway
: Postbox 1554 Vika, 0117 Oslo 1 (☎ 095 468 212444)

Singapore
: 24 Raffles Place, 20-01 Clifford Centre, Singapore 0104 (☎ 535 2966)

South Africa
: Lancaster Gate, Hyde Lane, Hyde Park, Sandton 2196 (☎ 011-325 0343)

Spain
: Torre de Madrid 6/5, Plaza de Espana 18, 28008 Madrid (☎ 91-541 13 96)

Sweden
: Klara Norra Kyrkogata 29, S 111 22 Stockholm (☎ 08-21 24 44)

Switzerland
: Limmatquai 78, CH-8001 Zürich (☎ 01-261 42 77)

USA
: 625 N Michigan Avenue, Suite 1510, Chicago IL 60611 (personal callers only)
: 551 Fifth Avenue, Suite 701, New York, NY 10176-0799 (☎ 1 800 GO 2 BRITAIN)

Other Information

There's no shortage of information on every aspect of life in London. The problem is wading through it.

Time Out, the London listings magazine issued every Tuesday (£1.70), is a mind-bogglingly complete listing of what's on where. The same company publishes the *Time Out Guide to Eating & Drinking in London* (£8.50), which lists over 1700 restaurants and bars.

The Saturday *Guardian* newspaper (70p) includes *The Guide*, a useful summary of what's happening during the week. Thursday's *Evening Standard* (30p) has its own weekly what's on magazine.

If you balk at paying for information, *TNT*, *Traveller* and *SA Times* are free magazines and papers available from pavement bins, especially in Earl's Court, Notting Hill and Bayswater. They have Australian, New Zealand and South African news and sports results but are invaluable for any budget traveller, with entertainment listings, excellent travel sections, and useful classifieds covering jobs, cheap tickets, shipping services and accommodation. *TNT* is the glossiest and most comprehensive; phone ☎ 373 3377 for the nearest distribution point.

Loot (£1.30) is a daily paper made up of classified ads that are placed free by sellers.

You can find everything from second-hand wrestling magazines to kitchen sinks and cars, as well as an extensive selection of flats and house-share ads. Also worth considering, if you're planning some serious shopping, is the *Time Out Guide to Shopping & Services* (£6).

Capital Radio has a number of useful helplines. For general information phone ☎ 388 7575.

For information on buses, trains and the tube, see the Getting Around chapter; for connections further afield, see the Getting There & Away chapter.

VISAS & DOCUMENTS

With a few notable exceptions (like for Iraq), London is an excellent place to gather information and visas.

Visas

A visa is a stamp in your passport permitting you to enter a country for a specified period of time. Visa regulations are always subject to change, so it's essential to check with your local British embassy, high commission or consulate before leaving home.

Currently, if you're a citizen of Australia, Canada, New Zealand, South Africa or the USA, you're given 'leave to enter' Britain at your place of arrival. Tourists from these countries are generally permitted to stay for up to six months, but are prohibited from working. If you're a citizen of the European Union (EU), you may live and work in Britain free of immigration control – you don't need a visa to enter the country. Other citizens will find it very difficult to get permission to stay for anything longer than a short holiday (see Work Permits for the exceptions).

The immigration authorities have always been tough, and this can only get worse; dress neatly and carry proof that you have sufficient funds to support yourself. A credit card and/or an onward ticket will help. People have been refused entry because they were carrying papers (such as references) that suggested they intended to work.

Several travel companies offer quick foreign visa services at a cost. Trailfinders (☎ 938 3999), 194 Kensington High St W8 (Map 8), handles visas and Top Deck, 131 Earl's Court Rd SW5 (Map 8), hosts the Rapid Visa Service (☎ 373 3026).

Visa Extensions

Tourist visas can only be extended in clear emergencies (following an accident, for example). Otherwise you'll have to leave Britain (perhaps going to Ireland or France) and apply for a fresh visa. However, too many such new visas are likely to arouse suspicion.

Student Visas

Nationals of EU countries can enter the country to study without formalities. Otherwise you need to be enrolled on a full-time course of at least 15 hours a week of weekday, daytime study at one educational institution to be allowed to stay as a student. For more details, you must consult the British Embassy or High Commission in your own country.

Work Permits

EU nationals don't need a work permit to work in London, but everyone else does to work legally. If the *main* purpose of your visit is to work, you basically have to be sponsored by a British company.

However, if you're a citizen of a Commonwealth country aged between 17 and 27 inclusive, you may apply for a Working Holiday Entry Certificate that allows you to spend up to two years in the UK and take work that is 'incidental' to a holiday. You're not allowed to engage in business, pursue a career, or provide services as a professional sportsperson or entertainer.

You must apply to the nearest UK mission overseas – Working Holiday Entry Certificates are *not* granted on arrival in Britain. It's not possible to switch from being a visitor to a working holidaymaker, nor is it possible to claim back any time spent out of the UK during the two-year period. When you apply, you must satisfy the authorities you have the means to pay for a return or onward journey, and will be able to maintain yourself without recourse to public funds.

If you're a Commonwealth citizen and have a parent born in the UK, you may be eligible for a Certificate of Entitlement to the Right of Abode, which means you can live and work in Britain free of immigration control.

If you're a Commonwealth citizen with a grandparent born in the UK, or if the grandparent was born before 31 March 1922 in what is now the Republic of Ireland, you may qualify for a UK Ancestry – Employment Certificate, which means you can work full time for up to four years in the UK.

Visiting students from the USA can get a work permit allowing them to work for six months; you have to be at least 18 years old and a full-time student at a college or university. It costs US$200 and is available through the Council on International Educational Exchange (☎ 212-661 1414), 205 East 42nd St, New York, NY 10017.

If you have any queries once you're in the UK, contact the Home Office, Immigration & Nationality Department (☎ 0181-686 0688), Lunar House, Wellesley Rd, Croydon CR2 (station: East Croydon). It's open Monday to Friday from 9 am to 4 pm. For information on employment opportunities, see under Work later in this chapter.

Photocopies

Copy your passport, air tickets, insurance policy, and serial numbers of your camera and travellers cheques before you leave home. Take one set of copies with you (keeping them separate from the original documents) and leave a second set with someone responsible in your home country.

Travel Insurance

Whichever way you're travelling, make sure you take out a comprehensive travel insurance policy which covers you for medical expenses and luggage theft or loss, and for cancellation or delays in your travel arrangements. Ticket loss should also be covered, but make sure you have a separate record of all the details – or better still, a photocopy of the ticket. There are all sorts of policies but the international student travel policies handled by STA Travel and other student travel organisations are usually good value. Some policies offer lower and higher medical expense options – unless you're eligible for free treatment under the NHS (see under Health later in this chapter), go for as much as you can afford. Others are cheaper if you forego cover for lost baggage.

Buy insurance as early as possible. If you buy it the week before you fly, you may find that you're not covered for delays to your flight caused by strikes or other industrial action. Always read the small print carefully for let-out loopholes for the insurers.

Paying for your ticket with a credit card often provides limited travel accident insurance, and you may be able to reclaim the payment if the operator doesn't deliver. In the UK, credit card providers are required by law to reimburse consumers if a company goes into liquidation and the amount in contention is more than £100.

Driving Licence & Permits

Unless you're hiring a car, you should always carry a Vehicle Registration Document as proof that you own the vehicle you're driving. Your normal driving licence is legal for 12 months from the date you last entered Britain; you can then apply for a British licence at post offices. It's not a bad idea to carry an International Driving Permit (IDP) as well. This should be obtainable from your local automobile association for a small fee.

Hostelling International Card

To stay in London's HI/YHA hostels you must be a member of the organisation. If not you'll be charged a £1.55 surcharge for the first six nights which will add up to becoming a member.

Student & Youth Cards

Most useful is the International Student Identity Card (ISIC), a plastic ID-style card with your photograph which costs £5 and can produce discounts on many forms of transport. Even if you have your own transport, the card will soon pay for itself through cheap or free admission to museums and sights, and cheap meals in some student restaurants.

There's a worldwide industry in fake student cards, and many places now stipulate a maximum age for student discounts or, more simply, substitute a 'youth discount' for a 'student discount'. If you're aged under 26 but not a student, you can apply for a Federation of International Youth Travel Organisations (FIYTO) card or a Euro26 Card which gives much the same discounts for the same £5 fee.

Both types of card are issued by student unions, hostelling organisations or student travel agencies.

London White Card

If you plan to do a lot of sightseeing the London White Card offers free admission to 15 museums and galleries. It costs £15 for three days or £25 for seven days. Family cards, offering free admission for up to two adults and four children, cost £30 and £50.

Tickets are available from tourist information centres, London Transport information centres and the London Visitor Centre at the Waterloo International terminal. They're also available at the participating museums: Apsley House (Wellington Museum), Barbican Art Gallery, Courtauld, Design Museum, Hayward Gallery, Imperial War Museum, London Transport Museum, Museum of London, Museum of the Moving Image, National Maritime Museum (with Old Royal Observatory and Queen's House), Natural History Museum, Royal Academy, Science Museum, Theatre Museum and Victoria & Albert Museum.

Seniors' Cards

Many attractions offer reduced price admission for people over 60 or 65; it's always worth asking even if you can't see a discount listed. The railways also offer a Senior Citizen Railcard (see Getting There & Away for details).

EMBASSIES

British Embassies Abroad

Some British embassies abroad are:

Australia – British High Commission
  Commonwealth Ave, Yarralumla, Canberra, ACT 2600 (☎ 02-6270 6666)

Canada – British High Commission
  80 Elgin St, Ottawa, Ont KIP 5K7 (☎ 613-237 1530)

New Zealand – British High Commission
  44 Hill St, Wellington 1 (☎ 04-472 6049)

South Africa – British High Commission
  91 Parliament St, Cape Town 8001 (☎ 27-21-461 7220)

USA – British Embassy
  3100 Massachusetts Ave, NW, Washington, DC 20008 (☎ 202-462 1340)

Foreign Embassies in London

Some foreign embassies in London are:

Australian High Commission
  Australia House, Strand WC2 (☎ 379 4334; tube: Temple; Map 3)

Belgian Consulate
  103 Eaton Square SW1 (☎ 470 3700; tube: Victoria)

Canadian High Commission
  Macdonald House, 38 Grosvenor St W1 (☎ 629 9492; tube: Bond St)

French Consulate General
  6A Cromwell Place SW7 (☎ 838 2050; tube: South Kensington)

German Embassy
  23 Belgrave Square SW1 (☎ 824 1300; tube: Hyde Park Corner)

Italian Consulate
  38 Eaton Place SW1 (☎ 235 9371; tube: Sloane Square)

Japanese Embassy
  101-04 Piccadilly, London W1 (☎ 465 6500; tube: Bond St)

New Zealand High Commission
  New Zealand House, 80 Haymarket SW1 (☎ 973 0363; tube: Piccadilly Circus; Map 3)

Royal Netherlands Embassy
  38 Hyde Park Gate SW7 (☎ 584 5040; tube: Gloucester Rd)

Russian Embassy
  5 Kensington Palace Gardens W8 (☎ 229 8027; tube: High St Kensington)

South African High Commission
  South Africa House, Trafalgar Square WC2 (☎ 930 4488; tube: Trafalgar Square; Map 3)

Spanish Consulate General
2 Draycott Place SW3 (☎ 581 5921; tube: Sloane Square)
US Embassy
5 Upper Grosvenor St W1 (☎ 499 9000; tube: Bond St; Map 2)

CUSTOMS

Britain has a two-tier customs system, the first for goods bought duty free, the second for goods bought in an EU country where taxes and duties have already been paid.

Tax & Duty Paid

The second tier is relevant because several products (including alcohol and tobacco) are much cheaper on the continent. Under the rules of the single market, as long as taxes have been paid somewhere in the EU there are no additional taxes to export the goods to another EU country – provided they're for individual consumption. A thriving business has developed, with many Londoners making day trips to France to load up their cars with cheap grog and cigarettes – the savings can more than pay for a trip, though the duty-free allowances are due to end in the summer of 1999.

If you purchase from a normal retail outlet, customs use the following maximum quantities as a guideline to distinguish personal imports from those on a commercial scale: 800 cigarettes or 1kg of tobacco, 10L of spirits, 20L of fortified wines, 90L of wine (of which not more than 60L are sparkling) and 110L of beer!

Duty Free

If you buy from a duty free shop, you're allowed to import 200 cigarettes or 250g of tobacco, 2L of still wine plus 1L of spirits or another 2L of wine (sparkling or otherwise), 60cc of perfume, 250cc of toilet water, and other duty-free goods (including cider and beer) to the value of £71 (EU countries) or £136 (non-EU countries).

MONEY

The British currency is the pound sterling (£), with 100 pence (p) to a pound. One and 2p coins are copper; 5p, 10p, 20p and 50p coins are silver; and the bulky £1 coin is gold (coloured). A new £2 was also due to be introduced in 1998.

Notes (bills) come in £5, £10, £20 and £50 denominations and vary in colour and size.

Carrying Money

However you decide to carry your funds, it makes sense to keep most of it out of easy reach of snatch thieves in a money-belt or similar. You might want to stitch an inside pocket into your skirt or trousers to keep an emergency stash; certainly it makes sense to keep something like £50 apart from the rest of your cash in case of an emergency.

Take particular care in crowded places like the London Underground, and never leave wallets sticking out of trouser pockets or daypacks.

Cash

Although nothing beats cash for risk, it's still a good idea to travel with some sterling cash, if only to tide you over until you get to an exchange facility. There's no problem if you arrive at any of London's five airports; all have good-value exchange counters open for incoming flights.

Travellers Cheques

Travellers cheques exist to offer protection from theft. Ideally your cheques should be in pounds, preferably issued by American Express or Thomas Cook which are widely recognised, well represented and don't charge for cashing their own cheques. Thomas Cook has offices and bureaux de change all over London. There are also plenty of Amex offices about town; look in the phonebook for the nearest branch.

Bring most cheques in large denominations. It's only towards the end of a stay that you may want to change a small cheque to make sure you don't get left with too much local currency.

In London, travellers cheques are rarely accepted outside banks or used for everyday transactions so you need to cash them in advance.

Lost or Stolen Travellers Cheques Keep a record of the cheque numbers and the cheques you have cashed, then if they're lost or stolen you will be able to tell the issuing agency exactly which cheques are gone. Keep this list separate from the cheques themselves.

As soon as you realise any cheques are missing, you should contact the issuing office or the nearest branch of the issuing agency. Thomas Cook (☎ 01733-318950) and American Express (☎ 01222-666111) can often arrange replacement cheques within 24 hours.

Cashpoint Machines (ATMs)

Plastic cards make the perfect travelling companions – they're ideal for major purchases and let you withdraw cash from selected banks and cashpoint machines or automatic telling machines (ATMs). ATMs are usually linked up internationally, so you can shove your card in, punch in a personal identification number (PIN) and get instant cash. But ATMs aren't fail-safe, especially if the card was issued outside Europe, and it's safer to go to a human teller – it can be a headache if an ATM swallows your card.

Credit cards usually aren't hooked up to ATM networks unless you specifically ask your bank to do this and request a PIN number. You should also ask which ATMs in England will accept your particular card. Cash cards, which you use at home to withdraw money directly from your bank account or savings account, are becoming more widely linked internationally – ask your bank at home for advice.

Credit, Debit & Charge Cards

Visa, MasterCard, American Express and Diners Club cards are widely accepted in London (Access is being phased out), although most B&Bs prefer cash. Businesses are allowed to make a charge for accepting payment by credit card so this isn't always the most economical way to pay. You can get cash advances using your Visa card at the Midland Bank and Barclays, or using MasterCard/Access at NatWest, Lloyds and Barclays. If you have an American Express card, you can cash up to £500 worth of personal cheques at American Express offices in any seven-day period.

If you plan to use a credit card make sure you have a high enough credit limit to cover major expenses like car hire or airline tickets. Alternatively, leave your card in credit when you start your travels.

If you're going to rely on plastic, go for two different cards – an American Express or Diners Club with a Visa or MasterCard. Better still, combine plastic and travellers cheques so you have something to fall back on if an ATM swallows your card or the bank won't accept it.

Lost or Stolen Cards If any of your cards are lost or stolen you should inform the police and the issuing company as soon as possible; provided you do so you shouldn't have to pay for purchases you didn't make. Here are some numbers for cancelling your cards:

American Express (☎ 01273-696933/689955)
Diners Club (☎ 01252-516261)
MasterCard (☎ 01702-362988)
Visa (☎ 0800-895082)

International Transfers

If you instruct your bank back home to send you a draft make sure you specify the bank and the branch to which you want your money directed, or ask your home bank to tell you where a suitable one is. The whole procedure will be easier if you've authorised someone back home to access your account.

Money sent by telegraphic transfer should reach you within a week; by mail, allow at least two weeks. When it arrives, it will most likely be converted into local currency – you can take it as it is or buy travellers cheques. The charge for this service is likely to be about £15.

You can also transfer money by American Express or Thomas Cook or by post office moneygram. Americans can also use Western Union although it has fewer offices in London from which to collect.

Changing Money

Changing money is never a problem in London, with banks, bureaux de change and travel agencies all competing for your business. What is harder is to be sure that you're getting the best possible deal. Be particularly careful using bureaux de change; they may seem to offer good exchange rates but frequently levy outrageous commissions (branches of Chequepoint charge 8% to cash a sterling travellers cheque) and fees. To be sure you're getting the best deal you need to check the exchange rate, the percentage commission and any minimum charge very carefully.

The bureaux at the international airports charge less than most high street banks and cash sterling travellers cheques free; on other currencies they charge 1.5% with a £3 minimum. They also guarantee that you can buy up to £500 worth of most major currencies on the spot.

There are 24-hour exchange bureaux in Heathrow Terminals 1, 3 and 4. Terminal 2's bureau is open daily from 6 am to 11 pm. Thomas Cook has branches at Terminals 1, 3 and 4. There are 24-hour bureaux in Gatwick's South and North Terminals and at Stansted; at Luton and the City airport bureaux will be open for arrivals and departures.

The main American Express office (☎ 930 4411), 6 Haymarket (tube: Piccadilly Circus; Map 3), is open for currency exchange Monday to Friday from 9 am to 5.30 pm, Saturday from 9 am to 6 pm, and Sunday from 10 am to 5 pm. Other services are available weekdays from 9 am to 5 pm and Saturday from 9 am to noon.

The main Thomas Cook office (☎ 499 4000), 45 Berkeley St (tube: Green Park), is open from 9 am (10 am on Thursday) to 5.30 pm Monday to Friday, and from 9 am to 4 pm on Saturday. There are many branches scattered around central London. The bureau at Victoria railway station, near the tourist office, is open daily from 6 am to 11 pm.

Bank hours vary, but you'll be safe if you visit between 9.30 am and 3.30 pm Monday to Friday (Friday afternoons get very busy). Some banks also open on Saturday, generally from 9.30 am till noon but sometimes all day.

Buying Currency & Travellers Cheques If you're buying currency or travellers cheques, the cost varies considerably depending on where you shop. Branches of American Express are often cheapest, charging 1% commission with no minimum charge. Main post offices also offer very competitive rates. The banks are usually more expensive and often want advance warning: NatWest charges 1% commission for sterling travellers cheques, with a £4 minimum charge; Lloyds, Midland and Barclays all charge 1.5% commission, with a minimum charge of £3.

Exchange Rates

Exchange rates at the time of going to press were:

Australia	A$1	=	£0.42
Canada	C$1	=	£0.42
France	1FF	=	£0.10
Germany	DM1	=	£0.34
Ireland	£1	=	£0.89
Japan	¥100	=	£0.46
New Zealand	NZ$1	=	£0.37
USA	US$1	=	£0.59

Costs

London prices can seem absolutely horrific, especially to anyone trying to stick to a tight budget. You will need to budget £22 to £30 a day for bare survival. Dormitory accommodation alone will cost from £10 to £20 a night, a one-day travel card is £3.60, and drinks and the most basic sustenance will cost you at least £6, with any sightseeing or nightlife costs on top. There's not much point visiting if you can't enjoy some of the city's life, so if possible add another £15 a day.

Costs will be even higher if you choose to stay in a central B&B or hotel and eat restaurant meals. B&B rates start at around £20 per person and a restaurant meal tends to average £10. Add a couple of pints of beer (£3) and entry fees to a tourist attraction or nightclub and you could easily spend £55 a day without being extravagant.

Tipping & Bargaining

If you eat in a restaurant you should expect to leave a 10 to 15% tip unless the service was unsatisfactory. Waiting staff are often paid derisory wages on the assumption that the money will be supplemented by tips. It's legal for restaurants to include a service charge on the bill, but this should be clearly advertised. You needn't add a further tip.

Some restaurants have been known to include the service charge in the total cost shown on a credit card voucher, then to leave a blank for a further tip. This is a scam – you only have to tip once.

London taxi drivers also expect to be tipped (just round the total up to the nearest 50p). It's less usual to tip minicab drivers. If you take a boat trip on the Thames you'll find the boatmen importuning for a tip in return for their commentary. Whether or not you pay is up to you.

Bargaining is virtually unheard of, even at markets, although it's fine to ask if there are discounts for students, young people, or youth hostel members. Some 'negotiation' is also OK if you're buying an expensive item such as a car or motorcycle.

London for Free

However you look at it, London is frighteningly expensive. But there's no need to despair...even now there are still plenty of things you can do without having to part with a penny.

At the time of writing some of London's finest museums and galleries were still holding out against charges and the coming of a new government makes it look likelier that they will be able to continue to do so. These were:

- British Museum
- National Gallery
- National Portrait Gallery
- Tate Gallery
- Wallace Collection

The South Kensington Museums, the Imperial War Museum and the Museum of London also offer free admission after 4.30 pm but it would take a lot of visits to see everything in these short free periods.

Smaller museums offering free admission include:

- Albert Memorial Visitor Centre
- Bank of England Museum
- Bethnal Green Museum of Childhood
- Burgh House
- Dulwich Picture Gallery
- Geffrye Museum
- Guildhall Museum
- Hogarth's House
- Horniman Museum
- Keats' House
- Leighton House
- London Docklands Visitor Centre
- Museum of Garden History
- Museum of the Order of St John
- National Army Museum
- North Woolwich Old Station Museum
- Orleans House Gallery

RACHEL BLACK

Keats' House is open free to visitors

Discounts

Most attractions (though not, for some reason, the Monument!) offer discounts to some of the following groups:

children under 12, 14 or 16
people under 25 or 26
students with ISIC cards (age limits may apply)
people over 60 or 65
disabled visitors
family groups

Sometimes the discounts form an impressive list by the ticket office, at other times there may just be a separate list price for 'concessions', in which case you'll need to ask if you're eligible. Throughout this book, where two prices are given (eg £7/3.50), the first is the adult (regular) charge, the second is the usual concession.

Opening a Bank Account

It's not easy to open a bank account, although if you're planning to work it may be essential. Building societies tend to be more welcoming and often have better interest rates. You'll need a permanent address in the UK, and it will smooth the way if you have a reference or introductory letter from your home bank manager, *plus* bank statements for the previous year. Owning credit/charge cards also helps.

Personal cheques are still widely used in

- Photographers' Gallery
- Pitshanger Manor
- Ragged School Museum
- Royal Hospital
- Royal Naval College
- Serpentine Gallery
- Sir John Soane's Museum
- Wellcome Centre for Medical Sciences
- Wellington Museum
- Whitechapel Art Gallery
- William Morris Gallery

You may have to pay to get into St Paul's Cathedral or Westminster Abbey but Southwark and Westminster cathedrals are open free, as are most of London's other churches, including Wren's masterpieces, St Bride's Fleet St and St Stephen Walbrook. The great Norman church of St Bartholomew's in Smithfield and the round church at Temple are also open free.

There are some places where you can hear music for free:

- The lobby of the National Theatre
- The parks, including the Embankment Gardens and St James's Park
- The Barbican Centre terrace on Wednesday and Friday lunchtimes in July and August
- St Katherine's Dock on Thursday lunchtime in July and August
- Many City churches (although donations are requested; see the Entertainment chapter)

Great fun can be had without having to spend a penny at the many street markets (see Markets in the Shopping chapter)

Many of London's festivals also involve free entertainment (for some suggestions see Special Events in the Facts for the Visitor chapter). You can also watch the Changing of the Guard without having to pay for the privilege.

Other less obvious possibilities for filling in a few hours without putting your hand in your pocket include visiting the House of Commons to watch Parliament in action; or visiting the Old Bailey or the Royal Courts of Justice to watch British justice in action.

For the complete lowdown on what you can see and do without paying for it, read Ben West's *London for Free* (Pan, £3.99). ■

England, but they're validated and guaranteed by a plastic card. Increasingly, retail outlets are linked to the Switch/Delta network, which allows customers to use a debit card (deductions are made directly from your current account). Look for a current account that pays interest, gives you a cheque book and guarantee and Switch/Delta card, and gives access to cashpoint machines.

Taxes & Refunds

Value-Added Tax (VAT) is a 17.5% sales tax levied on virtually all goods and services except food and books. Restaurant prices must by law include VAT.

It's sometimes possible to claim a refund of VAT paid on goods – a considerable saving. You're eligible if you've spent *less* than 365 days out of the two years prior to making the purchase living in Britain, and if you're leaving the EU within three months of making the purchase.

Not all shops participate in the VAT refund scheme, and different shops will have different minimum purchase conditions (normally around £40). On request, participating shops will give you a special form/invoice (they will need to see your passport first). This form must be presented with the goods and receipts to customs when you depart (VAT-free goods can't be posted or shipped home). After customs has certified the form, it should be returned to the shop for a refund less an administration fee.

Several companies offer a centralised refunding service to shops. Participating shops carry a sign in their window. You can avoid bank charges for cashing a sterling cheque by using a credit card for purchases and asking to have your VAT refund credited to your card account. Cash refunds are sometimes available at major airports.

DOING BUSINESS

Roughly five million people a year visit London to do business in what is one of the world's major commercial centres, home to the head offices of 118 of Europe's 500 largest companies. As a result most of London's biggest hotels depend on business travellers for their livelihood and come equipped with business centres with faxes, ISDN lines etc. More countries can be dialled direct from London than from anywhere else in Europe and international call rates are cheaper too. In any given week there are international flights to 255 different destinations, and 70 million people a year use Heathrow, the world's busiest international airport.

The main source of general information for businesspeople in London is the bilious pink *Financial Times*, a weekday newspaper; the *Economist* is a more detailed weekly. Other useful sources of information include:

London Chamber of Commerce & Industry, 33 Queen St EC4R 1AP (☎ 248 4444; fax 489 0391)

Westminster Chamber of Commerce, Mitre House, 177 Regent St W1R 8DJ (☎ 734 2851; fax 734 0670)

Bank of England, Threadneedle St EC2R 8AH (☎ 601 4846; fax 601 4356)

Board of Inland Revenue, Somerset House, Strand WC2R 1LB (☎ 438 6622)

British Overseas Trade Board, Department of Trade & Industry, Kingsgate House SW1E 6SW (☎ 215 4936; fax 215 2853)

Companies House, Crown Way, Maindy, Cardiff CF4 3UX (☎ 01222-388588; fax 380900)

Department of Trade & Industry, 1 Victoria St SW1H 0ET (☎ 215 5000; fax 8283258)

Confederation of British Industry (CBI), Centre Point, 103 New Oxford St WC1A 1DU (☎ 379 7400; fax 240 1578)

London World Trade Centre, International House, 1 St Katherine's Way E1 (☎ 488 2400)

Office of European Commission, 8 Storey's Gate SW1P 3AT (☎ 973 1992; fax 973 1900)

For anyone interested in finding out about the possibilities of Docklands, a special free 'Introduction to Docklands' coach tour leaves the London Docklands Visitors Centre, 3 Limehouse, Isle of Dogs E14 9TQ (☎ 512 1111), every Wednesday at 10 am.

If you need a translator, try AA Technical & Export Translation (☎ 583 8690; tube: Blackfriars); for word processing or secretarial services try Typing Overload, 67 Chancery Lane WC2 (☎ 4040 5464; tube: Chancery Lane).

The City airport was originally developed with business travellers in mind and is still the quietest, most relaxing place to wait for a flight. Full secretarial services are available from its business centre.

POST & COMMUNICATIONS

Post

Post office hours vary slightly, but most are open from 9 am to 5 pm, Monday to Saturday (smaller offices close at noon on Saturday).

Postal Rates Within England, 1st-class mail is quicker and more expensive (26p per letter) than 2nd-class mail (20p).

Postcards and letters up to 20 grams cost 26p within Britain and the EU; 31p to most of the rest of Europe; and 63p to the Americas/Australasia. Packets and parcels must be taken to the post office for weighing.

Air-mail letters to the USA or Canada generally take less than a week; to Australia or New Zealand, around a week.

Poste Restante Unless otherwise specified, poste restante mail is sent to the London Chief Office (☎ 239 5047), King Edward Building, King Edward St EC1 (tube: St Paul's; Map 6). It's open from 9 am to 6.30 pm, Monday to Friday.

It's more convenient to have your mail sent to Poste Restante, Trafalgar Square Post Office, 24-28 William IV St, London WC2N 4DL (tube: Charing Cross; Map 3). It's open daily except Sunday from 8 am to 8 pm. Mail will be held for four weeks; ID is required. American Express Travel offices will also hold clients' mail free. The London Adventure Centre (☎ 244 8641), 35 Earl's Court Rd SW5 9RH, will hold mail for members of the Deckers Club (see Australasian Clubs in the Useful Organisations section of this chapter).

Telephone

British Telecom's famous red booth survives in conservation areas only, notably Westminster. More usually you'll see two types of glass cubicle: one takes money, while the other uses prepaid, plastic debit cards and, increasingly, credit cards.

Since BT was privatised other companies have started competing for its business. This competition is at its fiercest in inner London where kiosk war has broken out between BT, New World and IPM Communications (Interphone). Now you can hardly move along main thoroughfares like Kensington High Street for the number of new phone booths.

All phones come with reasonably clear instructions. If you're going to make several calls (especially international), buy a phonecard first. These are widely available from all sorts of retailers, including post offices and newsagents. Phonecards can be bought in values ranging from £2 to £20; the phone continually indicates how much credit is left.

Some special codes worth knowing are:

☎ 0345
: local call rates apply

☎ 0500
: call is free to caller

☎ 0800
: call is free to caller

☎ 0891
: premium rates apply; 39p cheap rate, 49p at other times

☎ 0990
: national call rate applies

Beware of other codes which may indicate you're calling a mobile phone. This is usually considerably more expensive than calling a conventional phone.

Calling London London telephone numbers have two codes (0171 or 0181) before a seven-digit number. In general 0171 indicates a number in central London, 0181 a

Code Change
On Easter Saturday, 2000, the area code for all of London will change to 020, and subscribers will gain an extra digit at the front of their number: either 7 for 0171 numbers, or 8 for 0181 numbers. ■

number in greater London. Unless the text indicates otherwise, all numbers in this book should be prefixed with 0171, but it is only necessary to use the code if calling from outside the area. To call London from abroad, dial your country's international access code, then 44 (Britain's country code), then either 171 or 181 and the seven-digit phone number.

Local and National Calls in England Local calls are charged by time; national calls are charged by time and distance. Daytime rates are from 8 am to 6 pm, Monday to Friday; the cheap rate is 6 pm to 8 am, Monday to Friday; and the cheap weekend rate is from midnight Friday to midnight Sunday. The latter two rates offer substantial savings.

For directory inquiries ☎ 192. These calls are free from public telephones but will be charged at 25p if you call from a private phone. To get the operator call ☎ 100.

International Calls To call someone outside Britain dial 00, then the country code, area code (drop the first zero if there is one) and

CHARLOTTE HINDLE

CHARLOTTE HINDLE

PAT YALE

MARK HONAN

PAT YALE

PAT YALE

TOM SMALLMAN

A	B	C
	D	
E	F	G

A: Entering City of London, Canning St
B: St Stephen's Tower (Big Ben)
C: Byzantine striped tower of Westminster Cathedral
D: Notting Hill Carnival
E: Shot Tower at Chelsea
F: Tower of St Bride's Fleet St – the 'wedding cake' church
G: Nelson's Column, Trafalgar Square

RACHEL BLACK

DOUG McKINLAY

Top: Hampton Court Palace East Front & Gardens
Bottom: Buckingham Palace

number. International direct dial (IDD) calls to almost anywhere in the world can be made from most public telephones.

To make a reverse-charge (collect) call, dial ☎ 155 for the international operator. Direct dialling is cheaper, but some travellers prefer operator-connected calls. For international directory inquiries dial ☎ 153 (45p from private phones).

International Rates For most countries (including Europe, USA and Canada) it's cheaper to phone overseas between 8 pm and 8 am Monday to Friday and at weekends; for Australia and New Zealand, however, it's cheapest from 2.30 to 7.30 pm and from midnight to 7 am every day. The savings are considerable.

The private company CallShop etc offers cheaper international calls than BT. You can find them open until 1 am at 181a Earls Court Rd (☎ 390 4549; Map 8) and until 10 pm at 88 Farringdon Rd (☎ 837 7788; Map 6).

In CallShops you phone from a metered booth and then settle the bill. It's also possible to undercut BT international call rates by buying a special phonecard to use from any phone, even a home phone. The most widely available cards are available from newsagents and grocers by Swiftlink, but there are several other companies too; to decide which is best you really have to compare the rate each offers for the particular country you want.

Fax, Telemessage & Email

Fax CallShop etc (see the previous section) is the best place for sending or receiving faxes. It costs 25p a page to receive a fax. It may be useful to know that there's also a BT payfax machine at Victoria Coach Station.

Telemessage If you need to get a message overseas urgently, call ☎ 0800-190190.

Email See the information on Internet cafés in the Entertainment chapter.

BOOKS

London has innumerable good book and map shops (see Books in the Shopping chapter). In addition, the YHA Adventure Shop, 14 Southampton Row, Covent Garden; the British Travel Centre; and the London Tourist Board's Victoria station centre (see under Tourist Offices) stock a wide range of titles.

Lonely Planet

Lonely Planet also publishes *Britain* and *Walking in Britain*, which provide information for people planning to travel around the country.

Guidebooks

Innumerable guides cover every aspect of a stay in London. Culture vultures who want to find out more about the art and architecture should look for the *Blue Guide London* or *The Art & Architecture of London* (Phaidon), although the latter is in need of updating. American visitors might like to look out for *American Walks in London* (£9.99) which describes ten itineraries covering places with links to the USA. For hidden corners of the capital it's worth looking for anything by Geoffrey Fletcher whose books often come with pleasing sketches of the sights.

London for Free (£3.99) is the cheapskate's bible while the *Virago Women's Guide to London* (£9.99) is good for digging out otherwise forgotten snippets of women's history. Finally, to keep the kids amused, *I-Spy London* (Michelin, £1.99) comes with boxes to tick off the sights.

Travel

London doesn't seem to have inspired many modern-day travel writers to set pen to paper, although Bill Bryson recounted his exploits in the capital in his witty best-seller about Britain, *Notes From a Small Island*. Rolling back the years George Orwell's *Down and Out in Paris and London* described his experiences in the 1920s. Some citizens might claim not a lot has changed for the underclass since then.

History

A *Traveller's History of England* (£7.95) by Christopher Daniell offers a quick introduction to English history, useful for making sense of all those kings and queens.

It's a bit of a blockbuster but anyone interested in 17th century London (the Great Fire and all that) should try battling with Samuel Pepys' *Diary*, published in abridged form (still 1021 pages) by Penguin.

To find out how London turned into the cultural melting pot it is today look for *The Peopling of London* which describes 15,000 years of settlement from overseas. It was produced to support a Museum of London exhibition and that's the best place to buy a copy.

General

For a readable account of where Britain's at economically, try *The State We're In* (£7.99), *Observer* editor Will Hutton's analysis of Britain's position at the close of the 20th century, or its appendix *The State to Come* (£4.99).

NEWSPAPERS & MAGAZINES

Newspapers

The bottom end of the British newspaper market is occupied by the *Sun*, *Mirror*, *Daily Star* and *Sport*. The middle-market tabloids, the *Daily Mail* and *Daily Express*, are Tory strongholds. *The European* makes an honourable attempt to reconnect the British with the Continent.

Of the broadsheets, the *Telegraph* far outsells its rivals and its readership remains old fogeyish. The *Times* is still conservative and influential, and carries some of the best travel pages. The *Independent* tries to live up to its name but is struggling to stay afloat. The mildly left-wing *Guardian* is read by the chattering classes. The best travel pages are in the *Telegraph* and *Independent*.

The Sunday papers are an institution. *The Sunday Times* must destroy at least one rain forest per issue. The *Observer* was recently taken over by its soul mate, the *Guardian*. Almost every daily has a Sunday stablemate which shares its political views.

London has its own widely-read paper, the *Evening Standard*. In general this is as right-wing as most British dailies although it can become radical when matters directly affecting London are concerned. Its restaurant and entertainment reviews are usually worth reading.

Every district of London has its own local papers, some of them freebies. Particularly good is the *Ham & High* which serves the Hampstead and Highgate area of north London.

You can also buy the *International Herald Tribune* and many foreign-language papers in central London. For a particularly good selection, try the newspaper stands in the Victoria station shopping complex, in Charing Cross Rd, in Old Compton St and along Queensway.

Magazines

The weekly listings magazine *Time Out* (£1.70) is an institution with a history running back to the 1970s. This should be your first point of reference for anything to do with the cinema, theatre or concert halls, although it's also good on eating out and shopping possibilities. It's sold in many bookshops as well as in newspaper kiosks.

London sells an astonishing range of magazines on every subject under the sun. Good places to stock up are the kiosks in the main-line stations where *Time* and *Newsweek* are also available.

The weekly freebie *TNT* is worth picking up outside tube stations if you want to find out about cheap flights, shipping goods home etc. The other freebies thrust into your arms at tube stations or placed in the bins outside are of variable quality although *Midweek* is stuffed with (mainly permanent) job vacancies.

RADIO & TV

Radio

While in London you'll be able to pick up all the national BBC services, including Radio 1 (98.8kHz FM), the main pop music station, which has undergone a revival after some years in the doldrums. As Radio 1 has reached out to a younger market, Radio 2 (89.1kHz FM) has broadened its outlook and now plays the pops of the 60s, 70s and 80s alongside the older stuff.

Radio 3 (91.3kHz FM) sticks with classical music and plays, while Radio 4 (198kHz LW; 720kHz MW; 93.5kHz FM) offers a mixture of drama, news and current affairs; the *Today* Programme (Monday to Saturday, 6 to 9 am) is particularly popular. Radio 5 Live (693kHz AM), sometimes known as 'Radio Bloke', provides a mix of sport and current affairs. Lastly, the World Service (648kHz AM) offers brilliant news coverage and quirky bits and pieces from around the world.

There are also innumerable commercial radio stations, sometimes offering local news and chat alongside the music. Virgin (1215kHz AM; 105.8kHZ FM) is a commercial pop station. Classic FM (100.9mHz FM) does classical music with commercials; Kiss FM (100kHz FM) and Choice FM (96.9kHz FM) are the soul and dance stations; while the excellent Jazz FM (102.2kHz FM) caters for jazz and soul buffs. The much-hyped Talk Radio (1053kHz AM) brings tabloid news values to the radio dial; LBC (1152kHz AM) is a less sensationalist talk channel.

London's own radio stations include Capital FM (95.8kHz FM), the commercial version of Radio 1, and Capital Gold (1548kHz AM), which recycles golden oldies from the 60s, 70s and early 80s. GLR (94.9kHz FM) brings yet more talk, but with a London bias, to the ear. The latest offering is XFM on 104.9kHz FM, which bills itself as an alternative radio show.

TV

Britain still turns out some of the world's best TV, padding out the decent home-grown output with American imports, Australian soaps, inept sitcoms and trashy chat and game shows. There are five regular TV channels – BBC1 and BBC2 are publicly funded by a TV licence and don't carry advertising; ITV, Channel 4 and Channel 5 are commercial stations and do. These are now competing with Rupert Murdoch's satellite channel, BSkyB, which has a variety of programming but mostly churns out rubbish, and assorted cable channels.

That's TV Entertainment!

If you want to see your favourite British TV show in the making, send a stamped self-addressed envelope to BBC TV Ticket Unit, Room 301, Television Centre, Wood Lane, London W12 7RJ, or (for ITV, LWT and Carlton shows) to Ticket Unit, London Television Centre, Upper Ground, London SE1, as far ahead as you can. Tickets are free but the most popular shows get booked out up to a year ahead.

Tickets for recordings of BBC Radio shows can be obtained by sending an sae to BBC Radio Ticket Unit, Broadcasting House, London W1A 4WW. ■

ONLINE SERVICES

Britain is second only to the USA in its number of World Wide Web sites and there are lots of sites of interest to cyber travellers. Many sites offer general information. The Lonely Planet web site (www.lonelyplanet.com.au) offers a speedy link to many of them.

As for all things in London, Time Out is a good place to start. Their website is at www.timeout.co.uk

Many London tourist attractions have their own web sites. Worth trying are those for the Science Museum (www.nmsi.ac.uk), Buckingham Palace (www.royal.gov.uk), the British Museum (www.britishmuseum.ac.uk) and the Commonwealth Institute (www.commonwealth.org.uk).

Try www.artefact.co.uk for information about London art galleries and exhibitions.

Details of National Express services are available on www.nationalexpress.co.uk; you can make a credit-card booking via this site. Look up www.eurostar.com/eurostar/ for Eurostar information.

Although accurate at the time of going to press, the web site addresses given may change. Either use the Lonely Planet site for links or a good web engine to check the latest details. Lycos is at www.lycos.com/ and Yahoo at www.yahoo.com/. All the above site addresses must, of course, have the standard http:// prefix.

PHOTOGRAPHY & VIDEO

Since many tourist attractions sell videos as souvenirs it's worth bearing in mind that British videos are VHS rather than PAL. Check carefully that you're buying the right thing.

Film & Equipment

Although print film is widely available, slide film can be more elusive; if there's no specialist photographic shop around, Boots, the High St chemist chain, is the likeliest stockist. Thirty-six exposure print films cost from £4.30 for ISO 100 to £5 for ISO 400. With slide film it's usually cheapest to go for process-inclusive versions; 36 exposure slide films cost from £7 for ISO 100 to £10.50 for ISO 400. Jessop's offers a discount if you buy 10 films at once. There are branches at 11 Frognal Parade NW3 (☎ 794 8786) and 67 New Oxford St WC1 (☎ 240 6077).

Photography

With dull, overcast conditions common, high-speed film (ISO 200, or ISO 400) is useful. In summer, the best times of day for photography are usually early in the morning and late in the afternoon when the sun's glare has passed.

Many tourist attractions either charge for taking photos or prohibit it altogether.

Airport Security

You will have to put your camera and film through the X-ray machine at all British airports. The machines are supposed to be film-safe, but you may feel happier putting exposed films in a protective lead-lined bag.

TIME

One hundred years ago the sun never set on the British Empire, so the British could be forgiven for thinking that London (more specifically Greenwich) was the centre of the universe. Greenwich is still the location for the prime meridian which divides the world into eastern and western hemispheres.

Wherever you are in the world, the time on your watch is measured in relation to the time at Greenwich – Greenwich Mean Time (GMT) – although strictly speaking, GMT is used only in air and sea navigation, and is otherwise referred to as Universal Time Coordinated (UTC).

Daylight-saving time (DST), also known as British Summer Time (BST), muddies the water so that even London is ahead of GMT from late March to late October. To give you an idea, San Francisco is usually eight hours and New York five hours behind GMT, while Sydney is 10 hours ahead of GMT. Phone the international operator on ☎ 155 to find out the exact difference.

ELECTRICITY

The standard voltage throughout Britain is 240 volts AC, 50 Hz. Plugs have three square pins and adaptors are widely available.

LAUNDRY

Every high street has its laundrette – with rare exceptions a disheartening place to spend much time. The average cost for a single load is £1.60 for washing, and between 60p and £1 for drying. Try Forco at 60 Parkway in Camden Town; Bendix at 395 King's Rd in Chelsea; or Notting Hill Laundrette at 12 Notting Hill Gate.

WEIGHTS & MEASURES

In theory Britain has now moved to metric weights and measures although non-metric equivalents are likely to be used by much of the population for some time to come. Distances continue to be given in miles, yards, feet and inches.

Most liquids other than milk and beer (pints) are now sold in litres. For conversion tables, see the back of this book.

HEALTH

Aside from the threats posed by the nightlife and widely available liquids, herbs and chemical substances, London presents no major health hazards. Good personal hygiene and care over what you eat and drink should see you OK. Serious problems are unlikely, but mild stomach upsets as a result of a change in diet are not unknown.

Tap water is always safe so there's no need to pay the outrageous prices restaurants ask for bottled water. No jabs are needed to visit Britain. Whether you want to eat British beef after the BSE (mad cow disease) scare must remain a matter of personal choice.

Reciprocal arrangements with Britain allow Australians, New Zealanders and several other nationalities to receive free emergency medical treatment and subsidised dental care through the National Health Service (NHS); you can use hospital emergency departments, GPs and dentists (check any Yellow Pages phone book).

EU nationals can obtain free emergency treatment on presentation of an E111 form. Inquire about this at your national health service or travel agent. However, travel insurance is advisable because it offers greater flexibility over where and how you're treated, and covers expenses for ambulance and repatriation that won't be picked up by the NHS. Regardless of nationality, anyone should receive free emergency treatment if it's a simple matter like bandaging a cut.

Chemists can advise on minor ailments. There's always one local chemist that opens round the clock. Other chemists should display details in their window or look in a local newspaper. Since all medication is readily available either over the counter or on prescription there's no need to stock up.

Look in the phone book or phone ☎ 100 (free call) for the address of a local doctor or hospital. In an emergency phone ☎ 999 (free call) for an ambulance.

Between 10 am and 5 pm Monday to Friday you can call ☎ 0345-678444 to listen to one of the Healthline's 400 recordings. One call might save a lot of traipsing around.

Medical Services

The following hospitals have 24-hour accident and emergency (A&E) departments:

Guy's Hospital
St Thomas St SE1 (☎ 955 5000; tube: London Bridge; Map 6)

University College Hospital
Grafton Way WC1 (☎ 387 9300; tube: Euston Square; Map 5)

Charing Cross Hospital
Fulham Palace Rd W6 (☎ 0181-846 1234; tube: Hammersmith)

Hackney & Homerton Hospital
Homerton Row E9 (☎ 0181-919 5555; tube: Homerton BR)

Royal Free Hospital
Pond St NW3 (☎ 794 0500; tube: Belsize Park; Map 11)

Royal London Hospital
Whitechapel Rd E1 (☎ 377 7000; tube: Whitechapel)

To find an emergency dentist phone the Dental Emergency Care Service on ☎ 955 2186; or call into Eastman Dental Hospital (☎ 837 3646), 256 Gray's Inn Rd WC1 (tube: Chancery Lane).

Several travel companies offer medical (immunisation) services but at very different prices. Trailfinders (☎ 938 3999), 194 Kensington High St W8 (Map 8), has an immunisation centre. The International Medical Centre (☎ 486 3063) has two branches, including one at the Top Deck (Deckers) headquarters, 131 Earl's Court Rd SW5 (Map 8). Nomad (☎ 0181-889 7014), 3-4 Wellington Terrace, Turnpike Lane N8, sells travel equipment and medical kits, and gives immunisations (Saturday only).

HIV/AIDS Organisations

Help, advice and support are available from the National AIDS Helpline (☎ 0800-567123). The Terrence Higgins Trust (☎ 242 1010) is another worthwhile source of advice. Body Positive (☎ 373 9124) offers support to people who are HIV positive.

TOILETS

Although many city-centre toilets are still pretty grim (graffitied and with sandpaper toilet paper), those at main stations, bus terminals and attractions are generally good, usually with facilities for disabled people and those with young children. At the rail and coach terminals you usually have to pay 20p to use the facilities, more to have a shower (average £3). You also have to pay to use the Tardis-like concrete booths in places like Leicester Square.

In theory it's an offence to urinate in the streets (and men could be arrested for indecent exposure). However, as everywhere, those who've passed the evening in the pub happily make use of underpasses and alleyways, thereby rendering them unpleasant for other users.

Many disabled toilets can only be opened with a special key which can be obtained from the tourist offices or by sending a cheque or postal order for £2.50 to RADAR (see Disabled Travellers later in this chapter), together with a brief statement of your disability.

WOMEN TRAVELLERS

In general, London is a fairly laid-back place and you're unlikely to have too many problems provided you take the usual big-town precautions.

Attitudes to Women

The occasional wolf-whistle and groper on the London Underground aside, women will find the city reasonably enlightened. There's nothing to stop women going into pubs alone, although this is unlikely to be a comfortable experience; pairs or groups of women blend more naturally into the wallpaper. Some restaurants still persist in assigning the table by the toilet to lone female diners, but fortunately such places are becoming fewer by the year.

Safety Precautions

Solo travellers should have few problems, although commonsense caution should be observed, especially at night. It's particularly unwise to get into an Underground carriage with no-one else in it or with just one or two men (this advice probably applies as much to men as women), and there are a few tube stations, especially on the far reaches of the Northern Line, where you won't feel comfortable late at night. The same goes for some of the main-line stations in the south-east, which may well be unstaffed and pretty grim. If you can possibly afford it, take a cab for peace of mind.

Condoms are increasingly sold in women's toilets as well as men's. Otherwise, all chemists and many service stations stock them. The contraceptive pill is only available on prescription, as is the 'morning-after' pill (actually effective for up to 72 hours after unprotected sexual intercourse).

It can help to go on a women's self-defence course before setting out on your travels, if only for the increased confidence it's likely to give you.

Organisations

London's Well Women Clinic is at Marie Stopes House (☎ 388 0662), 108 Whitfield St W1. This is the place to come for advice on contraception and pregnancy (☎ 388 4843).

If worst comes to worst the Rape Crisis Centre phone line is open from 6 to 10 pm daily and from 10 am to 10 pm on weekends; call ☎ 914 5466.

GAY & LESBIAN TRAVELLERS

In general, Britain is fairly tolerant of homosexuality and London has a flourishing gay scene. Certainly it's possible for people to acknowledge their homosexuality in a way that would have been unthinkable 20 years ago; the current government has several openly gay MPs, including Chris Smith who is now Minister for Culture, Media and Sport. That said, there remain pockets of out and out hostility (you only need read the *Sun*, *Mail* or *Telegraph* to realise the limits of toleration) and overt displays of affection are not necessarily wise away from acknowledged gay venues and areas like Soho.

The age of homosexual consent is currently 18, although it's likely to be reduced to 16 in the near future.

For more information on London's gay & lesbian scene, see the boxed aside in the Entertainment chapter.

Information & Organisations

To find out what's going on in London pick up a free listings magazine like *The Pink Paper* or *Boyz*, or the *Gay Times* (£2) which also has listings. They're all available at Gay's The Word (☎ 278 7654), 66 Marchmont St, near Russell Square tube.

Another useful source of information is the 24-hour Lesbian & Gay Switchboard (☎ 837 7324) which can help with the most general inquiries. London Lesbian Line (☎ 251 6911) offers similar help but only from 2 to 10 pm on Monday and Friday and 7 to 10 pm on Tuesday and Thursday.

DISABLED TRAVELLERS

For many disabled travellers, London is an odd mix of user-friendliness and unfriendliness. These days few buildings go up without the need for wheelchair accessibility being acknowledged; large, new hotels and modern tourist attractions are therefore usually accessible. However, most B&Bs and guesthouses are in hard-to-adapt older buildings. This means that travellers with mobility problems may end up having to pay more for accommodation than their more able-bodied fellows.

It's a similar story with public transport. Newer buses sometimes have steps that lower for easier access, as do trains, but it's always wise to check before setting out. London Transport (☎ 918 3312) can give you detailed advice. They also publish *Access to the Underground* which indicates which stations have ramps and lifts (all DLR stations do); to receive a copy ahead of your visit write to London Transport Unit for Disabled Passengers, 172 Buckingham Palace Rd SW1 W9TN. Supermarkets and tourist attractions sometimes reserve parking spaces near the entrance for disabled drivers.

Many ticket offices, banks etc are fitted with hearing loops to assist the hearing impaired; look for the symbol of a large ear.

The 1995 Disability Discrimination Act makes it illegal to discriminate against people with disabilities in employment or the provision of services. Over the next decade barriers to access will have to be removed and the situation for wheelchair-users should slowly improve.

For more details, consult *Access in London* by Couch, Forrester and Irwin (Quiller, £7.95) or phone ahead before visiting. General information on wheelchair access is also available from Artsline on ☎ 388 2227.

Information & Organisations

If you have a physical disability, get in touch with your national support organisation and ask about visiting London. They can often put you in touch with specialist travel agents.

The Royal Association for Disability and Rehabilitation (RADAR) publishes *Access in London* (£4.10) which is required reading for visitors. Contact RADAR (☎ 250 3222) Unit 12, City Forum, 250 City Rd, London EC1V 8AF.

The Holiday Care Service (☎ 01293-774535), 2 Old Bank Chambers, Station Rd, Horley, Surrey RH6 9HW, publishes a *Guide to Accessible Accommodation and Travel* for Britain (£5.95) and can offer general advice.

British Rail theoretically offers a Disabled Persons Railcard (£16) but they don't make it easy to get. First you must fill out a form published in a booklet which you get from the Railcards Office, TRMC CP 328, 3rd Floor, The Podium, 1 Eversholt St, London NW1 1DN. You then post it to the Disabled Person's Railcard Office, PO Box 1YT, Newcastle upon Tyne, NE99 1YT, and wait.

The Corporation of London produces a leaflet with parking advice for disabled drivers; for a copy phone ☎ 332 1548.

LONDON FOR CHILDREN

Although London's crowds, traffic and pollution might be offputting to some parents, the city is jam-packed with things to entertain their offspring. The following attractions are particularly recommended for children:

- Battersea Park Children's Zoo
- Bethnal Green Museum of Childhood
- Brass Rubbing Centre, St Martin-in-the-Fields
- Coram's Fields' Children's Play Area
- London Aquarium

- London Dungeon, London Bridge (not suitable for very young children)
- London Toy & Model Museum
- London Zoo, Regent's Park
- Madame Tussaud's and the Planetarium, Baker St
- Museum of the Moving Image, South Bank
- Natural History Museum (including dinosaur galleries)
- Pollock's Toy Museum
- Science Museum basement galleries
- Segaworld in the Trocadero Centre, Leicester Square (for older children)
- Tower of London

For more details, prices and opening hours, see the main entries in the Things to See & Do chapter. The London Tourist Board also operates a 24-hour Children's Information line on ☎ 0839-123404, while *Time Out* issues a bimonthly supplement, *Kids Out* (£1.75), with all sorts of information for parents in search of something to entertain their offspring.

London has several theatres specially aimed at children. Try the Polka Theatre for Children (☎ 0181-543 4888), 240 The Broadway SW19 (tube: Wimbledon South); the Unicorn Theatre for Children (☎ 836 3334), 6 Great Newport St WC2 (tube: Leicester Square); or Little Angel Theatre (☎ 226 1787), 14 Dagmar Passage N1 (tube: Angel).

You may also like to know about a special children's hotel, *Pippa's Pop-Ins*; see the Places to Stay chapter for details.

Child-pleasing places within easy reach of London include Chessington World of Adventures, Legoland Windsor, Whipsnade Wild Animal Park and Woburn Safari Park. See the Excursions chapter for details.

USEFUL ORGANISATIONS

Membership of English Heritage (EH) and the National Trust (NT) are worth considering if you plan to travel around Britain and are interested in historical buildings. Both are nonprofit organisations dedicated to the preservation of the environment, and both care for hundreds of spectacular sites. If you're only visiting London, however, they're of limited use.

English Heritage
: Most EH properties cost nonmembers around £2 to enter. Adult membership is £20 and gives free entry to all EH properties, half-price entry to Historic Scotland and Cadw (Wales) properties, and an excellent guidebook and map. You can join at most major sites.

National Trust
: Most NT properties cost nonmembers from £1 to £5 to enter. Adult membership is £26, under age 23 is £13. It gives free entry to all English, Welsh, Scottish and Northern Irish properties, and an excellent guidebook and map. You can join at most major sites. There are reciprocal arrangements with the National Trust organisations in Scotland, Australia, New Zealand, Canada and the USA (the Royal Oak Foundation) – all of which are cheaper to join.

Great British Heritage Pass
: This pass gives you access to National Trust and English Heritage properties and some of the expensive private properties. A seven-day pass costs £25, 15 days is £36, one month is £50. It's available overseas (ask your travel agent or contact the nearest Thomas Cook office) or at the British Travel Centre in London.

Australasian Clubs
: The London Walkabout Club (☎ 938 3001), 7 Abingdon Rd W8; Deckers London Club (☎ 244 8641), 35 Earl's Court Rd SW5 9RH; and Drifters (☎ 402 9171), 22A Craven Terrace W2, all offer back-up services like mail holding, local information, discounts on film processing, freight forwarding and equipment purchase, and cheap tours. They're mainly aimed at Aussies and Kiwis, but anyone is welcome. Membership is around £15. The clubs are all associated with tour companies – they hope you will use them when you come to book.

Globetrotters Club
: If you'd like to meet other travellers it's worth going along to Globetrotters which holds meetings on the second Saturday of every month at the Friends Meeting House, 52 St Martin's Lane WC1 (Map 3) at 3.30 pm. Admission is £2.50.

LIBRARIES

London's most important library is the British Library, which has just moved into its new home in St Pancras. This is a copyright library which receives one copy of every British publication. Unfortunately it's not open to the general public; to use it you need to apply for a reader's pass to the British Library Reference Division, Great Russell St WC1B 3DG. In return you'll receive a form which must be filled out by yourself and a referee.

More user-friendly is Westminster Central Reference Library (☎ 798 2036), 35 St Martin's St (tube: Charing Cross), although you're free to use any local library for newspapers, books and magazines provided you don't want to take them away; consult the phonebook for the nearest branch.

The British Council also has a library which is free to users at 10 Spring Gardens SW1 (☎ 389 4989). The Chamber of Commerce & Industry Reference Library is at 33 Queen St EC4 (☎ 248 4444) and stocks all manner of commercial information.

DANGERS & ANNOYANCES

Crime

It would be possible to write an introduction to London so scary it would put you right off coming, but although city crime is certainly not unknown, most tourists spend their two weeks in the capital without anything worse happening than being overcharged for an ice-cream. Considering its size and the disparities in wealth, London is remarkably safe. That said, you should take the usual precautionary measures against pickpockets who operate in crowded public places like the London Underground. Always carry your daypack or other bag in front of you and don't put it down without keeping an eye on it, especially in a crowded pub. Never put a wallet in a back pocket – the thieves will be laughing all the way to the shops.

Take particular care at night. When travelling by tube, choose a carriage with other people and avoid some of the deserted suburban tube stations; a bus or cab is often a safer choice.

The most important things to guard are your passport, papers, tickets and money so carry these next to your skin or in a sturdy leather pouch on your belt. Use your own padlock for hostel lockers. Be careful even in hotels; don't leave valuables lying around in your room. Never leave valuables in a car, and remove all luggage overnight. Report thefts to the police and ask for a statement, or your travel insurance won't pay out; thefts from cars are often excluded anyway.

Traffic

More of a menace even than pickpockets are motorcycle couriers who belt down London roads, weaving in and out of the traffic at death-defying speeds. Keep your wits about you, especially if plugged into a Walkman while crossing the road.

Terrorism

At the time of writing a renewed IRA ceasefire held out hope for a more relaxed security environment. But since one such ceasefire has already collapsed it's as well to restate the ground rules. Never leave your bag unattended in case you trigger a security alert – you wouldn't want to come back and find your bag had gone the way of a controlled explosion, would you? If you see an unattended package, keep calm and alert those in authority and anyone nearby as quickly as possible. If asked to open your bag for inspection in museums etc, don't get stressed and argumentative – it's for your own safety ultimately.

Petty inconveniences attached to terrorism include transport hold-ups while suspicious packages are inspected and the sealing of left-luggage lockers at bus and train stations. At the time of writing the left-luggage facilities at the main bus and train stations were operating normally but the situation can change at short notice.

Lost Property

Every year thousands of items come adrift from their owners in London. Eventually most items found on buses and tube trains find their way to London Regional Transport's Lost Property office at 100 Baker St, NW1 5RZ, where you can call to collect them from Monday to Friday between 9.30 am and 2 pm. A charge of £2 per item is made; £1 if you retrieve it from a bus garage instead.

Items left on main-line trains should end up back at the main terminals but you'll be charged a fee to recover them which seems to relate to the value of what was lost.

If you leave something in a black taxi, phone ☎ 833 0996 to see if it's been handed in.

Touts & Scams

Hotel/hostel touts descend on backpackers at Underground and main-line stations such as Earl's Court, Liverpool St and Victoria. Treat their claims with scepticism and don't accept any offers of free lifts unless you know precisely where you're going (you could end up miles away).

Never accept the offer of a ride from an unlicensed taxi driver either – they'll drive you round in circles, then demand an enormous sum of money. Use a metered black cab, or phone a reputable minicab company for a quote.

In front of popular landmarks someone may approach and offer to take your photograph. If they don't disappear with your camera, they'll only remain friendly if you pay them for the privilege.

Every year foreign men are lured into Soho strip clubs and hostess bars and efficiently separated from unbelievable sums of money; refuse to pay and things may rapidly turn nasty. Do yourself a favour – just say no!

Cardsharping – where tourists are lured into playing a game that seems to be going all one way until they join in whereupon the luck changes sides – seems to be on the wane, but in its place have come the mock auctions that operate primarily out of Oxford St. You may be handed a flyer advertising an auction of electrical and other goods at unbelievably cheap prices. But just watch that word 'unbelievable' because that's just what they are. At the advertised venue you'll see attractive goods on display, sure enough. However, you'll be asked to bid for goods in black plastic bags or other packaging which you can't remove until the show's over. When you do remove it, you'll find your wonderful bargain has turned into fool's gold. Caveat emptor, as they say.

Beggars

These days London has a depressing number of beggars and it's difficult to know how best to deal with them. If you want to give, don't wave a full wallet around – carry some change in a separate pocket. However, it's probably better to give to a recognised charity. All the arguments against giving to beggars in developing countries apply in London too, although it takes a pretty insensitive soul to ignore an outstretched palm when you've just blown a fortune in some trendy bar or restaurant.

Shelter (☎ 253 0202), 88 Old St EC1, is a charity that helps the homeless and gratefully accepts donations. Also consider buying *The Big Issue* (80p), a weekly newspaper available from homeless street vendors who benefit directly from sales.

Racism

London is not without racial problems, particularly in some of the more deprived areas like Tower Hamlets, but generally tolerance prevails. Visitors are unlikely to have problems associated with their skin colour, but please let us know if you find otherwise.

Litter

Many first-time visitors are shocked at how dirty the capital is, with rubbish strewn everywhere. The glib excuse would be to say that litter bins have been removed in response to the threat of bombs. In reality, however, Londoners seem to be a pretty thoughtless bunch of litterbugs.

LEGAL MATTERS

Drugs

Although even possession of cannabis is still illegal, drugs of every description are widely available, especially in clubs where Ecstasy is at the heart of the rave scene; a recent report found that up to 87% of people in a dance club intended to imbibe one illegal substance or another during the course of their night out. Nonetheless, all the usual dangers associated with drugs apply and there have been several high-profile deaths associated with Ecstasy, the purity of which can't be tested in London as it is in Amsterdam. Possession of small quantities of cannabis usually attracts a small fine (still a criminal conviction) or a warning; other drugs are treated more seriously.

Much of London's crime is associated with drug dealing. Don't even think of getting caught up in it, and remember that the dodgiest bits of town are usually those associated with dealing.

Driving Offences

The laws against drink-driving have got tougher and are treated more seriously than they used to be. Currently you're allowed to have a blood-alcohol level of 35mg/100mL, but there's talk of reducing the limit to a single drink. The safest approach is not to drink anything at all if you're planning to drive.

The other laws of the road most likely to catch visitors out relate to speeding and parking. The current speed limits are 30mph (miles per hour) in built-up areas (indicated by the presence of street lighting), 60mph elsewhere and 70mph on motorways and dual carriageways. Other speed limits will be indicated by signs. Many side streets now come kitted out with speed humps and chicanes aimed at reducing the traffic flow to a crawl. Increasingly speed cameras are being installed to catch speedsters red-handed – it's hard to argue with the evidence of a film.

Parking in the wrong place may not be a criminal offence but can still cost you a fortune, especially if your car is clamped and you have to pay to retrieve it from a pound – you won't see much change from £100 if this happens to you. Car park charges may be a pain but they're cheaper than being clamped.

On-the-Spot Fines

In general you rarely have to cough up on-the-spot for your offences. The two main exceptions are trains (including London Underground trains) and buses where people who can't produce a valid ticket for the journey when asked to by an inspector can be fined there and then; £5 on the buses, £10 on the trains, no excuses accepted.

BUSINESS HOURS

Offices are usually open from 9 am to 5 pm, Monday to Friday, with shops opening on Saturday as well and often staying open much later. A growing number of shops also open on Sunday, perhaps from 10 am to 4 pm but phone to check before making a special trip. Late-night shopping in the West End is on Thursday.

In suburban areas there may be an early-closing day for shops – usually Tuesday or Wednesday afternoon.

PUBLIC HOLIDAYS & SPECIAL EVENTS

Public Holidays

Most banks and businesses are closed on public holidays: New Year's Day, Good Friday, Easter Monday, May Day Bank Holiday (first Monday in May), Spring Bank Holiday (last Monday in May), Summer Bank Holiday (last Monday in August), Christmas Day and Boxing Day.

Museums and other attractions may well observe the Christmas Day and Boxing Day holidays but generally stay open for the other holidays. Exceptions are those that normally close on Sunday; they're quite likely to close on bank holidays too. Some smaller museums close on Monday and/or Tuesday, and several places, including the British Museum, close on Sunday morning.

Special Events

Countless festivals and events are held in and around London. Look out for the BTA publications *Forthcoming Events* and *Arts Festivals*, which list most of the year's events with their exact dates.

New Year

Street Party – in Trafalgar Square

Lord Mayor's Parade – Mayors of Westminster and other London boroughs parade with floats, carriages and street theatre

Last Sunday in January

Charles I Commemoration – wreaths laid outside Banqueting House, Whitehall

Late January/early February

Chinese New Year – lion dances in Soho

Clowns' Service – clowns gather at Holy Trinity Church, Beechwood Rd, Dalston E8, to commemorate clown of clowns Grimaldi

Shrove Tuesday

Pancake Day Races – Lincoln's Inn Fields, Covent Garden and Spitalfields

Last week in March

Oxford/Cambridge University Boat Race – traditional rowing race; Putney to Mortlake

Head of the River Race – less well-known rowing race from Putney to Mortlake with 400-odd teams

Easter

Fair – Battersea Park

Early May

London Marathon – 26-mile race from Greenwich Park to Westminster Bridge via Isle of Dogs and Victoria Embankment

Mid-May

FA Cup Final – deciding match in major football tournament; Wembley

Royal Windsor Horse Show – major showjumping event

Last week in May

Chelsea Flower Show – premier flower show; Royal Hospital, Chelsea

Oak Apple Day – Chelsea Pensioners decorate statue of Charles II with oak leaves

First week in June

Beating Retreat – military bands and marching; Whitehall

Mid-June

Trooping the Colour – the Queen's birthday parade with spectacular pageantry; Whitehall

Spitalfields Festival – three-week celebration of East End through music, theatre, talks and walks

Greenwich Festival – similar fun and games in Greenwich

Late June

Wimbledon Lawn Tennis Championships – runs for two weeks

London Pride – Europe's biggest gay & lesbian march and festival

City of London Festival – music and theatre in City churches and squares

July

Hampton Court Palace International Flower Show – flowers galore in one of London's finest gardens

Doggett's Coat & Badge Race – rowing race from London Bridge to Albert Bridge

Mid-July

Clerkenwell Festival – fun and games shift to around Farringdon

Vintners' Company Procession – vintners in traditional costume parade from Upper Thames St to St James's Garlickhythe church

Late July

Royal Tournament – world's biggest military tattoo at Earls Court; phone ☎ 244 0244 for tickets

Late August (August Bank Holiday)

Notting Hill Carnival – Europe's biggest outdoor festival, a vast Caribbean carnival with music pounding out and gorgeous floats

Early to Mid-September

Open House – public admitted to buildings usually closed; call ☎ 0181-341 1371 for dates

Great River Race – barges, dragon boats and longships race 22 miles from Ham House in Richmond to Island Gardens on the Isle of Dogs

Late September

Horseman's Sunday – vicar on horseback blesses 100-plus horses outside church of St John & St Michael, Hyde Park Crescent, followed by horse-jumping in Kensington Gardens

Early October

Punch & Judy Festival – gathering of P & J fanatics in Covent Garden piazza

Costermonger's Pearly Harvest Festival – 100+ Pearly Kings and Queens attend service in St Martin-in-the-Fields

Mid-October

Trafalgar Day Parade – marching bands descend on Trafalgar Square to lay wreaths commemorating Nelson's victory in 1805

Late October/early November

State Opening of Parliament – Queen visits Parliament by state coach amid gun salutes

Early November

Guy Fawkes Day – on the 5th, commemorates an attempted Catholic coup with bonfires and fireworks around town; try Battersea Park, Primrose Hill, Blackheath or Clapham Common

London to Brighton Veteran Car Run – pre-1905 cars line up in Serpentine Rd, Hyde Park to race to Brighton

Mid-November

Lord Mayor's Show – Lord Mayor travels in state coach from Guildhall to Royal Courts of Justice, an excuse for floats, bands and fireworks

Remembrance Sunday – The Queen and members of government lay wreaths at Cenotaph to remember dead of world wars

WORK

Despite the fact that large numbers of Londoners continue to go jobless, if you're prepared to do anything and to work long hours for poor pay, you'll almost certainly find work. The trouble is that without skills, it's difficult to find a job that pays well enough to save money. You should be able to break even, but will probably be better off saving in your home country.

Traditionally, unskilled visitors have worked in pubs and restaurants and as nannies. Both jobs often provide live-in accommodation, but the hours are long, the work exhausting and the pay lousy. If you live in, you'll be lucky to get £110 per week; if you have to find your own accommodation you'll be lucky to get £150. Before you accept a job, make sure you're clear about the terms and conditions, especially how many hours (and what hours) you will be expected to work.

Accountants, nurses, medical personnel, journalists, computer programmers, lawyers, teachers and clerical workers (with computer experience) stand a better chance of finding well-paid work. Jobs have been scarce over the last few years but may now be picking up again. Even so, you'll probably need some money to tide you over while you search. Don't forget copies of your qualifications, references (which will probably be checked) and a CV.

Teachers should contact London borough councils, which administer separate education departments, although some schools recruit directly. To work as a trained nurse you have to register with the United Kingdom Central Council for Nursing, a process that can take up to three months; write to the Overseas Registration Department, UKCC, 23 Portland Place W1N 3AF. If you aren't registered you can still work as an auxiliary.

The free *TNT* magazine is a good starting point for jobs and agencies aimed at travellers. For au pair and nanny work buy the quaintly titled *The Lady*. Also check the *Evening Standard*, national newspapers and the government-operated Jobcentres. There's a central branch at 195 Wardour St W1; for others look under Manpower Services Commission in the phone book. Whatever your skills, it's worth registering with several temporary agencies.

Depending on your normal line of business, you might consider self-employment and/or starting your own company. Take professional advice first though.

For details on all aspects of short-term work consult the excellent *Work Your Way Around the World* (Vacation Work, £9.95). Their *Au Pair and Nanny's Guide to Working Abroad* (£8.95) sets out the regulations for au pairing in London and elsewhere.

Tax

As an official employee, you'll find income tax and National Insurance automatically deducted from your weekly pay packet. However, the deductions will be calculated on the assumption that you're working the entire financial year (which runs from April 6 to April 5). If you don't work as long as that, you may be eligible for a refund. Contact the tax office, or use one of the agencies who advertise in *TNT* (but check their fee or percentage charge first).

Getting There & Away

For information on getting to and from London's five airports, see the Getting Around chapter.

AIR

London has no fewer than five main airports: Heathrow is the largest, followed by Gatwick, Stansted, Luton and the City.

The Sunday papers and the *Evening Standard* carry ads for cheap fares. Also look out for *TNT* magazine – you can often pick it up free outside the main train and tube stations. For recommended travel agencies, see Travel Agents below.

Buying Tickets

The plane ticket may well be the single most expensive item in your budget, and buying it can be an intimidating business. There will be a multitude of travel agents hoping to separate you from your money, and it's always worth researching the current state of the market. Start early: some of the cheapest tickets must be bought months in advance, and some popular flights sell out early.

Cheap tickets are available in two distinct categories: official and unofficial. Official ones are advance-purchase (Apex and Superapex) tickets, budget fares or whatever other brand name the airlines care to use.

Unofficial tickets are discounted ones that the airlines release through selected travel agents, or consolidators. Airlines can supply information on routes and timetables, and their low-season, student and senior citizens' fares can be competitive, but they don't sell these discounted tickets. Bear in mind that normal, full-fare airline tickets sometimes include one or more side trips to Europe free of charge. Fly-drive packages can also be good value if you really want to bother with driving in London.

Discounted tickets are usually available at prices as low as or lower than the official Apex or budget tickets. When you phone around, find out the fare, the route, the duration of the journey, the stopovers allowed and any restrictions on the ticket and ask about cancellation penalties.

Return tickets usually work out cheaper than two one-ways – often *much* cheaper. In some cases, a return ticket can even be cheaper than a one-way. Round-the-World (RTW) tickets can also be great bargains, sometimes cheaper than ordinary return tickets. RTW prices start at about UK£900, A$1800 or US$1300 depending on the season.

Official RTW tickets are usually put together by two airlines, and permit you to fly anywhere on their route systems so long as you don't backtrack. There may be restrictions on how many stops you are permitted, and on the length of time the ticket will remain valid. Travel agents put together unofficial RTW tickets by combining a number of discounted tickets.

You're likely to discover that the cheapest flights are 'fully booked, but we have another one for just a bit more'. Or the flight is on an airline notorious for its poor safety standards and liable to leave you stranded in the world's least favourite airport for 14 hours in mid-journey. Or the agent claims to have the last two seats available, which s/he will hold for a maximum of two hours. Don't panic – keep ringing around.

If you are travelling from the USA or South-East Asia, or leaving Britain, you will probably find that the cheapest flights are advertised by small, obscure agencies. Many such firms are honest and solvent, but there are a few rogues who will take your money and disappear. If you feel suspicious about a firm, leave a deposit (no more than 20%) and pay the balance when you get the ticket. You could phone the airline direct to check you actually have a booking before you pick up the ticket. If the travel agent insists on cash in advance, go somewhere else or be prepared to take a very big risk.

You may decide to pay more than the

rock-bottom fare by opting for the safety of a better known travel agent. Firms like Council Travel in the USA, Travel CUTS in Canada and Trailfinders and STA Travel in London offer good prices to most destinations, and are competitive and reliable. Excellent discounts are often available to full-time students aged under 30 and all young travellers aged under 26 (you need an ISIC card or an official youth card) and are available through the large student travel agencies.

Use the fares quoted in this book as a guide only. They are likely to have changed by the time you read this.

Note that all domestic flights and flights to EU countries from London now attract a £10 departure tax. For flights to other international destinations you pay £20.

Travellers with Special Needs

If you have special needs of any sort – you've broken a leg, you require a special diet, you're taking the baby, or whatever – let the airline people know as soon as possible so that they can make arrangements. Remind them when you reconfirm your booking and again when you check in at the airport.

Children aged under two travel for 10% of the standard fare (or free on some airlines) if they don't occupy a seat, but they don't get a baggage allowance either. 'Skycots', baby food and diapers should be provided if requested in advance. Children aged between two and 12 usually get a seat for half to two-thirds of the full fare, and do get a baggage allowance.

The shortage of non-smoking seats on flights is a perennial source of irritation. All flights within the UK and Europe and on Concorde are now completely smoke-free. Smoking is also banned on some flights to Australia and South-East Asia. Otherwise you can ask your agent to put a request for a non-smoking seat in your booking, but there's no guarantee that you'll find one available at check-in unless you can produce a doctor's note certifying chronic emphysema.

The USA

The North Atlantic is the world's busiest long-haul air corridor and the flight options are bewildering. The *New York Times*, the *LA Times*, the *Chicago Tribune*, the *San Francisco Chronicle* and the *San Francisco Examiner* all produce weekly travel sections in which you'll find any number of travel agents' ads. Council Travel and STA Travel have offices in major cities nationwide. You should be able to fly New York-London return for around US$400 (low season) or LA-London from US$480. High season fares are usually about 30% higher.

Airhitch (☎ 212-864 2000) is worth contacting for one-way tickets and can get you to London (one way) for around US$330/450 from the east coast/west coast of the USA.

Another option is a courier flight, where you accompany a parcel or freight to be picked up at the other end. A New York-London return can be had for around US$360 or less. You can also fly one way. The drawbacks are that your stay in Europe may be limited to one or two weeks, your luggage is usually restricted to hand luggage (the parcel or freight you carry comes out of your luggage allowance), and you may have to be a resident and apply for an interview before they'll take you on (dress conservatively). Find out more about courier flights from As You Like It Travel (☎ 212-779 1771), 18 East St 41, NY 10017.

The *Travel Unlimited* newsletter, PO Box 1058, Allston, MA 02134, publishes monthly details of the cheapest airfares and courier possibilities for destinations all over the world from the USA and other countries, including the UK. It's a treasure trove of information. A year's subscription is US$25 (US$35 abroad).

Canada

Travel CUTS has offices in all major cities. Scan the budget travel agents' ads in the *Toronto Globe & Mail*, the *Toronto Star* and the *Vancouver Province*.

See the previous USA section for general information on courier flights. For courier flights originating in Canada, contact FB On Board Courier Services (☎ 905-612 8095) in Toronto. A courier return flight to London or Paris will set you back between C$375 and C$450 from Toronto or Montreal, around C$475 from Vancouver.

Australia

STA Travel and Flight Centres International are major dealers in cheap airfares. Check the travel agents' ads and ring around.

The Saturday travel sections of the *Sydney Morning Herald* and Melbourne's *Age* newspapers have many ads offering cheap fares to London, but don't be surprised if they happen to be sold out when you contact the agents: they're usually low-season fares on obscure airlines with conditions attached.

Discounted return fares on mainstream airlines through a reputable agent like STA Travel cost between A$1500 (low season) and A$2500 (high season), or as low as A$1400 to A$1900 on Garuda or Malaysian Airlines. Flights to/from Perth are a couple of hundred dollars cheaper. A Britannia charter service also operates between Britain and Australia/New Zealand. Between November and April, prices can drop as low as £499 return from London to Sydney and £698 return from Sydney to London. Contact UK Flight Shop (☎ 02-9247 4833), 7 Macquarie Place, Sydney, or, in the UK, Austravel (☎ 838 1011), 152 Brompton Rd, London SW3 1HX, or ☎ 734 7755 at their Knightsbridge office.

New Zealand

As in Australia, STA Travel and Flight Centres International are popular travel agents. Not surprisingly, the cheapest fares to Europe are routed through the USA, and a Round-the-World ticket can be cheaper than a return.

Africa

Nairobi, Kenya, is probably the best place in Africa to buy tickets to Britain, thanks to the many bucket shops and the strong competition between them. A typical one-way/return fare to London would be about US$550/800. If you're travelling to London from Cairo, it's often cheaper to fly to Athens and take a budget bus or train from there.

South Africa Student Travel, Rosebank, Johannesburg (☎ 011-447 5551; Cape Town, 021-418 6570), is primarily aimed at students and has youth fares to London from R3200 (low season) to R3500 (high). The Africa Travel Centre (☎ 021-235555), on the corner of Military Rd and New Church St, Tamboerskloof, Cape Town, also has keen prices.

Asia

Hong Kong is the discount plane-ticket capital of Asia, and its bucket shops are at least as unreliable as those of other cities. Ask the advice of other travellers before buying a ticket. Many of the cheapest fares from South-East Asia to Europe and London are offered by Eastern European carriers. STA Travel has branches in Tokyo, Singapore, Bangkok and Kuala Lumpur.

To/from India, the cheapest flights tend to be with Eastern European carriers like LOT and Aeroflot, or with Middle Eastern airlines such as Syrian Arab Airlines and Iran Air. Bombay is the air transport hub, with many transit options to/from South-East Asia, but tickets are slightly cheaper in Delhi.

Europe

Typical low season one-way/return flights from London start at Amsterdam £34/68, Athens £76/149, Frankfurt £56/99, Istanbul £100/172, Madrid £56/99, Paris £35/71 and Rome £93/169, but prices change all the time so there's no substitute for shopping around. EasyJet (☎ 0990-292929) offers one-way tickets to Nice and Barcelona from Luton for £59. Standard tickets with carriers like British Airways can cost a great deal more.

Rest of Britain

Most regional centres and islands are linked to London. However, unless you're going to the outer reaches of Britain, in particular northern Scotland, planes are only marginally quicker than trains if you include the time

DOUG McKINLAY

Nº4 STATE COACH HOUSE

PAT YALE

Top: Royal Albert Hall, South Kensington
Bottom: Queen's Coach, Royal Mews

PAT YALE

PAT YALE

PAT YALE

DOUG McKINLAY

Top Left: Victorian Gothic facade of St Pancras Station
Top Right : Old Railway Company badge at Blackfriars
Middle: Farewell to London
Bottom: Russell Square Underground Station

it takes to get to/from airports. Note that a £10 airport departure tax is added to the quoted price of tickets.

The main operators are British Airways (☎ 0345-222111), British Midland (☎ 0345-554554) and Air UK (☎ 0345-666777). Most airlines offer a range of tickets including full fare (very expensive but flexible), Apex (for which you must book at least 14 days in advance) and special offers on some services (British Airways calls these Seat Sale fares and also has occasional World Offer fares which may be even cheaper). There are also youth fares (for under 25s) but Apex and special-offer fares are usually cheaper.

Prices vary enormously. For example, a return ticket from London to Edinburgh on BA costs £256 full fare, £125 Apex (booked 14 days in advance), £106 Saver, £72 Domestic Saver and £59 Domestic Special Saver. Air UK and British Midland charge £59 return. All the cheaper fares are hung about with restrictions which a travel agent will explain; staying Saturday night or travelling midweek are two of the most common.

Examples of other BA Apex/Saver return fares from London include Inverness for £141/106, Aberdeen for £151/106, Kirkwall (Orkney) for £262/206 and Lerwick (Shetland) for £262/214. To Jersey in the Channel Islands you can sometimes get a return fare from Heathrow for £69.

EasyJet (☎ 0990-292929) now offers no-frills flights for £29 one-way between Luton and Edinburgh, Glasgow and Aberdeen. Tickets are sold direct, by phone, rather than through a travel agent. They're also sold on a first-come-first-served basis – when the £29 tickets are sold the price goes up to £39 and so on up to £59. EasyJet doesn't have the greatest record for punctuality – worth bearing in mind if you're booked on a late flight back to Luton; if you arrive in central London after the tube stops running, having to pay for a taxi home could wipe out what you've saved.

If you're flying into the UK on BA you may be eligible for a UK Airpass. This costs from an extra £55 per internal flight, and must be arranged at least seven days prior to arrival in the UK. Students may also be eligible for a Skytrekker UK Airpass; buy three domestic flights and they'll cost just £27 each. Your travel agent should have details.

Ireland

Dublin is linked to all the major London airports. There are also flights to various regional centres in the Republic of Ireland. The standard one-way economy fare from London to Dublin is £75, but with the advent of price-cutting Ryanair, return tickets are sometimes available for as little as £59.

There are regular connections between London and Belfast on the British Airways shuttle service from Heathrow. Costs on the shuttle range from £82 for a regular one-way ticket to £139 for an advance-purchase return. British Midland offers similar fares. Jersey European Airways has a £55 return fare from Gatwick or Stansted and BA Express has an £84 advance-purchase return from Luton.

Airline Offices

Most major airlines have ticket offices in London. The following are the ones you're most likely to want but others can be found in the London Business phone book.

Aer Lingus
: Aer Lingus House, 83 Staines Rd, Hounslow, Middlesex TW3 3JB (☎ 0645-737747)

Aeroflot
: 70 Piccadilly W1V 9HH (☎ 355 2233)

Air Canada
: Air Canada Complex, Radius Park, Middlesex TW14 0NJ (☎ 0990-247226)

Air France
: Colet Court, 100 Hammersmith Rd W6 (☎ 0181-742 6600)

Air New Zealand
: Elsinore House, 77 Fulham Palace Rd W6 8JA (☎ 0181-741 2299)

Air UK
: Stansted House, Stansted Airport, Essex CM24 1AE (☎ 0345-666777)

Alitalia
: 205 Holland Park Ave W11 4XB (☎ 602 7111)

American Airlines
    25-29 Staines Rd, Hounslow TW3 3HE (☎ 0345-789789)
British Airways
    PO Box 10, Heathrow Airport, Hounslow, Middlesex TW6 2JA (☎ 0345-222111)
British Midland
    Donington Hall, Castle Donington, Derbyshire DE74 2SB (☎ 0345-554554)
Canadian Airlines International
    25-29 Staines Rd, Hounslow, Middlesex TW3 3HE (☎ 0345-616767)
Cathay Pacific
    7 Apple Tree Yard, Duke of York St SW1Y 6LD (☎ 747 8888)
Continental Airlines
    1st floor, Beulah Crt, Albert Rd, Horley, Surrey RH6 7HP (☎ 0800-776464)
El Al
    185 Regent St W1 8EU (☎ 437 9255)
Iberia
    Venture House, 29 Glasshouse St W1R 6JU (☎ 830 0011)
KLM
    Piesman House, 190 Great South West Rd, Feltham, Middlesex TW14 9RL (☎ 0181-750 9000)
Lufthansa
    Lufthansa House, 10 Old Bond St W1X 4EN (☎ 0345-737747)
Olympic
    11 Conduit St London W1R 0LP (☎ 409 3400)
Qantas
    Qantas House, 395-403 King St W6 9NJ (☎ 0345-747767)
Ryanair
    Enterprise House, Stansted Airport, Essex CM24 8QL (☎ 0541-569569)
Sabena
    Gemini House, Second Floor, West Block, 10-18 Putney Hill SW15 6AA (☎ 0181-780 1444)
SAS
    52 Conduit St W1R 0AY (☎ 0345-010789)
Singapore Airlines
    580-86 Chiswick High Rd W4 5RP (☎ 0181-747 0007)
South African Airways
    St George's House, 61 Conduit St W1R 0NE (☎ 312 5000)
TAP
    Gillingham House, 38-44 Gillingham St SW1V 1JW (☎ 828 0262)
Thai
    41 Albermarle St W1X 4LE (☎ 499 9113)
Turkish Airlines
    11-12 Hanover St W1R 9HF (☎ 499 4499)
United
    United House, South Perimeter Rd, Heathrow Airport, Hounslow, Middlesex TW6 3LP (☎ 0181-990 9900)
Virgin Airways
    Crawley Business Quarter, Manor Royal, Crawley, West Sussex RH10 2NU (☎ 01293-747747)

Excess Baggage

Many people, but especially those who spend time working, accumulate considerably more baggage than the 20kg allowed by airlines (note that the routes to/from, or through, the USA have much more generous allowances than those to the east). The most economical solution is to contact one of the many shipping companies that advertise in *TNT* or *Traveller* magazines and arrange to have the surplus shipped or airfreighted home. This should not be a last-minute decision since most companies will often require a couple of days notice to arrange the delivery of cartons or tea chests and a pick-up time.

It is also worth giving yourself time to phone around for quotes. Be suspicious of companies that offer rates substantially below the average. Check that the one you choose is either a bonded member of an overseas division of the British Association of Removers, or the Association of International Removers. The shipping business does not have standard safeguards for its customers and in recent years a number of companies have collapsed or disappeared. This can mean losing possessions entirely, having bags stuck in Britain, or, if you're lucky, just paying twice.

Shipping is considerably slower and cheaper than airfreight and delivery dates are approximate at best. Most companies will quote eight to 12 weeks for shipping to Australasia, but the reality can be 16 to 20 weeks. Airfreight generally takes from one to two weeks. For shipping, the charges are based on volume; for airfreight, both weight and volume.

There are generally two other alternatives: door to door, or door to port/airport. Most companies deliver boxes and packing materials and pick up free in London, but you can choose whether you pick up goods from the port or airport at the goods' destination.

The additional cost of having a tea chest delivered door to door can add £50 to the charge (providing you live less than 30 miles from the port – more otherwise), but in most cases this is money well spent. It's easy to waste at least a day battling with bureaucracy and there are substantial fees you cannot avoid (port and unloading charges, plus customs charges).

Your goods can't be released until they've been cleared by customs. Generally, import duty will not be levied if the goods have been privately used for a reasonable period of time, but it's worth checking the regulations with your embassy or high commission in advance. If your goods are subject to import duty, you should make sure you're home before they are so you can provide the appropriate documentation.

If you will arrive after your goods, make sure a friend or relative can answer customs inquiries on your behalf. They'll need a photocopy of your passport, the date you left and plan to return, a list of contents and a letter authorising them to obtain the goods. In New Zealand, if a friend or relative clears the goods, import duty will automatically be levied, although you will be able to claim a refund when you get home.

If you plan to pick your goods up from the port or airport yourself, bear in mind that once the goods arrive you generally have only a couple of days grace before hefty storage charges are levied. Fortunately, most companies will store baggage in London (usually for a nominal charge) and ship it on a nominated date.

Insurance is recommended. Check (and that means reading the small print) that it covers loss, theft and breakage of individual items, not just the entire package, that claims can be settled at your destination and that the goods are insured for full replacement value.

BUS

Bus travellers to London arrive and depart from Victoria Coach Station (☎ 730 3466; tube: Victoria; Map 4), Buckingham Palace Rd, about 10 minutes walk south of the Victoria railway and tube station.

Europe

Even without using the Channel Tunnel, you can still get to Europe by bus – there's just a short ferry/hovercraft ride thrown in as part of the deal. Eurolines (☎ 0990-143219), a division of National Express (the largest UK bus line), has an enormous network of European destinations, including Ireland (from £29 return) and Eastern Europe (from £98 return).

You can book through any National Express office, including Victoria Coach Station and at many travel agents. It also has agents around Europe, including: Paris (☎ 01 49 72 51 51); Amsterdam (☎ 020-267 5151); Frankfurt (☎ 06979-03240); Madrid (☎ 91-530 7600); Rome (☎ 06-88 40840); and Budapest (☎ 1-1172 562).

Youth fares are available to holders of National Express Discount Coach Cards (see the Getting Around chapter) but the discount is quite disappointing in most cases.

The following single/return prices and journey times are representative: Amsterdam £36/49 (12 hours); Athens £126/218 (56 hours); Frankfurt £52/88 (18½ hours); Madrid £76/137 (27 hours); Paris £36/49 (10 hours); and Rome £85/129 (36 hours).

Eurolines also offers good-value explorer tickets which are valid up to six months and allow travel between a number of major cities. For example, you can visit Paris, Barcelona, Madrid and Avignon and return to London for £184.

Hoverspeed (☎ 0990-240241) claims the fastest coach service between London and Paris, with the 6½ hour journey costing from £39 return.

Eurobus (☎ 0118-936 2321; in the US ☎ (800) 727-2437) travels a pre-determined route around Europe with a hop-on-hop-off reservation service. Europe is divided into three zones; a ticket for one zone costs from £119 (plus £28 for a return link to London), a ticket for all three zones costs £269, with the link to London thrown in; those over 26 pay a little more.

Rest of Britain

Road transport in Britain is almost entirely

privately owned and run. National Express (☎ 0990-808080) runs the largest network – it completely dominates the market and is a sister company to Eurolines – but there are often smaller competitors on the main routes.

Long-distance express buses are usually referred to as coaches and most leave London from Victoria Coach Station (VCS). Note that tickets queues here can be horrendous; to wait an hour to be served is not at all exceptional. Do yourself a favour and book over the phone by credit card. You can then pick up the ticket from a separate window as long as you do so more than 30 minutes before the coach is due to depart.

Generally speaking, if you want to travel by coach it's cheaper to do so midweek. Booking a week ahead can also result in a discount. Absurdly, there are some routes where it can be several pounds cheaper to buy two singles than a return, even if it means standing in line twice to qualify.

National Express Discount Coach Cards can be bought from all National Express agents and are available to students studying full-time in the UK, to all young people between 16 and 25 and to people aged 60 and over. A passport photo is required; ISIC cards are accepted as proof of student status and passports for date of birth.

The National Express Britexpress Card is available to all overseas visitors on presentation of a passport. It can be bought overseas, at Heathrow or Gatwick, or at the National Express/Eurolines office (☎ 0990-808080), 52 Grosvenor Gardens, London (tube: Victoria).

There are also four National Express Tourist Trail Passes available to UK and overseas citizens, which can be bought overseas through travel agents, or at any National Express agent in the UK.

TRAIN

Since the Channel Tunnel opened in 1994 London's main rail terminus for Europe has been Waterloo International. It is linked by high-speed Eurostar trains with Brussels, Lille and Paris, providing connections all over Europe.

Rail/ferry links generally use Victoria, Liverpool or King's Cross stations, depending on your European destination. There are information centres at all the main stations. For rail information by phone, one overstretched inquiry number now covers all destinations in Britain: ☎ 0345 484950. For inquiries on European trains contact Rail Europe on ☎ 0990-300003.

If you plan to travel extensively by train, consider buying the *Thomas Cook European Timetable*, which gives a complete listing of train schedules and indicates where supplements apply and where reservations are necessary. It's updated monthly and is available from Thomas Cook outlets worldwide. You can also get train times from all over the world on the Internet.

Rail Privatisation

The old British Rail has been split into 25 train operating companies (TOCs), with a separate company, Railtrack, owning the track and stations. Where you should use a main-line train to get somewhere, this is differentiated from the tube in the text by the simple word 'station'.

Currently, companies using exactly the same route must charge the same fare but if they use a different route they can vary the price. Thus, between some stations, passengers can buy a cheaper ticket for a more roundabout journey or pay more for a direct route.

The main routes are served by excellent InterCity trains that travel at speeds of up to 125 mph and can whisk you from London to Edinburgh in just under four hours.

If you're planning a long journey (over 100 miles) and don't have a rail pass, the cheapest tickets on offer must be bought one or two weeks in advance. Buying an Apex ticket has the added advantage that you get a reserved seat – astonishing given that on some crowded routes people who've paid the full fare can find themselves standing! Phone ☎ 0345-000125 for advance credit-card bookings (8 am to 10 pm daily). For shorter journeys, it's not really necessary to purchase tickets or make seat reservations in advance. Just buy them at the station before you go.

London Main-Line Terminals

London has 10 main-line terminals, each serving a different geographical area of the UK:

Paddington
: South Wales, west and south-west England, and the South Midlands

Marylebone
: North-west London and the Chilterns

King's Cross
: North London, Hertfordshire, Cambridgeshire, north and north-east England, and Scotland

Euston
: North and north-west England, and Scotland

Liverpool Street
: East and north-east London, Stansted airport and East Anglia

St Pancras
: East Midlands and South Yorkshire

Victoria
: South and south-east England, Gatwick airport and Channel ports

Waterloo
: South-west London, and south and south-west England

Charing Cross
: South-east England

London Bridge
: South-east England

Recently a lot of work has been done to make the terminals more attractive. Most now have left-luggage facilities, toilets (10p or 20p) with showers (around £3), book and magazine shops, and a range of eating and drinking possibilities. In particular, Upper Crust sells good filled baguettes, while Costa Coffee shops serve, as the name suggests, good coffee. Victoria and Liverpool Street have entire shopping malls attached. At Victoria, BA also has advance check-in facilities for people using Gatwick airport.

Liverpool Street in particular has been restored to its Victorian splendour, with its wonderful wrought-iron roof beautifully repainted. It's almost worth a visit in its own right. Brunel's station at Paddington is likely to be much improved once work on building the Heathrow Express is completed, sometime in 1998.

Rail Classes

There are two classes of rail travel: 1st class, and what is now officially referred to as standard class. First class costs 30 to 50% more than standard and, except on very crowded trains, is not really worth the extra money, except at weekends when you can sometimes upgrade to 1st class on the train for a supplement of a few pounds.

Overnight trains between London and Plymouth or Penzance, and on the routes to Scotland, have sleeping compartments. To the West Country a 1st class berth is £30, a standard class berth £25; to Scotland they're £33 and £27 respectively, in addition to the cost of the ticket. Berths must be reserved in advance.

BritRail Passes

BritRail passes are the most interesting possibility for visitors, but they are *not available in Britain* and must be bought in your country of origin. Contact the BTA in your country for details.

Rail Rovers

The domestic version of the BritRail passes are BritRail Rovers: a seven-day All Line Rover is £410/250, and 14 days is £620/410, with reductions for railcard-holders. There are also regional Rovers and some Flexi Rovers to Wales, north and mid-Wales, the North Country, the north-west coast and Peaks, the south-west, and Scotland.

Railcards

You can get discounts of up to 34% on most off-peak fares (except Apex and Super Apex – see the following Tickets information) if you're aged 16 to 25, or over 60, or studying full-time, or disabled – but you must first buy the appropriate railcard. There are also railcards for families.

The cards are valid for one year and most are available from major stations. You'll need two passport photos, and proof of age (birth certificate or passport) or student status.

Young Person's Railcard – Costs £16 and gives you 34% off most tickets and some ferry services; you must be aged 16 to 25, or a student of any age studying full-time in the UK

Senior Citizen's Railcard – Available to anyone over 60, this card costs £16 and gives a 34% discount

Disabled Person's Railcard – Costs £14 and gives a 34% discount to a disabled person and one person accompanying them; for details of how to obtain this card, see Disabled Travellers in the Facts for the Visitor chapter

Family Railcard – Costs £20 and allows discounts of 34% (20% off Saver and SuperSaver tickets) for up to four adults travelling together, providing one of the card-holders is a member of the party. Up to four accompanying children pay a flat fare of £2 each. A couple of journeys can pay for the card

Network Card – If you're planning to stay in south-east London or do a lot of rail travel in southern England, a Network card is worth considering. This is valid for all main-line routes within London and the entire south-east of England, from Dover to Weymouth, Cambridge to Oxford. It costs £14, or £10 for holders of the Young Person's Railcard. Discounts apply to up to four adults travelling together provided one of the card-holders is a member of the party. Children pay a flat fare of £1. Travel is permitted only after 10 am Monday to Friday but at any time on the weekend. A couple of journeys can pay for the card.

Tickets

The main ticket variations are given below, but these are hangovers from the old British Rail days. Since privatisation, the system has become more complicated, so finding the best ticket for your journey isn't easy. The best thing to do is keep asking...

Children under five travel free; aged between five and 15 they pay half-price for most tickets, and full fare for Apex and Super Apex tickets.

Single ticket – Valid for a single journey at any time on the day specified; expensive

Day Return ticket – Valid for a return journey at any time on the day specified; relatively expensive

Cheap Day Return ticket – Valid for a return journey on the day specified on the ticket, but there may be time restrictions and it's usually only available for short journeys; often about the same price as a single. You're not usually allowed to travel on a train that leaves before 9.30 am

Open Return – For outward travel on a stated day and return on any day within a month

Apex – A very cheap return fare, rivalling National Express prices; for distances of more than 100 miles; you must book at least seven days in advance, but seats are limited so book ASAP

Super Apex – Cheapest return fare for journeys to and from north-east England or Scotland; you must book at least 14 days in advance, but seats are limited and not available on all trains so book ASAP

SuperSaver – A cheap return ticket with up to 50% savings; not available in south-eastern England; cannot be used on Friday, Saturday in July and August, or in London before 9.30 am or between 4 and 6 pm

SuperAdvance – For travel on Friday, and also Saturday in July and August; similarly priced to the SuperSaver, but must be bought before midday on the day before travel, or earlier

Saver – Higher priced than the SuperSaver, but can be used any day and there are fewer time restrictions

AwayBreak ticket – For off-peak travel in south-eastern England. Valid for four nights (five days) for journeys over 30 miles or 40 miles from London

StayAway ticket – As above but valid for one month

Telephone Bookings

The National Telephone Inquiries Line (☎ 0345-484950) is open 24 hours a day, but has been criticised for failing to answer all the calls put through to it. The operating companies have been warned to pull up their socks or face hefty fines. Watch this space.

Europe

European rail passes are only worth buying if you plan to do a fair amount of travelling within a short space of time. Otherwise travellers aged under 26 can pick up BIJ (Billet International de Jeunesse) tickets which cut fares by up to 50%. London to Zürich return costs from £148, London to Munich from £199.

Various agents issue BIJ tickets in London, including the Eurotrain department of Campus Travel (☎ 730 3402), 52 Grosvenor Gardens, London SW1 0AG (tube: Victoria;

Map 4). Eurotrain options include circular Explorer tickets, allowing a different route for the return trip: London to Madrid, for instance, takes in Barcelona, Paris and numerous other cities. The fare for this Spanish Explorer ticket is £175, valid for two months. Rail International (☎ 0990-848848) and Wasteels (☎ 834 7066), Platform 2, Victoria Station, London SW1, also sell BIJ tickets.

Channel Tunnel For the first time since the ice ages, Britain has a land link (albeit a tunnel) with mainland Europe. Two services operate through the Tunnel: Eurotunnel operates a rail shuttle service (Le Shuttle) for motorcycles, cars, buses and freight vehicles, between terminals at Folkestone in the UK and Calais in France; and the railway companies of Britain, France and Belgium operate a high-speed passenger service, known as Eurostar, between London, Paris and Brussels.

Le Shuttle Specially designed shuttle trains run 24 hours a day, theoretically departing up to four times an hour in each direction between 6 am and 10 pm and every hour between 10 pm and 6 am. From France twice-hourly services leave between 7 am and 10 pm.

Le Shuttle terminals are clearly signposted and connected to motorway networks. British and French Customs and Immigration formalities are carried out before you drive on to Le Shuttle. Total travel time from motorway to motorway, including loading and unloading, is estimated at one hour; the shuttle itself takes 35 minutes.

A ticket for a car and up to nine passengers costs from £149. You can make an advance reservation (☎ 0990-353535) or simply pay by cash or credit card when you arrive at a toll booth.

Eurostar Eurostar (☎ 0345-303030) runs up to 20 trains a day between London and Paris Nord, and up to 12 a day between London and Brussels. In London, trains arrive at and depart from the international terminal at Waterloo station, a fine piece of modern designwork by Nicholas Grimshaw. Some trains stop at Ashford International station in Kent, and at Frethun (near Calais) or Lille. Immigration formalities are completed on the train, but British Customs is at Waterloo.

The London to Paris journey takes three hours (which will drop to just 2½ hours when the high-speed track through Kent is finally completed). From London to Brussels takes two hours and 40 minutes (which will eventually drop to two hours and 10 minutes).

Get tickets from travel agents and major railway stations. The normal single/return fare to Paris is £89/169 but various special offers and advance purchase may reduce this to £99 or £119 return. To Brussels the normal single/return fare is £80/160, falling to £99 or £119 for fixed date returns. An Apex return direct to Disneyland Paris booked 14 days in advance costs £89.

Rail/Ferry Eurostar has eclipsed many of the more long-established rail/ferry links, but they still provide the cheapest cross-channel travel.

Non-Tunnel rail options will depend on whether you cross the Channel by hovercraft or ferry, or from Boulogne/Folkestone or Newhaven. The cheapest option to Paris is 2nd class via Newhaven and the Stena Line ferry; adult singles/returns are £36/59 and the journey takes nine hours. If you travel via Dover and Hoverspeed the fares rises to £45/59, but the journey time drops to six hours.

For Belgium and Germany you cross the Channel from Ramsgate in Kent. Direct services from Holland will bring you to Liverpool St station via Harwich, and Scandinavian Seaways ships from Hamburg, Esbjerg and Gothenburg also arrive in Harwich. A final option is for travellers to or from Norway; the Color Line ferry from Bergen, Haugesund and Stavanger arrives in Newcastle, three hours by train from King's Cross.

CAR & MOTORCYCLE

Getting to London by car or motorcycle couldn't be easier, although it's worth asking yourself if you really want to add to the traffic congestion there. From France or Belgium you can use the Channel Tunnel trains or the ferries, from Germany or the Netherlands the ferries. See the preceding Channel Tunnel section for information on services through the Tunnel and the following Boat section for details on ferry charges for cars. See the Getting Around chapter for information on buying a car or van.

Once in the UK there are good road connections from all the ports to London, which is ringed by the notorious M25 orbital road, useful for getting close to the area you want before trying to deal with normal London roads. If you are thinking of driving in or out of London it might be worth buying the *A-Z M25* road map which highlights the arterial red routes where no stopping is allowed.

BICYCLE

Bringing a bicycle to London is also perfectly straightforward. Ferries and Eurostar don't charge extra for this, but most airlines do; you need to contact each one individually to check what arrangements it wants you to make for carrying your bike.

HITCHING

Hitching is never entirely safe and we can't recommend it as a way of getting to London. That said, if you're determined to risk it, you can minimise the likelihood of problems by hitching with someone else and making sure someone knows where you're going and when you expect to arrive.

Both ferry and Le Shuttle fares are structured so that it doesn't always cost any more to carry extra passengers. This should make it easier to persuade a driver to give you a lift.

WALKING

Until recently walking to London would not have seemed a very bright idea, but now that the Thames Path National Trail has been mapped out there's nothing to stop you hiking all the way from its source near Kemble in the Cotswolds to the Thames Barrier, a distance of 180 miles/288km. Alternatively you could walk Britain's first National Waterway Walk which follows the Grand Union Canal from Little Venice in London to Gas St Basin in Birmingham, a distance of 145 miles/232km.

Thames Path

Full details of the Thames Path route appear in Lonely Planet's *Walking in Britain* guide, and also in the Countryside Commission National Trail Guide *The Thames Path* by David Sharp (£12.99) which divides the route up into 15 day-size walks as follows:

	Miles	*Kms*
Source to Cricklade	12¼	19.7
Cricklade to Lechlade	10¾	17.3
Lechlade to Newbridge	17	27.4
Newbridge to Oxford	14	22.5
Oxford to Culham	12	19.3
Culham to Cholsey	14½	25
Cholsey to Tilehurst	11¾	18.9
Tilehurst to Shiplake	10	16.1
Shiplake to Marlow	11	17.7
Marlow to Windsor	14½	23
Windsor to Shepperton	13¾	22.1
Shepperton to Teddington	11	17.7
Teddington to Putney (north)	14¼	22.9
Teddington to Putney (south)	11½	18.5
Putney to Tower Bridge (north)	10¼	16.5
Putney to Tower Bridge (south)	10	16.9
Tower Bridge to Thames Barrier (north)	5½	8.8
Tower Bridge to Thames Barrier (south)	9	14.5

The Thames Path National Trail booklet published by Benchmark Books (£2.99) lists accommodation possibilities along the route together with tourist offices and transport possibilities.

Ordnance Survey Landranger map Nos 163, 164, 174, 175, 176 and 177 cover the entire route on a scale of 1:50,000.

Unlike most of Britain's national trails, the Thames Path is accessible by public transport along most of its length. That means you could walk some of the way and catch trains or buses the rest of the way. Thames Trains sells special Thames Path Tickets which allow you to travel to one point along the path and return from another at a special fare.

Before setting out you should check that the stretch of path you intend to walk is actually open since there have been repeated problems with obstructive landlords.

Grand Union Canal Walk

British Waterways publishes a leaflet outlining the route of the Grand Union Canal Walk from Little Venice to Gas St Basin in Birmingham, which passes 150 locks, three aqueducts and three tunnels. *The Grand Union Canal Walk Trail Guide* (£9.99) gives full details, and British Waterways also publishes a list of places to stay within one mile of the trail; for a copy send £1.50 to The Toll House, Delamere Terrace, Little Venice, London W2 6ND (☎ 286 6101).

While you'll be on firm ground while passing through towns, you'll need sensible footwear for the stretches of towpath which run through the countryside.

BOAT

There is a bewildering array of ways of getting from Britain to mainland Europe by boat. This chapter outlines the main options, but it doesn't give a complete listing. The bible for sea travel is the *ABC Cruise & Ferry Guide*, published by the Reed Travel Group (☎ 01582-600111), Church St, Dunstable, Bedfordshire LU5 4HB. Good travel agents should have a copy.

Competing companies operate on the main routes, and the resulting service is comprehensive but complicated. The same ferry company can have a whole host of different prices for the same route, depending on the time of day or year, the validity of the ticket, or the size of a vehicle. Return tickets may be much cheaper than two single fares, and vehicle tickets may also cover a driver and passenger. Very cheap day-return tickets are also available (like Dover-Calais for £8), but they're strictly policed – if you don't come back the same day the company may charge you the full one-way fare.

It's worth planning (and booking) ahead where possible as there may be special reductions on off-peak crossings. Unless otherwise stated, the prices quoted for cars do not include passengers. The ferries/hovercraft all carry cars, motorcycles and bicycles.

France

On a clear day, you can actually see land across the Channel. A true budget traveller would obviously swim – it's only seven hours and 40 minutes if you can match the record.

The shortest ferry links are between Calais or Boulogne and Dover or Folkestone. Dover is the most convenient port for those who plan onward travel to London by bus or train. P&O (☎ 0990-980980), Stena Line (☎ 0990-707070), Sea France (0990-711711) and Hoverspeed (☎ 0990-240241) all operate between Dover and Calais every hour or so. It's worth checking prices for all three.

Fares are extremely volatile, but at the time of writing Stena Line was charging foot passengers £24 one way; cars and drivers from £48 to £94 including the driver (depending on the date and time); cars with up to four passengers from £64 to £126; and motorcycles and riders from £36 to £56. These fares are for their fast 45-minute catamaran service and the 90-minute ferry.

Prices for P&O and Hoverspeed are generally similar to those of Stena Line but special offers can make a big difference. The hovercraft operated by Hoverspeed only takes 35 minutes to cross the Channel.

In response to increasing competition from the Channel Tunnel, Stena Line and P&O have announced plans to create a new merged company, P&O-Stena Line, which will operate their Dover to Calais and Newhaven to Dieppe routes. At the time of going to press, they were still awaiting EU approval for this merger. Should they get it, their fleets are likely to be cut back and price rises on the short sea crossings to France are a distinct possibility.

Other routes across the Channel include Portsmouth or Poole to Cherbourg or Le Havre, Portsmouth to Caen or St Malo and Plymouth to Roscoff.

Ireland

There are many ferry services from Britain to Ireland using modern car ferries. Figures quoted are one-way fares for foot passengers and for cars with up to five occupants, but there are special deals, return fares and other money-savers worth investigating.

There are services from eight ports in England, Scotland and Wales to six ports in Ireland. Details of the most popular routes with travellers to and from London are given here. For details of the others see Lonely Planet's *Ireland* guide.

You can get to Rosslare in southern Ireland from Fishguard or Pembroke. These popular short crossings take 3½ hours (Fishguard via Stena Line) or 4½ hours (Pembroke via Irish Ferries). From Fishguard a foot passenger pays from £22 to £33, while a car and up to five passengers costs from £54 to £219 (marginally more on the speedier catamaran). From Pembroke a foot passenger pays from £20 to £25, while a car with five passengers costs from £59 to £159.

Foot passengers pay the same fare on the 3½-hour Irish Ferries crossing between Holyhead and Dublin as they do from Pembroke to Rosslare, but to take a car on this route will cost from £99 to £204 depending on the date. The fastest run is the Stena Line ferry between Holyhead and Dun Laoghaire which takes an hour and 40 minutes and costs slightly more than the Irish Ferries crossing.

Spain

From Plymouth, Brittany Ferries (☎ 0990-360360) operates at least one ferry a week to Santander on the north coast of Spain. The journey takes 24 hours; a foot passenger pays from £47 to £80 and a vehicle costs from £152 to £391, depending on the date and the number of passengers. Brittany also operates a service between Santander and Portsmouth that takes 30 hours. P&O (☎ 0990-980555) operates a service between Portsmouth and Bilbao at similar rates.

Other Routes

There are also ferry links with Esbjerg (Denmark) and Gothenburg (Sweden) from Harwich in Essex, operated by Scandinavian Seaways (☎ 01255-240240). Scandinavian Seaways also operates ferries to Hamburg (Germany) every two days, while Stena Line (☎ 0990-707070) has two ferries a day to the Hook of Holland in the Netherlands. All these crossings are longer than the ones to France and therefore cost more.

Sally Ferries (☎ 0990-595522) also operates six daily ferries and several jetfoils to Ostend. The ferry takes four hours and the jetfoil (passengers only) takes 95 minutes.

TRAVEL AGENTS

London is Europe's major centre for discounted long-haul airfares. There are countless travel agents, some of dubious reliability; the good ones include Trailfinders and branches of STA Travel and Campus Travel whose staff understand what a tight budget is and offer competitive, reliable fares (you don't have to be a student to use their services).

Trailfinders
: 194 Kensington High St W8 (for long-haul travel phone ☎ 938 3939; for first class and business class flights phone 938 3444); 215 Kensington High Street (for transatlantic and European travel phone ☎ 937 5400); 42-50 Earls Court Road, Kensington W8 (for long-haul travel phone ☎ 938 3366). Also, visa and passport service (☎ 938 3848); immunisation centre (☎ 938 3999); foreign exchange (☎ 938 3836); and information centre (☎ 938 3303). See Map 8

STA Travel
: 86 Old Brompton Rd SW7 (Map 8); 117 Euston Rd NW1; 38 Store St WC1; 11 Goodge St W1. For European inquiries phone ☎ 361 6161; for worldwide inquiries phone ☎ 361 6262; for tours, accommodation, car hire or insurance phone ☎ 361 6160

Campus Travel
: 52 Grosvenor Gardens SW1 (☎ 730 3402 – European; 730 8111 – worldwide); YHA Adven-

ture Shop, 174 Kensington High St W8 (☎ 938 2188); YHA Adventure Shop, 14 Southampton St, Covent Garden WC2 (☎ 836 3343). See Map 3

Council Travel

28A Poland St W1 (☎ 437 7767) – the USA's largest student and budget travel agency

Plenty of other agents advertise in the weekend newspapers, *TNT* and *Time Out*. All agents should be covered by an Air Travel Organiser's Licence (ATOL). This scheme, operated by the Civil Aviation Authority (CAA), means that if either the agent or airline goes bust you are guaranteed a full refund or, if you are already abroad, to be flown back more or less on schedule. It's worth noting that, under existing consumer protection legislation, the only way you can lose out is if you book direct from an airline; using an agent – even a 'bucket shop' – gives you more protection. But to be covered by the scheme, when you hand over the cash you must be given either the ticket or an official ATOL receipt showing the agent's number. If in doubt, call the CAA on ☎ 379 7311.

ORGANISED TOURS

Companies with trips pitched at a young crowd include Top Deck (☎ 244 8641), 131 Earls Court Rd SW5 (Map 8); Drifters (☎ 262 1292), 10 Norfolk Place W2; Contiki, (☎ 0181-290 6777), Wells House, 15 Elmfield Rd, Bromley BR1 1LS – all in London; and Tracks (☎ 01303-814949), 8 Evegate Park Barn, Smeeth, Ashford, Kent TN25 6SX.

If you don't fit into this category, try Shearings Holidays (☎ 01942-824824), Miry Lane, Wigan, Lancashire, WN3 4AG, which has a wide range of four to 12-day coach tours covering the whole country. They also offer Club 55 holidays for more mature holiday-makers – on their West Country tour you can expect resident entertainers, bingo every evening and wrestling one evening per week!

For the over-60s, Saga Holidays (☎ 0800-300500), Saga Building, Middleburg Square, Folkestone, Kent CT20 1AZ, offers holidays ranging from cheap coach tours and resort holidays to luxury cruises around Britain and abroad. Saga also operates in the USA (☎ 617-262 2262) at 222 Berkeley St, Boston, MA 02116, and in Australia (☎ 02-957 5660) at Level 1, 10-14 Paul St, Milsons Point, Sydney 2061.

Slowcoach

Slowcoach (☎ 01249-891959) is an excellent bus service specially designed for budget travellers. Buses run on a regular circuit between London, Windsor, Bath, Stratford, Manchester, the Lake District, Edinburgh, York, Nottingham, Cambridge and back to London, calling at youth hostels en route. You can get on and off the bus where you like without time limits and a ticket costs £99. Slowcoach picks up from the Earl's Court youth hostel (38 Bolton Gardens) every Monday, Wednesday and Saturday at 3.45 pm.

WARNING

This chapter is particularly vulnerable to change – prices for international travel are volatile, routes are introduced and cancelled, schedules change, special deals come and go, and rules and visa requirements are amended.

Airlines and governments seem to take a perverse pleasure in making price structures and regulations as complicated as possible. You should check directly with the airline or travel agent to make sure you understand how a fare (and any ticket you may buy) works.

The upshot of this is that you should get opinions, quotes and advice from as many airlines and travel agents as possible before you part with your hard-earned cash. The details given in this chapter should be regarded as pointers and are not a substitute for careful, up-to-date research.

Getting Around

THE AIRPORTS

The Airport Transfers (☎ 403 2228) minicab company delivers to and picks up from all of London's airports.

Heathrow

Heathrow is one of the largest, busiest airports in the world. In true British style, it has grown organically and now has four terminals, with a fifth at the planning stage. There are also two tube stations, one serving Terminals 1, 2 and 3, the other serving Terminal 4, so you need to be sure you get off at the right stop.

Although the place appears chaotic and it's hard to find anywhere pleasant for a farewell drink (though there are pubs or bars in all four terminals), it's really pretty well organised. Duty-free facilities are not especially impressive (they're particularly weak on photographic and electronic equipment), but each terminal has excellent, competitive currency-exchange facilities, and good information counters. There are also several accommodation booking counters.

There are several large 'international' hotels nearby and you may need to consider them if you're leaving or arriving at a peculiar time, even though none are cheap or particularly noteworthy. To get to these hotels you must take a Heathrow Hotel Hoppa bus costing £2/3.50 single/return. These buses run between 6 am and 11 pm, with service every 10 minutes at peak times, every 15 minutes otherwise. Services from Terminal 4 run every 30 minutes.

Even if the tube isn't running, those on a budget will do better to catch a minicab for cheaper accommodation in central London (perhaps in Earl's Court, which is on the right side of town).

Baggage Hold has left-luggage facilities in Terminal 1 (☎ 0181-745 5301) and Terminal 4 (☎ 0181-745 7460) from 6 am to 11 pm. The charge is £2.50 per item up to 12 hours and £3 per item up to 24 hours. Excess Baggage (☎ 0181-759 3344) offers a similar service in Terminals 2 and 3. Both companies also have a baggage forwarding service.

For general inquiries and flight information (except British Airways) phone ☎ 0181-759 4321. For British Airways ring ☎ 0990-444000. Other useful numbers are: Car Park Information ☎ 0800-844844, and Hotel Reservation Service ☎ 0181-759 2719.

Be warned that pickpocketing is a growing problem at Heathrow.

Which Heathrow Station do I Want?

Terminal 4
- Air Lanka
- Air Malta
- Atlantic Island Air
- All British Airways intercontinental flights
- British Airways flights to Amsterdam, Paris, Moscow and Athens
- Canadian Airlines International
- City Hopper
- KLM
- Qantas

Terminal 1, 2 & 3
- All British Airways domestic and European flights
- All other flights

Getting There & Away Until the new overland Heathrow Express rail route, which will whisk passengers from Paddington to Heathrow in 15 minutes, is completed (probably in the summer of 1998, but check on arrival), the airport is only accessible by bus, Underground or car. The Underground (Piccadilly Line) is the cheapest and most reliable way of getting there between 5.30 am and 11.30 pm. The station for Terminals 1, 2 and 3 is directly linked to the terminal buildings. Since there's a separate station for Terminal 4, you must check which terminal your flight uses when you reconfirm. The adult single fare is £3.30, or use an All Zone Travelcard which is £4.30. Note that you can buy tickets for the tube from machines in the baggage reclaim area of the Heathrow terminals so you don't have to queue up in the actual station. The journey to/from central London takes about an hour.

Airbus (☎ 0181-897 2688) services are also useful; there are two routes, the A1 which runs along Cromwell Rd to Victoria, and the A2 which runs along Notting Hill Gate and Bayswater Rd to Russell Square. Buses run every half-hour and cost £6/4 single. Once the motorway bus lane along the M4 opens it should be possible to drive to the airport from central London in less than an hour.

A minicab to/from central London will cost from around £25; a metered black cab around £35. Hotelink (☎ 01293-532244) and Golden Tours (☎ 233 9050) offer minibus transfers from central London hotels for £10 a head.

Gatwick

Gatwick is a large airport, but much smaller than Heathrow, so in many ways it's easier and more pleasant to use. Its only drawback is the relative expense of the rail link to Victoria, but this, too, is more pleasant than the tube to Heathrow.

There are two terminals, North and South, linked by an efficient monorail service, along with all the predictable stores, and several eating and drinking areas. For British Airways information phone ☎ 0990-444000.

Accommodation options close to the airport are expensive and unremarkable. If you need more information phone the central Gatwick Directory (☎ 01293-535 3530). This number will connect you to Thomas Cook who deal with hotel reservations, charging £5 a time.

Excess Baggage plc (☎ 01293-569 9900), in both the North and South terminals, has left-luggage facilities available daily from 6 am to 10 pm. The charge is £2.50 per item up to 12 hours and £3 per item up to 24 hours. It also has a baggage forwarding service.

Getting There & Away The Gatwick Express (☎ 0990-301530) runs nonstop between the main terminal and platforms 13 and 14 at Victoria train station from 5.20 am to 12.05 am, with hourly services through the night. Singles are £8.90 and the journey takes 30 minutes (35 minutes on Sunday). The Connex SouthCentral service takes a little longer but costs £7.70. British Airways and American Airlines customers can check in in advance at the office in the shopping arcade above Victoria station.

Flightlink buses (☎ 0990-747777) run from central London to Gatwick every hour from 7.15 am to 11.35 pm. A single from Victoria costs £7.50/6.

A minicab to central London will cost around £35, a black cab around £70. Hotelink (☎ 01293-532244) and Golden Tours (☎ 233 9050) offer minibus transfers from central London hotels for £16 a head.

London City Airport

While it's hardly Venice, the small London City airport (☎ 474 5555) has a wonderful waterside setting in Docklands. There are flights from here to some 20 European destinations, including Manchester, Edinburgh and Dublin. For the time being this is a relatively underused airport, where the calm of the departure lounge is in blissful contrast to the hubbub of Heathrow and Gatwick. A fully-equipped business centre is also available (☎ 476 3999).

Getting There & Away The airport is to the east of the Blackwall Tunnel in east London. A shuttle bus (☎ 476 6428) connects the airport with Liverpool St station (£4 single) and Canary Wharf (£2 single), between 6 am and 9 pm. Services are every 15 minutes from Monday to Friday, every 30 minutes on Saturday and every 20 minutes on Sunday, and the journey takes 25 minutes from Liverpool St and eight minutes from Canary Wharf. You can also use the North London Line and get off at Silvertown, close to the airport terminal (see the tube map for connections to this line). Alternatively, take the DLR (Docklands Light Railway) to Prince

Regent Lane and catch the No 473 bus from there.

Stansted

It's anticipated that eight million passengers a year will pass through Stansted by the end of this century, and there will be space to accommodate 15 million in the future. At the moment this is hard to believe, but if you're offered a ticket that arrives or departs from here don't be put off. From London's Liverpool St station you arrive under the airport building to be whisked up to the main concourse by escalator where you can appreciate the Norman Foster building – simplicity itself and one of the finest new buildings in Britain.

There's one number (☎ 01279-680500) for general inquiries, hotel reservations and rail information.

Getting There & Away The direct Stansted Skytrain to Liverpool St takes 40 minutes and costs £10, departing every half hour. You can change at Tottenham Hale for the Victoria Line (for which you need a separate ticket).

Flightline buses (☎ 0990-7474777) link central London with Stansted every hour from 6 am to 7 pm. A single from Victoria costs £9/8.

Minicabs to/from central London will cost about £35, a black cab around £75.

Luton

By London standards a small, remote airport, Luton (☎ 01582-405100) mainly caters for cheap charter flights. However, EasyJet (☎ 0990-292929) operates scheduled services from Luton (see Getting There & Away chapter for fare details).

Getting There & Away The Greenline 757 bus from Victoria serves Luton airport.

Alternatively catch the airport-station Luton Flyer bus outside the arrivals hall for a short trip to the railway station, then take the train to King's Cross or St Pancras (30 minutes); the all-in price is £9.90. There are regular services approximately every 20 minutes, starting early and finishing late.

LONDON UNDERGROUND

Normally the quickest and easiest way of getting round London is to take the Underground, or 'tube', which extends way out into the suburbs and as far afield as Amersham in Buckinghamshire and Epping in Essex. An estimated 2.5 million journeys are made by Underground every day but with the cheapest single ticket in central London costing £1.20, the Underground is one of the world's most expensive public transport systems. And as the ageing system suffers from decades of underfunding, delays are increasingly common.

London Regional Transport (LRT) is responsible for the Underground trains and

Mapping the Underground

The London Underground map is so familiar that it's sometimes used as a symbol for the city itself. Millions of people refer to it every year, mostly without giving a thought to Harry Beck, the engineering draughtsman responsible for this masterpiece of design.

It was Beck who realised that the entire network could be fitted into a realistic amount of space and be perfectly usable even if strict geography was ignored. After all, once underground you don't really need to know exactly where places are, just so long as you understand where they lie in relation to each other in the network.

Beck expanded the space devoted to the central London stations, redrew all the lines until they were horizontal, vertical or at 45 degrees to each other, and devised the colour coding system for the different lines. For his efforts he was paid the grand sum of five guineas but every London Underground map still carried his name until 1960. Even now the map is basically unchanged, bar additions to take account of new lines. ■

its information centres provide tickets and free maps. Among others, there are centres in each Heathrow terminal, and at Victoria, Piccadilly Circus, Oxford Circus, St James's Park, Liverpool St, Euston and King's Cross stations. There are also information offices at Hammersmith and West Croydon bus garages. Alternatively, phone ☎ 222 1234 for information.

Throughout this book the nearest Underground station is indicated by the word 'tube'.

Fares

One-day Travelcards usually offer the cheapest method of travelling, and can be used after 9.30 am on all London transport (tubes, main-line trains and buses). London is divided into concentric zones, and the Travelcard you need will depend on how many zones you cross. Most visitors will find that a Zone 1 & 2 card (£3.50) will be sufficient, but a card for Zones 1, 2, 3 & 4 costs £3.80 and one for Zones 2, 3, 4, 5 & 6 costs £3.20. A card to cover all six zones costs £4.30. A child's Travelcard costs £1.80 regardless of how many zones it covers. If you will need to catch a bus to the station in the morning it's worth noting that Travelcards can be bought several days ahead (you can't buy them on buses).

If you plan to start moving before 9.30 am you can buy a Zone 1 & 2 LT Card (London Transport Card) for £4.50/2.20 (£6/2.80 for Zones 1, 2, 3 & 4, and £7.30/3.20 for all Zones).

Weekly Travelcards are also available but require an identification card with a passport photo. A Zone 1 & 2 card costs £16.60; Zones 1, 2 & 3 is £20.90; Zones 1, 2, 3 & 4 is £26; Zones 1, 2, 3, 4 & 5 is £30.40; and an all Zones card costs £33. These allow you to travel at any time of day and on night buses, but before buying one decide whether you're really likely to travel much before 9.30 am; five one-day Travelcards plus a weekend card can work out cheaper than a weekly pass.

At £5.20 for Zones 1 & 2, Weekend Travelcards for Saturday and Sunday are 25% cheaper than two one-day cards. Family Travelcards are also available for groups of one or two adults travelling with between one and four children who need not be related to them; they start at £2.80 per adult and 50p per child for Zones 1 & 2.

If you will be making a lot of journeys within Zone 1, you can buy a carnet of 10 tickets for £10, a saving of £3.

Using the Underground

Times of the last tube trains vary from 11.30 pm to 12.30 am depending on the day, the station and the line; the times of the first and last trains are usually listed in the ticket office.

To find your way around the system first locate where you are on the Underground map. Each line has a different colour (red for the Central Line, yellow for the Circle etc), so note what line your station is on and what line the station you're travelling to is on. If they're both on the same line then all you need to do is note whether you're travelling north, east, south or west (known as northbound, eastbound etc by LRT) and head on down. If they're not on the same line, then you need to note the nearest station where the two lines meet and where you must change trains.

In the past as a rough rule of thumb you could assume it would take two minutes to travel between two stations and plan your journey accordingly. These days, however, it's a happy journey which doesn't involve any unscheduled halts in tunnels or other delays, so you must allow more time than you really think is necessary.

Different lines vary in their reliability and it's unfortunate that the Circle Line, which links most of the main-line stations and so is much used by tourists, has one of the worst records. Conversely, the Piccadilly Line to Heathrow is generally pretty good.

The extension of the Jubilee Line east to Canary Wharf and North Greenwich and north to Stratford is due to open in mid-1998 which is also when the East London Line is due to reopen. But other much-needed lines like the east-west Crossrail route, the Chelsea-Hackney Line and the Croxley Rail Link are all on hold pending the discovery of some pot of untapped financing.

If you're caught travelling on the Underground without a valid ticket you're liable for an on-the-spot fine of £10. Should your journey be delayed for more than 15 minutes for a reason under LRT's control you're theoretically entitled to compensation. Phone ☎ 918 4040...and good luck!

BUS

'First none came at all, then there were three at once' – it's the constant refrain of users of the London bus services.

If you're not in a hurry, travelling round by London's famous double-decker buses can be more enjoyable than using the tube, if only because you can get in some incidental sightseeing along the way. LRT is also responsible for the buses which are used by an estimated 3.8 million passengers a day. There are four types of tickets: single-journey bus tickets sold on the bus (minimum 60/40p), daily and weekly bus passes, single or return tickets (same as for the tube and sold at stations, sometimes from vending machines, minimum £1.30) and Travelcards (see the Underground section). A one-day all zones bus pass is great value at £2.70/1.40 for an adult/child.

There are 35 separate free bus maps of London although map sheet number one, which covers the whole of central London and the City of London, will suit most people's purposes. The LRT information centres in the Heathrow terminals, and at Victoria, Piccadilly and King's Cross stations can provide these maps; or phone ☎ 371 0247 to have one sent. For general information on London buses phone ☎ 222 1234 (24 hours); for news of how services are running call Travelcheck on ☎ 222 1200.

Trafalgar Square is the focus for a reasonable network of night buses, but services can be infrequent and only stop on request. LRT publishes a free timetable, *Buses for Night Owls*, which lists them all. One-day Travelcards aren't valid on night buses but Weekly Travelcards are.

Useful Bus Routes

One of the best ways to explore London is to buy a Travelcard and jump on a bus. From north to south, or vice versa, the No 24 is especially good. Beginning in Hampstead, it travels through Camden and along Gower St to Tottenham Court Rd. From Tottenham Court Rd it travels along Charing Cross Rd, past Leicester Square to Trafalgar Square, then along Whitehall, past the House of Commons, Westminster Abbey and Westminster Cathedral. It reaches Victoria station and then carries on to Pimlico, which is handy for the Tate Gallery.

Another north-south route worth trying – not least because Kentish Bus has a distinctive cream and chocolate livery and the route clearly marked on the side – is the No 19 which travels down Upper St in Islington, through Clerkenwell and Holborn, then along New Oxford St and down Charing Cross Rd. It then travels along Shaftesbury Ave and Piccadilly, bypassing Green Park before continuing down Sloane St and along King's Rd. If you get off at the far side of Battersea Bridge you'll be well-placed for Battersea Park.

From east to west, try the No 8. This is a 'Routemaster' bus (red, open-backed and with a conductor) and comes from Bethnal Green Market. It passes or runs close to the Whitechapel Art Gallery, Petticoat Lane Market, Liverpool St station, the City, the Guildhall and Old Bailey. It then crosses Holborn and enters Oxford St, travelling past Oxford Circus, Bond St, Selfridges and the flagship Marks & Spencer store at Marble Arch. Get off at Hyde Park Corner unless you wish to continue north-west up Edgware Rd to Willesden Green.

The wheelchair-accessible Stationlink bus service follows a similar route to the Circle line, joining up all the main-line stations. People with mobility problems and those with heavy luggage may find this easier to use than the tube, although it only operates once an hour. From Paddington there are

DOUG McKINLAY

TOM SMALLMAN

TOM SMALLMAN

PAT YALE

A	C
B	
D	

A: Trafalgar Square
B: Feeding the pigeons, Trafalgar Square
C: Resting on Landseer lion, Trafalgar Square
D: Frolicking in Trafalgar Square in summer

CHARLOTTE HINDLE

TOM SMALLMAN

PAT YALE

Top: Summer Festival, Festival Hall
Middle: Sunbathing in Hyde Park
Bottom: Modernist Penguin Pool at London Zoo

services clockwise (SL1) from 8.15 am to 7.15 pm, and anticlockwise (SL2) from 8.40 am to 6.40 pm.

MAIN-LINE TRAINS

Several rail companies now operate passenger trains in London; most lines interchange with the tube and Travelcards can be used on them.

If you're staying in south-east London where main-line trains are often more useful than the tube, it may be worth buying a one-year Network Card which offers one-third off most rail fares in south and east England and one-day Travelcards for all six zones (see Tickets under Train in the Getting There & Away chapter for more details).

CAR & MOTORCYCLE

If you can, avoid bringing a car into London. Traffic moves slowly and parking is expensive. Traffic wardens and wheel clampers operate with extreme efficiency and if your vehicle is towed away it'll cost you around £100 to get it back.

At around 66p per litre (equivalent to £2.20 for a US gallon), petrol is expensive by American or Australian standards; and diesel is a only few pence cheaper. Distances, however, aren't great.

Road Rules

If you do plan to drive you should first get hold of the *Highway Code* (99p), which is often available in TICs and is sold in bookshops. A foreign driving licence is valid in Britain for up to 12 months from the time of your last entry into the country. If you're bringing a car from Europe make sure you're adequately insured.

Briefly, vehicles drive on the left-hand side of the road; front-seat belts are compulsory and if belts are fitted in the back they must be worn; the speed limit is 30mph (48kmh) in built-up areas, 60mph (96kmh) on single carriageways, and 70mph (112kmh) on dual or triple carriageways; you give way to your right at roundabouts (traffic already on the roundabout has the right of way); and motorcyclists must wear helmets.

See Legal Matters in Facts for the Visitor for information on drink-driving rules.

Car Parking

If you're blessed/cursed with private transport, avoid peak hours (7.30 to 9.30 am, 4.30 to 7 pm), and plan ahead if you need to park in the centre.

Look out for yellow lines along the roadside. The only way to establish exactly what restrictions they indicate is to find the nearby sign that spells them out. A single line means no parking 8.30 am and 6.30 pm, five days a week; a double line means no parking at all; and a broken line means more limited restrictions. Single red lines on main routes in and out of central London indicate a ban on stopping, loading or parking between 7 am and 7 pm while a double red line means no stopping, loading or parking at all.

There are 'short-stay' and 'long-stay' car parks. Prices will often be the same for stays of up to two or three hours, but for lengthier stays the short-stay car parks rapidly become much more expensive. The long-stay car parks may be slightly less convenient but they're much cheaper.

Cars parked illegally will be clamped, which is as agonising as it sounds. A clamp is locked on a wheel and in order to have it removed you have to travel across town, pay an enormous fine, then wait most of the day for someone to come and release you. Phone National Car Parks (☎ 499 7050) for car park addresses; rates vary but are rarely cheap.

The City of London Information Centre can supply a leaflet on parking in the City for people with disabilities. For a copy phone ☎ 332 1548.

Rental

Car hire rates are expensive; often you'll be better off making arrangements in your home country for some sort of package deal. The big international rental companies charge from around £150 a week for a small car (Ford Fiesta, Peugeot 106).

The main companies include Avis (☎ 0990-900500), British Car Rental (☎ 278 2802), Budget (☎ 0800-181181), Europcar

(☎ 0345-222525), Eurodollar (☎ 0990-365365), Hertz (☎ 0345-555888) and Thrifty Car Rental (☎ 403 3458).

Holiday Autos (☎ 0990-300400) operates through a number of rental companies and generally offers excellent deals. A week's all-inclusive hire starts at £129 for the smallest car. For other cheap operators check the ads in *TNT* magazine. The tourist information centres stock lists of local car-hire companies.

Purchase

If you're planning to tour around when you leave London you may want to buy a vehicle. It's possible to get something reasonable for around £1000; a reliable van (see following section) could be up to twice as much. Check *Loot* (every weekday), *Autotrader* (Friday; includes photos) and the *Motorists' Guide* (monthly; lists models and average prices).

All cars require a Ministry of Transport safety certificate (MOT), valid for one year and issued by licensed garages; full third party insurance – shop around but expect to pay at least £300; registration – a standard form signed by the buyer and seller, with a section to be sent to the Department of Transport; and tax (£145 for one year, £79.75 for six months) – from main post offices on presentation of valid MOT, insurance and registration documents.

You're strongly advised to buy a vehicle with valid MOT and tax. MOT and tax remain with the car through a change of ownership; third party insurance goes with the driver rather than the car, so you will still have to arrange this (and beware of letting others drive the car). For further information about registering, licensing, insuring and testing your vehicle, contact a post office or Vehicle Registration Office for leaflet V100.

Van Vans provide a popular method of touring Britain, particularly for shoestring travellers. Often three or four people will band together to buy or rent a van. Look at the adverts in *TNT* magazine if you wish to form or join a group.

TNT carries ads for vans, as does *Loot*. The Van Market in Market Rd, London N7 (near Caledonian Rd tube station), is a long-running institution where private vendors congregate on a daily basis. Some second-hand dealers offer a 'buy-back' scheme for when you return, but buying and reselling privately is better if you have the time.

Vans usually feature a fixed high-top or elevating roof and two to five-bunk beds. Apart from the essential camping gas cooker, professional conversions may include a sink, fridge and built-in cupboards. You will need to spend at least £1000 to £2000 for something reliable enough to get you around Europe.

An eternal favourite is the VW Kombi; they aren't made any more but the old ones seem to go on forever, and getting spares isn't a problem.

Motoring Organisations

Consider joining a motoring organisation for 24-hour breakdown assistance. The two largest in the UK are the AA (☎ 0800-444999) and the RAC (☎ 0800-550550). One year's membership starts at £45 for the AA and £44 for the RAC. Both these companies can also extend their cover to include Europe.

If you're a member of a motoring organisation back home, you should check to see if it has a reciprocal arrangement with a British organisation.

TAXI

The black London taxi cab is as much a feature of the cityscape as the red bus, although these days it comes in a variety of colours and liberally bespattered with advertising.

Taking a taxi on your own is unlikely to be cheap, but with a group of five it can work out quite competitively and save the hanging around for trains and buses. Taxis also come into their own at night, although prices are higher. Cabs are available for hire when the yellow sign is lit. Fares are metered, kicking in at £2, and a 10% tip is expected. To order a cab try one of the radio taxi companies on (☎ 272 0272).

Drivers with The Knowledge

To get behind the wheel of a black cab in London, drivers need to earn a green badge (yellow for suburban drivers), study a blue book and put themselves severely in the red. Confused? Well spare a thought for what prospective cabbies must go through to become a licensed London taxi driver.

When you climb into one of London's 20,000 black cabs you can can rest assured you'll get where you want to go – by the quickest route possible – because all drivers must complete a rigorous learning and testing process known as 'The Knowledge' before they can hit the streets. For an 'All London' licence, this means buying a moped and a good map and spending up to two years studying (the 'blue book'), and memorising 25,000 streets within a six mile radius of Charing Cross.

But it's not just getting from street A to street B. Drivers are expected to know the locations of clubs, hospitals, hotels, theatres, railway stations, places of worship ... the list goes on. All this culminates in a series of 15 minute interviews and tests which may take months to pass. It means a lot of time, money and patience – which, says the Public Carriage Office, means only committed cabbies will join the 'noble trade'.

These days many of the black cabs are anything but black – some are daubed with a variety of colourful advertising slogans. While you're in London, look out for the Lonely Planet taxi ... and see our Spot the Taxi competition on page 273 of this book. ■

Minicabs are cheaper freelance competitors to the black cabs; anyone with a car can work, but they can only be hired by phone. Some have a very limited idea of how to get around efficiently (and safely) – you may find yourself being pressed to map read. They don't have meters, so it's essential to get a quote before you start. They can carry four people.

Small minicab companies are based in particular areas: ask a local for the name of a reputable company, or phone one of the large 24-hour operators (☎ 387 8888, 272 2612, 383 3333, 0181-340 2450, 0181-567 1111). Women travelling by themselves at night can choose Lady Cabs (☎ 272 3019), which has women drivers. Gays and lesbians can choose Freedom Cars (☎ ☎ 734 1313).

BICYCLE

Cycling around London is one way of cutting transport costs, but it can be a grim business, with heavy traffic and fumes detracting from the pleasure of taking exercise. The London Cycling Campaign (☎ 928 7220) is working towards improving conditions, not least by campaigning to establish the London Cycle Network which is up and running in some parts of the capital. The plan is that by the year 2000 there should be 1200 miles of bike route throughout the capital. For £4.95 they produce a pack including a map showing established cycle routes and advisory cycle routes, as well as green routes where cycling is actually pleasurable. The pack also includes a copy of *On Your Bike* with all sorts of info on bike maintenance etc.

If you want to buy a bike it might be worth heading for the auction (☎ 0181-870 3909) at 63 Garratt Lane SW18 (Wandsworth Town station) where the police offload bikes every Monday at 11 am. Less frequent bike auctions occur at 118 Putney Bridge Rd SW15; phone ☎ 0181-788 7777 for details. Second-hand bikes are also advertised in *Cycling Weekly*, *Loot* and *Exchange & Mart*.

If you prefer to hire, all the places listed below offer mountain or hybrid bikes in mint condition. Each demands at least £150 deposit (credit-card slips are accepted), however long you intend to hire for. It's advisable to wear a helmet and increasingly Londoners wear a face mask to filter out pollution.

London Bicycle Tour Company
: Gabriel's Wharf SE1 – £9.95 for the first day, £5 for subsequent days; or £29.95 the first week, £25 subsequent weeks (☎ 928 6838).

Bikepark
: 14½ Stukeley St WC2 – minimum charge is £4 for four hours; £10 for the first day, £5 the second day and £3 for subsequent days (☎ 430 0083).

Dial-a-Bike
18 Gillingham St SW1 – £6.99 per day and £29.90 per week (☎ 828 4040).

The London Bicycle Tour Company also organises cycle tours of London, costing £9.95 and lasting three and a half hours. Tours of the East End taking in the Globe Theatre, Tower Bridge, Tobacco Dock, the East End proper, the City and St Paul's Cathedral, depart from Gabriel's Wharf every Saturday at 2 pm. Tours of the West End, taking in the Houses of Parliament, Lambeth Palace, Kensington and Chelsea, the Royal Albert Hall, Buckingham Palace, St James's, Trafalgar Square and Covent Garden, depart from Gabriel's Wharf every Sunday at 2 pm.

Bikes can be taken on the District, Circle, Hammersmith & City, and Metropolitan tube lines outside the rush hours (ie after 10 am and before 4 pm, and after 7 pm). They can also travel on the overground sections of the suburban tube lines, but not on the deeper lines. No bikes can be carried on the Docklands Light Railway.

To get to Heathrow, take a main-line train from Paddington to Hayes & Harlington and then cycle the rest of the way, or (for Terminal 4) take a train from Waterloo to Feltham and cycle from there. Alternatively pick up the tube between Barons Court and Hounslow West and cycle the rest of the way. To get to Stansted take the train to Stansted Mountfitchet from Liverpool St and then cycle the rest of the way (bicycles aren't allowed on the direct Skytrain). Bikes can be carried on the trains to Gatwick airport, and will be allowed on the Heathrow main-line train from Paddington once it's completed. There's free bike parking in the airport car parks but it's not necessarily secure.

Now that British Rail has been privatised into innumerable smaller train operating companies you need to check with the relevant one before attempting to take a bike on a journey into or out of London.

There's a central bike park in Stukeley St, Covent Garden. It's open weekdays from 7.30 am to 8.30 pm and weekends from 8.30 am to 6.30 pm. To park your wheels there for four hours costs 50p.

WALKING

Although London is huge, many of the sights you'll want to visit are relatively close together in the centre and walking between them can be as pleasant as battling your way onto a tube or bus. Stock up on a good map (see Facts for the Visitor) or an A-Z atlas and you'll be well away.

Guided Walks

Several companies offer themed walking tours with guides. Popular themes include Dickensian London, Pepys' London, Shakespearean London, Wesley's London, legal London and Jewish London. Other walks will take you down hidden alleys and byways, round modern developments like Broadgate, or into hidden gardens and pubs. There are also various ghost and ghoul walks and, for those who don't think this too tacky, Jack the Ripper tours of Whitechapel.

Most walks take place between Easter and October, last around two hours, cost around £4 a head and leave from outside tube stations; *Time Out* will have details for the week ahead.

The main companies offering guided walks are:

London Walks (☎ 624 3978)
Cityguide Walks (☎ 01895-675389)
Historical Walks of London (☎ 0181-668 4019)
Capital Walks (☎ 0181-650 7640)
Ye Olde Walks of London (☎ 0181-672 5894)
Stepping Out (☎ 0181-881 2933)

Regular walks round Shakespeare's Bankside leave from outside the Globe Theatre in New Globe Walk on Friday, Saturday and Sunday at 11.30 am and 12.30, 1.30, 2.30, and 3.30 pm. They last 40 minutes and cost £2.

Clerkenwell Guides (☎ 638 4942) offer regular walks round Clerkenwell, leaving from outside Farringdon tube at 11 am on Wednesday, 6.30 pm on Thursday and 2 pm on Sunday. They also offer a Smithfield

Trail, leaving from outside Barbican tube on Saturday at 11 am, and an Angel Trail leaving from outside Angel tube on Sunday at 2 pm. All these walks cost £4.50.

The Greenwich Tour Guides Association offers a Meridian Walk at 12.15 pm and a Royal Greenwich Walk at 2.15 pm. These leave daily from the tourist information centre at 46 Greenwich Church St, last 1½ hours and cost £4/3. For more details phone ☎ 0181-858 6169.

From June to October the Society of Voluntary Guides offers walks round Richmond, Twickenham and Kew. Tours of historic Richmond leave the Old Town Hall at 11 am Monday to Friday. On Saturday the tours are of Richmond Hill, while on some Sundays Discovering Richmond walks amalgamate the highlights of the other tours. Tickets cost £2/1 and must be bought from Richmond TIC (☎ 0181-940 9125), Old Town Hall, Whittaker Ave, Richmond.

Kew Walks leave St Anne's Church on Kew Green at 11 am on Saturday. Twickenham Walks leave St Mary's Church, Church St, York House End, Twickenham on Sunday at 2.15 pm. Tickets (£2/1) can be bought from the guides.

Self-Guided Walks

You can also buy several booklets detailing self-guided walks. A good one to look out for is *The London Wall Walk* (£1.95) which takes you round 21 landmarks along the old Roman and medieval city wall. Altogether this 1¾ mile (2.8km) walk should take between one and two hours to complete.

The British Travel Centre sells a map (£1.20) showing the route of the 12-mile *Silver Jubilee Walkway* which starts in Leicester Square and runs through the City, along the South Bank and round Westminster, with silver boards describing the sights along the way.

The Theatre Museum sells *A Walk of Theatre land* (£1.50), with details not only of all the West End theatres but also of many famous theatrical personalities of the past. It should take around two hours to complete.

British Waterways also publishes an excellent short guide, *Explore London's Canals* (£1), with details of six walks along London's 40 miles of canal towpaths.

You'll find other ideas for walks in the Walks chapter.

BOAT

Although the main commuter waterbus along the Thames has ceased operating, there are still a few services on the river, and this can be one of the most enjoyable ways to get round on a sunny day.

City Cruises (☎ 237 5134) operates a May to September Pool of London ferry service, travelling from Tower Pier to London Bridge, City, Butlers Wharf and St Katherine's Pier every 15 minutes from 11 am to 5 pm daily. Tickets cost £2/1 and are valid for unlimited use all day.

The main starting points for cruises along the Thames are Westminster and Charing Cross piers (see the boxed aside Messing About on the River for details of boat trips to Greenwich, Kew Gardens and Hampton Court Palace).

Canal Trips

London has 40 miles of inner-city canals, most of them constructed in the early 19th century to transport goods from the industrial Midlands to the Port of London. After a long period of neglect, these canals are slowly being given a new lease of life as a leisure resource for boaters, walkers, anglers etc.

Regent's Canal loops round north London for 2½ miles from Little Venice in Maida Vale to Camden Lock, passing through London Zoo and Regent's Park on the way. Two companies offer boat rides along the canal; you can choose between travelling on an enclosed waterbus (London Waterbus Company) or on an open-sided canal cruiser (Jason's Trip). Jason's boats leave from opposite No 60 Blomfield Rd, Little Venice, while the waterbuses leave from a little further east across the Westbourne Terrace bridge.

The London Waterbus Company (☎ 482 2550) runs 80-minute trips between Camden

Lock (tube: Camden Town) and Little Venice (tube: Warwick Avenue). From April to October boats depart from the locks at Camden and Little Venice every hour between 10 am and 5 pm; the last return trip departs at 3 pm, the last one-way trip at 3.45 pm. From November to March boats only go at weekends; phone for exact times. One-way tickets are £3.70/2.30, return tickets £4.80/2.90.

If you want to go to the zoo a ticket including the admission fee and a ride from Little Venice costs £9.70/6.50, or £8/6 if you want to be ferried from Camden Lock. If you want to leave the zoo by boat, a one-way ticket to Camden Lock is £1.40/1, while to Little Venice it's £2.60/1.70. Boats from the zoo to Camden Lock leave at 10.35 am, then hourly until 5.35 pm; to Little Venice they leave at 10.15 am, then hourly to 5.15 pm. From June to September there are services every 30 minutes on Sunday.

Alternatively you can travel the same route with Jason's Trip (☎ 286 3428). Boats leave Little Venice at 10.30 am, 12.30 and 2.30 pm from April to September, with an extra 4.30 pm departure in June, July and August but no 10.30 am departure in October. Tickets cost £4.50/3.20 one way or £5.50/4 return. Jenny Wren (☎ 485 4433) offers a similar service out of Camden Lock.

Real canal enthusiasts might like to phone

Messing About on the River

For too long the River Thames has been London's most under-utilised asset, but recently there has been a resurgence of interest in getting around by water, not least because of traffic congestion on the roads. However, regular ferries have not been particularly successful and it's mainly the tour cruisers that cash in on the fine river scenery.

If you take the cruises to Greenwich and to Hampton Court they will quickly show up the staggering difference between east and west London. Although the trip from Westminster Pier to Hampton Court takes half a day, it's certainly worth taking the shorter trip east to Greenwich unless you're extremely pushed for time. It's likely to prove one of the highlights of your visit.

For information on boat services eastward call the Westminster Passenger Services Association on ☎ 930 1616; for services westward call ☎ 930 4721. Advance booking is rarely required.

East Along the Thames

Cruise boats leave Westminster Pier (beside Westminster Bridge) for Greenwich every half-hour from 10 am, passing the site of Shakespeare's Globe Theatre, stopping at the Tower of London and continuing under Tower Bridge and past many famous docks. Tickets to Greenwich cost £5.30/6.30 single/return.

West Along the Thames

River boats also run west from Westminster Pier, an enjoyable excursion although it takes much longer and is not, perhaps, as dramatic or interesting as the trip to the east.

The two main destinations are Kew Gardens and Hampton Court Palace, both highlights of a London visit, but to do them both justice you need to set aside more than one day. It's also possible to get off the boats at Richmond in July and August.

Boats to the Royal Botanic Gardens at Kew sail from Westminster Pier every 30 minutes from 10.15 am to 2.30 pm (from the Monday before Easter until the end of September). They take 1¾ hours and a single/return costs £6/10. Boats to Hampton Court Palace leave from Westminster Pier from April to October at 10.30 and 11.15 am and noon. The journey takes 3½ hours and costs £8/12. Children pay half fare but may get restless on such a long trip.

You can also get to Hampton Court from St Helena Pier, Water Lane, Richmond. From May to September, Turk Launches (☎ 0181-546 2434) has boats at 11 am, 2.15 and 6.15 pm Tuesday to Saturday. The journey takes 1¾ hours and tickets cost £5/6 a single/return. In April the boats leave on Sunday and bank holidays.

Two warnings about the boats. Firstly, the food and drink on board is inevitably expensive; pack a picnic if you don't want to pay over the odds. Secondly, the boatmen who give the commentaries insist that they're not professional guides (despite the fact that they do this day in, day out) and then solicit an 'appreciation for the commentary' (ie a tip). Whether or not you pay is up to you, but why this should be seen as an added 'extra' is something of a mystery. ■

the London Waterbus Company for details of occasional day trips to Limehouse Basin and back via Limehouse Cut and the Hertford Union Canal; or to Brentford via the Paddington Arm and the Grand Union Canal, passing across the North Circular Aqueduct and through the Hanwell Flight of six locks which raises the canal 16m in a third of a mile.

ORGANISED TOURS

Since travel round London by bus or train is so easy, there's little need to pay for organised tours. Still, if your time is limited and you prefer to travel in a group, companies are falling over themselves to offer organised sightseeing tours, many of them of the hop-on-hop-off variety and often in open-top buses – great if it's warm, wretched if it's not.

It makes more sense to book an organised tour if you want to see sights like Hampton Court Palace or Windsor Castle on the periphery of London, or to get out to Bath, Oxford, Stonehenge or Canterbury for the day.

Round London

The Original London Sightseeing Tour (☎ 222 1234), the Big Bus Company (☎ 0181-944 7810) and London Pride Sightseeing (☎ 01708-631122) all offer tours around the main sights in double-decker buses which allow you either to go straight round without getting off or to hop on and off at the sights along the way. They're all expensive (around £12/6) and probably only worth considering if you're only going to be in London for a day or two. Most companies can sell you advance tickets to the biggest attractions to save wasting time in queues.

Convenient starting points are in Trafalgar Square in front of the National Gallery, in front of the Trocadero on Coventry St between Leicester Square and Piccadilly Circus, and in Wilton Gardens opposite Victoria Station.

London Pride Sightseeing includes Docklands and Greenwich in one of its tours, while the Original London Sightseeing Tour has an express tour for those with limited time.

Day Trips

The Adventure Travel Centre (☎ 370 4555), 131 Earls Court Rd SW5 (tube: Earls Court), does Sunday day trips specifically aimed at the Australasian market. Each trip takes in two destinations (say Oxford and Blenheim Palace or Leeds Castle and Canterbury) and costs £12 (£10 to members of the Deckers Club; see Australasian Clubs under Useful Organisations in the Facts for the Visitor chapter).

Another company worth trying is Astral Tours (☎ 0700-0781016) whose Magical Tours in mini-coaches cover Bath, the Cotswolds, Old Sarum, Brighton, Salisbury, Stonehenge, Avebury and Glastonbury...not all on the same trip, of course! A day trip costs from £28 to £42, including all entrance fees and a pub lunch. There's also an £18 half-day tour to Windsor, Runnymede, Eton and Henley. Students and YHA members are eligible for discounts.

Evan Evans Tours (☎ 0181-332 2222) also offers excursions with pick-ups from most large London hotels. A trip to Windsor costs £18.50/14 (including admission to the castle) and leaves from the TIC at Victoria at 12.30 pm on Monday, Wednesday, Thursday and Friday. Other tours combine Windsor with Hampton Court Gardens, Oxford and Stratford. They also operate a tour to Bath and Stonehenge.

Sightseeing Flights

If you want to see London in style, what better way than to book a trip over the Thames in a hot-air balloon? Flights from the City airport or Stansted sail over the Thames Barrier, the Tower of London, St Paul's Cathedral, Buckingham Palace and Chelsea Harbour. Depending on the weather, flights leave between 9.30 am and 2.30 pm Monday to Saturday. On Sunday they leave Stansted airport from 9.30 am to 3.30 pm. Flights last for 30 minutes and cost £99 from the City airport and £79 from Stansted. Telephone ☎ 0345-697074 for more details.

Things to See & Do

Even more than most capital cities, London is stuffed with things to see and do. Fortunately most of them are clustered together in the centre of town, either in the City of London, the West End or Westminster, and you can easily walk between them, bearing in mind the need to conserve enough energy to cope with the museums and galleries. Alternatively there are plenty of buses and tube trains to get you around. You could even hire the odd taxi, especially if you're in a group to cut costs.

Other sights are further afield, which is when the tube really comes into its own. Unfortunately the south-east corner of London is not well served by the Underground, a situation that should gradually improve, especially once the station at Greenwich is built.

This chapter covers London's innumerable tourist attractions in the following sequence. First come the sights in central London, with those in the West End, Covent Garden, the Strand, Westminster & Pimlico and the City described first since these are the 'must sees' that visitors with limited time will want to take in. Immediately afterwards come the attractions in the remainder of central London, defined for the purposes of this guide as those areas covered by London Transport's Central London bus route map. Attractions are described as if moving in a clockwise direction with those in the north (St John's Wood, Marylebone & Regent's Park; Euston & King's Cross; Camden & Islington; Bloomsbury & Holborn; Clerkenwell) described first, followed by those in the east (East End & Docklands), the south (Bermondsey & Southwark; Waterloo & Lambeth; Battersea) and the west (Knightsbridge & Chelsea; Kensington & Holland Park; Notting Hill, Bayswater & Earl's Court; Hyde Park; Hammersmith & Fulham).

After that come the attractions in Greater London, again described in clockwise order, starting from the north (Wembley & Neasden; Hampstead & Highgate; Walthamstow), and heading south (Greenwich; Brixton; Wimbledon) and west (Richmond; Twickenham & Teddington; Chiswick & Kew; Brentford & Ealing).

Phone Codes

All phone numbers in this chapter should be prefixed with the code ☎ 0171 unless the text says otherwise.

If calling from within central London, it is not necessary to use the 0171 code. ■

SIGHTSEEING ITINERARY

With limited time you'll have hard choices to make about what to see and do. The following is a suggested itinerary for a first-time visitor with a week to spend in London:

Day One
: Visit Westminster Abbey and view the Houses of Parliament and Big Ben. Walk down Whitehall, passing Downing St, the Cenotaph and Horse Guards Parade. Cross Trafalgar Square to visit the National Gallery. Walk to Piccadilly Circus to see the statue of Eros. Dine out in Soho.

Day Two
: Visit the British Museum and go shopping in Oxford St. Take in a play or a musical.

Day Three
: Visit one of the South Kensington museums, then take a bus to Harrods. Have a look at Buckingham Palace and St James's Park. Eat out in Covent Garden.

Day Four
: Visit St Paul's Cathedral and the Museum of London. Attend an outdoor concert at Kenwood.

Day Five
: Visit the Tower of London and Tower Bridge. Use the Docklands Light Railway to see a newer side of London.

Day Six
: Visit Hampton Court Palace. Go clubbing.

Day Seven

Cross the Thames to visit the new Globe Theatre. Walk along the South Bank to the Museum of the Moving Image. Take in a foyer concert in the National Theatre.

With another week you could explore some of the London markets, take a boat to Greenwich to see the Cutty Sark and the National Maritime Museum, go to London Zoo and Camden Lock, and visit some of the smaller museums like the quirky Sir John Soane Museum in Lincoln's Inn Fields, Leighton House in Holland Park and the Old Operating Theatre near London Bridge. You could also head north to Hampstead to explore the heath and Freud and Keats' houses, both of them open to the public.

A third week would let you explore some of the outer suburbs like Chiswick and Richmond, perhaps taking in Ham House and Osterley House. A side trip to Windsor and Eton would be possible. You might also want to visit Hatfield House or St Albans with its Roman remains.

Highlights

- British Museum
- National Gallery
- Leighton House, Holland Park
- Outdoor concerts at Kenwood House
- Plays at the Globe Theatre
- Natural History Museum
- Courtauld Gallery
- Hampton Court
- Boat trip to Greenwich
- St James's Park

Lowlights

- London Dungeon
- Rock Circus
- Leicester Square
- The tat along Camden High St
- Litter-strewn streets
- Queuing for Planet Hollywood
- Last trains timed to leave you stranded after a night out
- Ticket barriers on London Underground
- Unintelligible station announcements on London Underground
- Pubs closing at 11 pm ■

Central London

WEST END (Map 3)

The West End of London is the area roughly centred on Piccadilly Circus and Trafalgar Square. It takes in Oxford St, Regent St and Tottenham Court Rd, a heady mixture of consumerism and culture. Several outstanding museums and galleries rub shoulders with tacky tourist traps while world-famous buildings and monuments share the streets with some of the capital's best shopping and entertainment possibilities. This is the London of the postcard stands and folk memory.

Trafalgar Square

Trafalgar Square (tube: Charing Cross) is the closest you'll get to the heart of London. This is where many great marches and rallies take place, and where the new year is seen in by thousands of drunken revellers. The riot in Trafalgar Square in 1990, which hammered one of the last nails into the coffin of the unpopular poll tax, is depicted in a painting on display in the Museum of London.

The square was designed by Nash in the early 19th century, and executed by Barry, who was also partly responsible for the Houses of Parliament. The 165ft-tall **Nelson's Column** commemorates Napoleon's defeat at sea in 1805. The four bronze lions round its foot were designed by Landseer and attract tourists and pigeons in equal numbers.

Although the traffic swirling past and the crowds of people often make it difficult to get much sense of perspective, the Square is virtually ringed with imposing buildings. To the north stands the National Gallery, with the church of St Martin's-in-the-Fields to the north-east. Directly to the east stands **South Africa House** (1933), where the stone heads of African wildlife once gazed down on non-stop protests against apartheid. To the south the square opens out and you catch glimpses down Whitehall through the traffic. To the south-west stands **Admiralty Arch**, with The Mall leading to Buckingham Palace beyond it. To the west is **Canada House**, designed by Sir Robert Smirke in 1824-7.

National Gallery

The porticoed front of the National Gallery (☎ 839 3321) extends along the north side of the square. With over 2000 paintings on display it's one of the world's finest art galleries...and the fact that admission is still free means you'll be able to visit more than once if you want to. The Salisbury Wing on the west side was only added after considerable controversy during the course of which Prince Charles put paid to one possible modernist design by describing it as like 'a carbuncle on the face of a much-loved friend.'

To make life easier for visitors, the paintings in the National Gallery were rehung in a continuous time line a few years ago. That means that by starting in the Sainsbury Wing and progressing west you could take in a collection of pictures painted between 1260 and 1920 in chronological order. In reality most people like some periods of art more than others, so if you're keen on the real oldies head for the Sainsbury Wing (1260-1510); if your tastes are for the High Renaissance head for the West Wing (1510-1600); if you prefer Rubens, Rembrandt and Murillo head for the North Wing (1600-1700); and if you're after Gainsborough, Constable, Turner, Hogarth and the Impressionists head for the East Wing (1700-1920).

If you were to seek out the highlights listed in the boxed aside they would certainly give you a good overview of what the National Gallery has to offer. But the list is by no means comprehensive and you'll have fun picking your own favourites. To find out more about any of the pictures borrow a National Gallery Soundtrack headset from the central hall. Beside each picture a number is listed. Feed this into the machine and it will skip to the appropriate place in the CD-Rom so you needn't even walk round following someone else's sequence.

It's also worth taking one of the free guided tours which introduce you to a manageable half-dozen paintings at a time.

Highlights of the National Gallery

Arnolfini Wedding	van Eyck
Rokeby Venus	Velasquez
Wilton Diptych	
Bathers	Cezanne
Venus & Mars	Botticelli
Virgin of the Rocks	da Vinci
Virgin & Child with St Anne & St John the Baptist	da Vinci
Battle of San Romano	Uccello
The Ambassadors	Holbein the Younger
Charles I	van Dyck
Le Chapeau de Paille	Rubens
The Hay-Wain	Constable
Sunflowers	van Gogh
The Water-Lily Pond	Monet
The Fighting Temeraire	Turner

Afterwards there's a branch of Pret-a-Manger or a brasserie for refreshments.

The gallery is open Monday to Saturday from 10 am to 6 pm (8 pm on Wednesday), and Sunday from 2 to 6 pm.

National Portrait Gallery

You visit the National Portrait Gallery not so much for the quality of its paintings but to put the faces to the famous and the not-so-famous names in British history. The pictures are displayed in chronological order, starting with the Tudors on the top floor and descending to the late 20th century on the ground floor. Everyone will have their own favourites, but the portraits of Elizabeth I in all her finery and of Byron in romantic oriental garb are particularly memorable. The portrait of Elizabeth II, which greets you as you mount the stairs, didn't go down well with royalists for showing her with fingers like podgy sausages.

The lower ground floor hosts small-scale temporary exhibitions. A new system of audio-guides enables you to listen to the voices of some of the people portrayed.

The NPG (☎ 306 0055) is open (free) from Monday to Saturday, 10 am to 6 pm (from noon on Sunday). It's round the corner from the National Gallery and opposite St Martin's church (tube: Charing Cross).

On the traffic island outside the NPG is a **statue of Edith Cavell** (1865-1915), the British nurse who helped Allied soldiers escape from Brussels during the WWI and was shot for her pains by the Germans.

St Martin-in-the-Fields

An influential early 18th century masterpiece by James Gibbs, this well-known church (☎ 930 0089) occupies a prime site at the north-eastern corner of Trafalgar Square. The wedding-cake spire is offset by the splendid visual harmony of white stone linking St Martin's and the National Gallery. When floodlit this becomes one of London's greatest vistas.

St Martin's has a long tradition of tending to the poor and homeless, running among other things a soup kitchen. This is a sociable church all round, with an adjoining craft market, and a brass rubbing centre, bookshop and café in the crypt. For details of lunchtime and evening concerts, see Churches in the Entertainment chapter.

It's open Monday to Saturday from 10 am to 6 pm, Sunday from noon to 6 pm.

Leicester Square

Despite efforts to smarten it up, and the presence of four huge cinemas, various nightclubs and pubs and restaurants ringing it, Leicester (pronounced lester) Square still feels more like a transit point between Covent Garden and Piccadilly Circus. You're bound to pass through at some point but it's hard to imagine a time when artists Joshua Reynolds and William Hogarth actually chose to live here.

The patch of green in the middle of the square is a barely acceptable picnic spot if you haven't got the energy to press on to St James's Park. The fountain in the centre commemorates Shakespeare and there's a small statue of Charlie Chaplin to one side. Plaques in the ground also list the distances from central London to the capitals of various Commonwealth countries. More plaques in the pavement outside incorporate the hand prints of various Hollywood stars (the cinemas here are where British film premieres take place).

The 12-mile **Silver Jubilee Walkway** starts in Leicester Square and loops round Lambeth Bridge in the west and Tower Bridge in the east. A map shows the entire route (see Guided Walks in the Getting Around chapter).

Chinatown

Immediately north of Leicester Square are Lisle St and Gerrard St, the heart of London's Chinatown where street signs come with Cantonese translations, and Chinese lanterns and dragon-adorned arches are commonplace. This is the place to come for an after-hours Chinese meal (Lisle St tends to be cheaper than Gerrard St) but to see it at its over-the-top best, time your visit for the Chinese New Year in late January/early February when the streets explode with lion dances.

Piccadilly Circus

Piccadilly Circus is the world-famous, neon-lit home of the statue of Eros. This used to be the hub of London, where flower girls flogged their wares and people arranged to meet or simply bumped into each other. Nowadays it's fume-choked and pretty uninteresting, overlooked by the Rock Circus, Tower Records and a disappointing Japanese department store. Eros itself is one of those monuments every tourist feels obliged to visit and photograph just to prove they've done so. In fact behind this not especially exciting statue of the Greek god of Love lies the romantic story of the Earl of Shaftesbury, a Victorian philanthropist who struggled to prevent women and children working in coalmines and whose memorial this is. At least no-one need risk life or limb to inspect the statue now that it has been moved out of the middle of the road.

Don't miss the nearby Criterion restaurant, attached to the theatre of the same name. This is one of London's big-name eateries, presided over by chef Marco Pierre White, famed for his good food and surliness in equal part (see the Places to Eat chapter for details).

The streets running off Piccadilly Circus are almost as famous as Eros. Running north-east is **Shaftesbury Ave**, named after the same Earl of Shaftesbury and the heart of London's theatreland. To the east Coventry St heads past Planet Hollywood and the Fashion Café to Leicester Square. To the south the Haymarket runs past the Design Centre and down to Pall Mall, while Lower Regent St passes the British Travel Centre to join up with Pall Mall. To the west Piccadilly itself leads past Fortnum & Mason, the Royal Academy and Green Park to end at Hyde Park Corner. From the north-west corner of the circus Regent St snakes north towards Oxford Circus, lined on both sides with elegant arcades of shops.

Rock Circus This is one of London's greatest mysteries. The Rock Circus (☎ 734 8025), London Pavilion, Piccadilly Circus W1 (tube: Piccadilly Circus), is one of the capital's most popular attractions, despite the fact that virtually none of those immortalised in wax would be unknown to the forty-something generation.

It won't take you long to eye up the images and absorb the few snatches of their greatest hits relayed to you through crackly headsets. Then you may have to queue for up to 15 minutes to see the show, the wait made tolerable only by the fine views down on the Circus through the circular windows.

In the video age, the show is even more enigmatic. You're whipped back to rock's cotton-picking origins so fast you barely have time to take in what's happening, after which you're treated to a succession of animated models who fail to lip-sync to their music while jerking their limbs around like puppets. The triumphant finale is Springsteen warbling to *Born in the USA*. Hardly cutting-edge stuff – Britpop might never have happened.

It's open daily from 10 am to 10 pm from late June to early September. Otherwise it's open Monday, Wednesday, Thursday and Sunday from 11 am to 9 pm; Tuesday from noon to 9 pm; Friday and Saturday to 10 pm; £7.95/6.50 (£1 discount for tickets bought at Madame Tussaud's).

Pepsi Trocadero & Segaworld The Pepsi Trocadero (☎ 439 1791), Piccadilly Circus W1 (tube: Piccadilly Circus), first opened as a men's tennis court in 1744 but is now an indoor entertainment complex with several hi-tech attractions, anchored by the Segaworld indoor theme park.

This is a good place to take youngsters who can't be sold on London's more educational attractions, but don't expect a cheap night out. There's a £2 admission charge to Segaworld (☎ 0990-505040) but you must then pay another £2 for each of the five rides and £3 for each of the two 3D simulators. Queues can be offputtingly long. Also inside the Trocadero you can scare yourself half to death on the Drop Ride (£3.50) or have a go at warfare Virtual World style (£2). A visit to the Emaginator 'cinema' costs another £3.75. Then there are assorted interactive games each costing 50p to £1 a shot. The centre is open from 10 am until midnight daily, staying open until 1 am on Friday and Saturday.

Piccadilly

Piccadilly is said to take its curious name from the 'piccadils', or ruffs, made by a 17th century tailor who built himself a house here. As you leave Piccadilly Circus look out for **St James's, Piccadilly** on the left. This was one of the churches designed by Sir Christopher Wren after the Great Fire of 1666, and it's another of those sociable London churches, churning out concerts and with its own excellent café (see Places to Eat for details).

On the right you'll come to the **Royal Academy of Arts** (☎ 439 7438), Burlington House, Piccadilly W1 (tube: Green Park), which tends to play poor relation to the Hayward Gallery, with international exhibitions that aren't quite as sexy or high profile – which is not to say that the displays can't be excellent, or that the crowds don't flock here. Each summer, the academy holds its traditional Summer Exhibition, an open show that anyone can enter. The quality can be mixed, but on the right day, amid the glorious setting of one of London's few remaining 18th century mansions, nobody seems to mind that much.

It's open daily from 10 am to 6 pm. Admission prices depend on what's on (check in *Time Out*) but expect to pay around £5. For the blockbuster exhibitions tickets are sold on a timed basis to prevent too many people crowding in at once and so queues don't get out of hand.

A little further along on the right you'll come to the **Burlington Arcade** which was built in 1819 and still recalls a bygone age – selling the kinds of things that only the very rich are likely to want. Watch out for the Burlington Berties, the uniformed guards who patrol the arcade, with a brief to prevent high spirits, whistling and the inelegant popping of bubble gum. Surprisingly, there's a low-key atmosphere, and this polite and genteel arcade is well worth strolling through. At the far side turn right and you'll see an imposing 19th century Italianate building which was, until recently, home to the **Museum of Mankind**. This is being returned to its original home in the British Museum but the move is unlikely to be completed much before the year 2000.

Keep heading west and you'll come to Old Bond St, where many of London's commercial art galleries can be found. The **Royal Arcade**, a covered thoroughfare lined with extremely expensive shops selling quintessential English ware like hunting jackets, pipe tobacco, cashmere jumpers and golfing knickerbockers, runs off Old Bond St. Built in 1879, it reflects that era's love affair with Gothic style.

Keep on going and on the left you'll see **The Ritz**, perhaps the most glitzy of London's upmarket hotels. This was one of the first steel-framed buildings to be erected in London, but that's unlikely to distract you much if you're coming here for tea (see boxed aside Time for Tea in the Places to Eat chapter). Immediately west of the Ritz is **Green Park**. Keep going and you'll come out at Hyde Park Corner.

Mayfair

Squeezed in between Hyde Park and Soho, Mayfair is one of London's most exclusive neighbourhoods – as everyone who's ever played Monopoly will know. At the heart of the district is **Grosvenor Square**, dominated by the US Embassy on the west side and with a memorial to Franklin D Roosevelt in the centre. The other famous Mayfair landmark is **Berkeley Square**, where nightingales might conceivably still sing amid the plane trees, although you'd never hear them for the traffic. The house at No 44 still retains its fine old iron railings, complete with snuffers for snuffing out the torches carried by footmen.

Regent St

Regent St owes its original design to John Nash, although the elegant shopfronts you see today only date back to 1925. Here you'll find such household-name shops as **Hamley's** and **Liberty**. If you cut down Beak St on the right you'll soon see **Carnaby St** on the left. Once thought to have outlived its sell-by date, Carnaby St has been given a breath of new life by the Oasis/Spice Girls/Cool Britannia enthusiasm for all things clad in the Union Jack.

Oxford St

What was once London's finest shopping street can come as a big disappointment, especially if you emerge from Oxford Circus tube and head east towards Tottenham Court Rd. It can sometimes feel as if you're running the gauntlet of permanent 'closing down' sales and spivvy shopfront salesmen who draw people in by offering dubious bargains, usually on electrical goods (see Scams in the Facts for the Visitor chapter). Things are much better if you head west towards Marble Arch. This is where you'll find the famous department stores, including Debenhams, John Lewis and massive Selfridges, particularly famous for its Santa's Grotto at Christmas but worth a visit at any time of year.

Beside the flagship HMV and Virgin record stores, Oxford Sreet's other great shopping institution is the big Marks & Spencer store near Marble Arch. A lot of people swear by this place, which isn't quite as unhip as you might glibly assume.

For more on the possibilities of Oxford St and Regent St, see the Shopping chapter.

For details on Marble Arch, at the west end of Oxford St, see the Hyde Park section later in this chapter.

Wallace Collection

West of Oxford Circus, the Wallace Collection (☎ 935 0687), Hertford House, Manchester Square W1 (tube: Bond St), is London's finest small gallery housing a treasure trove of high-quality paintings from the 17th and 18th centuries, including works by Rubens, Titian, Poussin, Frans Hals *(The Laughing Cavalier)* and Rembrandt in a splendidly Italianate mansion. There's also a collection of mind-bogglingly splendid, elaborate armour. The staircase is reckoned to be one of the best examples of French interior architecture. It was intended for the Banque Royale in Paris but was bought by Sir Richard Wallace and installed here in 1874. Vast canvases by Frances Boucher adorn the stairwell.

The collection was bequeathed to the nation towards the end of the last century. It's a well-kept secret where you can escape some of the hordes mobbing better-known galleries.

It's open (free) Monday to Saturday from 10 am to 5 pm, Sunday from 2 to 5 pm. Free guided tours take place daily; phone for exact times.

The BBC Experience

North of Oxford Circus along Regent St to Langham Place is the distinguished building that is Broadcasting House (1931), home to the BBC and decorated with sculptures by Eric Gill. The basement now houses a museum where you can see clips of popular BBC programmes and examine the Marconi Collection of early wireless equipment. Interactive displays let you take part in an episode of the long-running Radio 4 rural soap opera *The Archers* or direct an episode of the equally popular BBC1 urban soap *EastEnders*.

The BBC Experience (☎ 0870-603 0304) is open daily from 9.30 am to 5.30 pm. Admission is £5.75/4 (tube: Oxford Circus; Map 5).

Soho

East of Regent St and south of Oxford St is Soho, one of the liveliest, hippest corners of London – the place to come for fun and games after dark. Hard though it is to believe, this area was once under fields where hunting took place; 'so-ho' is thought to have been a hunting cry, a bit like 'tally-ho', hence the name. Ten years ago Soho was an extremely sleazy neighbourhood filled with strip clubs and peepshows where unwary males were easily separated from large sums of money. The strip joints are still there, of course, but these days they rub shoulders with some of London's trendiest clubs, bars and restaurants (see the Places to Eat and Entertainment chapters for more details) – come here late and it'll be a revelation to anyone who still thinks the Brits are staid.

Almost lost amid this homage to Mammon, at 9-10 Soho Square you'll find London's **Radha Krishna temple**, worth a quick look for its incense-filled interior or to eat at the vegetarian restaurant downstairs.

COVENT GARDEN (Map 3)

In the 1630s Inigo Jones converted something that had started life as a vegetable field attached to Westminster Abbey into the elegant Covent Garden piazza. In time it became the haunt of writers like Pepys, Fielding and Boswell in search of shady nightlife, but by Victorian times a fruit and vegetable market had established itself (it's immortalised in the film *My Fair Lady*, the screen adaptation of Shaw's play *Pygmalion*). When the fruit and veg was moved out to Nine Elms in Battersea in the 1980s, a stroke of planning genius saw the old market transformed into one of central London's liveliest hubs, with glitzy shops built into the old arcades.

Covent Garden (tube: Covent Garden) gets horribly overcrowded in summer, but is still one of the few bits of London where pedestrians rule, and there's always a corner of relative peace where you can watch the world, and the licensed buskers, go by. Unfortunately there are signs of a gradual slither downmarket, as Pizza Hut and Dunkin Donuts outlets open on the fringes.

Where stallholders once flogged fresh produce, they now sell antiques, clothes and overpriced bric-a-brac. At the junction of the piazza and Southampton St, the covered Jubilee Market sells cheap clothes and jewellery from Tuesday to Friday but becomes a more upmarket crafts fair at the weekend.

Tucked away in the basement of the piazza is the **Cabaret Mechanical Theatre** (☎ 379 7961), a treasure trove of automata with buttons to push and handles to turn, guaranteed to bring out the child in all of us. The best models are by Paul Spooner and Keith Newstead whose peacock with opening tail is a joy to behold. It's open Monday to Saturday from 10 am to 6.30 pm (from 11 am on Sunday) and costs £1.95/1.20. For those who get hooked there are more automata in the foyer for which you'll need a handful of 10p and 20p pieces.

Overlooking the piazza on the western side is the porticoed rear of **St Paul's Church**. Designed by Inigo Jones in the 1630s, it's little more than a stone rectangle with a pitched roof... 'the handsomest barn in England'. In the square in front, where Samuel Pepys watched England's first Punch and Judy show in 1662, you can still see buskers perform. For a quiet escape, head down King St or Henrietta St and look for the narrow entrances into a churchyard with trees, flowers and very little noise.

On the opposite side of the piazza stands the Victorian **Floral Hall**, currently under restoration as part of ambitious plans to redevelop and expand the adjoining **Royal Opera House**. Excavations carried out by the Museum of London have uncovered extensive traces of the Saxon settlement of Lundenwic, including wattle and daub housing. Work will continue in this north-east corner of the piazza for several years to come.

Beyond the piazza are lively streets of clothes shops and bars, restaurants and designer gift shops. Neal St, a narrow lane leading from Long Acre to Shaftesbury Ave, is particularly worth exploring. (See the Places to Eat chapter later for details on Neal's Yard, and Shopping for more details of what to buy in Covent Garden.)

For all things African, turn left down King St after leaving St Paul's for the Africa Centre (☎ 836 1973), 38 King St WC2. There are often African bands here as well as an excellent moderately-priced African restaurant, the Calabash – see Places to Eat for details.

A block further north is Floral St, where swanky designers like Paul Smith, Jigsaw, Jones and Agnès B have their main outlets. Another block north and you're in Long Acre which boasts Emporio Armani, Woodhouse, The Gap, and Flip (a true thrift shop selling 50s American clothing). Here too you'll find bookshops (including Stanford's for guidebooks and maps) and St Martin's College of Fashion & Design.

London Transport Museum

Tucked into the corner of Covent Garden between the Jubilee Market and Tutton's restaurant, the London Transport Museum (☎ 836 8557) tells how London made the transition from streets choked with horse-drawn carriages to the arrival of the Docklands Light Railway, a more interesting story than you might imagine. If you thought underfunding of public transport and the chaos of deregulation were unique to the late 20th century this is the place to come for re-education. Hordes of marauding school kids are the one mid-week drawback.

The museum (tube: Covent Garden) is open daily from 10 am to 5.15 pm (from 11 am on Friday) and admission costs £4.50/2.50. There's an excellent shop and a Transport Café where cheese and mushroom croissants take the place of the fry-ups associated with more normal transport caffs.

For details of talks on varied aspects of transport, phone ☎ 379 6344.

Theatre Museum

A branch of the Victoria & Albert Museum, the Theatre Museum (☎ 836 7891), Russell St, Covent Garden, displays costumes and artefacts relating to the history of the theatre, including memorabilia of great actors and actresses like David Garrick, Edmund Kean, Henry Irving and Ellen Terry. One exhibition shows how Kenneth Grahame's children's book *The Wind in the Willows* was adapted for the stage by Alan Bennett and then performed at the Royal National Theatre. Another shows how stage make-up is used (fun for kids, this). Finally, you can see recordings from the newly-compiled National Video Archive of Stage Performance before returning along a corridor where famous performers have left their hand prints in paint.

The museum (tube: Covent Garden) is open Tuesday to Sunday from 11 am to 6.30 pm and admission costs £3.50/2.

THE STRAND

Courtauld Gallery

Housed in the Strand Block of the splendid Palladian Somerset House, the Courtauld Gallery (☎ 873 2526), Strand WC2 (tube: Covent Garden; Map 3), displays some of the Courtauld Institute's marvellous collection of paintings in the partially furnished 1st floor rooms. Exhibits include work by Rubens, Bellini, Velasquez and Botticelli. However, for many visitors the most memorable display is of the Impressionist and post-Impressionist art by Van Gogh, Cézanne, Manet, Pissarro, Sisley, Rousseau, Toulouse-Lautrec, Gauguin, Renoir, Degas and Monet shown on the top floor. Rarely can so many world-famous paintings have been gathered together in one beautifully-lit, undivided room.

The gallery also has a small exhibition of paintings by the 20th-century Bloomsbury artists Duncan Grant, Vanessa Bell and Roger Fry, together with colourful furniture produced by the Omega Workshops (also in Bloomsbury) and influenced by newly discovered African masks and other ethnographical items.

A collection of 18th century Huguenot-made silverware is shown in a small room ringed with cartoons by contemporary artist Thomas Rowlandson (1756-1827).

By the time you read this the gallery should have reopened after a National Lottery-funded overhaul. The art bookshop will no doubt be as good as ever; the basement café may well have improved.

The gallery is open Monday to Saturday from 10 am to 6 pm, Sunday from 2 to 6 pm and costs £4/free. Admission is free after 5 pm and at all times to the temporary exhibitions housed in a separate set of rooms across the arcade from the main display.

Royal Courts of Justice

At the east end of the Strand, where it joins Fleet St, you'll see the Royal Courts of Justice (☎ 936 6000; Map 6), a gargantuan melange of Gothic spires and pinnacles and burnished Portland stone, designed by GE Street in 1874. This is where civil cases (libel and the like) are tried and where many famous appeals against conviction wind up, ensuring that the High Court, as it's also know, provides a backdrop for the television news virtually every night of the year. Criminal cases (murders, bank robberies and the like) are heard at the Old Bailey, near St Paul's (see the City of London).

Visitors are welcome to come in and watch cases in progress, although you must go through airport-style security checks first. No cameras can be brought inside the building; you can leave them at BK News across the road for £1.

WESTMINSTER & PIMLICO (Map 4)

Since a British city is defined as a town with a cathedral, London actually consists of two cities: Westminster and London, with Westminster Cathedral and St Paul's Cathedral respectively. It's the City of London that is known simply as 'the City' but Westminster is the centre of political power and most of its places of interest are defined

PAT YALE

TOM SMALLMAN

DOUG McKINLAY

Left: Bungee-jumping at Adrenalin Village, Battersea
Right: Posing for portrait, Leicester Square
Bottom: Big Ben & Houses of Parliament

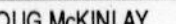
DOUG McKINLAY

DOUG McKINLAY

RACHEL BLACK

Left: Westminster Abbey
Top: Blues & Royals Squadron, Horse Guards Parade
Bottom: Guard of the Household Regiment

by their association with royal and/or parliamentary power. By way of cultural power, two notable institutions lie to the north and south: the ICA and the Tate Gallery respectively.

Westminster Abbey

Westminster Abbey (☎ 222 7110), Dean's Yard SW1 (tube: Westminster), is one of the most visited churches in the Christian world. It has played an important role in the history of the English church and, with the exception of Edward V and Edward VIII, every sovereign has been crowned here since 1066. Since Henry III, most kings and queens have also been buried here.

In September 1997, a large proportion of the world's population got to see the inside of Westminster Abbey when TV cameras were allowed in for Princess Diana's funeral service, though she was laid to rest at her family home at Althorp, Northamptonshire.

The abbey is a spectacular example of various styles of Gothic architecture. The original church was built by Edward the Confessor, later St Edward, who is buried at the east end. Henry III (1216-72) began work on the new building but didn't complete it. Only an expert would be able to tell that the French Gothic nave was finished off in 1375. Henry VII's Chapel was added in 1503.

The main entrance is through the west door, above which are two towers built by Sir Christopher Wren and his pupil Hawksmoor. Set in the floor immediately inside is the **Tomb of the Unknown Warrior**, surrounded by poppies in remembrance of those who died on the battlefields of WWI. Nearby is a stone commemorating Winston Churchill, prime minister from 1940 to 1945 and from 1951 to 1955.

Straight ahead of you a **screen** separates the nave from the choir; built in 1834, it is the fourth screen to be placed here. Against this stand monuments to Sir Isaac Newton and Lord Stanhope by Rysbrack. Above the

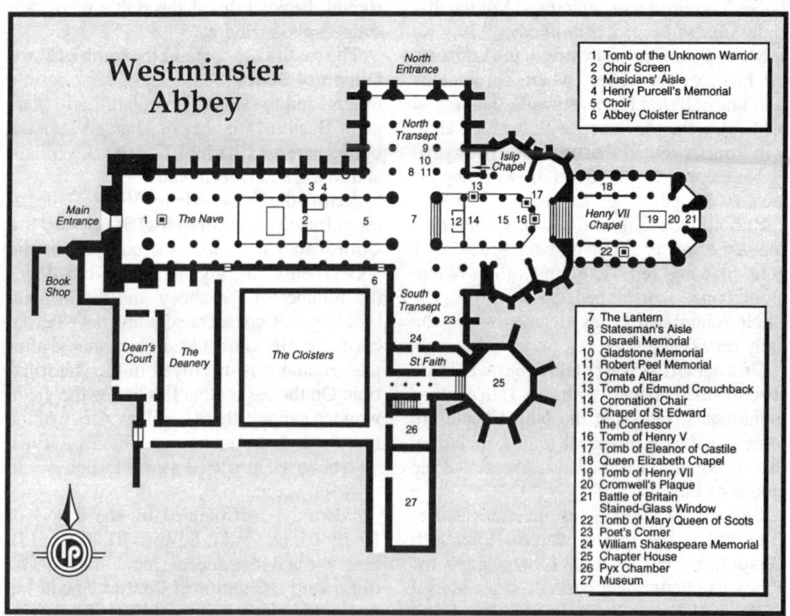

screen is the magnificent organ dating from 1730. Look up at the beautiful stone vaulted ceiling in the nave and at the fan-vaulted aisles.

Unfortunately you must pay to see the rest of the abbey; the turnstile is in the north aisle. Once through the gates you pass organ pipes as you enter the **Musicians' Aisle**, with memorials to musicians who served the abbey. Look out for memorials to Henry Purcell, a past organist at the abbey, and to Vaughan Williams, Edward Elgar and Benjamin Britten.

Continuing east, you come to the **Statesmen's Aisle** where politicians and eminent public figures are commemorated, often by staggeringly large marble statues redolent of a more confident age. Gladstone and Disraeli, the Whig and Tory prime ministers who dominated late Victorian politics, are ironically close together, with Robert Peel, who created the police force and gave the police their nickname 'Bobbies', nearby. Above them is a rose window, designed by Sir James Thornhill and depicting 11 of the disciples (Judas Iscariot is omitted).

Make your way eastwards to the **Lantern**, the heart of the abbey, where coronations take place. If you face east while standing in the centre, the sanctuary, with the high altar, is in front of you. The **ornate altar**, designed by Sir George Gilbert Scott in 1897, depicts the Last Supper.

Behind you Edward Blore's mid-19th century **choir** is a breathtaking structure of gold, blue and red Victorian Gothic. Where monks once worshipped, 20 boys from the Choir School and 12 lay vicars now sing the daily services.

On your left as you continue eastwards are several small chapels with fine 16th century monuments. Opposite the Islip Chapel are three wonderful medieval tombs, including that of Edmund Crouchback, founder of the House of Lancaster.

Beyond the chapels, up the steps and to your left is the narrow **Queen Elizabeth Chapel**. Here Elizabeth I, who gave the abbey its charter, and her half-sister Mary I share an elaborate tomb. In life, they didn't get on, which may be why there's no effigy of Mary. In front of the altar are memorials to the daughters of James I who died in childhood; Princess Sophia is shown, touchingly, as a baby in her cradle.

The most easterly part of the abbey is **Henry VII's Chapel**, added in 1503 and an outstanding example of late Perpendicular architecture with spectacular fan vaulting. At its entrance a plaque marks the spot where Oliver Cromwell's body lay until the Restoration, whereupon it was disinterred, hanged at Tyburn and beheaded. The magnificently carved wooden stalls, reserved for the Knights of the Order of the Bath, feature colourful headpieces bearing the chosen personal statement of their owners. Recent members of the order include Ronald Reagan and Norman Schwarzkopf.

Behind the altar, with a 15th century *Madonna and Child* by Vivarini, is the elaborate black-marble **sarcophagus** of Henry VII and his queen, Elizabeth of York, designed by the Florentine sculptor Torrigiani. Beyond this is the Battle of Britain stained-glass window.

The south aisle contains the **tomb of Mary Queen of Scots** (beheaded on her cousin's orders) and the stunning tomb of Lady Margaret Beaufort, mother of Henry VII. Also buried here are Charles I, Charles II, William and Mary, and Queen Anne.

Across the bridge, Henry V's tomb lies at the entrance to the **Chapel of St Edward the Confessor**, the most sacred spot in the abbey, behind the high altar. St Edward was the founder of the abbey and the original building was consecrated a few days before his death. His tomb was slightly altered after the original was destroyed in the Reformation. On the casket that lies below the green wooden canopy, there is still evidence of the mosaic and the niches in which pilgrims, who believed him to be a great healer, would pray for a cure.

Edward is surrounded by the tombs of Henry III, Edward I, Edward III, Richard II, Henry V and four queens, including the wife of Edward I, **Eleanor of Castile**. She lies in one of the oldest and most beautiful surviving bronze tombs, designed by the goldsmith William Torel in 1291 (see the boxed aside Crosses of Love in the Excursions chapter).

The **Coronation Chair** faces Edward's tomb and sits in front of an amazing stone screen portraying scenes from his life. The chair dates from around 1300 and is made of oak. Below it used to lie the Stone of Scone (pronounced skoon) – the Scottish coronation stone pilfered in 1297 by Edward. The stone was finally returned to Scotland in 1996, though the Scots had to agree to return it for any future coronations.

The **south transept** houses **Poet's Corner**, where many of England's finest writers are buried, a precedent established with Geoffrey Chaucer, although he was actually buried here because he had been Clerk of Works to the Palace of Westminster, not because he had written *The Canterbury Tales*. The practice actually began in earnest in 1700.

In front of medieval wall paintings of Doubting Thomas and St Christopher on the south wall stands the **memorial to William Shakespeare**. Like TS Eliot, Byron, Tennyson, William Blake (whose bronze head by Sir Jacob Epstein has very unnerving eyes) and various other luminaries, he wasn't actually buried here. Here, too, you'll find memorials to Handel (holding a score of the *Messiah)*, Edmund Spenser, Lord Tennyson and Robert Browning, as well as the graves of Charles Dickens, Henry James, Lewis Carroll and Rudyard Kipling.

St Faith's chapel is reserved for private prayer. Scraps of skin on the door belong to a thief who tried to rob the abbey in the 16th century; he didn't get far and was flayed for his crime.

The entrance in the north-east corner of the cloister dates from the 13th century, the rest of it from the 14th. East down a passageway off the cloister, the octagonal **Chapter House** has one of Europe's best preserved medieval tile floors and retains traces of religious murals. It was used as a chamber by the king's council, and as a meeting place by the 16th century House of Commons. To this day the government runs the Chapter House and the adjacent **Pyx Chamber**, once the Royal Treasury but now displaying the abbey's plate and the oldest altar in the building.

The **museum** exhibits the death masks of generations of royalty and there are wax effigies representing Charles II and William III (who is on a stool to make him as tall as his wife Mary).

To reach the 900-year-old College Garden, the oldest in England, enter Dean's Yard and the **cloisters** on Great College St.

Guided tours of the abbey last about 1½ hours (£7), or there's a portable tape-recorded commentary, which you can stop and start at leisure (£6). Access to the chapels costs £4/2 so both tour options are good deals as they include admission. There is half price admission on Wednesday from 6 to 7.10 pm and this is the only time when photographs may be taken.

Access to the nave used to be free but the sheer pressure of visitors means it is unlikely that you will be able to walk round without paying by the time you read this.

The abbey is open Tuesday to Thursday from 7.30 am to 6 pm, Wednesday from 7.30 am to 7.45 pm. The royal chapels and transepts are open Monday to Friday from 9 am to 3.45 pm, and Saturday from 9 am to 1.45 pm and 4 to 4.45 pm. Sunday is for services only.

The Chapter House, Pyx Chamber and Abbey Museum (☎ 222 5897) are open 10 am to 6 pm from April to September, closing at 4 pm between October and March. Admission costs £2.50/1.90 (free to English Heritage members). The College Garden is open April to September, Tuesday and Thursday from 10 am to 6 pm; October to March, Tuesday and Thursday from 10 am to 4 pm. The Brass Rubbing Centre (☎ 222 4589) is open Monday to Saturday from 9 am to 5.30 pm.

One of the best ways to visit the abbey is to attend a service, particularly evensong when the atmosphere and acoustics will send shivers down your spine. Evensong is on Monday, Tuesday, Thursday and Friday at 5 pm; on Saturday and Sunday at 3 pm.

Houses of Parliament

The Palace of Westminster accommodates the Houses of Parliament (☎ 219 4272), Parliament Square SW1 (tube: Westminster), made up of the House of Commons and House of Lords. Jointly built by Sir Charles Barry and Augustus Pugin in 1840 during the Victorian neo-Gothic frenzy, the original soft gold brilliance of the edifice was revealed after a thorough cleaning. Externally the most famous feature of the palace is St Stephen's Tower, commonly known as Big Ben. The real Ben, a bell named after Sir Benjamin Hall, the Commissioner of Works when the tower was completed in 1858, hangs inside. At the opposite end of the building the Victoria Tower was completed in 1860. The main Commons was gutted by bombs in 1941 and reconstructed in 1950.

The **House of Commons** is where Members of Parliament meet to propose and discuss new legislation and to question the prime minister and other ministers. The layout of the Commons Chamber is based on that of St Stephen's Chapel in the original Palace of Westminster. The current Chamber, designed by Sir Giles Gilbert Scott, replaces the earlier version which was destroyed by a bomb in 1941. Although there are currently 651 MPs, the Chamber of the House of Commons only has seating for 437 of them. Government members sit to the right of the Speaker and Opposition members to the left. The Speaker presides over business from a chair given by Australia while ministers speak from a despatch box donated by New Zealand.

Visitors are admitted to the Strangers' Gallery of the House of Commons after 4.15 pm from Tuesday to Thursday and from 10 am on Friday. Parliamentary recesses (holidays) last for three months over the summer and another few weeks over Easter and Christmas, so it's best to ring in advance to check that the houses are in session. To find out what's being debated on a particular day, look in the *Daily Telegraph*. The day's business is also posted up beside the entrance to the Strangers' Gallery. Expect to queue for an hour even when the debate is run-of-the-mill. No large suitcases or backpacks can be taken through the airport-style security arrangements, and even handbags and cameras will have to be checked into a cloakroom before you enter the gallery. Admission is free and watching the arcane rituals of the Commons makes a good way to while away a wet few hours.

As you're waiting for your bags to go through the X-ray machines, take a look to the left at the stunning hammerbeam roof of **Westminster Hall**, originally built in 1097-99 and today the oldest surviving part of the Palace of Westminster, main home of the English monarchy from the 11th to the early 16th century. Added between 1394 and 1401, the roof is the earliest known example of a hammerbeam roof and has been described as 'the greatest surviving achievement of medieval English carpentry'. As well as being used for banquets following medieval coronations, Westminster Hall also served as a courthouse until the 19th century. The trials of William Wallace (1305), Sir Thomas More (1535), Guy Fawkes (1606) and King Charles I (1649) all took place here. More recently it was used for the lying-in-state of several 20th century monarchs and of Sir Winston Churchill in 1965.

You can visit parts of the **Palace of Westminster** when the houses are not sitting, although arrangements must be made in advance through the Public Information Office, 1 Derby Gate, SW1A 2DG. Visit permits are free, but guides charge around £25 for a group of 16.

The Palace faces **Parliament Square** where swirling traffic makes it hard to appreciate the statues of past prime ministers and other worthies including Sir Winston Churchill and Abraham Lincoln. To the south of the square is Westminster Abbey with the tiny **St Margaret's church**, famous for society weddings, in front of it. To the west stands the elaborately decorated **Middlesex Guildhall** which now houses Middlesex Crown Court.

Jewel Tower

Once part of the Palace of Westminster, the

Jewel Tower (☎ 973 3479), immediately opposite the Houses of Parliament and beside Westminster Abbey, was built in 1365 to house Edward III's treasury. Originally it was surrounded by a moat but this was filled in in 1664. Later the tower served as an office for clerks of the House of Lords. Now it houses exhibitions describing the history of Parliament and showing how it works. There's also a 25-minute explanatory video where you can see some of the present-day Commons stars in action. It's well worth visiting before attending a Commons debate so you'll understand more of what you're seeing.

The Jewel Tower is open 10 am to 6 pm daily from 1 April to 31 October, closing at 4 pm in winter. Admission costs £1.50/80p (free to EH members).

Whitehall

This wide avenue lined with government buildings leads from Trafalgar Square to Parliament Square. What was once the administrative heart of the empire is still the focal point for British government, with the Admiralty and the Ministry of Defence at the north end, the Scottish and Welsh Offices in the middle, and Downing St and the Treasury at the south. Many of these buildings stand directly over the site of the Tudor Whitehall Palace, once the largest in the world, which burnt down in 1698.

Finest of the many striking edifices is Inigo Jones' splendid Banqueting House, scene of King Charles I's execution. Opposite is **Horse Guards Parade** where the mounted guard is changed twice daily, offering a more accessible version of the ceremony than the one outside Buckingham Palace.

Near the Parliament Square end of Whitehall, the **Cenotaph** ('empty tomb') is a memorial to Commonwealth citizens who were killed during the two world wars. Every November it becomes the focus of a commemorative service, with the Queen and other public figures laying poppies at its base.

One of the finest of the government offices is the newly-restored **Foreign & Commonwealth Office**, jointly designed in 1872 by Sir George Gilbert Scott and Matthew Digby Wyatt who was responsible for the glorious Durbar Court. Other impressive structures are the High Victorian Grand Staircase and the Grand Reception Room. To see inside these rooms, watch for the dates of the Heritage Open Days in mid-September.

Banqueting House Built in 1622, the imposing Banqueting House (☎ 930 4179), Whitehall SW1 (tube: Westminster), is the only surviving part of the old Whitehall Palace which once stretched most of the way along Whitehall but burnt down in 1698.

Inspired by what Palladio had done with porticoes and pilasters, the architect Inigo Jones (1573-c.1652) returned from a visit to northern Italy to build the Banqueting House, England's first Renaissance building. Despite the fact that it was designed to provide a venue for banquets and masques, the Banqueting House's greatest claim to fame is that it was on a scaffold built against a 1st floor window that King Charles I was executed on 30 January 1649. Despite the resumption of its original role on the Restoration of King Charles II, once the palace burnt down the Banqueting House fell from favour, becoming for a while the Chapel Royal. It's still occasionally used for state banquets, concerts and other events, and can sometimes be closed to the public.

Inside you can watch a video account of the Banqueting House's history before proceeding upstairs to the 1st floor, a huge, virtually unfurnished hall whose ceiling displays nine panels painted by Rubens in 1634. These portray the divine right of kings in general (the cause for which King Charles I later died) and of King James I in particular, and the union of Scotland with England which came about as a result of his reign (when Queen Elizabeth I died childless, she was succeeded by James VI of Scotland, son of Mary Queen of Scots, who became James I of England).

It's open Monday to Saturday from 10 am to 4.30 pm. Admission costs £3/2.25.

Downing Street Sir George Downing was a Dublin diplomat and supposedly the second man to graduate from Harvard. After his glory years in the American colonies, Downing came to London and built a row of sturdy-looking houses in a street off Whitehall which took his name. Four of the originals remain, but all you can do is peer through the huge iron gates.

Since 1732, when George II gave **No 10** to Robert Walpole, it has been the British prime minister's official residence. The chancellor of the exchequer (the country's senior economic and financial minister) lives next door at No 11. The other two houses are used as government offices. During Margaret Thatcher's time in office the gates were erected and the street closed off to the public for fear of IRA terrorist attacks. The fears later proved well-founded when an IRA mortar bomb came close to blowing up John Major's cabinet.

Cabinet War Rooms

During WWII the British Government took refuge underground, conducting its business from beneath 3m of solid concrete. It was from the Cabinet War Rooms (☎ 930 6961), Clive Steps, King Charles St SW1 (tube: Westminster), that Winston Churchill made some of his most stirring speeches, and you can hear extracts from some of them here. Restored to its 1940s condition, the bunker is a fascinating place to visit although its narrow corridors become uncomfortably crowded in summer. Indeed, even during the war years most officials preferred to take the risks above ground rather than sleep in such claustrophobic surroundings. Churchill himself rarely slept in his luxury pad despite its handsome furnishings.

The 40-minute recorded commentary certainly helps make sense of the maze of tunnels and doors. Particularly interesting are the actual Cabinet War Room where the Cabinet held more than 100 meetings during the war; the Map Room with charts showing the movements of troops and ships around the globe; the Telegraph Room, its door marked with a borrowed 'vacant/engaged' sign so that some people thought it was Churchill's private lavatory; and the bedrooms with their petty details of class segregation. Even people who're not much interested in military matters will find this a fascinating glimpse at a hidden world.

The War Rooms are open daily from 9.30 am to 5.15 pm (from 10 am October to March). Admission costs £4.20/2.10.

Institute for Contemporary Arts (ICA)

The Institute for Contemporary Arts (☎ 930 3647), The Mall SW1 (tube: Charing Cross), is a venue with a reputation for being at the cutting edge of all kinds of arts. In any given week this is the place to come for obscure films, dance, photography, art, theatre, music, lectures, video and book readings.

The complex includes a bookshop, art gallery, cinema, bar, café and theatre. There's invariably something worthwhile to see, the bar and restaurant are good value, and the ICA attracts an interesting and relaxed crowd.

It's open daily from noon to 1 am; a day pass is £1.50, £1 with any ticket purchase, 50p after 9 pm.

Up the steps beside the ICA you'll see the **Duke of York's Column**, commemorating the grand old duke, a son of George III. It was erected in 1834 but never caught the public imagination like the one in Trafalgar Square, not a hundred miles away.

St James's Park & St James's Palace

St James's Park (☎ 930 1793), The Mall SW1 (tube: St James's Park), is the neatest and most royal of London's royal parks, with the best vistas – of Westminster, Buckingham Palace, St James's Palace, Carlton Terrace and Horse Guards Parade. The flower beds are sumptuous and colourful, some of them newly replanted to mimic John Nash's original 'floriferous' beds mixing shrubs, flowers and trees. But what makes St James's so particularly special is the large lake that spans it and the collection of waterfowl that live on it, including a group of pelicans, descendants of birds who've been here since the reign of Charles II. Come here in early evening and you'll see Londoners whose lives revolve around the birds summoning them with imitation tweeting and whistling.

St James's Palace is not open to the public. The striking Tudor gatehouse, only survivor of a building initiated by the palace-hungry Henry VIII in 1530, is best approached from St James's St. It's never been much used, although foreign ambassadors are still accredited to the court of St James.

In nearby St James's Place, **Spencer House** (☎ 409 0526) was built for the first Earl Spencer, an ancestor of Princess Diana, in part-Palladian, part-neoclassical style between 1756 and 1766. The Spencers moved out in 1927 and eventually their grand house became an office with people typing away oblivious to the gilded palms and Classical statuary. Recently Lord Rothschild spent £16 million on a meticulous restoration of the house. The house is now open for tours from 11.45 am to 4.45 pm on Sunday except in July and August. Admission is £6/5.

Buckingham Palace

Buckingham Palace (☎ 930 4832) SW1 (tube: Victoria), is located at the end of The Mall, where St James's Park and Green Park meet at a giant traffic roundabout.

It was built in 1803 for the Duke of Buckingham and has been the royal family's London home since 1837 when St James's Palace was written off as too old-fashioned and insufficiently impressive. Eighteen rooms (out of 661) are open to summer visitors, but don't expect to see the Queen's bedroom – it's strictly state apartments only.

It's easy to be sniffy about the palace, especially given that neither exuberant white and gold decoration nor flock wallpaper are flavour of the decade. But, hell, we wouldn't really expect the Queen's front room to look like our own, would we? Anyway, all but the most hardened anti-monarchist should get a kick out of seeing what lies behind that expressionless facade. If nothing else it's fun to discover that such a familiar landmark does have other faces – and the view from the garden is much better than that from the front.

Most people will enjoy seeing the Throne Room, with his and hers thrones lined up under something like a theatre arch; the State Dining Room with a portrait of King George III looking extremely fetching in furs; and the Blue Drawing Room with a gorgeous fluted ceiling by John Nash. The paintings on display in the Long Gallery are also very

The Queen Victoria monument outside Buckingham Palace

fine, with several impressive Rembrandts, a Vermeer and a pair of van Dyck portraits of Charles I.

The palace is open daily from 9.30 am to 4.30 pm from early August to early October; for exact dates phone ☎ 839 1377. Admission costs £9/5. Tickets are sold from a booth in Green Park but you can also book by credit card on ☎ 321 2233.

What a shame it took the fire at Windsor Castle in 1993 to persuade the Queen to open the doors to her (cash-paying) subjects!

Royal Mews The Royal Mews (☎ 839 1327) is tucked away in Buckingham Palace Rd SW1, behind the palace. What started life as a home for falcons now houses all the flashy vehicles the royals use for getting around on ceremonial occasions, including the stunning Gold State Coach of 1761 used for every coronation since George IV's and the Glass Coach of 1910 which is used for royal weddings. Also interesting are a French charabanc given to Queen Victoria in 1844 and the miniature barouche and landau that round off the exhibition. Don't forget to look at the stables where the royal horses munch their oats in stalls designed by John Nash in the 1820s.

The Royal Mews is open from Easter to August, Tuesday to Thursday, from noon to 4 pm; from August to October from 10.30 am to 4.30 pm and on Monday; the rest of the year open Wednesday only. Admission costs £3.70/2.10.

Queen's Gallery A few doors on from the Royal Mews is the Queen's Gallery (☎ 930 4832) where paintings from the Queen's extensive collection go on display in regularly changed exhibitions. The gallery is pretty small, so if you're pressed for cash you might prefer to hang onto it.

The gallery is open daily from 9.30 am to 4.30 pm except when the exhibitions are being changed. Admission costs £3.50/2.50.

Changing the Guard This is one of those quintessentially English events visitors to London must see, although you'll probably go away wondering what all the fuss was about. The old guard comes off duty to be replaced by the new guard in the forecourt of Buckingham Palace, which gives tourists a chance to gawp at the bright red uniforms, bearskin hats (synthetic alternatives are being sought), shouting and marching. If you arrive early, grab a prime spot by the railings; more likely than not, however, you'll be 10 rows back and hardly see a thing. A similar ceremony takes place at Horse Guards in Whitehall.

Buckingham Palace
  From 3 April to 3 August daily at 11.30 am; August to April alternate days at 11.30 am.
Whitehall
  From Monday to Saturday at 11 am, Sunday at 10 am.

Green Park

Green Park adjoins St James's just across The Mall, and is a less fussy, more naturally rolling park, with trees and open space, sunshine and shade. Once a duelling ground and, like Hyde Park, a vegetable field during WWII, Green Park tends to be less crowded than its illustrious neighbour. If you need to get to Hyde Park Corner a stroll through the park is much more enjoyable than taking the tube or a bus.

Westminster Cathedral

Completed in 1903, Westminster Cathedral (☎ 798 9064), Ashley Place SW1 (tube: Victoria), is the headquarters of the Catholic Church in Britain, and the only good example of neo-Byzantine architecture in the city. Its distinctively striped red-brick and white-stone tower features prominently on the west London skyline, although remarkably few people think to look inside. For £2 you can take a lift up the tower for panoramic views of London from 9 am to 5 pm daily (closed Monday to Wednesday from December to March).

The interior is part splendid marble and mosaic and part bare brick – the money ran out although there are now plans to complete it. The highly regarded stone carvings of the

14 Stations of the Cross by controversial sculptor Eric Gill and the marvellously sombre atmosphere, especially in early evening when the mosaics glitter in the dark, make this a cherished haven from the traffic outside.

The cathedral is open daily from 7 am to 7 pm. There are eight masses daily from Monday to Friday, seven on Saturday and Sunday.

An Organ Festival (☎ 798 9055) is held every second Tuesday at 7 pm, from 18 June to 10 September; admission is £6/4.

Tate Gallery

The Tate Gallery (☎ 887 8000), Millbank SW1 (tube: Pimlico), is custodian to both the nation's international modern art collection and its historical archive of British art. A bright, modern gallery, it only has hanging space for a quarter of its treasures at any one time, and these are displayed in chronological order. Director Nicholas Serota gets round this problem by rehanging the pictures once a year, which means you can't be sure any one particular painting will be on display without calling first to check. Nevertheless, you can be sure that high-quality works by Picasso, Matisse, Cezanne, the two Johns, Rothko and Pollock will be on display – alongside stuffy Victorian paintings of thoroughbred racehorses and the sort of contemporary art that brings the Establishment out in a sweat (the Tate has never quite lived down an exhibition of workaday bricks laid out in lines that it was brave, or foolish, enough to show in the 70s). Likely highlights include the mystical paintings by William Blake in rooms 6 and 7, the Hogarths in room 2 and the Constables in room 8.

Adjoining the main building is the **Clore Gallery**, James Stirling's quirky stab at acceptable, post-modern architecture, where the bulk of JMW Turner's paintings can be found. Turner is perhaps the only British artist who would consistently and universally be counted among the all-time greats. For most people, the Clore, like the main gallery, will be a must-see.

An extension to the Tate is currently under construction in the old Bankside power station across the river. It's unlikely to open before the year 2000 but when it does there's likely to be some rationalisation of the collections at the National Gallery and the two Tates; all the pre-1900 pictures (apart from the Turners) are likely to wind up at the National, with the newer pictures in the Tates.

The Tate is open Monday to Saturday from 10 am to 5.50 pm, Sunday from 2 to 5.50 pm; free. Major special exhibitions have a separate admission rate from £4 to £7. The basement café, with a mural by Rex Whistler, is enormously popular and offers a wide range of hot and cold food at reasonable prices.

The City of London

The City of London (Map 6) is 'the one square mile' on the north bank of the Thames where the Romans first built a walled community 2000 years ago. The boundaries of today's City of London haven't changed much and you can always tell when you're within them because the coat of arms of the Corporation of London appears on the street name plates. This is the business heart of London where you'll find not only the Bank of England, but also the headquarters of many British and overseas banks and insurance companies. Only 6000 people actually live in the City but around 300,000 commute there to work every day.

St Paul's Cathedral and the Tower of London are both in the City of London. Here too you'll find the headquarters of many of London's livery companies (see the boxed aside The Livery Companies) and many of the churches built by Sir Christopher Wren after the Great Fire of 1666. The IRA exploded a huge bomb in the City in 1992; some of the damage is still being repaired.

A quiet weekend stroll when the banks and offices are closed offers a unique chance to appreciate the architectural richness of its many famous buildings. Bear in mind, though, that some of the sights close on Saturday and Sunday, as do the shops in Leadenhall Market.

St Paul's Cathedral

St Paul's Cathedral (☎ 236 4128) was built, amid much controversy, by Sir Christopher Wren between 1675 and 1710. It stands on the site of two previous cathedrals, the first of which dated back to 604.

St Paul's was one of the 50 commissions that Wren was given after the Great Fire of London. Plans for alterations had already been made, but the fire gave him the opportunity to build from scratch. Several plans were spurned before the authorities accepted the current design.

Despite being surrounded by some less-than-pleasant architecture (due for demolition), the dome still dominates the City and is only exceeded in size by St Peter's in Rome. Pictures of the cathedral miraculously surrounded by the devastation of WWII bombing can be seen in the Britain at War Experience (see the Southern Central London section); fortunately, the dome survived virtually unharmed, although other parts of the cathedral were not entirely unscathed. The windows were blown out (hence the quantity of clear glass) and various other parts were also damaged.

In 1981 it featured as the venue for the wedding of Prince Charles and Lady Diana Spencer. They broke with royal tradition, partly because Charles thought the acoustics were much better than those in Westminster Abbey. Time your visit to coincide with a service and judge for yourself; evensong takes place most weekdays at 5 pm and at 3.15 pm on Sunday.

A **statue of Queen Anne** stands in front of the cathedral. You enter via the west door and proceed up the nave until you reach the dome; 100ft above is the **Whispering Gallery** (the lower part of a triple dome), so called because if you talk close to the wall it carries your words around to the other side.

This gallery, and the **Stone** and **Golden galleries** above, can be reached by a staircase in the south transept. All in all there are 530 narrow steps as you ascend and 543 narrow steps when you descend, but even if you can't make it right to the top (the Golden Gallery) it's worth struggling as far as the Stone Gallery for one of the best views of London.

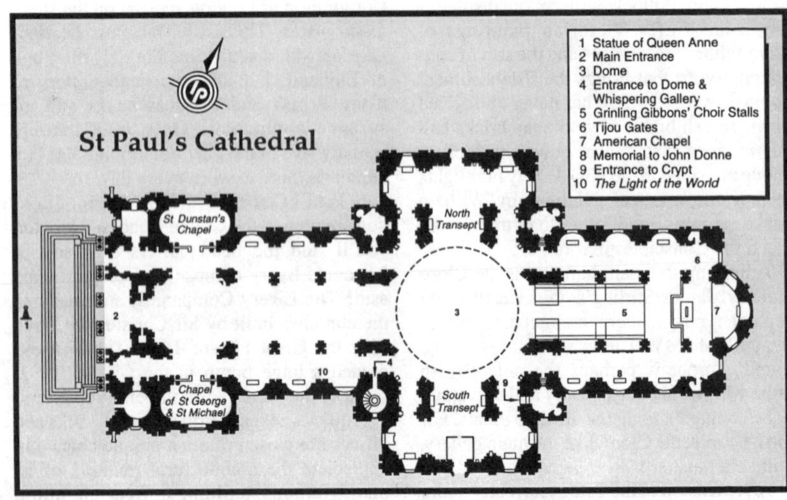

In the cathedral itself, look at the ornately carved **choir stalls** by Grinling Gibbons, and the **iron gates** by Jean Tijou, both of whom also worked on Hampton Court. Walk around the altar, with its outrageous canopy, to the **American Chapel**, a memorial to Americans killed during WWII.

As you walk round the south side of the ambulatory look for the **memorial to the poet John Donne** (1571-1631), once Dean of St Paul's, standing upright in his shroud.

At the west side of the south transept, close to a memorial to the painter JMW Turner, a staircase leads down to the **Crypt** and the **Treasury** . The Crypt has memorials to a number of military demigods including Wellington, Kitchener and Nelson, who is below the dome in a black sarcophagus. There are also effigies rescued from the previous cathedral that look rather the worse for wear – not surprisingly as they were saved from the fire. A niche exhibits Wren's controversial plans and his 'great' model. The most poignant memorial of all is to Sir Christopher Wren himself, adorned by his son's famous epitaph: *Lector, si monumentum requiris, circumspice* – Reader, if you seek his monument, look around you.

The Treasury displays some of the cathedral plate along with some spectacular needlework including Beryl Dean's Jubilee cope of 1977 showing spires of 73 London churches. Back in the body of the cathedral, walk down the south side of the nave and you'll spot Holman Hunt's famous painting *The Light of the World* which depicts Christ knocking at an overgrown door.

The cathedral (tube: St Paul's or Mansion House) is open Monday to Saturday from 8.30 am to 4 pm. Admission is £3.50/2, or £6/3 if you wish to visit the galleries. Recorded 45-minute tours are available for £2.50, and guided 90-minute tours leave the tour desk at 11, 11.30 am, 1.30 and 2 pm. A café should have opened in the crypt by the time you read this.

Museum of London

Despite it's unprepossessing setting amid the concrete walkways of the Barbican, the Museum of London (☎ 600 3699), 150 London Wall EC2 (tube: Barbican), is one of the city's finest museums, showing how the city has evolved from the Ice Age to the mobile-phone age. The sections on Roman Britain and Roman Londinium make use of the nearby ruins of a Roman fort discovered during road construction. Otherwise, the displays work steadily through the centuries, using audiovisuals to show major events like the Great Fire of London.

The focus is on people as much as on the buildings and streets; the days of Dickensian London, of mass prostitution, sweat-shop labour, unionisation and suffragettes make particularly poignant stories. The London Now gallery brings the story bang up to date (or at least as far as the watershed of the last election). John Bartlett's painting of the poll tax riot in Trafalgar Square in 1990 raised a few eyebrows, which seems odd since by the time you reach it you'll already have read about the Wat Tyler rebellion, the Gordon Riots and countless other episodes of urban unrest.

The museum is open Tuesday to Saturday from 10 am to 6 pm, Sunday from noon to 6 pm and costs £4/2 (free from 4.30 to 6 pm). Tickets are valid for three months, so you might want to come here at the start of your stay and then again just before you leave. There's a pleasant café opposite the entrance serving snacks like brie, grape and walnut-filled baguettes for £2.50. The excellent shop has a wide selection of fictional and factual accounts of London.

Barbican

Tucked into a corner of the City of London where there was once a watch-tower (or 'barbican'), the Barbican (☎ 638 8891), Silk St EC2 (tube: Barbican or Moorgate), is a vast urban development built on a large bomb site left over from WWII. The original ambitious plan was to create a terribly smart, modern complex for offices, housing and the arts.

Perhaps inevitably, the result was a forbidding series of wind tunnels with a dearth of

Going Up...

Although London's relatively few skyscrapers stick out like sore thumbs, they're not easily accessible to sightseers. The best views used to be had from the Telecom Tower off Cleveland St but that has been closed to visitors for years. Nor are visitors admitted to Canary Wharf or the NatWest Tower. Still, good views can be had from the following vantage points:

The Golden Gallery at St Paul's Cathedral (tube: St Paul's)
The walkways of Tower Bridge (tube: Tower Hill)
The viewing platform of the Monument in Fish St (tube: Monument)
The striped Byzantine tower of Westminster Cathedral (tube: Victoria)
The 8th floor viewing platform of the Oxo Tower (tube: Waterloo)

Those with a real head for heights can mount the 60m Chelsea Bridge Tower at Battersea (£5)...and bungee jump off if they so wish (£35)!

Provided they're not in use for a private function, the 1½-acre Kensington Roof Gardens (☎ 937 7994) provide a delightfully unexpected vantage point for peering down on the high street. To find them, head down Derry St and take the lift to the 6th floor.

Most of these views will cost you. Head for Parliament Hill on the south side of Hampstead Heath or for Primrose Hill to the north of Regent's Park, however, and you can see vast areas of London spread out below you without having to part with a penny. The same is true if you trek west to One Tree Hill in Greenwich Park.

...And Going Down

The quickest and easiest way of getting round London is by heading underground to catch the tube. London was the first city in the world to open an underground railway, when the Metropolitan Railway Company opened its first route between Paddington and Farringdon in 1863. Although none of the stations quite matches up to the Moscow Metro in splendour, the 1980s saw attempts to brighten up the platforms with themed tilework: Sherlock Holmes with pipe and deerstalker at Baker St, medieval masons working on the Eleanor Cross at Charing Cross and Eduardo Paolozzi's wild abstract design supposedly meant to represent the electrical goods shops at Tottenham Court Rd. The London Transport Museum offers occasional guided tours of Aldwych station which closed in 1994 (£7.50/5; ☎ 379 6344 for more details).

Other places where you can go underground include:

The crypts of St Paul's Cathedral, St Bride's Fleet St, All Hallows-by-the Tower and St John's Clerkenwell
The Cabinet War Rooms off Whitehall where wartime strategy was thrashed out beneath a hefty concrete beam
The Guildhall's medieval crypt (groups of 10 or more only; ☎ 332 1460 for more details)

London Walks (☎ 624 3978) offers occasional tours along the route of the old Fleet River which runs from Hampstead Heath beneath Farringdon St to join the Thames near Blackfriars Bridge.

You can also eat underground in the crypts of St Mary-le-Bow and St Martin-in-the-Fields churches. ■

shops, plenty of expensive high-rise apartments and an enormous cultural centre lost in the middle. Here you'll find the London home of the Royal Shakespeare Company (RSC), the London Symphony Orchestra and the London Classical Orchestra. There are also two cinemas, smaller theatrical auditoria, and ample gallery space, with possibly the best photographic shows in London. But be warned – even Londoners get here early to make sure of finding their way to the right spot at the right time.

For details of the theatres, cinemas and concert halls, see the Entertainment chapter. For details of the highly regarded Searcy's Brasserie, see the Places to Eat chapter.

Smithfield Market

Supposedly Europe's largest wholesale meat market, Smithfield, West Smithfield EC1 (tube: Farringdon), is central London's last surviving produce market and something of a vegetarian's nightmare. They stopped selling livestock here a century ago, around the same time that the main buildings were erected by Horace Jones, the man responsible for Leadenhall market, but on early weekday mornings Smithfield remains a hive of activity. Many local pubs open from the crack of dawn to cater for the stallholders' unsociable work hours; there's always a chance of joining the cockney meat sellers for an early-morning pint with your fried breakfast.

Smithfield is open Monday to Friday from 5 am to 10.30 am but at the time of writing the main sheds were still undergoing restoration. It remains to be seen whether the meat market can hang in here or whether it will be forced to follow the original Billingsgate fish market and Covent Garden fruit and vegetable market out to the suburbs. Already the surrounding streets are being tarted up, and the pavement cafés are moving in.

St Bartholomew-the-Great

One of London's oldest churches, adjoining one of London's oldest hospitals (presently threatened with closure), St Bartholomew-the-Great (☎ 606 5171), West Smithfield EC1 (tube: Barbican), is a stone's throw from the Barbican arts centre and more than worth a fleeting visit. The authentic Norman arches and detailings lend this holy space a kind of rustic calm.

Approaching from nearby Smithfield's Market through the restored 13th century archway is like walking into history. Film buffs might like to note that this is where Hugh Grant jilted Duck Features in the runaway hit film *Four Weddings & A Funeral*.

It's open Monday to Friday from 8.30 am to 5 pm, Saturday from 10.30 am to 1.30 pm and Sunday from 8 am to 8 pm.

Central Criminal Court (Old Bailey)

All Britain's major gangsters and serial killers eventually find their way to the Central Criminal Court, better known as the Old Bailey after the street in which it stands. Look up at the great copper dome and you'll see the figure of justice holding a sword and scales in her hand – although as the Birmingham Six and Guildford Four would probably testify, justice has occasionally been tilted against the defendants.

The old Newgate Prison, site of innumerable hangings, once stood here. Like most London prisons it was burnt down during the Gordon Riots of 1780, only to rise again from the ashes to incarcerate yet more prisoners until 1902.

Inns of Court

There are four Inns of Court all clustered around Holborn and Fleet St: **Lincoln's Inn** (☎ 405 1393), Lincoln's Inn Fields WC2 (tube: Holborn); **Gray's Inn** (☎ 405 8164), Gray's Inn Rd WC1 (tube: Holborn or Chancery Lane); **Inner Temple** (☎ 797 8250), King's Bench Walk EC4 (tube: Temple); and **Middle Temple** (☎ 353 4355), Middle Temple Lane EC4 (tube: Temple). The latter two are part of the Temple complex between Fleet St and Embankment.

All London barristers work from within one of the Inns, which boast a rollcall of former members ranging from Oliver Cromwell to Mahatma Gandhi, and from Charles Dickens to Margaret Thatcher. Anyone who believes Britain is becoming a more classless society should drop by one of these oases to have their illusions shattered; the aloof air of complacency and permanence that you see here suggests that not much has changed after all. You'll be even more convinced of it if you find a group of homeless men occupying Lincoln's Inn Fields.

It would take a lifetime spent working here

to grasp all the intricacies and subtleties of the arcane protocols of the Inns – they're a lot like the Freemasons (both organisations date back to the 13th century) and, needless to say, a lot of barristers are indeed Freemasons.

Both Gray's Inn and Lincoln's Inn have peaceful, picturesque lawns and quadrangles which offer the chance of a delightful stroll, especially early on weekday mornings before the hordes of self-important barristers in funny wigs and gowns have started to rush around.

All four Inns were badly damaged during the war. Lincoln's Inn is relatively intact, with original 15th century buildings, including the Tudor Chancery Lane Gatehouse – although the archway leading from the adjoining park, Lincoln's Inn Fields, is mock. Inigo Jones helped plan the chapel at Lincoln's Inn, which was built in 1621 and remains pretty well preserved.

Lincoln's Inn Grounds are open Monday to Friday from 9 am to 5 pm; Lincoln's Inn Chapel is open Monday to Friday from 12.30 to 2.30 pm; Gray's Inn is open Monday to Friday from 10 am to 4 pm; Inner Temple is open Monday to Friday from 10 am to 4 pm; Middle Temple is open Monday to Friday from 10 am to 4 pm.

Sir John Soane's Museum

Sir John Soane's Museum (☎ 405 2107), 13 Lincoln's Inn Fields, WC2 (tube: Holborn; Map 5), is partly a beautiful, if quirky, house and partly a small museum representing one man's personal taste.

Sir John Soane (1753-1837) was a leading architect who also designed the Bank of England, Dulwich Picture Gallery and Pitshanger Manor, drawing on ideas he'd picked up while on a Grand Tour of Italy. He married into money which he poured into customising two houses in Lincoln's Inn Fields, close to the Inns of Court. The building itself is a curiosity, with a glass dome bringing light to the basement, a lantern room filled with statuary, and a picture gallery where each painting folds away if pressed to reveal another one behind. Nothing is quite how it seems, which, along with Soane's ragbag collection, is its charm.

Soane's collection of Egyptiana predated the Victorian flirtation with all things pharaonic and includes a sarcophagus of Seti I. It also encompasses the original *Rake's Progress*, William Hogarth's set of cartoon caricatures of late 18th century London lowlife.

The museum is open (free) Tuesday to Saturday from 10 am to 5 pm.

Fleet Street

Fleet St used to be known as the Street of Shame, where clapped-out printing presses and equally clapped-out journalists padded out the nation's newspapers with gossip, speculation and lies.

Since Caxton's day, people round here had had ink on their fingers. But then the mid-1980s brought Rupert Murdoch, new technology and the Docklands redevelopment. Now that the action has moved east only ghosts linger on: El Vino's, the journos' No 1 watering hole, the glamorous former *Daily Telegraph* building (1930) now occupied by assorted banks, and the former *Daily Express* building (1932), London's first Modernist glass-box high-rise (the 'Black Lubianka') designed by Sir Owen Williams but now boarded up. It's to be hoped that plans to restore the facade and reopen the wonderful Art Deco entrance hall come to fruition soon.

St Bride's Church St Bride's (☎ 353 1301), Fleet St EC4 (tube: Blackfriars), is a small but perfect church, the fifth on the site and designed by Sir Christopher Wren between 1670-5. The add-on spire of 1701-03 may have inspired the design of the traditional English wedding cake. The church was hit by bombs in 1940 and the interior layout reflects a modern rethink when the time came to rebuild.

In the 16th century Wynkyn de Worde moved Caxton's printing press from Westminster to beside St Bride's, thus starting an association with the printing trade that has continued even though the newspapers

The Demon Barber of Fleet Street

In Thomas Peckett Priest's story which launched a thousand restaurants, Sweeney Todd ran a Fleet St barbershop with his assistant Tobias. Whenever casual customers appeared, Tobias was sent on an errand. Then, as Sweeney went to work, the barber's chair would swing back and the client would drop through a trapdoor into a cellar where he was murdered by a prisoner waiting below. Pieces of his body then found their way upstairs to become ingredients in Mrs Lovett's pies, famed for 'a flavour never surpassed and rarely equalled'.

Eventually Tobias left and his place was taken by Joanna, who had disguised herself as a boy to try to find out what had happened to her boyfriend after he visited the shop. She managed to catch Sweeney Todd out, whereupon the prisoner in the cellar, who was revealed as her boyfriend, miraculously escaped. ■

have drifted away to Docklands; a chapel in the north aisle honours journalists who have died in the course of their work, among them the Irish journalist Veronica Guerin, shot dead in Dublin in 1996.

Be sure to descend to the crypt which contains a small museum of the printing trade amid the foundations of previous churches and Roman remains found during post-war renovations. On display, too, is the party dress of Susannah Pritchard, wife of William Rich (1755-1811), the pastry cook credited with modelling his wedding cakes on the steeple.

It's open Monday to Friday from 8 am to 4.45 pm, Saturday from 9 am to 4.45 pm, and Sunday from 9 am to 12.30 pm and 5.30 to 7.30 pm.

Dr Johnson's House Dr Johnson's House (☎ 353 3745), 17 Gough Square EC4 (tube: Blackfriars), is the well-preserved Georgian town house where Johnson lived from 1748 to 1759. Johnson was a lexicographer who, along with six full-time assistants working in the attic upstairs, compiled the first-ever English dictionary.

Johnson is also famous for his witty, scathing aphorisms, all written down by his amanuensis and fellow Scot, James Boswell. It was Johnson who claimed that 'when a man is tired of London he is tired of life; for there is in London all that life can afford'.

The house is full of pictures of friends and intimates of Johnson, including his black manservant Francis Barber to whom he was surprisingly generous in his will, a copy of which is also on display. A video provides background information on Johnson and Boswell but the house is of rather specialist interest if you're short of time – although it's fun to see the anti-burglar devices fitted to the front door that prove 18th century Londoners were just as worried about crime as their 20th century counterparts.

It's open May to September, Monday to Saturday from 11 am to 5.30 pm; October to April, Monday to Saturday from 11 am to 5 pm. Admission costs £3/1.

For more information on what to see in Fleet St, see Walk 2 in the London Walks chapter.

Temple Church

Temple Church (☎ 353 1736), Inner Temple, King's Bench Walk EC4 (tube: Temple, or Blackfriars on Sunday), was originally planned and built by the secretive Knights Templar between 1161 and 1185. They modelled it on the Church of the Holy Sepulchre in Jerusalem, using Purbeck marble for the pillars, and the core of the building is one of only five round churches in Britain (the only one left in London). In 1240 a more conventional, if elongated Early English chancel was added on.

Although the Knights Templar were eventually suppressed for being too powerful and their lands were leased to the lawyers who set up the Inns of Court, stone effigies of notable 13th century knights still adorn the floors of the circular nave; some of them are cross-legged but contrary to popular belief this doesn't necessarily mean they were Crusaders. Look out, too, for the grotesque faces peeping down from above the blind arcading ringing the walls. In a couple of instances ears are being nibbled by mini monsters.

Externally the most interesting feature is the Norman west door with an elaborately moulded surround. It's set into a dip which shows how far the ground level has risen over the centuries.

The church was badly damaged during the last war, but has since been sensitively restored to serve as the private chapel of Middle and Inner Temple. It's open Wednesday to Saturday from 10 am to 4 pm, Sunday from 12.45 to 4 pm. Westminster Abbey and St Paul's Cathedral aside, this is possibly London's most interesting and architecturally important church. Don't miss it.

Guildhall

The Guildhall (☎ 606 3030), off Gresham St EC2 (tube: Bank), has been the City's seat of government for nearly 800 years. The present building dates from the early 15th century and the walls have survived both the Great Fire of 1666 and the Blitz of 1940, although surrounding development makes it hard to appreciate them from the outside.

Visitors can see the Great Hall where the Mayor and Sheriffs are still elected, a vast empty space with church-style monuments and the banners of the 12 great livery companies of London (see boxed aside The Livery Companies) lining the walls. The impressive wooden roof is a post-war reconstruction by Sir Giles Gilbert Scott. The minstrels gallery at the west end carries statues of Gog and Magog (see the boxed aside Gog & Magog in the London Walks chapter), modern replacements for 18th century figures destroyed in the Blitz.

Among the monuments look for those to Sir Winston Churchill (1874-1965), Admiral Nelson (1758-1805), the Duke of Wellington (1769-1852) and the two prime ministers Pitt the Elder (1708-78) and Younger (1759-1806).

The Guildhall's stained glass was blown out during the Blitz but a modern window in the south-west corner depicts the City's history; look out for Dick Whittington and his cat, old and new St Paul's, and modern landmarks like the Lloyd's building. Set into two nearby windowsills you can also see standard measures for feet, yards and metres.

The Livery Companies

In the Middle Ages most craftworkers belonged to guilds which organised apprenticeships and could be seen as embryo trade unions. The wealthier guilds built themselves magnificent halls and their leaders wore suitably fine costumes, or liveries, as a result of which the guilds became known as livery companies. These same bigwigs were eligible to stand for the chain of offices which culminated in one of them becoming Lord Mayor of the City of London.

A bit of arcane history? Perhaps, but while the old craft guilds may be no more, some 82 livery companies live on and their leading lights still stand for office at the Court of Common Council which runs the Corporation of London.

Although most of the original halls fell victim to the Great Fire or the Blitz, some have since been rebuilt and they're impressive, if largely inaccessible, places. One of the oldest and most interesting is the Merchant Taylors Hall in Threadneedle St which still retains its 15th-century kitchen. The wealthy Vintners Company has just been given a brand new neoclassical building on the waterside beside Southwark Bridge; you can admire its facade from the South Bank Walkway.

If you'd like to visit some of the halls you'll need to inquire at the City of London Information Centre (☎ 332 1456) weeks ahead of your intended visit; they receive stocks of tickets for the Goldsmiths', Fishmongers', Ironmongers', Tallow Chandlers', Haberdashers' and Skinners' Halls in February each year and they're snapped up pretty quickly.

Otherwise, the Guildhall is where the liverymen meet to choose two sheriffs in June and where they meet again in September to elect the Lord Mayor. ■

PAT YALE

Tourists gather at the Statue of Eros in Piccadilly Circus

PAT YALE

PAT YALE

TOM SMALLMAN

Top: Kew Gardens in summer
Middle: Flower paintings at the Marianne North Gallery, Kew Gardens
Bottom: Police patrol on horseback, Camberwell Green

Meetings are still held in the hall every third Thursday of each month (except August) and the Guildhall hosts an annual flower show and various ceremonial banquets including for the Booker Prize, the leading British literary prize.

Beneath the Great Hall is London's largest surviving medieval crypt with 19 stained-glass windows showing the coats of arms of the livery companies. The **Guildhall Clock Museum** houses more than 700 clocks and watches dating back over 500 years. A new **Guildhall Library** should have opened in Guildhall Yard by the time you read this.

The Guildhall is open (free) daily from 10 am to 5 pm, closed on Sunday between October and April. The Clock Museum is open Monday to Friday from 9.30 am to 4.45 pm.

Along one side of Guildhall Yard stands the church of **St Lawrence Jewry**, the church of the Corporation of London, originally built by Sir Christopher Wren in 1678 but virtually rebuilt after the WWII. The arms of the City of London adorn the organ case at the west end. In the northern Commonwealth Chapel a modern painting of the Madonna and Child incorporates images of the sins of the modern world: financial greed, use of drugs and pornography, and a preoccupation with living standards. It's open daily from 7.30 am to 5.15 pm.

Bank

One of the best tube stations for exploring the heart of the City is Bank, which brings you out at the point where six bank-filled streets converge. Take Prince's St north-west to get to the Guildhall, or head north-east along Threadneedle St for the Bank of England Museum and Lothbury Gallery.

Squeezed in between Threadneedle St and Cornhill to the east is the **Royal Exchange**, the third building on a site originally chosen in 1564 by Sir Thomas Gresham, whose grasshopper emblem appears on the weathervane. Until 1992 you could go inside to watch the London International Financial Futures Exchange in hectic action. Now, however, they've moved to newer premises and the Exchange is closed to the public, except for the rather pricey shops and restaurants that encircle it. The steps provide a great vantage point for observing the citadel that is the Bank of England.

Lombard St, named after the Italian bankers who ran London's money markets between the 13th and 16th centuries, heads off to the south-east. In the angle between it and King William St to the south you'll see the twin towers of Hawksmoor's **St Mary Woolnoth**, the huge Corinthian columns of its interior a foretaste of his even more splendid Christ Church in Spitalfields.

Between King William St and Walbrook stands the grand, porticoed **Mansion House**, the mid-18th century work of George Dance the Elder and now the official residence of the Lord Mayor of London. It's not open to the public.

Walbrook, which heads off south, is named after one of London's lost rivers. Here you'll find **St Stephen Walbrook**, which many would regard as the finest of Wren's City churches; it's certainly the one where he experimented with a dome before embarking on St Paul's Cathedral. Sixteen pillars with Corinthian capitals rise up to support the dome and ceiling, parting in the middle to provide a central open space now filled with an almighty travertine boulder, actually an altarstone by Henry Moore. This manages to look quite at home amid its Classical surroundings which is more than can be said for the dreary modern benches which encircle it and quite detract from the splendour.

Victoria St cuts south-west from Bank. A short way along it on the left you'll find all that remains of the Roman **Temple of Mithras**, excavated in 1954 and moved here from a short distance away. Mithras was a Persian god of light whose cult travelled round the Empire with the Roman legionaries. Although it's not much to look at, its great age offers it a certain poignancy. The finds from the temple can be seen in the Museum of London.

Due west of Bank is Poultry which runs into Cheapside, site of a great medieval market. On the left you'll see another of

The Wren Churches

After the Great Fire of 1666 had destroyed 86 of London's parish churches, Sir Christopher Wren was commissioned to rebuild 51 of them, as well as to create a new St Paul's Cathedral. The money was raised by clapping a tax on all the coal imported through the Port of London. Perhaps the most striking features of Wren's new designs were the graceful Renaissance steeples which were to take the place of the solid square towers of the medieval churches.

Wren later built another three churches in London but since 1781, 19 of his churches have bitten the dust. For a list of some of the surviving churches and their locations, see the City of London, Clerkenwell and Embankment map (Map 6). ■

Wren's great churches, this time **St Mary-le-Bow**, famous as the church whose bells dictate who is and is not a cockney. This was the most expensive of all the Wren churches and its delicate steeple is much admired. There's a good café in the basement, The Place Below (see the Places to Eat chapter).

Bank of England Museum

The Bank of England (☎ 601 5545), Threadneedle St EC2 (tube: Bank), is in charge of maintaining the integrity and value of sterling and of the British financial system. It was originally set up in 1694 when the government needed to raise money to finance a war with France. At first it was housed in the Mercers and Grocers Halls but in 1734 it moved to a new home on the present site. From 1788 to 1833 Sir John Soane was architect to the Bank of England and although much of his work was destroyed during rebuilding after the WWI, some of it was recently reconstructed.

The first room you come to is a reconstruction of Soane's 18th century banking hall, the Bank Stock Office, complete with mannequin clerks and customers. A statue of William III, who was king when the Bank was established, stands to one side. You can also inspect the caryatids which supported Soane's original rotunda in Sir Herbert Baker's later replacement.

The museum's various rooms trace the history of the Bank and of bank notes. Highlights include a pair of Roman gold ingots in the rotunda and a diorama showing an attack on the Bank during the Gordon Riots of 1780. Finally, if you ever fancied a career as a foreign exchange dealer, an interactive video lets you try your hand.

The museum is open (free) from Monday to Friday from 9 am to 5 pm.

The Monument

To the east side of King William St, near London Bridge, stands The Monument (tube: Monument), designed by Sir Christopher Wren to commemorate the Great Fire of 1666 which started in nearby Pudding Lane. The monument is 62m tall (the distance to Pudding Lane) and topped off with a copper vase of flames. If you're up to it, 311 steps lead to a platform offering panoramic views over the City.

It's open from April to September, Monday to Friday from 9 am to 6 pm and from 2 to 6 pm on weekends. For the rest of the year it closes at 4 pm and all day on Sunday. Admission costs £1/50p.

Leadenhall Market

There's been a market on this site in Whittington Ave, Gracechurch St EC1 (tube: Bank), since the year dot. It began life as a Roman forum, and in the 15th century Richard Whittington, the Lord Mayor of London, made it an official food market. Nowadays the Leadenhall arcades serve food and drink to hard-working City folk. Naturally the prices aren't cheap but the selection is excellent and the Victorian glass-and-iron structure is an architectural treat. It's open Monday to Friday from 7 am to 3 pm and gets packed around midday.

Lloyd's of London

Although it's the most famous house of insurance brokers in the world, where everything from planes to film stars' legs is insured, Lloyd's of London (☎ 327 6210), 1 Lime St EC3 (tube: Aldgate or Bank), wouldn't make much of a tourist mecca were it not for the building that houses it.

Right over on the east side of the City, Richard Rogers, doyen of post-modern architecture and architect of the Pompidou Centre in Paris, created one of London's most spectacular new buildings, for which he received scant thanks from an architecturally conservative population. Although Britain has produced some of the best modern architects practising today, many of their best buildings have been constructed elsewhere. Lloyd's, with its external pipes and ducts, is a triumphant exception, especially at night when it becomes a spectacular illuminated framework of yellow and blue.

Access to the equally excellent interior is restricted to professional groups who must still book in advance.

Tower of London

One of London's two World Heritage Sites, the Tower of London (☎ 709 0765), Tower Hill EC3 (tube: Tower Hill), has dominated the south-eastern corner of the City of London since 1078 when William the Conqueror laid the first stone of the White Tower to replace the earth and timber castle he'd already built on the site.

William II completed his father's work on the White Tower and between 1190 and 1285 two walls with towers and a moat were built around it. A riverside wharf was later added and since then the medieval defences have barely been altered.

Until the reign of Henry III (1216-72), the kings had been content to live within the White Tower itself but as well as strengthening the Tower's defences, Henry had a palace constructed between the White Tower and the river. He also started the Royal Menagerie, London's first zoo, after King Louis presented him with an elephant in 1255.

In the early Middle Ages, the Tower acted not just as a royal residence but also as a treasury, a mint, an arsenal and a prison. After Henry VIII moved to Whitehall Palace in 1529, the Tower's role as a prison became increasingly important, with Sir Thomas More, queens Anne Boleyn and Catherine Howard, Archbishop Cranmer, Lady Jane Grey, Princess (later Queen) Elizabeth and Sir Robert Devereux, Earl of Essex, just some of the most famous Tudor prisoners.

After the monarchy was restored in 1660, a large garrison was stationed in the Tower and the arsenal was expanded. For the first time the public was admitted to see the coronation regalia and the armoury.

When the Duke of Wellington became Constable of the Tower in 1826 he was worried that revolution might spread across the Channel from France and so set about reinforcing the Tower's military strength. The Royal Menagerie was closed and the public records moved out. A new barracks quickly replaced the Grand Storehouse when it burnt down in 1841.

Queen Victoria's husband, Prince Albert, saw things very differently and oversaw the demolition of some of the newer buildings and the repair or reconstruction of the medieval towers. From then on the Tower's gruesome and sometimes ferocious history became little more than a tourist attraction although prisoners were still occasionally housed here right up to WWII, most notably Rudolf Hess in 1941.

These days the Tower is visited by more than two million people a year, with impressive crowds even on cold winter afternoons. With hour-long queues to see the Crown Jewels in summer, you'll do yourself a favour if you visit out of season.

Tower Tour You enter the Tower via the West Gate and proceed across the walkway over the moat between the **Middle Tower** and **Byward Tower**.

Walking along Water Lane between the walls you come to **St Thomas's Tower** on the right. Built by King Edward I between 1275 and 1279, it stands immediately above

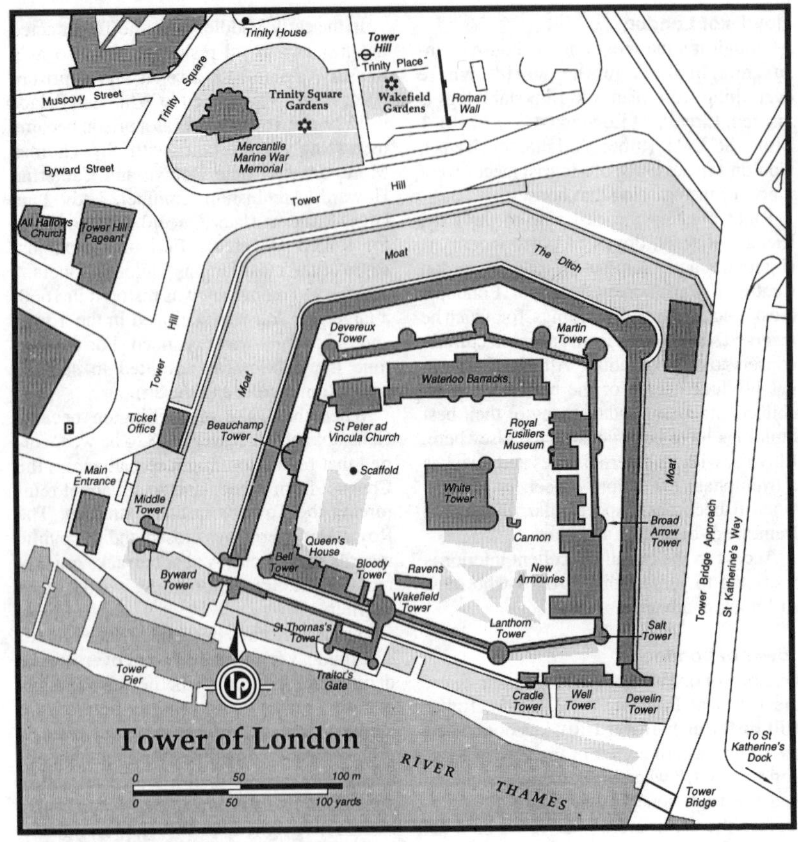

Traitor's Gate, the pathetic gateway through which prisoners being brought to the Tower by river entered their jail. Rooms inside the tower have been restored to show what the king's hall might once have looked like and also to show how archaeologists peel back the layers of newer buildings to find what went before.

Immediately opposite St Thomas's Tower is the **Wakefield Tower**, built by King Henry III between 1220 and 1240. The ground floor was once a guard house and has been restored to show its original stonework. In sharp contrast the upper floor has been furnished with a replica throne and huge candelabra to give an impression of how it might have looked in Edward I's day. It is believed that King Henry VI was murdered in its chapel in 1471.

Passing under Henry III's Watergate you come to the **Cradle Tower**, the **Well Tower** and **Develin Tower** on the right. On the left is the **Lanthorn Tower**, a Victorian copy of the original which burnt down in 1774. Passing through to the inner ward and turning right you'll come to the **Salt Tower**, built around 1238 and perhaps used to store saltpetre for gunpowder. On the 1st floor you

The Beefeaters

While at the Tower you're bound to see the Yeoman Warders – better known as Beefeaters – in their distinctive black and red costumes. But unless you visit on a ceremonial occasion you're unlikely to catch them in the more splendid gold and red costumes of the postcards, which are too heavy and hot for everyday use and also cost around £12,000 a shot.

The 38 Yeoman Warders have all spent at least 22 years in the Army, Royal Marines or Royal Air Force and reached the rank of sergeant-major. They can stay in the job until they're 60 and live within the Tower precincts.

The Beefeaters conduct guided tours of the Tower and also enact the age-old 'Ceremony of the Keys' each evening, in which the Tower gates are locked and the keys ceremoniously locked away in the Queen's House.

Their colourful nickname derives from the tradition whereby the Yeoman Warders received a daily ration of beef and beer. Since beef was a luxury beyond the reach of the poor, this generated much jealousy and the envious nickname which dates back to the 17th century. ■

can see graffiti carved into the wall by Tudor prisoners.

Beside the Salt Tower stand the **New Armouries** built in 1663-4. These now show an assortment of exhibits, including old prints of the Tower, pictures of the Royal Menagerie, the elaborately carved pediment of the Grand Storehouse which survived the 1841 fire, and a list of the Tower's most famous prisoners from Ranulf Flambard, Bishop of Durham, in 1100 to Josef Jakobs, a German spy who was executed by firing squad in 1941. On the lawn opposite is a magnificent **Flemish cannon** built in 1607 and brought from Malta in 1800. It bears the arms of the Order of St John of Jerusalem and of Grand Master Alof de Wignacourt, together with a pewter plaque showing St Paul shipwrecked off Malta.

Passing the **Hospital Block** built in 1699-1700 as houses for officials of the Board of Ordnance, you come to the **Royal Fusiliers Museum** for which a separate 50p charge is made. It contains information on the history of the Royal Fusiliers dating back to 1685, and models of several battles. A 10-minute video gives details of the modern regiment.

The **Martin Tower** houses an exhibition about the original coronation regalia. Here you can see some of the older crowns which were designed so that the jewels in them could be removed. The oldest surviving crown is that of George I which is topped with the ball and cross from James II's crown. The crown of King George IV (1821) was originally set with 12,314 cut diamonds.

It was from the Martin Tower that Colonel Thomas Blood attempted to steal the Crown Jewels in 1671 while disguised as a clergyman; disturbed, he had to abandon the sceptre and flee, only to be apprehended within minutes. The Martin Tower gives access to the **Wall Walk** along the 13th century ramparts. The **Broad Arrow Tower**, built in 1238, has been furnished as the bedchamber of Sir Simon Burley, tutor to the young King Richard II.

The most striking building in the Tower is undoubtedly the massive **White Tower** with its solid Romanesque architecture and four turrets. Unfortunately refurbishment of the Tower to provide a picture gallery, a Spanish armoury and better presentation of the Chapel of St John the Evangelist will be taking place until at least 1999. In the meantime temporary exhibitions show some gruesome instruments of torture and punishment including the last block (used to execute the 80-year-old Simon Fraser, Lord Lovat in 1747) and some of the Royal Armoury's collection including a child's suit of armour designed for James I's young son Henry. You can also see pieces that have survived from the old Line of Kings, a set of models of the monarchs on horses, dating back to 1660. These, too, will receive better treatment in the refurbished White Tower.

Facing the White Tower is the **Waterloo Barracks**, the neo-Gothic barracks introduced by the Duke of Wellington which now houses the Crown Jewels. Queues in summer are so long that the lines are provided with entertainment boards and videos. When you do finally make it through the massive steel doors to the inner sanctum you'll find a moving pavement which will whisk you past the jewels in next to no time.

Beside the Waterloo Barracks stands the **Chapel Royal of St Peter ad Vincula** (St Peter in Chains) which can only be visited in a group or after 4.30 pm; if you aren't already part of a group you can hang around until one shows up and then tag on. This is the third church on the site and a rare example of Tudor church architecture, but is most interesting as the burial place of the unfortunates executed on the scaffold outside or on nearby Tower Hill. Buried without much care at the time, these bodies were disinterred and reburied with proper memorials in Victorian times. Services take place on Sunday morning at 9.15 and 11 am.

What looks quite a peaceful, picturesque corner of the Tower is in fact one of its most tragic. On the small green in front of the church stood the **scaffold**, set up during Henry VIII's reign. On it were executed his two allegedly adulterous wives, Anne Boleyn and Catherine Howard, together with Jane Rochford, lady-in-waiting to Catherine Howard. Also executed here was Margaret Pole, Countess of Salisbury. The fact that she was 70 and guilty of no particular offence except being descended from the House of York couldn't protect her from Henry's wrath.

Lady Jane Grey, on the other hand, was only 16 when she was executed here during the reign of Henry's daughter, Queen Mary I. Proclaimed queen on the death of King Edward VI to ensure that a Catholic wouldn't recover the crown, Jane came to the Tower to await her coronation but lasted only nine days before Mary's supporters rose against her. From her room overlooking Tower Green, Jane watched her husband being taken away for execution on Tower Hill before she too was dragged to her fate.

These five women were executed within the Tower precincts largely to spare the monarch the embarrassment of their public execution. The only two men executed here were William, Lord Hastings, in 1483, and Robert Devereux, the Earl of Essex, once favourite of Queen Elizabeth I. Although he had betrayed her it was believed to be a mark of her continued affection that he was spared public execution...although the authorities may also have feared a popular uprising in his support as well.

Overlooking the scaffold site is the **Beauchamp Tower**, built in about 1281 and taking its name from Thomas Beauchamp, Earl of Warwick, who was imprisoned here from 1397 to 1399. The walls, especially of the upper chamber, are densely carved with graffiti. A numbered list is available to help you pick out the most interesting scribblings.

The attractive half-timbered Tudor houses set around Tower Green are now home to Tower personnel. The **Queen's House**, where Anne Boleyn is believed to have been imprisoned, is now home to the Resident Governor; if and when Prince Charles succeeds the Queen, its name will change to the King's House.

Beside the Wakefield Tower stands the **Bloody Tower**, probably the best known part of the Tower. On the 1st floor you can see the windlass that controlled the portcullis in the gatehouse with a 17th century wooden screen separating it from a room furnished with artefacts dating from 1520 to 1620. It was here that Sir Walter Raleigh was imprisoned for 12 years and where he wrote his *History of the World* (a copy is on display).

A Tudor Whodunnit

When King Edward IV died in 1483, his heir was his 12-year-old son Edward. His uncle Richard, the Duke of Gloucester, was appointed Protector and Edward was taken to the Tower of London to await his coronation.

Within three months Richard managed to persuade the queen to let her other son, the Duke of York, join his brother in the Tower. At first the two boys were seen playing there but gradually their appearances grew shorter and less frequent. Eventually they vanished altogether and their uncle was appointed king as Richard III.

Although it was widely assumed that the boys had been smothered in the Garden Tower (henceforth known as the Bloody Tower), there were no witnesses to the fact and imposters later emerged, claiming to be one or other boy. The most famous is Perkin Warbeck, a young Belgian who tried to spur an uprising in Scotland in 1495, saying he was the Duke of York. He was hanged at Tyburn in 1499.

In 1674 workmen found a chest containing the skeletons of two children near the White Tower. These were assumed to be the 'Princes in the Tower' and were reburied in Innocents' Corner in Westminster Abbey.

But assuming that the boys were murdered, who was the guilty party? The finger has always pointed at Richard, who had a direct motive for wishing to remove the two people who stood ahead of him in line to the throne. Shakespeare's play *Richard III* confirmed the image of the embittered hunchback king as murderer. However, Shakespeare is sometimes held to have been a propagandist for the Tudors and other historians have pointed out that King Henry VII also had a motive for doing away with the boys; although he had won the crown at the Battle of Bosworth in 1485, the boys, if still alive, would have been potential rivals.

Even Poirot couldn't have solved this one decisively. For a fictionalised, easy to read account of the arguments look in second-hand bookshops for Josephine Tey's detective story *A Daughter of Time*. ■

The upstairs room is similarly equipped with 16th century bedchamber furnishings, including a fine oak four-poster bed.

Once called the Garden Tower, the Bloody Tower acquired its unsavoury nickname from the story that the 'Princes in the Tower', Edward V and his younger brother, were murdered here. The blame is usually laid at the door of their uncle King Richard III but there are those who prefer to finger King Henry VII for the crime (see boxed aside A Tudor Whodunnit).

Don't leave the Tower without taking a look at the stretch of green in front of the White Tower where the Great Hall once stood. Here you'll find one or more of the Tower's famous ravens. Historically there had always been ravens here, scavengers on the lookout for scraps chucked from the tower windows (and feasting on the bodies of executed traitors which were displayed as a deterrent to others). However, by the 17th century the numbers had become so great that it was proposed to kill them all, until someone remembered the legend that the White Tower would crumble and a great disaster befall England if ever the ravens left it. The newly restored King Charles II was sufficiently superstitious to take note of this and a compromise was agreed. Now there are never fewer than six ravens in residence, all with their wings clipped so that they can't fly away.

The clipping of their wings makes their normal courtship displays impossible so for many years no ravens bred at the Tower. In 1989 the first chick was successfully reared. A competition on the television programme *Blue Peter* to find a suitable name came up with ... Ronald Raven.

The tower is open March to October, Monday to Saturday from 9.30 am to 6 pm, Sunday from 10 am to 6 pm; November to February, Monday to Saturday from 9 am to 5 pm. Admission is £8.30/6.25.

Note that although there is disabled access to the Crown Jewels, much of the Tower would be tricky, if not impossible, to get around with a wheelchair. There are two Pret-à-Manger sandwich bars on the wharf outside the Tower, but only a coffee shop inside. Bus Nos 15, 25, 100 and D1 pass by.

Despite the Tower's World Heritage Site status, the area immediately to the east is thoroughly disappointing. Immediately outside Tower Hill station a giant modern **sundial** depicts the history of London from AD 43 to 1992. It stands on a platform offering a view of the neighbouring **Trinity Gardens**, once site of the Tower Hill scaffold and now home to Lutyens' **memorial** to the marines and merchant sailors lost during the WWI. A gap in the subway under the main road lets you inspect a stretch of the original Roman wall with a modern statue of the Emperor Trajan standing in front of it.

From then on it's all downhill and the area immediately beside the Tower entrance is particularly dispiriting. The Tower Environs Scheme is currently assessing ways to improve things. In the meantime you may find it more atmospheric to arrive by boat at Tower Pier (see Messing about on the River in the Getting Around chapter for times).

All Hallows by the Tower

Despite its proximity to the point where the Great Fire of 1666 started, All Hallows by the Tower survived virtually unscathed, only to fall victim to German bombs. All that remains of the pre-Fire building is the brick tower and the church's outer walls. The spire was added in 1957 to make the church stand out more in an area flattened by bombs. Notice the pulpit taken from a lost Wren church and a beautiful 17th century font covered with cherubs and a dove. Several people beheaded nearby were buried here, including Sir Thomas More and Archbishop William Laud. William Penn, founder of Pennsylvania, was baptised here and John Quincy Adams, sixth President of the United States, was married here in 1797. Pepys records watching the Fire lapping the City from the tower of All Hallows – 'the saddest sight of desolation that I ever saw'.

A small undercroft museum (☎ 481 2928) reveals remnants of a Roman pavement and of the 7th century Saxon church on the site. It's open from 10 am to 4.30 pm and an audio-tour costs £2.50.

Tower Hill Pageant

Almost hidden amid the unprepossessing surrounds of the Tower, you'll find Tower Hill Pageant (☎ 709 0081), 1 Tower Hill Terrace, EC3 (tube: Tower Hill), the Museum of London's attempt to make London's history more immediately accessible by whizzing you round a series of tableaux in a 'time car'. Purists may not care for this sort of thing. On the other hand, if you're feeling confused about who came when, the taped commentary helps you get it all sorted out in a matter of minutes. Madame Tussaud's does the same thing more colourfully – but for historical accuracy this is the better deal.

At the end of the ride you get a chance to inspect some of the finds made along the London waterfront during the 1980s and 1990s when many of the old warehouses were torn down to make way for new offices. Perhaps most interesting are the remains of Billingsgate's Roman quay and of a Roman ship found at Blackfriars. Also on display is a skeleton dug up nearby in the only Black Death cemetery so far uncovered.

The Pageant is open daily from 9.30 am to 5.30 pm (4.30 pm from October to March). Admission costs £6.95/4.95.

Tower Bridge

Tower Bridge (☎ 403 3761) was built in 1894 when London was still a thriving port. Until then London Bridge was the most easterly crossing point and congestion was so bad that ship owners were forced to agree to a new bridge equipped with an ingenious *bascule* (seesaw) mechanism which can clear the way to oncoming ships in under two minutes. The 25m-high twin towers were given a steel frame and then faced with stone.

Now that London's port days are over you rarely see the bridge do its stuff (except in American movies) but its walkways afford excellent views across the City and Docklands. A lift takes you up into the north tower where the story of its building is recounted.

Afterwards, the basement engine room and engineers' gallery are well worth visiting, although the re-enactment of the royal opening of the bridge could be skipped if time is tight. Rumour has it that some naughty visitors have rebelled against the tour and made off on their own to see the views.

The Bridge (tube: Tower Hill) is open April to October, daily from 10 am to 6.30 pm; November to March, daily from 9.30 am to 6 pm. Entry costs £5.50/3.75.

St Katherine's Dock

If you pass under Tower Bridge from the Tower of London you'll come to St Katherine's Dock, created by Thomas Telford with a west and east basin in 1825 and the first of the docks to be renovated. It's a pleasant haven from the bustle around the Tower, a good place to come for a drink in the Dickens Inn or a bite to eat in one of the restaurants or snack bars serving city folk. You can even opt to stay here in the Tower Thistle Hotel (see the Places to Stay chapter).

Northern Central London

The northern reaches of central London stretch in a broad arc from St John's Wood in the west to Highbury and Islington in the east, those two districts exemplifying the great economic divide that exists in the capital: St John's Wood all monied gentility, areas of Islington around the Angel the run-down opposite. In between, Regent's Park and its Primrose Hill northerly extension offers the largest expanse of open space. Regent's Canal winds round the north of the Park, offering a pleasant way to sidestep the traffic en route to Camden market.

ST JOHN'S WOOD, REGENT'S PARK & MARYLEBONE (Map 2)

Marylebone Rd is north of Oxford St and home to the capital's number one tourist trap, Madame Tussaud's. Fortunately, it's also close to Regent's Park which provides a haven of peace in the city as well as being close to the hustle and bustle of Camden Town which lies just to the east. North-west of Marylebone Rd is posh St John's Wood, a leafy suburb of genteel houses to which the comfortably off retreat. Art lovers may want to divert here to see the Saatchi Gallery, one of those pace-setting collections that can leave the non-cognoscenti scratching their heads in an 'is-it-art-or-isn't-it?' quandary. Cricket-lovers will want to hotfoot it instead to Lord's Cricket Ground. Slightly south-west is Maida Vale and pretty Little Venice, the place to come for canal trips to London Zoo and Camden (see Canal Trips in Getting Around).

Saatchi Gallery

The Saatchi Gallery (☎ 624 8299), 98a Boundary Rd NW8 (tube: St John's Wood), is the private collection of contemporary art owned by Charles Saatchi, until recently co-chairman of Saatchi & Saatchi, once the world's biggest advertising agency.

Saatchi is a serious collector with the money to be extremely influential. When Saatchi buys a batch of Julian Schnabel, Schnabel becomes a big star with a bigger bank balance. But, when Saatchi unloads his Schnabel collection, it's all downhill for Schnabel.

This is not the place to come if your tastes run to Constable or Monet. Here you're more likely to find yourself confronting giant pools of oil reflecting the ceiling or models of human figures so lifelike you're almost afraid they'll jump and start talking. Saatchi it was who patronised Damien Hirst, the formaldehyde king, and Rachel Whiteread who turned an entire house into a work of sculpture only to see it torn down shortly afterwards. Despite the quibbles, the exhibition space is light, airy and large. Time a visit for Thursday when it's free and you're unlikely to be disappointed.

It's open from Thursday to Sunday from noon to 6 pm; admission is £3.50, free on Thursday. To get to the gallery, exit St John's Wood station and turn right along Finchley

Rd. Cross over and turn left along Marlborough Place, then third right along Abbey Rd (where the Beatles had their recording studio). Boundary Rd is the fifth turning on the left.

Lord's Cricket Ground

Daily tours of Lord's Cricket Ground take in the famous Long Room where members watch the games surrounded by portraits of cricket's great and good. There's also a museum which contains cricket memorabilia and offers cricket fans the chance to pose next to the famous urn containing the Ashes – however many times Australia wins the Ashes, they still remain in English hands! In the grounds look out for the famous weathervane in the shape of Old Father Time. Tours leave from the Grace Gates in St John's Wood Rd at noon and 2 pm, as well as at 10 am on county match days (no tours when major matches are on). They cost £5.50/4 and last 1½ hours; to book phone ☎ 432 1033.

Regent's Park

Regent's Park (tube: Baker St or Regent's Park), north of Marylebone Rd and west of Camden was, like all other London parks, once used as a royal hunting ground, subsequently farmed and then revived as a place for fun and leisure during the 18th century.

Soon after, John Nash was employed by the Prince Regent to do something grand and architectural. Nash's architectural brief was the closest London has ever come to a grand plan, with Regent St carving its way from the park all the way down to the Mall. Most of Regent St was torn down by the Victorians, but Nash's contribution – the immaculate stuccoed terraces around the perimeter of Regent's Park – survives.

With London Zoo, the **Regent's Canal** at the northern side, an **open-air theatre** where Shakespeare is performed during the summer months, ponds and colourful flower beds, football pitches and summer softball games, Regent's Park is a lively but serene, local but cosmopolitan haven in the heart of the city. The **Queen Mary Rose Gardens** are particularly spectacular and there's an adjoining café.

On the eastern side of the park is the impressive **London Central Islamic Centre & Mosque**, a huge white edifice with glistening dome. Provided you take your shoes off and dress modestly you're welcome to go inside, although the interior is disappointingly simple, not a patch on the splendour of the Blue Mosque in Istanbul or other such wonders.

To the north-east of Regent's Park, across Prince Albert Rd, is **Primrose Hill**, which, besides being less touristy and conventionally pretty, also has a spectacular view over London.

London Zoo

One of the oldest zoos in the world, London Zoo (☎ 722 3333), Regent's Park NW1 (tube: Camden Town), is, like the London Underground, a victim of its great age. It is saddled with many buildings which are historically interesting but no longer meet the expectations of animal-rights-minded modern visitors. After a long period in the doldrums, when at one stage it seemed that only a £1 million cash injection from the Emir of Kuwait was saving it from closure, the zoo has now embarked on a 10-year, £21 million programme to prepare it for the next millennium. The emphasis is now firmly on conservation and education, with fewer species kept, wherever possible in breeding groups.

In the short term this means a lot of upheaval and if you're keen to see one species in particular it's worth ringing ahead to check that it's still on show. Safe bets are the enclosures housing the big cats, the elephants and rhinos, the apes and monkeys, the small mammals and most of the birds. The Children's Zoo is also open, although the Aquarium is due for a complete refit. The old Mappin Terraces have just reopened but already one of the bears living there seems less than happy with its new home. Don't miss the elegant and cheerful Penguin Pool, one of London's foremost Modernist struc-

Not tonight, said Josephine

The grand old lady of London Zoo is not, as you might expect, a tiger or an elephant, but Josephine the Great Indian Hornbill who has been living in the Tropical Bird House since she was rescued from a New Brighton circus back in 1945.

But however keen the zoo may be on its captive breeding programme, Josephine resolutely refused the attentions of the two suitors arranged for her, most recently in 1953. When she did finally lay an egg in 1989, her keepers decided it was the result of hormone changes and whipped out her oviducts.

These days Josephine is living out her old age in peace and quiet, oblivious to her status as probably the zoo's oldest resident. ■

tures designed by Berthold Lubetkin in 1934.

The zoo is open from March to the end of October, daily from 10 am to 5.30 pm; November to March, daily from 10 am to 4 pm. Admission is £8/6 (family ticket £24). A special large print map is available for anyone who needs it.

The nicest way to get to the zoo is by canal boat from Little Venice or Camden (see Canal Trips in Getting Around) but you can also walk along the canal from Camden Lock.

Madame Tussaud's & the Planetarium

Madame Tussaud's (☎ 935 6861), Marylebone Rd NW1 (tube: Baker St), is one of London's most visited sights and, in summer at least, one of its most hideously overcrowded; expect long queues.

Madame Tussaud's dates back over 200 years and Madame T herself started life modelling the heads of people killed during the French Revolution; the new 200 Years exhibition shows her working on a model of Napoleon in her original studio alongside a modern waxworker creating a cast of model Jerry Hall.

Much of the modern Madame Tussaud's is made up of the Garden Party exhibition where you can have your picture taken alongside sporting greats like Muhammad Ali and comedians like Lenny Henry. The Grand Hall is where you'll find models of world leaders past and present, and of the Royal Family, now minus Fergie, the disgraced Duchess of York, and with the departed Princess Diana on the sidelines.

The latest addition to Madame Tussaud's is a **Spirit of London** time ride. You sit in a mock-up of a black taxi cab and are whipped through a five-minute summary of London's history. The models are great but it's irritating if you land the cab whose commentary is still dealing with the Great Fire as you're passing the panorama devoted to Swinging London.

Tucked away in the basement and certainly not for very young children or anyone particularly squeamish is the revamped **Chamber of Horrors** where models of contemporary prisoners like Denis Nilson ('the Muswell Hill Murderer') sit uneasily alongside tacky, not to say tasteless, representations of historic horrors – the mutilated corpse of one of Jack the Ripper's victims is particularly unpleasant.

The **Planetarium** presents 30-minute spectaculars on the stars and planets livened up with special effects which, sadly, can't match those you'd find at the Staffordshire theme park Alton Towers. While you're waiting you can inspect waxworks of the great scientists from Copernicus to Stephen Hawkings and find out more about the universe on assorted computer consoles.

It's open June to September, daily from 9 am to 5.30 pm; October to May, Monday to Friday from 10 am to 5.30 pm, Saturday and Sunday from 9.30 am to 5.30 pm. An all-inclusive ticket costs £11.20/7.10. Madame Tussaud's only is £8.95/5.90; the Planetarium only £5.65/3.70. Arrive early in the morning or late in the afternoon to avoid the worst of the queues.

Sherlock Holmes Museum

Just around the corner is the small Sherlock Holmes Museum (☎ 935 8866) which gives its address as 221b Baker St, although the house in which Sherlock Holmes famously resided is actually the Abbey National building further down the road. Fans of the books will enjoy looking at the three floors of reconstructed Victoriana but the building is too small to cope comfortably with the summer crowds. At £5 a head (£3 child) it's also horribly expensive. The museum is open from 9.30 am to 6 pm daily and has a Victorian-themed restaurant called Hudson's attached (see the Places to Eat chapter).

EUSTON & KING'S CROSS (Map 5)

Euston Rd links Euston Station to King's Cross and St Pancras stations. This is not an especially inviting area to visit although it's one that you're likely to pass through en route to or from the north of England. Attractions are thin on the ground, although St Pancras Station itself is a Victorian masterpiece, recently restored so that its splendour is more obvious.

Although some effort has been made to clear up the street prostitution and drug-dealing around King's Cross, this is still a distinctly seedy district best avoided after dark.

What would have been the most imposing sight at Euston was Philip Hardwick's vast Doric arch which was ripped down in 1947 before the conservation movement got into its stride and when flamboyant Victorian buildings were generally viewed with suspicion. Outrage at this act of vandalism was a spur to the creation of the Victorian Society.

With time on your hands while waiting for a train at Euston you could nip across the road to the imposing **Wellcome Building** and take in the free Science for Life exhibition.

St Pancras Station

Together with Barry and Pugin's Houses of Parliament, St Pancras station is the pinnacle of the Victorian Gothic revival. Whether you go for the style or not, beautifully restored St Pancras is something special: there's a dramatic glass-and-iron train shed at the back, engineered by the great Brunel, and a fantastically pinnacled hotel designed by Sir George Gilbert Scott at the front.

Though the railway station is still active, the hotel has been disused for years, which means your only chance to see the immense central staircase and superb detailing is on a Heritage Open Day tour in September. Next door is the new **British Library** building, its stark, prison-like, red-brick architecture in blatant contrast to the station next door. After 15 years and £500 million, the library has finally opened to readers, taking over from the British Museum as London's copyright library and stocking one copy of every British publication.

St Pancras Church

Other than the station, the most striking building along Euston Rd is the church of St Pancras which has a tower designed to imitate the Temple of the Winds in Athens, a portico with six Ionic columns like the Erectheum and a wing decorated with caryatids, again like the Erectheum. When it was built in 1816 St Pancras was the most expensive new church to have been erected in London since St Paul's Cathedral. Unfortunately it's usually locked.

CAMDEN TOWN & ISLINGTON (Maps 10 & 2)

From Euston station you can walk up Eversholt St to Camden, a tourist mecca that is especially lively at weekends. Twenty years ago Camden Town was home to a large Irish community, but yuppification has changed all that and nowadays parts of it at the Chalk Farm end blend in more harmoniously with the sedate middle class character of Hampstead further to the north. Not that you'll notice that if you just come for the market ...

Islington is an up-and-coming (some would say come now that Tony Blair's home has been sold for around £750,000) area of north-east London which you're most likely to visit to eat in one of Upper St's many restaurants or to take in a show at the Almeida Theatre (see the Entertainment chapter). Antique-lovers will also want to explore Camden Passage which runs parallel with Upper St just north of the Angel tube station.

Camden Market

In just over 20 years Camden Market has developed into London's second most visited tourist attraction (after the British Museum). What started out as a collection of attractive craft stalls by Camden Lock (on the Grand Union Canal) now extends most of the way from Camden Town tube station northwards to Chalk Farm tube. How much you like it probably depends on your tolerance for crowds, but the junky stalls at the Camden end and the sight of people gorging themselves on sausages and chips out of polystyrene boxes is not a pretty one.

The best time to see the market in full swing is at the weekend – Sunday is particularly busy. But if crowds and mayhem aren't your idea of fun, a lot of the stalls function throughout the week, increasing in number as you get to Thursday and Friday.

If you arrive at Camden Town tube station, take the right-hand exit and turn right again on to Camden High St (which becomes Chalk Farm Rd). For more details of what's where, see Markets in the Shopping chapter.

To escape the crowds, head for the canal towpath which provides a lovely walk, especially heading west past London Zoo to Little Venice in Maida Vale. For boat trip details see Canal Trips in the Getting Around chapter.

Camden Passage

Don't confuse this Islington art and antiques paradise (tube: Angel) with the better-known Camden Market in Camden Town. The best time to visit is Saturday when a multitude of stalls sell more affordable items than the serious shops that specialise in heavy duty antiques (see Antiques in the Shopping chapter for more details).

BLOOMSBURY (Map 5)

East of Tottenham Court Rd and north of Holborn, elegant Bloomsbury is an area of fine Georgian squares and neat Victorian terraces, home to the British Museum and London University.

Between the world wars these pleasant streets were colonised by the group of artists and intellectuals known as the Bloomsbury Group. The novelists Virginia Woolf and EM Forster, who lived in Tavistock Square and Brunswick Square respectively, and the economist John Maynard Keynes are perhaps the best known Bloomsbury Group members. Others included the biographer Lytton Strachey; the art critic Roger Fry, who organised the first-ever London show of the French Impressionists and has been rather dubiously credited with coining the movement's name; Vanessa Bell, sister of Virginia Woolf; and Duncan Grant, who painted mediocre pictures.

The heart of literary Bloomsbury was **Gordon Square** where, at various times, Lytton Strachey lived at No 51, Vanessa and Clive Bell at No 37, and Maynard Keynes and the Woolf family at No 46. Lytton Strachey, Ralph Patridge, Dora Carrington and Lydia Lopokova (later wife of Maynard Keynes) all took turns living at No 41.

Until recently, lovely **Bedford Square** was home to many London publishing houses now swallowed up by American conglomerates and moved out to west London. They included Jonathan Cape, Chatto and the Bodley Head (set up by Woolf and her husband Leonard). These publishers were part-conspirators in creating and sustaining the Bloomsbury Group legend, churning out seemingly endless collections of letters, memoirs and biographies.

Not far from the British Museum in Bloomsbury Way is **St George's Bloomsbury**, another creation of Nicholas Hawksmoor and notable not just for its portico of Corinthian capitals but for its steeple which is topped with a statue of King George I in Roman dress. This steeple can just be made out in the background of Hogarth's influential print of the goings-on in *Gin Lane*.

British Museum

The British Museum (☎ 636 1555), Great Russell St WC1 (tube: Tottenham Court Rd or Russell Square), is Britain's largest museum and one of the oldest in the world. It's also the most visited tourist attraction in London. Six million people can't be wrong so make sure you don't miss it.

The collection is vast, diverse and amazing; so vast, diverse and amazing in fact that it can seem pretty daunting, especially on a stuffy summer's day when it seems that all six million have chosen the same day to visit. To make the most of the museum don't plan on seeing too much in one day; the fact that admission is still free means you can come back several times and appreciate things at your leisure.

Although people are usually in too much of a hurry to get inside to appreciate it, the British Museum is, in itself, a striking building, designed by Sir Robert Smirke between 1823 and 1847 and gradually added to over the years. The collections inside originated with that of Sir Hans Sloane (of Sloane Square, of course) which the physician left to the nation in 1753. They, too, have been added to over the years and still are, as and when funds allow.

The British Museum has two entrances: the imposing Smirke-designed, porticoed main entrance off Great Russell St, and the sneaky back entrance off Montague Place which tends to be less congested. Assuming you come in with the masses through the front entrance, head straight for the information desk at the back of the main hall and ask for a list of the free Eye Opener tours of individual galleries. These last an hour and generally take place between 11 am and 3 pm Monday to Saturday and between 3.30 and 4.30 pm on Sunday. The museum itself lays on 90-minute tours of the highlights but these cost £6 and can get booked up.

Highlights of the British Museum

- Benin Bronzes
- Elgin Marbles
- Egyptian mummies
- Rosetta Stone
- Magna Carta
- Lindisfarne Gospels
- Sutton Hoo Treasure
- Lewis chessmen
- Mildenhall Treasure
- Battersea shield & Waterloo helmet
- Lindow Man
- Oxus Treasure
- Portland Vase ■

If you don't want to be shown around by anyone else, use the plan of the museum to find your way around. The most obvious strategy is to home straight in on the highlights but bear in mind that most people will do the same thing. If you don't like crowds head for the less visited galleries housing Japanese arts, Chinese and South-East Asian arts or the antiquities of Western Asia.

From the main hall you can choose to go left, right or upstairs. This whip-round the museum assumes you start by turning left and bypassing the cramped book and gift shop to arrive in the galleries housing Egyptian sculptures, the famous mummies and the trilingual **Rosetta Stone**, discovered in 1799 and used to decipher Egyptian hieroglyphics. While all this is undoubtedly impressive, it's well worth sidetracking to look at the Ancient Assyrian finds from Nimrud, Nineveh and Khorsabad in rooms 19 to 21. Most striking are the vast human-headed, winged bulls which used to guard the temple of Ashurnarsipal II but the carved reliefs dating back to the 7th century BC are almost as fascinating.

West of these rooms you'll come to the galleries housing finds from the Classical Greek, Roman and Hellenistic empires (rooms 3-15). Best-known of the exhibits here are the **Elgin Marbles**, pilfered on frail pretext from the walls of the Parthenon on the Acropolis in Athens by Lord Elgin in

1801-06. The marbles used to provide the frieze round the top of the temple and fill its pediments. They are thought to show the great procession to the temple that took place during the Panathenaic Festival but have been pretty battered and beaten by the centuries. The Greek government would like its marbles back but almost the first act of the new Labour government was to confirm that they'll be staying put.

The great fame of the Elgin Marbles shouldn't prevent you appreciating some of the other fine monuments on display here, including the reconstructed facade of the **Nereid Monument** from Xanthos in modern Turkey. The Turks would like this back too but that's another story. In room 6 you can see one of the caryatids (female figures) from the portico of the Erectheum in Athens, while room 12 has sculptures from the Mausoleum of Halicarnassus and from the Temple of Artemis at Ephesus, two of the Seven Wonders of the Ancient World and both in modern-day Turkey, although there's little left to see at either site.

Heading up the west stairs you'll arrive in the galleries with exhibits from Greece and Rome themselves. Returning to the main hall and turning right you'll walk through the Grenville Library to the Manuscript Saloon where documents as diverse as **Magna Carta**, the charter of 1215 which set out the rights of the nobility vis-à-vis the monarch, and original Beatles' lyrics are on display. The British Museum also owns the 4th century **Codex Sinaiticus**, a version of the Bible in Greek rescued from a rubbish bin at the Monastery on Mt Sinai in1844, and the **diary of Scott of the Antarctic**, written on the unlucky Polar expedition of 1912. A quick left and you'll be walking through the wooden-floored King's Library which contains cases full of illuminated manuscripts as well as fine old leather bookbindings and delicate oriental miniatures.

At the far end of the King's Library you'll find the Mexican Gallery tucked behind the east stairs, with the fine **Mask of Tzcatlipoca**, with a turquoise mosaic laid over a real skull on display. Beyond that is the British Museum's collection of big-breasted Indian goddesses, dancing Shivas and serene cross-legged Buddhas. At the top of the east stairs turn left for the galleries devoted to Western Asia (rooms 51-2). Here you'll find the stunning **Oxus Treasure**, a collection of 7th to 4th century BC pieces of Persian gold rescued from bandits in a Rawalpindi bazaar. It's believed that they originally hailed from the Ancient Persian capital at Persepolis. Here, too, you'll discover the **finds from Ur** of the Chaldees, including a beautiful model of a goat on its hind legs peering through gold leaves. These artefacts are believed to date back to the third millennium BC, placing them among the oldest exhibits in the museum.

Rooms 49 to 51 contain finds from Roman Britain and from Bronze Age and Celtic Europe. This is where you'll find the stunning **Mildenhall Treasure**, a 28-piece silver dinner service dating back to the 4th century, and the **Snettisham Treasure**, a hoard of gold and silver torcs (neck rings) dating back to Celtic times. Also here are the **Battersea shield** and **Waterloo helmet** dredged from the Thames near the bridges whose names they bear. The Battersea shield dates from around 350-150 BC. It's believed that it was thrown into the Thames as an offering to the gods or during a funeral rather than falling in accidentally. The horned helmet, the only one of its kind ever found, dates from around 150-50 BC.

This is also where you'll find **Lindow Man**, an Iron Age unfortunate who seems to have been garrotted before having his throat cut in an apparent ritual killing. The Cheshire peat-bog preserved his gruesome, leathery remains until 1984 when he was sliced in half by a peat-cutting machine and uncovered.

Eventually you'll arrive in a group of rooms (41-3) showing medieval European art. Particularly interesting for the visitor to London are the fragmentary **murals from St Stephen's Chapel** in the Palace of Westminster, now the Houses of Parliament. The chapel burnt down in 1834 but these scenes from the Book of Job were rescued. Two panels from the ceiling of the King's

Get in Training

Pre-visit warm-up exercises, half-hour breathers, a mobile seat, bottled water and an energy-giving banana ... it might sound as if you're preparing for a trek up the Eiger but these were some of the tongue-in-cheek-but-only-just recommendations for tackling London museums offered in a recent edition of the London museums and galleries magazine.

The British Museum alone has two and a half miles of corridors and over seven million exhibits – and that's without the six million-plus visitors jostling to see them all in a limited amount of time. Hardly surprising, then, that many people feel worn out almost before they've crossed the threshold.

It certainly makes sense to wear comfortable footwear and make use of the free cloakrooms to avoid walking around weighed down with heavy coats and bags. But if you don't want to risk the funny looks that would greet an outbreak of aerobics in the Reading Room, it makes better sense to accept that you won't be able to see everything in a single visit. Pick up a free ground plan of any of the big museums and galleries and decide what you most want to see and where it is. Then head straight there and try not to get sidetracked along the way. You can always come back another time for the also-rans.

Another way to make sure you see the highlights without expiring from exhaustion is to join a guided tour. Many of these are free, though the British Museum charges £6 for its highlights tour. ■

State Bedchamber, known as the Painted Chamber because of its 14th century murals, were rediscovered in Bristol in 1993. They show a seraph and a prophet.

Here, too, you'll see the finds from **Sutton Hoo**, an Anglo-Saxon ship burial site in Suffolk which was excavated in 1939. Inside the remains of the wooden ship were found wonderful gold and cloisonné garnet shoulder clasps and purse decorations. Perhaps the most evocative sight is the helmet of the presumed king, reconstructed so that he looks like the Man in the Iron Mask.

Also worth seeking out is the 67-piece **walrus ivory chess-set** (or sets) found in the sandbanks on the Isle of Lewis in 1831 and dating back to the mid-12th century; and the tiny **Dunstable Swan Jewel**, a 15th century gold masterpiece with its feathers picked out in white enamel.

The *objets d'art* in rooms 44 to 48 would seem more at home in the Victoria & Albert, but it's worth inspecting the late 16th century Bohemian 'nef' or **ship-clock** where you'll be hard pressed to spot the clockface tucked away at the foot of the main mast of a miniature ship. The Hull-Grundy jewellery collection, which includes pieces by Tiffany, Boucheron and other masters, is also pretty unmissable.

On the landing leading up from the main stairs you'll see the stunning 4th century **Roman mosaic** from Hinton St Mary which incorporates the Christian *chi-rho* symbol. Look down into the stairwell and on the wall you'll see the 17th century **Benin Bronzes**, plaques depicting soldiers, musicians and other scenes from everyday life which were stolen from the king and his chiefs in 1897 when a British company seized Benin City and overthrew the ruler. Needless to say, the Benin government would like its bronzes back ...

Across the corridor you'll see more finds from the Greek and Roman empires in southern Italy and Cyprus (rooms 69-73), including the blue and white glass **Portland Vase**, most famous because it was smashed into 200 pieces by a deranged visitor in 1845 and then painstakingly put back together again. It also provided the inspiration for Keats' *Ode on a Grecian Urn*, written in 1820. More antiquities from Egypt and from Western Asia line the corridor between the east and west stairs. Room 66 has exhibits from Coptic Egypt, and beyond that lies a temporary exhibition gallery which often has fine free displays from the prints and drawings collection. Beyond that is a gallery (91) devoted to Korean art. Continue upstairs and you'll come to the peaceful new Japanese Galleries (rooms 92-4).

RACHEL BLACK

RACHEL BLACK

PAT YALE

Left: Elaborate entrance to Green Park near Buckingham Palace
Right: Hampton Court Palace Clock Tower
Bottom: Detail from the Coronation Coach, Royal Mews

PAUL STEEL

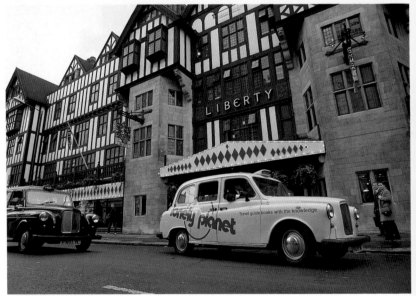

DOUG McKINLAY

Top: Tower Bridge at dusk
Bottom: Liberty in Regent Street

At the heart of the museum, the **British Library Reading Room** is a grand structure where Bernard Shaw and Gandhi studied and where Karl Marx wrote *Das Kapital*. The British Library has now been moved to its new home at St Pancras and work has started on modernising the museum to ease the congestion in the main hall. Eventually the ethnographical collections which used to be housed in the Museum of Mankind will be displayed in new galleries here.

Note that work on the new Great Court may cause disturbance to the usual exhibitions. If you can't find a particular item, most of the custodians will be pleased to direct you. Until the work is complete the museum's café will seem cramped and overpriced. It's much better to head off along Museum St in search of sustenance (see Bloomsbury & Holborn in the Places to Eat chapter).

The museum is open Monday to Saturday, from 10 am to 5 pm and on Sunday from 2.30 to 6 pm. Admission is free, but donations of £2 are requested. Information for visitors with disabilities is available by phoning ☎ 637 7384.

Dickens' House

Charles Dickens' House (☎ 405 2127), 49 Doughty St WC1 (tube: Russell Square), is the only surviving residence of the many the great Victorian novelist occupied before moving to Kent. While living here from 1837 to 1839 he wrote *Pickwick Papers*, *Nicholas Nickleby* and *Oliver Twist*, between bouts of worry over debts, deaths and the burden of an ever-growing family.

In Dickens' day, Doughty St was an exclusive neighbourhood with porters in gold-laced livery guarding gates at each end. These days you'll be hard-pressed to snatch a snapshot that doesn't include parking meters. Inside, two desks illustrate Dickens' own rags-to-riches story. The rough-hewn wooden table where he worked as a 15-year-old Gray's Inn lawyer's clerk for 13s 6d could hardly stand in sharper contrast to the velvet-topped desk he later used on reading tours of England and America.

It's open Monday to Saturday from 10 am to 5 pm and admission costs £3.50/1.50.

CLERKENWELL

Immediately north-east of the City, Clerkenwell was until recently a quiet backwater. Famous in Victorian times for its appalling slums and street crime, Clerkenwell was settled by Italians whose mark can still just be made out in some of the surviving cafés. The Italian revolutionary Mazzini settled here and Garibaldi dropped by in 1836. The great tenor Caruso also performed on the steps of St Peter's church.

Recently Clerkenwell has decided to capitalise on its proximity to the City; this is now a trendy corner of the capital, with the usual batch of pricey restaurants. The area around the Green is very attractive, with St James's church looming over the houses, and the Clerkenwell Conference Centre housed in the 18th century Sessions House, supposedly haunted by a woman whose lover had been transported.

St John's Church and Gate

What looks like a toy-town medieval gate cutting across St John's Lane (tube: Farringdon; Map 6) turns out to be the real thing, albeit restored in the 19th century. During the Crusades of the Middle Ages the Knights of St John of Jerusalem were soldiers who took on a nursing role. In Clerkenwell they established a priory which originally covered around 10 acres of land. Their church, in St John's Square, had a round nave like the Temple church and you can still see some of the outline picked out in brick in the street outside.

The gateway was built as a grand entrance in 1504, only just before Henry VIII suppressed the priory along with all the others in the country. Although most of the buildings were demolished, the gateway lived on to have a very varied afterlife, not least as a Latin-speaking coffee house run, without much success, by William Hogarth's father in the 18th century. The restoration dates from the period when it housed the Old Jerusalem Tavern.

Inside is a small and fairly pedestrian museum recounting the history of the Knights and their properties around the world, and of the modern British Order of St John which has taken its place. There's also a mock-up of the coffee house.

To get the most out of a visit try and time it for 11 am or 2.30 pm on Tuesday, Friday or Saturday when you'll be given a guided tour taking in the restored church in St John's Square. This has a fine Romanesque crypt with a sturdy alabaster monument commemorating a Castilian knight (1575), a battered monument showing the last prior William Weston as a skeleton in a shroud, and stained glass windows showing the main figures in the story.

Back at the main building you'll be shown the Chapter Hall where the Chapter General of the Order meets every three months. Over the fireplace is a portrait of the Queen in her robes as Sovereign Head of the Order and round the walls are the names of all the Grand Priors up to the Duke of Gloucester, the current title holder. The most interesting piece of a furniture is a 17th century cabinet with no less than 50 hidden drawers.

Above the gate itself you'll see other rooms linked up by a wooden spiral stairway dating back to 1502. One is full of mementos of the knights' stay in Malta after they were evicted first from the Holy Land and then from Rhodes. Opening hours for the museum are Monday to Friday from 10 am to 5 pm, Saturday from 10 am to 4 pm. Admission is free.

House of Detention

From 1616 to 1890, when it was demolished to make way for a school, a prison stood in what is now Clerkenwell Close. Visitors to the House of Detention (☎ 493 1089) can descend into a murky, damp-smelling basement to inspect the old kitchen and laundry and some refitted cells with details of a tide of criminality to make you think twice before complaining about modern pickpockets. Here you'll learn how it was once thought wise to keep prisoners in darkened, solitary cells, wearing masks whenever they were let out. It's well done (better than the Clink, for example)...and you'll probably be very glad to escape to the outside again.

The museum is open from 10 am to 6 pm daily. Admission costs £4/2.50. It's not that easy to find but there are signs from Clerkenwell Green, notorious as the place where Fagin introduced Oliver Twist to the fine art of silk handkerchief-stealing.

Eastern Central London

The eastern reaches of central London are taken up with the sprawl of Docklands, an odd mix of the old and decaying, and the rampantly new. The East End, immediately east of the City, has also been included here.

EAST END (Maps 2 & 6)

The East End districts of Shoreditch & Hoxton, Spitalfields and Whitechapel may lie within walking distance of the City, but the change of pace and style is quite extraordinary. Traditionally, this was working-class London, an area settled by wave upon wave of immigrants, giving it a curiously mixed Irish/Huguenot/Bangladeshi/Jewish culture. Run down and neglected in the early 1980s, the East End is starting to look up in places, especially where it rubs right up against the City and Liverpool St station in Spitalfields. Here some of the Georgian houses have been snapped up by city suits with a few grand to spare for tarting them up. Developers have also spotted the area's potential and have moved in with their grandiose complexes.

Hoxton, to the north of Shoreditch, has also had new life injected into it by young artists who've snapped up its old buildings to create New York-style lofts.

But the tarting up still coexists with appalling squalor and deprivation which, while not exactly Dickensian in its scale, should still give anyone with a conscience pause for thought.

For anyone interested in modern, multicultural London, it's well worth venturing a look at the East End. Alongside a couple of interesting museums you'll find some of the best-value Asian cuisine in London (see the Places to Eat chapter) as well as some of its most colourful markets (see Markets in the Shopping chapter). You may also want to pop into Whitechapel Art Gallery to see what's on or to eat in its excellent café (see Galleries later in this chapter).

For more detailed information on the East End, see Walk 4 in the Walks chapter.

Geffrye Museum

The Geffrye Museum (☎ 739 9893) Kingsland Rd, Dalston E2 (tube: Old St; leave by exit 2 and take bus No 243), was originally built to provide homes for the elderly poor by Robert Geffrye, a late 16th century mayor of London who had made a fortune from the slave trade. His statue stands above the main entrance.

When the occupants were moved to healthier surroundings outside London, the house became a school for carpenters and artisans. It's now a museum of domestic interiors, with each room furnished to show how homes would have looked from Elizabethan times right through to the 1950s. The original chapel also survives. New 20th century rooms should have opened by the time you read this.

It's open (free) Tuesday to Saturday from 10 am to 5 pm, and Sunday from 2 to 5 pm. Bus Nos 22A, 22B, 67, 149 and 243 pass by. There's a small café and you can picnic in the grounds.

Bethnal Green Museum of Childhood

The Bethnal Green Museum of Childhood, (☎ 0181-983 5200), Cambridge Heath Rd E2 (tube: Bethnal Green), is guaranteed to bring memories of childhood rushing back. Set in a rather grungy 19th century building, it's packed with numerous dolls, dolls' houses, train sets, model cars, children's clothes, old board games, children's books, toy theatres and puppets. The upstairs gallery attempts to provide a context for the toys by tracing the stages of childhood from babyhood to leaving home.

It's open (free) from Monday to Thursday and Saturday from 10 am to 5.50 pm, Sunday 2.30 to 5.50 pm, closed Friday. There's a small café serving tea and sandwiches, and lockers operated by a returnable £1 coin. Bus Nos 8, D9, 26, 48, 55, 106, 253 and 309 pass by.

DOCKLANDS (Map 7)

The Port of London was once the greatest port in the world, the hub of the British Empire and its enormous worldwide trade. In the 16th century there had been 20 cargo quays to the east of London. By the 18th century these were hard-pressed to cope with the quantity of cargo flowing through and in the 19th century new docks were opened: West India Dock opened in 1802, London Dock in 1805, East India Dock in 1806 and Victoria Dock in 1855. Even these proved inadequate as goods from the British Empire poured in and out and a new wave of dock building kicked off with Millwall in 1868, followed by the Royal Albert in 1880 and Tilbury in 1886. Finally, this century the King George Dock VI was built in 1921.

However, in 1940 25,000 bombs fell on the area over 57 consecutive nights. Already reeling, the docks were in no state to cope with the post-war technological and political changes as the empire evaporated, and enormous new bulk carriers and container ships demanded deepwater ports and new loading and unloading techniques. From the mid-1960s dock closures followed each other as fast as the openings had done in the 19th century and the number of jobs available slumped from around 50,000 in 1960 to just 3000 by 1980. Almost one-eighth of the land area of London slowly succumbed to dereliction.

This was the area Mrs Thatcher saw as ripe for development. The builders moved in, the Docklands Light Railway was constructed to link it to the rest of London, and yuppification proceeded apace. In a rush of activity new offices were built and new toy-town houses were thrown up beside new marinas. Places like the beautiful **Tobacco Dock** (☎ 702 9681), The Highway E1 (tube: Wapping), were transformed into shopping malls full of delicatessen food and designer clothes. It was all very controversial, with those of a left-wing bent complaining that for all the money spent, very little filtered down to the local population who watched with awe and irritation as the London Docklands Development Corporation (LDDC) made all the decisions for them.

Of course, when the recession of the early 1990s arrived, the bubble burst. The offices stood empty, the yuppies lost their jobs, their apartments wouldn't sell, and the trendy shops hung up For Sale signs. Over it all towered the flagship development of Canary Wharf which had already come a financial cropper before the IRA bomb of 1996 devastated the area immediately around it. Now, however, things are moving along nicely again and Canary Wharf, once an apparent white elephant, is full of newspaper people: the home of the *Telegraph* and *Independent* newspapers, it has been described as a vertical Fleet Street and makes a striking focal point visible for miles around. Sadly, Tobacco Dock remains an empty shell (at the time of writing the Dock was awaiting yet another reincarnation).

Getting around was always the Docklands' Achilles heel. In the Thatcherite 80s, it was thought philosophically unsound for government to underwrite development by providing decent transport infrastructure. However, the Docklands Light Railway has got over its teething problems and now provides an excellent way of seeing what's going on from on high. Things will get even better when the Jubilee Line is eventually extended to Canary Wharf and beyond.

Whisper it, but history may eventually conclude that Docklands was Mrs Thatcher's greatest stroke of genius.

A Short Tour of Docklands

The obvious starting point for a tour of Docklands is Tower Hill, where the Underground system connects with the DLR at the aptly named Tower Gateway. Just behind Tower Hill is **St Katherine's Dock**, the first of the rejuvenated docks, once at the vanguard of change and a symbol of Docklands optimism. Of all the dockland developments this is the one which most clearly took tourism into consideration. Cafés and tourisy shops ring the waterside where several old ships have been given a new home. The Dickens pub was also restored with an eye as much to the tourists as to the workers from the nearby World Trade Centre.

If you head east along the river from St Katherine's Dock you'll come to **Wapping** and Wapping High St, home to Rupert Murdoch's media empire and the scene of pitched battles between police and printers in the mid-1980s. The ancient Prospect of Whitby (☎ 481 1095) at 57 Wapping Wall is a very popular riverside pub. Nearby is Shadwell station, where you can catch the DLR across to the Isle of Dogs.

The next DLR station is at Limehouse Basin, the centre of London's Chinatown in the last century. The only reminders are street names like Ming and Mandarin St. It's easy to forget the long history of the Docklands, especially when it is buried by enormous developments like Canary Wharf, three stops further on. **Canary Wharf** (DLR: Canary Wharf), until recently the largest building site in Europe, is dominated by Cesar Pelli's tower – a square prism with a pyramidal top. When building stopped there were more than two million sq yards of unlet office space in London, and over 500,000 of them were in Canary Wharf. But the Cassandras who forecast disaster and thought their prophecies had come true when the developers went bust in 1992, are having to eat their words as the floors fill up and the surrounding areas come to life. Marco Pierre White is opening MPW, the first of a planned string of franchised brasseries, here which just about says it all.

Continue on the DLR to Island Gardens, across the river from Greenwich. Alternatively, change at West India Quay station for a northbound DLR train to All Saints station. At 240 East India Dock Rd E14 (DLR: All Saints), you'll see a building that amply illustrates the ups and downs of life in Docklands. A brilliant Nicholas Grimshaw creation of metal and glass, it originally housed the ***Financial Times* Print Works**. Now, however, the newspaper has moved on and the building stands empty, awaiting the arrival of a new, wealthier, owner.

Further east is the Thames Flood Barrier, built to protect London from the great tidal river that made this city what it is. The massive floodgates are supported by a row of concrete piers capped with gleaming metal, like an extraordinary sculpture. The Victoria, Royal Albert and George VI docks that are close by were the largest and last docks to be built and the last to capitulate. This is the location for the London City airport, originally built to cater for businessfolk from the City but now a good starting point for trips to north European cities with nothing of the hassle of Heathrow and Gatwick.

London Docklands Visitor Centre

The London Docklands Visitor Centre (☎ 512 1111), 3 Limeharbour, Isle of Dogs E14 (DLR: Crossharbour), is a good place to find out both about what went on in the area in the past and what is likely to happen in the future. Inevitably its ownership ensures a rosy presentation which concentrates on the good works of the LDDC in providing new health centres, watersports facilities etc. Still, in the past the Docklands development has been so widely slated that it's interesting to listen to people trumpeting the one bit of London which certainly can't be accused of pandering to the heritage industry.

The visitor centre is open (free) Monday to Friday from 8.30 am to 6 pm and at weekends from 9.30 am to 5 pm. The bookshop is a good source of literature both on modern Docklands and on the East End. If you're spending time in the area it's worth investing in *Eating Out in Docklands* (£2).

Southern Central London

As recently as 10 years ago, the southern part of central London was the city's forgotten underside; run down, neglected and offering little for foreign visitors once they'd visited the South Bank arts venues. Recently, however, all that has changed and parts of London immediately south of the river can seem as exciting as anywhere further north. The new Globe Theatre has already opened to considerable acclaim and the new Tate Gallery at Bankside should be up and running for the Millennium. A spate of new museums and exhibitions have opened in and around Southwark, and the success of the new restaurant in the old Oxo Tower has served to consolidate the area's popularity. As development continues apace this part of the capital is likely to become ever more of a drawcard.

For more details on the area south of the Thames from Hungerford Bridge to Tower Bridge, see Walk 3 in the London Walks chapter.

BERMONDSEY & SOUTHWARK (Map 6)

Originally settled by the Romans, Southwark (pronouced sutherk) became an important thoroughfare for people travelling to London in the Middle Ages. For centuries London Bridge, with its houses and shops, was the only crossing point on the Thames and so travellers congregated in Southwark where many inns opened to cater for them. In Tudor times the City authorities refused to permit theatres to be built in the City and so it was on Bankside in Southwark that the Globe, the Rose, the Swan and the Hope theatres were established. At that time Southwark had a thoroughly raffish air, with plentiful 'stews' (brothels-cum-bathhouses), several prisons and innumerable bear-baiting pits.

Victorian Southwark flourished on the back of the trade passing through the docks. Processing and packaging firms set up nearby, many of them household names like Crosse & Blackwell, Jacob's, Peek Frean's and Courage. However, Southwark suffered terribly during WWII and even worse in the post-war years when the docks closed and the trade on which it had prospered moved away.

Although Southwark is still pretty run down, it's worth coming here to visit Southwark Cathedral. The back streets are also well worth exploring for their many small museums and attractions, including HMS *Belfast*, the London Dungeon, the Britain at War exhibition and the excellent Old Operating Theatre Museum. Sam Wanamaker's Globe Theatre is the real jewel in the crown, although no doubt the new Tate at Bankside will put up fierce competition when it opens around the year 2000.

A little further east is Bermondsey where you might want to visit Sir Terence Conran's Design Museum. Antique-lovers will also want to explore the Friday morning antiques market (see Antiques in the Shopping chapter for details). It was only in the 1980s that life began to return to the run-down, decaying warehouses. Although parts of Bermondsey still look pretty dejected, there are also pockets of refurbishment, even gentrification, especially along the waterfront.

Design Museum

The brainchild of Sir Terence Conran, the bright, white Design Museum (☎ 378 6055), Shad Thames, SE1 (tube: London Bridge), offers displays which show how product design evolves over time and how it can make the difference between success and failure for items intended for mass production. Try a set of chairs for comfort and then use a computer to help you design a new-look toothbrush. The 2nd floor hosts temporary exhibitions which might tell you how, for example, the Dyson cyclonic cleaner was developed, while on the 1st floor you can gaze in awe at cutting-edge phone and camera technology.

The museum is open Monday to Friday from 11.30 am to 6 pm, and Saturday and Sunday from noon to 6 pm. Admission costs £4.75/3.50. There's a coffee shop and gift shop, while the adjacent Blue Print Café offers wonderful river views and prices to match (see the Places to Eat chapter for details).

Bramah Tea & Coffee Museum

The Bramah Tea & Coffee Museum (☎ 378 0222), The Clove Building, Maguire St SE1 (tube: London Bridge), traces the story of tea and coffee drinking in Britain beside Butler's Wharf where 5000 chests of tea a day were once handled. Teapots abound in every shape you can imagine and many you probably wouldn't – a cactus plant, a ball of wool with knitting needles, Daniel Lambert (the fattest man who ever lived), a rubbish bin, a Channel Tunnel train. Look out, also, for the largest teapot ever made which would weigh 154kg if anyone were foolish enough to fill it.

The museum is open from 10 am to 6 pm daily and admission costs £3.50/2. In the excellent tea shop your tea is served with an egg timer so you can get the infusion just right.

HMS Belfast

The HMS *Belfast* (☎ 407 6434), Morgan's Lane, Tooley St SE1 (tube: Tower Hill or London Bridge), is a large, light cruiser built with 16 six-inch guns in 1936. It took its name from the Harland & Wolff shipyard in Belfast where it was built. During WWII, the *Belfast* escorted merchant shipping on the Arctic convoy, and took part in the 1943 Battle of the North Cape when the German *Scharnhorst* was sunk during the last large-scale gun battle between ships fought in Europe; only 36 of the 1963 men on board the *Scharnhost* survived. Hit by a mine in 1939, the *Belfast* was out of action until 1942 but then took part in the Normandy landings, before being moved to the Far East to repatriate prisoners-of-war and internees at the end of the war. Later it saw 404 days action during the Korean War.

In 1952 the *Belfast* returned to the UK and was comprehensively refitted before setting off on a round-the-world voyage. In 1963 it returned to Devonport docks and was only saved from the scrapyard when the Imperial War Museum bought it to serve as a museum.

It probably helps to be keen on military manoeuvres, but the *Belfast* is surprisingly interesting anyway for what it shows of the way of life on board a cruiser. Finding your way about the eight zones on board can be rather confusing even with a map to help you, and you need to be prepared for a lot of scrambling up and down steep ladders.

In the zone three Operations Room models and sound effects attempt to bring the Battle of the North Cape to life, while a fixed exhibition, HMS *Belfast* in War and Peace, in zone five gives more details and shows a video of the battle. A second exhibition, the Modern Royal Navy, is more propagandist, with information, for example, on Britain's nuclear deterrent. But almost anyone should enjoy looking around zone seven where you can see the ship's galley, hospital, chapel, dentist's surgery and laundry. Even more interesting are the messdecks of zone four, where some poor sods had to hang their hammocks amid the machinery of the capstan space.

The ship is open March to October, from 10 am to 5.15 pm daily; November to March, from 10 am to 4.15 pm daily. Admission costs £4.40/2.20.

Southwark Cathedral

There was already a church on this site in 1086 but this was rebuilt in 1106 and then for a third time in the 13th century. During the Middle Ages it was part of the Priory of St Mary Overie, becoming the local parish church in 1539 after the dissolution of the monasteries. By the 1830s it had fallen into decay and much of what you see today is actually Victorian; the nave was rebuilt in 1897, although the central tower dates back to 1520 and the choir to the 13th century. In 1905 the Collegiate Church of St Saviour (☎ 407 3708) became a cathedral with its own bishop.

You enter via the south-west door and immediately to the left is a **memorial** to the 51 people who died in the *Marchioness* disaster of 1987 when a pleasure cruiser on the Thames hit a dredger and sank. Against the west wall are a series of **15th century bosses** taken from the original nave ceiling; one shows the devil swallowing Judas Iscariot.

Walk down the north aisle and you'll come to the brightly coloured **canopied tomb** of John Gower (d. 1408), regarded as the first English poet because his *Confessio Amantis* was written in English.

In the north transept you'll see several 17th and 18th century monuments and a fine 17th century wooden **sword-rest** from the lost church of St Olave. Opening off on the east side is the Harvard Chapel, originally the chapel of St John the Evangelist but now named after John Harvard, founder of Harvard University, who was baptised here in 1607.

In the north choir aisle look out for a gruesome **medieval monument** showing a skeleton in a shroud and for a rare but heavily restored 13th century **wooden effigy** of a knight in chain mail armour. Immediately opposite is a **17th century monument** to Richard Humble which shows him kneeling towards the altar with his two wives behind him.

Crossing the retro-choir behind the high altar and returning along the south choir aisle, look out for the fine **17th century monument** to Lancelot Andrews, Bishop of Winchester. It was restored and redecorated by Sir Ninian Comper in 1930. A few steps further and you'll see a **Roman statue** of a hunter god found in a nearby well and probably dating from the second or third century AD.

Cross into the choir to admire the Early English arches and vaults, and the **16th century screen** separating the choir from the retro-choir; the statues in the niches were added in 1905.

Return to the south choir aisle and continue to the south transept, noting the fine **organ** designed by Lewis in 1897 and rebuilt in 1952.

Stand beneath the 16th century crossing tower and look up at the finely painted ceiling. The **brass candelabrum** hanging from it dates back to 1620. The crown, mitre and dove incorporated in the design are said to reflect contemporary concern about the relationship between Church and State.

Returning along the south aisle, stop and look at the alabaster **monument to William**

Shakespeare, the playwright whose great works were originally written for the Bankside playhouses. Shakespeare is actually buried at Stratford-upon-Avon and this memorial was only erected in 1912. The background depicts the Globe theatre and Southwark Cathedral, while the stained-glass window above shows characters from *A Midsummer Night's Dream*, *Hamlet* and *The Tempest*. Right beside Shakespeare's monument is a memorial to Sam Wanamaker (1919-93), the Canadian film director who was the brain behind the newly rebuilt Globe Theatre.

The cathedral is open daily. A donation of £2 is requested. Sung evensong is at 5.30 pm on Tuesday and Friday and 3 pm on Sunday. A Pizza Express restaurant in the Chapter House is open from 10 am to 4 pm daily. Lunchtime concerts take place on Monday and Tuesday at 1.10 pm.

Winchester Palace & Clink Prison Museum

Close to the cathedral is Clink St, once the heart of the huge Winchester Palace complex started by Henry de Blois, half-brother of King Stephen, in 1144. Today the scant remains include the fine 14th century rose window of the Great Hall.

The Clink Prison, a private prison attached to the Palace, was used to detain debtors, whores, thieves, martyrs and even actors until 1780 when it was burnt down during the Gordon Riots. This is where we got the expression 'in the clink' from. The small, rather half-hearted Clink Prison Museum (☎ 403 6515) reveals the wretched life of the prisoners who were forced to pay their gaolers for their food and accommodation and sometimes had to resort to catching and eating mice. It's open daily from 10 am to 6 pm and admission costs £3.50/2.50 (tube: London Bridge).

London Dungeon

Located under the arches of London Bridge station in Tooley St, the Dungeon (☎ 403 0606) must be London's most tasteless 'attraction', supposedly developed after a mother's children found Madame Tussaud's Chamber of Horrors insufficiently frightening. Here you can watch people hanging on the Tyburn gallows, listen to the speaking head of Anne Boleyn before it was cut from her body, observe St Thomas à Becket's murder and wonder at an assortment of ingenious methods of torture. These sections are bad enough, and the reconstruction of the French guillotine in action is even worse. But for real bad taste you can hardly sink lower than the section dealing with Victorian serial killer Jack the Ripper and his five unfortunate victims, depicted in gruesome detail with their entrails hanging out. It says everything for the sensitivity of the London Dungeon that you emerge straight from watching the guillotine to a bright and breezy Pizza Hut.

The Dungeon (tube: London Bridge) is open daily from 10 am to 4.30 pm from March to October, until 5.30 pm in summer. Despite the Dungeon's tackiness you may well have to queue for entry in July and August.

Britain at War Experience

Under another Tooley St railway arch you'll find the Britain at War Experience (☎ 403 3171). This aims to educate the younger generation about the effect WWII had on daily life while simultaneously playing on the curious nostalgia of the war generation who sit in the mock-up Anderson air-raid shelter listening to the simulated sounds of warning sirens and bombers flying overhead with extraordinary detachment.

You descend by lift to a reproduction Underground station fitted with bunks, tea urns, even a lending library, as some of the stations really were, and then progress through rooms which display wartime newspaper front pages, posters and ration books. Mannequins illustrate the ways in which women tried to get around a shortage of fabric, and there's a model of an iced cardboard wedding cake with a small drawer at the bottom for a tiny piece of real fruit cake. Finally, you emerge amid the wreckage of a shop hit by a bomb with the smoke still eddying around and a burst pipe pumping out water.

It's open from October to March from 10 am to 4.30 pm (5.30 pm in summer). Admission costs £5.50/2.95.

Old Operating Theatre & Herb Garret

If the London Dungeon is all about shock-horror grotesquery, you don't have to walk far to find an exhibition which focuses on the more mundane nastiness of 19th century hospital treatment. The Old Operating Theatre Museum (☎ 955 4791), 9A St Thomas St, SE1 (tube: London Bridge), is in the top of the tower of St Thomas church which was built in 1703. The garret was used by the St Thomas' Hospital apothecary to store medicinal herbs and now houses an atmospheric medical museum delightfully hung with bunches of herbs which go some way to soften the impact of the nasty devices displayed in the glass cases.

Even more interesting is the 19th century operating theatre attached to the garret. An adjoining building used to house the surgical ward of St Thomas' and the church's roof space provided an ideal position for the theatre – high enough to take advantage of the natural light and isolated enough to provide soundproofing. In the days before the importance of an antiseptic environment was understood, students crowded round the operating table in what looks like a modern lecture hall. A box of sawdust was placed beneath the table to catch the blood and contemporary accounts record the surgeons wearing frockcoats 'stiff and stinking with pus and blood'.

The museum is open Tuesday to Sunday from 10 am to 4 pm and admission costs £2.50/1.70.

Shakespeare Globe Centre & Theatre

The Shakespeare Globe Centre (☎ 928 6406), Bear Gardens, Bankside SE1 (tube: London Bridge), presently consists of the new Globe Theatre and an exhibition opened in the shell of a 17th century Inigo Jones theatre, also due to be rebuilt. A visit to the exhibition includes a guided tour of the Globe Theatre itself. The exhibition is open daily from 10 am to 5 pm; £5/3.

The original Globe (Shakespeare's 'wooden O') was built in 1598-9, burnt down in 1613 and immediately rebuilt. In 1642 it was finally closed by the Puritans who regarded theatres as dreadful dens of iniquity. Despite the worldwide popularity of Shakespeare, that was still the state of affairs when Canadian producer Sam Wanamaker came searching for the Globe in 1949. Undeterred by the fact that the foundations of the theatre had vanished beneath a row of listed Georgian houses, Wanamaker set up the Globe Playhouse Trust in 1970 and began fundraising for a memorial theatre. Work started in 1987 but sadly Wanamaker died in 1993 before it could be completed.

The new Globe opened in 1997 to great acclaim. Unlike other venues for Shakespearean plays, this theatre has been designed to resemble the original as closely as possible – even if that does mean leaving the arena open to the skies and expecting the 500 'groundlings' to stand. Despite all this you shouldn't necessarily assume that the productions you'll see will be terribly conservative – Shakespeare in untranslated Zulu was one first-season offering! For ticket details see Theatre in the Entertainment chapter.

WATERLOO & LAMBETH (Maps 2 & 4)

The area immediately around Waterloo station is currently a mess of run-down streets and concrete walkways. However, this is where you'll find the area known as the South Bank, with several important theatres and concert halls. The South Bank Walkway also provides stunning views across the Thames. A lot of work is being done to brush things up – in the short term that may make matters worse, in the long term it can only be good news. Emerging from Waterloo station you'd be well advised to follow the signs for Festival Hall rather than walking through the concrete Bullring to Waterloo Bridge. For many years this wretched underpass has suffered the nickname 'Cardboard City' because of the number of homeless people living in its soulless confines

Lambeth is the district immediately south of Westminster Bridge where you'll find the old County Hall, now housing the London Aquarium, Lambeth Palace with the Museum of Garden History just beside it, and St Thomas' Hospital, with the Florence Nightingale Museum inside the grounds.

The South Bank

Across the Thames from Embankment, the South Bank (see inset map) is a labyrinth of arts venues strung out on rain-stained concrete walkways between Hungerford Railway Bridge and Waterloo Bridge (tube: Waterloo). Almost no-one has a good word to say for the architecture and a complete overhaul, which will roof over the Hayward Gallery, the Queen Elizabeth Hall and the Purcell Room, is finally on the cards. Expect work to have begun by the time you visit. In the meantime the concrete slopes and buttresses host a mixed bag of art lovers, skateboarders and homeless people.

The **Festival Hall** was built in 1951 for the Festival of Britain and now hosts classical, opera, jazz and choral music. Alongside a range of pricey cafés and restaurants and a good music shop, it also has a foyer where free recitals take place most evenings. The smaller **Queen Elizabeth Hall** and **Purcell Room** host similar concerts.

Tucked almost out of sight is the **National Film Theatre**, or NFT, built in 1958 and due to get a new café and restaurant. The popular, and much newer, Museum of the Moving Image (MOMI) next door tells the story of film and television. A second-hand book and print market takes place immediately in front of the NFT on the river side.

The **Hayward Gallery**, built in the mid-1960s, caters for blockbuster modern art exhibitions. Finally, the **Royal National Theatre**, a love-it-or-hate-it complex of three theatres, is the nation's flagship theatre. Dismissed by Prince Charles as resembling a 'disused power station', the National was designed in 1976 by the Modernist architect Denys Lasdun, a great fan of concrete and horizontal lines. Work on modernising the National started in 1997.

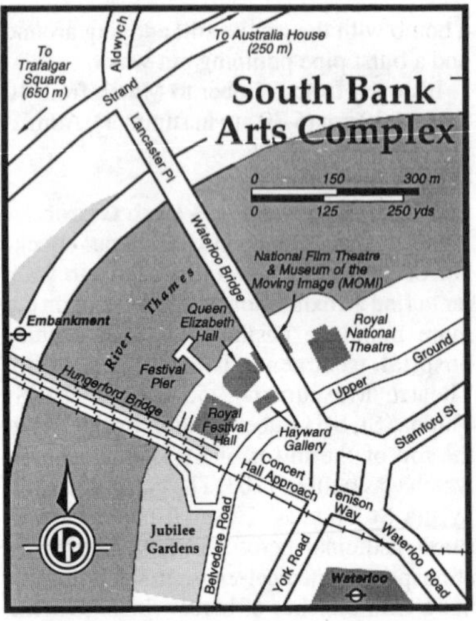

A short walk east along the South Bank is **Gabriel's Wharf**, a cluster of craft shops which forms part of local residents' successful attempt to resist further large-scale development in the area. From the South Bank Walkway you look across the river to stunning views of St Paul's, Lloyds, Canary Wharf and so on – a veritable Manhattan-on-Thames.

Museum of the Moving Image Tucked away among the South Bank's high-brow arts venues, the Museum of the Moving Image (MOMI) (☎ 401 2636), South Bank SE1 (tube: Waterloo), offers the chance to have a bit of fun, skilfully mixing up showbiz glamour and education so you hardly realise you're learning.

MOMI's 44 rooms work their way chronologically through from the early days of zoetropes, magic lanterns and other idiosyncratic ways of making images move, to the glory days of the silent movies and then the talkies. Along the way you can find out about the development of censorship, about surrealism in film and about the pioneers of European cinema like Gance and Eisenstein. Eventually you fetch up in the modern world of television and video, with the chance to get yourself interviewed with TV film critic Barry Norman and to rewatch your favourite TV ads. Actor-guides are on hand to explain oddities like the Russian agitprop train, and children get the chance to try their hand at cartooning or acting in their own movie. Throughout you can watch clips from old films and television shows...beware the nasty eye-cutting sequence in Bunuel's *Un Chien Andalou* though.

MOMI is open daily from 10 am to 6 pm. Admission costs £5.95/4. Allow about two hours for a visit.

Hayward Gallery The Hayward Gallery (☎ 928 3144), Belvedere Rd SE1 (tube: Waterloo), is London's premier exhibition space for major international art shows. Some love the grey concrete building, an integral part of the South Bank arts centre, others can't say a nice thing about it. Whichever camp you fall into, you can hardly deny that it makes an excellent hanging space for contemporary and 20th century art. If the media has gone to town on a show, you need to arrive early – or pack a picnic and expect to join a queue.

Between exhibitions the Hayward is sometimes closed, so check before turning up. Generally, it's open Monday and Thursday to Sunday from 10 am to 6 pm, Tuesday and Wednesday from 10 am to 8 pm. Admission depends on what's showing but assume around £5/3.50. There's a branch of the Aroma coffee shop here but only for those who've paid the admission fee.

Imperial War Museum

The Imperial War Museum (☎ 416 5000), Lambeth Rd SE1 (tube: Lambeth North), is housed in a striking building dating back to 1815 and given a magnificent copper dome in 1845. Originally this was the site of the Royal Bethlehem Mental Hospital, commonly known as Bedlam, hence the modern word for a chaotic situation. The hospital had stood on the site since the 13th century but was moved to Kent in 1926, whereupon Viscount Rothermere bought the old building and gave it to the nation to house a museum. Look out for a chunk of the Berlin Wall to the left of the main entrance.

Although there's still plenty of military hardware on show and the core of the museum is a chronological exhibition on the two world wars, these days the Imperial War Museum places more emphasis on the social cost of war: the Blitz, the food shortages and the propaganda. Especially distressing is a small room where film footage of the discovery of the Bergen Belsen concentration camp is shown. Children under 14 are not admitted without adults...and with good reason. The top floor is devoted to war paintings by the likes of Henry Moore, Paul Nash and John Singer Sargent.

Particularly popular exhibits are the Trench Experience which depicts the grim day-to-day existence of a WWI foot soldier, and the Blitz Experience which lets visitors sit inside a mock-up bomb shelter during an air raid and then stroll a set of the ravaged streets of the East End. This 'experience' lasts only 10 minutes but you may have to queue to get in, especially during school hours. Also very popular is the Secret History exhibition which takes a look at the work of the secret services, with video footage of the siege of the Iranian Embassy in Knightsbridge in 1980, brought to a dramatic end by balaclava-clad SAS commandos in an 11-minute assault.

Alongside the permanent exhibitions, temporary ones cover topics like war reporting and fashion in the post-war years. Those none too keen on the tanks and guns may find these more gripping.

The museum is open daily from 10 am to 6 pm for £4.70/2.35 (free after 4.30 pm). It's particularly popular with school groups; visit early in the morning or late in the afternoon to avoid them.

Museum of Garden History

Within walking distance of the Imperial War Museum is the Museum of Garden History (☎ 401 8864), Lambeth Palace Rd SE1 (tube: Lambeth North), housed in the church of St Mary-at-Lambeth. The museum was inspired by the work of John Tradescant and his son, also called John, who were gardeners respectively to Kings Charles I and II. The Tradescants roamed the globe and brought back many exotic plants together with a collection of 'all things strange and rare' which they housed in The Ark, their South Lambeth Road house. This collection eventually formed the basis for the Ashmolean Museum in Oxford, Britain's oldest true museum.

Although the tower of St Mary's dates back to the 14th century, the nave was rebuilt in the 19th century and now provides exhibition space for information on the Tradescants' lives and on the inspirational 20th century gardener Gertrude Jekyll. A knot garden has been planted in the small churchyard which also shelters the tombs of the Tradescants and of William Bligh, the ship's captain famously cast adrift during the mutiny on the *Bounty* in 1789. The Tradescants' tomb is well worth a look for the carvings of crocodiles seemingly swimming in a primeval swamp on the side.

The museum is open (free) Monday to Friday from 10.30 am to 4 pm and on Sunday until 5 pm (closed Saturday). There's a café in what was once the chancel.

The redbrick Tudor gatehouse immediately beside the church leads to **Lambeth Palace**, the London home of the Archbishop of Canterbury. Although the palace is not usually open to the public, the gardens occasionally are; check with the tourist office for details.

London Aquarium

Immediately across Westminster Bridge from the Houses of Parliament stands County Hall, home to the Greater London Council (GLC) until its final disagreement with Mrs Thatcher in 1985. The grand building with its curved, colonnaded facade was built in 1922. After more than a decade of wrangling over its future it's finally started to acquire new life with the opening of a vast aquarium in the basement. While this is certainly better than what London Zoo currently has on offer, the Aquarium is curiously disappointing, partly because its basement position is so dark but also because the fish on display are generally of the less colourful variety. There's also an uncomfortable discrepancy between the huge tanks with their shark inhabitants and the side tanks which are so small that it only takes one inconsiderate home-video-maker to put them off-limits to everyone else. If you've been to Sea World in Florida or even to one of England's Sea Life Centres you may well be disappointed.

The Aquarium (☎ 967 8000) is open daily from 10 am to 6 pm, opening at 9.30 am and closing at 7.30 pm from June to August. Admission costs £6.50/4.50 and there's a café and huge shop attached. Future development should see all sorts of leisure facilities and a hotel opening on the upper floors of the Hall.

Beside County Hall are the **Jubilee Gardens**. Outline plans for celebrating the Millennium envisage the world's largest ferris wheel being built here.

As you walk across Westminster Bridge (tube: Westminster) to get to County Hall look out for the **statue of Boadicea** on the left. As Queen of the Iceni she led the resistance to the Romans in 60 AD, razing the first city of London to the ground. When the Romans rallied and fought back Boadicea poisoned herself.

Florence Nightingale Museum

Within walking distance of the Aquarium and attached to St Thomas' Hospital is the Florence Nightingale Museum (☎ 620 0374), 2 Lambeth Palace Rd SE1 (tube: Westminster), which tells the story of everyone's favourite war heroine, a feistier character than her 'lady of the lamp' image sometimes suggests. The museum will be rather wordy for some but the video about Nightingale's life is certainly interesting.

It's open Tuesday to Sunday from 10 am to 5 pm (last admission at 4 pm) and costs £2.50.

BATTERSEA (Map 2 & 14)

In between Brixton and Wandsworth is Battersea, not the most inspiring of London districts but boasting a fine Thamesside park with a children's zoo, a pagoda, Adrenalin Village (see bungee-jumping under Activities later in this chapter) and the shell of the old Battersea Power Station.

Battersea Park

Stretching out between Battersea Bridge and Chelsea Bridge is Battersea Park, a 200-acre park filled with attractions and distractions, most prominently the **Japanese Peace Pagoda**, erected in 1985 by the Nipponzan Myohoji sect of Buddhists who aim to complete similar pagodas all over the world. Golden Buddhas sit in the niches on all four sides and a pinnacle soars 10m into the air.

Boats can be hired (£3.50 an hour) to get around the small lake, and there's a mile-long running track. The small **children's zoo** is open from Easter to October from 10 am to 5 pm and admission costs £1.10/60p. Over public holidays there'll usually be a funfair here, the sound carrying right the way across the river.

Battersea Power Station

Familiar from a million Pink Floyd album covers and loved and loathed in equal measure, Battersea Power Station is the building looking rather like an upturned table that's visible from Chelsea Bridge. Originally built by Sir Giles Gilbert Scott in 1933, it was decommissioned in 1983, and since then there have been innumerable schemes to give it new life. The latest idea envisages a 32-screen Warner cinema occupying the main hall which stands, for the time being, exposed to the elements with its insides ripped out.

Western Central London

Much of west London is high-class territory – Knightsbridge, Chelsea, Kensington and Holland Park – into which more dilapidated areas like Paddington and Earl's Court seem to have been dropped by accident. This is where you'll find some of London's best-known museums as well as the shopping emporia of Harrods and Harvey Nichols (see the Shopping chapter).

CHELSEA & KNIGHTSBRIDGE (Maps 8 & 2)

Until the 18th century Chelsea was a village harbouring the grand country houses of the rich. Nowadays, of course, it's well and truly part of London although its riverside setting ensures that it's still a favoured place for the wealthy to live. During the 60s Chelsea was fashionable with the trendsetters who frequented King's Rd. The heyday of punk brought a brief, colourful renaissance but even if Chelsea is no longer at the forefront of fashion this is still one of London's classier and most exclusive districts, with tree-lined streets of architecturally striking houses. One look at the cars parked outside them is enough to reveal the incomes of those living within. **Cheyne Walk**, in particular, is a delightful road which follows the river from Battersea Bridge to Albert Bridge and then turns inland. The *Middlemarch* author George Eliot died at No 4, while the artist Dante Rossetti and the poet Algernon Swinburne both lived at No 16. Where Cheyne Mews now stands was once the site of one of Henry VIII's manor houses. It was pulled down on the death of its last resident, Sir Hans Sloane, the British Museum benefactor who died in 1753 and is buried in nearby Chelsea Old Church.

The best shops lie a little to the north, especially in Knightsbridge which is virtually synonymous with Harrods in many minds, although these days Harvey Nichols has an almost equally high profile in the mental map of shopaholics.

Chelsea Royal Hospital

Well known as the site of Chelsea's annual Flower Show, the Royal Hospital (☎ 730 5282), Royal Hospital Rd SW3 (tube: Sloane Square), is a superb building designed by Sir Christopher Wren during the reign of King

Charles II whose statue, in Roman dress, adorns an inner courtyard. It was a home for veteran soldiers and still houses 420 Chelsea Pensioners – you may see them around town in their striking scarlet (summer) or blue (winter) jackets and black pillbox hats.

You can stroll in the grounds and visit the elegantly simple Chapel and the Great Hall which is really, in spite of the flags and royal portraits, a glorified canteen prone to smelling of fish. Visible across the river are the four white chimneys of the old Battersea Power Station.

The Royal Hospital is open (free) Monday to Saturday from 10 am to noon and from 2 to 4 pm; on Sunday it's open in the afternoon only.

National Army Museum

Right beside the Royal Hospital but designed with sublime disregard for its elegant neighbour, the ugly National Army Museum (☎ 730 0717), Royal Hospital Rd SW3 (tube: Sloane Square; Maps 8 & 14), does its best to inject life into its military exhibits. Unfortunately you have to be pretty keen on war and what goes with it to find much to detain you here. All sorts of displays deal with the history of weapons, armies, artillery and tactics, and there's even some scorched weaponry fresh from the Gulf War. Women turned off by all things military may yet find something to interest them on the 2nd floor where a permanent display looks at the female role in the forces.

The museum is open (free) daily from 10 am to 5.30 pm. Bus No 239 stops right outside.

Chelsea Physic Garden

A peaceful oasis hidden behind a high brick wall (tube: Sloane Square; Maps 2 & 14), the Chelsea Physic Garden (☎ 352 5646) was created by the Society of Apothecaries in 1673 to study the ways in which botany related to medicine, then known as the 'physic art'. It's one of the oldest botanic gardens in Europe with many rare trees and plants. The rock garden is also said to be one of the oldest in existence and incorporates chunks of black lava brought from Iceland in 1773. Individual corners of the garden are given over to world medicine, and plants suitable for dyeing and aromatherapy.

Unfortunately it's only open from April to October on Wednesday from 2 to 5 pm and Sunday from 2 to 6 pm. In the weeks of the Chelsea Flower Show and the Chelsea Festival it opens Monday to Friday from noon to 5 pm. Admission costs £3.50/1.50. The entrance is in Swan Walk. Teas with excellent cakes are served from 2.30 to 4.45 pm (5.45 pm on Sunday).

Carlyle's House

From 1834 the great essayist and historian Thomas Carlyle (1795-1881) lived at 24 Cheyne Row SW3 (tube: Sloane Square; Maps 2 & 14), a three-storey terrace house built in 1708. Here he wrote his famous history of the French Revolution and many other works. Legend claims that when the manuscript was complete, a maid mistakenly threw it on the fire, whereupon the diligent Thomas duly wrote it all again.

While it's not particularly large, this is a charming house which has been put on show to the public much as it would have been when the Carlyles were still living there – there's a keen sense that you might turn round and find them beside you and it's not hard to see how it became an artists' hangout, popular with the likes of Chopin, Thackeray and Dickens. There's a small garden at the rear.

Carlyle's House (☎ 352 7087) is open from the end of March to October, Wednesday to Sunday from 11 am to 4.30 pm. Admission costs £3/1.50 (free to National Trust (NT) members).

Chelsea Old Church

As you walk along Cheyne Walk you'll spot a colourful statue of Sir Thomas More (1478-1535), the politician who was executed for his opposition to King Henry VIII's plans to make himself Head of the Church of England after his divorce from Catherine of Aragon. More and his family used to live in Chelsea and immediately behind him is Chelsea Old Church, which dates back to the 14th century but was flattened by two land mines in 1941 and rebuilt shortly afterwards.

Step inside and you'll be pleasantly surprised to find that the red-brick exterior conceals an interior which retains many of its fine Tudor monuments. Most interesting is the More Chapel to the south-east which was built by Sir Thomas More in 1528 and retains its wooden ceiling and column capitals, examples of a fledgling Renaissance style. At the west end of the south aisle don't miss the only chained books in a London church (chained, of course, to stop anyone making off with them), including a copy of Foxe's *Book of Martyrs* dating back to 1684.

King's Rd

In the 17th century King Charles II set up a lovenest for his mistress, the orange-seller Nell Gwyn, in Chelsea. Returning from her house to Hampton Court he would make use of a farmer's track which inevitably came to be known as the King's Rd.

Even today when the hippies and punks have moved on, King's Rd is still a mightily fashionable place where you'll see cars like spaceships parked outside designer bars and restaurants. Midway along on the left as you walk up from Sloane Square look out for the **Old Town Hall**, built in 1886 and now the venue for a Saturday antiques market.

Michelin Building

Even if you can't afford to eat in Bibendum, Terence Conran's lovely restaurant at 81 Fulham Rd, it's still worth passing by just to take a decko at the astonishingly lighthearted Art Deco architecture, more reminiscent of a seaside pier than a factory. It was designed for Michelin in 1905 by Francois Espinasse and the famous roly-poly Michelin Man appears in the modern stained-glass. The open-fronted ground floor provides space for upmarket fish and flower stalls, while the lobby is decorated with tiles showing off cars of the early 20th century. Just off it is an oyster bar and the Conran Shop (see Furnishing & Household Goods in Shopping chapter). Upstairs is a fine restaurant (see Places to Eat).

HYDE PARK AREA (Maps 2, 8 & 9)

At the far west end of Piccadilly, Hyde Park is one of those areas where posh hotels and prestigious shops have long since squeezed out the hoi polloi. If you're driving, you'd do well to avoid the nightmare of Hyde Park Corner roundabout – although trying to find the right exit from the Underground isn't all that much easier!

Apsley House (Wellington Museum)

After Buckingham Palace, London's most prestigious address would surely be No. 1 London, although to most people this striking 18th century mansion overlooking the nightmarish Hyde Park Corner roundabout is better known as Apsley House or the Wellington Museum (☎ 499 5676; Map 4). Apsley House was designed by Robert Adam between 1771 and 1778 for Baron Apsley but was eventually sold to the first Duke of Wellington, victor at the Battle of Waterloo and later prime minister. The Corinthian portico was an afterthought of 1828. In 1947 the house was given to the nation. Unlike most 18th century London town houses, Apsley House retains most of its furnishings and collections and still has the descendants of the original family in residence.

The ground floor displays an astonishing collection of china, including a dinner service decorated with Egyptian scenes, and some of the Duke of Wellington's silverware including the stunning Waterloo Vase and Shield. The stairwell is dominated by Canova's staggering 3.26m statue of Napoleon, naked but for the obligatory fig leaf – try not to laugh when you see the portrait of the un-Adonis-like real man on the landing. The 1st floor rooms have fine plaster ceilings and a collection of paintings by Landseer, Goya, Rubens, Brueghel and Murillo.

Perhaps the most striking exhibit is the 1000-piece Portuguese silver-gilt table centrepiece partly on display in the dining room. This used to be brought out for the annual Waterloo Banquets to commemorate the victory of 1815.

The cramped basement gallery contains Wellington memorabilia, including some entertaining old cartoons. The house is open Tuesday to Sunday from 11 am to 5 pm. Admission is £4/2.50.

Hyde Park

At 360 acres, Hyde Park is central London's largest royal park. Acquired from the church by Henry VIII, it became a hunting ground for kings and aristocrats, and then a venue for duels, executions and horse racing. In 1851 the Great Exhibition was held here, and during the war it became an enormous potato field. More recently, it has served as a venue for concerts by the likes of Queen, the Rolling Stones and Pavarotti. The park is a riot of colour during spring, and full of lazy sunbathers in summer. Boating on the Serpentine Lake is an option for the relatively energetic.

Besides sculptures by Henry Moore and Jacob Epstein, and the statue of Peter Pan (Map 9), Hyde Park boasts its own art gallery. The **Serpentine Gallery** (☎ 402 6075; Maps 8 & 9), beautifully sited just south of the lake and west of the main road that cuts through the park, specialises in contemporary art. By the time you read this it should have reopened after extensive restructuring. It will probably open from 10 am to 6 pm daily and hopefully will still be free.

Speaker's Corner (near Marble Arch) started life in 1872 as a response to serious riots. Every Sunday anyone with a soapbox can hold forth on whatever subject takes their fancy. Provided you don't go along expecting Churchillian oratory, it's still an entertaining experience.

Hyde Park is open daily from 5 am to midnight, but like all big city parks, it's much less welcoming at night. It's not as bad as New York's Central Park, but you should certainly steer clear once darkness falls.

Marble Arch

The north-eastern corner of Hyde Park is marked by Marble Arch (tube: Marble Arch; Map 2), a huge arch designed by John Nash in 1828 which originally stood in front of Buckingham Palace. Near here used to stand the **Tyburn Gallows** where thousands of unfortunates were executed between 1196 and 1783. Many of them had been dragged all the way to the scaffold from the Tower of London or Newgate Prison. At 8 Hyde Park Place, off Bayswater Rd, is **Tyburn Convent** (☎ 723 7262) where the chapel contains relics of 105 martyrs killed at Tyburn. Free 40-minute tours to see them take place at 10.30 am, 3.30 and 5.30 pm.

KENSINGTON & HOLLAND PARK (Map 8)

Kensington is another of those thoroughly desirable London neighbourhoods where you'll not get much change from a million pounds if you want to buy a family-sized house. South Kensington is the place to come for the big-name museums – the Victoria & Albert Museum, the Science Museum and the Natural History Museum – while High St Kensington is a shoppers' paradise. It's also the kicking off point for visits to Kensington Palace with its state apartments.

Holland Park lies west of Notting Hill and High St Kensington. In the heart of a residential district of elegant town houses is the well-wooded park, once belonging to Holland House, a sprawling, pinnacled mansion destroyed during WWII. Here you'll find a youth hostel, a playground and a restaurant, and some delightful formal gardens, at their most glorious in summer. The old orangery is usually open as an exhibition space for young artists.

Victoria & Albert Museum

The Victoria & Albert Museum (☎ 938 8441), Cromwell Rd SW7 (tube: South Kensington), is a vast, rambling, wonderful museum of decorative art and design, part of Prince Albert's legacy to Londoners in the aftermath of the successful Great Exhibition of 1851.

Like the British Museum, this is one that needs careful planning if you're to get the most out of your visit. Sadly, the fact that you must pay to come in makes repeat trips a less practical option unless you invest in a London White Card (see Discounts in the Facts for the Visitor chapter). As soon as you're through the turnstile look at the floorplan and decide what you're most interested in; then stick to that plan unless you want to find the time has flown by and you're still inspecting the plastercasts of Classical statues! Alternatively, take one of the free guided tours that introduce you to the galleries. Amazingly, most of the V&A's four-million-piece collection is actually on display, but you've no hope of seeing everything and it's best to admit that at the outset.

The main entrance to the V&A, as it's affectionately nicknamed, is from Cromwell Rd although you can also enter from Exhibition Rd. The ground floor is mostly devoted to art and design from India, China, Japan and Korea, and to European art. There's a fine new room devoted to costume – everything from absurd 18th century wigs and whalebones to the platform shoes that brought Naomi Campbell crashing to the ground on the Paris catwalk.

One entire room is devoted to Raphael's seven cartoons – not, as you might think, early satirical drawings but great paintings commissioned by Pope Leo X as designs for tapestries which now hang in the Vatican Museum, Rome. The finest are those showing Christ's *Charge to Peter* and *The Miraculous Drought of Fishes*. The cartoons became part of Charles I's great art collection, were pawned by Charles II, redeemed by William III and hung in Hampton Court Palace until Queen Victoria agreed to their transfer to the museum (17th century copies now hang at Hampton Court).

Also on the ground floor are the V&A's three original refreshment rooms dating back to the 1860s. The gorgeous Green Dining Room was designed by William Morris with help from his friend Edward Burne-Jones. Next to it is the Gamble Room, whose tiles, marble statuary and frieze with quotations from the Book of Ecclesiasticus would cast London's most stylish modern restaurants into the shade. Finally there's the Poynter Room, designed by Edward Poynter and still with its grill for turning out chops in place.

Highlights of the Victoria & Albert
- Raphael Cartoons
- Great Bed of Ware
- Music Room from Norfolk House
- Morris, Gamble and Poynter Refreshment Rooms
- Tippoo's Tiger
- Shah Jahan's wine cup
- Throne of Maharaja Ranjit Singh
- Canova's *Three Graces*
- Becket Casket ■

On the 2nd floor you'll find collections of ironwork, stained glass and jewellery, together with a wonderful exhibition of musical instruments. In the British rooms you could hardly fail to notice the late 16th century Great Bed of Ware, big enough to sleep five and designed as an attention-grabbing gimmick for a Ware inn. But the highlight of this floor must surely be the new silver galleries. Even if silver isn't your thing, the goblets and chalices are displayed in a lovely Victorian gallery, approached up a delightful tiled staircase which was narrowly saved from destruction in the days when full-blown Victoriana was thought the height of bad taste.

On this floor you'll also find displays of textiles, arms and armour and 20th century furniture, including the famous sofa in the shape of Mae West's lips. Up on the 3rd and 4th floors are displays of British art and design, ceramics and porcelain from Europe and the Far East.

The Henry Cole Wing is an add-on at the Exhibition Rd side of the museum. Here you'll find displays of prints and printmaking techniques and of European paintings and miniatures. The collection of Constable paintings seems to have come adrift from the National Gallery.

The museum is open Monday from noon to 5.50 pm, Tuesday to Sunday from 10 am to 5.50 pm; admission is £5/3 (free after 4.30 pm). The restaurant in the Henry Cole Wing serves snacks and light meals to keep you going throughout your visit; on Sunday there's also a jazz brunch between 11 am and 3 pm. When the V&A ran an advertising campaign describing itself as 'an ace café with a rather nice museum attached' it was widely felt to have taken its eye off the ball.

Science Museum

The Science Museum (☎ 938 8008), Exhibition Rd, South Kensington SW7 (tube: South Kensington), has had a complete makeover since the days when it was a rather dreary place for machine boffs and reluctant school children. The ground floor looks back at the history of the Industrial Revolution via examples of its machinery and then looks forward to the exploration of space. There are enough old trains ('Puffing Billy' among them) and cars to keep the boys well and truly happy. Up a floor and you can find out about the impact of science on food, up another one and you're into the world of computers. The 3rd floor is the place to come for the old aeroplanes, among them the ones in which Alcock and Brown first flew the Atlantic in 1919 and in which Amy Johnson flew to Australia in 1930. Finally on the 4th and 5th floors you'll find exhibits relating to the history of medicine.

Look out for a version of Foucault's famous pendulum hanging in the hall. As the day wears on the pendulum seems to change direction. In fact, because the earth is moving beneath it, it really stays in the same place all the time. Thus it was that Foucault illustrated how the earth rotates on its own axis.

The basement has imaginative hands-on galleries specifically for children: The Garden is for three to six-year-olds, Things is for seven to 11-year-olds.

The museum is open daily from 10 am to 6 pm. Admission costs £5/2.60 (free after 4.30 pm); if you think you might like to come back, consider buying a London White Card (see Discounts in Facts for the Visitor chapter). Information for disabled visitors is available on ☎ 938 9788.

Highlights of the Science Museum

- Boulton & Watt Steam Engine
- Foucault's Pendulum
- Apollo 10 Command Module
- Robert Stephenson's *Rocket*
- Gas Drilling Rig
- Watson & Crick's DNA model
- Amy Johnson's *Gypsy Moth*
- Alcock & Brown's Vickers Vimy ■

Natural History Museum

The Natural History Museum (☎ 938 9123), Cromwell Rd, South Kensington SW7 (tube: South Kensington), is one of London's finest Gothic Revival buildings. It was designed by Alfred Waterhouse between 1873 and 1880 with a grand cathedral-like main entrance, a gleaming brick and terracotta frontage, thin columns and articulated arches, and carvings of plants and animals crawling all over it.

In recent years the Natural History Museum has changed out of all recognition, not least because it has absorbed the old Geological Museum in Exhibition Rd; the two collections are now divided between the adjoining Life and Earth Galleries. Where once there were dreary glasscases you'll now find wonderful interactive displays on themes like Human Biology and Creepy Crawlies, alongside the crowd-attracting exhibition on dinosaurs (some of them moving and roaring) and mammals.

In term-time the Life Galleries tend to be overrun with screaming schoolkids whose place is taken in holidays by equally large, if not so noisy, crowds of tourists. Luckily the schoolkids flock to see the dinosaurs, leaving more space on the wondrous mammal balcony, at the Blue Whale exhibit, or in the spooky ecology gallery (a moonlit replica rainforest). The old glasscases containing the bird exhibits are overtly apologetic at not having received their makeover yet.

But in some ways it's the Earth Galleries that are most staggering. Enter from Exhibition Rd and you'll find yourself facing an escalator which slithers up and into a hollowed-out sphere. Around its base single fine samples of different rocks and gems are beautifully displayed.

Upstairs there are two main exhibits: The Power Within and the Restless Surface which explains how wind, water, ice, gravity and life itself impact on the earth. The Power Within includes an extraordinary mock-up of what happened to one shop during the Kobe earthquake in Japan in 1995 which killed 6000 people. As you stand on a surface that shakes harder and harder, it's impossible not to contemplate the fine line that separates explanation from entertainment.

To avoid the crowds it's best to visit early in the morning or late in the afternoon. It's impossible to do justice to everything in just one visit; if you think you might like to come back consider buying a London White Card (see Discounts in Facts for the Visitor chapter) to save money. The museum is open Monday to Saturday from 10 am to 5.50 pm, Sunday from 11 am to 5.50 pm. It costs £5.50/2.80, but is free after 4.30 pm on weekdays and after 5 pm on weekends.

Kensington State Apartments & Gardens

Sometime home to Princess Margaret and the late Princess Diana, Kensington Palace (☎ 937 9561), Kensington Gardens W8 (tube: High St Kensington; Maps 8 & 9), dates back to 1605 when it was home to the second Earl of Nottingham. In 1688 when William of Orange arrived to take over as king from James II, he found the old palace at Whitehall too close to the river to suit his asthmatic lungs. He and wife Mary bought the house in the park from Nottingham and had it adapted by Sir Christopher Wren and Nicholas Hawksmoor. When George I arrived from Hanover to succeed Queen Anne, the childless last Stuart monarch, he recruited William Kent to modernise the palace. Much of the interior decor you see today is Kent's sometimes clumsy handiwork. Later Queen Victoria was born here in 1819 and one room is preserved as a memorial to her, with a painting of her marriage to Prince Albert.

Hour-long tours of the palace take you round the small, wood-panelled state apartments dating back to the Stuart period and the much grander, more spacious apartments of the Georgian period.

Displayed under low lights in some of the rooms you'll see costumes from the Court Dress Collection, including dresses with skirts so ludicrously wide that they made it impossible for their wearers to sit down and ensured that rooms had to be sparsely furnished, lest they knock over the tables and chairs.

Most striking of all is the Cupola Room where the ceremony of initiating men into the exclusive Order of the Garter took place; you can see the Order painted on the *trompe d'oeil* domed ceiling. The room is ringed with marbled columns and niches in which stand gilded Roman-style statues. In the centre of the room a clock stands on a stepped plinth. It used to play the music of Handel and Corelli but no more.

The King's Long Gallery displays some of the royal art collection, including the only known painting of a Classical subject by Van Dyck; it shows Cupid and Pysche and is, apparently, the painting which would be removed first should fire break out. On the ceiling William Kent painted the story of Ulysses but slipped up by giving the Cyclops two eyes!

The King's Drawing Room is dominated by an extraordinarily ugly painting of Cupid and Venus (looking like an all-in wrestler), this time by Giorgio Vasari, better known for his books on art. Through the window you can see the **Round Pond**, once full of turtles for turtle soup but now popular for sailing model boats, and a **statue of the young Queen Victoria**, sculpted by her daughter, Princess Louise.

The King's Staircase is decorated with striking murals by William Kent who painted himself in a turban on the fake dome. A prominent figure of a Highlander was included at a time when the threat from the Jacobites in Scotland was by no means dead.

Also included is a portrait of Peter the Wild Boy who had been discovered in the woods of Hanover and brought to England to entertain jaded court tastes.

The **Sunken Garden** near the palace is at its prettiest in summer. Also nearby is **The Orangery**, designed by Hawksmoor and Vanbrugh and with carvings by Grinling Gibbons. Tea here is a pricey treat (see Time for Tea in the Places to Eat chapter).

The State Apartments are open from May to October from 9 am to 5 pm Monday to Saturday and from 11 am on Sunday. Admission costs £6/4.

Albert Memorial & Visitor Centre

On the southern edge of the park, the Albert Memorial is an over-the-top monument to Queen Victoria's German husband Albert (1819-61). Said to have been inspired by the Eleanor Crosses (see the boxed aside Crosses of Love in the Excursions chapter), the 53m memorial was designed by Sir George Gilbert Scott, and decorated with 178 figures representing the continents, the arts, industry and science, and with mosaics designed by the renowned church artists Clayton and Bell.

Until recently the monument was slowly crumbling. Work to restore it is now underway and is unlikely to finish before the summer of 1999. While the monument itself is under gigantic wraps English Heritage has provided a visitor centre which explains Albert's role in the development of South Kensington ('Albertopolis') and allows you to watch the work in progress. It's open (free) daily from 10 am to 6 pm, opening at 9 am and closing at 3.30 pm from October to March.

Royal Albert Hall

The huge red-brick amphitheatre facing the Albert Memorial is the Royal Albert Hall (☎ 589 8212; tube: South Kensington), built in 1867-71 and adorned with a frieze of Minton tiles.

The Royal Albert Hall is best known for the annual 'Prom' concerts (see the Entertainment chapter for ticket information). Unfortunately the only way to see inside this wonderful venue is by attending a concert.

Royal Geographical Society

Across the road at 1 Kensington Gore is the home of the Royal Geographical Society, a red-brick edifice of 1874 easily identifiable by the statues of explorers David Livingstone and Sir Ernest Shackleton outside. Non-members of the Society can come in to see a small exhibition of historic maps.

Linley Sambourne House

Tucked away at 18 Stafford Terrace W8, just behind High St Kensington, is the Linley Sambourne House (☎ 0181-742 3438), home from 1874 to 1910 of the *Punch* cartoonist Linley Sambourne, great grandfather of Princess Margaret's ex-husband Lord Snowdon. This is one of those freakish houses whose owners never redecorated or threw anything away; what you'll see is the virtually unmodernised home of a reasonably well-to-do Victorian family, all dark wood, Turkish carpets and rich stained glass – a gem for anyone who couldn't bear to see a space on a table without placing an ornament on it.

It's open from March to October on Wednesday from 10 am to 4 pm and on Sunday from 2 to 5 pm. Admission costs £3/1.50.

Leighton House

Near Holland Park and Kensington but frequently overlooked is Leighton House (☎ 602 3316), 12 Holland Park Rd W14 (tube: High St Kensington). A gem of a house designed by George Aitchison between 1864 and 1879, it was once the home of Lord Leighton (1830-96), a pre-Raphaelite painter who decorated parts of it in Middle Eastern style. Finest of all the rooms is the exquisite Arab Hall, densely covered with blue and green tiles from Rhodes, Cairo, Damascus and Iznik (Turkey) and with a fountain tinkling away in the centre. Even the wooden latticework of the windows and gallery came from Damascus. The house contains notable pre-Raphaelite paintings by

Burne-Jones, Watts, Millais and Lord Leighton himself.

By the time you read this the upstairs studio should have been returned to its original splendour, with the central screen which Lord Leighton used for storing his brushes and paints reinstated. Work may also have begun on restoring the back garden to its Victorian glory.

It's open (free) Monday to Saturday from 11 am to 5.30 pm.

Commonwealth Institute

On the High St Kensington side (south) of Holland Park an open space with fountains and flagpoles fronts the Commonwealth Institute (☎ 371 3530), designed in 1962 to resemble a large tent and created from materials gathered from all over the British Commonwealth. The rather pedestrian interior is being revamped to extol the virtues of the 50-odd countries making up the Commonwealth. The resulting exhibition (the Commonwealth Experience), spread over three floors, has an atmosphere midway between that of the old Museum of Mankind and the Earl's Court holiday show – if you're planning to head on overseas this could be a good place to come for inspiration.

The basement is children-friendly with lots of hands-on exhibits and a new heliride which simulates a flight over Kuala Lumpur and Malaysia. The café charges £1 for a cup of tea, and individuals are expected to pay 50p to leave their bags, which seems unfair when there are three free cloakrooms for groups.

The Experience (tube: High St Kensington) is open daily from 10 am to 5 pm and admission costs £4.45/2.95.

NOTTING HILL, BAYSWATER & EARL'S COURT (Maps 8 & 9)

The great popularity of the Notting Hill Carnival at the end of August reflects the multicultural appeal of this area of west London. In the 1950s Notting Hill became a focus for immigrants from Trinidad. Today it's a thriving, vibrant corner of London separated from the West End by the expanse of Hyde Park and best visited on Sunday morning for the Portobello Rd Market (see Markets in the Shopping chapter).

Bayswater and Earl's Court are lively, cosmopolitan parts of town, with large, mobile populations. They're a funny mix of the smart and the scruffy, although Bayswater is undoubtedly the classier of the two areas. This is the place to come to buy paintings on Sunday mornings (see Art in the Shopping chapter) or to unwind in the Porchester Spa (see Public Baths later in this chapter).

HAMMERSMITH & FULHAM

Hammersmith is not an especially inviting borough, dominated as it is by the hideous flyover and the chaos of the roundabout. There are no specific sights here, although you might want to visit the Riverside Studios or the Lyric Theatre (see Entertainment). That said, things are getting better, with the tube station much improved and King St quite presentable. With time to spare there's a good set of riverfront pubs on the Chiswick side of Hammersmith Bridge plus a pleasant two-mile walk along the Thames from the mall beside the Bridge to Chiswick itself.

Fulham is more immediately inviting than Hammersmith, with Fulham Road in particular a good place for a night out.

Riverside Studios

Riverside Studios (☎ 0181-741 2255), Crisp Rd W6 (tube: Hammersmith), is west London's equivalent of the ICA, a mixed-media arts centre with two good-sized auditoria which cater to film, theatre, modern dance and about a dozen art shows per year featuring the occasional well-known overseas artist.

It's open Monday to Saturday from 9 am to 11 pm, Sunday from noon to 11pm.

Fulham Palace

In Bishop's Park, running alongside the Thames on the Fulham side of Putney Bridge, stands Fulham Palace (☎ 736 3233; tube: Putney Bridge; Map 13), summer home of the Bishops of London from 704 to 1973. It originally boasted a mile-long moat, making it the largest moated site in Europe. The oldest part to survive is the dinky red-brick Tudor gateway, but the main building you see today dates from the mid-17th century and was remodelled in the 19th century. There's a pretty, walled garden and, detached from the main house, a Tudor Revival chapel designed by Butterfield in 1866.

The museum describes the history of the palace and is open Wednesday to Sunday from 2 to 5 pm for 50/25p. On the second Sunday of every month 90-minute tours (£2) take place at 2 pm, taking in the Great Hall, the chapel, Bishop Sherlock's dining room and the museum.

North London

North London's main attraction is the wild expanse of Hampstead Heath, where it's as easy to forget you're in a big city as it is to get completely lost. The other main drawcards are Highgate Cemetery and – for football fans at least – Wembley Stadium, but it also has a handful of smaller, interesting attractions. Long-term visitors to London may well find themselves living in a North London suburb.

WEMBLEY & NEASDEN

Football-minded tourists will want to head out north-west to Wembley to see the famous stadium with its twin towers (guaranteed to survive a remodelling of the entire complex). Neasden, on the other hand, is hardly the most obvious destination for a tourist. However, anyone interested in seeing the impact being made on the London skyline by its ethnic minority communities will want to brave the wastes of Tesco and IKEA-land to see the Shri Swaminarayan Mandir.

Wembley Stadium

A tour of Wembley Stadium includes the opportunity to walk down the players' tunnel onto the pitch, as well as to go up and receive the Cup to the (taped) roar of the crowd. Tours take place daily (☎ 0181-902 8833) between 10 am and 4 pm (3 pm in winter) and cost £6.95/4.75. To get to the stadium take the tube to Wembley Park and walk straight down Olympic Way towards the twin towers. Alternatively, turn right along Bridge Rd, taking the left fork at the roundabout into Empire Way. The stadium is on the left, just past Wembley Arena.

Shri Swaminarayan Mandir

In the unlikely setting of Neasden, Britain's Hindu community has built Europe's first traditional *mandir*, or temple, an astonishing sight with its icing-sugar towers and pinnacles, only the absence of rampaging monkeys and scabby dogs acknowledging its distance from the subcontinent. The temple was constructed out of Bulgarian limestone and Italian marble, all shipped to India to be carved by traditional craft workers and then shipped back to London for erection. Some of the carvings on the pillars seem relatively crude but the dome is a masterpiece, so finely carved it looks more like lace than marble. The work took three years to complete and cost around £7.5 million, with much of the labour carried out by volunteers. The temple opened in 1995.

It receives visitors from 9 am to noon and from 4 to 6 pm. You must leave your shoes in racks near the door, and women in short skirts will be asked to wrap up in a sheet.

To get there, take the tube to Neasden, turn left and walk to the big roundabout to catch a No 16 bus to Tesco's. There you pick up bus No 206 or PR2 to the temple.

HAMPSTEAD & HIGHGATE (Map 11)

Perched on a hill four miles north of the City, Hampstead is an exclusive suburb attached to an enormous, rambling heath which just about gets away with calling itself a village. You can lose yourself on Hampstead Heath and forget that you're in one of the world's largest, noisiest cities – something harder to forget when walking up Hampstead High St, or Heath St, both inundated with pricey shops and bumper-to-bumper traffic.

Nonetheless, Hampstead still keeps its charm and character – part left-wing intelligentsia, part arty bohemia. Ex-Labour Party leader Michael Foot lives here and Hampstead's MP is the actress-turned-politician Glenda Jackson. Famous people have been making their home here since the 18th century, among them poets Coleridge, Keats and Pope; Charles II's mistress, Nell Gwyn; General de Gaulle; Sigmund Freud; and painters John Constable and William Hogarth. More recently Oasis songwriter Noel Gallagher took up residence in a house called Supernova Heights in Belsize Park on the southern edge of Hampstead.

Architecturally, Hampstead is a harmonious balance of Georgian and early Victorian, speckled with a few notable examples of Modernist architecture. The excellent *Hampstead Town Trail* (£1), available from second-hand bookshops in Flask Walk and in Keats House, will take you along the prettier back streets. You'll soon realise why there was an uproar when McDonald's announced they wanted to open a branch in Hampstead. They got their way, of course, but the golden arches had to be cut down to a little logo on a black fascia.

The heath boasts woods, meadows, hills, bathing ponds and, most important of all, space. An outdoor concert in the grounds of Kenwood House is likely to prove a highlight of your trip (for details, see the Entertainment chapter).

With the exceptions of Freud's House and Highgate Cemetery, the nearest tube station for all the attractions described below is Hampstead. You could easily spend a day poking round Hampstead and Highgate, but if you want to see all the various houses open to the public it's best to avoid Monday, Tuesday or Wednesday when several are closed.

Keats House

Just seconds from the heath, this elegant Regency house (☎ 435 2062) in Keats Grove was home to the golden boy of the Romantic poets. Never short of generous pals, Keats was persuaded to take refuge here by Tom Armitage Brown during the years 1818-20 and it's here that he met his fiancée Fanny Brawne. Sitting under a plum tree in the garden, Keats wrote his most celebrated poem, *Ode to a Nightingale*, in 1819; a new tree has since been planted on the spot.

Apart from many mementos, including original manuscripts and Keats' collection of works by Shakespeare and Chaucer, you can peek at some of his love letters. Unfortunately the house is not very well-maintained, with damp dripping down the bedroom walls. Refurbishment was due to take place at the time of writing, so things may be looking better by the time you visit.

It's open April to October, Monday to Friday from 10 am to 1 pm and 2 to 6 pm, closing at 5 pm on Saturday and all Sunday morning. The rest of the year it only opens in the afternoon except on Saturday when it's also open from 10 am to 1 pm. Admission is free but there's a box for donations.

No 2 Willow Rd

Fans of modern architecture may want to pop into this nearby house (the central one in a block of three) which was designed by Erno Goldfinger in 1939 as his family home (☎ 435 6166). Despite the claim that he was following Georgian principles in creating it, many people will think it looks uncannily like the sort of mundane 1950s architecture we all know and hate around town. Still, the interior, with its cleverly designed storage space and collection of artworks by the likes of Henry Moore and Bridget Riley, is certainly interesting.

It's open for guided tours from mid-April to October on Thursday, Friday and Saturday from noon to 4 pm. Admission is £3.60/1.80 (free to NT members).

Fenton House

In Hampstead Grove you can visit one of Hampstead's oldest houses, a 17th century merchant's house with a walled garden and a fine collection of musical instruments. It's open from April to October on weekends from 11 am to 5.30 pm and on Wednesday, Thursday and Friday from 2 to 5.30 pm. In March it opens on weekend afternoons too. Admission costs £3.60/1.80 (free to NT members).

Burgh House

In New End Square you can visit this late 17th century mansion which houses the Hampstead Museum of local history. Admission is free but it's only open Wednesday to Sunday from noon to 5 pm.

Hampstead Heath & Kenwood House

The heath itself covers 800 acres of land, most of it wild but with some sections laid out for sports like football and cricket. There are several bathing ponds but they're only recommended for strong, competent swimmers. One is for men only, one for women only; both have had their controversial moments so you might prefer to stick with the mixed pond. Walk up Parliament Hill for fine views over London. This is where kite fliers come to play with their toys on windy days.

Kenwood House (☎ 0181-348 1286), on the north side of the heath, is a magnificent neoclassical house rejigged by Robert Adam in 1764 and stuffed with fine paintings by the likes of Rembrandt, Vermeer and Van Dyck. It's open (free) from 10 am to 6 pm, April to September, closing at 4 pm for the rest of the year.

For a drink after walking, the best known pubs are The Spaniards, Jack Straw's Castle and The Old Bull & Bush (see the Entertainment chapter for more details). The link between drink and rioting has a long-standing tradition. The first two of these hostelries played their part in famous early uprisings; Jack Straw's Castle is named after Wat Tyler's companion in arms of the Peasants' Revolt, while some of the Gordon Rioters of 1780 popped by The Spaniards for a drink before continuing on to attack Kenwood House.

Freud's House

Sigmund Freud lived at 20 Maresfield Gardens NW3 (☎ 435 2002) for the last 18 months of his life after it became clear that it was no longer safe for him to stay in Nazi-occupied Vienna in 1938. Here you can see the original psychiatrist's chair from which sprang all later models, together with all his Greek and oriental artefacts and, of course, his books. A photo shows how carefully he attempted to reproduce his Viennese home in the unfamiliar surroundings of London.

Later the house was occupied by Freud's daughter, Anna, a child psychologist of note in her own right; one room upstairs has mementos of her, including a loom which is still in use today.

It's open Wednesday to Sunday from noon to 5 pm. Admission costs £3/1.50. A shop sells all sorts of histories, biographies and other books to do with all aspects of the psyche. To get there take the tube to Finchley Rd, from where it's a short walk. Better still, get out at Swiss Cottage and cast your eye over the unlikely wooden chalet which gave the junction its name, before walking up Fitzjohn's Ave and turning left into Maresfield Gardens.

Highgate Cemetery

This is the final resting place for Karl Marx, the novelist George Eliot and lots of other ordinary mortals who lie beneath eccentric and extraordinary tombs. Highgate Cemetery (☎ 0181-340 1834), Swain's Lane N6 (tube: Highgate), has wild, hectic acres of absurdly overdecorated Victorian tombs, catacombs and family plots linked in a ring and based on ancient Egyptian burial sites, all topped off by spooky cypresses.

It's divided into two parts. The only way to see the western section is on a tour (£3), possible on Saturday and Sunday all year on the hour from 11 am to 4 pm; or Monday to Friday, March to November, at noon, 2 and 4 pm.

Marx's tomb can be found in the comparatively uninteresting eastern part, which is open daily from 10 am to 4 pm (to 5 pm from April to October). Admission is another £1.

WALTHAMSTOW

Walthamstow, in north-east London, is probably best known as the birthplace of East 17, the only pop group to have named themselves after their post code (E17). However, 19th century Walthamstow, then a village on the outskirts of London, was also birthplace to the socialist designer and campaigner William Morris. A plaque on Forest Rd fire station commemorates Elm House where he was born in 1834.

William Morris Gallery

The William Morris Gallery (☎ 0181-527 3782), Lloyd Park, Forest Rd E17 (tube: Walthamstow Central), is housed in a delightful Georgian house where the Morris family lived from 1848 to 1856. The downstairs rooms tell the story of Morris' life and his working relationship with pre-Raphaelite artists like Burne-Jones. They're also full of gorgeous Morris-designed wallpapers, chintzes and furniture, together with tiles and stained glass designed by his friends. The upstairs gallery houses a selection of pre-Raphaelite paintings and an exhibition about the designer AH Mackmurdo (1851-1942) and the Century Guild.

The gallery is open (free) Tuesday to Saturday from 10 am to 1 pm and from 2 to 5 pm. It's also open on the first Sunday of each month from 10 am to noon and from 2 to 5 pm. To get there take the tube to Walthamstow Central and then bus No 97, 97A or 215 along Hoe Rd to the Forest Rd turnoff. Alternatively, it's a 10-minute walk from the station. Lloyd Park is a good spot for a picnic afterwards.

South London

Londoners still sometimes talk as if the Thames was the big barrier between north and south that it was in the Middle Ages. That's all nonsense, of course, and usually springs from parochial affection for one particular neighbourhood, although until the extension to the Jubilee line opens in 1998, those living in the south-east have some reason to feel they've been shortchanged on the transport front.

For tourists the single biggest reason to venture south of the Thames is to visit Greenwich, but you can also have fun exploring Brixton's colourful Caribbean market or visiting the excellent Horniman Museum in Forest Hill or the Soane-designed Picture Gallery in Dulwich.

GREENWICH

Packed with beautiful architecture, Greenwich (pronounced grenitch) has strong connections with royalty, the sea and science. It lies to the south-east of central London, where the Thames widens and deepens, and there's a sense of space rare in the big city. Quaint and villagey in its own right, and boasting the magnificent *Cutty Sark*, Greenwich is a delightful place which has been proposed, although not yet accepted, as a world heritage site. A trip there will be one of the highlights of any visit to London, and you should certainly allow at least a day to do it justice, particularly if you want to head on down the river to the Thames Barrier.

Greenwich is home to an extraordinary interrelated cluster of classical buildings; all the great architects of the Enlightenment made their mark here, largely thanks to royal patronage. Henry VIII and his daughters Mary and Elizabeth I were all born here. Charles II was particularly fond of the area and had Christopher Wren build both the Royal Observatory and part of the Royal Naval College, which Vanbrugh then completed in the early 17th century.

A 371m foot-tunnel dating back to 1902 runs under the Thames to connect Greenwich with the Isle of Dogs, where new office developments, yuppie housing and inner-city squalor rub shoulders uneasily. The entrance to the tunnel offers exquisite views of Greenwich's architectural heritage.

It's worth timing your visit for Friday, Saturday or Sunday when the arts & crafts and antiques markets will be in full swing (see Markets in the Shopping chapter). If you don't want to have to walk far a shuttle bus from the pier to the Old Observatory, Fan Museum and Ranger's House costs £1/50p.

There's a TIC (☎ 0181-858 6376) at 46 Greenwich Church St.

Cutty Sark

The *Cutty Sark* (☎ 0181-858 3445) is in King William Walk, right beside Greenwich Pier. It was once the fastest ship that had ever sailed the seven seas and remains one of the most beautiful ever built.

Launched in 1869, it's the sole surviving example of the clippers which dominated mid-19th century trade in tea and wool across both the Pacific and Atlantic. The *Cutty Sark* sailed its last journey in 1938 and retired to Greenwich in the 50s. You can stroll on the decks and peep in the refitted cabins, then read up on the history below deck and inspect the world's largest collection of ship's figureheads in the hold.

When it's not crowded, wandering around can be very enjoyable. You don't have to be a salty old sea dog to find this graceful thoroughbred captivating.

It's open April to September, Monday to Saturday from 10 am to 6 pm, Sunday from noon to 6 pm; October to March, Monday to Saturday from 10 am to 5 pm, Sunday from noon to 5 pm. Admission costs £3.50/2.50.

Gipsy Moth IV

Nearby, *Gipsy Moth IV* (☎ 0181-853 3589) was the boat Francis Chichester used to complete the first solo circumnavigation of the world by an Englishman in 1966-7. Chichester was 64 at the time and endured 226 days in this pokey, bath-sized craft. Later he was given a knighthood and various civic plaudits.

Royal Naval College

If you walk straight ahead from the *Cutty Sark* you'll come to the entrance to the Royal Naval College (☎ 0181-858 2154), off King William Walk on the left. Despite its splendour, this Christopher Wren masterpiece is largely off-limits to the public and its future, once the navy moves out, is the subject of much speculation. There have even been suggestions that it could become a university campus!

The Naval College was built on the site of the old Greenwich palace between 1696 and 1701 as a thank you from William III and Queen Mary for the naval victory over the French at La Hogue in 1692. Intended to provide a retirement home for navy veterans in the same way that the Chelsea Royal Hospital provided one for army veterans, it was designed in two separate halves so as not to spoil the view of the river from the Queen's House, Inigo Jones' miniature masterpiece of neo-Palladian harmony.

You can visit the chapel, which was completed 20 years after Wren's death, only to be gutted by fire in 1779. When it was redecorated it was in lighter, airier rococo style. The east end of the chapel is dominated by a painting by the 18th century American artist Benjamin West showing *The Preservation of St Paul After Shipwreck at Malta*.

Even more wonderful is the Painted Hall which is also open to the public. As soon as you step inside, your eye will be drawn ceilingwards to marvel at the paintings by James Thornhill. These show William and Mary enthroned amid symbols of the Virtues. Beneath William's feet, you can see the defeated French king Louis XIV grovelling. Up a few steps is the Upper Hall where George I is depicted with his family on the west wall. At the bottom right Thornhill drew himself into the picture too.

Wren designed the hall as the hospital dining room, but it soon proved too small and was vacated. Until 1806 it stood empty until Admiral Nelson's body was brought here to lie in state.

The college is open (free) daily from 2.30 to 5 pm. It's due to appear as a backdrop in the forthcoming film of *The Avengers* starring Sean Connery and Ralph Fiennes.

National Maritime Museum

Further along King William Walk you'll come to the National Maritime Museum (☎ 0181-858 4422), Romney Rd SE10, a massive collection of boats, maps, charts, uniforms and miscellaneous bits and pieces designed to tell the long and pickled history of Britain as a seafaring nation. Some galleries are likely to be closed for some time while they're given an overhaul for the Millennium, but the exhibition on 20th century seapower should be open; look out for its bland account of the controversial sinking of the Argentinian ship, the *Belgrano*, during the Falklands War.

Upstairs the Nelson Gallery is interesting enough to grab the imagination even of those not much interested in naval history. Videos tell the story of the Battles of the Nile and Trafalgar, and there's an impressive display of early Nelson memorabilia.

Otherwise, the best thing about the museum is the building itself. Designed by Inigo Jones and completed by Wren, it slots in behind the Naval College quite neatly, and from its colonnaded walkways you'll get fine views up One Tree Hill to the Royal Observatory.

The museum is open from 10 am to 5 pm daily. The admission fee of £5.50/3 includes admission to the Queen's House and the Royal Observatory.

Queen's House

The Palladian-style Queen's House (☎ 0181-858 4422) is a continuation of the National Maritime Museum on the eastern side. Inigo Jones started work on the house for Anne of Denmark, wife of James I, in 1616 but it wasn't completed until 1635 when it became the home of Charles I and his wife, Henrietta Maria.

Rooms open off a Great Hall which originally had a ceiling painted by Orazio Gentileschi and his daughter Artemisia, one of the few early women artists to achieve much celebrity. Sadly it was later moved and what you see are laser photographs instead.

Most of the original furniture has also been lost so the rooms are perhaps not as exciting as the building's exterior might lead you to expect.

It's open daily from 10 am to 5 pm. Admission is included in the ticket for the National Maritime Museum.

Greenwich Park & Old Royal Observatory

Greenwich Park is one of London's loveliest parks, with a grand avenue, wide open spaces, a rose garden and rambling, picturesque walks. It's partly the work of Le Nôtre who landscaped the palace gardens of Versailles.

In 1675 Charles II had the **Old Royal Observatory** (☎ 0181-858 4422) built in the middle of the park, intending that astronomy be used to establish longitude at sea. The Octagon Room, designed by Wren, is where John Flansteed, the first astronomer royal, made his observations and calculations, and where he was visited by Tsar Peter the Great of Russia. This is one of the few Wren interiors known to have survived intact.

Thereafter Greenwich became accepted as Prime Meridian, or zero hour, and from 1884 onwards the whole world accepted Greenwich Mean Time (GMT) as the universal measurement of standard time. Here the globe divides between east and west and you can place one foot either side of the meridian line and straddle the two hemispheres. For £1 a machine will generate a certificate confirming that you've done just that. Nearby a clock accurate to one-millionth of a second is counting time down towards the Millennium.

The observatory is open daily from 10 am to 5 pm. You can get in free with your National Maritime Museum ticket, but if you just want to visit the Observatory it costs £4/2.

From the observatory, or from the statue of James Wolfe just outside, there's a spectacular view over Greenwich and across the river to the city and the Docklands, with Canary Wharf tower looming in the middle distance.

Attached to the Observatory is **Greenwich Planetarium** where you can see the night sky projected on a dome for £1.50/1. There are showings every 30 minutes from 11.30 am to 4 pm.

Further south you'll come to the **Ranger's House** (☎ 0181-973 3479), a stately home built for Admiral Francis Hosier in 1700 and later used to house the park's ranger. Inside there's not a great deal to detain you, although the Jacobean portraits, including some by Lely and Kneller, are striking for their size if nothing else. You can also ascend to Admiral Hosier's rooftop gazebo but as you're not allowed out on the roof the views you'll get are rather oblique – not worth the climb if you've already been to the Observatory.

The Ranger's House is open April to September from 10 am to 6 pm, closing at 4 pm for the rest of the year. It's also closed between 1 and 2 pm daily. Admission is £2.50/1.50 (free to EH members).

Continue past the Ranger's House and out through the Chesterfield Gate and you'll come to **Blackheath**, an expanse of open common where Wat Tyler camped in 1381 before marching on London and where Henry VIII fought off Cornish rebels in 1497. Later it became the haunt of highwaymen.

Getting There & Away

The best way to get to/from Greenwich is by boat. The boats drop you off at Greenwich pier close to both the *Cutty Sark* and *Gipsy Moth IV*. They leave from Westminster Pier (beside Westminster Bridge; Map 4) every half hour from 10 am to 4 pm; singles cost £5.50/3, returns £6.70/3.50. Last boats return from Greenwich at 5 or 6 pm, depending on demand.

Alternatively, there are trains from Charing Cross station to Greenwich station, which are quicker and cheaper, or you can catch the Docklands Light Railway from Tower Gateway to Island Gardens and walk through the pedestrian tunnel to the south side of the river. There can be longish gaps between trains at weekends and you should check the time of the last train if planning a late return (the lifts down to the tunnel stop at 7 pm so you'll have to walk down after that).

Catamaran Cruises also link Charing Cross Pier and Tower Pier with Greenwich. From Charing Cross singles cost £6/3.50, returns £7/3.80; from the Tower singles cost £3.30/2.80, returns £6.30/4.95.

THAMES BARRIER

The Thames Barrier, between Greenwich and Woolwich, was built between 1972 and 1983 to protect London against the risk of flooding. It consists of 10 separate movable gates supported between concrete piers with silver roofs which house the operating machinery. They make a surreal sight, straddling the river in the lee of a giant Tate & Lyle warehouse.

You might well ask why London should suddenly need such defences when the site has been occupied since Roman times without disaster. The answer is that the water level has been gradually rising, by perhaps 75cm every century, at the same time as the river itself has been narrowing – in Roman times it was probably around 800m wide while now it's barely 250m, with constant pressure to develop the foreshores. The Thames tide rises and falls quite harmlessly twice a day, and once a fortnight there's also a stronger spring tide. The danger comes when the spring tide coincides with an unexpected surge which pushes tons of extra water upriver. The barrier has been built to prevent that water pouring over the riverbanks and flooding nearby houses.

The barrier is closed for checking roughly once a month; phone ☎ 0181-305 4188 for exact dates and times.

The visitor centre is open daily from 10 am to 5 pm (5.30 pm on weekends) and tells the story of the Thames through history, of the building of the barrier and of recent attempts to clean up the Thames. Admission costs £3.40/2, although if you just want to see the barrier there's no charge for that. There's a small, reasonably priced café and picnic benches outside.

Getting There & Away

The nicest way to get to the barrier is probably by boat from Greenwich Pier. From April to October boats (☎ 0181-305 0300) leave at 11.15 am, 12.30, 2 and 3.30 pm and take 35 minutes to get there (the last departure doesn't leave time to take in the visitor centre). Tickets cost £3/1.75 single and £4.50/2.50 return. In winter the 11.15 am service doesn't operate and in January there are no boats at all.

Alternatively, you can get to within 15

minutes walk of the barrier by train from London Bridge to Charlton station. When you get there turn left out of the station and follow the sign to the Thames Path, then head east along it for half a mile to its end at the barrier. It's not the prettiest stretch of the path, but it's better than walking along Woolwich Rd.

From Romney Rd in Greenwich you can catch bus Nos 177 and 180 to within walking distance of the barrier.

DULWICH & FOREST HILL (Map 13)

Tucked away in that part of south-east London which the tube fails to reach, Dulwich (pronounced dullitch) is one of those suburbs with some claim to the title 'village' – it's leafy and quiet with some fine architecture and an air of gentility. You might want to venture out here to see the Dulwich Picture Gallery, a work of that idiosyncratic 19th century architect Sir John Soane.

Also a bit off the beaten track and lacking Dulwich's cohesiveness, Forest Hill boasts one attraction well worth venturing onto a main-line train to reach – the Horniman Museum.

Dulwich Picture Gallery

Sir John Soane designed the Dulwich Picture Gallery (☎ 0181-693 5254), College Rd SE21 (North Dulwich station), in 1817 to house paintings collected by Noel Desenfans and Sir Francis Bourgeois. Perhaps uniquely, the gallery doubles as their mausoleum, its *'lumiére mystérieuse'* in sharp contrast with the top-lit rooms containing the paintings. Masterpieces by Rembrandt, Rubens, Reynolds, Gainsborough, Lely and others are hung in fetchingly old-fashioned style, very close together. Temporary exhibitions by modern artists generally get more space.

The gallery is open Tuesday to Friday from 10 am to 5 pm, from 11 am on Saturday and from 2 pm on Sunday. Admission costs £3/1.50. In summer you may find a tea tent set up in the garden outside. To get there take a train to North Dulwich and turn left out of the station. Cross over East Dulwich Grove and walk down Dulwich Village until the road divides. Take the left fork which is College Rd; the entrance is on the right, opposite Dulwich Park.

Horniman Museum

The Horniman is an extraordinary little museum, originally the collection of Frederick John Horniman, the son of a wealthy tea merchant, who had the Art Deco building with clock-tower and mosaics specially designed to house it in 1901. The top floor of the Horniman (☎ 0181-699 1872), 100 London Rd SE23 (Forest Hill station), is a reminder of how most museums used to be, with a collection of ethnic masks jumbled in alongside cases of stuffed animals. Downstairs, however, it's a very different picture. There's a superb collection of musical instruments, each displayed with computerised recordings and headsets, and a wonderful room devoted to the nomad lifestyle, with reconstructed tents and yurts. The small aquarium fits rather oddly with the other exhibits but the way it follows the line of the steps is rather fun. Until the collections from the Museum of Mankind go on display again in the British Museum, the Horniman is London's best ethnographical museum.

It's open (free) Tuesday to Saturday from 10.30 am to 5.30 pm and on Sunday from 2 pm. To get there, take the train to Forest Hill, turn left out of the station along Devonshire Rd and then right along London Rd. The Horniman is on the right. Alternatively, take the P4 bus from Dulwich which stops right outside the museum.

BRIXTON

At the end of the Victoria tube line, Brixton is home to many Londoners of Caribbean descent – the place to come to shop for interesting fruits in the market (see Markets in the Shopping chapter) and to listen to hopping music in the clubs. Ever since the Brixton riots of 1981 there's been a slight edge to the place, and when times are tense you'd do well to steer clear of the Railton Rd 'front line'. But since then, soaring house prices have sent househunters foraging in

Brixton and pockets of gentrification sit alongside the more run-down streets.

WIMBLEDON (Map 13)

This leafy southern suburb will be forever associated in most minds with the lawn tennis championships that have been taking place here every June since 1877. The rest of the year you can still visit the Wimbledon Lawn Tennis Museum and Wimbledon Common, one of London's more uninhibited open spaces and a great place for a picnic.

Wimbledon Lawn Tennis Museum

This museum (☎ 0181-946 6131), Church Rd SW19 (tube: Southfields), is inevitably of fairly specialist interest, dwelling as it does on the minutiae of the history of tennis playing, traced back here to the invention of the lawnmower in 1830 and of the India rubber ball in the 1850s. Nonetheless it's a state-of-the-art presentation, with plenty of video clips to let fans of the game relive their favourite moments.

It's open Tuesday to Saturday from 10.30 am to 5 pm and Sunday from 2 to 5 pm. During the tournament visiting hours are more restricted so phone before showing up. Admission costs £2.50/1.50.

Wimbledon Common

Running on into Putney Heath, Wimbledon Common covers 1100 acres of south London, a wonderful expanse of open space for walking, nature trailing and picnicking, although for many Londoners thought of the Common is tainted by memory of the vicious murder of Rachel Nickell, a sobering reminder of the slight risk attached to every large, open space.

There are a few specific sights on the Common, most unexpectedly **Wimbledon Windmill**, a fine smock windmill dating back to 1817. It was during a stay in the mill that Baden-Powell was inspired to write parts of his *Scouting for Boys* in 1908. The mill is open from 2 to 5 pm on weekends from April to October. Admission costs £1/50p. The Windmill Tea Rooms just beyond are more fruitcake and sausage roll than ciabatta and pesto, and service can be dreadfully slow. Still, for a Sunday brunch (£4.50) it might be worth considering.

On the south side of the common, **Caesar's Camp** is a prehistoric earthwork which proves that Wimbledon was settled before Roman times.

Buddhapadipa Temple

Popping up unexpectedly at 14 Calonne Rd, half a mile from Wimbledon village, you'll find as authentic a Thai temple as ever graced these parts. Buddhapadipa Temple (☎ 0181-946 1357) opened in 1982 and boasts a traditional *bot* or chapel decorated by two leading Thai artists who've incorporated scenes of English life into otherwise traditional scenes. To get there take the tube or main-line train to Wimbledon and then take bus No 93 up to Wimbledon Parkside. Calonne Rd is on the right.

West London

If visitors make one foray into London's western hinterland, then it should really be to Hampton Court, although Kew Gardens runs a close second and nearby Syon House is not far behind. Other stately piles worth visiting include Osterley House, Ham House and Chiswick House. Then there's Richmond Park, one of the finest expanses of wild, open space that London has to offer.

RICHMOND (Map 14)

If anywhere in London could be described as a village without provoking guffaws of laughter, then Richmond, with its delightful green and riverside vistas, just about fits the bill. There are plenty of good places to eat and drink, including the White Cross pub, which is so close to the river that drinkers occasionally have to paddle out. Of Richmond Palace, where Queen Elizabeth I died in 1603, only a red-brick gatehouse and a courtyard survive. To cap it all Richmond Park is the largest and most rural of the royal parks. You can get to Richmond on foot from

Kew by following the river towards Twickenham.

Richmond Park

One of London's finest and wildest parks, Richmond Park (☎ 0181-948 3209) covers 2500 acres and is home to all sorts of wildlife including herds of red and fallow deer, and more elusive foxes and badgers. It's a great place for birdwatchers too, with a wide range of habitats, from neat gardens to woodland and assorted ponds. The philosopher Bernard Russell (1872-1970) grew up in Pembroke Lodge, now a tearoom with fine views from the terrace at the back. Edward VIII was born in the 18th century White Lodge. The Isabella Plantation is at its most spectacular in April/May when the rhododendrons and azaleas are in bloom.

The park is open daily from dawn to half an hour before dusk.

Getting There & Away It's easier to get to the park with your own transport, although parking can be tricky on weekends. To get there from Richmond station, turn right along the high street which winds round towards Richmond Bridge and then forks. Take the left fork up Richmond Hill, pausing to soak up views so magnificent that they spurred Reynolds and Turner to canvas, until you reach the Star & Garter, a home for men disabled in 20th century conflicts from the WWI to the Gulf War. Across the road (a dangerous crossing) is Richmond Gate and the park.

Ham House

This Hampton Court in miniature was actually built in 1610 and became home to the first Earl of Dysart, an unlucky individual who had been employed as 'whipping boy' to Charles I, taking the punishment for all the king's wrongdoings. Inside it's furnished with all the grandeur you might expect; the Great Staircase is a magnificent example of Stuart woodwork. Look out for ceiling paintings by Antonio Verrio, who also worked at Hampton Court, and for a miniature of Queen Elizabeth I by Nicholas Hilliard. Other notable paintings are by Constable, Reynolds and Kneller.

The grounds of Ham House slope down to the Thames but there's also a pleasant 17th century formal garden as well.

From Easter to October, the house (☎ 0181-940 1950) is open Monday to Wednesday from 1 to 5 pm, and from noon on Saturday and Sunday. The gardens are open daily (except Friday) from 10.30 am to 6 pm. Admission costs £4.50/2 (free to NT members). To get there take a train or tube to Richmond and then a No 65 bus heading south. Alternatively, there's a ferry (foot passengers only) from Marble Hill House to Ham House between 10 am and 6 pm daily (40p).

TWICKENHAM, TEDDINGTON & HAMPTON (Map 14)

Just across the bridge from Richmond, Twickenham is another of those London boroughs which will always be associated with a sport, in this case, of course, rugby. Otherwise there's not much to detain visitors unless they want to visit Marble Hill House which overlooks the Thames.

Out in London's south-western outskirts, Teddington is another riverside borough, with 1000-acre Bushy Park stretching away on its south side. Hampton Court Park adjoins Bushy Park, but is in Hampton rather than Teddington proper.

The Twickenham Experience

Another state-of-the-art museum that will appeal to sports lovers but leave everyone else cold, the Twickenham Experience (☎ 0181-892 2000), Rugby Rd, Twickenham (station: Twickenham), is tucked in behind the east stand of the new Twickenham stadium. Relive those highlights of old matches in the video theatre and then take a tour of the grounds.

The Museum of Rugby is open Tuesday to Saturday from 10.30 am to 5 pm and Sunday 2 to 5 pm. Admission is £2.50/1.50. Tours (also £2.50/1.50) must be prebooked and don't take place during the days around matches. Joint tickets for the museum and

Bridging the Thames

With the Thames slicing right through the capital, finding ways to cross from one side to the other has been crucial throughout its history. Today there are 28 road, rail and foot bridges between Teddington Lock and the Tower of London, with the 29th about to come on line at Dartford and a 30th planned for the Millennium. In central London you're rarely far from a bridge, but they get further apart the further west you go. Many of the bridges are striking landmarks in their own right with interesting histories behind their piers and abutments.

Heading east from Richmond these are the main bridges you'll come to:

Richmond Bridge
: Linking Richmond with East Twickenham, five-arched Richmond Bridge was designed by James Paine between 1774 and 1777 and is the oldest of the existing structures. Views from the bridge are relatively rustic, and there's an inviting towpath underneath. To the right of the bridge on the south side don't miss Quinlan Terry's pastiche Georgian development à la architectural school of Prince Charles.

Twickenham Bridge
: Twickenham's otherwise prosaic bridge was designed by Maxwell Ayrton in 1933 with fine bronze lampstands and railings.

Kew Bridge
: A renowned bottleneck during hot spells, Kew Bridge has a graceful profile that's not easy to appreciate when you're stuck in traffic. It's much better to descend to the east of the bridge where you can gaze up at it from several very pleasant waterside pubs at Strand-on-the-Green. The current bridge, the third on the site, was opened in 1903.

Chiswick Bridge
: Opened on the same day in 1933 as the Twickenham and Hampton Court bridges, triple-arched Chiswick Bridge marks the end point of the Oxford & Cambridge Boat Race.

Hammersmith Bridge
: The attractive suspension bridge at Hammersmith was designed by the great Victorian engineer Sir Joseph Bazelgette in 1887. At the time of writing it was closed for repairs which were expected to extend into 1998.

Putney Bridge
: The bridge at Putney is famous as the starting point for the annual Oxford & Cambridge boat race which has been splashing off from here since 1829. Although there had been a bridge here since 1729, the current one is another Joseph Bazelgette model of 1884. The 15th century tower of St Mary's church on the Putney side of the bridge is more or less mirrored by that of All Saints church on the Fulham side. In a sign of the times, the old public conveniences on the Fulham side now house a sandwich shop!

Wandsworth Bridge
: The current bridge was erected in 1938 to replace an earlier model of 1873.

Battersea Bridge
: The bridge portrayed by Turner and Whistler was an earlier wooden model dating back to 1772. It was Bazelgette who once again came up with the designs for the current brightly painted bridge which was built in 1890.

Albert Bridge
: One of the most striking of London's bridges, the Albert is a cross between a cantilever and a suspension bridge which was buttressed to strengthen it as an alternative to closure in the 1960s. It was designed by Roland Mason Ordish in 1873 but later modified by the ubiquitous Bazelgette. With fairylights adorning its cables it can look jauntily festive when lit up at night. The booths at either end survive from the days when tolls were charged to cross it.

Chelsea Bridge
: The existing suspension bridge opened in 1937 to replace an earlier model of 1858.

Vauxhall Bridge
: The present bridge of 1906 is decorated with figures intended to represent Learning, Engineering, the Fine Arts, Astronomy, Agriculture and Architecture. It replaced an earlier iron bridge of 1816 which had been the first to carry trams across the Thames. Beside the bridge on the north side stands an extraordinary stepped building designed by Terry Farrell for MI6, the British intelligence service, in 1992.

Lambeth Bridge
: Look out for pineapples carved at each end of this bridge of 1929. They commemorate the Tradescants, buried in nearby St Mary's church, who had introduced the fruit to Britain.

Westminster Bridge

Linking Westminster and Lambeth, the seven-arched Westminster Bridge was designed by Thomas Page in 1862 and replaced an earlier bridge of 1747, only the second to be erected and the cause of vociferous complaint by the shopkeepers on older London Bridge. When Wordsworth crossed the bridge in a coach in 1802, the view inspired him to compose the sonnet *Upon Westminster Bridge.* This suggests a very different panorama from the one you'll see today:

Earth has not anything to show more fair:
Dull would be he of soul who could pass by
A sight so touching in its majesty:
This city now doth, like a garment, wear
The beauty of the morning; silent, bare,
Ships, towers, domes, theatres and temples lie
Open unto the fields, and to the sky;
All bright and glittering in the smokeless air.

Hungerford Bridge

Few people have a good word to say about the current Hungerford Bridge, a train and foot bridge which replaced a 15-year-old Brunel suspension bridge in 1860. Although plans exist to replace the bridge they're not expected to come to fruition before the end of 2000.

Waterloo Bridge

Five-arched Waterloo Bridge was the first London bridge to be built out of concrete and was constructed, to the design of Sir Giles Gilbert Scott, in 1944, mainly by women workers while the men were away at war. Those who find it graceless will be disappointed to learn that it replaced a 19th century model designed by Sir John Rennie and regarded by the sculptor Canova as the most beautiful bridge in the world.

Blackfriars Bridge

Blackfriars Bridge was built in 1869 to the designs of James Cubbit with pulpit-like buttresses on each side; it was widened in 1909 to allow trams to cross. Squeezed in between this bridge and the adjacent railway stand a row of truncated red struts, all that remain of the Alexandra Railway Bridge, torn down in 1985.

Millennium Bridge

As yet just a dream in architect Norman Foster's eye, the Millennium Bridge should be in place by spring 2000.

Southwark Bridge

The present bridge was designed by Sir Ernest George in 1921 and replaced an early 19th century version by Sir John Rennie, referred to by Dickens in *Little Dorrit* as the 'Cast Iron Bridge'.

London Bridge

Of all London's bridges, it is London Bridge that has had the most interesting history, stretching right back to Roman times. The *Anglo-Saxon Chronicle* records a supposed witch being drowned off London Bridge in the 10th century, and it has been suggested that the children's nursery rhyme 'London Bridge is Falling Down' refers to an attack on the bridge by King Olaf of Norway in support of King Ethelred the Unready in 1015. In 1176 Peter of Colechurch began work on what is believed to have been the first post-Roman stone bridge in Europe; the work wasn't completed until 1209. The new bridge stood on 19 piers but was only just wide enough for two carts to pass each other. Despite that fact, by 1358 there were already 139 shops clinging to its sides. Until 1749, when Westminster Bridge was built, this was the sole crossing point on the Thames. Shortly after, in 1758, the old shops were swept away. In 1823 work began on a new bridge designed by Sir John Rennie and worked on by his son. In 1973 this bridge was, in turn, replaced with another, this time a flattened concrete number with three arches designed by Harold Knox King. Rennie's old bridge was carefully dismantled and shipped to the United States where it now forms the centrepiece of the park at Lake Havusu in Arizona.

Tower Bridge

The most famous of all London bridges, Tower Bridge is the one with the twin towers and the movable walkways that links the Tower of London to Shad Thames; for more details see under City in Things to See & Do. The story goes that the Americans who bought London Bridge thought they were getting Tower Bridge – probably an urban myth but none the less amusing! ■

tour cost £4/2.50. From the station take bus No 281 to the grounds.

Marble Hill House

Marble Hill House is an 18th century Palladian-style lovenest, built originally for George II's mistress Henrietta Howard and later occupied by Mrs Fitzherbert, the secret wife of George IV. The poet Alexander Pope had a hand in designing the park which stretches down to the Thames. Inside you'll find an exhibition about the life and times of Henrietta, and a collection of early Georgian furniture.

The house is open from Easter to October, 10 am to 6 pm, closing at 4 pm and all day Monday and Tuesday in winter. Admission costs £2.50/1.90 (free to EH members).

To get there take a train to St Margaret's station and turn right along St Margaret's Rd. Then take the right fork along Crown Rd and turn left along Richmond Rd. Turn right along Beaufort Rd and walk across Marble Hill Park to the house. Alternatively, take the foot ferry from Ham House (see above).

Across Orleans Rd is the **Orleans House Gallery**, housed in the early 18th century Octagon designed by James Gibbs for Orleans House. It shows temporary art exhibitions (free) Tuesday to Saturday from 1 to 5.30 pm.

Hampton Court Palace

In 1515 Thomas Wolsey, Cardinal and Lord Chancellor of England, decided to build himself a palace in keeping with his sense of self-importance. Unfortunately even Wolsey couldn't persuade the pope to grant Henry VIII a divorce from Catherine of Aragon and relations between king and chancellor rapidly soured. Given that background, you only need to take one look at Hampton Court Palace to realise why Wolsey felt obliged to present it to Henry, a monarch not too fond of anyone trying to muscle in on his mastery of all he surveyed. The hapless Wolsey was charged with high treason but died before he could come to trial.

As soon as he acquired the palace Henry set to work to expand it, adding the Great

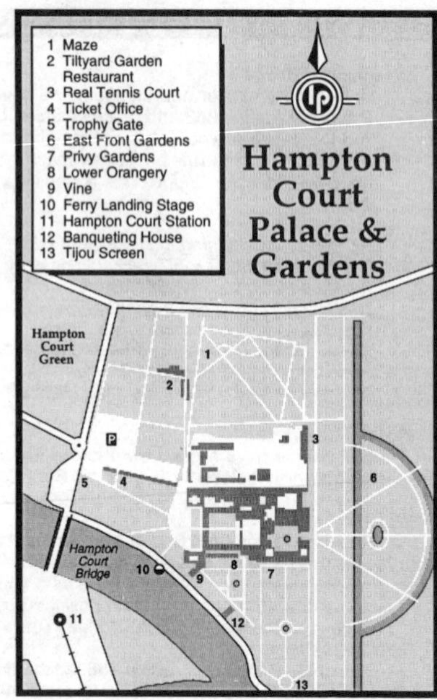

Hall, the Chapel and the sprawling kitchens. By 1540 this was one of the grandest and most sophisticated palaces in Europe. In the late 17th century, William and Mary employed Sir Christopher Wren to build extensions, the result being a beautiful blend of Tudor and neoclassical architecture.

Today the palace is England's largest and grandest Tudor structure, knee deep in history, and with superb gardens and a famous 300-year-old maze. You should set aside plenty of time to do it justice, bearing in mind that if you come by boat the trip will have eaten up half the day already.

Tickets are on sale in an office to the left of the main Trophy Gate. Here you should pick up a leaflet listing the daily programme which will help you plan out your visit; this is important since many of the free guided tours require advance booking.

As you walk up the path towards the palace you'll have a fine view of the lengthy red-brick facade with its distinctive, twisted

Tudor chimneys and sturdy gateway. Passing through the main gate you arrive in the **Clock Court**, so named for the fine 16th century astronomical clock which still shows the sun revolving round the earth. Here you can follow signs to the six main sets of rooms in the complex.

Stairs inside Anne Boleyn's Gateway lead up to **Henry VIII's State Apartments**, including the Great Hall, the single largest room in the palace, hung with tapestries and with a spectacular hammerbeam roof from which tiny painted faces peep down on visitors. A hallway hung with antlers leads to the Great Watching Chamber where guards controlled access to the king; this is the least altered of all the rooms dating from Henry's day. Leading off from the chamber is the smaller Pages' Chamber and the Haunted Gallery. Arrested for adultery and detained in the palace in 1542, Henry's fifth wife Catherine Howard managed to evade her guards and ran screaming down the corridor in search of the king. Her wretched ghost is said to do the same all these centuries later.

Further along the corridor you'll come to the beautiful Chapel Royal. A Royal Pew forming part of the state apartments looks down over the altar below. The blue and gold vaulted ceiling was originally intended for Christchurch, Oxford, but was installed here instead, while the 18th century reredos was carved by Grinling Gibbons.

Also dating back to Henry's day are the **Tudor Kitchens**, again accessible from Anne Boleyn's Gateway and originally able to rustle up meals for a royal household of some 1200 people. The kitchens have been fitted out to look as they might have done in Tudor days. Don't miss the Great Wine Cellar which could originally cope with the 300 barrels of ale and the same again of wine consumed here annually in the mid-16th century.

Returning yet again to the Clock Court and passing under the colonnade to the right you'll reach the **King's Apartments** built by Wren for William III towards the end of the 17th century. These apartments were badly damaged by fire in 1986 but have now been extensively restored; more rooms can now be visited than were open beforehand.

A tour of the apartments takes you up the grand King's Staircase painted by Antonio Verrio in about 1700 and flattering the king by comparing him to Alexander the Great. You'll emerge into the King's Guard Chamber which is decked out with guns, bayonets and swords and leads to the King's Presence Chamber. This room is dominated by a throne backed with scarlet hangings and by an equestrian portrait of William III by Sir Godfrey Kneller.

Next on the tour is the King's Eating Room where William would sometimes have dined in public, beyond which you'll find the King's Privy Chamber where ambassadors would have been received; the chandelier and throne canopy have been carefully restored after suffering terrible damage in the fire. Beyond this is the King's Withdrawing Room, where more intimate gatherings took place, and the King's Great Bedchamber, a splendid room, its bed topped with ostrich plumes, where the king was ceremonially dressed each morning. William actually slept in the Little Bedchamber beyond.

The back stairway beyond the King's Closet leads to three more wood-panelled closets furnished with paintings and more Grinling Gibbons' carvings. You then walk through an orangery to the King's Private Drawing Room and Dining Room which is decorated with Kneller's paintings of the *Hampton Court Beauties*; the table here is piled high with fruit for just three diners.

William's wife, Mary II, had her own separate **Queen's Apartments** which are accessible up the Queen's Staircase, decorated by William Kent. When Mary died in 1694 work on these rooms was incomplete. Queen Anne had more work done on them but it wasn't until the reign of George II that they were finally completed. The rooms are shown as they might have been when Queen Charlotte used them for entertaining between 1716 and 1737.

In comparison with the King's State Apartments, those for the queen seem rather austere, although the Queen's Audience

Chamber has a throne as imposing as the king's. Passing through the Queen's Drawing Room you arrive in the State Bedchamber where the queen took part in public levées rather than sleeping. The Queen's Gallery is hung with a set of 18th century tapestries depicting the adventures of Alexander the Great.

Also upstairs and ringing Wren's graceful Fountain Court are the **Georgian Rooms** used by George II and Queen Charlotte on their last visit to the palace in 1737. The first rooms you come to were designed to accommodate George's second son, the Duke of Cumberland, whose bed is laughably tiny for its grand surroundings. The Wolsey Closet was restored and repanelled in 1888 to give an idea of what one of the palace's smaller rooms might have looked like in Tudor times. The Communications Gallery was built for William III and is decorated with Sir Peter Lely's portraits of the *Windsor Beauties*, the most beautiful women at the court of Charles II. Beyond that is the Cartoon Gallery where the Raphael Cartoons now in the Victoria & Albert Museum used to hang; nowadays you have to make do with late 17th century copies.

Beyond the Cartoon Gallery are the queen's private rooms: her drawing room and bedchamber where she and the king would sleep if they wanted to be alone. Particularly interesting are the Queen's Bathroom, with its tub set on a floor cloth to soak up any mess, and the Oratory, with its 16th century Persian carpet.

Once you're finished with the palace interior there are still the wonderful gardens to appreciate. Look out for the **Royal Tennis Court**, dating back to the 1620s and designed for 'real tennis', a rather different game to the one associated with Wimbledon. The award-winning **Privy Gardens** have recently been restored and are a spectacularly beautiful mix of the grand and the intimate. Here you'll find the Great Vine planted in 1768 and still producing around 300kg of grapes a year; the Lower Orangery housing Andrea Mantegna's nine *Triumphs of Caesar* paintings, bought by Charles I in 1629; and the Banqueting House designed for William III and painted by Antonio Verrio. Look out, too, for the iron screens designed by French blacksmith Jean Tijou and slowly being repainted.

Of course, no-one should leave Hampton Court without risking being lost for ever in the famous half-mile-long, hornbeam and yew **maze**, planted in 1690. In case you're wondering, the average visitor takes 20 minutes to reach the centre. If you're unlucky you may arrive to find it closed since a replanting to fill yawning gaps has been ordered.

Hampton Court Palace (☎ 0181-781 9500) is open April to October, Monday from 10.15 am to 6 pm and Tuesday to Sunday from 9.30 am to 6 pm; late October to March, Monday from 10.15 am to 4.30 pm and Tuesday to Sunday from 9.30 am to 4.30 pm. An all-inclusive ticket costs £8/5.75, but if you just want to visit the gardens you can come in free until dusk. In that case you would pay 50/25p to go into the tennis court, £2/1 to see the Privy Gardens and £1.70/1 for the maze. Refreshments are available in the Privy Kitchen and the Tiltyard Tea Room, but they're not especially cheap so bring a picnic.

Carriage rides round the gardens cost £13 (up to six people) and are available from 10 am to 5.30 pm.

Getting There & Away There are trains every half-hour from Waterloo to Hampton Court station (£3.90 return, Zone 6).

Alternatively, the palace can be reached by river boat from Westminster Pier to Hampton Court Pier. Ferries depart from April to October at 10.30 am, 11.15 am and noon, and take 3½ hours to complete the journey via Richmond and Teddington Locks (children may find this a long time to be stuck on a boat). Tickets cost £8/4 one way.

CHISWICK & KEW (Map 14)

Despite the abomination of the A4 which slices through Chiswick (pronounced chisick), cutting off the riverside roads from the shopping centre, this is still a pleasant suburb – the High Rd is wide enough to accommodate a succession of cafés and restaurants which can set up tables on the pavements without impeding the flow of pedestrians. That said, the prettiest streets are those so cruelly severed from where it's all happening by a road that sounds so much nicer when described as the Great West Rd. Most people come to Chiswick to visit Palladian Chiswick House and the home of the artist Hogarth. There's also a very pleasant riverside walk all the way to Hammersmith.

Kew will be forever associated in most minds with Kew Gardens, headquarters of the Royal Botanical Society and boasting one of the world's finest plant collections. But Kew Green is also a pretty place where cricket sometimes takes place in summer, and 18th century Kew Church, should you be able to get inside it, would certainly be worth a look.

Chiswick House

Chiswick House (☎ 0181-995 0508), Chiswick Park W4 (tube: Turnham Green), is a fine Palladian pavilion with octagonal dome and colonnaded portico which was designed by the third Earl of Burlington (1694-1753) when he returned from his Grand Tour of Italy, fired up with enthusiasm for all things Roman. Lord Burlington used it to entertain friends and to house his library and art collection, but in 1788 the fifth earl had it turned into a more conventional home by adding wings on either side. Pictures inside the house suggest that these were perfectly in keeping with the building, but in 1951, when the house was collapsing into dereliction, they were ripped down.

Inside, the ground floor has details of the restoration work that took place recently and also accommodates several statues brought in from the park to protect them. Upstairs some of the rooms have been completely restored to a grandeur some will find overpowering. But there's no denying the splendour of the main saloon, where the dome has been left ungilded and the walls are decorated with eight enormous paintings. In the Blue Velvet Room (blue flock wallpaper!), look for the portrait of Inigo Jones, an architect much admired by Lord Burlington, over one of the doors. The ceiling paintings are by William Kent who also decorated the Kensington State Apartments.

Lord Burlington also planned the original gardens around the house, now Chiswick Park, but they have been much altered since then and may be changed even more if a funding application to the National Lottery succeeds. In particular the Cascade, which stopped working years ago, may eventually be set flowing again. Burlington's Café is not an inspiring building but it does offer excellent food, especially for vegetarians. Breakfasts cost £4.50 and there are ciabatta sandwiches for lunch from £2.30. It's open from 10 am to 4.30 pm.

Chiswick House is open daily from Easter to October, 10 am to 6 pm, closing at 4 pm for the rest of the year. Admission is £2.50/1.50 (free to EH members).

The house is quite a walk from the station, but bus No E3 from under the bridge outside will drop you nearby. Ask the driver to tell you when to get off as it's not that obvious.

Hogarth's House

Robbed of its setting by the thundering traffic on the A4, Hogarth's House (☎ 0181-994 6757), Hogarth Lane, Great West Rd W4 (tube: Turnham Green), nevertheless offers an opportunity to see inside a small 18th century house with pistachio-coloured panelled walls and a dinky garden.

William Hogarth (1697-1764) was an artist and engraver who specialised in satire and what might be thought rather heavy-handed moralising these days. He lived in this house from 1749 to 1764 and although very little original furniture survives, the walls are decorated with Hogarth's evocatively-named engravings of life in Georgian London, *The Rake's Progress*, *The Harlot's Progress*, *Marriage-à-la-Mode* and, most famously, *Gin Lane* and *Beer Street*. *Gin Lane* was produced as part of a campaign to have gin distillation made a crime (as it was under the Gin Act of 1751) so the poor wouldn't spend their last pennies on spirits. It shows drunkards lolling about in the parish of St Giles, with the church of St George's Bloomsbury clearly visible in the background.

The house is open (free) Tuesday to Friday from 1 to 5 pm (on Saturday and Sunday to 6 pm), closing an hour earlier from November to March. To see Hogarth's tomb in **St Nicholas churchyard**, come out of the house, turn right and walk up to Hogarth roundabout. Use the underpass to come out by Church St, a street of lovely houses which leads to the church and then to the river. With time to spare, it's a very pleasant two-mile riverside stroll to Hammersmith from here.

Kew Gardens

Kew Gardens (☎ 0181-940 1171), Kew Rd, Kew, Surrey (tube: Kew Gardens), is one of the most visited sights on the tourist itinerary, which means it can get very crowded during summer, especially at weekends. Spring is probably the best time to visit, but at any time of year this expansive array of lawns, formal gardens and botanical greenhouses has delights to offer. As well as being a park, Kew is an important botanical research centre and it maintains its reputation as the most exhaustive botanical collection in the world.

The wonderful plants and trees aside, there are several specific sights within the gardens. Assuming you come by tube and enter via **Victoria Gate**, you'll come almost immediately to a large pond overlooked by the wonderful **Palm House**, a metal and glass hothouse designed by Decimus Burton and Richard Turner between 1844 and 1848 and housing all sorts of exotic tropical greenery. Lined up in front of it are stone statues of the heraldic beasts, including the white horse of Hanover which appears in painted form on the ceilings of Kensington Palace. Just north-west of the Palm House is the tiny but irresistible **Waterlily House**, dating from 1852.

If you head north, you'll come to the **Princess of Wales Conservatory**, opened in 1987 and housing plants from 10 different computer-controlled climate zones – everything from desert to cloud forest. Beyond that you'll come to the **Kew Gardens Gallery**, which houses exhibitions of paintings and photos on a broadly botanical theme. It's open daily from 9.30 am to 5.30 pm (closed from 1 to 2 pm).

Heading west from the gallery you'll arrive at the red-brick **Kew Palace**, once a royal residence dating from the early 1600s, and very popular with George III and his family (his wife Charlotte died here in 1818); it's furnished as it might have been when they lived there. The gardens surrounding the palace are especially pretty.

If you cut south from the palace across the lawns you'll pass a lengthy **lake**. Follow it round and head west to reach **Queen Charlotte's Cottage**, a wooden summerhouse used, again, by George III and his family and surrounded by bluebells in spring.

Due east of the cottage you'll find the new **Japanese Gateway** and then the famous **Pagoda**, designed by Sir William Chambers in 1761. Unfortunately you can't go inside.

Heading north again you'll arrive at the **Temperate House**, another wonderful iron and glass hothouse (although not so hot this time) designed by Decimus Burton in 1860 and completed in 1899. On the west side a small **Evolution House** shows how plants have evolved over the millennia.

Due east of the Temperate House is the **Marianne North Gallery**. Marianne North was one of those indomitable Victorian women travellers who rejected the stay-at-home option in favour of roaming the globe. From 1871 to 1885 she ranged the continents, painting their plants and trees. The results of her labour now paper the walls of this small purpose-built gallery.

By now you should be worn out, in which case head north-west again for the **Orangery** where cream teas are served from 2 pm (£3.95).

Kew Gardens is open November to January, daily from 9.30 am to 4.30 pm; February, daily from 9.30 am to 5 pm; March, daily from 9.30 am to 6 pm; April to

August, Monday to Saturday from 9.30 am to 6.30 pm and Sunday from 9.30 am to 8 pm; September to mid-October, daily from 9.30 am to 6 pm. Admission costs £4.50/3. Note that most of the hothouses close at 5.30 pm in summer, earlier in winter.

At the time of writing Kew Palace (☎ 0181-332 5189) was closed for renovation. It was expected to reopen sometime during the summer of 1998. Normally it's open April to September daily from 11 am to 5.30 pm for 80p. If you want to go into the gardens as well, a joint ticket is £4.80/2.80.

Getting There & Away You can get to Kew Gardens by tube or main-line train. Come out of the station and walk straight ahead, crossing Kew Gardens Rd and continuing straight along Lichfield Rd which winds up opposite the Victoria Gate.

Alternatively, boats sail from Westminster Pier to Kew Gardens at 10.15 and 2 pm from March to September. In July and August there are additional sailings at 11 am and 2.30 pm, with an extra sailing at 1 pm if there's enough demand. They take 1¾ hours and a single costs £6/3, a return £10/5.

ISLEWORTH, BRENTFORD & EALING (Map 14)

Isleworth is a quiet Thamesside suburb without much to draw a visitor bar Osterley House and its fine park to the north, and the London Apprentice pub by the river (see Pubs & Bars in the Entertainment chapter).

Equally nondescript is Brentford, which links Kew to Osterley and Ealing. Again you're unlikely to want to hang about, although magnificent Syon House is well worth a look.

Ealing is popular with flat-seekers, partly because it's linked to the Central and District Underground lines and to the Paddington main line, but also because it's reasonably leafy, with pockets of moderate affluence. Film buffs will remember the Ealing Film Studios on The Green with nostalgic affection (*Passport to Pimlico* and all that), but although the BBC still makes occasional use of them they're not normally open to visitors. The one specific sight you might want to visit is Pitshanger Manor, the country retreat designed by Sir John Soane. While you're out Ealing way it's also fun to shop in Western Ave Tesco's, a carefully converted Hoover factory of 1932 with lovely Art Deco details.

The London Borough of Ealing also includes Southall, an area settled first by Sikh immigrants from the Punjab in the 1950s and 60s and then by African Asian refugees from Uganda and Kenya in the 1970s. This is a lively area, with excellent curry houses (see boxed aside Out for a Curry in the Places to Eat chapter) and shops selling videos and music from the subcontinent. The Saturday market is awash with glittering saris and there are several Hindu temples here.

Osterley House & Park

Osterley House (☎ 0181-560 3918) started life in 1575 as the country retreat of Thomas Gresham, the man responsible for the Royal Exchange, but was extensively remodelled in the 18th century by Robert Adam. The wonderful plasterwork, furniture and paintings are all worth seeing, but many people rate the downstairs kitchen even more interesting.

It's open from Easter to October, Wednesday to Sunday from 1 to 5 pm and admission costs £3.80/1.90 (free to NT members); a £1 discount for travelcard-holders encourages people to arrive by public transport. The Tudor stable is also open on summer Sundays. The park, with its ornamental lake, is open from 9 am to sunset. The ghastly M4 slashes the park in two and injects a distant drone of traffic into the peace, but there are still large areas where you can forget its existence.

To get there take the tube to Osterley, walk along Osterley Avenue and turn left along Thornbury Rd which will bring you out opposite the park entrance.

Syon House

Syon House (☎ 0181-560 0881), Syon Park, Brentford (tube: Gunnersbury; station: Syon Lane), is a superb example of the English stately home. The house where Lady Jane Grey ascended to the throne for her nine-day-long monarchy in 1554 was remodelled by Robert Adam in the 18th century, and possesses plenty of Adam furniture and oak panelling. The interior was designed along gender-specific lines, with pastel pinks and purples for the ladies' gallery, and mock Roman sculptures for the men's dining room. The gardens, including an artificial lake, were landscaped by Capability Brown and now contain the London Butterfly House, open daily from 10 am to 5 pm (£2.90/1.85).

Syon House is open April to September, Wednesday to Sunday from 11 am to 4.15 pm; October to mid-December it's open Sunday only from 11 am to 4.15 pm. Admission costs £5.50/4.

Pitshanger Manor

The books have been booted out of what used to be Ealing Library, and Pitshanger Manor (☎ 0181-567 1227) in Mattock Lane W5 (tube: Ealing Broadway), is now open to fans of architect Sir John Soane who built it as a Regency-style country retreat; a video in the basement tells the story. Parts of the manor now house a collection of pottery designed by the Martin Brothers of Southall in the 19th century. Not everyone will care for their grotesque designs, although the owl-jars with swivel heads are undoubtedly fun. A Martinware fountain rescued from vandals in Southall Park has also found a refuge here.

The manor is open (free) from 10 am to 5 pm Tuesday to Saturday.

Other Attractions

MUSEUMS & PUBLIC BUILDINGS

As well as those described above, London has many smaller museums and buildings open to the public. Some are of specialist interest or have severely restricted opening hours. These include:

Alexander Fleming Laboratory
: St Mary's Hospital, Praed St, Paddington W2 (☎ 725 6528; tube: Paddington); reconstruction of the laboratory where Fleming discovered penicillin in 1928. It's open Monday to Thursday from 10 am to 1 pm

Brass Rubbing Centre
: St Martin-in-the-Fields WC2 (☎ 930 1862; tube: Charing Cross; Map 6); replica church brasses kept in the crypt; rubbings cost from £2.99

Brunel's Engine House
: Railway Ave, Rotherhithe SE16 (☎ 0181-318 2489; tube: Rotherhithe; Map 7); engine house designed by Brunel to drain water out of the Thames Tunnel, the world's first major underwater road (1825-43), now a railway tunnel. It's open on the first Sunday of the month from noon to 4 pm. Admission costs £1.50/50p

Fan Museum
: 12 Crooms Hill, Greenwich SE10 (☎ 0181-305 1441; station: Greenwich; Map 12); collection of fans from the 17th century and from around the world displayed in a small 18th century townhouse. It's open Tuesday to Saturday from 11 am to 5 pm and Sunday from noon. Admission is a steep £3/2

Gunnersbury Park Museum
: Pope's Lane W3 (☎ 0181-992 1612; tube: Acton Town); large Regency house containing a local history museum and a collection of carriages. It's open (free) from 1 to 5 pm daily (6 pm on weekends, 4 pm in winter)

Handel House Museum
: 25 Brook St, W1 (tube: Bond St) by the time you read this a new museum devoted to the life of the 18th century composer Handel should have opened in the house where he lived for 36 years and where he composed his famous *Messiah*

House Mill
: Three Mill Lane E3 (☎ 0181-980 4626; tube: Bromley-le-Bow); Britain's largest surviving tidal mill (1776), used for making flour and powering the distillery. It's open from mid-May to October on Sunday only from 2 to 4 pm. Admission is £2

Jewish Museum
: 129 Albert St, Camden Town NW1 (☎ 284 1997; tube: Camden Town); museum explaining Judaism and the history of the Jewish community in Britain. It's open daily except Friday and Saturday from 10 am to 4 pm. Admission costs £3/1.50

Kew Bridge Steam Museum
: Green Dragon Lane, Brentford (☎ 0181-568 4757; station: Kew Bridge); restored 19th century pumping station with five Cornish beam engines, two of which steam away at weekends.

It's open daily from 11 am to 5 pm. Admission costs £3.25/2.80

London Canal Museum
12 New Wharf Rd N1 (☎ 713 0836; tube: King's Cross); Victorian warehouse with small museum about life on the canals. It's open daily except Monday from 10 am to 4.30 pm. Admission costs £2.50/1.25

London Toy & Model Museum
21 Craven Hill, Bayswater W2 (☎ 706 8000; tube: Queensway); five floors of old toys and models, plus a roundabout in the garden. Admission costs £4.95/2.50

Musical Museum
368 High St, Brentford TW8 (☎ 0181-560 8108; station: Kew Bridge; Map 14); converted church housing a collection of mechanical musical 'instruments'. It's open for 90-minute tours from April to October at weekends from 2 to 5 pm (Wednesday 2 to 4 pm in July and August). Admission is £3.20/2.50

North Woolwich Old Station
Pier Rd E16 (☎ 474 7244; station: North Woolwich); small preserved railway station likely to interest rail fanatics. It's open (free) Friday and Sunday 2 to 5 pm, and Saturday 10 am to 5 pm from April to September

Pollock's Toy Museum
1 Scala St W1 (☎ 636 3452; tube: Goodge St); collection of old model theatres. Admission costs £2.75

Ragged School Museum
46 Copperfield Rd E3 (☎ 0181-980 6405; tube: Mile End); small East End museum with information on the Dr Barnado homes and education. It's open (free) Wednesday and Thursday from 10 am to 5 pm, and the first Sunday of the month from 2 to 5 pm

Royal Air Force Museum
Grahame Park Way, Hendon, NW9 (☎ 0181-205 2266; tube: Colindale); huge museum in the old Hendon Aerodrome displaying 70 planes and flying machines alongside a flight simulator. It's open daily from 10 am to 6 pm and costs £5.70/2.85

Sutton House
2 & 4 Homerton High St, Hackney E9 (☎ 0181-986 2264; station: Homerton); Tudor red-brick house with 18th century additions and gardens. It's open from February to November on Wednesday and Sunday from 11.30 am to 5pm, and Saturday from 2 to 5 pm. Admission is £1.80/50p (free to NT members)

Wellcome Trust
183 Euston Rd NW1 (☎ 611 7211; tube: Euston); 'Science for Life' exhibition on biomedicine and History of Medicine Gallery. It's open (free) Monday to Friday from 9.45 am to 5 pm, and Saturday until 1 pm

John Wesley's House & Museum of Methodism
49 City Rd EC1 (☎ 253 2262; tube: Old St); well-kept chapel, museum and house filled with Wesley memorabilia. It's open Monday to Saturday 10 am to 4 pm, Sunday noon to 2 pm. Admission is £4/2

GALLERIES

As well as the galleries described earlier in this chapter, London has many smaller, often commercial galleries which host changing exhibitions throughout the year. Recently it's become quite fashionable to visit even the poshest of the Bond St galleries. Provided you've got the nerve to brave the horsey accents and snooty stares there's nothing to stop you spending a very enjoyable day or so taking in these temples to art. The free monthly publication *Galleries* will tell you exactly what's on where. You can pick it up at many galleries around town but if you're having trouble tracking it down call ☎ 0181-740 7020 for guidance.

The following are just suggestions. Wander up and down Cork St or New/Old Bond St and you'll find many other possibilities:

Agnew's (☎ 629 6176), 43 Old Bond St W1 (tube: Bond St)
Bankside Gallery (☎ 928 7521), 48 Hopton St SE1 (tube: Blackfriars)
Berkeley Square Gallery (☎ 493 7939), 23A Bruton St W1 (tube: Green Park)
Brixton Artists' Collective (☎ 733 6957), 35 Brixton Station Rd SW9 (tube: Brixton)
Chinese Contemporary (☎ 734 9808), 11 New Burlington Place W1 (tube: Piccadilly Circus)
Colnaghi (☎ 491 7408), 15 Old Bond St W1 (tube: Bond St)
Crafts Council (☎ 278 7700), 44A Pentonville Rd N1 (tube: Angel)
Fine Art Society (☎ 629 5116), 148 New Bond St W1 (tube: Bond St)
London Institute Gallery (☎ 514 6127), 65 Davies St W1 (tube: Bond St)
Lothbury Gallery (☎ 726 1642), 41 Lothbury EC2 (tube: Bank; Map 6)
Mall Galleries (☎ 930 6844), The Mall SW1 (tube: Charing Cross)
Marlborough Fine Art (☎ 629 5161), 6 Albemarle St W1 (tube: Green Park)

October Gallery (☎ 242 7367), 24 Old Gloucester St WC1 (tube: Holborn)
Photographers' Gallery (☎ 831 1772), 5 Great Newport St WC2 (tube: Leicester Square; Map 3)
Sackville Gallery (☎ 734 8014), 26 Sackville St W1 (tube: Piccadilly Circus)
Spink & Son (☎ 930 7888), 5 King St SW1 (tube: Piccadilly Circus)
Tracey Emin Museum (☎ 401 2692), 221 Waterloo Rd SE1 (tube: Waterloo)
Whitechapel Art Gallery (☎ 522 7878), 80-82 Whitechapel High St E1 (tube: Aldgate East)

PUBLIC BATHS

If you're visiting London during a hot, muggy summer you may well want to find a place to cool off. Medieval and Tudor London boasted innumerable public baths which were called 'stews' and had a distinctly dodgy reputation. Even in 1879 the capital still boasted more than a dozen Turkish baths, but today hardly any survive. Those that do are well worth seeking out.

One possibility is the **Porchester Spa** (☎ 792 3980), the Porchester Centre, Queensway W2 (tube: Bayswater or Queensway; Map 9), where a small plunge pool sits in the middle of a tiled Art Deco lounge. You can relax here and then take advantage of the Turkish hot rooms, Russian steam rooms, Finnish sauna and whirlpool bath. A full range of massages is available although the prices are pretty offputting. The spa is open daily from 10 am to 10 pm (last admission at 8 pm). Monday, Wednesday and Saturday are for men, Tuesday, Thursday, Friday and Sunday until 4 pm for women. From 4 to 10 pm on Sunday couples can use the facilities. Admission is £17.60.

Another, cheaper, possibility is to head east to the **Ironmonger Row Baths** (☎ 253 4011), 1 Ironmonger Row EC1 (tube: Old St), the closest London gets to a real Turkish bath. Monday, Wednesday, Friday and alternate Sundays are for women, Tuesday, Thursday, Saturday and alternate Sundays for men. The baths stay open until 10 pm, with last admissions at 8 pm. Admission costs £9.60 (£5.70 if you go in the morning), and a Turkish-style body scrub and massage would cost another £7. It's not as classy as Porchester but the atmosphere was inviting enough to inspire Nell Dunn to write her play *Steaming* as a protest against the wave of bath closures in the 1970s.

Incidentally, there are conventional swimming pools at both these baths.

A third, women-only, option is to visit The Sanctuary (☎ 240 9635), 12 Floral St WC2 (tube: Covent Garden), but with a day's membership costing £47.50 this is definitely for special treats only. The Sanctuary is open daily from 10 am to 6 pm, and for your money you can use the sauna, steam room, whirlpool and twin pools all day.

Activities

SWIMMING POOLS

Almost every London borough has its own swimming pool; to find the address of the nearest one look in the phonebook or *Yellow Pages* or call Sportsline on ☎ 222 8000. One particularly popular and central pool is **The Oasis**, 32 Endell St WC2 (tube: Covent Garden), which is open from 6.30 am to 9 pm on weekdays and from 9.30 am to 5 pm on weekends. Admission costs £2.45/85p.

From Easter to September you can also swim at the outdoor **Lido** (Map 9) beside the Serpentine in Hyde Park. A dip costs £1.50. Hardy souls head up to Hampstead Heath to swim in the pools there.

TENNIS

Although most London parks have tennis courts, they are often booked up for weeks ahead. The Lawn Tennis Association produces the useful *Where to Play Tennis in London* which they'll send you on receipt of a stamped addressed envelope; write to Queen's Club, Palliser Rd W14 (☎ 381 7000). Alternatively, call Sportsline on ☎ 222 8000 for advice.

GOLF

If you really can't leave the clubs behind, the capital has a couple of leafy golf courses on its outskirts. For details of the **Brent Valley Course**, Church Rd, Cuckoo Lane W7 (station: Hanwell), phone ☎ 0181-567 1287; for details of **Richmond Park Course**, Roehampton Gate SW15 (station: Barnes), phone ☎ 0181-876 3205.

HORSE RIDING

If you'd like to go riding in Hyde Park, horses can be hired for £25 from **Hyde Park Stables**, 63 Bathurst Mews W2 (tube: Lancaster Gate). Phone ☎ 723 2813 for costs and details of riding lessons.

WATERSPORTS

You can go boating on the Serpentine in Hyde Park, but for a wider range of watersports Docklands is shaping up as the place to go, with jetskiing, waterskiing and windsurfing all available. For details of what's possible in *Watersports London* send an sae to the Visitor Centre, 3 Limeharbour E14 9TJ, or contact the Docklands Watersports Club, King George VI Dock, Woolwich Manor Way E16 (☎ 511 7000).

BUNGEE-JUMPING

Bungee-jumping (☎ 720 9496) is just one of the sports available to visitors to Adrenalin Village, squeezed in beside the Thames between Battersea Park and the Power Station (Maps 2 & 14). To jump from a 300ft tower will cost you £35 plus £15 first-jump insurance (valid for one year); you'll need to be between 18 and 50 to avoid requirements for parental consent forms or doctor's go-ahead letters.

Courses

No matter whether you want to study sculpture or Sanskrit, circus skills or computing, someone somewhere in London is going to be running a course, and your starting point for information should be *Floodlight* (£3.50), published in July annually and listing most of the regular courses around town.

LANGUAGE

Every year thousands of people come to London to study English and there are centres offering tuition all round town. The problem is to identify a reputable one which is where the British Council (☎ 930 8466), 10 Spring Gardens SW1, comes in. They produce a list of accredited colleges which meet minimum standards for facilities, qualified staff and pastoral back-up which is free to would-be students. They can also offer general advice to overseas students on educational opportunities in the UK since many normal colleges and universities now offer courses aimed at students from abroad. Most colleges offer courses leading to Cambridge or IELTS exams and most will help their students find accommodation.

The British Council has offices all round the world which can provide the same starting-out information so you don't have to wait until you get to London to ask for help in choosing a college. The British Tourist Authority also produces a brochure for people wanting to study in England.

The following are recognised schools you might find useful. All offer courses aimed at every level which can be studied full-time or part-time and lead to Cambridge University Preliminary, First Level and Proficiency qualifications. They also offer intensive summer courses and private tuition. A four-week full-time course is likely to cost from £120 to £180, while a 12-week course will cost between £300 and £400, depending in part on how many hours you'll be studying.

Central School of English
1 Tottenham Court Rd W1 (☎ 580 2863)
English in Central London
Peter St W1 (☎ 437 8536)
Frances King School of English
195 Knightsbridge SW7 (☎ 838 0200)
Hampstead School of English
553 Finchley Rd NW3 (☎ 794 3533)
Holborn English Language Services
14 Soho St W1 (☎ 734 9989)
Kingsway College
Vernon Square WC1 (☎ 306 5880)
London Study Centre
Munster House, 676 Fulham Rd SW6 (☎ 731 3549)

London Walks

London is a huge and often overwhelming city, but the central area is compact enough to make walking an excellent way of seeing the sights.

The four walks described in this chapter are designed to enable you to explore widely different areas of London and get the feel not just of the tourist highlights but also of the more workaday modern city.

The first walk takes you round the 'must see' sights from St Paul's Cathedral to Trafalgar Square; if you're pressed for time this is one you'll probably want to go for. The second concentrates on the Strand and Fleet St, two famous thoroughfares which link Westminster with the City and were the haunt of such famous London luminaries as Samuel Pepys, Dr Johnson and Charles Dickens. This walk also gives you the chance to take in some Christopher Wren masterpieces other than St Paul's.

The third walk lets you discover the south bank of the Thames, one of the most happening areas of London where change and modernisation are taking place at a staggering pace. Here you can see some fine modern buildings like Terence Conran's Design Museum as well as exploring some of the murkier bits of Southwark around the old Clink Prison.

The fourth walk takes you even further off the beaten track, into the East End of London, an area which is still very run-down in parts and not so immediately attractive to the visitor. Take the trouble to explore it, however, and you'll get a glimpse of London's rich cultural diversity as well as seeing how pockets of renewal continue to rub shoulders with miserable dereliction.

WALK 1: ST PAUL'S CATHEDRAL TO TRAFALGAR SQUARE

One of the best ways to get your bearings is to walk around the city centre where some of the most famous sights can be found. The following tour could be covered in a day, although that wouldn't allow you time to explore any of the individual sights in detail. It will, however, give you a good introduction to the West End and Westminster. For details of the individual sights see their entries in the Things to See & Do chapter.

Start at **St Paul's Cathedral** (1), the Wren masterpiece that was completed in 1710, and climb to the top of the Golden Gallery for one of the best views of London. Then, unless you're feeling very energetic and want to walk all the way along Fleet St and the Strand (see Walk 2 below), save on foot leather by catching bus No 501 or 521 from Newgate St (behind St Paul's station) to Covent Garden.

Covent Garden (2), once London's fruit and vegetable market, has been restored to a bustling piazza. It's one of the rare places where pedestrians rule the roost, with plenty of places to sit out and eat and drink. The **Royal Opera House** (3) (currently under refurbishment) is on the north-east corner, with the Theatre Museum facing it and the London Transport Museum round the corner in the piazza.

Walk north-west up James St to Covent Garden tube station and turn left into Long Acre. Stroll along the road looking out for Stanfords map and travel bookshop on your left, and then continue across Charing Cross Rd to **Leicester Square** (4) with the green in the centre fighting to be noticed amid the first-run cinemas, nightclubs and fast-food outlets. Note the Leicester Square Theatre Ticket Booth to the south side which sells half-price tickets on the day of performance.

Continue along Coventry St, past the **Trocadero Centre** (5), with its indoor theme park and entertainments, and the **Rock Circus** (6), to arrive in **Piccadilly Circus** (7), dominated by the famous statue of Eros. To the west is Tower Records, one of London's best music shops. Shaftesbury Ave, the heart of theatreland, exits the circus at the north-eastern corner where you'll see a cluster of

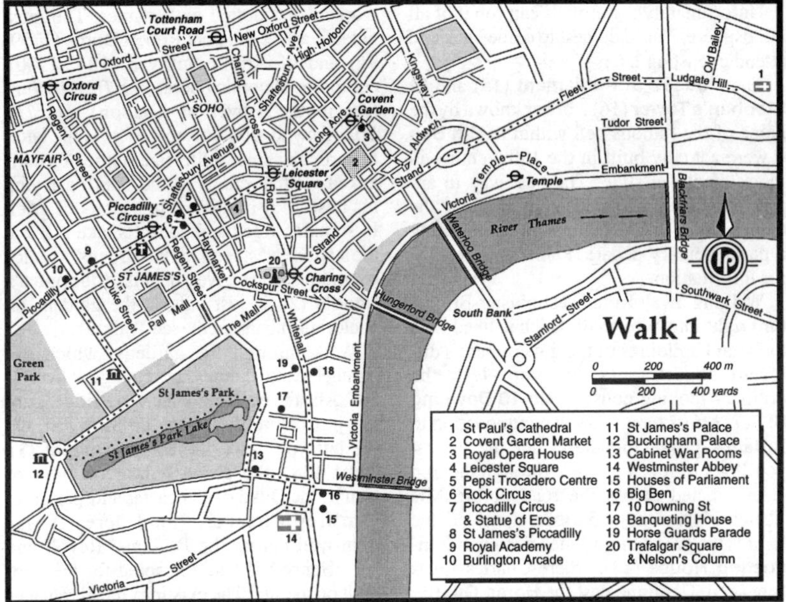

cheap kebab/pizza counters, and runs back into Soho, with its myriad restaurants and flourishing nightlife. Regent St curves out of the north-west corner up to Oxford Circus.

Continue west along Piccadilly to **St James's church** (8) (with its excellent cheap restaurant) and the **Royal Academy** (9) which has regular temporary art exhibitions, some of them blockbusters for which you must book in advance. Detour right into the extraordinary **Burlington Arcade** (10), just after the academy, but beware the Burlington Berties (private 'police') who are supposed to stop you whistling or otherwise misbehaving.

Return to Piccadilly and continue until you reach St James's St on your left (south). This takes you down to the red-brick **St James's Palace** (11), the royal residence from 1660 to 1837 when Queen Victoria upped and moved to Buckingham Palace. Skirt around its east side and you emerge in The Mall.

Trafalgar Square is to the east (left) and **Buckingham Palace** (12) to the west. If you want to watch the Changing of the Guard, it takes place daily at 11.30 am from April to August and on alternate days from August to April. The best place to position yourself is by the gates of Buck House, but the crowds are awesome. Cross back into beautiful St James's Park and follow the lake to its east end. Turn right onto Horse Guards Rd which takes you past the **Cabinet War Rooms** (13), offering an extraordinary insight into the dark days of WWII.

Continue south along Horse Guards Rd, then turn left on Great George St, which leads to Westminster Abbey, the Houses of Parliament and Westminster Bridge. **Westminster Abbey** (14) is so rich in history you need half a day to do it justice. The coronation chair where all but two monarchs since 1066 have been crowned is behind the altar, and many greats – from Darwin to Chaucer – have been buried here.

Unfortunately the crowds can rob it of all atmosphere. You'd do best to come back and attend evensong later.

The **Houses of Parliament** (15) and **St Stephen's Tower** (16) – better known by the name of the famous bell within it, **Big Ben** – were actually built in the 19th century in mock medieval style. The best way to appreciate what goes on inside is to attend the Commons or Lords visitors' galleries during a parliamentary debate. Phone ☎ 219 4272 for information.

Walking away from Westminster Bridge, turn right into Whitehall which is lined with the grand buildings of the government's different departments. On your left, the ordinary-looking house at **No 10 Downing St** (17) offers temporary accommodation to Britain's prime ministers, but the closest you'll get to it is a glimpse through the iron gates erected across the road during Mrs Thatcher's tenancy. Further along on the right is the grand Inigo Jones-designed **Banqueting House** (18), where Charles I was beheaded. Continue past the **Horse Guards** (19) on the left, where you can watch a less crowded changing of the guard at 11 am Monday to Saturday and 10 am on Sunday.

Finally, you arrive in **Trafalgar Square** (20) with Nelson's Column plopped down in the centre. The National Gallery and National Portrait Gallery are on the north side, St Martin-in-the Fields and the South African Embassy to the east and Admiralty Arch to the south-west. If you can't walk another step, Charing Cross station is handily positioned to the south-east.

WALK 2: EMBANKMENT STATION TO LUDGATE CIRCUS

This walk takes you along the Strand and Fleet Street, two of London's most famous streets which straddle the junction between Westminster and the City of London.

Take the tube to Embankment station (District and Circle lines). When you come through the ticket barriers turn left so you emerge in Villiers St, then turn immediately right into **Victoria Embankment Gardens** (1), popular as a lunch spot with local workers and dotted with statues. The most notable are of the poet Robert Burns (1759-96) and of Arthur Sullivan (1842-1900), composer of comic operas like *Trial by Jury* (set in the Tower of London) and *The Mikado*; you won't be able to miss the latter in particular since a life-size statue of a half-naked woman clings to the plinth carrying his bust, as if in the last transports of grief. In summer, free band concerts take place at the station (west) end of the gardens; a notice by the entrance gives details. **Cleopatra's Needle** (2), is just outside the gardens on Victoria Embankment (see Walk 3).

Walk through the gardens, which run parallel to the Thames, and emerge at the east end. Ahead you'll see Waterloo Bridge. Turn left just before the bridge up Savoy St. On the left you'll see the **Savoy Chapel** (3). Until 1381 the grand palace of John of Gaunt, the Duke of Lancaster and patron of Geoffrey Chaucer, stood here. It was destroyed during the Peasants' Revolt and later Henry VII had a hospital for the poor built on the site. The existing chapel replaces one that was attached to the hospital but burnt down in 1864; what you see now is a Victorian replica. A few ancient monuments survive in the chancel but it's worth dropping in to see the fine heraldic stained glass and panelled ceiling. The chapel is open Tuesday to Friday from 11.30 am to 3.30 pm.

Continue along Savoy St, passing the Australia Shop on the left. When you emerge on the Strand, turn right and cross over Lancaster Place. Shortly afterwards you'll come to **Somerset House** (4) on the right. This elegant building, designed by Sir William Chambers in 1774 and finally completed in 1835, now houses assorted government offices as well as the Courtauld Gallery with some of the finest paintings in London.

Even if you don't have time to visit the gallery it's worth wandering round the courtyards to admire the graceful Palladian architecture (fine views of the water-facing side can be had from Waterloo Bridge). Parts of Somerset House are due to become an arts complex which will allow visitors to see more of the 18th century plasterwork inside.

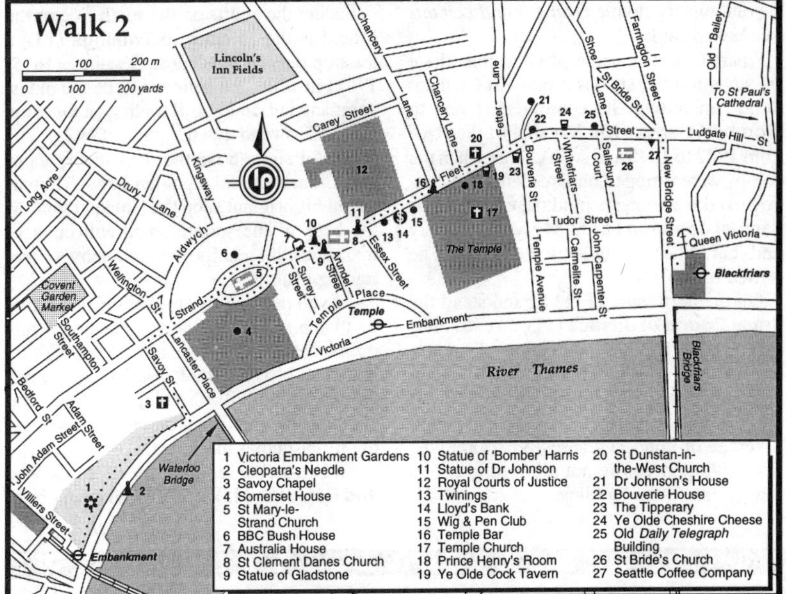

The 18th century Strand was a fashionable district lined with the grand houses and palaces of the nobility, a place to promenade at midday. Unfortunately some of the buildings put up in the 1960s did nothing to perpetuate the street's traditional elegance.

Walk east along the Strand with the ugly 60s building of King's College on your right. Cross into the middle of the road to visit **St Mary-le-Strand** (5), designed by James Gibbs between 1715 and 1724. The elaborately plastered ceiling is in marked contrast to the dowdy beige walls; the lofty windows were intended to reduce the noise from the traffic outside.

Continue along the Strand with **Bush House** (6), built in 1920, on your left. Part of it houses the BBC World Service. A little further along is **Australia House** (7), designed by Marshall Mackenzie between 1912 and 1918 and with huge statues by Harold Parker gracing the facade.

Once again a church stands on a road island. This time it's **St Clement Danes** (8) with a statue of **William Ewart Gladstone** (9), prime minister in 1868-74, 1880-85, 1886 and 1892-94, in front.

The old St Clement Danes was designed by Sir Christopher Wren in 1682, with the steeple added to the tower by James Gibbs in 1719. Unfortunately it was almost completely destroyed by bombs in 1941; only the walls and steeple survived. In 1958 the church was rebuilt for the Royal Air Force; 800-plus slate badges of different squadrons and units of the RAF are set into the nave pavement. Its curious name is a reminder of a 9th century church on the same site. At that time seafaring Danes who had married Englishwomen were only allowed to live between Westminster and Ludgate. Unsurprisingly, when they built their own church, they named it after St Clement, the patron saint of mariners.

Time your visit for 9 am, noon, 3 or 6 pm and you'll hear the church bells chime out the old nursery rhyme *Oranges and Lemons* (see boxed aside).

Apart from the statue of Gladstone there are several other statues around St Clement Danes, including the controversial one to **'Bomber' Harris** (10), Marshal of the RAF from 1942 to 1945 and so in charge when the bombs were dropped on Dresden. Less controversial is the one behind the church to **Dr Samuel Johnson** (1709-84) who famously said that 'when a man is tired of London he is tired of life' (11).

On the north side of the Strand stand the **Royal Courts of Justice** (12), an extraordinary Gothic Revival confection of arches, turrets and spires. This is where many landmark cases wind up and the High Court often forms the backdrop to television news coverage of important cases. Visits are possible although you're not allowed to take a camera inside the building.

Facing the courts on the south side of the Strand is the entrance to **Twinings** (13), a teashop opened by Thomas Twining (1675-1741) in 1706 and believed to be the oldest company in London still trading on the same site and owned by the same family. The colourful sign above the door incorporates two Chinamen and a golden lion – Thomas called his original shop the Golden Lyon. At the back of the shop a small collection of memorabilia recalls the company's long trading history.

As you proceed east towards Fleet St look up to appreciate the fine architecture. A few doors east of Twinings the Law Courts branch of **Lloyd's Bank** (14) has carved fish twined around its circular windows and elaborate tiles adorning the recess now housing its cashpoint machines.

Still on the same side of the street, the **Wig and Pen Club** (15) at 229 Strand dates back

Oranges & Lemons and Other Church Chimes

Oranges & lemons, say the bells of St Clements
Bulls eyes & targets, say the bells of St Margarets
Pokers & tongs, say the bells of St Johns
Pancakes & fritters, say the bells of St Peters
Two sticks & an apple, say the bells at Whitechapel
Old Father Baldpate, say the bells at Aldgate
Maids in white aprons, say the bells of St Catherines
Brickbats & tiles, say the bells of St Giles
Kettles & pans, say the bells at St Annes
You owe me five farthings, say the bells of St Martins
When will you pay me, say the bells of Old Bailey
When I grow rich, say the bells of Shoreditch
Pray, when will that be, say the bells of Stepney
I'm sure I don't know, says the great bell at Bow
Here comes a candle to light you to bed
Here comes a chopper to chop off your head.

St Giles Cripplegate in the City

Academics have long pointed out that nursery rhymes and games are much more than the childish nonsense we might suppose. One of their favourites has always been *Oranges & Lemons*, the nursery rhyme that seems to incorporate the names of many City of London churches and other landmarks and which first surfaced in 1744.

It's generally agreed that St Clements was St Clement Danes and St Martins was St Martin-in-the-Fields, while the bells of Old Bailey belonged to St Sepulchre, Holborn, the bells of Shoreditch to St Leonards, Shoreditch, and the bells of Stepney to St Dunstan, Stepney. The great bell at Bow belonged to St Mary-le-Bow and was the one whose range decided who was and wasn't technically a cockney.

Beyond that, however, is only guesswork and it has been suggested that the writer just plucked out of the air the names of saints that happened to rhyme with the chosen phrase. That theory is lent support by the fact that the names of the churches are not always the same. In some surviving versions of the rhyme, for example, Shoreditch is Fleet Ditch and Bow has become Paul. ■

RACHEL BLACK

CHARLOTTE HINDLE

DOUG McKINLAY

Left: Beefeaters at the Tower of London
Right: The Golden Hinde, St Mary Overie Dock, Southwark
Bottom: Hyde Park Corner

DOUG McKINLAY

CHARLOTTE HINDLE

TOM SMALLMAN

Left: Royal Courts of Justice, Strand
Right: Base of Monument to the Great Fire in Pudding Lane
Bottom: British Museum

to 1625 and is the only Strand building to have survived the Great Fire of 1666. It's now an exclusive restaurant but you can admire the symbolic wigs and pens in the external plasterwork.

In the centre of the road a griffin bestriding an elaborately carved plinth marks the site of the original **Temple Bar** (16) where the City of Westminster becomes the City of London. The plinth is decorated with statues of Queen Victoria and husband Albert together with symbols of Art and Science, War and Peace and portrayals of processions.

A little further along the road you'll come to a newsagents' stand and an arch leading off to the right. Duck under it and you'll find yourself in the Temple, one of the Inns of Court. At different times playwright Oliver Goldsmith, novelist William Thackeray and diarist John Evelyn all lived here. According to Shakespeare the Wars of the Roses also broke out after the Dukes of York and Lancaster plucked white and red roses to represent their respective sides in Temple Gardens. The fountain in Fountain Court was immortalised by Charles Dickens in *Martin Chuzzlewit*.

Just inside the arch is a plan of the Temple. Take your time to look around an area which is as close to the atmosphere of an Oxbridge college as you'll get in London. Those buildings marked with a lamb and flag belong to Middle Temple, those with the winged horse Pegasus to Inner Temple

You can't go inside most of the Temple buildings. The one glorious exception is **Temple Church** (17), one of London's few surviving medieval churches dating back to 1185 and one of only five round churches in the whole of Britain.

Return to Fleet St via the same archway and immediately to the right stairs lead up to **Prince Henry's Room** (18) which dates back to the 16th century but was extensively remodelled as a tavern with an overhanging half-timbered facade in 1610-11. Since the tavern was called *The Princes Arms*, the feathers of the Prince of Wales appear in the external woodwork. The 1st floor room boasts the best Jacobean plaster ceiling surviving in London and some original wooden wall panelling. Prince Henry's Room is open (free) Monday to Saturday from 11 am to 2 pm.

A little further east on the same side of the road is **Ye Olde Cock Tavern** (19), Fleet Street's oldest pub (built in 1549). The coloured cockerel that acts as its sign is said to have been designed by Grinling Gibbons, whose work adorns many London churches. Past patrons include Pepys, Dr Johnson, Goldsmith and Dickens.

Across the road stands octagonal **St Dunstan-in-the-West church** (20) which was built by John Shaw in 1832 and boasts a spectacular lantern tower. On the facade look out for the statue of Queen Elizabeth I (the only such outdoor statue in London) and for the figures of Gog and Magog on the clock (see boxed aside); time your visit for the hour and you'll see them swing round and club the bells beside them. Inside, St Dunstan's is an ecumenical church with a Romanian Orthodox congregation, hence the fine 19th century iconostasis closing off the chapel to the left of the altar; this was brought from Bucharest in 1966 but fits the archway as snugly as if it had been designed to stand there.

In 1667 Samuel Pepys recorded a visit to St Dunstan-in-the West church in his diary:

> 'Stood by a pretty, modest maid whom I did labour to take by the hand and body; but she would not, but got further...from me and at last I could perceive her to take pins out of her pocket to prick me if I should touch her again.'

As you continue east along Fleet St the dome of St Paul's Cathedral comes into view. Cross over Fetter Lane and turn left along Johnson's Court, one of many narrow alleyways surviving on both sides of the street. This leads eventually to Gough Court where you can visit **Dr Johnson's House** (21), home of the famous dictionary-maker whose parish church was St Clement Danes. The wooden chair on which he used to drink at Ye Olde Cock Tavern is preserved on the 1st floor landing.

Gog & Magog

According to a 12th century historian, Britain was once inhabited by giants who were conquered by the Trojans around 1200 BC. After becoming king of Cornwall, the Trojan general Corineus killed all the local giants. Last to go was Gogmagog, a 12ft monster whom he hurled into the sea.

By the 18th century Gog and Magog were thought to have been the last two surviving giants, forced to work for the Trojan Brutus in his palace on the site of the Guildhall in what was, believe it not, called New Troy in this version of history. ■

Return to Fleet St and continue east. On the north side you'll pass **Bouverie House** (22), once home to the *Sun* newspaper in the days when Britain's national newspapers were all printed in Fleet St (most are now printed in Docklands). Across the road is **The Tipperary** pub (23) which stands on the site of a medieval monastery whose inhabitants were brewers. The original pub on the site, The Boar's Head, was built in 1605 and survived the Great Fire, only to be bought in 1700 by a firm of Dublin brewers who turned it into the first Irish theme pub outside Ireland. In 1918 printers returning from war renamed it The Tipperary.

A little further east on the north side you'll see another famous London pub, **Ye Olde Cheshire Cheese** (24), rebuilt after the Great Fire and popular with Dr Johnson and Charles Dickens. The entrance is along Wine Office Court where the excise office stood until 1665 and which retains several Georgian houses. While living at No 6, Goldsmith wrote parts of *The Vicar of Wakefield*.

The Cheshire Cheese is a delightfully atmospheric pub with wood-panelled walls, and is best frequented outside peak lunch hour when it's packed. A sign over the cramped bar reads 'Gentlemen only served in this bar', a reminder of the days not too long ago (and thankfully now gone) when women were routinely prevented from ordering a drink in many central London pubs.

Back on the north side of Fleet St and still heading east you'll pass **135-141 Fleet St** (25), Tommy Tait's superb 'Egyptian-style' building of 1929 which once housed the *Daily Telegraph* and now accommodates Credit Agricole and a branch of Goldman Sachs.

Cross the road and a gateway on the right leads to **St Bride's Church** (26), designed by Christopher Wren and nicknamed the 'wedding cake church' for its graceful tiered spire which is thought to have launched a million icing-sugar reproductions.

By this time Ludgate Circus is in sight. There's a handy branch of the **Seattle Coffee Company** (27) at 91 Fleet St for refreshments before catching the tube at Blackfriars (Circle and District lines).

WALK 3: THE SOUTH BANK FROM HUNGERFORD BRIDGE TO TOWER BRIDGE

This walk lets you see some of the development that has been taking place along the south bank of the Thames east of the Royal National Theatre. For much of the way you'll be following the route of the Silver Jubilee Walkway, marked out in 1977 to celebrate Queen Elizabeth II's Silver Jubilee and adorned with plaques identifying riverside landmarks.

Take the tube to Embankment station. When you come out into the ticket hall turn right out onto the Victoria Embankment. On your right you'll see **Hungerford Bridge**, an ugly cast-iron structure due to be replaced. From the bridge you'll have a view upriver towards the City. Look along on the left and you should see **Cleopatra's Needle** (1), an Egyptian obelisk which started life as a monument to the Pharaoh Thotmes III in c. 1500 BC but was transported to London in 1879. The 'needle' had nothing at all to do with the Cleopatra of asp fame. Instead it was conveyed from Alexandria in a metal cylinder called Cleopatra which was in turn attached to a steamer called Olga. En route to England it ran aground off the Bay of Biscay and six men were killed in the effort to refloat it.

Immediately on your left is **Charing Cross Pier** (2), and to the right is the restaurant ship *Hispaniola* (3). Once across the bridge turn left (east) along the river and you'll pass in front of the **Royal Festival Hall** (4), built in 1951 as the centrepiece for the Festival of Britain, and the **Queen Elizabeth Hall** (5), built in 1967. Soon you'll reach **Waterloo Bridge**; it's well worth diverting onto it to look at the views along the river, west to the Houses of Parliament and east to the Tower of London.

Immediately beside Waterloo Bridge on the east side is the much derided **Royal National Theatre** (6) designed by Denys Lasdun in 1976 with no apparent thought for the grim appearance of streaky wet concrete. Continue eastwards and you'll pass the South Bank Television Centre before arriving at **Gabriel's Wharf** (7). This is where local people started to strike back against the postwar redevelopment of the South Bank which had seen shops and schools close down and the price of land rise until only large companies like IBM could afford to build there.

In 1900 the population of Waterloo had been around 50,000. However, the area was devastated by the Blitz and the ensuing slum clearances. By 1970 only around 4000 people were still living there. In the 1970s locals lobbied the then Greater London Council and Southwark and Lambeth councils for a change of approach which would see more normal development taking the place of showcase buildings. The GLC was then part owner of the land around Gabriel's Wharf and planned to build Europe's tallest skyscraper on it.

The Coin St Action Group demanded affordable housing and a riverside park instead and in 1983 the government finally approved their plans. The GLC then bought out the other owners of the land and had it redesignated for housing and recreational use, thus reducing its value to developers. The non-profit-making Coin St Community Builders group then bought the land and demolished the remaining derelict buildings. In their place they completed the South Bank Walkway, laid out the Bernie Spain Gardens (a small park) and created a craft market at Gabriel's Wharf.

Right beside it stands the splendid **Oxo Tower** (8), built in 1928 with the letters 'OXO' picked out in the windows in a barefaced attempt to get round a ban on outdoor advertising. These days the tower consists of apartments owned by a housing co-op, with the super-posh Oxo Tower Restaurant & Brasserie owned by the Harvey Nichols department store on top. Although the two user-groups have had their run-ins – residents have complained about the noise made by departing diners – the restaurant has been one of London's great success stories. You won't get a table unless you book five weeks in advance ... unless your name is Liam Gallagher, of course!

Continue east towards Blackfriars Bridge and you'll come to **Doggett's Coat & Badge pub** (9). Thomas Doggett was an 18th century Irish comedian who set up what is believed to be the oldest rowing competition in the world in 1715. Ever since then six men have set out from London Bridge to race downriver to Chelsea Bridge at the start of August each year. The winner is rewarded with a red jacket and a silver badge. For the precise date and details phone ☎ 626 3531.

A path leads underneath **Blackfriars Bridge** and on to the **Bankside Gallery** (10), home to the Royal Watercolour Society (☎ 928 7521). If there's an exhibition on it will be open on Tuesday from 10 am to 8 pm, Wednesday to Friday until 5 pm and on Sunday from 1 to 5 pm. Shortly afterwards you'll see the vast bulk of the old **Bankside Power Station** (11) looming on your right. This was designed by Sir Giles Gilbert Scott after WWII but was decommissioned in 1986 and is due to become the second London home of the Tate Gallery.

A little further east and you'll see a terrace of Georgian houses set at an oblique angle on the right. Immediately beside and behind them is the extraordinary new **Globe Theatre** (12), standing as close as it could do to the original site of Shakespeare's Globe, now partly buried beneath the houses. You should certainly pause for a tour of the theatre. Better still, stay and take in a show.

Continue under **Southwark Bridge** and you'll pass the **Anchor pub** (13) which has been standing here in one guise or another since the 18th century and offers good views across the river. Divert inland following signs to the Clink Prison Museum. This will take you along Clink St where there are slight remains of a **palace of the Bishop of Winchester** (14), including a fine medieval rose window. The **Clink Prison** (15) stood just past the palace, hence the modern expression 'in the clink' for in jail.

Continue along the road until you emerge in St Mary Overie Dock where a replica of the **Golden Hinde** (16), the boat in which Sir Francis Drake circumnavigated the globe between 1577 and 1580, is moored. You can go on board from 9 am to sunset every day (£2.30/1.50). It's quite fun to see the replica Tudor fittings and cannons but watch your head on the low ceilings of the gun deck.

Wind your way round the ship to walk along Montague Close and up onto the approach to London Bridge. Keep left under the railway arches and head east along Tooley St. To your left, **St Olave's House** (17) is one of London's finest Art Deco buildings, a diminutive riverside office block built in 1932 and fronted with gold mosaic lettering and bronze relief sculptures. Further along on the other side of Tooley St are the **London Dungeon** (18) and the **Britain at War Experience** (19). The entrance to **Hay's Galleria** (20) is on the left. Cut through into this upmarket warehouse development where a fake Victorian iron-and-glass roof covers an atrium surrounded by a mix of offices, shops and cafés.

Continue eastwards along the south bank, passing the **HMS *Belfast*** (21), moored just offshore and open for visits. **Tower Bridge** now looms ahead of you, its twin towers offering one of those quintessential images of London. Walk under the bridge and along

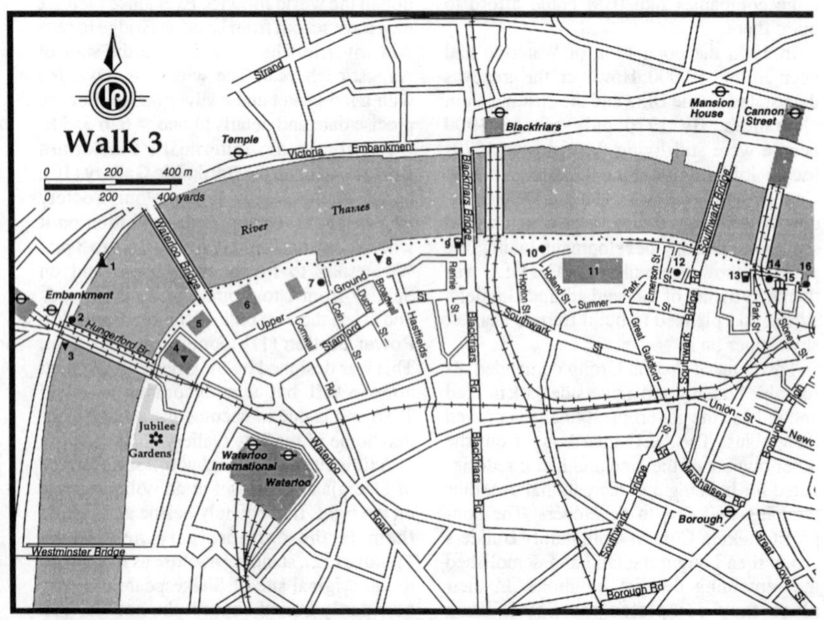

Shad Thames, past old warehouses which have been tarted up and turned into cafés and pricey shops. Eventually the road opens out into Butler's Wharf and you'll see the **Design Museum** (22) on the right. This stark modernist structure is filled with objects ranging from the superb to the downright silly. Its café, the Blue Print, is well worth frequenting if you can afford it.

If you can't, never fear. Turn right beside the Design Museum, down Maguire St, and in the converted Clove Building you'll find the **Bramah Tea & Coffee Museum** (23), the perfect place to relax over a perfectly brewed cup of tea.

WALK 4: THE EAST END FROM LIVERPOOL ST TO TOWER GATEWAY

This walk takes you through the streets of Spitalfields and Whitechapel, areas which have offered a home in turn to communities of Huguenots, Jews and Bengalis, each of whom has left their mark. During the late 1980s this area saw considerable redevelopment, both around Liverpool St station and around Tower Gateway, the access point for the Docklands Light Railway. If you're keen on street markets or curries this is a great corner of the capital to explore, especially at the weekend.

Come out of Liverpool St station and pause to marvel at the brand-new high-rise **Broadgate Centre** (1) behind you; an open-air skating rink operates here in winter. Then turn left into Bishopsgate at the **Hamilton Hall pub** (2). Cross the road and walk past the turning for Spital Square where the medieval hospital ('spittle') which gave its name to the area originally stood. Sadly, there's little to see on the site today. Turn right into Folgate St, lined with fine Georgian houses. It was in this area that Protestant Huguenots, who left France after the Edict of Nantes guaranteeing them freedom of worship was revoked in 1685 chose to settle, bringing with them their skills as silk

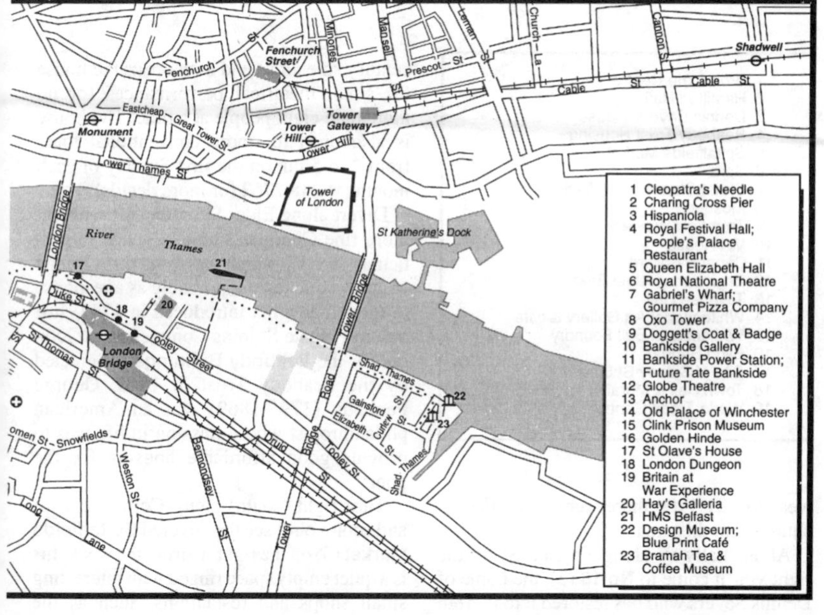

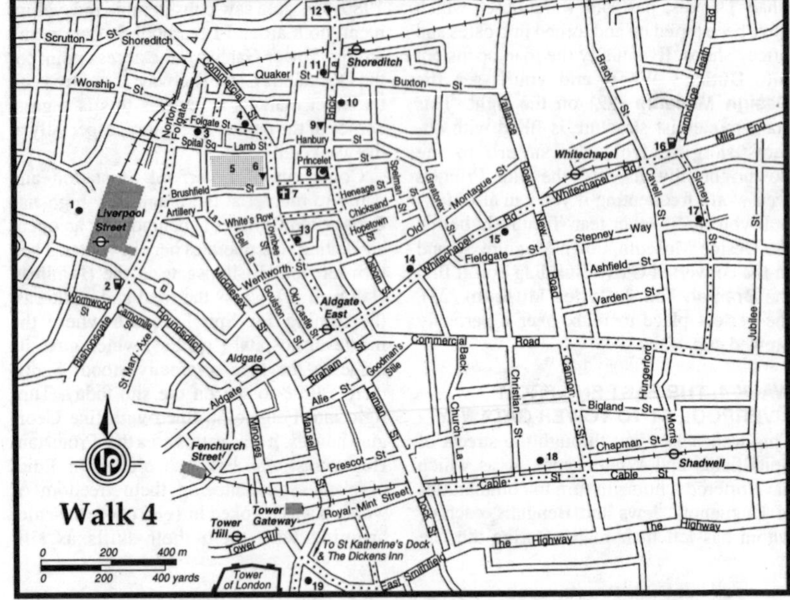

1 Broadgate Centre
2 Hamilton Hall
3 Dennis Severs' House
4 Peabody Trust Housing
5 Spitalfields Market
6 Spitz
7 Christ Church Spitalfields
8 Mosque
9 Truman's Brewery
10 Vat House
11 Cannon Bollard
12 Brick Lane Beigel Bake
13 Toynbee Hall
14 Whitechapel Art Gallery & café
15 Whitechapel Bell Foundry
16 Blind Beggar
17 Site of Sidney St Siege
18 Town Hall & Mural
19 World Trade Centre

weavers. By 1700 there were seven French churches in this area.

About halfway along Folgate St on the right you'll come to **No 18** (3), the home of Dennis Severs who has restored it to its 18th century splendour and now opens the house for small theatrical performances for no more than eight people at a time. The house is also open for more conventional tours from 2 to 5 pm on the first Sunday of each month (☎ 248 2762 for more details).

Divert along Elder St on the left with yet more fine Georgian houses. Notice in particular No 17 which has had three of its windows bricked up, probably as a response to the window tax introduced in 1742. Just before Folgate St joins Commercial St look out for the **Peabody Buildings** (4) erected by the Peabody Trust in 1863. George Peabody (1795-1869) was an American philanthropist whose mission in life was to provide good affordable housing for the poor.

Turn right (south) along Commercial St and soon you'll see the covered **Spitalfields Market** (5) on the right. During the week this is a quiet empty space ringed with interesting small shops and restaurants, such as the

Spitz (6), but on Sundays one of London's more interesting and varied markets takes place in the arena (see Markets in the Shopping chapter). A market of some sort has been taking place here since 1682 but the present building only dates from 1887. It was designed by Robert Horner who had started his working life as a porter in the fruit and vegetable market on the site.

On Commercial St, virtually opposite the market, you can't miss the striking porticoed facade of **Christ Church, Spitalfields** (7), designed by Nicholas Hawksmoor and completed in 1729. Ongoing restoration work ensures that the church's exterior, said to resemble a Venetian window, will still be covered in scaffolding, but it's well worth timing your visit for the brief opening hours (Monday to Friday from noon to 2.30 pm; ☎ 247 7202) since Christ Church has one of the most breathtaking interiors of all London's churches. It's hard to credit that until very recently the church was virtually abandoned.

Turn down Fournier St, to the left (north) of Christ Church, admiring the beautifully restored Georgian houses with wooden shutters reminiscent of Swiss chalets. Most of them were built between 1718 and 1728 for wealthy London merchants, only to be taken over by silk weavers and their families. By the 19th century Fournier St was run-down, neglected and crime-ridden. These days Georgian houses like these, within walking distance of the city, are expensively desirable again. No 2 Fournier St was designed by Hawksmoor as the rectory for Christ Church. On the left look out for the unusually numbered house – Eleven and a Half.

At the Brick Lane end of Fournier St is one of the most interesting buildings in the whole of Spitalfields, epitomising as it does the waves of immigrants who have settled in the area. The **New French Church** (8) was built for the Huguenots in 1743 and the contemporary sundial facing Fournier St reads 'Umbra Sumus' (We are Shadows). In 1899 the church became the Great Synagogue for Jewish refugees who had fled from the pogroms of Russia and Central Europe and settled in Spitalfields. Finally in 1975 it changed religion yet again, becoming the Great Mosque (Jamme Masjid) of the Bengali community who moved in as the Jews moved out. Pass by at prayer times and see the men emerging in skullcap and *shalwar kameez* and you could be forgiven for thinking you'd skipped east a few continents.

Turn left (north) into Brick Lane, a wonderful street of small curry and balti houses intermingled with shops selling brightly coloured fabrics, the ingredients for cooking your own curries and the paraphernalia of Islam: rosary beads, Koran stands, prayer rugs etc. In 1550 this was just a country road leading to brickyards, hence its name. By the 18th century it had been paved and lined with a mixture of houses and cottages inhabited by the Spitalfields weavers, some of whom rioted against the introduction of automated looms. These days many of the Bengalis also make a living from the clothes trade and there are many sweatshops where people slave for long hours and poor wages in the streets around.

Cross over Hanbury St and on the left you'll come to **Truman's Brewery** (9), the biggest brewery in London by the mid-18th century. Today the director's house stands to the left and the head brewer's house to the right of a small courtyard; Ben Truman's house dates back to 1740 but the brewer's house was only built in the 19th century, although it was designed to blend in with the earlier buildings. The brewery closed in 1989 and there's a modern café on the site.

Across the road notice the old **Vat House** (10), which dates back to the turn of the 19th century and has a hexagonal bell tower. Next to it stands the Engineer's House of 1830 and a row of former stables, all given new uses. At the junction with Quaker St look out for a **bollard** (11) made from a redundant 18th century cannon. Further along is the **Brick Lane Beigel Bake** (12) (see Places to Eat).

Head back down Brick Lane (south) and cross over Princelet St, with more fine 18th century houses. Turn right along Fashion St and then left along Commercial St. On the left you'll pass **Toynbee Hall** (13), founded in 1884 to bring educational opportunities to the East End. Courses continue today and the courtyard offers a peaceful escape from the grubby commercialism outside.

Commercial St eventually joins Whitechapel High St, which Monopoly players will remember as one of London's shabbier neighbourhoods. If you need a break and something to eat it's worth turning left along Whitechapel Rd and visiting **Whitechapel Art Gallery** (14), which puts on interesting temporary exhibitions but also has a pleasant upstairs café. The wonderful recessed entrance with turrets on either side was designed by Charles Harrison Townshend in 1897.

From here on, the streets get much more run-down and depressing, so you might want to call it a day and catch the tube home from Aldgate East. If not, continue east along Whitechapel Rd. At No 32-4 you'll see the **Whitechapel Bell Foundry** (15) which has been standing on this site since 1738, although an earlier foundry nearby is known to have been in business in 1570. More creepily, you're now in Jack the Ripper country. Although the serial killer's actual identity remains a mystery (with some new crackpot theory rolling off the presses every year), that hasn't stopped a dubious trade in Jack the Ripper walks and models growing up around his legend. What is certain is that in 1888 he murdered five prostitutes in the wretched backstreets of the Victorian East End; Mary Anne Nichols died in Bucks Row (now Durward St), Annie Chapman in Hanbury St, Elizabeth Stride in Berner St (now Henriques St), Catherine Eddowes in Mitre Square and Mary Kelly in Miller's Court.

Continue east to the junction with Cambridge Heath Rd and you'll see the **Blind Beggar pub** (16), notorious as the place where Ronnie Kray shot George Cornell in 1966 in a feud between the Kray and Richardson gangs for control of the East End's organised crime. The film *The Krays* (1990), starring Martin and Gary Kemp of Spandau Ballet, tells the story of the Krays, hardened criminals who somehow managed to recast themselves as lovable rogues.

The pub's name commemorates the more romantic story of Bessie, daughter of Henery de Montfort, who had been blinded at the Battle of Evesham in 1265 and became a London beggar. His beautiful barmaid daughter was wooed by a wealthy knight who was prepared to ignore her father's wretched circumstances. In a Cinderella conclusion, her father arrived at the wedding, cast off his rags and produced a £3000 wedding present, the proceeds of his begging.

Cross over and walk south down Sidney St, noting **No 100** (17), the scene in 1911 of the Siege of Sidney St when two Russian anarchists who had killed three policemen during a botched burglary were cornered by a group of Scots Guards. Winston Churchill was a witness to the ending of the siege when the house was burnt down and the anarchists killed.

At the end of Sidney St turn right along Commercial Rd and then left along Cannon St. At the end of Cannon St turn right into Cable St and look for the **town hall** (18). On the wall a mural commemorates a famous episode in East End history when the fascist Sir Oswald Mosley led a bunch of Blackshirts into the area to intimidate the local Jewish population in 1936. Locals fought back and the Blackshirts were driven out.

Continue to the end of Cable St, which becomes Royal Mint St; the Royal Mint stood here from 1811 until 1968 when it moved to Llantrisant in Wales (before then coins were minted in the nearby Tower of London). Turn left along Cartwright St and then right into East Smithfield, with the **World Trade Centre** building (19) on the left. Just beyond it the road winds round into St Katherine's Dock, in the shadow of the Tower of London and Tower Bridge, a good place to wind up your walk with a drink at the Dickens pub before catching the tube home from Tower Hill.

Places to Stay

Whichever way you do it, accommodation is going to make a huge hole in your budget. Especially at the bottom end of the market, demand can also outstrip supply, so it's worth prebooking a night or two's accommodation, especially in July and August.

The English Tourist Board operates a classification and grading system which covers London; participating hotels, guesthouses and B&Bs have a plaque at the front door. If you want to be confident that your accommodation reaches basic standards of safety and cleanliness, the first classification is 'Listed', which denotes clean, comfortable accommodation. One crown means each room will have a washbasin and its own key. Two crowns means washbasins, bedside lights, and a TV in a lounge or in bedrooms. Three crowns means at least half the rooms have private bathrooms and that hot evening meals are available. And so on up to five crowns.

In addition there are gradings ('approved', 'commended', 'highly commended' and 'deluxe'), which may actually be more significant since they reflect a subjective judgment of quality.

All this sounds useful, but in practice there's a wide range within each classification and some of the best B&Bs don't participate at all because they have to pay to do so. A high-quality 'listed' B&B can be 20 times nicer than a low-quality 'three crown' hotel. Actually seeing the place, even from the outside, will give a clue as to what to expect. Always ask to look at your room before you check in.

As ever, single rooms are in short supply and many accommodation suppliers are reluctant to let a double room, even when it's quiet, to one person without charging a hefty supplement.

The London Tourist Board publishes *Where to Stay in London* (£2.95), which lists approved hotels, guesthouses, apartments and B&Bs. It also produces a separate pamphlet called *Accommodation for Budget Travellers*.

The area code for all telephone and fax numbers in this section is ☎ 0171 unless the text states otherwise.

Booking Offices

It's possible to make same-day accommodation bookings at the TICs at Victoria station and Heathrow airport, although they charge £5 for a hotel/B&B and £1.50 for hostels; the queues at Victoria in particular can be alarmingly long in summer. The telephone bookings hot line is ☎ 824 8844.

Alternatively, the British Hotel Reservation Centre (☎ 0800-726298) has a booking office on the main Victoria station concourse. It charge £3 per hotel/hostel booking.

Thomas Cook also operates a hostel and hotel reservation service, charging £5 per booking. There are kiosks at Paddington (☎ 723 0184), Charing Cross (☎ 976 1171), Euston (☎ 388 7435), King's Cross (☎ 837 5681) and Victoria (☎ 828 4646) railway stations; at Earl's Court (☎ 244 0908) and South Kensington (☎ 581 9766) tube stations; and at Gatwick airport (☎ 01293-529372) railway station.

The YHA operates a central reservations system (☎ 248 6547; fax 236 7681) to help match people with beds. Although you still pay the individual hostel directly, the staff on this line will know what beds are available where and will be able to sort things out if you can't get through on the direct numbers – very possible in July and August! You can also email to YHALondonReservations@compuserve.com or write to YHA Central Reservations at 36 Carter Lane, London EC4V 5AB.

If you want to stay in a B&B, bookings for a minimum of three days can be made free through London Homestead Services (☎ 0181-949 4455; fax 0181-549 5492), Coombe Wood Rd, Kingston-upon-Thames, Surrey KT2 7JY. Bed & Breakfast (GB)

(☎ 01491-578803), PO Box 66, Henley-on-Thames RG9 1XS, specialises in central London. Host & Guest Service (☎ 731 5340), Harwood House, 27 Effie Rd SW6 1EN, will look for student accommodation as well. Primrose Hill B&B (☎ 722 6869), 14 Edis St NW1 8LG, deals with select properties in or near Hampstead.

PLACES TO STAY – BUDGET

With camping sites thin on the ground, budget travellers will be fighting each other for beds in the youth hostels, some of them run by the YHA/HI, a few of them independent. Over the Christmas and Easter holidays and in July and August, beds are also available in rooms vacated by their regular student occupants. The YMCA has a few big central hostels but they book up way ahead and often to long-stayers. A few B&Bs also just about scrape into the budget accommodation category.

Camping

For obvious reasons camping is not a particularly realistic option when visiting London.

Tent City (☎ 0181-743 5708), Old Oak Common Lane W3 (tube: East Acton), is the cheapest option short of sleeping rough. Beds in dormitory-style tents cost £6. It's open from June to September and you're advised to book. There are also a few tent sites but there is no space for caravans or camper vans.

A second *Tent City* (☎ 0181-985 7656), in Millfields Rd, Hackney (station: Clapton), north-east London, has space for tents or vans for £5.

Lee Valley Park (☎ 0181-345 6666), Picketts Lock Sport & Leisure Centre, Picketts Lock Lane, Edmonton N9 (tube: Tottenham Hale, then bus No 363), has 200 pitches for tents or caravans. It's open all year and the nightly charge is £5/2.10 (adult/junior) per person plus £2.20 for electricity.

YHA/HI Hostels

Nine London area hostels are affiliated to Hostelling International (HI), still known mainly as the Youth Hostel Association (YHA) in Britain. Membership of the YHA gives you access to a network of hostels throughout England, Wales and Scotland – and you don't have to be young, or single, to use them.

You can join the association at the YHA Adventure Shop (☎ 836 8541), 14 Southampton St WC2 (tube: Covent Garden; Map 3), where there's also a bookshop, outdoor equipment shop and a branch of Campus Travel. Membership costs £9.50/3.50 for a year. Alternatively you can join in your home country. If you aren't a member you'll be given a card to fill up with six nightly stamps, each costing £1.55. Once the card's full, you pay the same price as a member. National offices include:

Australia
: Each state has its own YHA. The National Administration Office is the Australian Youth Hostels Association, Level 3, 10 Mallett St, Camperdown, NSW 2050 (☎ 02-9565 1699)

Canada
: Canadian Hostelling Association, 1600 James Naismith Drive, Suite 608, Gloucester, Ontario K1B 5N4 (☎ 613-748 5638)

New Zealand
: Youth Hostel Association of New Zealand, PO Box 436, 173 Gloucester St, Christchurch 1 (☎ 03-379 9970)

USA
: Hostelling International, PO Box 37613, Washington, DC 20013-7613 (☎ 202-783 6161)

The biggest advantages of staying in hostels are price (although the difference between a cheap B&B and an expensive hostel isn't huge) and the chance to meet other travellers. The disadvantages are that you usually sleep in bunks in single-sex dormitories and may find the atmosphere somewhat institutional – although things are more relaxed than they used to be, partly in response to the success of the independent hostels.

London itself currently has seven YHA hostels, but they're very crowded in summer. An eighth is out in Epping Forest. At a push you could even try the Windsor hostel (for more on Windsor & Eton see the Excursions chapter). They all take advance bookings by phone (if you pay by Visa or MasterCard). They also hold some beds for those who wander in on the day, but come early and be prepared to queue. All but one offer 24 hour access and all have a bureau de change. Most have facilities for self-catering and some offer cheap meals. Adults will pay £15 to £19.75, juniors £12.80 to £16.55.

The excellent *City of London YHA* (☎ 236 4965; fax 236 7681), 36 Carter Lane EC4 (tube: St Paul's; Map 6), is virtually next door to St Paul's Cathedral in a pleasantly restored building which was the cathedral choir's school. Rooms are mainly four, three or two beds and only two are en suite. There's a licensed cafeteria but no kitchen. Rates vary from £16 to £22.75, depending on the room (£12.50 to £19.15 for juniors). This part of town is pretty quiet outside working hours.

Earl's Court (☎ 373 7083; fax 835 2034), 38 Bolton Gardens SW5 (tube: Earl's Court; Map 8), is a Victorian town house in a tacky, though lively, part of town. Rooms are mainly 10-bed dorms with communal showers, although there's one triple and five family rooms. This is not the best equipped of the hostels but there's a café and kitchen. Rates are £18/15.80.

Hampstead Heath (☎ 0181-458 9054; fax 0181-209 0546), 4 Wellgarth Rd NW11 (tube: Golders Green; Map 11), is in a beautiful setting with a well-kept garden, although it's rather isolated. The dorms are comfortable, and each room has a washbasin. There's a rather average, though licensed, café and a kitchen. Rates are £15/12.80.

Holland House (☎ 937 0748; fax 376 0667), Holland Walk, Kensington W8 (tube: High St Kensington; Map 8), has a great location built around the remains of a Jacobean mansion in the middle of Holland Park. It's large, very busy and rather institutional, but the position can't be beaten. There's a café and kitchen. Rates are £18/15.80.

Right in the centre of town, *Oxford St* (☎ 734 1618; fax 734 1657), 14-18 Noel St W1 (tube: Oxford Circus; Map 3), is the most basic of the London hostels, with a large kitchen but no meals. Rates are £18/14.65. There are only 89 beds so book ahead.

St Pancras International (☎ 248 6547; fax 236 7681), Euston Rd N1 (tube: King's Cross, St Pancras; Map 5), is London's newest hostel. The area isn't great, although it's certainly convenient if you want to head east or north afterwards. The hostel itself is a state-of-the-art affair, with kitchen, restaurant, lockers, cycle shed and lounge. Rates are £20.50/17.20.

Rotherhithe (☎ 232 2114; fax 237 2919), Salter Rd SE16 (tube: Rotherhithe; Map 7), is a highly recommended purpose-built hostel. Unfortunately, it's a bit far out and the area isn't great, although transport is reasonable. Rooms are mainly six-bed, with some fours and a few doubles; all have attached bathroom. There's a licensed restaurant as well as kitchen facilities. B&B rates are £19.75/16.55. Six rooms are specially adapted for disabled visitors.

Epping Forest (☎ & fax 0181-508 5161), High Beach, Loughton, Essex (tube: Loughton), is over 10 miles from central London and a good two mile walk from the nearest tube station, so it's only worth considering if all else is full. Rates are £6.75/4.60 (but allow for the tube fares). There's a small shop at the hostel. If you're staying out here it's worth noting that as well as having the forest on your doorstep you'll be well positioned for visiting Waltham Abbey and Queen Elizabeth's Hunting Lodge, a fine half-timbered building in Chingford.

Even further out but still worth remembering is the hostel at *Windsor* (☎ 01875-861710; fax 01753-832100), Edgeworth House, Mill Lane (station: Windsor & Eton Central), which is 18 miles from central London but only 10 miles from Heathrow. Housed in a Queen Anne building with a fine garden, the hostel has its own kitchen. Beds cost £9.10/6.15, mainly in nine-bed dorms. Reception is closed from 10 am to 1 pm.

Independent Hostels

London's independent hostels tend to be more relaxed and cheaper than the YHA places although standards are more hit and miss; expect to pay around £10 per night in a basic bunkroom. Like the YHA hostels they're great places to meet other travellers.

In terms of facilities, most hostels don't vary much. Most have three or four small bunk beds jammed into a room, a small kitchen and some kind of lounge. Some have budget restaurants and a bar. Problems with theft are relatively unusual, but be careful with your possessions and deposit your valuables in the office safe. In the past, some hostels have had an irresponsible attitude to fire safety – check that fire escapes are accessible.

Apart from noise levels, safety and cleanliness, the most important variable is the atmosphere. This can change by the week, as to some extent it depends on the people who are staying. If you're not happy with the first place you try, move on quickly.

Most private hostels are in Earl's Court (SW5), hence its bustling backpacker scene, but there are also some in Paddington and Bayswater (W2), Notting Hill and Holland Park (W11), Bloomsbury (WC1), Pimlico (SW1), Battersea (SW8) and Southwark (SE1). With the possible exceptions of Notting Hill, Holland Park, Bloomsbury and bits of Bayswater, all these areas are pretty seedy but they're also quite central and well served by public transport.

Notting Hill The *Palace Hotel* (☎ 221 5628; fax 243 8157), 31 Palace Court W2 (tube: Notting Hill Gate; Map 9), has dorm beds for £12. It has a pleasant, convenient location and isn't quite as run down and manic as some places.

The *London Independent Hostel* (☎ 229 4238), 41 Holland Park W11 (tube: Holland Park; Map 9), is well positioned on an elegant street. It's also good value, with dorms for £8, quads for £9, triples for £10, and doubles for £11 per person.

Paddington & Bayswater The friendly *Quest Hotel* (☎ 229 7782; fax 727 8106), 45 Queensborough Terrace W2 (tube: Bayswater; Map 9), is just around the corner from the Queensway action and a minute from Hyde Park, but it gets pretty crowded. There are kitchen facilities and a pool table. Dorm beds are £11.50 and £12.50; a few beds are available on a weekly basis for about £2 a night less.

Next door, the *Royal Hotel* (☎ 229 7225), 43 Queensborough Terrace, is much like many other hostels, but does try not to overcrowd the rooms. As a result, many people stay for quite long periods. A very basic double is £10 per person, and quads are £9 per person.

Earl's Court The relaxed, friendly *Curzon House Hotel* (☎ 581 2116; fax 835 1319), 58 Courtfield Gardens SW5 (tube: Gloucester Rd; Map 8), is one of the better private hostels. Dorms are £13 per person, singles/doubles with facilities are £23/36.

The *Chelsea Hotel* (☎ 244 6892; fax 244 6891), 33 Earl's Court Square SW5 (tube: Earl's Court; Map 8), is a classic hostel, with hundreds of cheery backpackers wandering around. They have some good-value singles and doubles as well as dorms. A dorm bed is £12, a twin is £35 to £40 and a single is £25. The restaurant offers basic meals.

Regency Court Hotel (☎ 244 6615), 14 Penywern Rd SW5 (tube: Earl's Court; Map 8), is in need of renovation and some travellers don't care for it. Dorms are £10, doubles £20, triples £40 and quads £50. A better bet is *Windsor House* (☎ 373 9087) next door at No 12. A dorm bed is £10, a single £28, a double £38 and a triple £48, all including breakfast.

The *Court Hotels* (tube: Earl's Court; Map 8), at 194-196 Earl's Court Rd SW5 (☎ 373 0027) and 17-19 Kempsford Gardens (☎ 373 2174; fax 912 9500), are under Australasian management and have well-equipped kitchens and a TV in most rooms. Dorm beds cost £11, singles/doubles are £21/24. Weekly rates are available.

Pimlico The *Victoria Hotel* (☎ 834 3077; fax 932 0693), 71 Belgrave Rd SW1 (tube: Victoria; Map 4), is a 15 minute walk from Victoria station and has been criticised for being overcrowded and poorly maintained. Still, it may be worth considering if you arrive late, or have to leave early in the morning. Reception is open 24 hours. Beds are around £14.

Bloomsbury The slightly shambolic *Museum Inn* (☎ 580 5360; fax 636 7948), 27 Montague St WC1 (tube: Russell Square or Tottenham Court Rd; Map 5), has an excellent position opposite the British Museum. It has a small kitchen and lounge, and a few rooms have colour TVs. A basic breakfast is included in the price: £17 per person in the one twin; £15 in a four bed dorm; £14 in a 10 bed dorm.

The *International Students House* (☎ 631 8300; fax 631 8315), 229 Great Portland St W1 (tube: Great Portland St; Map 5), is more like a university residential college. The single and double rooms are ordinary but clean, and there are excellent facilities and a friendly atmosphere – you don't have to be a student. It's open all year. B&B ranges from £27.50 for a single to £9.99 for a dorm. Book in advance.

Southwark *St Christopher's Inn* (☎ 407 1856), 121 Borough High St SE1 (tube: London Bridge), is conveniently positioned if you want to explore up-and-coming south London, but attracts a lot of long-stay tenants; you'll need to book ahead in summer. Beds in eight-bed dorms cost £10 including continental breakfast; it's £14 in a three bed dorm. There's a small concrete veranda and a lounge. St Christopher's is attached to a pub and claims to be run by 'travellers who know how to party'.

Chelsea The *New Ark Backpackers Flotel* (☎ 720 9496), Adrenalin Village, Queenstown Rd SW8 (tube: Sloane Square; Maps 2 & 14), comes recommended as 'a very funky place' and is certainly different. A converted lighter (flat-bottomed barge) sleeps up to 40 people in four-bunk cabins with each bunk costing just £12 a night. There's a 24 hour bar and quayside barbecues. What's more, you're within heart-stopping distance of the Chelsea Wharf Tower with its bungee-jumping opportunities. But bear in mind that the cabins are small and cramped, without proper doors, so they wouldn't suit anyone wanting peace and quiet.

University Accommodation

University halls of residence are let to non-students during the holidays, usually from the end of June to mid-September. They're a bit more expensive than the youth hostels, but you usually get a single room (there are a few doubles) with shared facilities, plus breakfast.

University catering is usually reasonable and includes bars, self-service cafés, takeaways and restaurants. Full-board, half-board, B&B and self-catering options are available.

The London School of Economics (Room B508, LSE, Houghton St WC2A 2AE) lets several of its halls at Easter and summer. *Carr Saunders Hall* (☎ 323 9712; fax 580 4718), 18-24 Fitzroy St W1 (tube: Warren St; Map 5), is not in the greatest part of town, but is near Oxford St and so fairly central. It's open over Christmas, Easter and July/August; singles/doubles with full breakfast are £17/31 over Easter, £22.50/48 in the summer. Self-catering flats of different sizes are also available on a weekly basis in the summer only, ranging from £238 for a two person flat to £539 for five people. The central *High Holborn* (☎ 379 5589; fax 379 5640), 178 High Holborn WC1 (tube: Holborn; Map 3), has self-catering singles/doubles for £27/45, with continental breakfast, in the summer only. *Passfield Hall* (☎ 387 3584; fax 387 4364), Endsleigh Place WC1 (tube: Euston; Map 5), consists of 10 late-Georgian houses in the heart of Bloomsbury. B&B costs £18/38/51 a single/double/triple. Similar rates apply at *Rosebery Avenue Hall* (☎ 278 3251; fax 278 2068), 90 Rosebery Ave EC1 (tube: Angel; Map 5).

The *Imperial College of Science & Technology* (☎ 594 9494; fax 594 9505), 15 Prince's Gardens SW7 (tube: South Kensington; Map 8), is brilliantly positioned near the South Kensington museums. It's open Easter and summer, and B&B costs £26.50/42.

Regent's College (☎ 487 7483; fax 487 7524), Inner Circle, Regent's Park NW1 (tube: Baker St; Map 2), is a converted Regency manor right in the middle of beautiful Regent's Park, convenient for Camden and central London. It's open over Christmas and from May to September. Singles/doubles cost £25/36.

John Adams Hall (☎ 387 4086; fax 383 0164), 15-23 Endsleigh St WC1 (tube: Euston; Map 5), is a row of Georgian houses with its own swimming pool. It's open Christmas, Easter and summer, and B&B costs from £20/34 a single/double.

King's Campus Vacation Bureau (☎ 351 6011; fax 352 7376), 552 Kings Rd SW10 0UA (tube: Fulham Broadway), administers bookings for several central King's College residence halls. The *Hampstead Campus* (☎ 435 3564; fax 431 4402), at Kidderpore Ave NW3 (tube: Finchley Rd; Map 11), has 392 beds from £12.80/22.30 a single/double. It's open from June to September.

Finsbury Residences (☎ 477 8811; fax 477 8810), Bastwick St EC1 (tube: Angel/Old Street; Map 2), comprises two modern halls belonging to City University. Bed and continental breakfast is £19.50 per person, £97.50 a week. It's open over Christmas, Easter and the summer. Evening meals are available on request.

University of Westminster (☎ 911 5000), 35 Marylebone Rd NW1 (tube: Baker St; Map 2), has beds in singles or doubles for £18.50 per person under 26, £22.50 over 26. Continental breakfast is sometimes available for another £3.

YMCAs

The National Council for YMCAs (☎ 0181-520 5599) can supply you with a list of all their London hostels, where rooms cost from £20/35 a single/double. The main ones to know about are the *Barbican* (☎ 628 0697), 2 Fann St EC2 (tube: Barbican; Map 6), with 240 beds; the *London City Hostel* (☎ 628 8832), 8 Errol St EC1 (tube: Barbican; Map 6), with 111 beds; and the *Central Club* (☎ 636 7512), 16 Great Russell St WC1 (tube: Tottenham Court Rd; Map 5), with 240 beds.

Bed & Breakfasts (B&Bs) & Guesthouses

B&Bs are a great British institution and the cheapest private accommodation around. At the bottom end you get a bedroom in a private house, a shared bathroom and an enormous cooked breakfast (juice, cereal, bacon, eggs, sausage, baked beans and toast). Small B&Bs may have just one room to let, and you can really feel like a guest of the family. They're often excellent value, although if you're after something around the £18 to £20 mark you'll probably have to settle for something way out of town or pretty crummy.

In central London most cheaper accommodation is in guesthouses, often just large converted houses with half a dozen rooms which tend to be less personal than B&Bs. They range from £30 to £60 a night, depending on the quality of the food and accommodation. Double rooms often have two single beds (twins) rather than a double bed, so you don't have to be cuddling up to share a room.

Bloomsbury (WC1), Bayswater (W2), Paddington (W2), Pimlico (SW1) and Earl's Court (SW5) are the main centres for budget hotels.

In this section you'll find B&Bs/guesthouses where you can expect to pay £25/30 for basic singles/doubles without a bathroom, or £30/40 with a bathroom. You'll be lucky to find anything really pleasant for much less than £35/50 (for a better standard see Places to Stay – Middle).

Outside the high season, prices are often negotiable; don't be afraid to ask for the 'best' price and for a discount if you're staying more than a couple of nights or don't want a cooked breakfast. In July, August and September prices can jump by 25% or more, and it's definitely worth phoning ahead to book. Many of the cheapies don't take credit cards.

Some of the cheapest places are occupied by homeless families who are being 'temporarily' housed by local authorities. They're not in the market for foreign visitors at all...which is one reason why it may be wise to stick with tourist board-approved places.

Paddington Paddington is a pretty seedy area, and although there are lots of cheap hotels, single women in particular will probably feel more comfortable elsewhere. Nevertheless, it's convenient and there are a few decent places at decent prices.

Right in the centre of the action, *Norfolk Court & St David's Hotel* (☎ 723 4963; fax 402 9061), 16 Norfolk Square W2 (tube: Paddington; Map 9), is a clean, comfortable, friendly place with the usual out-of-control decor. Basic singles/doubles have wash-basin, colour TV and telephone and cost £30/46. With shower and toilet, prices jump to £56 for a double. A big plus in summer is Norfolk Square itself, just outside and a small oasis of greenery. The *Camelot Hotel* (☎ 723 9118; fax 402 3412) at No 45 is another good choice but slightly more expensive. Should these be full, the square is ringed with similar places.

Bayswater Bayswater is extremely convenient and, as a result, can feel as if it's under constant invasion. Some of the streets immediately to the west of Queensway – which has an excellent selection of restaurants – are depressingly run down.

Sass House Hotel (☎ 262 2325; fax 262 0889), 11 Craven Terrace W2 (tube: Lancaster Gate; Map 9), is fairly threadbare but singles/doubles with continental breakfast cost from £22/28.

One of Bayswater's best options is the *Garden Court Hotel* (☎ 229 2553; fax 727 2749), 30 Kensington Gardens Square W2 (tube: Bayswater; Map 9). It's a well-run, well-maintained family hotel, with well-equipped rooms with telephone and TV. Singles/doubles without bathroom are £32/48, with bathroom £45/66. You can save a couple of pounds by forgoing breakfast, although these are actually good value.

Manor Court Hotel (☎ 729 3361; fax 229 2875), 7 Clanricarde Gardens W2 (tube: Queensway; Map 9), is off Bayswater Rd – a good location. It may not be spectacular, but you could do worse for the money. Singles with private showers are from £30, doubles with private bathroom from £45.

Earl's Court For years Earl's Court has been a hang-out for refugees from the empire's far-flung corners. These days Africans, Arabs and Indians are more conspicuous than Australians but most people seem to be in transit, and it shows in the grubby, unloved streets (although some smartening up of the side streets could see things improve). It's not really within walking distance of many places you'll want to be, but Earl's Court tube is a busy interchange, so getting around is a cinch.

The *St Simeon* (☎ 373 0505; fax 589 6412), 38 Harrington Gardens SW7 (tube: Gloucester Rd; Map 8), is within walking distance of the South Kensington museums and has dorms as well as singles and doubles. Prices start at around £18 per person but seem to be negotiable.

The *Boka Hotel* (☎ 370 1388), 33 Eardley Crescent SW5 (tube: Earl's Court; Map 8), is a relaxed place where guests have use of a kitchen. Singles/doubles start at £25/40 (mostly without bathroom) and there's also a dorm with beds from £16.

Pimlico & Victoria This may not be the most attractive part of London, but you'll be very close to the action and, despite the large transient population, the quality of the hotels is reasonably good. In general the cheap hotels (around £30 per person) are better value than their Earl's Court counterparts.

If only all London's budget hotels were like the *Luna-Simone Hotel* (☎ 834 5897; fax 828 2474), 47 Belgrave Rd SW1 (tube: Victoria; Map 4), which is central, spotlessly clean, comfortable and without offensive decor. Singles/doubles without bathroom are from £28/50; a double with bathroom is £65.

Facilities vary from room to room, but a full English breakfast is included. There are free storage facilities if you want to leave bags while you go travelling.

The *Brindle House Hotel* (☎ 828 0057; fax 931 8805), 1 Warwick Place North SW1 (tube: Victoria; Map 4), is in an old building off the main thoroughfares. Although the decor is a mess, the light, clean rooms are more pleasant than the foyer suggests. Singles are £30 (shared facilities), doubles are £42/38 (with/without facilities).

The *Romany House Hotel* (☎ 834 5553; fax 834 0495), 35 Longmoore St SW1 (tube: Victoria; Map 4), is pleasingly old-fashioned, in line with a history that includes tales of highwaymen. You'll share a bathroom but breakfasts are good and rooms cost from £25/35.

Bloomsbury Bloomsbury is a peculiar mix of London University, British Museum, beautiful squares, Georgian architecture, traffic, office workers, students and tourists – and it's very convenient, especially for the West End.

The *Hotel Cavendish* (☎ 636 9079), at 75 Gower St (Map 5), and the *Jesmond Hotel* (☎ 636 3199; fax 580 3609), at No 63, are fairly basic, but clean and entirely adequate, with singles/doubles for £28/38 including breakfast. You share a bathroom, although all rooms have a washbasin. The nearest tube is Goodge St.

The *Repton Hotel* (☎ 436 4922; fax 636 7045), 31 Bedford Place WC1 (tube: Russell Square; Map 5), is pretty good value considering that Bedford Place isn't nearly as busy as Gower St. Singles/doubles with TV and telephone are £48/63. There's also a dorm with six beds at £15 a head.

Chelsea & Kensington Real cheapies are at a premium in these trendy, expensive areas.

The *Magnolia Hotel* (☎ 352 0187; fax 352 3610), 104-5 Oakley St SW3 (tube: South Kensington; Map 8), has a good position and is remarkably good value. The rooms, all with colour TV, are pleasant, but try and get one at the back, away from traffic noise. Singles are from £35, doubles from £45 without bathroom and £60 with bathroom. Triples are £60. The only drawback is the hike to the tube.

PLACES TO STAY – MIDDLE

The better B&Bs are often in beautiful old buildings and some have private bathrooms with showers or baths. Guesthouses and small hotels are more likely to have private bathrooms and TVs but tend to be less personal. Good showers continue to be elusive.

Places in this section offer singles/doubles for between £40/60 and £60/70. Before booking accommodation in this category (or top end), it's worth checking whether you can get a better deal by booking a package including transport from home.

Notting Hill

Notting Hill has become increasingly trendy and expensive over the last few years, but is still a great place to stay, with several interesting bars and restaurants and Portobello Rd Market at the weekend.

Holland Park Hotel (☎ 792 0216; fax 727 8166), 6 Ladbroke Terrace W11 (tube: Notting Hill Gate; Map 9), has a great position on a quiet street near Holland Park and the hubbub of Notting Hill. The rooms are very pleasant and it's particularly good value; singles/doubles without bathroom are £40/54, with bathroom £54/72.

At the south end of Portobello Rd, the *Gate Hotel* (☎ 221 2403; fax 221 9128), 6 Portobello Rd W11 (tube: Notting Hill Gate; Map 9), is an old town house with classic frilly English decor and lovely hanging baskets. Singles/doubles, all with bathroom, are from £40/65.

Paddington & Bayswater

Paddington isn't the most inspiring place to stay but it is very handy if you're heading for the West Country afterwards. Bayswater can be more appealing, provided you pick your street carefully.

Sussex Gardens in Paddington is lined with small hotels but unfortunately it's also a major traffic route. The *Balmoral House*

PAT YALE

PAT YALE

PAT YALE

JUDI SCHIFF

A	B
C	D

A: The Dickens Inn at St Katherine's Dock
B: Bag o'Nails near Victoria – how names change over the centuries!
C: The Three Kings in Clerkenwell – papier – mâché paradise
D: Caffé Uno

DOUG McKINLAY

PAT YALE

JUDI SCHIFF

Left: Michelin Building & Bibendum Restaurant, Fulham Road
Right: Brick Lane shop, East End
Bottom: The Shakespeare's Head, Carnaby Street

Hotel (☎ 723 7445; fax 402 0118), at No 156 (tube: Paddington; Map 9), is immaculate and very comfortable, with TV in all rooms. Singles with/without bathroom cost £40/35, doubles with facilities cost £60 (breakfast extra). All rooms at the clean, quiet *Europa House Hotel* (☎ 723 7343; fax 224 9331) at No 151 (Map 9) come with bathroom, TV and telephone. Singles/doubles cost £45/60.

The *Oxford Hotel* (☎ 402 6860; fax 706 4318), 13 Craven Terrace W2 (tube: Lancaster Gate; Map 9), is reasonable value; singles and doubles with TV cost £65 which reduces to £48 if you rent for eight days.

Earl's Court

Mid-range places in Earl's Court are generally perfectly acceptable; if the one you've set your heart on is full, there will be plenty more nearby.

The *Shellbourne Hotel* (☎ 373 5161; fax 373 9824), 1 Lexham Gardens W8 (tube: Gloucester Rd; Map 8), is tatty but clean, and the rooms are well equipped for their price, complete with TVs, showers and direct-dial telephones. Singles/doubles/triples with full breakfast are £35/55/65.

York House Hotel (☎ 373 7519; fax 370 4641), 27 Philbeach Gardens SW5 (tube: Earl's Court; Map 8), is relatively cheap, but you get what you pay for. The rooms are basic, although some have showers. Singles/doubles without bath are £28/45; doubles/triples with bath are £62/75.

The pleasant *London Town Hotel* (☎ 370 4356; fax 370 7923), 15 Penywern Rd SW5 (tube: Earl's Court; Map 8), has singles/doubles with bathroom and TV from £38/62.

The unpretentious *Merlyn Court Hotel* (☎ 370 1640; fax 370 4986), 2 Barkston Gardens SW5 (tube: Earl's Court; Map 8), has a good atmosphere. Clean, small singles/doubles with bathroom cost £50/55; without they're £25/35. Triples and quads with/without bathroom are £65/70.

West End

Cheapies in the town centre are like gold dust and you usually get more for your money elsewhere.

Glynne Court Hotel (☎ 262 4344; fax 724 2071), 41 Great Cumberland Place W1 (tube: Marble Arch), is fairly typical. Singles/doubles are from £45/50, but you only get a continental breakfast. All rooms have TV and telephone.

Ripe for a makeover but pretty cheap for its position right beside Piccadilly Circus is the *Regent Palace Hotel* (☎ 734 7000; fax 734 6435; Map 3), where rooms without bath or breakfast start at £49/75 a single/double.

Pimlico & Victoria

If you can afford to pay a bit more, Pimlico is more appealing than Earl's Court, with some good-value places to stay. Victoria is extremely convenient transportwise, although it's not the most characterful quarter of town and can be noisy.

The *Hamilton House Hotel* (☎ 821 7113; fax 630 0806), 60 Warwick Way SW1 (tube: Victoria; Map 4), has singles/doubles with private bathroom, TV and telephone for £48/58. The doubles are certainly worth considering. At No 142, the *Windermere Hotel* (☎ 834 5163; fax 630 8831; Map 4) is another good choice with small, clean rooms from £34/48 and its own restaurant.

The *Winchester Hotel* (☎ 828 2972; fax 828 5191), 17 Belgrave Rd SW1 (tube: Victoria; Map 4), is clean, comfortable and welcoming. For the area it's pretty good value. Doubles and twins with private bathroom, TV and phone cost £65.

The *Woodville* (☎ 730 1048; fax 730 2574), 107 Ebury St SW1 (tube: Victoria; Map 4), has 12 simple but clean and comfortable rooms with shared bathroom and use of a kitchen. Singles/doubles cost £38/58. It's a friendly, good-value place owned by the same people who run the slightly more expensive *Morgan House* (☎ 730 2384; fax 730 8842) at 120 Ebury St (Map 4).

Camden

At 78 Albert St NW1, *Peter & Suzy Bell* (☎ 387 6813; fax 387 1704; Map 10) offer three comfortable double rooms in a quiet street well placed for exploring Camden

Market. B&B costs £70 (£40 for single occupancy).

Bloomsbury

Tucked away in Cartwright Gardens to the north of Russell Square you'll find some of London's most comfortable, attractive and best-value hotels within walking distance of the West End (tube: Russell Square). They're on a crescent around a leafy garden, and are certainly worth it if you can afford them. *Jenkin's Hotel* (☎ 387 2067; fax 383 3139), at No 45 (Map 5), has attractive, comfortable rooms with style. All have washbasin, TV, telephone and fridge, and prices include an English breakfast. Singles/doubles are £45/55; doubles with private facilities are £65. Guests can even use the tennis courts in the gardens across the road. The bigger *Crescent Hotel* (☎ 387 1515; fax 383 2054), at No 49 (Map 5), is a high-standard family-owned operation, with prices more or less the same as Jenkin's. The nearby *Euro Hotel* (☎ 387 4321; fax 383 5044) and *George Hotel* (☎ 387 8777; fax 387 8666) are also good and cost about the same.

A row of places along Gower St (tube: Goodge St or Euston Square) are also pretty fair value but not all of them have double-glazing, which is essential if you're sensitive to traffic noise. Insist on one of the back rooms overlooking the garden, which are the nicest anyway. The *Arran House Hotel* (☎ 636 2186; fax 436 5328), at No 77 (Map 5), is friendly and welcoming, with a great garden and laundry facilities. Singles range from £31 to £41 (with shower and toilet), doubles from £46 to £61, and there are also triples and quads. Their front rooms are sound-proofed, and all have colour TV and telephone.

The family-run *St Margaret's Hotel* (☎ 636 4277; fax 323 3066), 26 Bedford Place WC1B (tube: Russell Square or Holborn; Map 5), is in a classic Bloomsbury town house. It's not particularly inspiring but it is clean and all rooms have TV and telephone. Singles/doubles (some with private bathroom) are £42.50/54.50. Overall it's not bad value.

The *Ruskin Hotel* (☎ 636 7388), 23 Montague St WC1, and its nearby sister hotel *Haddon Hall Hotel* (☎ 636 2474; fax 580 4527), 39 Bedford Place WC1 (tube: Russell Square or Holborn), are fairly basic places with ordinary decor, but the locations are good and they're entirely adequate. Doubles with bathroom are £67; singles/doubles without are £39/55.

The *Royal National Hotel* (☎ 636 8401; fax 837 4653), Woburn Place WC1 (tube: Russell Square; Map 5), has just been refurbished and now offers clean, modern rooms for £62/75 a single/double.

Chelsea & Kensington

These classy neighbourhoods offer easy access to the museums and some of London's best shops.

The *Swiss House Hotel* (☎ 373 2769; fax 373 9383), 171 Old Brompton Rd (tube: Gloucester Rd; Map 8), is a clean, good-value hotel, nudging Earl's Court. Singles/doubles without bathroom are from £36/68; doubles with shower are £68, which is rather a lot since you only get continental breakfast. Still, rooms do have TV and direct-dial phone.

The *Vicarage Private Hotel* (☎ 229 4030; fax 792 5989), 10 Vicarage Gate W8 (tube: High St Kensington; Map 8), is well placed near Hyde Park and between Notting Hill and Kensington. It's pleasant and well kept, with good showers and some charm. Singles/doubles are £38/60. Since it's recommended in several guidebooks you have to book ahead. *Abbey House* (☎ 727 2594), 11 Vicarage Gate, is a particularly good-value small hotel which modestly describes itself as a B&B. The decor is decent and the welcome warm. Singles/doubles are £38/60. Again, booking is recommended.

Hampstead

Classy Hampstead retains a village atmosphere. Although it can feel cut off from central London, it's still handy by tube and you get the added bonus of the heath.

La Gaffe (☎ 794 7526; fax 794 7592), 107 Heath St NW3 (tube: Hampstead; Map 11), is a small, rather eccentric, but nonetheless comfortable hotel in an 18th century cottage. The Italian restaurant here has been going forever. Singles/doubles with bathroom are from £50/75.

The *Sandringham Hotel* (☎ 435 1569), 3 Holford Rd NW3 (tube: Hampstead; Map 11), is a pleasing small hotel whose top-floor rooms look over the city. Breakfasts have an American flavour, reflecting the owners' origins. If you call room service in the evening what you'll get will probably come from La Gaffe. Singles/doubles cost from £65/90.

Greenwich

Although it's a little cut off from the centre of the action, Greenwich is another very pleasant part of town with a village feel; Greenwich Park and Blackheath are distinct pluses.

The *Ibis Hotel* (☎ 0181-305 1177; fax 0181-858 7139), 30 Stockwell St SE10 (station: Greenwich; Map 12), is one of the new brand of standardised modern hotels where all rooms cost the same regardless of whether one or two people occupy them – good for couples but a real downer for solos. Here they cost £52 and you could certainly do a lot worse. There's plenty of parking and a Café Rouge is attached.

The Airports

Heathrow and Gatwick in particular have masses of accommodation, most of it pretty undistinguished and pricey – do yourself a favour and head on into town if you possibly can. But if you're arriving late or leaving early you may need to stop over, in which case the Ibis hotels are worth knowing about.

The *London Heathrow Ibis* (☎ 0181-759 4888), 112-114 Bath Rd, Hayes, Middlesex, charges £53 for a room, with a coach link to Terminals 1, 2 and 3. The *London Gatwick Skylodge* (☎ 01239-611762), London Rd, Lowfield Heath, Crawley, Sussex, has rooms for £38. The *Luton Airport Ibis* (☎ 01582-424 488), Spittlesea Rd, Luton, has rooms for £42. These prices are the same regardless of whether one or two people occupy the room.

PLACES TO STAY – TOP END

The term 'hotel' covers all sorts of accommodation, from pleasant, small places not that different from B&Bs to the poshest, most expensive places frequented by the business community and the hyper-wealthy. The very best hotels are magnificent places, often with restaurants to match.

Some hotels in large converted houses are virtually indistinguishable from guesthouses. Others are big, old-style, residential hotels. More purpose-built chain hotels are also appearing in the city centre. Most depend on business trade and offer competitive weekend rates to attract tourists.

Good-quality hotels are scattered around, but there are some excellent places in Notting Hill, Marble Arch, the West End and Bloomsbury. In this section you'll find the pricier hotels where doubles cost upwards of £75.

Notting Hill

Hillgate Hotel (☎ 221 3433; fax 229 4808), 6 Pembridge Gardens W2 (tube: Notting Hill Gate; Map 9), has a great position in a quiet street and rooms with all the facilities you'd expect in a good hotel. Singles/doubles are £70/94. Along the road at No 20, *Abbey Court* (☎ 221 7518; fax 792 0858) has individually decorated rooms, some with fine views over the rooftops. Snack meals are available throughout the day. Singles/doubles cost from £88/130.

The *Portobello* (☎ 727 2777; fax 792 9641), 22 Stanley Gardens W11 (tube: Notting Hill Gate; Map 9), is a beautifully appointed place in a great location. It's not cheap but most people think the £80/140 money well spent. Nearby at 34 Pembridge Gardens W2 is the *Pembridge Court Hotel* (☎ 229 9977; fax 727 4982), another handily located and immaculately kept hotel which will especially suit anyone missing their cat – Spencer and Churchill, the resident gingers, are something of a local institution. Once again it's not cheap, especially if you're travelling alone, with singles/doubles from £110/135.

Portobello Gold (☎ 460 4910; fax 460 4911), 95 Portobello Rd W11 (tube: Notting Hill Gate; Map 9), was the first hotel in London to offer a computer with email link-up in every room. There's a classy ground-floor restaurant and a pleasing 1st floor bar. Singles/doubles are from £45/55 without bath, £60/80 with bath.

Paddington & Bayswater

The *Gresham Hotel* (☎ 402 2920; fax 402 3137), 116 Sussex Gardens W2 (tube: Paddington; Map 9), is a stylish, small hotel with well-equipped rooms. Expect to pay £60/75 a single/double.

The *Inverness Court Hotel* (☎ 229 1444; fax 706 4240), Inverness Terrace W2 (tube: Queensway; Map 9), would make a good choice for the history-lover; it was built by a Victorian gentleman for his actress mistress and comes complete with a private theatre, now the cocktail bar. Some bedrooms overlook Hyde Park. Singles/doubles cost £70/90.

Earl's Court

Midway between Kensington and Earl's Court, the *Amber Hotel* (☎ 373 8666; fax 835 1194), 101 Lexham Gardens W8 (tube: Earl's Court; Map 9), is pretty good value for its position, with fully equipped rooms for £75/95 in July/August. Across the road, the *London Lodge Hotel* (☎ 244 8444; fax 373 6661), at No 134 (Map 9), has fully equipped rooms and does an excellent breakfast from £75/85 a single/double.

The nameless B&B at *47 Warwick Gardens* (☎ & fax 603 7614) offers just three comfortable double rooms in a basement opening onto a patio for £75 each. It's a homely place, not too far from Earl's Court tube, but you have to stay at least two nights and must book ahead.

Victoria

Refurbished and pricier than it used to be, the *Rubens* (☎ 834 6600; fax 828 5401), 39 Buckingham Palace Rd SW1 (tube: Victoria; Map 4), has a brilliant position overlooking the walls of Buckingham Palace. Singles/doubles, all with private bath, start at £110/135 without breakfast. The Rubens is popular with groups.

Knightsbridge, Chelsea & Kensington

Hotel 167 (☎ 373 0672; fax 373 3360), 167 Old Brompton Rd SW5 (tube: Gloucester Rd; Map 8), is small, stylish and immaculately kept, and has (for England) an unusually uncluttered and attractive decor. All rooms have private bathroom. Singles are from £65, doubles range from £82 to £90.

For really stylish luxury you could hardly better *Blakes* (☎ 370 6701; fax 373 0442), 33 Roland Gardens SW7 (tube: Gloucester Rd), five Victorian houses knocked into one and decked out with four-posters and antiques on stripped floorboards. Such comfort doesn't come cheap, of course; you're looking at from £150/175 a single/ double.

Two excellent places on Sumner Place fail to hang out signs. There's not much to distinguish them, but *Five Sumner Place* (☎ 584 7586; fax 823 9962), 5 Sumner Place SW7 (tube: South Kensington; Map 8), has won several awards and is the cheaper. The rooms are comfortable and well equipped (all have bathroom, TV, phone, drinks cabinet and more) and there's an attractive conservatory and garden. Singles start at £81, doubles at £111.

Hotel Number Sixteen (☎ 589 5232; fax 584 8615), at No 16 (Map 8), shares all the attributes of No 5. Singles range from £80 to £105, doubles from £140 to £170, but ask about weekend specials from £50 per person.

Lovers of Victoriana might want to try the *Gore* (☎ 584 6601; fax 589 8127), 189 Queen's Gate SW7 (tube: Gloucester Rd), where aspidistras run wild amid thousands of fading prints and Turkish carpets. Some will love the antique-style bathrooms, but not all have actual baths. Singles/doubles cost from £111/156.

Annandale House Hotel (☎ 730 5051; fax 730 2727), 39 Sloane Gardens, Sloane Square SW1 (tube: Sloane Square; Map 8), is a discreet, traditional small hotel in a fashionable part of London – expect real linen napkins and tablecloths. Singles/doubles with phone and TV cost from £45/70.

Right in Knightsbridge, *Basil Street Hotel* (☎ 581 3311; fax 581 3693; tube: Knightsbridge) is a surprisingly unpretentious, antique-stuffed hideaway, perfectly placed for carrying back the shopping parcels. Singles/doubles start at £70/110 but a few still lack bathrooms.

West End

There are tremendous advantages to staying in the centre of town – as the real estate agents say, location, location and location. Unfortunately, such a privilege doesn't come cheap.

Right in the heart of London, *Hazlitt's* (☎ 434 1771; fax 439 1524), 6 Frith St, Soho Square W1V (tube: Tottenham Court Rd; Map 3), is one of London's finest hotels with efficient personal service. Built in 1718, it comprises three linked Georgian houses. All 23 rooms have names and are individually decorated with antique furniture and prints. Singles/doubles are from £127/162; booking is advisable.

The *Fielding Hotel* (☎ 836 8305; fax 836 8305), 4 Broad Court, Bow St WC2 (tube: Covent Garden; Map 3), is remarkably good value considering that it's in a pedestrian walk, almost opposite the Royal Opera House. The hotel looks like an old pub, but the rooms are clean and well run. Most have private bathroom, TVs and telephones. Singles/doubles are £65/85.

Wigmore Court Hotel (☎ 935 0928; fax 487 4254), 23 Gloucester Place, Portman Square W1 (tube: Marble Arch), has pretty horrible decor, although someone must love it. On the other hand, it's a well-organised place whose guests have access to a kitchen and self-service laundry. Well-equipped singles/doubles with bath are £45/79 in peak season, about 10% cheaper out of season. All in all, it's good value.

The small, comfortable *Edward Lear Hotel* (☎ 402 5401; fax 706 3766), 30 Seymour St W1 (tube: Marble Arch), was formerly the home of Victorian painter and poet Edward Lear. All rooms have TV, tea and coffee facilities and telephone. Singles/doubles without bathroom cost from £39.50/54.50, with bathroom £70/84.50.

Just behind the Wallace Collection and excellently placed for shopping, the luxurious *Durrants Hotel* (☎ 935 8131; fax 487 3510), George St W1 (tube: Marble Arch), is a large hotel that, amazingly, was once a country inn and still retains something of the feel of a gentleman's club. Comfortable singles/doubles with bathroom start at £90/108, but breakfast is extra.

Bryanston Court (☎ 262 3141; fax 262 7248), 55 Great Cumberland Place W1 (tube: Marble Arch), also has something of a club atmosphere, with leather armchairs and a formal style. It's particularly aimed at business people, and all rooms have private bathroom, TV and phone. It's expensive during the week at £73/90, but offers special weekend deals between December and February when doubles sink to £75.

Handy for Oxford St and the British Museum, the *Academy Hotel* (☎ 631 4115; fax 636 3442), 21 Gower St (tube: Goodge St; Map 2) is in a rather busy street, although double-glazing keeps the noise down. Rooms are pale and pretty, and there's a pleasant back garden. Singles/doubles cost from £90/115.

The big *Strand Palace* (☎ 836 8080; fax 836 2077), Strand WC2 (tube: Charing Cross; Map 3), went through a bad patch but has had some work done to improve things. Its position, close to Covent Garden, is excellent but the price tag (from £94/121 without breakfast) is still pretty steep. Look out for a package deal.

The City

The *Tower Thistle Hotel* (☎ 481 2575; fax 481 3799), St Katherine's Way E1 (tube: Tower Hill; Map 7), has a superb waterside position in St Katherine's Dock, right beside Tower Bridge and the Tower of London. It's not the prettiest building from the outside, but inside, of course, the views make up for a lot. B&B costs from £154/186 a single/double and there's plenty of parking space.

Wimbledon

It may be out on a limb but Wimbledon has a gem of a hotel in *Cannizaro House* (☎ 0181-879 1464; fax 879 7338), Westside, Wimbledon Common SW19 (tube: Wimbledon), a restored Georgian house with 46 comfortable rooms with all mod cons and individual decor. Prices start at £137/158 a single/double without breakfast. For peace and quiet, ask for a room overlooking Cannizaro Park rather than Wimbledon Common.

PLACES TO STAY – DELUXE

Some of central London's hotels are so venerable and luxurious they're tourist attractions in their own right. These are the places to come for hyper-comfortable bedrooms, and restaurants and bars which can compete with the best in town – although not necessarily on price! Despite their often old-world splendour all these places are geared for the needs of business travellers, so expect fax machines, modem connections, secretarial services – the whole ball game.

Claridges (☎ 629 8860; fax 499 2210), Brook St W1 (tube: Bond St; Map 2), is one of the greatest of London's five-star hotels, a leftover from a bygone era, where you could easily bump into the people who grace the pages of *Hello* magazine. The Art Deco suites were designed in 1929 and have log fires in winter. Expect to pay £258/348 for a single/double.

Another stunner of a five-star is *Brown's* (☎ 493 6020; fax 493 9381), 30 Albemarle St W1 (tube: Green Park; Map 3), which was originally created out of 11 houses. Not that you'd know that now, of course. Service is tip-top, and even the ladies' powder room (for once aptly named) is an experience.

London's most famous hotel, the *Ritz* (☎ 493 8181; fax 493 2687), 150 Piccadilly W1 (tube: Green Park; Maps 3 & 4), has a spectacular position overlooking Green Park. Rooms cost a staggering £253/306 a single/double for which you get all the luxury you would quite rightly expect. The Terrace Restaurant is decked out like a tart's boudoir but the food doesn't necessarily live up to the exorbitant prices.

The *Connaught* (☎ 499 7070; fax 495 3262), Carlos Place W1 (tube: Green Park), brushes aside fads and fashions, concentrating instead on a style appropriate to a hotel which has one of the best restaurants in London. This serves solid French and English cuisine with the dignified confidence that comes of having held onto a chef for a quarter of a century. The rooms are similarly old-fashioned in the grand way – which is not to say you won't have access to all the faxes and mod cons you require. Singles/doubles start at £233/311.

In a similar class is the *Savoy* (☎ 836 4343; fax 240 6040), Strand WC2 (tube: Charing Cross; Map 3), which stands on the site of the old Savoy Palace, burnt down during the Peasants' Revolt of 1381. The rooms here are so comfortable and have such great views that some people have been known to take up permanent residence. Some have Art Deco decor and all have modem connections and voice-mail phones. Rooms are £240/285 a single/double. Prices at the Savoy Grill reflect its largely corporate clientele but the Art Deco American Bar is worth frequenting for its cocktails. Or you could just drop by for tea in the capacious, chandeliered Thames Foyer (see boxed aside Time for Tea in the Places to Eat chapter).

There's more Art Deco on display in the ballroom at the *Park Lane Hotel* (☎ 499 6321; fax 499 1965), Piccadilly W1 (tube: Green Park; Map 4), another jazzy place which needs triple-glazing to keep the noise of the modern world at bay. Most rooms have been refurbished in a light, modern style but Sheraton has just taken it on board so more changes can be expected. Singles/doubles start at £200/217.

The *Waldorf* (☎ 836 2400; fax 836 7244), Aldwych WC2 (tube: Charing Cross; Map 3), is another grand oldie, glorying in an Edwardian splendour typified by the liveried doormen and the wonderful Palm Court

Lounge where tea dances take place at weekends. Singles/doubles start at £185/200 without breakfast.

You can't get more central than the *Hampshire* (☎ 839 9399; fax 930 8122), Leicester Square (tube: Leicester Square; Map 3). It's part of the Radisson Edwardian group, which has a number of luxury hotels scattered around London. The Hampshire tends to be full of rich, retired Americans and top-flight business people. Singles/doubles are £230/265.

Forget the braided uniforms and chandeliers – the *Halkin* (☎ 333 1000; fax 333 1100), 5 Halkin St SW1 (tube: Hyde Park Corner), is for business travellers of a minimalist bent. Bedrooms are wood-panelled and stylishly uncluttered; you press buttons to control the heating and doors, giving the rooms a space-age feel. Waiters strut about in Armani, which goes some way to explaining the £259 minimum price tag for a room.

Just as modern but rather less brash is the *Covent Garden Hotel* (☎ 806 1000; fax 806 1100), 10 Monmouth St WC2 (tube: Covent Garden), a newcomer which prefers to use antiques and beautiful fabrics to stake out its individuality. There's a bar, brasserie and café, and rooms start at £176/206.

SPECIALIST HOTELS

Gay Hotels

Philbeach Gardens SW5 (tube: Earl's Court; Map 8) is a pleasingly quiet yet central side street with a couple of hotels catering for a gay clientele. *Philbeach Hotel* (☎ 373 1244; fax 244 0149), at No 30, is a pleasant, well-decorated place, popular with males and females. There's a decent restaurant and bar and a nice garden. Rooms without bathroom are £45/55; with bathroom they're £50/70.

Next door, the *New York Hotel* (☎ 244 6884), at No 32, caters to a male gay clientele and charges £50/70 in comfortable single/doubles with TV. It has a jacuzzi and garden.

Children's Hotel

Pippa's Pop-Ins (☎ 385 2457), 430 Fulham Rd SW6 (tube: Fulham Broadway; Map 13), exists to give parents a break from their children. It offers 24 hour childcare by trained nannies and entertainment for children aged two to 12; overnighters get a midnight feast as well as dinner, bed and breakfast. A stay here costs £40 a head.

SELF-CATERING

Families may prefer to rent a flat rather than stay in a hotel or B&B. A couple of agencies can help track something down. Aston's (☎ 370 0737), 39 Rosary Gardens SW7, and Holiday Flats Services (☎ 373 4477), 140 Cromwell Rd SW7, both near Gloucester Rd tube, have a range of flats on their books.

The Landmark Trust (☎ 01628-825925), Shottesbrooke, Maidenhead, Berkshire SL6 3SW, is an architectural charity established to rescue historic buildings, a process partly funded by renting out the properties to self-caterers after they've been restored. Unfortunately they only have four properties available in London. Two of them are in Cloth Fair, Smithfield E1 (tube: Farringdon), a short terrace of 18th century houses; No 43 sleeps two and to hire it for a week in July would cost £501, while No 45A sleeps four and would cost £643. At Hampton Court (station: Hampton), Fish Court sleeps six and would cost £1276 for a week in July or August, falling to £939 in winter. The Georgian House sleeps eight and would cost £1386 in July and August, falling to £1020 in winter. You can contact the Landmark Trust in the USA (☎ 802-254 6868) at 28 Birge St, Brattleboro, Vermont 05301.

RENTING A HOUSE OR FLAT

In general, prices for rented accommodation are high and standards low, but on the plus side, most places are fully furnished (including linen and crockery) so you won't have to buy much.

At the bottom end of the market, bedsits are single furnished rooms, usually with a shared bathroom and kitchen, although some have basic cooking facilities. Expect to pay £50 to £100 per week. The next step up is a studio, which normally has a separate bathroom and kitchen, for between £75 and

£120. One-bedroom flats average between £90 and £135. Shared houses and flats are probably best value, with bedrooms for between £40 and £60 plus bills. Most landlords demand a security deposit (normally one month's rent) plus a month's rent in advance.

For help in finding a flat phone ☎ 388 5153 or call into the foyer of Capital Radio at 29/30 Leicester Square WC2 and pick up their flatshare list; new lists appear at 4 pm every Friday and the best places will go fast. Saturday's *Guardian* contains a useful supplement, *The Guide*, which reproduces this list. Rooms and flats are also advertised at the *New Zealand News UK* office in the Royal Opera Arcade behind New Zealand House, in *TNT*, *Time Out*, the *Evening Standard* and *Loot*. When you inspect a flat it's wise to take someone else with you, both for safety reasons and for help in spotting any snags.

A few things to check before signing a tenancy agreement:

- the cost of gas, electricity, the phone, the TV and how they're to be paid for
- whether there's street parking or how near the tube is
- what arrangements are made for cleaning the house
- whether you can have friends to stay

If you prefer to use an agency, check that it doesn't charge fees to tenants; Jenny Jones (☎ 493 4381) and Derek Collins (☎ 930 2773) are free.

Places to Eat

In some parts of town it can seem as if there's not a square inch of pavement that isn't occupied by a restaurant, café or snack bar. London is England's undisputed culinary capital and there's no doubt that the blossoming of good restaurants and cafés plays a big part in the city's famed 'coolness'. It doesn't matter what you fancy eating, there's bound to be a restaurant serving it, albeit often at a price you may be less keen to pay; you'll be lucky to get a decent meal and a glass of wine for less than £10 per head, except in pubs where the food is rarely that great.

The dilemma for anyone on a tight budget will be how to balance the need to economise against the fact that you'll certainly be missing out if you don't try any of the happening restaurants. Many places mentioned in this chapter will seem outrageously expensive to someone on a tight budget. However, they're so much part of the London scene that no guidebook worth its salt could afford to leave them out. To keep costs down, resist the lure of alcohol, which can be frighteningly expensive; few restaurants will let you bring your own grog. Watch out, too, for the price of bottled water; if no price is listed, think before drinking.

Restaurant chains like Pizza Express, Garfunkel's, Nachos and Stockpot guarantee good-value food in pleasant surroundings, but perhaps the biggest shock wave to hit London's diners came with the arrival of the new café chains like Café Rouge, Café Flo, Caffé Uno, Dôme and particularly Pret-à-Manger which serve everything from sandwiches to hot meals, often in stylish settings and at very reasonable prices. As its name suggests, the Pâtisserie Valerie chain specialises in mouthwatering cakes ... they'll cost you but you won't go away disappointed. The Seattle Coffee Company and Aroma coffee houses have also made a difference, although their emphasis is on civilised drinking rather than eating.

Pizza and pasta places can still be good value and the Caffé Uno chain has brought a reasonably varied Italian menu, mixing familiar spaghetti dishes for around £5 with less familiar gnocchi and linguini, to most high streets. Several branches of the long-running Pizza Express still manage to dish up better than average pizzas, sometimes in fine buildings (look out for the new branch about to open in King's Rd).

Chinese restaurants are also a good bet, especially if you head for Chinatown behind Leicester Square or eat out in the suburbs. Look out, too, for the many Thai, Indonesian and Vietnamese restaurants. But these days the cutting-edge eateries are often Japanese sushi bars which are opening faster than corner shops are closing down. The Sofra restaurant chain is also helping to persuade the British that Turkish cookery transcends the familiar kebab.

Oddly enough, it's most difficult to track down really good traditional English cooking. Instead what you'll usually find is Modern British cuisine, a mix-and-match style of cooking with prices that start high and head for the stratosphere.

Restaurants are often clumped together in the West End. Good areas to try include around Covent Garden, especially north-east between Endell St and St Martin's Lane; around Soho, especially north-west of the intersection of Shaftesbury Ave and Charing Cross Rd (including Old Compton St and Frith St); and north of Leicester Square on Lisle and Gerrard Sts (Chinatown).

Camden Town's cosmopolitan restaurants and cafés can become very crowded at weekends. Clerkenwell and Islington are also stuffed with good places to eat. The hotel zone around Bayswater is well served by moderately priced restaurants along Queensway and Westbourne Grove. Other interesting possibilities are clustered around Notting Hill, although the Earl's Court eateries are pretty uninspiring.

Restaurants featuring the cuisine of the

Indian subcontinent are consistently good value, especially away from central London, although they often tone down their spices for English tastebuds. Drummond St has some excellent South Indian places which are particularly good for vegetarians. Brick Lane in the East End has plenty of good, cheap Bangladeshi restaurants. Church St in Stoke Newington has a row of interesting restaurants, some of them Indian. Further out in suburbia, Southall, with its large Indian community, is choc-a-block with Indian restaurants.

Theme restaurants are currently all the rage. A family atmosphere and plenty of distractions are the main ingredients for their success, but they also serve good old American burgers, salads, fries, ice cream and shakes. Granddaddy of them all is the Hard Rock Café by Green Park. Others include Planet Hollywood and the Fashion Café, side by side on Leicester Square, and the Sports Café and Football Football nearby in Haymarket. Just behind Kensington High St is Sticky Fingers, ex-Rolling Stone Bill Wyman's attempt to muscle in on the burger action.

Of the guides to London restaurants, the best is probably the *Time Out Eating & Drinking in London Guide* (£8.50), although it doesn't have much for shoestringers and can be difficult to navigate. The *Evening Standard Restaurant Guide* (£9.99) draws on the expertise of the newspaper's admired restaurant reviewer Fay Maschler. For more down to earth prices Harden's *Good Cheap Eats* (£4.95) is an annual guide to budget establishments.

Note that the trendier places get booked up weeks in advance. Some places will want a credit card number to confirm a booking. Be warned that if you don't show up they may charge a cancellation fee to your card.

In this section cafés and restaurants listed as budget conscious are those where you should be able to eat for less than £10 a head, sometimes for considerably less. At those listed as moderately priced the bill is likely to fall between £10 and £20 a head. The splash-out places are those where you're looking at more than £20 a head. Still, it's worth remembering that some of the more expensive places offer cheaper lunch and/or early evening menus.

The area code for all telephone and fax numbers in this section is ☎ 0171 unless the text states otherwise.

If you're interested in a particular style of cuisine, see the boxed aside Eat Your Way Around the World for a sampling of London's international offerings and refer to the district (eg Soho) given in brackets to locate it in the text.

Vegetarian Food

Once regarded as outrageously faddish, vegetarianism is now an accepted part of the restaurant scene. These days it's rare to find somewhere which doesn't offer something for non-meat-eaters, although it helps if you're the kind of demi-vegetarian who manages to overlook the aliveness of fish.

There are also a fair smattering of places that cater specifically for vegetarians. *Cranks* is the best-known and longest lived vegetarian/vegan restaurant chain with branches at 8 Adelaide St WC2; 23 Barrett St W1; 17 Great Newport St WC2; 1 The Market, Covent Garden WC2; 8 Marshall St W1; and 9 Tottenham Court Rd W1. A full meal will probably cost you around £10, but eat fewer portions and you'll get away with less.

The listings below include other one-off vegetarian places. As ever, restaurants serving the food of the Indian subcontinent make a good bet for non-meat-eaters. Most pizzerias feature basic cheese and tomato margaritas, and Pizza Express' fiorentinas always go down a treat although not, sadly, with vegans.

THE WEST END & SOHO (Map 3)

These days Soho is London's gastronomic heart with numerous restaurants and cuisines to choose from. The liveliest streets tend to be Greek St, Frith St, Old Compton St and Dean St, where tables often spill out onto the pavements. Some of the cafés and bars attract an almost exclusively gay clientele. In

Eat Your Way Around the World

There's no doubt about it – London's chefs can dish you up a meal featuring the cuisine of pretty much any corner of the globe. If you're after a particular style or nationality, the following ABC of eateries should help. Simply use the district given in brackets to locate the restaurant in the main text.

African
: Calabash (Covent Garden)

American
: Fatboy's Diner (City); Sticky Fingers (Kensington); Hard Rock Café (Hyde Park); Planet Hollywood, Fashion Café, Sports Café, Football Football (West End)

Belgian
: Belgo Centraal (Covent Garden); Belgo Noord (Camden)

British
: Arcadia (Kensington); The Ivy (Soho); RS *Hispaniola* (Embankment); Hudson's (Marylebone); Newens Maids of Honour (Kew); Porters, Rules (Covent Garden); St John (Clerkenwell); Simpson's-in-the Strand (Covent Garden); Sweeting's (City); Veronica's (Bayswater)

Chinese
: Mr Wu, Poons, Wong Kei, Chuen Cheng Ku, Jade Garden (Soho); New Culture Revolution (Camden, Chelsea); Mr Wing (Earl's Court); Four Regions (Lambeth)

Colombian
: El Pilon Quindiano (Brixton)

Cuban
: Cuba Libre (Islington); Bar Cuba (Kensington); Havana (Fulham)

Dutch
: My Old Dutch (Holborn, Chelsea, Ealing)

European (Modern)
: Apprentice, Pont de la Tour, Blue Print Café (Bermondsey); Criterion, Mezzo (West End); Searcy's Brasserie (City); The Canteen (Chelsea); Oxo Tower, People's Palace (Waterloo); The Collection, Daphne's, Bibendum (South Kensington); Mange-2 (Clerkenwell); All Saints (Ladbroke Grove *see* Notting Hill); Kensington Place (Notting Hill Gate)

European (Eastern)
: Primrose Brasserie (Camden)

French
: Maison Bertaux, Quo Vadis (Soho); Le Montmartre, Sacre Coeur (Islington); Aubergine (Chelsea); Novelli W8 (Notting Hill Gate); Chez Lindsay (Richmond)

German
: Prost (Notting Hill Gate)

Greek
: Costa's Grill (Notting Hill Gate); Kalamaras Taverna (Bayswater)

Hungarian
: Gay Hussar (Soho)

Indian
: Gopal's (Soho); Nazrul, Aladin (East End); Raj (Camden); Modhuban (Notting Hill Gate), Khan's (Bayswater); Jai Krishna (Finsbury Park)

Indonesian
: Nusa Dua, Melati (Soho)

Italian
: Kettners (Soho); Gourmet Pizza Company (Waterloo); Uno, O Sole Mio (Pimlico); Marine Ices (Camden); Mille Pini, Spaghetti House (Holborn); Pizza on the Park (Hyde Park); Pizzeria Castello (Elephant & Castle, see under Waterloo & Lambeth); La Porchetta Pizzeria (Finsbury Park); Assagi (Notting Hill Gate); River Café (Hammersmith)

Japanese
: Tokyo Diner, Yo Sushi, Wagamama (Soho); Inaho (Bayswater)

Mauritian
: Chez Liline (Finsbury Park)

Mexican
: Cafe Pacifico (Soho); Nachos (Notting Hill Gate)

Mongolian
: Mongolian Barbecue (Camden, Ealing)

Moroccan
: Momo (Soho)

Polish
: Wodka, Daquise (Kensington)

Portuguese
: Nando's (Earl's Court)

Spanish
: El Parador (Camden); Churreria Espanola (Bayswater); Café Gaudi (Clerkenwell)

Swedish
: Emma's (Camden)

Thai
: Chiang Mai (Soho); Silk & Spice (Camden); Tuk Tuk (Islington); Vong (Knightsbridge); Jim Thompson's (Chelsea); Krungtap (Earl's Court); Thai Bistro (Chiswick)

Turkish
: Sofra (Soho, Mayfair) ■

striking contrast are Gerrard and Lisle St with their Chinese community.

Cafés

For coffee and a cake *Pâtisserie Valerie* (☎ 823 9971), 44 Old Compton St W1 (tube: Leicester Square or Tottenham Court Rd), is a Soho institution, famous for its artistic and calorie-busting cakes, though you'll be lucky to get a seat. Nearby is *Maison Bertaux* (☎ 437 6007), 28 Greek St W1, which some rate more highly even than Pat Val for its mouthwatering confections. It stays open until 8 pm every evening and you won't be allowed to miss its French affiliation.

The unexpectedly cosy *Living Room* in Bateman St, between Frith and Greek Sts (tube: Tottenham Court Rd), is favoured by the young and the hip of Soho, but still manages to behave as if it's what it calls itself – someone's living room. Basically it's a less chi-chi coffee shop that sells sandwiches, but the comfortable sofas at the back encourage you to linger and read papers or magazines.

For details of Bar Italia and the Monmouth Coffee Company, see the boxed aside titled '...or Coffee'.

Budget Conscious

Leicester Square can be frantically crowded but does have a cluster of cafés where you can get a cup of coffee and slice of pizza for just a couple of pounds. On the east side of the square itself the *Capital Radio Café* (☎ 484 8888) is stylishly trendy but inevitably pricier, with salads from £7.95 and designer sandwiches from £6.95. The menu mixes Italian, American, Greek, Thai and Chinese dishes with postmodern abandon.

Bunjies Coffee House (☎ 240 1796), 27 Litchfield St WC2 (tube: Leicester Square), is a folk club tucked away off Charing Cross Rd where you can also get cheap and reasonable vegetarian food. Most main dishes are around £4. There's also a fish menu.

Café in the Crypt (☎ 839 4342), St Martin-in-the-Fields, Trafalgar Square (tube: Charing Cross), is in an atmospheric crypt under the church. The food is good with plenty of offerings for vegetarians, but it can be hectic and noisy. Most main dishes are from £5 to £6. Dinner is served daily between 5 and 7 pm.

Heading into Chinatown, a 10 course all-you-can-eat Chinese lunch or dinner buffet costs £4.50 at *Mr Wu* (☎ 839 6669) 6-7 Irving St WC2 (tube: Leicester Square). Even if the price goes up a bit, this is still a good deal for anyone with a big appetite.

Tiny *Poons* (☎ 437 4549), 27 Lisle St WC2 (tube: Leicester Square), is where the upmarket Poons empire started. It offers exceptional food at very good prices and specialises in superb wind-dried meats. The dried duck is heavenly, and the steamed chicken equally sensational. If you're hungry, start with soup and order perhaps two dishes and rice – you'll pay around £9. Be prepared to queue at busy times and to be hustled out again pretty quickly.

Wong Kei (☎ 437 6833), 41 Wardour St W1 (tube: Leicester Square), is famous for the rudeness of the waiters. Some find this adds to the experience, but even if you don't, you might be tempted by the cheap and good Cantonese food. Set menus start at £5.80 for a minimum of two people.

New Tokyo Diner (☎ 287 8777), 2 Newport Place WC2 (tube: Leicester Square), comes recommended as a good-value place to stop for a quick bowl of noodles or plate of sushi before the cinema or theatre. The Japanese fixtures and fittings distinguish it from the stripped and stranded look of other Japanese diners. A meal is likely to cost around £8, although their set bento boxes start at £9.50.

Pollo (☎ 734 5917), 20 Old Compton St W1 (tube: Leicester Square), attracts an art-student crowd with numerous pastas for around £3. It can be very busy, as can *Stockpot* at No 18 which does a long list of basic dishes for less than £5 (see the boxed aside Eating on a Budget for other branches).

Whether you'll want to risk *Garlic & Shots* (☎ 734 9505), 14 Frith St W1 (tube: Leicester Square), probably depends on your tolerance for garlic with everything, even the cheesecake and the brandy. Main courses clock in at around £8.50 a shot, but don't expect to make many friends afterwards.

Sofra (☎ 930 6090), 17 Charing Cross Rd (tube: Leicester Square), is one of a chain of Turkish restaurants and cafés originally set up by a Cappadocian and now franchised. Other branches are at 18 Shepherd St, Mayfair W1 (☎ 493 3320) and 36 Tavistock St WC2 (☎ 240 3972). Particularly worth sampling is the set £9.95 array of mezes. Turkish cuisine is generally thought of as unmitigatedly meaty but Sofra does a surprisingly good job of catering for vegetarians too.

Across the road *Gaby's Continental Bar* (☎ 836 4233), at No 30, is a wonderful snack bar right beside Wyndham's theatre (tube: Leicester Square). It's been there forever and attracts queues for staples like hummus and felafel for £3.20 and couscous royale for £7.50. Juices are pricey at £1.70 but generally this is a great value place.

Yo Sushi (☎ 287 0443), 52 Poland St W1 (tube: Oxford Circus), is one of London's livelier sushi bars where the drinks trolley moves by itself on magnetic rails. Dishes cost from £1.30 to £3.50; you should be able to get away with around £10 a head.

Nusa Dua (☎ 437 3559), 11 Dean St W1 (tube: Tottenham Court Rd), is a rather garish Indonesian restaurant, but the prices are reasonable and the food superb. Share a few main courses and you'll spend around £10 each. The tofu and tempeh are excellent and there are plenty of vegetarian offerings.

The branch of *Pizza Express* (☎ 437 9595) at 10 Dean St is unusually worthwhile. At street level you get cheap, good-quality pizzas and a glass of wine for £2.10; downstairs you eat to the accompaniment of excellent jazz (admission downstairs is between £8 and £20).

Mildred's (☎ 494 1634), 58 Greek St W1 (tube: Tottenham Court Rd), is so small that you may have to share a table. The chaos is worth it, however, because the vegetarian food is both good and well priced. Expect to pay around £5.10 for a large main course with delicious fresh flavours, £2.30 for a glass of wine.

Govinda's (☎ 437 4928), 9-10 Soho St W1 (tube: Tottenham Court Rd; Map 5), advertises pure vegetarian food cooked with love and devotion. That's because it's attached to London's Hare Krishna temple; pop upstairs for a discreet peek before you eat. For £4.99 an excellent eat-as-much-as-you-like buffet is available between 11 am and 8 pm.

Another reliable cheapie is the *Star Café* (☎ 437 8778), 22 Great Chapel St W1 (tube: Tottenham Court Rd), which serves up good old bangers and mash for £3.95 and soups for £1.75. It's been going since the 1930s and you can't say fairer than that.

Stepping into the *New Piccadilly* (☎ 437 8530), 8 Denman St (tube: Piccadilly Circus), is like stepping into a time warp – nothing, except the prices, has changed since it first opened in the 1950s. Even the prices haven't changed as much as you would expect: pastas and pizzas are around £3.50, chicken and steaks weigh in at around £4.50.

Melati (☎ 437 2745), 21 Great Windmill St W1 (tube: Piccadilly Circus), is an acclaimed Indonesian restaurant with excellent food and a good range of vegetarian options. The sweet corn fritters for £2.95 are delicious. Various noodle and rice dishes cost around £6. Expect to spend around £10 without wine.

Brash and busy *Wagamama* (☎ 292 0990), 10A Lexington St W1 (tube: Piccadilly Circus), does great Japanese food but is hardly the place for a quiet dinner. You have to share tables and, having queued to get in, may feel pressured to move on again quickly. Main dishes range from £4 to £7.

No prizes for guessing the theme at the 330-seater *Football Football* (☎ 930 9970), 57-60 Haymarket (tube: Piccadilly Circus). Be prepared to fork out around £10 for a burger followed by ice cream and coffee, but the videos etc come free. Bookings for days when England plays the rest of the world kick off a month in advance so you'll need to plan well ahead.

Fans of other sports should continue down the road to *The Sports Café* (☎ 839 8300), at No 80, which boasts a restaurant, dance floor, ski simulator, basketball court and acres of memorabilia. Not surprisingly there's no escaping sport here: tableside TVs keep you occupied with favourite memories while you await burger and chips for around £8. From 5 to 7 pm the early-bird menu lets two eat for the price of one.

Moderate

If you fancy something more one-off than Pizza Express, *Kettners* (☎ 734 6112), 29 Romilly St W1 (tube: Leicester Square), manages to serve up pizzas of a similar standard and price but in a wonderful atmosphere of gently fading grandeur. It's a big place on two floors with prints on the walls, a grand piano and all sorts of gaudy mirrors.

A particularly good way to sample the best of Chinese cuisine is to try a Cantonese dim sum where you select numerous small dishes and wash them down with a pot of jasmine tea. If you're unsure what to choose, the *Chuen Cheng Ku* (☎ 437 1398), 17 Wardour St W1 (tube: Leicester Square), is ideal because all the dishes – dumplings, paper-wrapped prawns and numerous other delicacies – are trundled around on heavily laden trolleys. The same kind of fare can be found next door at the *Jade Garden* (☎ 439 7851) where you order from the menu. A set meal for two at both places is around £15.

Arnie, Bruce and Sly's venture into the restaurant world has been an international success. Be prepared to queue at *Planet Hollywood* (☎ 287 1000), 13 Coventry St W1 (tube: Piccadilly Circus), for standard American fare at Beverly Hills prices. Nearby at 5-6 Coventry St, supermodels Naomi Campbell, Claudia Schiffer, Christy Turlington and Elle MacPherson are doing their bit for the girls at the *Fashion Café* (☎ 287 5888). Heading in the other direction, yet another chance for a burger crops up at the *Rock Island Diner* (☎ 287 5500), 2nd Floor, London Pavilion W1 (tube: Piccadilly Circus), where a resident DJ plays 60s and 70s hits. The food is typically American and there's dancing in the aisles. You'll pay around £15 for a meal.

The kasbah comes to London at *Momo* (☎ 434 4040), 25 Heddon St (tube: Piccadilly Circus), a recommended Moroccan restaurant where you can either eat at traditional tables or round circular trays. This is a popular place where those without reservations may have to queue to sample beautifully cooked tajines and couscous. Although the menu is inevitably meaty, there's a vegetarian couscous for £7.50.

Gopal's of Soho (☎ 434 0840), 12 Bateman St W1 (tube: Tottenham Court Rd), is quite cramped but offers delicately spiced food at affordable prices. Thalis (set meals) are good value; £10.75 for vegetarian and £1 more for the meat equivalent. A glass of house wine is £1.95.

Splashing Out

The *French House Dining Room* (☎ 437 2477), 49 Dean St W1 (tube: Leicester Square or Tottenham Court Rd), is on the first floor of a typically old-fashioned Soho pub. Upstairs is a tiny, high-ceilinged room with a convivial atmosphere. The short menu changes daily and offers robust English food. Typical examples are roast duck for £12 and grilled lamb chump and lentils for £9.50. They have an excellent range of British cheeses. Booking is advised.

There can't be many restaurants that start life with demonstrations against their tasteless artwork, but *Quo Vadis* (☎ 437 9585), at 26-29 Dean St, made the mistake of displaying some of the 'art' of Damien Hirst, famous for his exhibitions of dead cows preserved in formaldehyde – thereby outraging the animal-loving fraternity. That said, the food, by the increasingly ubiquitous Marco Pierre White, is reliably French at a price that ain't at all bad (£14.95 for a set two course lunch) for the location. Marx is said to have worked in the vodka bar upstairs.

Chiang Mai (☎ 437 7444), 48 Frith St W1 (tube: Tottenham Court Rd), is a top-class Thai restaurant with a separate vegetarian menu and a wide range of soups. Meat eaters should try kratong tong (curried meat wrapped in cases of batter). Set menus for two cost from £40/30.

Enormous *Dell 'Ugo* (☎ 734 8300), 56 Frith St W1 (tube: Tottenham Court Rd), gets fluctuating reports on its food, but many people love it. There's a café and bar on the ground floor, then a bistro on the second floor and a restaurant on the third. The menu is the same throughout: expect to pay around £25 for a Mediterranean-flavour meal.

The Gay Hussar (☎ 437 0973), 2 Greek St W1 (tube: Tottenham Court Rd), keeps to a familiar format which brings its clients coming back for more. Now in its fifth decade, it offers a wide range of Hungarian dishes. Firm favourites include the veal goulash which costs £14.25 (vegetables extra, which could make this an expensive trip), but there are vegetarian choices too. This is a unique gastronomic experience within a rich and decorous setting.

So big you might never find your dinner

date, *Mezzo* (☎ 314 4000), 100 Wardour St W1 (tube Piccadilly Circus), is another of Terence Conran's ventures which attracts London's media crowd and those with aspirations. Nevertheless, it's a fun place to eat. Upstairs is more casual and better value at about £6 for a main course. At weekends it often does over 1000 covers an evening, but then it is open until 3 am!

The *Atlantic Bar & Grill* (☎ 734 4888), 20 Glasshouse St W1 (tube: Piccadilly Circus), boasts high ceilings, a large dining area and two bars which make it a very buzzy, atmospheric place to eat. Food is expensive (£14 for a main course, and drinks quickly push the bill up) and booking is a must at weekends (last sitting 11.30 pm); a cheaper bar menu is available until 2 am.

Right on Piccadilly Circus, *The Criterion* (☎ 930 0488) has a spectacular interior, all chandeliers, mirrors and marble, and quite an atmosphere, so you won't feel comfortable unless you dress up accordingly. The menu offers Marco Pierre White's fashionable Mediterranean-style food (typically, sauteed goat's cheese and roasted peppers), but there are also some British classics like fish & chips. Although this is a pricey place where you won't have much change from £30 for dinner, set two course lunches cost £14.95 and three course lunches £17.95. Portions tend to cuisine minceur dimensions.

L'Odéon (☎ 287 1400), 65 Regent St W1 (tube: Piccadilly Circus), would be worth a visit just for the views of Regent St from its lofty windows. The food, the handiwork of Bruno Loubet, also comes in for good reports, especially if you go for the £14.50 two course set lunch or dinner (5.30 to 7 pm only).

With its liveried doorman, *The Ivy* (☎ 836 4751), 1 West St WC2 (tube: Leicester Square), is a showbizzy event in itself and you need to book ahead. A modern British menu lists dishes like steak tartare, cumberland sausages, onions and mash. Fillet of sea trout is £16.75, eggs benedict £5. It's a pricey outing (expect to pay £30 per person) but perfect for a special occasion.

You can also take to the water to eat on the RS *Hispaniola* (☎ 839 3011), an ex-Scottish islands passenger ferry moored beside Hungerford Bridge and offering Modern British cuisine carefully presented for around £20 a head.

COVENT GARDEN (Map 3)

Right beside Soho and technically part of the West End, Covent Garden is also densely packed with places to eat. The following are all accessible from Covent Garden tube unless otherwise stated.

Budget Conscious

There's a cluster of enjoyable New Age cafés in Neal's Yard. The *Beach Café*, *World Food Café*, *Neal's Yard Salad Bar* and *Paprika* all offer a similar diet of wholesome dishes like cheese breads and home-made noodles in pleasing surroundings, but space fills up quickly. Neal's Yard is off Short's Gardens and Monmouth St and is signposted from Neal St. Lunch in any of these places should cost less than £5 if you choose carefully.

Tiny *Food for Thought* (☎ 836 0239), 31 Neal St, is a reliable, nonsmoking vegetarian café whose menu features dishes like spinach and mushroom South Indian bake for £2.90, or stir-fried vegetables for £2.70. Get there early to grab a table and avoid the queues.

For Mexican food in a cheerful atmosphere try *Café Pacifico* (☎ 379 7728), 5 Langley St, which still manages a daily lunch special for £3.75. If you're hooked you can always move on to *La Perla del Pacifico Bar* (☎ 240 7400), 28 Maiden Lane, which is owned by the same people and boasts healthy lunches and not quite so healthy rare and premium tequilas.

Diana's Diner (☎ 240 0272), 39 Endell St, is very basic, but also very cheap. While not inspiring, the food is OK. Spaghetti is from £3.50 and you'll find a range of grills and roasts for around £4.50. A few doors down at No 27, *Designer Sandwiches* dishes up award-winning sandwiches for under £3.

Rock & Sole Plaice (☎ 836 3785), 47 Endell St, is a no-nonsense fish & chip shop with basic formica tables. Delicious cod or

Eating on a Budget
If London restaurant prices look terrifying, never fear – there are still ways to eat without having to take out a mortgage.

The best way to keep prices down is, of course, to cater for yourself. If you're staying in a hostel you will probably have access to cooking facilities, but provided the weather's good, London's parks also provide excellent picnic sites. Beware some of the smaller grocer's shops where prices are marked up alarmingly. Look instead for a branch of *Tesco Metro*, the town-based version of Britain's most successful supermarket chain. Tesco Metro has branches at 21 Bedford St, Covent Garden; 76 Cheapside; 25-9 Upper St; 311 Oxford St; 224 Portobello Rd; 29 George St, Richmond; Cabot Place, Canary Wharf; 326 Shopping Centre, Elephant & Castle; and Broadway Centre, Hammersmith.

Branches of Safeway, Sainsbury, Somerfield and Waitrose are equally competitively priced.

Breakfast
If you're staying in a B&B, breakfast will be included in the price. If not, the hostel may well offer breakfast for around £3. Alternatively, some of the department stores do big, sustaining breakfasts for very reasonable prices. *BHS* in Oxford St, for example, serves a breakfast of six items for £1.50 up to 10.30 am, and then a brunch for £2.50 up to 11.30 am. Nearby *Debenhams* does a five-item breakfast until 11 am for £1.25.

Other good places to breakfast can be found round Smithfield Market. You don't get more budget conscious than *Ferrari's Cafe*, a 24-hour greasy spoon café immediately opposite the market at 8 West Smithfield EC1. A mug of tea here costs just 35p, a banana sandwich £1, and the fry-ups are substantial enough to keep the marketfolk going through the morning.

For a bagel and a mug of tea you could hardly do better than head for the round-the-clock *Brick Lane Beigel Bake*, at the Bethnal Green Rd end of Brick Lane (see East End for details).

Even the most unpromising areas can turn up something if you look hard enough. *Franx Snack Bar* at 192 Shaftesbury Ave is at the end of trendy Neal's Yard, but still manages to dish up staples like eggs & bacon for £2.40.

Lunch
Assuming you don't want to put together your own sandwich, London's most ubiquitous sandwich

haddock in batter is £5. It's unlicensed but you can BYO.

Pies have long been a staple of English cooking but don't tend to figure on trendy menus. *Porters* (☎ 836 6466), 17 Henrietta St, does its best to make up with a menu that features lamb and apricot, chicken and broccoli and assorted other pies for £7.95. Steak and kidney pudding or roast beef are £8.

Moderate

Café Pelican (☎ 379 0309), 45 St Martin's Lane (tube: Leicester Square), functions as a restaurant, brasserie and café-bar. Its location, close to the English National Opera, is fantastic and it's a great people-watching spot, particularly in fine weather when you can sit at pavement tables. Inside it's rather like an ocean liner. There are reasonably priced snacks in the brasserie. More substantial French dishes are available from the restaurant where confit de canard is £9.25 and a good, complete meal costs around £20.

Calabash (☎ 836 1976), in the Africa Centre, 38 King St, serves food from all over Africa and has a menu which describes dishes to the uninitiated. A typical dish is yassa (£6.50), chicken marinated with lemon juice and peppers and hailing from Senegal. There are beers from all over Africa and wines from Algeria, Zimbabwe and South Africa. A glass of house wine costs £1.60, an average meal £15.

Taking the elevator down to the basement and walking through the kitchens is all part of the fun at *Belgo Centraal* (☎ 813 2233), 50 Earlham St, where the waiters dress up as monks. This being a Belgian restaurant, moules, spit-roasts and lager are the specialities and this is the only restaurant in shop is *Pret-à-Manger* which now has around 40 branches; for a list call ☎ 827 6300 or look in the phone directory. Get there early before the cheaper combinations are snapped up.

Chain stores like *Boots the Chemist* also sell sensible sandwiches for sensible prices; brie and walnut on ciabatta is all very well but you'll pay a third of the price for good old Cheddar and tomato between two slices of Hovis.

Dinner

If you really can't afford to part with a penny, *Govinda's* (☎ 437 4928), the Hare Krishna restaurant, 9 Soho St W1 (tube: Tottenham Court Rd), may be persuaded to serve you a vegetarian meal gratis. Don't show your face more than once unless you're serious about studying the religion though.

Assuming you're on for paying to eat out, there are several restaurant chains which hold out hope of food for a fiver. *Stockpot* has been going since 1953 so it's had time to refine cheapie standbys like gammon, egg and chips. There are branches at 18 Old Compton St; 40 Panton St; 273 King's Rd; 50 James St; and 6 Basil St. The *Chelsea Bun*, 98 King's Rd, and the *West End Kitchen*, 5 Panton St, are from the same stable.

A newer-comer to the cheap eating scene is *Pierre Victoire*, which has branches at 42 New Oxford St, Notting Hill Gate and 86 The Broadway, Wimbledon. Set three-course lunches cost £4.90, set three-course dinners £9.90 except on Sunday. The food is French in approach and can be astonishingly good value.

Branches of *Dôme* also offer daily set three-course menus for £4.99. There are branches at 58 Heath St NW3; 35A Kensington Court W8; 341 Upper St N1; 57 Old Compton St W1; 354 King's Rd SW3; 91 High St SW19; 32 Long Acre WC2; 26 Hill St TW9; 57 Charterhouse St WC1; 194 Earls Court SW5; and 8 Charing Cross Rd WC2; as well as inside Selfridge's in Oxford St.

Between Meals

If you're the type of eater who needs to graze throughout the day, you'll be well-served by the corner of Cranbourn St leading into Leicester Square where a cluster of cafés offer a wedge of pizza for £1. Similar places crop up at the junction of Shaftesbury Ave with Piccadilly Circus, along Oxford St and at the junction with Tottenham Court Rd, although the price sometimes rises to £1.50 a slice.

Before checking into a cinema or theatre, head for the supermarket to stock up or you'll find yourself paying three or four times over the odds for sweets, ices and cold drinks. ■

town to boast 100 different flavoured lagers including banana, peach and cherry. There's a set lunch menu for £5; and from Monday to Friday from 5.30 to 8 pm you can try their 'Beat the Clock' menu – the time you sit down decides the price you pay for your main dish (sit down at 6.15 pm and pay £6.15; minimum charge £6).

Splashing Out

Café des Amis du Vin (☎ 379 3444), 11-14 Hanover Place, is handy for pre or post-theatre meals. Each of its three floors has a different price range. The ground-floor brasserie is reliable and offers all the favourites: steak frites, quiches and omelettes cost between £6 and £9. Upstairs, in the more expensive eatery, a set meal, lunch or dinner, is £17.95.

Long-established *Joe Allen* (☎ 836 0651), 13 Exeter St WC2, is a star-spotter's paradise. Theatre posters adorn the walls and the tables are covered by gingham at lunchtime and white tablecloths and candles at night. There's a buzz here and it gets crowded, so book. Starters and main dishes (lamb chops, grilled halibut, vegetarian etc) are varied. A three course meal will come to at least £20.

Rules (☎ 836 5314), 35 Maiden Lane WC2, is very posh and very British; in its wonderful Edwardian interior waiters proudly wear starched white aprons. The menu is inevitably meat-oriented but fish dishes are also available. Puddings are traditional: trifles, pies and an abundance of custard. The quality and feel of the place make up for the steep prices (main courses start from £14).

For traditional English roasts, the place to

go is probably *Simpson's-in-the-Strand* (☎ 836 9112), 100 Strand (tube: Charing Cross), where they've been dishing up hot meats in a fine panelled dining room since 1848. Supposedly 25 loins of beef, 23 saddles of lamb and 36 ducklings are demolished every day. Beef and Yorkshire pud will set you back £17.50, lamb and redcurrant jelly or duck and apple sauce £14.50.

WESTMINSTER & ST JAMES'S

Budget Conscious

A stone's throw from Westminster Abbey and the Houses of Commons (tube: Westminster), the *Footstool Restaurant* (☎ 222 2779; Map 4) is housed in the crypt of 18th century St John's, Smith Square, now a concert hall. Choose between a buffet with soups for £3 and casseroles for £6.50 and a more formal restaurant for à la carte lunches (skate wing and crab for £10.75) and post-concert set dinners (£10 for two courses).

The *Wren at St James* (☎ 437 9419), 35 Jermyn St SW3 (tube: Piccadilly Circus; Map 3), is the perfect escape from the West End but is only open during the day. It adjoins St James's church (which often has free lunchtime concerts) and in summer tables spill out into the shady churchyard. There are plenty of vegetarian dishes for around £3.50, and excellent home-made cakes.

Splashing Out

Quaglino's (☎ 930 6767), 16 Bury St W1 (tube: Green Park or Piccadilly Circus; Map 4), has stayed popular since its relaunch back in 1993. The food is good but still manages to be outdone by the atmosphere which is busy, fun and glamorous. Main dishes start at £13.

PIMLICO & VICTORIA (Map 4)

Budget Conscious

If you're waiting for a coach at Victoria, don't hang about the coach station but head across Eccleston Place to *The Well* (☎ 730 7303), a church-run enterprise which has been dispensing tea and cakes, as well as soups and light meals, to travellers since time immemorial. It's open until 6 pm on weekdays and until 5 pm on Saturday but closed Sunday.

Uno (☎ 834 1001), 1 Denbigh St SW1 (tube: Victoria), offers pastas from £5.50 in a largely black and white interior. Low fat and vegetarian tastes are also catered for.

O Sole Mio (☎ 976 6887), 39 Churton St SW1 (tube: Victoria), is a standard, decent-value Italian restaurant with pizzas and pastas for around £6. Next door, *Grumbles* is a pleasant wine bar with, among other things, stuffed aubergine for £6.45, kebabs for £7.25 and sirloin steak for £9.95.

Mackintosh's (☎ 821 1818), 46 Moreton St SW1 (tube: Pimlico), is a second branch of the popular Chiswick restaurant (see later in this chapter). Breakfasts cost £4.95 and set two course lunches £8.50.

Moderate

Mekong (☎ 834 6896), 46 Churton St SW1 (tube: Victoria), is reputed to be one of the best Vietnamese restaurants in London. They have a set meal for £12 for a minimum of two persons, and house wine is reasonable at £1.70 per glass. Booking is advised.

THE CITY (Map 6)

Budget Conscious

In the crypt below St Mary-le-Bow (the cockney church) you'll find *The Place Below* (☎ 329 0789; tube: St Paul's or Mansion House), a pleasant vegetarian restaurant, open from 7.30 am to 2.30 pm; come between 11.30 am and noon and you'll get £2 discount on most main dishes. Salads cost £6.95, spicy lentil soup £2.95. There are a few tables in the courtyard for sunny days.

For those who like their burgers served American-style, *Fatboy's Diner* (☎ 375 2763), 296 Bishopsgate EC2 (tube: Liverpool St), will come as a real treat. Burgers, hot dogs, eggs, bacon and hash browns, are all served up here, with a quality to make McDonald's weep. Expect to spend between £3.50 and £5 on a main course plus another £2.75 if you succumb to dessert.

Moderate

Sweeting's Oyster Bar (☎ 248 3062), 39 Queen Victoria St EC4 (tube: Mansion House), is a wonderfully old-fashioned place, with a mosaic floor and waiters in white aprons standing behind narrow counters serving up all sorts of traditional delights like summer pudding. Something like wild smoked salmon costs £9, so you're likely to run up a bill of around £15 to £20. Oysters are still sold in season (ie from September to April).

Splashing Out

Finding *Searcy's Brasserie* (☎ 588 3008) in the Barbican Centre EC2 (tube: Barbican) is an achievement in itself. Chef Richard Corrigan is one of those arch exponents of Modern British cooking who can whip up a lobster lasagne to leave you begging for more. Unfortunately, unless you're up for a bill exceeding £35 a head, you'll have to stick with the two course set meal for £17.50 (three courses £20.50). Oh yes, it's on Level 2 of the virtually unnavigable Arts Centre building.

EAST END

Budget Conscious

Brick Lane is wall-to-wall cheap Bangladeshi restaurants, including *Aladin* (☎ 247 8210) at No 132 and *Nazrul* (☎ 247 2505) at No 130 (tube: Aldgate East; Map 6). Both are unlicensed, but you should eat for around £7 and can BYO. Many people rate this as the best subcontinental food in London. For more details, see boxed aside Out for a Curry.

Brick Lane Beigel Bake (☎ 729 0616), at No 159, is at the Bethnal Green Rd end of Brick Lane – and open 24 hours. You won't find bagels better, fresher or cheaper; the salmon and cream cheese version for 90p is just heavenly. A cup of tea is a mere 25p.

The Spitz (☎ 247 9747), 109 Commercial St EC1 (tube: Aldgate East; Map 6), is at the east side of Spitalfields Market and makes a great place to stop for a quick but classy snack while shopping at the Sunday market (although it's open the rest of the week too).

The café upstairs in *Whitechapel Art Gallery* (☎ 522 7878), 80-82 Whitechapel High St E1 (tube: Aldgate East), serves dishes like carrot filo strudel and salad for £4.65. It's

Out for a Curry

Central London has some excellent, headline-grabbing curry houses, like the *Red Fort* (☎ 437 2525), 77 Dean St W1 (tube: Leicester Square) and the *Bombay Brasserie* (☎ 370 4040), Courtfield Rd SW7 (tube: Gloucester Rd). The trouble is that these places tend to be as expensive as any other West End restaurants – and they don't have much ethnic atmosphere to go with them. For something cheaper and arguably more authentic you need to head east to Brick Lane or west to Southall, both areas with large populations from the Indian subcontinent.

Brick Lane is the more easily accessible of the two areas but this has one drawback; you may find your chosen eatery full of loud-talking City types with mobile phones. Still, reliable favourites include *Nazrul* and the *Clifton* (see East End in Places to Eat chapter). If you're prepared to delve a little deeper off the beaten track into Whitechapel even better choices might be the *Lahore Kebab House* (☎ 481 9738), 2 Umberston St E1 (tube: Whitechapel), a fine Pakistani restaurant which serves excellent brown dahl and tandoori rotis for just £3.50 in a less-than-upmarket dining room; or *Café Spice Namaste* (☎ 488 9242), 16 Prescot St (tube: Tower Hill), which, as its name might imply, is a posher place serving Goan treats like diced pork kidney and liver for £9.75.

Getting to Southall is nothing like as easy. To get to Southall Broadway you catch a main-line train to Southall from Paddington, but some of the best places are a bus ride on from there. Fairly central at 157 The Broadway is a branch of *Sagoo & Takhar* (☎ 0181-574 3476), aka the Asian Tandoori Centre, which concentrates on the cuisine of the Punjab. A wholesome meal is unlikely to cost more than £10. If you're prepared to push on to Western Rd on bus No 105, 195 or 232, you'll find the very different cuisine of Southall's Kenyan Asians being served up at the *Brilliant* (☎ 0181-574 1928), at No 72-74. Sunday is the best day to come if you want to join the family groups tucking into whole chickens with cassava chips. The bill will come to more than at the Tandoori Centre, but not by very much. ■

open 11 am to 5 pm Tuesday to Sunday (8 pm on Wednesday).

Most of the above East End eateries can also be found on Walk 4 map in the London Walks chapter.

MARYLEBONE

Moderate

Hudson's (☎ 935 3130), 221b Baker St NW1 (tube: Baker St; Map 2), is attached to the Sherlock Holmes Museum and offers lunches, dinners and teas amid mock Victorian gentility. Although the menus look tasty, they won't take you for less than a two course lunch, so afternoon tea may be the best bet.

CAMDEN & ISLINGTON

Camden High Street is lined with good places to eat, although to watch the Sunday trippers snacking on takeaway sausages and burgers you'd hardly credit it. See Map 10 for Camden eateries.

Trendy Islington is another good place for a night out. At the last count there were more than 60 cafés and restaurants between the Angel and Highbury Corner, and the Granita in Islington High St shot to fame as the place where Tony Blair and Gordon Brown met to plot the future of the Labour Party. Most of the action centres on Upper St where there are branches of Nachos and Pizza Express as well as the places mentioned here.

Lonely Planet UK's Top Nine Dines

The staff at Lonely Planet's London office have a few tips of their own for eating out in the capital. Their dining experiences have produced this diverse list of personal favourites:

The Standard (☎ 727 4818), 21-23 Westbourne Grove W2 (tube: Bayswater) – Indian food was never my first choice but I can't stay away from this place. Located next door to the famous Khan's restaurant, The Standard serves the most delicious and good value Indian food I have ever tasted. (£10 per head) – Victoria Wayland

Tiger Lil's (☎ 376 5003), 500 King's Rd SW10 (tube: Fulham Broadway) – Lively Thai restaurant where you create your own food by selecting ingredients and taking them up to the energetic chefs who cook them for you in a giant wok. You can keep creating all night as the price is all-inclusive, so take small platefuls and concoct a variety of dishes. There are also branches at 16a Southside, Clapham Common SW4 and 270 Upper St N1. (£11 per head) – Sara Yorke

Quo Vadis (☎ 437 9585), 26-29 Dean St W1 (tube: Tottenham Court Rd) – Eating sumptuous food surrounded by weird sculptures and Damien Hirst creations is a surreal experience. Don't worry though, formaldehyde appears to be off the menu! (dinner only; £30 per head) – Sarah Long

Osteria Basilico (☎ 727 9372), 29 Kensington Park Rd W11 (tube: Notting Hill Gate or Ladbroke Grove) – Good mix of Italian rustic charm and West London chic, with an authentic menu and lively, relaxed atmosphere. The tables by the window are best, but you will need to book. (£10 per head) – Claire Gibson

The Criterion Brasserie (☎ 930 0488), 224 Piccadilly W1 (tube: Piccadilly Circus) – This is a fabulously opulent restaurant smack in the middle of Piccadilly Circus. Its jewelled interior is like eating in a Fabergé egg and the food is amazing. (£25 per head) – Jennifer Cox

The Gate (☎ 0181-748 6932), 51 Queen Caroline St, Hammersmith W6 (tube: Hammersmith) – Attention subversive veggies! This is the place to convert your carnivorous counterparts. Beautifully presented, mouth-wateringly delicious, totally satisfying food at a fine price. Winner of numerous 'Vegetarian Restaurant of the Year' awards. (£20 per head) – Sarah Bennett

Pizzeria Castello (☎ 703 2556), 20 Walworth Rd SE1 (tube: Elephant & Castle) – Ask any South Londoner to direct you to London's best pizzeria and you'll end up here. It's been going for years, is family owned, very friendly and extremely popular. They do a fantastic Quattro Formaggio and the pizzas have a thick base. (£11 per head) – Charlotte Hindle

The Jaishan (☎ 0181-340 9880), 19 Turnpike Lane N8 (tube: Turnpike Lane) – This authentic Indian restaurant is by far the most delicious place I have ever eaten in. The location is not ideal, but the menu is mouth-watering...don't miss it. (£13 per head) – Helen McWilliam

Langan's Brasserie (☎ 491 8822), Stratton St W1 (tube: Green Park) – Good traditional British food in a stylish, yet relaxed, environment. Owned by actor Michael Caine, this is a firm favourite with many; always busy and rarely dull. (£35 per head) – Joanna Clifton ■

Budget Conscious

A quiet place in Camden Town is the *El Parador* (☎ 387 2789), 245 Eversholt St (tube: Camden Town), where the good vegetarian selection includes empanadillas de espinacas y queso (spinach and cheese dish) for £3.50, with meat and fish dishes just a little more expensive.

The Raj (☎ 388 6663), 19 Camden High St (tube: Camden Town), is a small Indian vegetarian place with eat-all-you-can lunch and dinner buffets for £3.50 and £3.75 respectively.

Ruby in the Dust (☎ 485 2744), 102 Camden High St (tube: Camden Town), is a cheerful, atmospheric bar/café. The menu includes Mexican snacks, soup for £2.90 and mains like bangers and mash or fish & chips for £6.45.

Silks & Spice (☎ 267 2718), 28 Chalk Farm Rd NW1 (tube: Camden Town), is a Thai/Malay restaurant doing express lunches for £4.95. Potent Caribbean cocktails cost £4 at the *Cottons Rhum Shop, Bar & Restaurant* (☎ 482 1096), further along at 55 Chalk Farm Rd (tube: Chalk Farm).

Bar Gansa (☎ 267 8909), 2 Inverness St NW1 (tube: Camden Town), is an arty but fun tapas bar with dishes around £3. Service is good and the staff friendly. Breakfast costs £3.95.

Bintang (☎ 284 1640), 93 Kentish Town Rd NW1 (tube: Camden Town), is a small, rather tackily decorated South-East Asian restaurant which nevertheless manages to dispense delicious, reasonably priced food. Service can leave something to be desired but with mixed seafood at £5.95 and BYO (£2 corkage) it's worth experiencing. It's open Tuesday to Sunday from 6 to 11.30 pm.

As the name suggests, *Marine Ices* (☎ 485 3132), 8 Haverstock Hill NW3 (tube: Chalk Farm), started out as a Sicilian ice-cream parlour but these days it does some savoury dishes as well. Whether you indulge in a meal or not it's imperative to try one of the amazing ice creams; sundaes start at £2.40. The nearby *Marathon* (☎ 485 3814) is a source of late night kebabs and beer.

Primrose Brasserie/Trojika Russian Tea Room (☎ 483 3765), 101 Regents Park Rd NW1 (tube: Chalk Farm), serves good-value Eastern European food, such as salt beef. Starters cost from £2.50, main dishes from £5.50, and it's BYO.

Close to Primrose Hill, *Lemonia* (☎ 586 7454), 89 Regent's Park Rd NW1 (tube: Chalk Farm), is often busy so it's wise to book. It offers good-value food and a lively atmosphere. Meze cost £12.25 per person and both the vegetarian and meat moussakas for £7.50 are particularly tasty.

Heading into Upper St, Islington N1 (tube: Angel; Map 2), *Tuk Tuk* (☎ 226 0837) at No 330 offers reliable Thai food for not too outrageous prices; a bowl of noodles with peanuts, prawns, egg and bean sprouts costs £4.95. Singha beer is available.

At No 331, *Café Flo* (☎ 226 7916) offers reliable French food like Alsatian hotpot for £8.50, plus an area for sipping coffee and cakes and watching the world go by.

At No 324 the *Upper St Fish Shop* (☎ 359 1401) doles out classy fish like half a dozen Irish oysters for £5.90. Even cod and chips costs £7. Still, if you're keen on seafood this is a good place to come.

Ravi Shankar (☎ 833 5849), 422 St John St EC1 (tube: Angel; Map 5), is a small but inexpensive restaurant favoured by vegetarians – the all-you-can-eat lunchtime buffets for £4.50 are extremely popular. There's another branch at 133 Drummond St NW1 (tube: Warren St or Euston Square).

Moderate

Belgo Noord (☎ 267 0718), 72 Chalk Farm Rd NW1 (tube: Chalk Farm), is a beautifully designed Belgian fish restaurant/bar. Waiters wear monks' habits and despite the place's popularity the food is excellent value. If you're unsure, go for the set menu: a starter, a beer, a bowl of mussels and chips for £12. Despite the three sittings it's still necessary to book in advance. There's another branch in Covent Garden.

The *Mongolian Barbecue* (☎ 482 6626), 88 Chalk Farm Rd NW1 (tube: Chalk Farm), is one of a rapidly spreading chain of restaurants where you select your ingredients and hand them to a chef who stir-fries them while you watch. A three course dinner without alcohol is likely to cost around £15 but you'll need the booze to get into the spirit of the thing.

Café Delancey (☎ 387 1985), 3 Delancey St NW1 (tube: Camden Town), offers the chance to get a decent cup of coffee with a snack or a full meal in a large, relaxed European-style brasserie complete with newspapers. Main dishes are from £7 to £13 and wine starts at £6.50 for a half-bottle. The cramped toilets seem suitably Parisian too.

Cuba Libre (☎ 354 9998), 72 Upper St N1 (tube: Angel), is a themed Cuban restaurant with a very popular bar serving mojitos and Cuba libres. The restaurant offers tapas and more filling dishes like moros and christianos (beans and rice); expect to pay around £18. Sadly, Cuban music has been displaced by thudding rock. Happy hour is from 5 to 8 pm and the bar stays open until 2 am.

The award-winning *Le Montmartre* (☎ 359 3996), 26 Liverpool Rd N1 (tube: Angel), is a minuscule and very popular French bistro whose reasonable prices attract the crowds; booking is advisable. A big bowl of fish soup followed by salmon, mushroom and chive pasta washed down with wine will set you back about £15.

Part of the same chain, the *Sacre Coeur* (☎ 354 2618), 18 Theberton St N1 (tube: Angel; Map 2), offers similarly reliable French food in similarly cramped surroundings. The moules et frites for £4.95 are excellent value but the overall bill will still top £10.

Splashing Out

Emma's (☎ 284 1059), 257 Royal College St NW1 (tube: Camden Town), is a Swedish restaurant tucked away off the beaten track. Here you can sample such delicacies as pea soup and smoked reindeer for about £17 a head. The cloudberry ice cream alone makes this place worth tracking down.

Vegetarian Cottage (☎ 586 1257), 91 Haverstock Hill NW3 (tube: Chalk Farm), is a good-quality vegetarian restaurant. The delicious cottage special combines mushrooms, lotus roots, Buddha's cushion fungus, nuts and vegetables wrapped up in a lotus leaf. Expect to pay around £15 for a full meal.

BLOOMSBURY & HOLBORN (Map 5)

Budget Conscious

If you're visiting the British Museum it's worth knowing that Museum St (tube: Tottenham Court Road) is packed with places to eat where you'll get better value for your money than in the museum café. *Ruskin's Coffee Shop* at No 41 does soup for £1.80 and filled jacket potatoes from £2.85. *Uncle Sam's Deli* does felafel feasts for £2.80. The tiny *Garden Café* at No 32 has cakes to kill for. Best of all is the tremendously popular *Coffee Gallery* (☎ 436 0455) at No 23 where dishes like grilled sardines and salad can be savoured in a bright, cheerful room with modern paintings on the walls.

Wagamama (☎ 323 9223), 4A Streatham St off Coptic St WC1 (tube: Tottenham Court Rd), is a deservedly successful, if spartan, non-smoking Japanese restaurant where people share long tables as in a canteen. You may well have to queue to get in. Main dishes cost around £5 and portions are generous, delicious and cheap.

The Greenhouse (☎ 637 8038), 16 Chenies St WC1 (tube: Goodge St), is underneath the Drill Hall. It's busy, so expect to share a table. The reason it's busy is the excellent vegetarian food, with main courses for £3.95.

The *North Sea Fish Restaurant* (☎ 387 5892), 7 Leigh St WC1 (tube: Russell Square), sets out to cook fresh fish and potatoes well – a limited ambition in which it succeeds admirably. Fish (deep-fried or grilled) and a huge serving of chips will set you back between £6 and £7.50.

The highly thought of *Mille Pini* (☎ 242 2434), 33 Boswell St WC1 (tube: Russell Square or Holborn), is a true Italian restaurant with reasonable prices. You'll waddle out, but will only have spent about £10 for two courses and coffee.

My Old Dutch (☎ 242 5200), 132 High Holborn (tube: Holborn), is a long-lived pancake restaurant, serving plate-sized sweet and savoury pancakes seven days a week for less than £10 a head. There's another branch at 221 King's Rd (☎ 376 5650) and one at 53 New Broadway, Ealing (☎ 0181-567 4486).

The *October Gallery Café* (☎ 242 7367), 24 Old Gloucester St WC1 (tube: Russell Square or Holborn), is, as the name suggests, inside a small gallery. It's only open for lunch but its varied daily menu caters for both meat-eaters and vegetarians. On warm days, take advantage of the small courtyard. Light lunches are around £7.

There's a big branch of *Spaghetti House* (☎ 405 5215), Vernon Place WC1 (tube: Holborn), in pretty Sicilian Ave, a pedestrianised cut between Southampton Row and Vernon Place. While you can never really escape the sound of traffic in central London, here at least it's relatively muted which makes sitting outside in summer very pleasant. Pasta dishes kick off at £5.95 and they're more than passably good.

Splashing Out

The *Museum Street Café* (☎ 405 3211), 47 Museum St WC1 (tube: Tottenham Court Rd), is packed at lunchtimes but less busy in the evening. The food, like the interior, is straightforward. Freshly cooked ingredients are combined to offer dishes like char-grilled fish and snappy salsas. Set lunches are cheaper but a three course evening meal will cost £23.50 (two courses £18.50). It's licensed but you can BYO for a £5 corkage charge.

CHELSEA & SOUTH KENSINGTON

Budget Conscious

King's Rd (tube: Sloane Square or South Kensington) has all sorts of eating possibilities. If the weather is decent make for the Chelsea Farmers' Market (Map 8) just off King's Rd in Sydney St where several small stalls spill out into a pleasant outdoor area. Among them, the *Market Place Restaurant-Bar* does soup (£3) inspired by what was on sale at the market that morning, and a big hangover breakfast including steak and eggs for £6.50. The *Il Cappuccino* has coffee for £1, while *La Delicia* does pizzas from £5.20 and the *Chelsea Deli* does filled baguettes from £1.80 and vegetarian ravioli for £4.

At 305 King's Rd SW3, *New Culture Revolution* (☎ 352 9281; tube: Sloane Square; Map 2), is a trendy, good-value dumpling and noodle bar. Top to bottom windows at the front mean that the restaurant is bright – you eat in full view of passers-by. Main dishes cost around £6. There's another branch at 43 Parkway NW1 (☎ 267 2700; tube: Camden Town).

The *Chelsea Kitchen* (☎ 589 1330), 98 King's Rd (Map 8), has some of the cheapest food in London, although the surroundings are pretty spartan. Minestrone soup is 80p, spaghetti is £2.40 and apple crumble is 99p. A set meal costs £4.20 – and you can't get much cheaper than that.

Further up King's Rd at No 249, *Made in Italy* (☎ 352 1880) serves pizzas from £4.50. The interior decor is streamlined and swish, but the fact that it opens onto the street in summer is the biggest plus. Even further along at No 273, a branch of *Stockpot* serves fish & chips for £3.50 and spaghetti bolognese for £2.40.

Popular *Henry J Bean's* (☎ 352 9255), at No 195 King's Rd (Map 8), is an American bar and restaurant, one of the few London places to have a garden complete with fans and heaters. Music and a happy hour give this place a fun atmosphere. Main dishes are from £5 to £7. Nearby at No 221 is *My Old Dutch* (☎ 376 5650) which sells over 100 different types of pancakes and waffles, most of them enormous.

Owned by members of the England rugby team, *Shoeless Joes* (☎ 384 2333), at No 555 (tube: Fulham Broadway; Map 2), is yet another sports-theme restaurant with a more imaginative approach to the menu than is shown by its competitors in Haymarket.

A British version of the American diner, the *Chelsea Bun* (☎ 352 3635), Limerston St SW10 (tube: Earl's Court; Map 2), is brilliant value. Breakfast is served all day, and there's seating on an upstairs veranda. Main dishes cost between £4 and £7.

If you're looking for a late-night meal

head straight for *Vingt Quatre* (☎ 376 7224), 325 Fulham Rd SW10 (tube: South Kensington), an extremely popular 24 hour burger bar which serves drinks until midnight.

Near the museums in South Kensington, *Spago* (☎ 225 2407), 6 Glendower Place SW7 (tube: South Kensington; Map 8), is an excellent value restaurant with a good range of pastas and pizzas from £4.

Daquise (☎ 589 6117), 20 Thurloe St SW7 (tube: South Kensington; Map 8), is very close to the museums. It's a rather shabby-looking Polish place, but with a good range of vodkas and reasonable food. A set lunch is £6.80.

Moderate

With its wicker chairs and mirrors, *Oriel* (☎ 730 2804), 50 Sloane Sq SW1 (tube: Sloane Square; Map 8), makes a perfect place to meet before going shopping in King's Road. The brasserie has tables overlooking the square. Main dishes cost from £5 to £11.

Named after the man who introduced silk production to Thailand and then vanished in the Cameron Highlands, *Jim Thompson's* (☎ 731 0999), 617 King's Rd SW6 (tube: Fulham Broadway; Map 14), offers mixed oriental fare rather than straightforward Thai food. What with the dense greenery, the candles and the swathes of silk, you could easily imagine yourself far away from central London, although the £15 or so you can expect to pay is more than you would in the real orient.

Splashing Out

Terence Conran's latest venture is the *Bluebird* (☎ 559 1000), 350 King's Rd SW3 (tube: Fulham Broadway; Map 14), where a vast restaurant and bar sit above an upmarket food market and the smaller Café Bluebird.

The Canteen (☎ 351 7330), Chelsea Harbour SW10 (tube: Fulham Broadway), is Michael Caine's well-known restaurant in the uninspiring Harbour Yard shopping centre. A good traditional British and French menu averages out at £25 but the decor – based on a playing card theme – may not be to everyone's taste.

Aubergine (☎ 352 3449), 11 Park Walk SW10 (tube: Sloane Square), is one of those restaurants whose chef, Gordon Ramsay, has made his mark way beyond the usual gourmet circles. The cooking's French, but not dyed-in-the-wool French; dishes like cappuccino de haricots blancs are all Ramsay's own, as is the delicious rhubarb souffle. Food like this doesn't come cheap; a set three course dinner costs £40, more if you go for the seven course blowout.

The Collection (☎ 225 2641), 64 Brompton Rd SW3 (tube: South Kensington; Map 8), has a wonderful location in a converted gallery, with the main restaurant on a balcony overlooking the bar; snacks cost about £5 but drinks are expensive. This is another haunt of people who want to see and be seen.

In a pretty setting in the heart of South Kensington, *Daphne's* (☎ 589 4257), 110-112 Draycott Ave (tube: South Kensington; Map 8), is small enough to be cosy but not claustrophobic. It serves delicious Mediterranean-style food, with main courses from around £12. It's very popular with the who's who crowd and booking is a must.

In what must be one of London's finest settings, *Bibendum* (☎ 581 5817), 81 Fulham Rd SW3 (tube: South Kensington; Map 8), is Terence Conran's superb restaurant in what used to be a Michelin factory. The ground floor accommodates a popular oyster bar where you really feel at the heart of the Art Deco finery. Upstairs it's all much lighter and brighter, and at weekends you'll need to have booked two weeks ahead to stand much chance of getting a table. The food is Modern British, with dishes like breast of guinea fowl costing £10. Eating here is likely to set you back around £50 a head with wine. Of course, you could just appreciate the architecture from the outside.

Kartouche (☎ 823 3515), 329 Fulham Rd SW10, (tube: South Kensington), is Fulham Rd's most popular restaurant for the 20-40s age group. Food and service are both good and the downstairs bar stays open until 2 am. Main courses, which plunder something

Time for Tea ...

Given the vital role that tea plays in their culture, it should be no surprise that going out for 'afternoon tea' is something dear to the souls of the English. But forget stewed tea and a Rich Tea biscuit...a traditional tea comes with a selection of delicate sandwiches (cucumber and smoked salmon are favourites), gooey cakes and scones with cream and jam. Oh, and lashings of tea too.

The following are all great places to try out the tea ritual:

The Ritz

The Ritz (☎493 8181), Piccadilly W1 (tube: Green Park; Map 3), is probably the best known place to take tea, although these days it's become something of a production-line process despite the splendour of the surroundings. Afternoon tea is served daily between 2 and 6 pm and costs £21 per person. You need to book a month ahead for weekdays and a ridiculous three months for weekends, and a strict dress code applies.

Fortnum & Mason

On the 4th floor of the department store, Fortnum's Fountain (☎734 8040), 181 Piccadilly W1 (tube: Piccadilly Circus; Map 3), serves afternoon tea for £10.50 and high tea with champagne for £15.75 between 3 and 5.15 pm (not on Sunday).

Brown's Hotel

Brown's (☎493 6020), 33-4 Albermarle St W1 (tube: Green Park; Map 3), dispenses tea in the downstairs lounge with a pianist to soothe away any lingering stress from the bustling streets outside. A sizeable tea will set you back £16.95 a head.

Claridge's

Claridge's (☎629 8860), Brook St W1 (tube: Bond St; Map 2), serves tea in its grand 18th century foyer from 3 to 5.15 pm daily. It'll cost you £16.50 a head.

Waldorf Meridien

Tea at the Waldorf Meridien (☎836 2400), Aldwych WC2 (tube: Covent Garden; Map 3), is served in the splendidly restored Palm Court Lounge between 3.30 and 6 pm at weekends. In this case tea comes with a chance to take part in the old-fashioned pleasure of tea dancing. It costs £22 and you must book ahead.

Savoy

The Savoy, Strand WC2 (tube: Charing Cross; Map 3), serves tea in its enormous Thames Foyer between 3 and 5.30 pm daily. It costs £17 a head.

The Orangery

The early 18th century, white-walled Orangery (☎376 0239) in Kensington Gardens (tube: High St Kensington; Map 9), makes a splendid setting for afternoon tea, although service doesn't match up to what you'll get in the hotels. On the other hand prices are considerably lower, with a choice of summer tea with cucumber sandwiches or traditional tea with scones for £6, or a combination tea with sandwiches and scones for £7.50.

Jane Asher Tea Shop

Actress Jane Asher, best known for her past liaison with ex-Beatle Paul McCartney, has developed a lucrative second line as a cake-maker. Try out her offerings over tea at her shop at 24 Cale St SW3 (☎584 6177; tube: South Kensington) for £10.50 a head. ■

from most of the world's cuisines, average £10.

KNIGHTSBRIDGE & KENSINGTON

Budget Conscious

There's a definite continental feel to *Pâtisserie Valerie* (☎ 823 9971), 215 Brompton Rd SW5 (tube: Knightsbridge; Map 8), a wonderful place to stop for a coffee and pastry or light snack after a trip to the V&A. Breakfast is popular at the weekend (£4.80 for full English) and newspapers are provided.

Pizza on the Park (☎ 235 5273), 11 Knightsbridge SW5 (tube: Hyde Park Corner; Map 4), is popular for its pizzas and jazz in the basement. There's also a spacious restaurant upstairs and, if you're lucky, a few tables overlooking Hyde Park. Pizzas average £6.50.

The original *Hard Rock Café* (☎ 629 0382), 150 Old Park Lane W1 (tube: Hyde Park Corner; Map 4), is now over 25 years old and as popular as ever. It serves a tried and tested diet of burgers and fries (from £6.95) and despite the competition you may still have to queue. Linda McCartney recently injected some veggie dishes into the menu.

Wodka (☎ 937 6513), 12 St Albans Grove W8 (tube: High St Kensington; Map 8), lies in a quiet residential area away from the hustle and bustle of the High St. Its decor is plain, its food Polish. Blinis (pancakes) average £6.50 and a large array of vodkas is available.

Sticky Fingers (☎ 938 5338), 1A Phillimore Gardens W8 (tube: High St Kensington; Map 8), is where ex-Rolling Stone Bill Wyman has chosen to hang up his gold discs and other memorabilia but it's still a rather good burger bar, with prices kicking off at £6.95. Service is excellent and there's nothing wrong with a bit off rockabilia to study while you're waiting.

More or less opposite the Royal Garden Hotel at the Kensington Gardens end of High St Kensington, Kensington Court (Map 8) is a little side turning with a number of good places to eat. Right on the corner *Dallas Pizza & Pasta* (☎ 938 1286) has a few pavement tables and pretty standard cheapie pizzas. There's a branch of *Dôme* immediately opposite or you could try *Bellini's* (☎ 937 5510) at No 47 which serves three course lunches for £9.50 in a stylish restaurant with a few pavement tables and views of a flower-filled alley.

Bar Cuba (☎ 938 4137), 11 Kensington High St (tube: High St Kensington; Map 8), offers a wide selection of tapas (from £2.75), steak sandwiches – even roasts, all reasonably priced. It's a trendy, friendly restaurant. Downstairs there's a live band or a DJ every night and dancing until 2 am. A three course meal with wine for two people is about £35.

Splashing Out

The Fifth Floor Café (☎ 235 5250) at Harvey Nichols, Knightsbridge SW1 (tube: Knightsbridge; Map 8), is the perfect place to drop after you've shopped. It's expensive – main courses served between noon and 3 pm cost between £10 and £15 – but you could just come here for coffee and a cake.

Thai cooking is now so popular that there are Thai restaurants where the seeing and being seen is almost as important as the food. *Vong* (☎ 235 1010), Berkeley Hotel, Wilton Place SW1 (tube: Knightsbridge; Map 8), is just such a super-trendy place, although most people will find the food, with its French input, as memorably enjoyable as the decor is unexpectedly spartan. But for the average £30 a head you pay for a meal here you could have three equally memorable Thai meals at, say, the Thai Bistro in Chiswick.

During July and August it's sometimes possible to enjoy a jazz supper in *The Orangery* in Kensington Gardens (Map 9). Tickets for a three course dinner with jazz entertainment (but no alcohol) cost £35 plus a £1.50 booking fee and must be bought in advance by phoning ☎ 316 4949. The music starts at 7 pm.

Launceston Place (☎ 937 6912), 1A Launceston Place W8 (tube: High St Kensington; Map 8), is tucked away in the Kensington back streets. It's a pretty, intimate restaurant, perfect for dinners à deux. The food is continental and quite expensive, although there are set dinners for £14.50 and £17.50.

In Kensington Court, *Arcadia* (☎ 937 4294) at No 35 is the most upmarket of a cluster of restaurants and cafés and its interior, with a pair of macaws showing off amid the murals, is classy and distinctive. The menu features dishes like rack of lamb with sauteed spinach, best sampled via the set two course lunch at £12.95. Vegetarians don't get much of a choice here.

EARL'S COURT (Map 8)

Budget Conscious

Benjy's, 157 Earl's Court Rd SW5 (tube: Earl's Court), is an institution. It's really nothing more than a fairly traditional café, but it's always busy and although the food is nothing to write home about, it's cheap and filling. Serious breakfasts with as much tea or coffee as you can drink are around £3.50, 50p less for vegetarians.

Nando's (☎ 259 2544), 204 Earl's Court Rd SW5 (tube: Earl's Court), serves Portuguese-style cooking concentrating on flame-grilled chicken dishes. A meal with a drink costs around £5.

Krungtap (☎ 259 2314), 227 Old Brompton Rd SW10 (tube: Earl's Court), is a busy, friendly Thai and generally oriental restaurant. Most dishes are in the £3 to £4 range. Portions are generous although beer is expensive.

The *Troubadour* (☎ 370 1434), 265 Old Brompton Rd (tube: Earl's Court), has an illustrious history as a coffee shop and folk venue. Among others it has hosted Dylan, Donovan and Lennon. These days it still occasionally has bands, plus good-value food. Service is slow, but the wait is worthwhile; order at the counter. Vegetable soup is £2.10, pasta £4.

Splashing Out

Mr Wing (☎ 370 4450), 242-244 Old Brompton Rd (tube: Earl's Court), is one of London's best Thai and Chinese restaurants. Make sure you get a seat in the jungle-styled basement. The food is pricey (bird's nest soup with scallops, prawns and squid for £10.95), but very good.

NOTTING HILL, BAYSWATER & MAIDA VALE (Map 9)

Notting Hill has all sorts of interesting places to eat, and there are literally dozens of places lining Queensway and Westbourne Grove, with everything from cheap takeaways to good quality restaurants. Surprisingly, there are even some decent restaurants on the 2nd floor of the vast Whiteley's shopping centre, although they're not particularly cheap.

Budget Conscious

Portobello Rd has plenty of trendy bars and restaurants; *Café Grove* at the Ladbroke Grove end of Portobello has a veranda overlooking the action and cheap and cheerful vegetarian food at around £5.

Costa's Grill (☎ 229 3794), 14 Hillgate St W8 (tube: Notting Hill Gate), is a reliable Greek place, with dips at £1.50 and mains like souvlaki for £4.50. Unusually, it has almost nothing a true vegetarian could eat. Nor do the staff like having this pointed out.

Nachos (☎ 221 5250), 147 Notting Hill Gate W11 (tube: Notting Hill Gate), is a popular Mexican joint with better than average quality at decent prices. A couple of tortillas will cost you around £8, but a full meal works out almost twice that.

Prost (☎ 727 9620), 35 Pembridge Rd W11 (tube: Notting Hill Gate), is a small one-up, one-down restaurant serving traditional German cuisine. Main courses are under £10; venison in red wine with blueberry sauce, for example, is £8.25 but between 5.30 and 11 pm any two courses are £8.95.

... Or Coffee

Coffee houses first hit London's streets in the mid-17th century. However, they gradually fell from favour and until recently modern coffee-lovers got a pretty raw deal in London. Fortunately, things are looking up, thanks in no small part to two chains, the Seattle Coffee Company and Aroma, which produce coffee good enough to convert even erstwhile Nescafe queens. Make sure you know the lingo though. Suddenly London is as awash with café lattes and hazelnut steamers as Seattle itself.

The *Seattle Coffee Company* has branches at 25A Kensington High St W8; 14 James St W1; 163 Fulham Rd SW3; 87 King William St EC4; 44 New Kings Rd SW6; 26 Pembridge Rd, Notting Hill Gate W11; 47 Queensway W2; 355 The Strand WC2; 137 Victoria St SW1; 27 Berkeley St W1; 365 Cabot Place East, Canary Wharf E1; 116 Cannon St EC4; 74 Cornhill; 51 Long Acre, Covent Garden WC2; 20 Eastcheap; 18 Eldon St EC2; 90-1 Fleet St EC4; 34 Great Marlborough St W1; 3 Grosvenor St W1; and 11 Heathmans Rd, Parsons Green SW6. There are also branches inside Books etc at 421 Oxford St and in the food court of The Plaza, 120 Oxford St W1.

There are branches of *Aroma* inside the Hayward Gallery and the Festival Hall, as well as at 36A St Martin's Lane WC2 (☎836 5110).

If you'd prefer to frequent a one-off coffee shop, head straight for the *Monmouth Coffee Company* at 2 Monmouth St WC2 (tube: Covent Garden) to sample Nicaraguan and Guatemalan blends in a diminutive café. Another great favourite is Bar Italia, 22 Frith St, Soho W1 (tube: Leicester Square), which is open round the clock and has a wonderful 1950s decor. It's always packed – your best chance of a seat might be after 1 am! ■

Dinner is served daily but it's only open for lunch on Saturday and Sunday.

Modhubon (☎ 243 1778), 29 Pembridge Rd W11 (tube: Notting Hill Gate), has been recommended for its inexpensive Indian food. Main dishes are under £5, set lunch is £3.90 and an eat-as-much-as-you-like Sunday buffet is £5.90.

Geales (☎ 727 7969), 2 Farmer St W8 (tube: Notting Hill Gate), is a popular old-fashioned fish restaurant, with the fish priced according to weight and season, and always fresh. Fish & chips cost about £7 a person, which is a lot more than you'd usually pay, but worth it. It's closed on Sunday.

The Mandola (☎ 229 4734), 139 Westbourne Grove W2 (tube: Bayswater), offers vegetarian Sudanese dishes like tamia, a kind of felafel, for £4 and meat dishes for £7. The portions are small so it would be better value if a couple were sharing dishes.

Kalamaras Taverna (☎ 727 9122), 76 Inverness Mews W2 (tube: Bayswater), is the cheaper sibling of the Mega-Kalamaras in the same mews, parallel to Queensway. Conditions are a bit micro, but the food is macro. Main courses are around £7.50.

Khan's (☎ 727 5420), 13 Westbourne Grove W2 (tube: Bayswater), is a vast and popular Indian restaurant where diners eat amid palms and pillars; it's authentic, the decor is smart and it's good value. There are vegetarian dishes and a selection of meat curries for around £3.

Churreria Espanola (☎ 727 3444), 179 Porchester Rd W2 (tube: Bayswater), is an unexpected café serving that old Spanish breakfast special, chocolate and churros, for £1.75.

The Waterside Café, Warwick Crescent, Little Venice W9 (tube: Warwick Avenue), is a cluster of tables alongside a narrowboat near where the London Waterbus leaves for the zoo. Here you can get a cream tea for £3.95 or a canalman's lunch for £4.60.

Moderate

All Saints (☎ 243 2808), 12 All Saints Rd W11 (tube: Westbourne Park), is a funky place which is especially popular on Saturday during the Portobello Rd Market. If you can make yourself think over the pounding music you'll realise you're in another of those Modern British places where a meal is likely to cost you around £20.

In a quiet suburban street *The Chepstow* is a conspicuously inviting bar, with large, brightly decorated rooms. Upstairs, the *Assagi* (☎ 792 5501), 39 Chepstow Place W2 (tube: Notting Hill Gate), provides proof that Italian cookery books contain more than just recipes for pasta. This is the place to try dishes like squid stuffed with risotto or lamb cutlets with aubergine. A meal is likely to cost £25 a head but it's well worth it.

Stylish *L'accento* (☎ 243 2201), 16 Garway Rd W2 (tube: Bayswater), offers a two course set menu for £11.50 which could include mussel stew in white wine and fresh herbs, followed by grilled pork chop filled with sundried tomatoes and leeks. Once you step away from this menu it becomes more expensive.

Veronica's (☎ 229 5079), 3 Hereford Rd W2 (tube: Bayswater), is trying to establish that England does have a culinary heritage while, at the same time, promoting healthy eating. There are some fascinating dishes (Cornish thunder and lightning, for example) and the restaurant has won many awards. A three course set menu is £16.50 and you'll have fun studying the annotated menu.

While waiting to take a boat along Regent's Canal to the zoo you might want to lunch at *Jason's* (☎ 286 6752), opposite 60 Blomfield Rd W9 (tube: Warwick Avenue), which serves fish dishes with a Mauritian, Indian and Chinese twist while you enjoy pleasant views out over the Little Venice boats. Midweek a set lunch costs £12.95, but a set dinner pushes up a price bracket to £21.50.

Splashing Out

Inaho (☎ 221 8495), 4 Hereford Rd W2 (tube: Bayswater), is a tiny Japanese restaurant where a tempura set dinner of an appetiser, soup, mixed salad, yakitori, sashimi, tempura, rice and seasonal fruits costs £20. A teriyaki equivalent is £22.

Kensington Place (☎ 727 3184), 201 Kensington Church St W8 (tube: Notting Hill Gate), has an impressive glass front and a design-conscious interior, which has made it the perfect place for settling business deals. Starters cost from £4 and main courses from £9; a meal is likely to cost around £25 a head unless you settle for the set three course lunch for £14.50. Not everyone rates this place as highly as it rates itself.

The *Sugar Club* (☎ 221 3844), All Saints Rd W11 (tube: Westbourne Park), defies its insalubrious surroundings to serve some of London's most fashionable food. Chef Peter Gordon is a New Zealander who concentrates on 'Pacific Rim cookery' – dishes like grilled kangaroo loin and roast pigeon breast on wok-fried black beans which cleverly mix and match traditions of east and west. This place is so popular that even Madonna was turned away when she didn't book. You have been warned.

W11 (☎ 229 8889), 123A Clarendon Rd W11 (tube: Holland Park), produces a menu of excellent modern British/European food despite its weird Egyptian-style interior. An average meal, including house wine, will set you back £20 to £25 a head.

Novelli W8 (☎ 229 4024), 122 Palace Gardens Terrace W8 (tube: Notting Hill), serves good-quality French food, with main courses for around £20 in a romantic hideaway restaurant. Booking is recommended. There's another branch on Clerkenwell Green (☎ 251 6606).

HAMMERSMITH & FULHAM

Budget Conscious

You can hardly miss *Havana* (☎ 381 5005), 490 Fulham Rd SW6 (tube: Fulham Broadway), a brash blue and yellow bar/restaurant with zebra-striped seating. You could stick with the set meal for £4.90 but the temptation to succumb to alcohol and force up the bill is likely to prove too strong to resist. Happy hour is from 6 to 8 pm.

Deals (☎ 0181-563 1001), The Broadway Centre W6 (tube: Hammersmith Broadway), offers good value food (£8 for a main dish) and a menu for everyone. There's some seating outside, a cocktail bar upstairs and an early-evening happy hour.

Splashing Out

The River Café (☎ 381 8824), Thames Wharf, Rainville Rd W6 (tube: Hammersmith), is a very buzzy, see-and-be-seen restaurant which owes its fame as much to the cookbook it spawned as to the food actually eaten here. The River serves probably the best nouvelle Italian cuisine in London but the café label is misleading – main dishes start at a very restaurant-like £17 and you're unlikely to have much change from £40 once you've added a pricey pud and wine.

CLERKENWELL (Map 6)

Pushed up against the City as it is, Clerkenwell was only ever biding its time before the developers spotted its potential. Nowadays it has well and truly arrived on the eating-out map, even if the surroundings still leave something to be desired. All these places are accessible from Farringdon tube.

Budget Conscious

The Greenery (☎ 490 4870), 5 Cowcross St EC1, is a small vegetarian café hanging on amid the gentrification. A salad platter is £3.95, a chickpea and coriander chapati £1.80.

Splashing Out

Café Gaudi (☎ 608 3220), 61 Turnmill St EC1, takes liberties with the genius of the Catalan architect Gaudi to provide a backdrop for a classy restaurant specialising in what has been dubbed New Spanish cuisine. Fish plays a big, if not exclusive, part in meals here, and you're probably looking at around £30 a head. At weekends there's a nightclub in the basement.

St John (☎ 251 0848), 26 St John St EC1, is the place to come if you fancy sampling old-fashioned British staples like tripe and trotters (£9.80) or pigeon and radishes (£10.50). It's a very pared-down, white-washed place which boasts a bar and a sweet-smelling bakery that's open from 9 am. Well worth a try.

Mange-2 (☎ 250 0035), 2-3 Cowcross St EC1, is a maniacally trendy, rather flashy place which should be fun provided not too many of the mobile-phone brigade are in the place. It's not an exclusively fish restaurant but there's some excellent seafood. Who could resist seafood sausage in lobster sauce unless the £13.75 price tag acts as a deterrent?

FINSBURY PARK & CROUCH END

A thoroughly cosmopolitan area of north London, Finsbury Park has a good mix of restaurants at very reasonable prices. Adjacent Crouch End is one of those up and coming corners of town where good places to eat are one of the attractions.

Budget Conscious

If you can be bothered to go out of your way for a pizza, tasty home-made versions are available at *La Porchetta Pizzeria* (☎ 281 2892), 147 Stroud Green Rd N4 (tube: Finsbury Park). The fiorentina for £4.70 is delicious and the non-pizza dishes look good too. There are pavement tables for good days, although Stroud Green Rd is hardly one of London's more picturesque main drags.

Jai Krishna (☎ 272 1680), a few doors further north at No 161, is an Indian vegetarian café. You won't be writing home about the decor, but the prices – masala dosa for £2.50, mixed bhajiya £1.75 – are noteworthy.

The *World Café* (☎ 0181-340 5635), 130 Crouch Hill N8 (tube: Finsbury Park, then W2 or W7 bus), comes in for rave reviews for its food and choice of world beers. Set two course meals cost £8.95, three courses are £10.95. It opens for breakfast too, although you may think £1.95 rather a lot for an orange juice.

Moderate

Cats (☎ 281 5557), 79 Stroud Green Rd, N4 (tube: Finsbury Park), is a delightful Thai restaurant serving some especially tasty starters, but with good noodle dishes as well. The furnishings are made from unimaginably heavy wood – the sort of decor you'll love or loathe. A meal with wine should cost you around £15.

Splashing Out

It doesn't look much from the outside but *Chez Liline* (☎ 263 6550), 101 Stroud Green Rd N4 (tube: Finsbury Park), has been serving up excellent fish dishes with a Mauritian flavour for 10 years. The assiette creole at £9.95 offers a good way to get to grips with what's what.

Pie 'n' Mash

Ciabatta and pesto may be all the rage in central London, but head for the East End and you may still stumble across cafés selling good old pie 'n' mash.

London's original 18th century itinerant piemen sold pies stuffed with spiced and stewed eels. Then in the 19th century their place was gradually taken by proper shops. One of the best known pie shops was not in the East End at all but in Twickenham where its name lingers on at Eel Pie Island. Most of the eels came from the Thames, but as the river became increasingly polluted, some had to be imported from the Netherlands. In 1860 there were roughly 20 eel pie shops, by 1890 over 100.

Most of the 80-odd surviving pie shops now stuff their pastries with meat rather than eels, although some still sell jellied eels as a sideline.

The oldest pie shop still trading is *Manze's* at 87 Tower Bridge Rd, Bermondsey SE1, which has been going strong for over a century and is handy for anyone heading for Bermondsey Market. In its pleasantly tiled interior jellied eels cost £2, pie and mash £1.85, and pie and liquor £1.35. Don't get excited at the thought of 'liquor' though...what will land up on your plate is not beer but a traditional parsley sauce! ■

BERMONDSEY

Moderate

The Apprentice (☎ 234 0254), 31 Shad Thames SE7 (tube: Tower Hill; Map 6), is so named because trainee chefs practice here. Prices are lower than at the neighbouring Conran restaurants, with a set lunch for £9.50 and a set dinner for £17.50. It closes at 8.30 pm (6 pm on weekends).

Splashing Out

Furniture retailer and restaurateur, Terence Conran, who set up the Design Museum in the Docklands, also located some of his excellent, expensive restaurants nearby. These include the stylish *Blue Print Café* (☎ 378 7031), which is actually on top of the Design Museum (Map 6) with spectacular views of the river. Modern British cooking is the order of the day and you won't see much change from £35 for dinner with wine.

Alternatively you could try *Le Pont de la Tour* (☎ 403 8403), Butlers Wharf Building, 36D Shad Thames SE1 (tube: Tower Hill), which has more spectacular river views, a Frenchish menu and a 30-page wine list. Expect dinner to cost around £25 a head.

WATERLOO & LAMBETH

This part of south London is not immediately attractive as a place to eat out, although the cafés and restaurants in the Festival Hall, the Royal National Theatre and the National Film Theatre (currently under renovation) are popular places to meet, with reasonable food.

Budget Conscious

It may not look much but the *Gourmet Pizza Company* (☎ 928 3188), Gabriel's Wharf SE1 (tube: Waterloo), usually has queues for its pizzas, which come with such outlandish toppings as Thai chicken (£7.50) and Italian sausage (£6.60). Standard cheese and tomato pizzas kick in at £4.70.

For great pizzas, venture a mile south to Pizzeria Castello (☎ 703 2556), Walworth Rd, Elephant & Castle (tube: Elephant & Castle). Prices are low and booking is essential if you want to avoid a long wait for a table.

Moderate

The conversion of the old County Hall continues apace, with a branch of *Four Regions* (☎ 928 0988), Westminster Bridge Rd SE1 (tube: Waterloo or Lambeth North), now ensconced inside the old building alongside the London Aquarium (Map 4). The food here is said to be garnered from the four main cuisines of China (Cantonese, Szechwan, Peking and Shanghai) and made without resort to MSG, but it fetches rather mixed reviews; best try it out with a set meal for £15.50. No-one is going to quibble over one of the finest river views in London.

The immensely popular *Fire Station* (☎ 401 3267), 150 Waterloo Rd SE1 (tube: Waterloo), is in a part of town that was once a culinary desert, despite the proximity of the South Bank. The bar is pleasant enough to make the wait for a table enjoyable and there's a varied menu with reasonable prices (£7 to £10 for main courses).

For a quieter, more intimate atmosphere try the *Bar Central* (☎ 928 5086) at 131 Waterloo Rd E1 (tube: Waterloo). Despite the name, this is actually a restaurant with a small bar. Main courses cost around £7 and the service is efficient.

Splashing Out

The big news in eating out in 1997 was the conversion of the old Oxo Tower (Map 6) on the South Bank into housing with a restaurant at the top. The *restaurant* (☎ 803 3888), Barge House St SE1 (tube: Waterloo), is owned by the Harvey Nichols department store and its venue and river views have ensured it a popularity that means five-week waits for a dinner table. A set lunch costs £24.50, dinner more like £40 a head. Although some reviewers have turned up their noses at the food, only jaded gourmets are likely to be disappointed. If you can't get into the restaurant, there's also a cheaper brasserie, with a bistro downstairs.

Easy to miss inside the Festival Hall and boasting the same fine views is *The People's*

Palace (☎ 928 2355), the rather deceptively named 3rd floor restaurant where the bill for a pre-concert meal featuring such delights as roast rabbit will cost a good £20.

HAMPSTEAD (Map 11)

Budget Conscious

Coffee Cup (☎ 435 7565), 74 Hampstead High St NW3 (tube: Hampstead), is a popular and good-value café offering everything from bacon & eggs to pasta.

The *Everyman Café* (☎ 431 2123), Holly Bush Vale NW3 (tube: Hampstead), is attached to the cinema of the same name. If you're looking for a quiet place to eat in Hampstead, with reasonable food, this is a good choice. The three course set menu is £7.

GREENWICH (Map 12)

Budget Conscious

Greenwich Church St has a couple of decent cheap cafés, and there's a branch of *Café Rouge* attached to the Ibis Hotel at the end of the road. The *Millennium Café* will do you a Cornish pasty for £3.50, while *Peter de Wit's Café* serves cream teas for £3.80 in what it describes as its tiny courtyard.

In the covered market the *Meeting House Café* does ploughman's lunches for £3.50 and milk shakes for £1.30. There's a minimum £2 charge at weekends when it closes promptly at 5 pm.

The *Beachcomber Restaurant* (☎ 0181-853 1155) does set two course lunches for £5.90 and there are a few rather cramped outdoor tables, the flower baskets making up in profusion for any lack of space below.

BRIXTON

Budget Conscious

Pizzeria Franco (☎ 738 3021), 4 Market Row, offers arguably the best pizzas and cappuccinos in south London, while the *Phoenix*, 441 Coldharbour Lane, is a classically reliable caff.

El Pilon Quindiano (☎ 326 4316), Brixton Market, is a Colombian café serving such authentic delicacies as tamales (stuffed maize) for £4.50 and a full lunch for £6. Nearby, the *La Terraza* bar is run by the same people.

Also in the market is *Café Pushkar* (☎ 738 6161), a small but cosy vegetarian place serving dishes like pumpkin and ginger soup for £2.40, and jolly good cakes. There's a noticeboard with details of all things alternative too.

Brixton is the closest tube for all these places.

RICHMOND

There are several places to eat along Richmond high street which runs south-west from the railway/tube station towards the river, but many of the more interesting places are clustered together in Hill Rise, just east of Richmond Bridge. Here you'll find branches of Café Rouge and Caffe Uno.

Budget Conscious

Pierre Victoire (☎ 0181-940 0999), 7 Hill Rise TW10 (tube: Richmond), is one of the most successful branches of the chain which brought reasonably priced French food to English towns.

Crusts (☎ 0181-940 1577), Hill Rise TW10 (tube: Richmond), is a long-standing burger and grill café with appealingly homy decor and tables outside on a platform overlooking busy Richmond roundabout. Burgers cost from £4.65, steaks from £7.95, a set brunch £4.95.

Moderate

Chez Lindsay (☎ 0181-948 7473), 11 Hill Rise TW10 (tube: Richmond), is an inviting French restaurant which specialises in crêpes to be downed with Normandy cider or wine. Alongside the crêpes there's also a more conventional French menu which means you can eat according to your budget: the plainer crêpes on a cheapskate day, the more elaborate ones or a meat or fish dish when you feel like splashing out.

CHISWICK & KEW

Chiswick High Rd is another happy hunting

PAT YALE

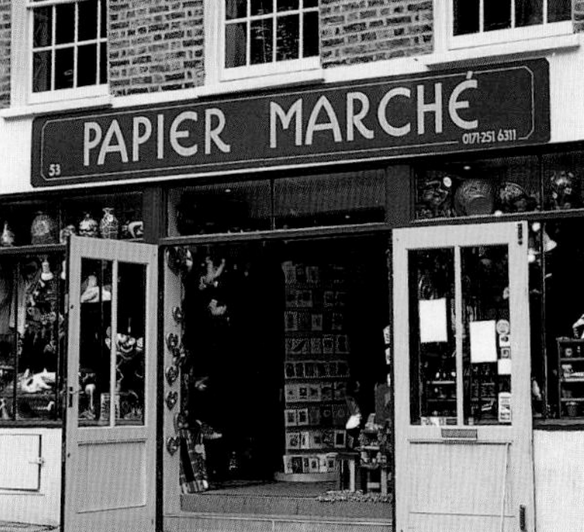

PAT YALE

PAT YALE

DOUG McKINLAY

Left: Chinatown, near Leicester Square
Top: Ye Olde Cheshire Cheese – haunt of Dickens & Dr Johnson
Middle: Clerkenwell shop
Bottom: Spitalfields Market – largest organic food market in London's East End

PAT YALE

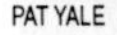

PAT YALE

PAT YALE

PAT YALE

PAT YALE

PAT YALE

A	B
C	D
E	F

A: Exotic fruit & vegetables at Brixton Market, South London
B: Shop on Camden High Street
C: Paraphernalia of tourism
D: Bermondsey Market – antiques paradise
E: Twinings Tea Shop in Fleet Street
F: Camden High Street

ground, with restaurants and cafés to suit all purses.

Budget Conscious

Mackintosh's (☎ 0181-994 2628), 142 Chiswick High Rd (tube: Turnham Green), is a deservedly popular brasserie with some tables on the pavement in good weather. The menu offers a fairly conventional mix of burgers, salads and grills, but portions are large and puddings are a treat; the key lime pie and banoffi pie at £2.95 each are especially moreish.

Tootsies (☎ 0181-747 1869), 148 Chiswick High Rd W4 (tube: Turnham Green), is just one branch of a mini chain also to be found in Old Brompton Rd, Haverstock Hill, New King's Rd, Holland Park Ave and Wimbledon High St. Its menu features a fairly standard choice of burgers, grills and baguettes but the bill shouldn't amount to more than £10. On a balmy evening this branch has the plus of tables on the pavement outside.

Newens Maids of Honour (☎ 0181-940 2752), 288 Kew Rd (tube: Kew Gardens), is a pleasantly old-fashioned tearoom that wouldn't seem out of place in a Cotswold village. It owes its particular fame to a special pudding supposedly concocted by Henry VIII's second wife Anne Boleyn out of puff pastry, lemon, almonds and curd cheese. A 'maid of honour' will cost you £1 but don't plan on sampling it on Monday afternoon or Sunday when the tearoom is closed.

Moderate

The *Thai Bistro* (☎ 0181-995 5774), 99 Chiswick High Rd W4 (tube: Turnham Green), serves delicious Thai food that will leave you begging for more, in stylishly simple black and white surroundings – you may have to share a long table but one mouthful of the mushroom tom yam het soup (£2.95) and that will be forgotten. Vatcharin Bumichitr, the bistro's owner, drew up the main and vegetarian menus from his own cookbooks, *The Taste of Thailand* and *Thai Vegetarian Cooking*.

Splashing Out

Despite its unimaginative name and rather spartan decor, *The Chiswick* (☎ 0181-994 6887), 131 Chiswick High Rd W4 (tube: Turnham Green), is an outstanding example of Modern British cuisine, its menu making free with all sorts of combinations of artichokes, aioli and anchovies. This is a deservedly popular place and if you're put off by the prospect of main courses at around £10 a throw, it's worth knowing that you can get away with £8.50 for two courses at lunchtime and until 8 pm at night.

Entertainment

Few cities in the world can have as much entertainment on offer as London. You'll be spoilt for choice and, expense aside, your biggest problem is likely to be transport to get you home afterwards. The last Underground trains leave between 11.30 pm and 12.30 am (check notices in the station for last services), forcing you to wrestle with the night buses or pay for a taxi.

The area code for all phone and fax numbers in this section is ☎ 0171 unless the entry indicates otherwise.

ENTERTAINMENT GUIDES

To find out what's on you need to buy the comprehensive listings magazine *Time Out* (£1.70), which is published every Tuesday and covers a week of events. Alternatively you can use the London Tourist Board's Visitor Call system; to find out what's on this week phone ☎ 0839-123400; for what's on for the next three months ☎ 0839-123401; for what to do on Sunday ☎ 0839-123407; and for rock and pop concerts ☎ 0839-123422. (These are premium-rated calls costing 49p a minute plus any surcharge your hotel may make for using the phone.)

THEATRES

London is one of the world's great centres for theatre lovers. Few cities offer comparable variety or quality, or such reasonable prices. It would be a crime not to organise tickets for one or two of the best productions even if you're not normally a theatre-goer.

How to Book

If you're booking ahead the best thing to do is to phone the theatre box office and see if you can buy tickets direct from them without having to pay commission to middlemen. Most box offices are open Monday to Saturday from 10 am to 8 pm. If the production is sold out you might be able to buy a returned ticket on the day of the performance, although for something popular like *Starlight Express* you might need to start queuing before the returns actually go on sale.

Student stand-by tickets are sometimes available on production of identity cards one hour before the performance starts. Phone ☎ 379 8900 for more details.

Tickets for the subsidised theatres (the Royal National, the Barbican and the Royal Court) can only be bought from the theatre box offices (see below).

On the day of performance you can buy half-price tickets for West End productions from the Leicester Square Half-Price Ticket Booth, on the south side of Leicester Square. It opens daily from noon to 6.30 pm and charges £2 commission per ticket. Note that you can't buy tickets for musicals like *Cats* and *Starlight Express* here. Nor can you buy tickets for *The Mousetrap*, although the boards showing availability at West End shows also indicate the odds on getting a ticket at one of these blockbusters.

Many theatre agencies also sell tickets, especially for popular musicals like *Cats*, but most charge a hefty commission. Be particularly wary of commercial booths near Leicester Square (like the one opposite the Hippodrome on Cranbourne St) which advertise half-price tickets without mentioning the commission added to the price. The worst possible option is to buy from a tout selling tickets in the street.

The Society of London Theatre (☎ 836 0971) offers the following advice for people buying tickets from an agency:

- Find out the normal prices for the show first.
- Ask the agent what the ticket's face value is and how much commission is being added.
- Ask to be shown where you'll be sitting on a seat plan.
- Don't pay for the tickets until you've seen them.
- Don't agree to pick the tickets up later or to have them sent to you.

Royal National Theatre

The nation's flagship theatre is the Royal

National Theatre (☎ 928 2252; tube: Waterloo), with three auditoria on the South Bank (the Olivier, the Lyttleton and the Cottesloe). It showcases classics and contemporary plays, and hosts guest appearances by the world's best young companies.

Tickets for evening performances at the Olivier and Lyttleton cost from £10 to £32.50. Visitors to the box office can sometimes buy one or two tickets for same-day performances for £10 or £11.50. Stand-by tickets are sometimes available two hours before the performance for £13; students with ID pay just £7 but must wait until 45 minutes before curtain up. You can save money by going to a weekday matinee performance, when prices range from £8 to £16.

Under-18s pay from £7.50 to £10.50 for matinees and senior citizens from £10 to £12.50. Registered disabled visitors are eligible for discounts at all performances.

Most tickets at the smaller Cottesloe cost £16, although some seats with restricted views cost £12.

Barbican

The *Barbican* (☎ 638 8891; tube: Barbican), Silk St EC2 (Map 6), is the London home of the Royal Shakespeare Company, with two auditoria, the Barbican Theatre and the smaller Pit, in the much-criticised and confusing Barbican Centre. Midweek matinee tickets start at £6 at the Barbican and £10 at the Pit. Tickets are half-price to anyone under 25 on Monday nights. There are also price reductions for anyone over 60 at Saturday matinees.

Royal Court

The *Royal Court* (☎ 730 1745) is operating temporarily out of the Duke of York and Ambassadors theatres until its own Sloane Square theatre has been rebuilt. It tends to favour the new and the anti-establishment – various enfants terribles from John Osborne to Caryl Churchill got their first break here.

Globe Theatre

The *Globe Theatre* (☎ 401 9919; tube: London Bridge; Map 6), a replica of Shakespeare's 'wooden O', now dominates Bankside where most of the Elizabethan theatres stood. Come here for a very different theatrical experience. Although there are wooden bench seats in tiers around the stage, many people will emulate the 17th century 'groundlings' who stood in front of the stage, moving around as the mood took them. The Globe makes few concessions to modern sensibilities. With no roof, it is open to the elements; you should wrap up warmly and bring a flask, although no umbrellas are allowed. Performances of plays by Shakespeare and his contemporaries are staged from May to September only.

Tickets for seats cost from £10 to £20. The 500 standing spaces per performance cost £5 each and can be booked, although you may find a few unsold on the day.

West End Theatres

Every summer the 50-odd West End theatres stage a new crop of plays, musicals and other performances. For full details, consult *Time Out*. Addresses and box office phone numbers of the West End theatres are as follows:

Adelphi Strand WC2 (☎ 344 0055; tube: Charing Cross)

Albery St Martin's Lane WC2 (☎ 369 1740; tube: Leicester Square)

Aldwych Aldwych WC2 (☎ 416 6003; tube: Holborn)

Ambassadors West St WC2 (☎ 565 5000; tube: Leicester Square)

Apollo Shaftesbury Ave W1 (☎ 494 5072; tube: Piccadilly Circus)

Apollo Victoria 17 Wilton Rd SW1 (☎ 416 6054; tube: Victoria)

Cambridge Earlham St WC2 (☎ 494 5083; tube: Covent Garden)

Comedy Panton St SW1 (☎ 369 1731; tube: Piccadilly Circus)

Criterion Piccadilly Circus W1 (☎ 369 1737; tube: Piccadilly Circus)

Dominion Tottenham Court Rd W1 (☎ 656 1888; tube: Tottenham Court Rd)

Drury Lane Catherine St WC2 (☎ 494 5000; tube: Covent Garden)

Duchess Catherine St WC2 (☎ 494 5075; tube: Covent Garden)

Duke of York St Martin's Lane, WC2 (☎ 565 5000; tube: Leicester Square)

Fortune Russell St WC2 (☎ 836 2238; tube: Covent Garden)

Garrick Charing Cross Rd WC2 (☎ 494 5085; tube: Charing Cross)
Gielgud Shaftesbury Ave W1 (☎ 494 5557; tube: Piccadilly Circus)
Haymarket Haymarket SW1 (☎ 930 8800; tube: Piccadilly Circus)
Her Majesty's Haymarket SW1 (☎ 494 5400; tube: Piccadilly Circus)
Labatt's Apollo Hammersmith Queen Caroline St W6 (☎ 416 6050; tube: Hammersmith)
London Palladium Argyll St W1 (☎ 494 5020; tube: Oxford Circus)
Lyceum Wellington St WC2 (☎ 656 1800; tube: Covent Garden)
Lyric Hammersmith King St W6 (☎ 0181-741 2311; tube: Hammersmith)
New London Drury Lane WC2 (☎ 405 0072; tube: Holborn)
Old Vic Waterloo Rd SE1 (☎ 928 7616; tube: Waterloo)
Palace Shaftesbury Ave W1 (☎ 434 0909; tube: Leicester Square)
Phoenix Charing Cross Rd WC2 (☎ 369 1733; tube: Tottenham Court Rd)
Piccadilly Denman St W1 (☎ 369 1734; tube: Piccadilly Circus)
Prince Edward Old Compton St W1(☎ 447 5400; tube: Leicester Square)
Prince of Wales Coventry St W1(☎ 839 5987; tube: Piccadilly Circus)
Royal Court Downstairs St Martin's Lane WC2 (☎ 565 5000; tube: Leicester Square)
St Martins West St, Cambridge Circus WC2 (☎ 836 1443; tube: Leicester Square)
Savoy Strand WC2 (☎ 836 8888; tube: Charing Cross)
Strand Aldwych WC2 (☎ 930 8800; tube: Covent Garden)
Vaudeville Strand WC2 (☎ 836 9987; tube: Charing Cross)
Victoria Palace Victoria St SW1 (☎ 834 1317; tube: Victoria)
Wyndham's Charing Cross Rd WC2 (☎ 369 1736; tube: Leicester Square)

London's longest running show – indeed the longest running in the world – is *The Mousetrap*, a rendition of the Agatha Christie detective story now into its 46th year at St Martins.

On a sunny day it's fun to take in a

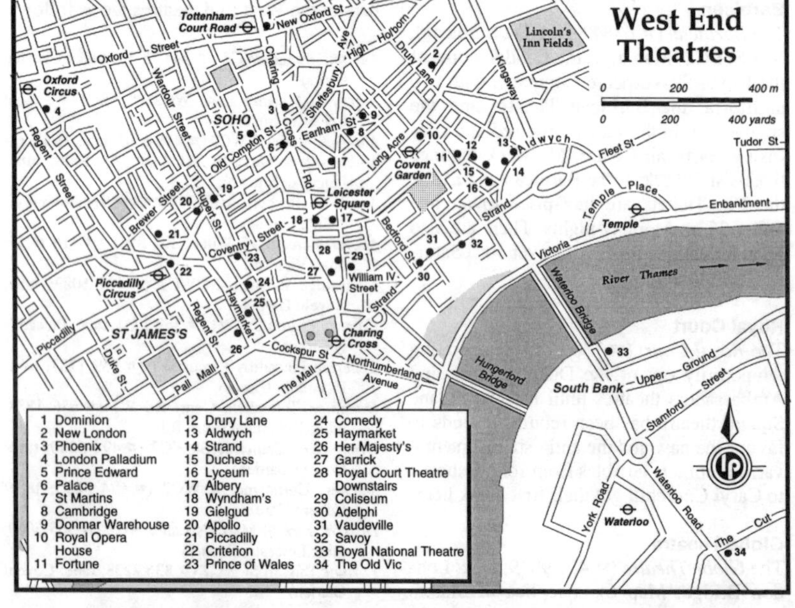

Shakespearean play or musical at the *Open Air Theatre* (☎ 486 2431; tube: Baker St) in Regent's Park, although it's safe to assume some of the dialogue will be drowned out by passing aircraft.

As if all this wasn't enough, at any time of the year London's many off-West End and fringe theatre productions offer a selection of the amazing, the boring, the life-enhancing and the downright ridiculous. Some of the better venues to try include:

Almeida Almeida St N1 (☎ 359 4404; tube: Highbury & Islington)
Donmar Warehouse Earlham St WC2H 9LD (☎ 369 1732; tube: Covent Garden)
Hampstead Theatre Avenue Rd NW3 (☎ 722 9301; tube: Swiss Cottage)
Tricycle Theatre 269 Kilburn High Rd NW6 (☎ 328 1000; tube: Kilburn)
Young Vic 66 The Cut SE1 (☎ 928 6363; tube: Waterloo)

CINEMAS

During the 50s and 60s many of London's great Art Deco and Art Nouveau cinema houses shut down. The late 80s saw the coming of the first multiplex cinemas and the revival continues to this day. Although these cinemas offer more choice of films at the one site and much more comfortable seating arrangements, they also tend to be expensive and serve up primarily mainstream American fare. Although full-price tickets are around £7, afternoon shows are usually cheaper, and on Monday several places offer half-price tickets all day.

Every year, in November, the National Film Theatre pops up from its South Bank bunker to host the London Film Festival (☎ 420 1122).

For less mainstream fare the following central London cinemas are most promising:

Barbican Silk St EC2 (☎ 382 7000; tube: Barbican)
Curzon Mayfair Curzon St W1 (☎ 369 1720; tube: Hyde Park Corner)
Curzon Phoenix Charing Cross Rd WC1 (☎ 369 1721; tube: Tottenham Court Rd)
Curzon West End Shaftesbury Ave W1 (☎ 369 1722; tube: Leicester Square)
Everyman Holly Bush Vale NW3 (☎ 435 1525; tube: Hampstead; Map 11)
Gate Notting Hill Gate W1 (☎ 727 4043; tube: Notting Hill Gate)
ICA Nash House, The Mall SW1 (☎ 930 3647; tube: Charing Cross)
Minema 45 Knightsbridge SW1 (☎ 369 1723; tube: Knightsbridge)
National Film Theatre South Bank SE1 (☎ 928 3232; tube: Embankment)
Renoir Brunswick Square WC1 (☎ 837 8402; tube: Russell Square)
Rio Kingsland High St E8 (☎ 254 6677; station: Dalston/Kingsland)
Ritzy Brixton Oval, Coldharbour Lane SW2 (☎ 733 2229; tube: Brixton)
Riverside Studios Crisp Rd W6 (☎ 0181-741 2255; tube: Hammersmith)
Screen on Baker St 96 Baker St NW1 (☎ 935 2772; tube: Baker St)
Screen on the Green Islington Green N1 (☎ 226 3520; tube: Angel)
Screen on the Hill 203 Haverstock Hill NW3 (☎ 435 3366; tube: Belsize Park)

The *Prince Charles* (☎ 437 8181; Map 3) in Leicester Place is central London's cheapest cinema, with tickets for new release films from only £1.75. It shows several films each day so check the programme carefully.

At the time of writing, the old *Electric Cinema* at 191 Portobello Rd W11 was closed pending a refit which should give it comfy seats, a bar and a bookshop.

To check disabled access to these cinemas call Artsline on ☎ 388 2227.

CLUBS

It may come as a surprise to discover that most pubs still close at 11 pm. Luckily there are clubs where you can carry on partying, although you'll have to pay to get in and the drinks are always expensive.

Late-night venues often have a 'club' licence, which means you have to be a member to enter. In practice, they usually include the membership fee as part of the admission price. Many venues have clubs that only operate on one night a week and cater for a specific market – whether for the type of music or the kind of people they let in.

Clubs can change with bewildering speed and sometimes use the membership requirement to exclude people they don't like the look of. *Time Out* and *Mixmag* have the details and some Soho record shops, like Black Market Records, 25 D'Arblay St, stock flyers and details of events. Many clubs have a gay night (see the boxed aside on Gay & Lesbian London).

Entry prices vary from £10 to £15 for most clubs, plus about £3 for one alcoholic drink. The most happening clubs don't kick off until midnight and often stay open until 4 or 5 am. Dress can be smart (no suits) or casual; the more outrageous you look the better chance you have of getting in!

At the time of writing it was still technically illegal to charge people to club on Sundays, a problem sometimes got round by levying membership fees instead. However, it's likely that the law will soon be changed, and the number of clubs opening on Sundays looks set to rise.

Aquarium 256 Old St EC1 (☎ 251 6136; tube: Old St) – converted gym with pool and jacuzzi and cool atmosphere. Opens on Sunday.

Bagley's Studios Kings Cross Freight Depot, off York Way N1 (☎ 278 2777; tube: Kings Cross) – a huge converted warehouse with five dance floors, four bars and an outside area for the summer. The music varies from room to room and the atmosphere is excellent.

Bar Rumba 36 Shaftesbury Ave W1 (☎ 287 2715; tube: Piccadilly Circus; Map 3) – varied nights including salsa. Small but very popular club; Thai food served all night.

Blue Note 1 Hoxton Square N1 (☎ 729 8440; tube: Old St) – relaxed club with live sets, funk, jazz and soul; opens from Sunday lunchtime too.

Browns 4 Great Queen's St WC2 (☎ 831 0802; tube: Holborn; Map 3) – the stars' after-party hang-out. Though slightly pretentious, it's a lively, fun club – if you can get in.

Café de Paris 3 Coventry St W1 (☎ 734 7700; tube: Piccadilly; Map 3) – completely revamped, this is London's newest dining bar. If you'd rather just be a spectator, the immense building has a galleried restaurant overlooking the dancefloor.

Cloud 9 67 Albert Embankment SE1 (☎ 735 5590; tube: Vauxhall) – brash, noisy club under two railway arches, good for a Saturday night.

The Cross Good Ways Depot, off York Way N1 (☎ 837 0828; tube: King's Cross) – one of London's leading venues, hidden under the arches. Brilliant DJs and a great ambience guarantee a good night.

Dingwalls The East Yard, Camden Lock NW1 (☎ 267 0545; tube: Camden Town; Map 10) – comedy acts at weekends, music during the week and clubbing every night. Upstairs there's a terrace bar which gives you an aerial view of the lock and the market; food is available.

Dog Star 389 Coldharbour Lane SW9 (☎ 733 7515; tube: Brixton) – as laid-back as you'd expect so dressing to kill isn't imperative.

Emporium 62 Kingly St W1 (☎ 734 3190; tube: Oxford Circus; Map 3) – very popular with the beautiful set, Emporium is one of the trendiest clubs in town.

The End 16A West Central St WC1 (☎ 419 9199; tube: Holborn) – modern industrial decor; free water fountain. For serious clubbers who like their music underground.

The Fridge Town Hall Parade SW2 (☎ 326 5100; tube: Brixton) – a wide variety of club nights in an excellent venue which is not too big, not too small. Saturday is gay night.

Gardening Club 4 The Piazza WC2 (☎ 497 3154; tube: Covent Garden; Map 3) – a varied crowd; this cave-like club tends to attract fun-loving out-of-towners.

Hanover Grand 6 Hanover St W1 (☎ 499 7977; tube: Oxford Circus; Map 3) – split-level venue, voted 'Best Club in London' two years running; worth queuing for.

Heaven Under the Arches, Craven St WC2 (☎ 930 2020; tube: Charing Cross; Map 3) – long-standing, popular gay nightclub.

Hippodrome Hippodrome Corner WC2 (☎ 437 4311; tube: Leicester Square; Map 3) – notorious for its glitzy dance floors and bright lights. Expensive and very popular with tourists.

HQ Club West Yard, Camden Lock NW1 (☎ 485 6044; tube: Camden Town) – predominantly a garage and house club. The cover charge averages around £5, depending on the day of the week.

Iceni 11 White Horse St, off Curzon St W1 (☎ 495 5333; tube: Green Park; Map 4) – three floors of contrasting music and a friendly atmosphere make this one of the more accessible clubs.

Legends 29 Old Burlington St W1 (☎ 437 9933; tube: Green Park; Map 3) – very suave-looking interior and separate bars mean that Legends is more sociable than other clubs. Good for people-watching.

Leopard Lounge The Broadway, Fulham Rd SW6 (☎ 385 0834; tube: Fulham Broadway) – large safari-themed club which attracts those who want to go a little wild as well as those looking to sit down and chatter.

Madame Jo Jo's 8 Brewer St W1 (☎ 734 2473; tube: Piccadilly Circus) – beautiful transvestite waiting staff in keeping with Soho's old image, but there's nothing sleazy about this place; opens Sunday.

Ministry of Sound 103 Gaunt St SE1 (☎ 378 6528;

tube: Elephant & Castle; Map 2) – now renowned internationally, this cavernous club attracts hard-core clubbers as well as people who just want to chill out, although rumour has it that it's past its finest hour. It's open until 9 am. Don't expect to do any talking in the box room.

Po Na Na The Hedgehog, 259 Upper St N1 (☎ 359 6191; tube: Highbury & Islington) – relatively low-key, if leopard-printed, gathering every other Thursday.

Velvet Underground 143 Charing Cross Rd WC2 (☎ 734 4687; tube: Tottenham Court Rd; Map 3) – an intimate, friendly club swathed in red velvet.

COMEDY

Central London plays host to several clubs whose *raison d'être* is comedy, as well as to others which set aside specific nights for funniness. As usual, the place to look for day-to-day details is *Time Out* but the following are long-standing venues where belly laughs are virtually guaranteed:

Comedy Store 1A Oxendon St SW1 (☎ 01426-914433; tube: Piccadilly Circus; Map 3)

Jongleurs Battersea The Cornet, 49 Lavender Gardens SW11 (☎ 924 2766; station: Clapham Junction)

Jongleurs Bow Wharf 221 Grove Rd E3 (☎ 924 2766; tube: Mile End)

Jongleurs Camden Lock Dingwalls, Middle Yard, Chalk Farm Rd, Camden Lock NW1 (☎ 924 2766; tube: Camden Town; Map 10)

MUSIC

Classical Music

London is Europe's classical music capital, with five symphony orchestras, various smaller outfits, brilliant venues, reasonable prices and high standards of performance.

There's so much on that you may have troubling deciding what to pick. On any night of the year the choice will range from traditional crowd-pleasers to new music and 'difficult' composers. Opera can be more problematic because it's costly to produce and so costly to attend.

South Bank Venues The *Royal Festival Hall*, *Queen Elizabeth Hall* and *Purcell Room* (☎ 960 4242; fax 401 8834) are three of London's premier venues for classical concerts. Depending on who's performing and where you, sit prices vary from £5 to £50. The box office is open from 10 am to 9 pm daily.

Wigmore Hall The *Wigmore Hall* (☎ 935 2141; tube: Bond St), 35 Wigmore St W1, offers intimacy and variety. The Sunday-morning recitals are particularly good.

Barbican The *Barbican* (☎ 638 8891; tube: Barbican), Silk St EC2 (Map 6), is home to the London Symphony Orchestra. Prices vary but stand-by tickets for £6.50 and £8 are sometimes available just before the performance to students and over-60s.

Royal Albert Hall The *Royal Albert Hall* (☎ 589 8212; tube: South Kensington), Kensington Gore SW7 (Map 8), is a splendid Victorian concert hall that, from mid-July to mid-September, plays host to the Proms – one of the world's biggest and most democratic classical music festivals. Tickets cost from £5 to £32 depending on what's on, but the real 'prom' experience means queuing for one of the 1000-odd standing (or promenading) tickets that go on sale one hour before the start of each concert for £3 each. You can choose to stand in the gallery or the arena and there are two separate queues accordingly.

The Last Night of the Proms is one of those quintessentially English affairs, all waving Union Jacks, drunken chanting of Elgar's *Land of Hope and Glory* and argument over whether the programme was too modern. For the last few years the action has been relayed onto screens in nearby Hyde Park to let more people join in; tickets cost £8.50.

Royal Opera House (ROH) Despite constant money problems, the *Royal Opera House* (☎ 304 4000), Covent Garden WC2 (tube: Covent Garden; Map 3), maintains its reputation for excellence, regularly bagging superstars like Pavarotti and Domingo for performances. For the best seats you normally need to be prepared to take out a mortgage although a really bad seat can be had for as little as £2 and the cheapest seats with clear views of the stage range from £7.50 to £29. Unfortunately, during the life of this book the Royal Opera House will be closed for redevelopment and if you do get to see a performance it will be in a temporary venue (possibly the Shaftesbury Theatre or the Barbican), ultimately in the Sadler's Wells Theatre in Rosebury Ave.

Coliseum The *London Coliseum*, home of the English National Opera (☎ 632 8300; tube: Leicester Square), St Martin's Lane WC2 (Map 3), is more reasonably priced and presents opera in English. From 10 am on the day of performance balcony seats go on sale for £5; expect a long queue. The Coliseum hopes to move to a new home but this is likely to take a couple of years.

Kenwood House A highlight of a sunny summer is certainly to attend an outdoor concert in the grounds of *Kenwood House* (☎ 413 1443; tube: Hampstead; Map 11) on Hampstead Heath. People sit on the grass, eat strawberries, drink chilled white wine and listen to classical music.

Churches

Many churches host evening concerts or lunchtime recitals. Sometimes they're free, with a suggested donation requested; at other times there are fixed prices. A few redundant churches now serve as concert halls.

All Hallows by the Tower
: Organ recitals on Thursday at 1.15 pm; donation requested (Map 6).

St George's Bloomsbury
: Tuesday lunchtime concerts at 1.10 pm; donation requested. Sunday evening concerts at 5.20 pm; £2 (Map 5).

St James's, Piccadilly
: Daily lunchtime concerts at 1.10 pm; donation requested. Evening concerts at 7.30 pm; £12 (Map 3).

St John's, Smith Square
: Lunchtime concerts on Mondays at 1 pm; tickets cost £6. Evening concerts (☎ 407 2276) start at 7.30 pm; tickets cost from £6 to £18 (Map 4).

St Lawrence Jewry
: Piano recitals on Monday, organ recitals on Tuesday at 1 pm. Evening concerts (☎ 344 9214) at 7.30 pm; tickets £6 (Map 6).

St Martin-in-the-Fields
: Lunchtime concerts on Monday, Tuesday, Wednesday and Friday at 1.05 pm; donations requested. Evening concerts (☎ 839 8362) by candlelight (Map 3).

St Mary-le-Strand
: Lunchtime concerts on Wednesday and Friday at 1.05 pm; donations requested. Evening concerts (☎ 0181-980 2948) cost £4/2.

Southwark Cathedral
: Lunchtime organ recitals on Monday at 1.10 pm; other music recitals on Tuesday at 1.10 pm (☎ 407 3708; Map 6).

Temple Church
: Lunchtime concerts on Wednesday at 1.15 pm (Map 6).

Rock & Pop

London also boasts a wide range of rock and pop venues, and you can hear everything from megastars raking in the bucks at Wembley, Earl's Court and similar hangar-sized arenas, to hot new bands at the Astoria in Charing Cross Rd, Subterania in Notting Hill, the Brixton Academy in Brixton or The Forum in Kentish Town. Pub rock is also loud and kicking at Islington's Powerhaus or Garage.

Capital FM radio station has a useful ticket hotline (☎ 420 0958), or Ticketmaster has a 24 hour credit-card booking line on ☎ 0990-344444. Tickets are also available from HMV or Tower Records, from the Camden Ticket Shop attached to the Jazz Café, or from the London Tourist Board at Victoria Station.

Here are some addresses you're likely to need:

Astoria 157 Charing Cross Rd WC2 (☎ 434 0403; tube: Tottenham Court Rd; Map 3) – dark, sweaty and atmospheric, with good views of the stage; cheap gay nights (£1) on Thursday.

Brixton Academy 211 Stockwell Rd SW9 (☎ 924 9999; tube: Brixton) – enormous venue with good atmosphere.

Earl's Court Exhibition Centre Warwick Rd SW5 (☎ 373 8141; tube: Earl's Court; Map 8) – venue for blockbuster concerts, the type that tend to sell out well ahead.

Forum 9-17 Highgate Rd NW5 (☎ 344 0044; tube: Kentish Town) – formerly the Town & Country club, and still an excellent roomy venue.
Hackney Empire 291 Mare St E8 (☎ 0181-985 2424; tube: Bethnal Green) – superb Edwardian theatre; an excellent venue.
London Arena Limeharbour, Isle of Dogs E14 (☎ 538 1212; Crossharbour DLR) – occasional outsize gigs.
Royal Albert Hall Kensington Gore SW7 (☎ 589 8212; tube: South Kensington; Map 8) – huge, historic auditorium which attracts big-name performers for one-off events.
Shepherd's Bush Empire Shepherd's Bush Green W12 (☎ 0181-740 7474; tube: Shepherd's Bush) – one of the best venues in London.
Wembley Arena Empire Way, Middlesex (☎ 0181-900 1234; tube: Wembley Park) – huge venue with little to recommend it bar its high profile.

Smaller places with a more club-like atmosphere that are worth checking for interesting bands include:

Barfly at the Falcon 234 Royal College St NW1 (☎ 485 3834; tube: Camden Town) – the small club, then called Splash, where Oasis played their first London gig still gives a succession of small-time artists their big break.
Borderline Orange Yard, off Manette St W1 (☎ 734 2095; tube: Tottenham Court Rd; Map 3) – small, relaxed venue, with a reputation for big-name bands playing under pseudonyms.
Rock Garden The Piazza WC2 (☎ 240 3961; tube: Covent Garden; Map 3) – small basement venue, often packed with tourists but also hosting good bands.
Subterania 12 Acklam Rd W10 (☎ 0181-960 4590; tube: Ladbroke Grove; Map 9) – atmospheric place showcasing up-and-comers.
Underworld 174 Camden High St NW1 (☎ 482 1932; tube: Camden Town; Map 10) – beneath the World's End pub, a small venue featuring new bands.

Jazz

London has always had a thriving jazz scene and, with its recent resurgence thanks to acid-jazz, hip-hop, funk and swing, it's stronger than ever.

Jazz Café 5 Parkway NW1 (☎ 344 0044; tube: Camden Town; Map 10) – very trendy restaurant/venue; best to book a table
Pizza Express 10 Dean St W1 (☎ 437 9595; tube: Tottenham Court Rd; Map 3) – beneath the main restaurant, a small basement venue
Ronnie Scott's 47 Frith St W1 (☎ 439 0747; tube: Leicester Square; Map 3) – operating since 1959; seedy and enjoyable but expensive if you're not a member (£45 a year); £15 between Monday and Thursday and £14 at weekends. There's no obligation to drink or eat but wine is from £12.50 a bottle, £1.40 for half a pint of beer, and food from £5
100 Club 100 Oxford St W1 (☎ 636 0933; tube: Oxford Circus; Maps 3 & 5) – legendary London venue, once showcasing the Stones and at the centre of the punk revolution, now concentrating on jazz

Blues & Folk

Three places well worth checking out are:

Biddy Mulligans 205 Kilburn High Rd NW6 (☎ 624 2066; tube: Kilburn) – a traditional Irish pub, with live music at weekends
Bunjies 27 Litchfield St WC2 (☎ 240 1796; tube: Leicester Square) – long-lived folk club with a good-value restaurant
Mean Fiddler 24 High St, Harlesden NW10 (☎ 0181-961 5490; tube: Willesden Junction) – legendary venue for top-quality acoustic folk

PUBS & BARS

Pubs are perhaps the most distinctive contribution the English have made to urban life and nothing really compares to a good one. Traditionally the 'local' has been at the hub of the community, and in some parts of London this tradition is still very much alive with people treating pubs as virtual extensions of their homes. The 'regulars' become members of an extended gregarious family, although, curiously, relationships don't always extend beyond the door of the pub. Finding a local where you feel comfortable is the first step to being a real Londoner.

These days traditional pubs are thin on the ground. If you're after something authentic, steer clear of pubs with the words 'slug', 'lettuce', 'rat', 'carrot', 'firkin', 'newt', 'parrot' or any combination of the above in their name. It's not that there's necessarily anything wrong with them, just that they're the ones most likely to come with antipodean bar staff and noisy 'fruit' machines competing with a TV and a jukebox. (They're also guilty of scrapping perfectly good historic names in favour of meaningless marketing make-ups, but that's another story...) Most will sell a good range of beers, and cheap and filling bar food; the more traditional the pub, the more limited the range of food is likely to be.

Bars are starting to outnumber pubs in some parts of London. You pay more for a drink (beer may not be on tap) and the fridges are full of imported designer drinks. However, the stylish decor, late opening hours and more upmarket atmosphere attract the upwardly-mobile 20-35s. Some bars have a DJ at weekends and make a door charge. Pitcher & Piano (Balham Hill, Chiswick High Rd, Dean St, Fulham Rd, William IV St and Wimbledon High St) and All Bar One (Canary Wharf, Chiswick, Dean St, Fulham Rd, Hanover St, Islington, Leicester Square, Ludgate Hill, Richmond, Regent St, St John's Wood and Wimbledon) are fast-growing chains. Dôme and Café Rouge are more like continental brasseries – you can just drink, have a snack or eat a decent meal.

If you're the sort of person who likes pubs but doesn't like the noise or the smoky atmosphere, it's worth knowing about the Wetherspoon chain which has been trying to lure back drinkers who've drifted away by offering nonsmoking areas, decent food and even some pubs without jukeboxes. Ironically the old Marquee Club in Charing Cross Rd, which showcased many punk acts in the 1970s, is now a music-free Wetherspoon pub, *The Moon Under Water*. A clue is the word 'moon' in the name, as in *JJ Moon's*, *The Moon and Stars* and so on. To find out where these pubs are phone ☎ 01923-477774 or look up their web site at www.jdwetherspoon.co.uk

Sampling a range of pubs and bars is an essential duty for every visitor to London. The following list gives a few clues but there's no substitute for careful individual research. For more suggestions look for the *Evening Standard Pub Guide* (£9.99). The London Docklands Visitor Centre also sells a handy guide to the area's waterside pubs (£2), a strange mix of the old and atmospheric, and the brashly new.

If you're on a tight budget it's worth noting that the Pitcher & Piano chain charges an outrageous £2.40 for a pint of lager – head for a Wetherspoon pub and you'll find prices up to £1 cheaper.

West End (Map 3)

All Bar One, Leicester Square (tube: Leicester Square), is a designer bar on the west side of the square with big plate-glass windows through which you can watch the goings on outside. To supplement the walls of bottles, blackboard menus offer sandwiches from £3.50 and a choice of small or big plate meals for around £5 and £7 respectively.

The Moon Under Water, Leicester Square (tube: Leicester Square), is one of the new Wetherspoon enterprises with no-smoking areas and reasonable pub food. This one is good for checking out the history of the square, with old photos and documentation lining the walls.

The *Cork & Bottle*, 44-46 Cranbourn St (tube: Leicester Square), is hidden downstairs on the left as you head to Leicester Square from the tube station. It's always packed to the hilt after work but the food's good, the wine list commendable and the ambience, with several hideaway alcoves, enjoyable.

The Polar Bear, 30 Lisle St WC2 (tube: Leicester Square), is a favourite with Australasians and handily placed for an after-hours Chinese.

Waxy O'Connors, 14 Rupert St W1 (tube: Leicester Square), is a large multi-level Irish pub with a quirky Gothic interior. It's always crowded and has a friendly, sociable atmosphere.

The Salisbury, 90 St Martin's Lane WC2 (tube: Leicester Square), was once an almost exclusively gay hang-out. Now that the action has moved Sohowards there's nothing to stop anyone dropping by to admire the beautifully etched and engraved windows and elaborate decor of a Victorian pub that has somehow escaped the moderniser's hand.

The Flamingo Bar, Hanover St W1 (tube: Oxford Circus), is a Latin American theme bar which often has live sets and is good for pre-Hanover Grand drinks (see Clubs section).

The friendly *ICAfé*, The Mall SW1 (tube: Piccadilly Circus), in the ICA arts centre, has a licence to 1 am.

You're certainly not going to find another pub called *I am the Only Running Footman*, however hard you look. This old-world-looking pub at 5 Charles St W1 (tube: Green Park) has been extensively refitted, so none of the 18th century running footmen who used to gather here in the past would recognise it, but it's none the less pleasant for that. And the running footman? Well, he was employed by a wealthy man to run in front of his carriage lighting the way and shifting any obstacles.

Gay & Lesbian London

The London gay scene is doing so well you could easily feel overwhelmed by the number of places to visit. Gay London has a livelier, more eclectic scene than most other European cities.

The best starting point is to pick up a free listings magazine like *The Pink Paper* or *Boyz*, available from most gay cafés, bars and clubs. Magazines like *Gay Times* (£2) and the lesbian *Diva* (£2) also have listings. *Time Out* is another excellent source of information.

London's bars and clubs cater for every predilection, but there's a growing trend towards mixed gay/straight clubs. There are also men or women-only nights; check the press for details.

In the 'gay village' of Soho, bars and cafés are thick on the ground. Walk down Old Compton St, from Charing Cross Rd. On your right at No 34 is the friendly, sometimes frantic, 24-hour *Compton St Café*. *Balaans*, at No 60, is a moderately-priced, popular, continental-style café. Further up the street are numerous gay-owned bars, shops and eateries. *Soho Men*, above *Clone Zone* at No 64, offers a 90-minute facial for £35. Further into Soho you'll find the hyper-trendy *Freedom Café*, 60 Wardour St, serving food and drink for a mixed clientele. At 57 Rupert St *The Yard* has a pleasant courtyard where you can eat and drink.

Near Tottenham Court Rd tube, the long-established, friendly *First Out*, 52 St Giles High St, is a mixed lesbian-gay café serving vegetarian food and with periodic exhibitions.

Café de Paris, 3 Coventry St (tube: Leicester Square), is an intimate club playing mainly house and garage. Just beyond Long Acre is Europe's largest gay bar, *The Base*, 167 Drury Lane (tube: Covent Garden). There's also the *Gardening Club*, 4 The Piazza (tube: Covent Garden), where the most popular nights are Club for Life (Saturday) and Queer Nation (Sunday).

The further you go from the West End, the more local the clientele becomes. *The Black Cap*, 171 Camden High St (tube: Camden Town), is a late-night bar with a good drag reputation. Further out on Hampstead Heath, a popular cruising spot, *The King William IV*, 75 Heath St (tube: Hampstead Heath), is a friendly pub with sofas and log fires. Also in north London, *The Central Station*, 37 Wharfdale Rd (tube: King's Cross; Map 5) has a bar with special one-nighters, including a women-only night called the Clit Club – depending on the night it's very popular. Further east at the Angel tube station, *The Angel*, open from midday, is a vegetarian café bar tucked away at 65 Graham St (Map 2), also good for women.

Despite being overshadowed by Soho, Earl's Court still has a few places of interest. There's the excellent *Wilde About Oscar* restaurant in the *Philbeach Hotel* (Map 8), 31 Philbeach Gardens, and *The Coleherne*, 261 Old Brompton Rd (Map 8), one of London's oldest pubs.

Love Muscle at the *Fridge*, Town Hall Parade, Brixton Hill (tube: Brixton), has dance music on Saturday nights with a mixed crowd. *Heaven*, Villiers St (tube: Charing Cross), in the West End, is London's most famous gay club with three dance floors. Every night has a different slant, so check the press for details.

Turnmills, 55B Clerkenwell Rd EC1 (tube: Farringdon; Map 6), has three gay nights. From 10 pm to 3 am on Saturday it's Pumpin Curls, a women's club. From 3 am onwards it's Trade, London's first all-nighter, which goes until 12.30 pm on Sunday; breakfast is served at 6 am. On Sunday, at the same venue, ff runs until 8 am on Monday with techno and trance music.

Before hitting the clubs, it's worth picking up advertising flyers (available in most bars), which will give you a reduced entry price. Any saving is worthwhile, because clubbing can be expensive. Places tend to be packed at the weekends, but you can party nonstop from Friday into Monday.

If the club scene's not for you, you can also make new friends at the myriad social, sport and dance groups and classes. *Time Out* and the gay press have the details. ■

Although the staff would throw their hands up in horror at the idea of being associated with pubs, those who're smartly dressed and don't suffer from vertigo might like to buy a pricey drink in *Windows on the World* (☎ 493 8000), the 28th floor bar on top of the Hilton Hotel, Park Lane W1. The prices are steep (£3.50 for a bottle of lager) and the interior tacky but the bar is open until late and the view over Hyde Park and across to the river is superb.

Soho & Covent Garden (Map 3)

Coach & Horses, 29 Greek St W1 (tube: Leicester Square), is a small, busy pub that has a regular clientele, but is nonetheless hospitable to visitors. It was made famous by the famously alcoholic *Spectator* columnist Jeffrey Bernard. Since being refurbished the nearby *Three Greyhounds* at 25 Greek St has become more continental in style. It serves good food and several varieties of ale.

The French House, 49 Dean St W1 (tube: Leicester Square), is very popular despite only serving halves (half pints); there's a posh restaurant upstairs (see Places to Eat). *The Pitcher & Piano* down the road at No 70 is one of a growing chain. If you're used to Soho's hustle and bustle, then the pace will come as no surprise. Lots of beer, lots of people and lots of conversation.

The *Dog & Duck*, 18 Bateman St W1 (tube: Tottenham Court Rd), is tiny, but it retains much of its old character and has loyal locals. *Riki Tik*, nearby at No 23, is famous for its flavoured vodka shots (Rolo and Toblerone are to die for) and half-price jugs of cocktails before 8 pm during the week, but this is a cool and trendy place where they expect you to dress the part.

The 'O' Bar, 83-85 Wardour St W1 (tube: Piccadilly Circus), has two main drinking floors with a DJ downstairs at the weekend (£5 cover charge). It's at its best during the week when it serves half-price pitchers of cocktails before 8 pm.

The pleasantly unchanged *Lamb & Flag*, 33 Rose St WC2 (tube: Covent Garden), lies low down a narrow alleyway between Garrick and Floral Sts. Food is available but it gets packed out at lunchtime.

The *Walkabout Inn*, 11 Henrietta St (tube: Covent Garden), is a popular Australiana-themed bar with live music and cheap midweek drink specials. Expect it to be packed to the hilt from Thursday to Sunday.

The *Punch & Judy* is right inside the Covent Garden marketplace. While not the most beautiful (or cheap) of pubs, it is nonetheless extremely well positioned and has a balcony which lets you look down on the buskers with drink in hand.

Freud, 198 Shaftesbury Ave (tube: Covent Garden), is a small basement bar with the sort of beige walls that could look just plain dirty but here are purposefully arty with pictures to complement the heavy church candles. The beers aren't cheap but it's very atmospheric.

Westminster

The Sherlock Holmes, Northumberland St WC2 (tube: Charing Cross; Map 4), is tucked away just off Northumberland Ave and so doesn't get quite as busy as it otherwise might. Come here for the Holmes memorabilia as much as for the alcohol.

Gordon's, 47 Villiers St WC2 (tube: Embankment; Map 3), is as near as you'll get to drinking in the London Dungeon. It's a wonderfully atmospheric wine bar in ancient vaults beneath the street, but spilling out into the Embankment Gardens in summer. The cold buffets are marvellous but you'll need to nip in quickly after work to get a table.

City

The entrance to *Ye Olde Cheshire Cheese*, Wine Office Court EC4 (tube: Blackfriars), is via a picturesque alley off Fleet St. Cross the threshold and you'll find yourself in a wood-panelled interior no less picturesque and divided up into various bars and eating areas. This was one of Dickens' watering holes (for more details see Walk 2 in the Walks chapter).

The busy *Eagle*, 159 Farringdon Rd EC1

(tube: Farringdon), was one of the first of the new-style pubs and serves delicious food and a good range of beers.

Hamilton Hall, Bishopsgate (tube: Liverpool St; Map 6), is a huge warehouse of a pub right beside Liverpool Station – handy for a drink while you wait for your train. It started life as the ballroom of the Great Eastern Hotel (1901) but has been given the Wetherspoon treatment, with libraries of faded books amid the grand decor.

The Cock Tavern, The Poultry Market, Smithfield Market EC1 (tube: Farringdon; Map 6), is a local for people working in Smithfield meat market. A 40 oz steak is the house speciality (£16.50) and there's a free bottle of wine for anyone who finishes it (the record is 13 minutes!). It's open from 5.30 am for breakfast.

East End

Canteloupe, 33 Charlotte Rd (tube: Old St), in newly trendy Hoxton, manages to feel arty enough to justify its location without being overwhelming. There's a small restaurant at the back.

Overlooking St Katherine's Dock near the Tower of London is the *Dickens Inn* (tube: Tower Hill; Map 7), an 18th century wooden-framed brewery uncovered when a warehouse was being demolished for new houses. The facade is a modern replica but the interior is still full of character. There's a pizzeria on the 1st floor, a branch of *Wheeler's* fish restaurant on the 2nd floor and bar snacks to be going on with on the ground floor.

In recent years *The Bricklayers Arms*, Rivington St EC2 (tube: Old St), has become a pretty hip place as a result of all the artists moving into Hoxton and Shoreditch. Some say it's already passed its prime but on a pleasant summer evening, when the crowds spill out onto the pavement, it's still a good place to come.

Maida Vale

The Warrington, 93 Warrington Crescent W9 (tube: Maida Vale), was once a brothel and is now an ornate Art Nouveau pub with heaps of character and a very laid-back atmosphere. There's seating outside and a good-value, authentic Thai restaurant.

Camden, Islington & Primrose Hill

The *Crown & Goose*, 100 Arlington Rd NW1 (tube: Camden Town; Map 10), is a new-style pub attracting a youngish crowd with good no-nonsense food.

The *Lansdowne*, 90 Gloucester Ave NW1 (tube: Chalk Farm; Map 10), is another new-style pub with bohemian style and excellent if reasonably pricey food. On Sunday the set menu is £15 but it's very popular, so book if you feel inclined to spoil yourself.

Cuba Libre, 72 Upper St (tube: Angel), has a lively bar at the back of the restaurant. Despite the fact that they've dropped the Latin sounds, the cocktails are still worth sampling. Space is limited so get there early.

The Engineer, 65 Gloucester Ave NW1 (tube: Chalk Farm), is a pretty Victorian place converted into a highly successful pub and restaurant which attracts the trendy north London set.

Bloomsbury & Holborn (Map 5)

The *Lamb*, 94 Lamb's Conduit St WC1 (tube: Russell Square), has a well-preserved Victorian interior of mirrors, old wood and 'snob screens'.

The Queen's Larder, 1 Queen's Square WC1 (tube: Russell Square), offers a handy retreat on the corner of the square, with outside benches and pub grub.

After a hard day's work in the British Museum Reading Room, Karl Marx used to repair to *The Museum Tavern*, 49 Great Russell St WC1 (tube: Tottenham Court Rd), a capacious pub where you can sup your pint with his shade.

Truckle's, Pied Bull Yard (tube: Tottenham Court Rd), is in a modern courtyard just off Museum St and so handy for a post-British Museum pick-up. The interior is pleasantly broken up so it doesn't seem too impersonal but you can drink outside if the weather's good. The pub lunches also make a good alternative to the museum's overpriced fare.

The *Princess Louise*, 208 High Holborn

(tube: Holborn), is a delightful and eternally popular example of Victorian pub decor with fine tiles, etched mirrors, columns and plasterwork. The beer's good and it makes a change to drink it in a listed building (ie one that the pub redesigners can't get their hands on).

Clerkenwell

The *Three Kings*, 7 Clerkenwell Close EC1 (tube: Farringdon), is a stone's throw from Clerkenwell Green. Its walls are densely decorated with papier-mâche models and there's a giant rhino head above the fireplace – a model, of course!

On the corner of Cowcross St near Farringdon tube station you'll find the *Castle* (Map 6), the only pub in London which is also a licensed pawnbroker's (look for the symbol of the three gold bails hanging above the sign). This dual function dates back to a time when George IV was in urgent need of a float to pay off his gambling debts and got one from the innkeeper. Don't bother asking behind the bar though – the present-day staff don't seem to have cottoned on.

Docklands

At the *Mayflower*, 117 Rotherhithe St SE16 (tube: Rotherhithe; Map 7), you can sit on the jetty and watch the Thames from one of the few pubs to survive the encroaching new development.

The *Prospect of Whitby*, 57 Wapping Wall E1 (tube: Wapping; Map 7), is one of London's oldest surviving drinking houses. It's firmly on the tourist trail, but there's a good terrace overlooking the Thames.

Southwark

The *George Inn*, 77 Borough High St SE1 (tube: London Bridge; Map 6), is that rare thing – a National Trust pub. It's London's last surviving galleried coaching inn facing a courtyard and makes a beautiful but busy after-work drinking hole.

The Anchor, Bankside (tube: London Bridge), is an 18th century riverside pub with great views across the Thames from its terrace. In summer it hosts occasional barbecues.

Chelsea

The *Po Na Na Souk Bar*, 316 King's Rd SW3 (tube: Sloane Square; Map 2), is an African-style fun bar where you can drink in little tented alcoves, seated on leopard skin sofas or chairs, playing backgammon. Even the cigarette machine is painted like a zebra.

Described as a 'designer dungeon bar', *Come The Revolution*, 541 King's Rd SW6 (tube: Fulham Broadway; Map 2), has an Italianate interior with murals and wrought-iron tables and chairs. Despite its size it can get very crowded, although there's a garden to escape to in summer.

The Cooper's Arms, 87 Flood St SW3 (tube: Sloane Square), is a great find, just off the King's Rd and with a stuffed bear as its focal point. Newspapers are provided and the food is excellent.

The King's Head & Eight Bells, 50 Cheyne Walk, (tube: Sloane Square), is an attractive corner pub pleasantly hung with flower baskets in summer. There's food and a wide range of beers, and you're just seconds away from the Victoria Embankment.

The Antelope, 22 Eaton Terrace SW1 (tube: Sloane Square), offers English tradition at its best. This quiet, charming pub has been around longer than any of the neighbouring buildings and could no doubt tell a tale or two.

Kensington

The cave-like *Fez Bar*, 222 Fulham Rd SW6 (tube: South Kensington), is in the livelier part of Fulham Rd and stays open until 2 am at the weekend. The £5 cover charge could put some people off.

The Abingdon, 54 Abingdon Rd W8 (tube: Kensington High St), is a light, airy bar, simply decorated with polished floorboards and huge sofas. Mediterranean-style meals are available.

Notting Hill & Earl's Court

Beach Blanket Babylon, 45 Ledbury Rd W11 (tube: Notting Hill Gate; Map 9), boasts an extraordinary Gaudiesque decor, and is a great place for watching Notting Hill trendies. The food's expensive though.

The Churchill Arms, 119 Kensington Church St W8 (tube: Notting Hill Gate), is a traditional English pub renowned for its Winston memorabilia and incredible Thai food.

Market Bar, 240A Portobello Rd W11 (tube: Ladbroke Grove; Map 9), has an interesting decor, entertaining crowd and relaxed atmosphere.

Windsor Castle, 114 Campden Hill Rd W11 (tube: Notting Hill Gate; Map 9), has a pleasant garden and good pub food including half a dozen oysters and a half bottle of champagne for £15.

The Westbourne, 101 Westbourne Park Villas W2 (tube: Westbourne Park; Map 9), is a trendy pub where the Notting Hill crowd congregates. The large forecourt is great in summer and there's good-value bar food.

The Cow, 89 Westbourne Park Rd W2 (tube: Notting Hill Gate), is owned by Tom Conran, son of restaurateur-extraordinaire Sir Terence. It's wildly popular and fresh oysters in the bar are a speciality.

The *Prince of Teck*, 161 Earl's Court Rd SW5 (tube: Earl's Court; Map 8), is an infamous Australasian pub. Further along the road at No 314, *Blanco's* (Map 8) is a lively, authentic Spanish tapas bar serving Spanish beer. It stays open until midnight.

Hammersmith & Fulham

Pitcher & Piano, 873 Fulham Rd (tube: Parsons Green), is a new-style stripped pine bar with a front that opens onto the street for sunnier days. Some find these places bland, others thoroughly enjoy them.

Bootsy Brogans, 1 Fulham Broadway SW6 (tube: Fulham Broadway), is a newly renovated Irish pub favoured by travellers.

The *Dove*, 19 Upper Mall W6 (tube: Ravenscourt Park), is a small 17th century building close to the Thames, serving good food and fine ales.

Hampstead (Map 11)

The *Flask*, 14 Flask Walk NW3 (tube: Hampstead), is a friendly local handy for the tube, with real ale and good food.

The *Holly Bush*, 22 Holly Mount NW3 (tube: Hampstead), is an idyllic pub with a good selection of beers, but rather ordinary food.

The *Spaniards Inn*, Spaniards Rd NW3 (tube: Hampstead), dates back to 1585. In winter you can warm up around an open fire, in summer you can enjoy the garden. Other favourites around the heath are *Jack Straw's Castle* at the junction of Spaniards Rd and West Heath Rd, and the *Old Bull & Bush* in North End Rd.

Greenwich (Map 12)

Right on the waterfront, just past the Royal Naval College, the *Trafalgar Tavern* is a cavernous pub with big windows opening onto the Thames on nice days. It stands above the site of the old Placentia Palace where Henry VIII was born. Prime ministers Gladstone and Disraeli used to come here to dine on whitebait; you can follow in their footsteps for a mere £3.75 a portion.

Richmond, Putney & Wandsworth

The *White Cross Hotel*, Water Lane Riverside, TW9 (tube: Richmond), is enormously popular thanks to its riverside location, good food and fine ales. When the river's at its highest the pub gets virtually cut off.

In Old Palace Lane, leading from Richmond Green to the river, the *White Swan* is another pleasant pub which serves food and has a garden. Facing the Green itself, the *Prince's Head* and the *Cricketers* are good for pre-theatre drinks or for sitting outside on a sunny day.

Bar M, 4 Lower Richmond Rd SW15 (tube: Putney Bridge), is a newly renovated café/bar with a pleasant riverside location. The environment is cool and relaxed and there's a spacious seating area.

Bar Coast, 50 High St SW15 (tube: Putney Bridge), is a trendy, up-tempo bar favoured by local young professionals. It has an interesting range of beers and a simple menu.

The Ship, 41 Jews Row SW18 (station:

Wandsworth Town), is trickier to get to, but worth the struggle. Relax with a drink and some pleasant food and enjoy the river views.

Chiswick

The City Barge, 27 Strand on the Green, Chiswick W4 (tube: Kew Gardens), was built in 1484 and perched dangerously close to the river's edge. It serves basic English food. The nearby *Bull's Head* is another good choice but both get uncomfortably full on pleasant summer evenings.

The Tabard, 2 Bath Rd W4 (tube: Turnham Green), was designed in 1880 by Norman Shaw as part of Bedford Park, London's first garden suburb. Despite restoration after a fire in 1971 it still boasts panels of William Morris wallpaper and William de Morgan tiles. The small Thai restaurant at the back gets good reviews, and there's a theatre upstairs (☎ 0181-995 6035).

Isleworth

It's worth venturing out as far as Isleworth if for no other reason than to visit *The London Apprentice*, a riverside pub dating back to the early 17th century which boasts its own Hogarths on the walls. The name commemorates apprentices who used to row upriver to the pub on their days off. Henry VIII is thought to have rendezvoused with fifth wife-to-be, Catherine Howard, at an earlier tavern on the site, and smugglers are believed to have lugged their booty through a tunnel from the pub to the crypt of the neighbouring church. Come here for a pint after exploring nearby Syon House.

INTERNET CAFÉS

Being online is more than a hobby for some. If you can't break the addiction, the following places could prove useful:

Cyberia Cyber Café (☎ 209 0983), 39 Whitfield St W1 (tube: Goodge St; Map 5), was the first Internet café in London. It has full Internet access with 10 terminals in the café (£2.50 for half an hour) and 12 in the training room. Weekday training costs £30 for two hours and needs to be booked in advance. The food's good with specials from £4 to £5. There's another branch at 73 New Broadway, Ealing W5 (tube: Ealing Broadway).

Webshack (☎ 439 8000), 15 Dean St W1, is the most central of the internet cafés.

Spider Café (☎ 229 2990), 195 Portobello Rd W11 (tube: Notting Hill Gate), has computers upstairs and downstairs and serves food and milk shakes. Internet access costs £2.50 a half-hour. If you need tuition it's £5.95 for half an hour or £35 for a more comprehensive two hour session.

Portobello Gold (☎ 460 4910), 95 Portobello Rd, is a classy hotel/restaurant whose upstairs bar has terminals available for customer use (see the Places to Stay chapter).

The Bean, 126 Curtain Rd (☎ 739 7829) is a Hackney coffee shop cum Internet access point.

Check out Lonely Planet's award-winning web site: www.lonelyplanet.com.au for travel information.

BALLET & DANCE

London is home to five major dance companies and a host of small and experimental companies. The *Royal Ballet* (☎ 240 1066) shares the Royal Opera House in Covent Garden (Map 3), and presents the best classical ballet in Britain. Like the Royal Opera, the Royal Ballet will have to lead a nomadic existence while the Opera House is being redeveloped. You may be able to catch it at Labatt's Apollo in Hammersmith (☎ 416 6022; tube: Hammersmith) or at the Festival Hall (☎ 960 4242; tube: Waterloo). Once the Sadler's Wells Theatre reopens, the Royal Ballet will take up temporary residence there.

Sadler's Wells has a long dance history, but its theatre in Rosebury Ave will be closed for rebuilding until 1998. *The Peacock Theatre* (☎ 312 1996), Portugal St WC2 (tube: Holborn; Map 3), will now host the London Contemporary Dance Theatre and London City Ballet. The Royal Sadler's Wells Ballet is now the Birmingham Royal Ballet.

The *Riverside Studios* and *ICA* (see the

CHARLOTTE HINDLE

CHARLOTTE HINDLE

CHARLOTTE HINDLE

Top: Theatre Royal, Haymarket
Middle: Shakespeare's Globe Theatre, Southwark
Bottom: Garrick Theatre, Charing Cross Road

CHARLOTTE HINDLE

CHARLOTTE HINDLE

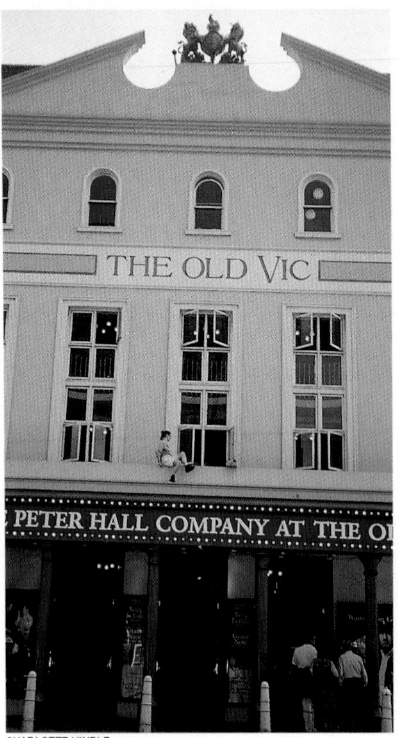

CHARLOTTE HINDLE

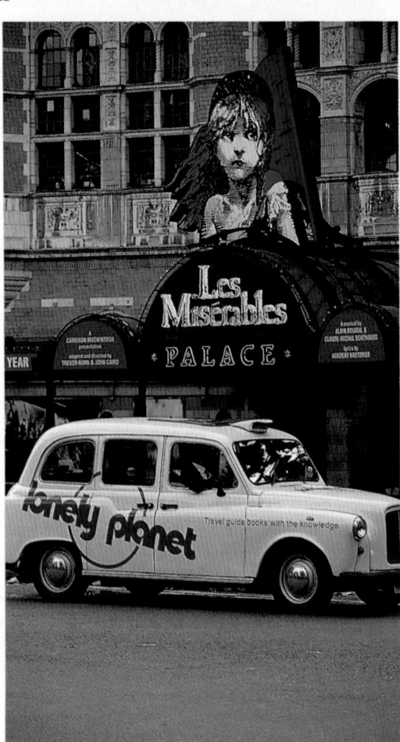

DOUG McKINLAY

Top Left: Strand Theatre, Aldwych
Top Right: Her Majesty's Theatre, Haymarket
Bottom Left: The Old Vic, Waterloo Road
Bottom Right: Palace Theatre, Shaftesbury Avenue

Cinemas section earlier in this chapter) are the most important venues for small experimental companies.

ORGANISED ENTERTAINMENT

Inevitably there are a few places where you can play the full tourist bit over a themed dinner, with entertainment, food and drink all laid on for one inclusive price. London Entertains (☎ 224 9000) has three venues offering such shows at 7.15 pm nightly for £39.50 a head. Tacky as they might sound, they can be quite fun if you're with the right group of people and in the right frame of mind. Interested? Then the places to try are:

Cockney Cabaret
: Three-course traditional English dinner with a cabaret featuring music hall and musical numbers; 161 Tottenham Court Rd W1 (tube: Tottenham Court Rd)

Talk of London
: Dinner and floorshow; New London Theatre, Drury Lane, Parker St WC2 (tube: Holborn)

Beefeater by the Tower
: Five-course medieval banquet, with jesters, fighting knights and minstrels; Ivory House, St Katherine's Dock E1 (tube: Tower Hill)

It's also possible to sign up for lunch or dinner cruises on the Thames, complete with dancing and live music. Bateaux London (☎ 925 2215) offers lunch cruises for £19.50, dinner cruises for £53 and Sunday lunch cruises for £26. The lunch cruises board at 12.15 pm, the dinner cruises at 7.30 pm. Departures are from Temple or Charing Cross piers on the Victoria Embankment.

Catamaran Cruises (☎ 987 1185) does Captain's Table dinner cruises on Wednesday, Friday and Sunday (8 pm) from May to September. They cost £35 and depart from Charing Cross Pier. Four-hour weekend Disco cruises kick off at 7 pm on Friday and Saturday and cost £12.50 a head.

SPECTATOR SPORT

All year round London plays host to myriad events. As always *Time Out* is the best source of information on fixtures, times, venues and ticket prices.

Football

Even if you're not much interested in sport, the 'beautiful game' is on such a roll you might be tempted to dip a toe in the water.

Wembley (☎ 0181-902 8833) is the home of English football, the place where the English national side plays international matches and where the FA Cup final takes place in mid-May. For details of tours see Wembley Stadium in the Things to See & Do chapter.

There are a dozen league teams in London and usually around six enjoy the big time of the Premier League, meaning that any weekend of the season, from August to mid-May, quality football is just a tube ride away.

These are the current Premier Leaguers:

Arsenal
: Avenell Rd, Highbury N5 (☎ 704 4040; tube: Arsenal) – tickets are available one month in advance for around £15; for credit card bookings ☎ 413 3366

Chelsea
: Stamford Bridge, Fulham Rd SW6 (☎ 385 5545; tube: Fulham Broadway; Map 2) – tickets cost from £18 to £50; for credit card bookings ☎ 386 7799

Crystal Palace
: Selhurst Park, Whitehorse Lane SE25 (☎ 0181-768 6000; station: Selhurst) – tickets cost from £12 to £27; for credit card bookings ☎ 0181-771 8841

Tottenham Hotspur
: White Hart Lane, 748 High Rd, Tottenham N17 (☎ 0181-365 5000; station: White Hart Lane) – tickets cost from £16 to £35; for credit card bookings ☎ 396 4567

West Ham United
: Boleyn Ground, Green St, Upton Park E13 (☎ 0181-548 2748; tube: Upton Park) – tickets cost from £18 to £31; for credit card bookings ☎ 0181-548 2700

Wimbledon
: Selhurst Park, Whitehorse Lane SE25 (☎ 0181-771 2233; station: Selhurst) – tickets cost £18; for credit card bookings ☎ 0181-771 8841

Hooliganism isn't much of a problem these days. Since the Hillsborough Stadium tragedy of 1989, in which nearly 100 fans died in a Cup-tie crowd crush, most stadia are all-seaters and the mood at most matches has cooled accordingly. The only thing that holds people back these days is the exorbitant prices although you'll pay considerably less if you patronise the less well-known teams. Note that all the above teams have some spaces for fans in wheelchairs and headsets for those with visual problems, but it's wise to phone ahead and book.

If you want to see behind the scenes at Chelsea, ground tours (tube: Fulham Broadway) take place on Friday at 11 am. They're free and last roughly 1½ hours.

Cricket

Cricket continues to flourish, despite the dismal fortunes of the England team. Test matches take place at Lord's (☎ 289 8979; Map 2) and the Oval (☎ 582 6660; Map 2) cricket grounds. Sadly, tickets cost a fortune and tend to go fast. You're better off looking out for a county fixture. Middlesex plays at Lord's, Surrey plays at the Oval and tickets cost around the £8 mark.

For details of tours of Lord's, see Lord's Cricket Ground in the Things to See & Do chapter.

Rugby Union

For rugby union fans south-west London is the place to be, with a host of good-quality teams like Harlequins, Richmond and Wasps. Each year, starting in January, the four nations of the British Isles, and the French compete in the Five Nations Rugby Union Championship. This guarantees two big matches at Twickenham (☎ 0181-892 8161), the shrine of English union football.

For details of tours of Twickenham, see The Twickenham Experience in the Things to See & Do chapter.

Rugby League

Rugby league fans would be advised to get on a train and head for the north of England, or settle for watching the London Broncos, the only rugby league side in southern England. In May, the rugby Challenge Cup final is held at Wembley.

Tennis

Tennis and Wimbledon (☎ 0181-946 2244) are synonymous, but queues, exorbitant prices, limited ticket availability and cramped conditions can turn a Wimbledon dream into a nightmare. Although a limited number of seats for the Centre Court and Court Nos 1 & 2 go on sale on the day of play, the queues are painfully long. The nearer to the finals it is, the higher the prices; a Centre Court ticket that costs £22 a week before the final will cost twice that a week later. Prices for the outside courts cost less than £10 and are reduced fter 5 pm.

Between August and December each year there's a public ballot for tickets for the best seats at the next year's tournament. Between those dates send a stamped addressed envelope to The All England Lawn Tennis & Croquet Club, PO Box 98, Church Rd, Wimbledon SW19 5AE for details.

If you haven't got a show court ticket and you don't want to camp out all night, go along in the late afternoon and take your chances on buying a returned ticket for £5. Otherwise you might try the pre-Wimbledon tournament at Queen's (☎ 381 7000) which attracts many of the top male players.

Unfortunately, these days many of the people who do land Centre Court tickets are there on corporate hospitality packages which have more to do with swigging champagne and socialising than watching the games. In recent years when rain in June has seen the tournament extended and the courts thrown open to everyone on 'People's Sundays' the atmosphere has been completely different, with real tennis fans given a chance to see the action.

It's estimated that 23 tonnes of strawberries and 12 tonnes of salmon are consumed during Wimbledon, along with 285,000 cups of tea and coffee and 190,000 sandwiches.

For details of the Wimbledon Lawn Tennis Museum, see Wimbledon in the Things to See & Do chapter.

Athletics

Athletics meetings attracting major international and domestic stars take place regularly throughout the summer at Crystal Palace National Sports Centre (☎ 0181-778 0131), Ledrington Rd SE19 (station: Crystal Palace). Tickets are from £10.

Racing
If you're looking for a cheap and thrilling night out, consider sampling greyhound racing. Entry to 'The Dogs' costs as little as £3 for a 12 race meeting. A few small bets will mean guaranteed excitement, and you'll rub shoulders with a London subculture that's gregarious and more than a little shady.

Catford Stadium, Adenmore Rd SE6 (☎ 0181-690 8000; station: Catford Bridge)
Walthamstow Stadium, Chingford Rd E4 (☎ 0181-531 4255; station: Highams Park)
Wembley Stadium, Stadium Way, Wembley (☎ 0181-902 8833; tube: Wembley Park)
Wimbledon Stadium, Plough Lane SE19 (☎ 0181-946 8000; tube: Wimbledon Park)

Alternatively, there's horse racing with plenty of top-quality courses lying just south of the city. Ascot in June can be nice if rather posh; Epsom on Derby Day can be a crushing experience in more ways than one. Windsor, by the River Thames, is an idyllic spot for an afternoon of racing and a summer evening picnic. Sandown is another top racecourse.

Shopping

Napoleon famously described the British as a nation of shopkeepers. These days it would be equally true to describe them as a nation of shoppers. Either way, London is the UK's shopping mecca; if you can't find it here you probably can't find it at all.

Some of London's shops are more or less tourist attractions in their own right. Few visitors come away without popping into Harrods and Fortnum & Masons, even if only to gawp. Since *Absolutely Fabulous* brought Edina and Patsy steaming onto our screens, Harvey Nichols ('Harvey Nicks') has become another must-see attraction.

There are also whole shopping streets whose fame has more to do with their past than what they have to offer today. Carnaby Street still reeks of the 60s although it's had something of a revival since the 'Cool Britannia' kick brought Union Jack dresses back into fashion. The last punks have long since slunk away from Chelsea's King's Rd but there are still plenty of interesting shops slipped in amid the high-street chains. The Peter Jones department store at the Sloane Square end also has its avid fans, not least because of its claim to unbeatable prices.

Covent Garden epitomises the entrepreneurial spirit of the 80s which saw new retailing opportunities in every other derelict landmark. For all that, the shops and stalls inside the old market building tend to be pricey and tourist-oriented, while the streets running off it remain a happy hunting ground for shoppers, with Neal St and Neal's Yard in particular offering a range of interesting one-off shops.

Oxford St and classier Regent St come into their own in the six weeks running up to Christmas when they're festooned with lights. At other times of the year Oxford St can be a great disappointment. Selfridge's is up there with Harrods as a place to visit and the flagship Marks & Spencers at the Marble Arch end has its fans, but the further east you go the tackier and less interesting it gets.

Although most things can be bought in most parts of town, there are also streets with their own specialities; Tottenham Court Rd, for example, is one long electrical goods shop, while Charing Cross Road is still the place to come for offbeat books.

Many tourist attractions have excellent shops selling good-quality souvenirs like mugs, pens, pencils, stationery and T-shirts, often with themes to match their content (war books and videos at the Imperial War Museum, designer fans at the Fan Museum, William Morris-designed rugs at the William Morris Gallery). By buying from these shops you help contribute towards the building's maintenance, especially important in the case of those without entry charges. You can often visit the shop even if you aren't going to look round the attraction.

True shopaholics should get the annual *Time Out Shopping Guide* (£6), with details of nearly every shopping opportunity in the capital.

DEPARTMENT STORES

Harrods

This famous store (☎ 730 1234), Brompton Rd SW1 (tube: Knightsbridge; Map 8), is a real one-off. It's a pain because it is so crowded, and because the security staff tell you how to carry your daypack. On the other hand, the toilets are fab, the food hall (complete with classical musicians) is enough to make you swoon, and if they haven't got what you want, it probably doesn't exist. No other store has such a sense of sheer, outrageous abundance. Don't miss it, although you may be wise to leave your credit cards somewhere safe. It's open on Monday, Tuesday and Saturday from 10 am to 6 pm, Wednesday to Friday to 7 pm.

Harvey Nichols

Harvey Nichols (☎ 235 5000), 109-125 Knightsbridge SW1 (tube: Knightsbridge; Map 8), is the city's heart of high fashion with a great food hall, an extravagant perfume department and jewellery to save up for. But with all the big names from Miyake to Lauren, Hamnett to Calvin Klein, and a whole floor of up-to-the-minute menswear, it's fashion that Harvey Nichols really does better than the rest. The selection is unrivalled and the prices high, although during sales there are some great bargains, and the store's own clothing line is reasonable. It's open Monday, Tuesday, Thursday and Friday from 10 am to 7 pm; Wednesday to 8 pm; Sunday from 2 to 5 pm.

Fortnum & Mason

Fortnum & Mason (☎ 734 8040), 181 Piccadilly W1 (tube: Piccadilly Circus; Map 3), is noted for its exotic, old-world food hall, but it also carries plenty of overpriced and stuffy fashion wear. All kinds of strange foodstuffs can be purchased here, along with the famous food hampers that cost an arm and a leg. This is where Scott of the Antarctic stocked up before heading off to the wilderness. These days you'd be better advised to buy your travel provisions elsewhere and settle for a small, gift-wrapped box of chocolates for a show-off present. It's open Monday to Saturday from 9.30 am to 6 pm.

Liberty

Almost as unique and amazing as Harrods, *Liberty* (☎ 734 1234), Regent St W1 (tube: Oxford Circus; Map 3), has high fashion, great modern furniture, a wonderful luxury fabrics department and those inimitable silk scarves. It was born at the turn of the century out of the influential Arts & Crafts Movement – in Italy Art Nouveau was called Liberty Style after the store. Both its appealing interior design (it's sometimes hard to tell what's for sale and what's just decoration) and the helpful sales staff add to the pleasure of shopping here. It's particularly good during the January and summer sales. It's open Monday to Wednesday, Friday and Saturday from 10 am to 6.30 pm; Thursday from 10 am to 7.30 pm.

Peter Jones

Peter Jones (☎ 730 3434; Map 8), at Sloane Square more or less facing the tube station, is a Londoners' institution – the place to know about if you're planning the sort of extended stay that requires stocking up on household goods. It has been described as the 'best corner shop in Chelsea', but that hardly starts to describe the wide range of goods on sale; everything from electrical goods through china and glass to towels and bedding. But the reason Peter Jones is such a fave place is its famous slogan... 'never knowingly undersold'. If you find the exact same thing on sale in another shop but for a lower price within the next week you can show the receipt and get the difference refunded. If you can drag your eyes from the contents it's worth noting that the building, too, is regarded as being among the best of its kind.

MARKETS

One of the great pleasures of a sunny Sunday morning is to visit one of London's many markets and then have lunch in a nearby restaurant. There are several markets widely spread out around the capital and each has its own individual character. Many of them also take place on Friday and Saturday. For Bermondsey antiques market, see Antiques below. For the complete lowdown on the markets look out for *The London Market Guide* (Metro Publications, £3.99), which gives details of local markets, and car boot (second-hand goods) sales too.

Berwick St Market

Tucked away between Oxford and Old Compton Sts, Berwick St Market (tube: Oxford Circus/Tottenham Court Rd; Map 3) is a fruit and vegetable market which has somehow managed to hang onto its prime location, even though the stallholders' sales patter has to compete with a babble of sounds from the surrounding record shops. This is a great place to put together a picnic to eat in one of the parks, even better if you're cooking your own meals.

Portobello Rd Market

Camden Market aside, Portobello Rd (tube: Notting Hill Gate, Ladbroke Grove or Westbourne Park; Map 9) is London's most famous (and crowded) weekend street market. Starting near the Sun in Splendour pub in Notting Hill, it wends its way northwards to wind up past the Westway flyover in Ladbroke Grove.

As you head north along Portobello Rd what you'll find on sale slowly changes, with the antiques, hand-made jewellery, paintings and ethnic stuff concentrated at the Notting Hill Gate end. Later the stalls dip down-market and you'll find more fruit and veg, second-hand clothing, cheap household goods and bric-a-brac. Beneath the Westway a vast tent covers yet more stalls selling cheap clothes, shoes and CDs, while the Portobello Green arcade is home to some cutting-edge clothes designers. On Friday and Saturday bric-a-brac goes on sale here too.

Portobello certainly has character and colour but it's too well known for there to be much chance of a bargain other than on cheap T-shirts. Nonetheless it's a fun place to while away a few hours, especially if you get there early before people-gridlock sets in. As you stroll along you can also observe how pockets of London's very different lifestyles rub shoulders with each other; at the Notting Hill end of the road the side streets are full of neat mews houses with window boxes and sleek cars parked outside; further north the noise levels rise and the range of people in the shops starts to reflect the city's ethnic mix; by the time you reach the Westway you're well and truly into bedsit land.

At the Ladbroke Grove end, fruit and vegetables are on sale all week, with an organic market on Thursday. The other stalls are rolled out for the weekend, with most of the antiques on sale on Saturday from 5.30 am to 5 pm and a flea market on Portobello Green on Sunday morning.

Since most people walk up Portobello Rd from Notting Hill Gate, the Ladbroke Grove and Westbourne Park tube stations are likely to be much less congested.

Petticoat Lane Market

Petticoat Lane (tube: Aldgate, Aldgate East or Liverpool St; Map 6) is east London's celebrated Sunday morning market on Middlesex St, which borders the City and Whitechapel. These days, however, it's all pretty run-of-the-mill with faintly bemused tourists struggling to get past locals sifting through the stalls of cheap T-shirts and underwear. By 2 pm it's all over.

Brick Lane Market

A few streets east of Petticoat Lane, Brick Lane Market (tube: Aldgate East; Map 6) is more fun although it, too, is probably past its prime. Activity kicks off at around 5 am on Sunday and spreads out along Bethnal Green Rd to the north, and the many side streets. Once again, by 2 pm it's all over. There's a mix of stalls selling clothes, fruit and veg, household goods and paintings, but you'll also see people picking through piles of dirt cheap shoes for whom finding a bargain is more a necessity than a bit of fun.

The big plus of heading out here is that you can round off a visit with lunch in one of the many curry houses or with a bagel in one of the bakeries (see East End in the Places to Eat chapter). Car parking in Brick Lane costs £2 on Sunday.

Spitalfields Market

More interesting than Brick Lane itself is Spitalfields undercover market off Commercial St (tube: Liverpool St; Map 6). Not only is this market weatherproof but there's a great mix of arts and crafts, organic fruit and veg, stylish and retro clothes, and second-hand books, with genuinely interesting ethnic shops ringing the central area and a football pitch and children's model railway (50p) to keep nonshoppers entertained. Shops to look out for include *Conservas Rainha Santa* (☎ 247 2802) which sells attractive Portuguese pottery, together with olives, oil and honey, and *2WO* (☎ 377 2454) which sells tribal weavings and central Asian jewellery.

It's open on Sunday from 8 am to 5 pm. Unfortunately developers have their beady eyes fixed on this piece of prime London territory and the market's future was uncertain at the time of writing.

Columbia Rd Market

Although visitors may have little need of geraniums or pelargoniums, a stroll up to Columbia Rd Flower Market (tube: Old St) is an excellent way to round off the Sunday morning market experience. To get there walk north along Brick Lane and then along Virginia Rd. Turn right when you emerge on Columbia Rd and the market is about 100m along the road past a tower block. The action takes place between 8 am and 2 pm and, as well as the flower stalls, a couple of basic cafés and several arty shops throw open their doors. You can sample cockles, mussels, whelks and other fishy titbits at *Lee's Seafoods* stall, 134 Columbia Rd, which opens on Friday and Saturday from 8.30 am to 8 pm and on Sunday until 2 pm.

Camden Market

These days Camden Market (Map 10) stretches most of the way from Camden Town tube station north to Chalk Farm tube station. To see it at its most lively, time your visit for a weekend, although most days there'll be some stalls up and running.

First off as you head north from Camden Town station is the **Electric Market** in an old ballroom. A busy studenty club on Friday and Saturday night, it's transformed into a market on Sunday. Sometimes there are record sales, but 60s clothes usually dominate. Opposite is a covered area with stalls selling a mishmash of leather goods, army-surplus stuff and a café. Next up is **Camden Market** (open from Thursday to Sunday), which houses stalls for fashion, clothing and jewellery.

Continue north, past the bootleg music sellers and hair plaiters, and over the bridge. On the right is the **Camden Canal Market**, with bric-a-brac from around the world. On the left, and beyond the comparatively new indoor market, is the small section where the market originated. This area, right next to the canal lock, houses a diverse range of food, ceramics, furniture, oriental rugs, musical instruments, designer clothes and so on.

From here you can walk along the **Railway Arches**, which mainly contain second-hand furniture. A slow meander eventually leads to **The Stables**, the northernmost part of the market, where it's possible to snap up antiques, eastern artefacts, rugs and carpets, pine furniture, and 50s and 60s clothing. If you want to get straight to The Stables there's an entrance on Chalk Farm Rd; this route passes *Thanh Binh*, 14 Chalk Farm Rd, which serves delicious takeaway noodles for £1.50.

Chapel Market

Every Tuesday, Wednesday, Friday and Saturday there's an excellent, if not necessarily very adventurous, all-day fruit and vegetable market in the street called Chapel Market in Islington (tube: Angel), just off Liverpool Rd. On Thursday and Saturday the stallholders pack up and go home at 12.30 pm.

Greenwich Market

Every Friday, Saturday and Sunday, from 9.30 am to 5.30 pm, Greenwich (station: Greenwich BR) hosts an undercover arts and crafts market (Map 12). You'll find it squeezed in between King William Walk and Greenwich Church St. It's not necessarily the place to come to find a bargain, but if you need to buy someone a present, this is an excellent place to start looking for decorated glass, rugs, prints, wooden toys etc.

Further along, opposite St Alfege Church, there's also a small antiques market. Needless to say this comes with the obligatory mix of stalls selling second-hand clothes and handmade jewellery. Some books, plants and household bric-a-brac can also be found. As with most of the weekend markets, some stuff is good, but most of the best bargains were snapped up five years ago.

Covent Garden

While the shops in Covent Garden piazza (tube: Covent Garden; Map 3) are open every day, several markets also take place in the Jubilee Hall on specific days: Monday is for antiques and a flea market which kicks off at 5 am; and from Tuesday to Friday a general market offers clothes, records, books, sweets, you name it. At weekends a craft market migrates into the piazza itself – nice things but you won't be able to afford many of them.

Brixton Market

Brixton Market (tube: Brixton; Map 14) is a cosmopolitan treat which mixes everything from The Body Shop and reggae music to slick Muslim preachers, halal meat, and fruit and exotic veg. In Electric Ave and the covered Granville Arcade you can buy wigs, unusual foods like tilapia fish and Ghanian eggs (really vegetables), weird spices and homeopathic root cures, rare records and dreadful end-of-the-line furnishings.

It's open Monday to Saturday from 8.30 am to 5.30 pm, closing at 1 pm on Wednesday. To find it, come out of Brixton station and turn left, and then first left again for Electric Ave.

For the bargains without the hustle, try the more workaday markets at Walthamstow and Wembley.

For information on the Smithfield and Leadenhall markets, see the City of London section in the Things to See & Do chapter.

CLOTHING

Behind Oxford Circus tube station near Liberty, **Carnaby St** (Map 3), was the centre of the world in the swinging 60s and is experiencing something of a revival on the back of the Britpop/cool Britannia mood. If you still think it's too tacky, near Carnaby St is the more salubrious west Soho, with plenty of groovy outlets for hip designers like *Pam Hogg* and the *Duffer of St George*.

It's easy to be intimidated by London's indoor fashion markets and to believe that only the most trendy fashion victims will be made welcome. However, designers at *Hyper-Hyper* (☎ 938 4343), 26-40 Kensington High St W8 (Map 8), and the *Garage* (☎ 352 8653), 181 King's Rd SW3, are mostly struggling types, more than a little keen to sell their imaginative glad rags. So, mosey along and see the great, the ridiculous and the eminently wearable, and note the bloody cheap price tags. Hyper-Hyper is open Monday to Wednesday, Friday and Saturday from 10 am to 6 pm; Thursday from 10 am to 7 pm. The Garage is open Monday to Saturday from 10 am to 6 pm.

Three storey *Kensington Market* (☎ 938 4343), 49-53 Kensington High St W8 (Map 8), is something of a dinosaur, and a hot, sticky shambles in summer but a lot of fun. It's more leather and patchouli oil than high fashion – the place to come for second-hand Levis, army jackets, chain-mail bikinis and hand-made jewellery. It's open Monday to Saturday from 10 am to 6 pm.

The following designer clothes shops are windowshoppable even if you can't avoid their fripperies:

Agnès B (☎ 379 1992), 35 Floral St WC2
Betty Jackson (☎ 589 7884), 311 Brompton Rd SW3
Comme des Garcons (☎ 493 1258), 59 Brook St W1
Donna Karan (☎ 499 8089), 27 Old Bond St W1
Emporio Armani (☎ 823 8818), 187 Brompton Rd SW3
Gianni Versace (☎ 499 1862), 34 Old Bond St W1
Gucci (☎ 629 2716), 32 Old Bond St W1
Hermès (☎ 823 1014), 179 Sloane St SW1
Jean-Paul Gaultier (☎ 584 4648), 171 Draycott Ave SW3
Karl Lagerfeld (☎ 493 6277), 173 New Bond St W1
Katherine Hamnett (☎ 823 1002), 20 Sloane St SW1
Nicole Farhi (☎ 240 5240), 55 Long Acre WC2
Paul Costelloe (☎ 589 9480), 156 Brompton Rd SW3
Paul Smith (☎ 379 7133), 40 Floral St WC2
Red or Dead (☎ 240 5576), 1 Thomas Neal's Centre, Earlham St WC2
Vivienne Westwood (☎ 629 3757), 6 Davies St W1
Zandra Rhodes (☎ 749 3216), 85 Richford St W6

For more traditional apparel head for *Burberry* (☎ 930 3343), 18-22 Haymarket SW1 (tube: Piccadilly Circus), or for *Aquascutum* (☎ 734 6090), 100 Regent St W1 (tube: Piccadilly Circus), both famed for their macs.

ANTIQUES

Antique-hunters may still find something worthwhile at Portobello Rd (Chepstow Villas end) but better pickings are to be had at Camden Passage or Bermondsey Market.

Camden Passage
At the junction of Upper St and Essex Rd, near Islington Green (tube: Angel; Map 2), you'll find this Aladdin's cave of antique shops and stalls, selling pretty well anything to which the label 'antique' could reasonably be attached. The stallholders know their stuff, so real bargains are few and far between, but it's still a fun place to browse. Wednesday is the busiest day when the action kicks off at 7 am and is all over by 2 pm. On Saturday it's worth coming along until 4 pm. Thursday sees a second-hand book market in full swing from 7 am to 4 pm.

Bermondsey Market
Bermondsey Market (Map 2) in Bermondsey Square (tube: Borough) is the place to come if you're after old opera glasses, bowling balls, hat pins, costume jewellery, porcelain or anything else that could loosely be described as an antique. The main market takes place outdoors in Bermondsey Square although adjacent warehouses shelter the more vulnerable furnishings. For a bargain you need to be up with the lark; the market kicks off at around 4.30 am on Friday; by lunchtime it's more or less over.

If you don't find what you want on the stalls, take a turn along Bermondsey St which is lined with antique shops. It's an interesting street in a conservation area, some of its warehouses still boasting their original winching gear. As you turn from Bermondsey Square into Bermondsey St, look out for an old watch-house in the grounds of St Mary Magdalene. This dates back to the 19th century craze for grave-robbing and is being restored by English Heritage.

FURNISHINGS & HOUSEHOLD GOODS

The Conran Shop
The Conran Shop (☎ 589 7401), Michelin House, 81 Fulham Rd SW3 (tube: South Kensington; Map 8), is the brainchild of Terence Conran, who created Habitat and several classy restaurants. Now his retro-style farmhouse interiors, furniture and kitchenware are available more exclusively, with more exclusive prices to match.

The shop's great appeal is partly its setting in beautiful Michelin House, a pre-WWI building that has been impeccably restored (see Michelin Building under Chelsea & Knightsbridge in the Things to See & Do chapter). It's open Monday, Thursday and Friday from 9.30 am to 6 pm, Tuesday from 10 am to 6 pm, Wednesday from 9.30 am to 7 pm, Saturday from 10 am to 6.30 pm, and Sunday from noon to 5.30 pm.

CAMPING AND BACKPACKING EQUIPMENT

The *YHA Adventure Shop* (☎ 836 8541), 14 Southampton St WC2 (tube: Covent Garden; Map 3), is an excellent place to stock up on all sorts of camping and walking gear. There's another branch at 174 Kensington High St W8 (☎ 938 2948; Map 8).

You could also try *Trekmate* (☎ 373 2363), 137 Earl's Court Rd SW5 (tube:

London's Auction Houses
Fancy a spot of upmarket shopping without the hassle of fixed price tags? What better than to pop into one of London's auction houses, those household-name powerhouses where van Goghs routinely change hands for silly money but which sometimes lower themselves to handle sales of more affordable ephemera. The following are the best known:

Christie's (☎ 839 9060), 8 King St SW1 (tube: South Kensington)
Sotheby's (☎ 493 8080), 34 New Bond St W1 (tube: Bond St)
Phillip's (☎ 629 6602), 7 Blenheim St W1 (tube: Bond St)
Bonhams (☎ 393 3900), Montpelier St SW7 (tube: Knightsbridge) ■

Earl's Court), which is next door to the Adventure Travel Centre and sells a wide range of Gore-Tex clothing, backpacks, boots and all the other paraphernalia of an overland or trekking trip. Members of the Deckers Club (see Australasian Clubs in Useful Organisations in the Facts for the Visitor chapter) get discounts on purchases here.

Taunton Leisure (☎ 924 3838), 557 Battersea Park Rd SW11 (station: Clapham Junction), and *Cotswold – the Outdoor People* (☎ 0181-743 2976), 42 Uxbridge Rd W12 (tube: Shepherd's Bush), also have good reputations, while *Nomad Traveller's Store & Medical Centre* (☎ 0181-889 7014) 3-4 Wellington Terrace, Turnpike Lane N8 (tube: Turnpike Lane), stocks all the other bits and bobs (mozzy nets, money belts etc) that an intending traveller could possibly want.

MUSIC

If you're after bog-standard CDs and tapes you'll probably find what you're after in one of London's three goliath-sized music shops, all in the West End (Map 3):

Tower Records (☎ 439 2500), 1 Piccadilly Circus W1 (tube: Piccadilly Circus)
HMV (☎ 631 3423), 150 Oxford St W1 (tube: Oxford Circus)
Virgin Megastore (☎ 631 1234), 14-30 Oxford St W1 (tube: Tottenham Court Road)

Tower Records is the easiest to find and stays open the latest. Its jazz, world music and soundtrack sections are pretty good, but overall it's hectic and difficult to negotiate. HMV is great for orders, classical music and specialist categories, but again the shop is loud and crowded. The Virgin Megastore near Tottenham Court Rd is by far the most pleasant and relaxed of the rival giants. The layout is a tad bewildering but it's worth persevering for some excellent bargains.

London also has a range of excellent specialist stores. *Ray's Jazz Shop* (☎ 240 3969), 180 Shaftesbury Ave WC2, speaks for itself. There's rare and recent jazz and the staff are helpful and knowledgeable.

Also worth trying are:

Black Market (☎ 437 0478), 25 D'Arblay St W1 (tube: Oxford Circus; Map 3)
Dub Vendor (☎ 223 3757), 274 Lavender Hill SW11
Honest Jon's (☎ 0181-969 9822), 278 Portobello Rd W10
Rough Trade (☎ 229 8541), 130 Talbot Rd W11 (tube: Ladbroke Grove; Map 9)
Trax (☎ 734 0795), 55 Greek St W1

For second-hand and rare vinyl tracks try:

Reckless Records (☎ 437 4271), 30 Berwick St W1
UFO Music (☎ 636 1281), 18 Hanway St W1
Kensington Market (☎ 938 4343), 49-53 Kensington High St W8 (Map 8)

BOOKS

For those who read the book or saw the movie *84 Charing Cross Rd*, Charing Cross Rd will need no introduction. This is where to go when you want reading matter.

Foyle's (☎ 437 5660), 119 Charing Cross Rd W1 (tube: Tottenham Court Road; Map 3), is the biggest and by far the messiest and most confusing bookshop in London. It has to be seen, whereupon you'll feel free to escape to the better-organised *Waterstones* (☎ 434 4291), 121-131 Charing Cross Rd, or *Books etc* (☎ 379 6838) next door. The Waterstones chain has transformed book-buying for Londoners. Their many stores are well stocked and smartly appointed, and the staff are knowledgeable and keen to help. Books etc tends to lag a bit behind its neighbour but has a slight edge where alternative and avant-garde titles are concerned.

There are also plenty of specialist bookshops in the area, from the self-explanatory *Sportspages* (☎ 240 9604), 94-96 Charing Cross Rd; to the broadest selection of crime fiction at *Murder One* (☎ 734 3485), 71-73 Charing Cross Rd; and *Zwemmer* (☎ 379 7886), 24 Litchfield St, for all kinds of art books. *Helter Skelter* (☎ 836 1151), 4 Denmark St, focuses on popular music. For anything written by a woman, try *Silver Moon* (☎ 836 7906), 64-48 Charing Cross Rd WC2 (tube: Leicester Square; Map 3), which describes itself as 'a world of women writers'. It's open Monday to Saturday from 10 am to 6.30 pm (8 pm on Thursday).

Further afield, *Dillons* (☎ 636 1577), 82 Gower St WC1 (Map 5), has the edge on academic titles. *Gay's the Word* (☎ 278 7654), 66 Marchmont St, Russell Square WC1 (Map 5), stocks, unsurprisingly, male gay writing; *Compendium* (☎ 485 8944), 234 Camden High St NW1 (Map 10), serves as the focus for left-wing, alternative and hard-to-find titles. *Books for Cooks* (☎ 221 1992), 4 Blenheim Crescent W11 (tube: Ladbroke Grove; Map 9), has an enormous collection of cookery books; there's also a small attached café where you can sample some of the recipes.

The major chains make adequate sources for guidebooks and maps, but there are also several specialist travel bookshops. *Stanfords* (☎ 836 1321), 12 Long Acre WC2 (tube: Covent Garden; Map 3), has one of the largest and best selections of maps and guides in the world; there are also branches in Regent St and attached to Campus Travel in Victoria. The *Travel Bookshop* (☎ 229 5260), 13 Blenheim Crescent W11 (Map 9), across the road from Books for Cooks, has all the new guides, plus a selection of out-of-print and antiquarian gems. *Daunts Books* (☎ 224 2295), 83 Marylebone High St W1, has a wide selection of travel guides and other subjects in a beautiful old shop. For antiquarian travel books it's also worth trying *Beaumont Travel Books* (☎ 637 5862), 31 Museum St WC1.

For half-price second-hand books one of the best places to look is the book market immediately in front of the National Film Theatre, which theoretically takes place every day, although few stallholders bother when the weather's bad. Modern novels tend to go for around £2.50, more for popular choices, less for anything obscure.

JEWELLERY

If you're just after a pair of common or garden studs, you'll be able to pick them up at any of the markets or at stalls in the main-line stations. But of course some occasions call for the sort of trinkets you need to win the lottery to afford. Once again, if you can't afford to buy, you may still want to eyeball.

Cartier (☎ 493 6962), 175 New Bond St W1
Garrard's (☎ 734 7020), 112 Regent St W1
Mappin & Webb (☎ 734 3801), 170 Regent St W1
Tiffany's (☎ 409 2790), 25 Old Bond St W1

If you want to get some part of your body pierced or tattooed, *Into You* (☎ 253 5085), 144 St John St EC1, promises that everything, but everything, is sterilised.

ART

Bond St is the place to head if you want to ogle the sort of paintings you won't be able to afford.

A more realistic place to start looking for something to buy is Bayswater where, every Sunday, hopeful artists hang their paintings on the railings of Hyde Park and Kensington Gardens. What you'll find here is mainly pretty derivative, with an eye to the tourists. Still, having a look costs nothing and it's a fun way to while away any bits of Sunday (from 9.30 am to 4 pm) when you're not chasing after the markets.

FOOD & DRINK

Obviously run-of-the-mill food shops are ten a penny all over London, but the food halls at Harrods and Fortnum & Mason's are world-famous, and it's well worth tracking down some of the more specialist stores.

The *Oil and Spices Shop* (☎ 403 4030), Shad Thames SE1 (tube: London Bridge), has the delightful aroma of an oriental bazaar and a dazzling array of different oils in beautifully shaped bottles. It's part of the Le Pont de la Tour complex, which also incorporates a fine bakery and wine shop.

Neal's Yard Dairy (☎ 379 7646), 17 Short's Gardens WC2 (tube: Covent Garden), is the place to go to sample some of Britain's more esoteric cheeses. A mail-order service is available if you can't make it to the shop. Also good for cheeses is *Paxton & Whitfield* (☎ 930 0250), 93 Jermyn St SW1 (tube: Piccadilly Circus), which claims to stock 300 different varieties.

Simply Sausages (☎ 287 3482), 93 Berwick St W1 (tube: Oxford Circus), is a great place to stock up for a picnic. Among the many meats on sale are Balinese bangers and vegetarian mushroom and tarragon sausages. Afterwards, pop out to the street market for the fruit and veg to go with them.

The *Algerian Coffee Stores* (☎ 437 2480), 52 Old Compton St W1 (tube: Leicester Square), is *the* place to go to buy all sorts of teas and coffees, including Maragogype, the biggest coffee bean in the world.

Gerry's (☎ 734 4215), 74 Old Compton Rd W1 (tube: Leicester Square), stocks a frightening array of alcohol garnered from far-flung parts. Come here if you just can't manage without a bottle of Cuban rum or Chilean pisco. Whether you'll want to sample bison grass vodka is more debatable.

The Tea House (☎ 240 7539), 15 Neal St WC2 (tube: Covent Garden), has a great range of teas plus the pots to put them in and all sorts of associated paraphernalia.

The Hive (☎ 924 6233), 53 Webbs Rd SW11 (tube: Clapham South), boasts a choice of more than 40 different types of honey, plus a cutaway section through a hive so you can see the bees going about their business.

SPECIALIST STORES

Hamleys (☎ 734 3161), 188 Regent St W1 (tube: Oxford Circus; Map 3), is an Aladdin's cave of a toy shop, the place to come to see every imaginable toy in the universe. But prices can be high, and you can probably buy more cheaply elsewhere. The crowds in the weeks leading up to Christmas, all fighting over this year's 'in' toy, must be experienced to be believed.

Playing cards with everything on the reverse can be bought at *Jack Duncan Cartoons & Books* (☎ 242 5335), 44 Museum St WC1 (tube: Tottenham Court Rd). With prices ranging from around £4 to £10 the cards would make excellent gifts to take home. You can also buy old newspaper cartoons of the Steve Bell kind here.

Covent Garden and the streets running off it (especially Neal St) remain a happy hunting ground for offbeat, one-off shops. Fancy taking home a model of a Victorian theatre? Then try *Benjamin Pollock's Toy Shop* (☎ 379 7866), 44 The Market, Covent Garden WC2 (tube: Covent Garden).

How about a kite? Then the *Kite Store* (☎ 836 1666), 48 Neal St, Covent Garden WC2 (tube: Covent Garden), stocks at least 100 different models. The nearby *Comic Showcase* (☎ 240 3664) at No 26 is nirvana for comic freaks.

For fish-shaped slippers, artificial aquaria and all things piscean, head straight for *Just Fish* (☎ 240 6277) in Short's Gardens, Covent Garden WC2 (tube: Covent Garden). A second shop opens in Colombia Rd on Sunday morning.

Papier Marché (☎ 251 6311), 53 Clerkenwell Close EC1 (tube: Farringdon), sells, as its name would suggest, all manner of birds made out of papier-mâche – gannets, pelicans, penguins, you name it. This is also the place to come if you're after a fur-lined mirror.

Compendia (☎ 0181-293 6616), 10 The Market, Greenwich SE10 (Greenwich BR), is piled high with board and other games, including a good selection of travel games. Nearby, the *Linen & Lace Company* (☎ 293 9407) stocks just what you'd expect – beautiful things made out of linen and lace.

For all things South American, try *Tumi* (☎ 485 4152), 23 Chalk Farm Rd NW1 (tube: Chalk Farm; Map 10), a company which has been trading for 17 years and has a good reputation for playing fair by its suppliers.

If you know someone who'd like a ship's clock or a ship's bell or even a jigsaw of HMS *Victory*, head straight for *Nauticalia* (☎ 480 6805) in St Katherine's Dock (tube: Tower Hill).

Finally, the *Museum Store* (☎ 240 5760), 37 The Market, Covent Garden WC2 (tube: Covent Garden), sells a wide variety of souvenirs from British and overseas museums, and is a good place to browse for a present.

Excursions

Since Britain is relatively small and most of its transport systems fan out from London, hardly anywhere is impossibly far away. However, there are several attractions and towns within a 50 mile radius of the city which could easily be visited on a day trip. Several companies organise excursions if you're pressed for time to do it yourself. See Organised Tours in the Getting Around chapter.

Immediately west of London, Windsor and Eton are so close that they're almost part of the capital. Whipsnade Wildlife Park and Woburn Abbey and Safari Park are off the M1 north-west of London, but you'll need two days to visit all three.

Hatfield House and St Albans are easy day trips north by train from King's Cross; Waltham Abbey is even closer to town, as is the wonderful Epping Forest. Bedford, too, can easily be seen in a day.

Charles Darwin's home at Down House is in Orpington, just to the south-east of London in Kent. A little further out, near Sevenoaks, you'll find Ightham Mote and Knole, two beautiful but very different historic houses. Hever and Leeds castles, near Tonbridge and Maidstone respectively, are also just south-east of London. Canterbury is due east of the capital with just the right amount to see and do in one day.

Brighton is directly to the south, a popular and fun place to escape to on a sunny day or for a weekend. The Chessington World of Adventures zoo and theme park is just south-west of London.

This chapter assumes you'll be returning to London after looking around. For details of places to stay and for information on other places to visit, including Oxford, Cambridge, Bath, Salisbury and Stonehenge, and Stratford-upon-Avon, see Lonely Planet's *Britain* guide.

If you're taking the train to destinations in the south-east of England, you can get worthwhile discounts with a Network Card (see Railcards in the Getting There & Away chapter).

WINDSOR & ETON

Windsor Castle is one of Britain's premier tourist attractions and since it is only 20 miles from central London, and easily accessible by rail and road, it crawls with tourists. If possible, avoid weekends and the peak months of July and August.

Orientation & Information

Windsor Castle overlooks the River Thames and the town of Windsor spreading out to the west. Eton is essentially a small village linked to Windsor by a pedestrian bridge over the Thames. You can easily visit both on the same trip.

The TIC (☎ 01753-852010) at 24 High St is open daily from 9.30 am to 5 pm, closing at 6.30 pm in July and August.

If you wish to stay in Windsor, the *Windsor Youth Hostel* (☎ 01753-861710) is at Edgworth House, Mill Lane, Clewer. Otherwise, there are several centrally located B&Bs or the TIC can help with booking accommodation.

Windsor Castle

Standing on chalk bluffs overlooking the Thames, Windsor Castle (☎ 01753-831118) has been home to British royalty for over 900 years and is one of the greatest surviving medieval castles. It started out as a wooden motte and bailey in 1070, was rebuilt in stone in 1165 and successively extended and rebuilt right through to the 19th century.

Castle areas to which the public are admitted are generally open March to October, 10 am to 5.30 pm (last entry 4 pm), closing an hour earlier the rest of the year. In summer, weather and other events permitting, the changing of the guard takes place at 11 am (not on Sunday). The State Apartments are closed when the royal family is in residence,

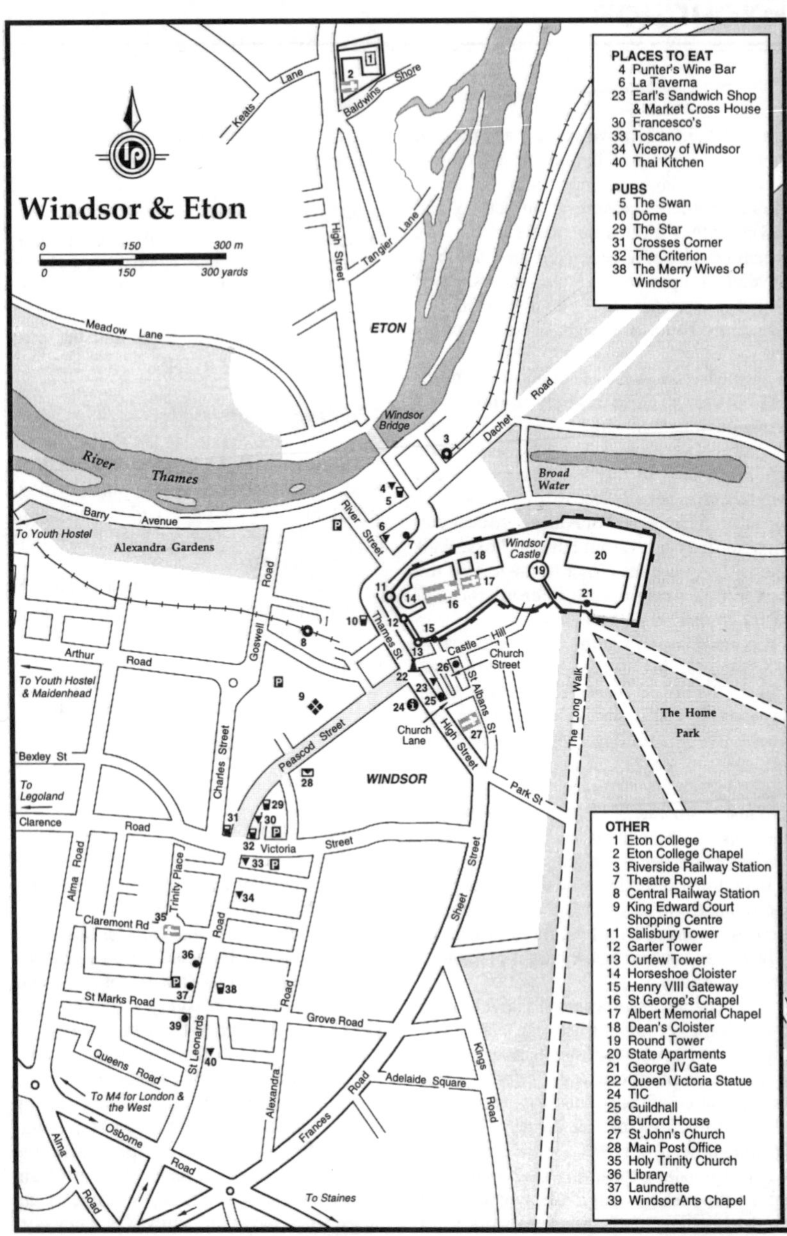

Windsor & Eton
0 150 300 m
0 150 300 yards
PLACES TO EAT
4 Punter's Wine Bar
6 La Taverna
23 Earl's Sandwich Shop & Market Cross House
30 Francesco's
33 Toscano
34 Viceroy of Windsor
40 Thai Kitchen
PUBS
5 The Swan
10 Dôme
29 The Star
31 Crosses Corner
32 The Criterion
38 The Merry Wives of Windsor
OTHER
1 Eton College
2 Eton College Chapel
3 Riverside Railway Station
7 Theatre Royal
8 Central Railway Station
9 King Edward Court Shopping Centre
11 Salisbury Tower
12 Garter Tower
13 Curfew Tower
14 Horseshoe Cloister
15 Henry VIII Gateway
16 St George's Chapel
17 Albert Memorial Chapel
18 Dean's Cloister
19 Round Tower
20 State Apartments
21 George IV Gate
22 Queen Victoria Statue
24 TIC
25 Guildhall
26 Burford House
27 St John's Church
28 Main Post Office
35 Holy Trinity Church
36 Library
37 Laundrette
39 Windsor Arts Chapel
ETON
WINDSOR
River Thames
Windsor Bridge
Windsor Castle
Broad Water
The Home Park
The Long Walk
Alexandra Gardens
To Youth Hostel
To Youth Hostel & Maidenhead
To Legoland
To M4 for London & the West
To Staines
Keats Lane
Baldwins Shore
High Street
Tangier Lane
Meadow Lane
Dachet Road
Barry Avenue
River Street
Goswell Road
Thames St
Castle Hill
Church Street
St Albans St
Church Lane
Peascod Street
Arthur Road
Charles Street
Bexley St
Clarence Road
Victoria Street
Park St
Sheet Street
Alma Road
Trinity Place
Claremont Rd
St Marks Road
Grove Road
Queens Road
St Leonards Road
Alexandra Road
Kings Road
Adelaide Square
Frances Road
Osborne Road

the most regular occasion being during the Ascot horse-racing meeting in June.

Entry to the castle is £8.80/4.60, except on Sunday when entry is £6.70/3.60 because St George's Chapel, a prime attraction, does not open until 2 pm.

St George's Chapel One of Britain's finest examples of late-Gothic architecture, the chapel was commenced by Edward IV in 1475 but not completed until 1528.

The nave is a superb example of the Perpendicular style with beautiful fan vaulting arching out from the pillars. The chapel is packed with the **tombs of royalty** including George V and Queen Mary, George VI and Edward IV. The **wooden oriel window**, built for Catherine of Aragon by Henry VIII, is a fine example of the Tudor style. The **garter stalls** are the chapel's equivalent of choir stalls. Dating back to 1478-85, the banner, helm and crest above each stall indicates the current occupant. Plates carry the names of earlier knights who have occupied the stalls since the 14th century.

Located between the garter stalls, the **Royal Vault** is the burial place of George III, George IV and William IV. Another **vault** between the stalls contains Henry VIII, his favourite wife Jane Seymour, and Charles I, reunited with his head which was detached after the Civil War. When the Knights of the Garter gather here the Queen and Prince of Wales always join them. The gigantic **battle sword** of Edward III, founder of the Order of the Garter, hangs on the wall. Henry VI and Edward VII and Queen Alexandra also have their **tombs** on this side.

From the chapel you enter the Dean's Cloister and the adjacent Albert Memorial Chapel. This originated in 1240 and became the first chapel of the Order of the Garter in 1350 but fell into disuse when St George's Chapel was built. It was completely restored after the death of Prince Albert in 1861.

State Apartments & Other Areas The State Apartments are a combination of formal rooms and museum-style exhibits. In 1992 a fire badly damaged St George's Hall and the adjacent Grand Reception Room. Restoration work is almost finished.

Like other parts of the castle, the State Apartments have gone through successive reconstructions and expansions, most notably under Charles II who added lavishly painted ceilings by Antonio Verrio and delicate woodcarvings by Grinling Gibbons. Further extensive modifications were made under George IV and William IV in the 1820s and 30s. A remarkable art collection adorns the walls.

Created to commemorate the Battle of Waterloo, the Waterloo Chamber is used for formal meals. The Garter Throne Room is used for investing new Knights of the Order of the Garter. The King's Drawing Room is also known as the Rubens Room, after the three paintings hanging there. The King's State Bedchamber has paintings by Canaletto and Gainsborough, but Charles II actually slept in the adjacent King's Dressing Room. Some of Windsor's finest paintings are hung here including works by van Dyck, Holbein, Rembrandt, Rubens and Dürer. The King's Closet was used by Charles II as a study and has works by Canaletto, Reynolds and Hogarth.

From the king's rooms the route continues into the queen's rooms. The Queen's Ballroom has a remarkable collection of van Dycks. Only three of the 13 Antonio Verrio ceiling paintings from Charles II's time survive, one of them in the Queen's Audience Chamber. More Gobelins tapestries and another Verrio ceiling can be found in the Queen's Presence Chamber.

Queen Mary's Dolls' House was the work of architect Sir Edwin Lutyens and was built on a 1:12 scale in 1923. It's complete in every detail, right down to running water to the bathrooms. Entry to the Dolls' House costs an additional £1.

Legoland Windsor

If you've got kids who're likely to tire of too many state rooms, Legoland (☎ 0990-040404) is the latest antidote. An updated version of the parent park in Denmark, Legoland features some pretty tame rides and miniature versions of famous European landmarks made from Lego among other standard theme-park fare.

It's open from Easter to September from 10 am to 6 pm daily; until 8 pm in August; weekends only in October. Admission costs a pretty steep £15/12. If you come by South West train a combined rail/admission ticket costs £20.50/14.75. To get there take the shuttle bus from Windsor & Eton Riverside railway station.

Around Town

On High St beside Castle Hill, Windsor's fine **Guildhall** was built between 1686-9, its construction completed under Christopher Wren's supervision. The central columns in the open area don't actually support the 1st floor; the council insisted upon them despite Wren's conviction that they were unnecessary. The inch or two of clear air proved his point.

Some of the oldest parts of Windsor lie along the cobbled streets behind the Guildhall. The visibly leaning **Market Cross House** is right next to the Guildhall. Charles II kept Nell Gwyn, his favourite mistress, in **Burford House** on Church St.

Eton College

Cross the Thames by the pedestrian Windsor Bridge to arrive at another enduring symbol of Britain's class system: Eton College, a famous public (meaning private) school that has educated no less than 18 prime ministers and now counts Prince William among its 1250-odd pupils. Several buildings date from the mid-15th century when Henry VI founded the school.

The college (☎ 01753-671177) is open to visitors during term from 2 to 4.30 pm, and during the Easter and summer holidays from 10.30 am. Entry is £2.50/2. Guided tours at 2.15 and 3.30 pm cost £3.50/3.

Places to Eat

Next to the Guildhall on High St, the *Earl's Sandwich Shop* turns out excellent sandwiches and French sticks for £2 to £3 from the tiny, precarious-looking Market Cross House.

Peascod St and its extension St Leonards Rd are good restaurant hunting grounds. *Francesco's* (☎ 01753-863773) at 53 Peascod St is a very popular pizza, pasta and cappuccino specialist with meals for around £6. The *Crosses Corner* (☎ 01753-862867) at 73 Peascod St also attracts the crowds.

Old Windsor's cobbled streets shelter numerous restaurants, particularly along Church St and Church Lane. There are more restaurants along Eton High St.

Getting There & Away

Windsor is 20 miles by road or rail from central London. It only takes about 15 minutes by car from Windsor to Heathrow airport.

Bus Bus Nos 700, 701, 702 or 718 for Windsor depart from London's Victoria Coach Station about every hour. No 192 (Monday to Saturday) or No 170 (Sunday) connects Windsor with Heathrow airport. On Sunday the No 701 London service also goes via Heathrow.

Train There are two Windsor and Eton railway stations – Central station on Thames St, directly opposite the Windsor Castle entrance gate, and Riverside station near the bridge to Eton.

From London, trains run to the Riverside station from Waterloo every half hour (hourly on Sunday) and take 50 minutes. Services from Paddington to Central station require a change at Slough, five minutes from Windsor, but only take about half an hour. The fare is £5.40 day return on either route.

Getting Around

Guide Friday open-top double-decker bus tours of the town cost £6.50/2; combined train and tour tickets cost £9.40/3.70. French Brothers (☎ 01753-851900) operates boat trips from Windsor and Runnymede (where the Magna Carta was signed in 1215). Half-hour trips cost £2.90/1.45.

WHIPSNADE

Whipsnade Wild Animal Park (☎ 01582-872171) in Dunstable is an offshoot of London Zoo which was originally established to breed endangered species in captivity. Most of the animals are in large enclosures and Whipsnade claims to release 50 animals into the wild for every one captured. The 2500 animals in the 600 acre site can be viewed by car, on the park's railway, or on foot. It's open daily all year from 10 am to 6 pm (until 7 pm on Sunday; closing at 4 pm November to March); entry is £8.50/6, plus £6.50 for a car if you want to drive round, although there's a free double-decker bus.

In summer you can get to Whipsnade by Green Line bus from near Victoria Coach Station (☎ 0181-668 7261).

WOBURN ABBEY & SAFARI PARK

Not really an abbey but a grand stately home built on the site of a Cistercian abbey, Woburn Abbey (☎ 01525-290666) has been the seat of the dukes of Bedford for the last 350 years. The house dates mainly from the 18th century, when the building was enlarged and remodelled into a vast country mansion. In 1950, half had to be demolished because of dry rot but it remains impressive.

The abbey is stuffed with furniture, porcelain and paintings, including a famous portrayal of Elizabeth I with the wrecked ships of the Spanish Armada in the background.

The surrounding 3000 acre deer park contains nine species of deer, including the largest breeding herd of Pére David deer, extinct in their native China for a century (although a small herd was returned to Beijing in 1985).

The abbey is open daily from late March to October, 11 am to 4 pm; weekends only from January to March. Entry is £7/2.50. It's easily accessible off the M1 motorway.

One mile from the abbey is Woburn Safari Park (☎ 01525-290407), the country's largest drive-through animal reserve. It's open from late March to October from 10 am to 5 pm; from 11 am to 3 pm on weekends only in winter. Entry is £9/6.50, reducing to £5.50/4.50 in winter. If you visit the abbey first you qualify for a 50% discount.

WALTHAM ABBEY

Just north of London on the dreaded M25 ring road, Waltham Cross gets surprisingly few visitors. With time to spare it's worth venturing out here to visit the abbey which gave it its name and one of the last remaining Eleanor Crosses (see the boxed aside Crosses of Love).

Despite being a hotchpotch of architectural styles, the nave of Waltham Abbey is still lined with fine Norman columns reminiscent of Durham Cathedral. The Victorian ceiling is painted with the signs of the zodiac and a handy mirror on wheels lets you inspect them without getting a crick in your neck. In the 14th century Lady Chapel the stained glass incorporates the image of an Old English sheepdog watching over the

Crosses of Love

When Edward I's wife Eleanor died in 1290, the grief-stricken king arranged for memorial crosses to be erected at every place where the body passed the night on its way from Harby in Nottinghamshire to London for burial in Westminster Abbey. Of the 12 crosses, only three originals survive.

One of them can be seen at Waltham in north London where it stands in the middle of the road with traffic swirling round it.

London's second Eleanor Cross is a meticulous Victorian reproduction which stands in the courtyard of Charing Cross station, all but ignored by the commuters racing for their trains (Charing is a corruption of 'Chère Reine'). The original stood in Whitehall until 1647. A statue of King Charles I now stands on that site. ■

manger, while a Trafalgar Square pigeon saunters past a fountain in another panel. It's worth looking for the tomb of Sir Edward Dennys which dates from 1600 and shows his 10 children with the boys grouped to one side and the girls to the other. Two have their arms locked together, possibly suggesting they were twins.

Waltham Abbey was originally founded by the same King Harold who met such an ignominious end at the Battle of Hastings in 1066. The site of his tomb is marked out in the grass behind the abbey.

Getting There & Away

Trains leave Liverpool St for Waltham Cross roughly every half hour (£4 day return).

EPPING FOREST

North of Waltham Abbey you come to Chingford and then to Epping Forest, 6000 acres of untamed forest strung out between the Lea and Roding valleys. The forest was a popular royal hunting ground in Tudor times and Henry VIII built a house here which daughter Elizabeth turned into the pretty half-timbered **Hunting Lodge** (☎ 0181-529 6681) in Rangers Rd. It now houses a small museum (50p), open Wednesday to Sunday from 2 to 5 pm.

Elizabeth also introduced fallow deer to the forest and you can still see around 500 of them in Birch Hall sanctuary. Otherwise, the forest makes a marvellous escape for a walk and a picnic, provided you're not the sort to worry about stories of the ghost of Dick Turpin, the 18th century highwayman who made the forest his own.

You can get to Epping very easily from Liverpool St to Chingford, for £3.40 day return.

ST ALBANS

Just 25 minutes train ride to the north, the cathedral city of St Albans makes a pleasant day trip from London. To the Romans, St Albans was Verulamium, and their theatre and parts of the ancient wall can still be seen to the south-west of the city.

The town centre is St Peter's St, 10 minutes walk west of St Albans railway station. The cathedral lies to the west, off High St, with the ruins of Verulamium even further to the west.

The TIC (☎ 01727-864511) in the grand town hall on Market Place sells the useful *Discover St Albans* town trail (95p).

St Albans Abbey & Cathedral

In 209, a Roman citizen named Alban was put to death for his Christian beliefs, becoming Britain's first Christian martyr. In the 8th century King Offa of Mercia founded an abbey on the site of his martyrdom. The Norman abbey church was built in 1077, incorporating parts of the Saxon building and many Roman bricks, conspicuously in the central tower. After the Dissolution of the Monasteries in 1538 the abbey church became the parish church. Considerable restoration took place in 1877 when it was redesignated a cathedral.

The heart of the cathedral is St Alban's shrine immediately behind the presbytery and overlooked by a wooden watcher's loft, where monks stood guard to ensure pilgrims didn't pilfer relics. Look out for a particularly fine 14th century mural of St Wilfrid on a nearby column.

The Norman nave columns are painted with 13th and 14th century crucifixion scenes.

Around Town

The **Verulamium Museum** (☎ 01727-819339), an interesting museum of everyday life in Roman Britain, is in St Michael's St and is open daily from 10 am to 5.30 pm (afternoon only on Sunday); admission free. In the surrounding streets and adjacent Verulamium Park you can also inspect the remains of a basilica, theatre and bathhouse.

The Museum of St Albans (☎ 01727-819340) in Hatfield Rd gives a quick rundown of the city's history since Roman times. It's open (free) Monday to Saturday from 10 am to 5 pm and Sunday from 2 to 5 pm.

The **Gardens of the Rose** (☎ 01727-850461) are three miles south-west of St

Albans. With about 30,000 specimens, these gardens contain the world's largest rose collection. They're open from June to mid-October for £4 (children free). You can get there on bus No 321 from the centre of St Albans.

Getting There & Away

There are eight trains an hour from King's Cross (Thameslink) to St Albans (£5.70).

HATFIELD HOUSE

Only 25 minutes north of London by rail, Hatfield House is England's most impressive Jacobean house, a graceful red-brick and stone mansion, full of treasures and built between 1607 and 1611 for Robert Cecil, first Earl of Salisbury and secretary of state to both Elizabeth I and James I. Of an earlier Tudor palace where Elizabeth spent much of her childhood, only the restored great hall and one wing converted into stables survive.

Inside, the house is extremely grand. Two storeys high, running the width of the house and clad in carved oak panels, the Marble Hall is most impressive. There are famous portraits of Elizabeth and, in the dining room, numerous English kings. The oak Grand Staircase is decorated with carved figures, including one of John Tradescant, the 17th century botanist responsible for the gardens.

Five-course Elizabethan banquets, complete with minstrels, court jesters and saucy ditties, are held in the great hall at 7.30 pm on Tuesday, Friday and Saturday, and also on Thursday from April to September. Phone ☎ 01707-262055 for tickets (£27 to £29.25 depending on the day) and information about coaches from London.

Hatfield House (☎ 01707-262823) is 21 miles from London. It is open Tuesday to Saturday from noon to 4 pm, Sunday from 1 to 4.30 pm, although the grounds are open from 10.30 am to 8 pm; admission is £5.50/3.40. The entrance is opposite Hatfield railway station, and there are numerous trains from King's Cross station (25 minutes, £5.50 day return).

BEDFORD

Fifty miles north of London, Bedford is a pleasant riverside town with links to the preacher and writer John Bunyan.

The TIC (☎ 01234-215226), just off the High St at 10 St Paul's Square, stocks *John Bunyan's Bedford*, a guide to places in the Bedford area with a Bunyan connection.

The Bunyan Meeting

The Bunyan Meeting (☎ 01234-358870) in Mill St is a church built in 1849 on the site of the barn where Bunyan preached from 1671 to 1678. Bronze doors inspired by Ghiberti's doors for the Baptistry in Florence show scenes from *The Pilgrim's Progress*. As a hostage in Beirut, envoy Terry Waite took comfort from a postcard of the stained-glass window showing Bunyan in jail. From April to October, the church is open to visitors Tuesday to Saturday from 10 am to 4 pm. The small museum of Bunyan memorabilia is open afternoons only at present but plans exist to expand it so people can see some of the 169 editions of *The Pilgrim's Progress* from around the world. Admission costs 50/30p.

Getting There & Away

The best way to reach Bedford is by rail from London, with frequent departures from King's Cross Thameslink (one hour, £12.60 day return). Most trains stop at Midland station, a 10 minute, well-signposted walk west of High St.

National Express has direct links between Bedford and London. The bus station is half a mile west of High St.

DOWN HOUSE

Charles Darwin, the great Victorian evolutionary theorist, lived at Down House (☎ 01689-859119), Luxted Rd, Orpington, Kent. It has been restored recently to show his study and lounge to better effect. Temporary exhibitions are housed upstairs and you can explore the garden of this fine Victorian house.

It's open Wednesday to Sunday from 1 to

5.30 pm and admission is £2.50/1 (free to English Heritage members).

To get there take a train from Victoria to Bromley South and then catch a No 146 bus.

KNOLE HOUSE

In a country full of extraordinary country houses, Knole (☎ 01732-450608) is outstanding.

Substantially dating from 1456, it's not as old as some of the great houses that incorporate medieval fortresses but is more coherent in style. It seems as if nothing much has been changed since the early 17th century, something the Sackville family, who have owned it since 1566, can take credit for.

Vita Sackville-West, Sissinghurst's co-creator, was born here in 1892, and her friend Virginia Woolf based the novel *Orlando* on the history of the house and family.

The house is vast, with seven courtyards, 52 staircases and 365 rooms, so the excellent guidebook (£1.50) is recommended. It's open from April to October on Wednesday, Friday, Saturday and Sunday from 11 am to 5 pm, and on Thursday from 2 to 5 pm (last entry 4 pm). Admission costs £5/2.50 (free to National Trust members who also get to park for free; everyone else pays £2.50). The grounds are open all year.

Getting There & Away

Knole is to the south of Sevenoaks, east of the A225. The railway station is on the Charing Cross to Tonbridge line, a 1½ mile walk from the house. A day return costs £10.

IGHTHAM MOTE

For six and a half centuries Ightham Mote (☎ 01732-810378) has lain hidden in a narrow wooded valley in the Weald. Not only has it survived, it has grown more beautiful – as the stone mellowed, a wing was added here, a room converted there...

Somehow it has survived wars, storms, changes in ownership, and generation after generation of occupants. This is all the more remarkable since it's not an aristocratic mansion full of priceless treasures but a small medieval manor house surrounded by a moat.

Although parts date from around 1340, the present building is like an architectural jigsaw puzzle, and you need a guide to unravel which bit belongs to what century. Some of the additions and alterations seem haphazard, but the materials (wood, stone, clay), the building's scale, and its watery frame add up to a harmonious whole.

The location is picturesque, the building extraordinary. It's six miles east of Sevenoaks off the A25, 2½ miles south of Ightham off the A227. It's open from April to October, daily except Tuesday and Saturday, from noon to 5.30 pm, and Sunday from 11 am to 5.30 pm. Admission is £4/2 (National Trust members free).

CANTERBURY

Canterbury, in Kent, is 58 miles from London and makes an easy day trip. Its greatest treasure is its magnificent cathedral, the successor to the church St Augustine built after he began converting the English to Christianity in 597. After the martyrdom of Archbishop Thomas à Becket in 1170, the cathedral became the focus for one of Europe's most important medieval pilgrimages, immortalised by Geoffrey Chaucer in *The Canterbury Tales*.

Today Canterbury is one of Britain's most impressive and evocative cathedrals and one of the country's World Heritage sites. Not even baying packs of schoolchildren can completely destroy the atmosphere, although try to visit late in the day to avoid them.

Canterbury was badly damaged by bombing during WWII and parts have been rebuilt insensitively. However, there's still plenty to see and the bustling centre is atmospheric and alive.

The city centre is enclosed by a medieval city wall and a modern ring road. It's easy to get around on foot, but virtually impossible to get around by car.

The TIC (☎ 01227-766567), 34 St Margaret's St, is open daily from 9.30 am to 5.30 pm. Guided walks leave from the TIC at 2 pm daily from 6 April to 3 November and also at 11 am, Monday to Saturday, in July and August. The walks cost £2.50, take about 1½ hours and explore the cathedral precincts, King's School and the town's medieval centre.

Canterbury Cathedral

Like most great cathedrals, Canterbury Cathedral (☎ 01227-762862) evolved over the centuries and reflects several architectural styles. To see everything, including the beautiful cloisters, can easily absorb half a day.

Since there are treasures tucked away in corners and a trove of associated stories, a tour is highly recommended. One-hour tours start at 10.30 am, noon, and 2 and 3 pm and cost £2.80. If the crowd looks daunting, you can take a Walkman tour for £2.50 (30 minutes). On weekdays and Saturday the cathedral is open from 9 am to 7 pm from Easter to September, and from 9 am to 5 pm from October to Easter; choral evensong is at 5.30 pm, 3.15 pm on Saturday. On Sunday it is open from 12.30 to 2.30 pm and 4.30 to 5.30 pm; choral evensong is at 3.15 pm. Admission is £2/1.

The traditional approach to the cathedral is along narrow Mercery Lane – which used to be lined with small shops selling souvenirs to pilgrims – to Christ Church Gate. Once inside the gate, turn right and walk east to get an overall picture.

St Augustine's original cathedral burnt down in 1067. The first Norman archbishop began construction of a new cathedral in 1070, but only fragments remain. In 1174 most of the eastern half of the building was again destroyed by fire but the magnificent crypt beneath the choir survived.

The fire presented the opportunity to create something in keeping with the cathedral's new status as England's most important pilgrimage site. In response, William of Sens created the first major Gothic construction in England, a style now described as Early English. Most of the cathedral east of Bell Harry tower dates from this period.

In 1391 work began on the western half of the building, replacing the south-west and north-west transepts and nave. The new Perpendicular style was used, and work continued for over 100 years, culminating in 1500 with the completion of Bell Harry. Subsequently, more has been subtracted than added, although the exterior has not been substantially changed.

The main entrance is through the **south-west porch**, built in 1415 to commemorate the English victory at Agincourt. From the centre of the nave there are impressive views east down the length of the church, with its ascending levels, and west to the **window** with glass dating from the 12th century.

From beneath **Bell Harry**, with its beautiful fan vault, more impressive glass that somehow survived the Puritans is visible. A 15th century screen, featuring six kings, separates the nave from the choir.

Becket is believed to have been murdered in the north-west transept. A modern **altar and sculpture** mark the spot. The adjoining **Lady Chapel** has beautiful Perpendicular fan vaulting. Descend a flight of steps into the Romanesque crypt, the main survivor of the Norman cathedral.

The Chapel of Our Lady at the western end of the crypt has some of the finest Romanesque carving in England. St Thomas was entombed in the Early English eastern end until 1220. This is where King Henry II allowed himself to be whipped in penance for having provoked Becket's murder with the infamous words 'who will rid me of this turbulent priest', and is apparently the site of many miracles. The **Chapel of St Gabriel** features 12th century paintings, while the **Black Prince's Chantry** is a beautiful Perpendicular chapel, donated by the prince in 1363, now used by Huguenots (French Protestants).

In the south-west transept the **Chapel of St Michael** includes a wealth of tombs, including that of Archbishop Stephen Langton, one of the chief architects of the Magna Carta. The superb **12th century choir** rises in stages to the **High Altar** and Trinity Chapel. The screen around the choir stalls was erected in 1305 and evensong has been sung in this inspiring space every day for 800 years. **St Augustine's Chair**, dating from the 13th century, is used to enthrone archbishops.

The stained glass in Trinity Chapel is mostly 13th century and celebrates the life of St Thomas. **St Thomas' shrine** no longer exists, but you can still see the alabaster tomb of Henry IV, buried with his wife **Queen Joan of Navarre**, and the **Black Prince's tomb** with its famous effigy along with the prince's shield, gauntlets and sword.

Opposite **St Anselm's Chapel** is the **tomb for Archbishop Sudbury** who, as Chancellor of the Exchequer, was held responsible for a hated poll tax – he was beheaded by a mob during the Peasants' Revolt of 1381.

Go around the eastern end of the cathedral and turn right into Green Court, which is surrounded on the east (right) side by the Deanery and on the north side (straight ahead) by the early 14th century Brewhouse and Bakehouse. In the north-west corner (far left) is the famous Norman Staircase (1151).

Around Town

The Canterbury Tales (☎ 01227-454888), St Margaret's St, is an automated historical recreation of Chaucer's famous stories. It's open all year from 9.30 am to 5 pm and admission costs £4.85/3.75.

The heavily restored but still charming Tudor **Weavers' Houses** were once home to Huguenot refugees who established a silk-weaving industry in Canterbury.

The only remaining city gate, the **West Gate**, dates from the 14th century and survived because it was used as a prison; it now houses a small museum featuring arms and armour. It's open all year, Monday to Saturday from 11 am to 12.30 pm and 1.30 to 3.30 pm, for 60/40p.

Founded in 1267, the **Greyfriars Monastery** was England's first Franciscan (the Grey Friars) monastery. The picturesque building spans a small branch of the River Stour, and includes an upstairs chapel, open to the public from mid-May to September, Monday to Saturday from 2 to 4 pm.

The **Canterbury Heritage Museum** (☎ 01227-452747), in a converted 14th century building in Stour St, gives good, though rather dry, coverage of the city's history. The building, once the Poor Priests' Hospital, is worth visiting in its own right. It's open all year from 10.30 am to 5 pm, but Sunday only from June to October and only from 1.30 to 5 pm. Admission is £1.90/95p, although a joint ticket covering the Roman and Westgate museums costs £3.40/1.70.

At the **Roman Museum** (built underground around the remains of a Roman town house, in Butchery House, opposite the Shakespeare Inn) you get to smell the aromas of a Roman kitchen, visit the marketplace, handle artefacts and take a computer-generated tour of the town house. It's open all year, Monday to Saturday, from 10 am to 5 pm, and on Sunday from June until the end of October from 1.30 to 5 pm. Admission costs £1.90/95p.

Henry VIII acted with thoroughness when **St Augustine's Abbey** (☎ 01227-767345) was demolished in 1538 – only foundations remain. Admission is £1.50/75p (free to English Heritage members).

Places to Eat

Il Vaticano (☎ 01227-765333), 35 St Margaret's St, has excellent Italian food, in particular a wide range of pastas from £4.25 to £7.95. The *Three Tuns Hotel* at the end of St Margaret's serves good-value pub meals from around £4. Some consider *Tuo e Mio Restaurant* (☎ 01227-761471), 16 The Borough, Canterbury's best restaurant. It serves high-quality Italian food with main dishes around £8.

Flap Jacques Cafe Creperie, 71 Castle St, opposite the Castle Court Guest House, serves French-style pancakes from £1.80 to £4.95. It's small but has a sunny atmosphere.

Getting There & Away

There are numerous buses from London with National Express (☎ 0990-808080). A day return costs £8.

There are two railway stations: East, accessible from Victoria, and West, accessible from Charing Cross and Waterloo. The journey takes about 1¾ hours and costs £15 day return.

SISSINGHURST CASTLE GARDEN

Sissinghurst (☎ 01580-715330), off the A262 between Biddenden and Cranbrook, is an enchanted place where Vita Sackville-West and her husband Harold Nicholson (of the infamous Bloomsbury Group) created a superb garden in 1930 in and around a ruined Elizabethan mansion. The castle and gardens are surrounded by a moat and rolling wooded countryside. All the elements come together to create an exquisite, dreamlike English beauty. Anyone who has ever doubted the seductiveness of the English landscape hasn't visited Sissinghurst in spring or summer.

The gardens are open from April to mid-October, Tuesday to Friday from 1 to 6.30 pm, and on Saturday and Sunday from 10 am to 5.30 pm. The ticket office opens at noon from Tuesday to Friday. Admission is £6/3 (free to National Trust members).

Getting There & Away

The nearest railway station is Staplehurst on the line between Tonbridge and Ashford; a day return from Charing Cross is £9.30. Maidstone & District's Maidstone to Hastings bus service (No 4/5) passes the station and Sissinghurst.

CHARTWELL

Chartwell (☎ 01732-866368) is the large country house just north of Edenbridge that Winston Churchill bought in 1922 and which remained the family home until his death. It's stuffed full of important memorabilia.

The house (only) is open from late March to October on Saturday, Sunday and Wednesday from 11 am to 4.30 pm. The house, garden and studio are open from April to October, on Tuesday, Wednesday and Thursday from 11 am to 4 pm, and Saturday and Sunday from 11 am to 5.30 pm. Entry to the house and garden costs £5/2.50 (free to NT members). To get there take a train from Victoria to Bromley South and then a metrobus No 746 to the house.

HEVER CASTLE

Idyllic Hever Castle (☎ 01732-865224) near Edenbridge, a few miles west of Tonbridge, was the childhood home of Anne Boleyn, mistress to Henry VIII and then his doomed queen. The moated castle was built in the 13th and 15th centuries and restored in the early 1900s by William Waldorf Astor. The exterior is unchanged from Tudor times, but the interior now has superb Edwardian woodwork. The castle is surrounded by a garden, again the creation of the Astors, that incorporates a formal Italian garden with classical sculpture.

It's open from March to late November daily from noon to 6 pm; admission to the castle and gardens is £6.50/3.30, and to the gardens only, £4.90/3. The nearest railway station is Hever on the Uckfield line, a mile from the castle itself (£12.20 day return from Victoria).

LEEDS CASTLE

Just east of Maidstone, Leeds Castle (☎ 01622-765400) is justly famous as one of the world's most beautiful castles. Like something from a fairy tale, it stands on two small islands in a lake surrounded by rolling wooded hills. The building dates from the 9th century, but Henry VIII transformed it from a fortress into a palace. It's open daily from 10 am to 5 pm, but is overrun by families, especially at the weekend. Admission is £8.50/5.50.

Getting There & Away

National Express (☎ 0990-808080) has one bus a day direct from Victoria station, leaving at 10 am; it must be prebooked and the combined cost of admission and travel is £15/11.25. The nearest railway station is Bearsted on the Kent Coast Line to Ashford. A combined admission and travel ticket from Victoria or Charing Cross stations costs £15.90/7.90.

BRIGHTON

Just an hour from Victoria by train, Brighton, with its heady mix of seediness and sophistication, is every Londoner's favourite seaside resort and the venue for many a dirty weekend. It's 53 miles due south of London.

The town's character essentially dates from the 1780s when the dissolute, music-loving Prince Regent (later King George IV) built his outrageous summer palace for lavish parties by the sea. Brighton still has some of the hottest clubs and venues outside London, including the largest gay club on the south coast, a vibrant population of students, excellent shopping, a thriving arts scene, and countless restaurants, pubs and cafés.

The TIC (☎ 01273-333755), 10 Bartholomew Square, should have copies of Brighton's listings magazine, *The Punter* (70p). If not, pick up a copy from any good newsagent.

Royal Pavilion

The Royal Pavilion (☎ 01273-603005) is an extraordinary fantasy – all Indian palace on the outside and Chinese brothel on the inside. It began with a seaside affair, when the Prince Regent came here to hang out with his wayward uncle, the Duke of Cumberland. He fell in love with both the seaside and a local resident, Maria Fitzherbert, and decided that this was the perfect place to party.

The first pavilion, built in 1787, was a classical villa. It wasn't until the early 1800s, when everything Eastern became the rage, that the current creation began to take shape. The final Indian-inspired design was produced by John Nash, architect of Regent's Park and its flanking buildings, and was built between 1815 and 1822. George is said to have cried when he first saw the Music Room, which confirms what a strange man he was. The whole over-the-top edifice is not to be missed.

It's open June to September daily from 10 am to 6 pm, October to May to 5 pm for £4.10/2.50. The *Queen Adelaide Tea Rooms* on the top floor make a pleasant spot to recuperate; simple meals like a ploughman's lunch are around £2.80.

Around Town

Originally built as an indoor tennis court, the **Brighton Museum & Art Gallery** (☎ 01273-603005) houses a quirky collection of Art Deco and Art Nouveau furniture, archaeological finds, surrealist paintings and costumes. The most famous exhibit, Salvador Dali's lips-shaped sofa, is often away on loan. It's open (free) daily (except Wednesday) from 10 am to 5 pm, 2 to 5 pm on Sunday.

The **Palace Pier**, with its Palace of Fun, is the very essence of Brighton. In this case, fun means takeaway food and a thousand machines, all with flashing lights and all swallowing your money. This is *the* place to stick your head in a cardboard cut-out of a royal, and the best spot to buy sticks of famous Brighton Rock candy. It's open daily and the deckchairs are free.

South of North St (and north of the TIC), **the Lanes** are a maze of narrow alleyways crammed with antiques, jewellery and fashionable clothes shops. Some of the best restaurants and bars are around here too.

Places to Eat

Brighton is jam-packed with good-value eating places. Wander around the Lanes or head down to Preston St, which runs back from the seafront near West Pier, and you'll turn up all sorts of interesting, affordable possibilities. *Food for Friends* (☎ 01273-202310), 17 Prince Albert St, is the most enduring vegetarian haunt, with main meals for around £5. The similarly priced *Dorset Street Bar* (☎ 01273-605423), 28 North Rd, is a friendly pub in the heart of the buzzy North Laine area. The *Yum Yum Noodle Bar* (☎ 01273-606777), 22 Sydney St, has good-value Chinese, Malay, Thai and vegetarian specials from £3.50.

Getting There & Away

National Express has 15 buses a day from London; a day return costs £8. There are also over 40 fast trains a day from Victoria (50 minutes, £13.80 day return) and slower Thameslink trains from King's Cross or Blackfriars.

CHESSINGTON WORLD OF ADVENTURES

Chessington World of Adventures (☎ 01372-727227), Leatherhead Rd, Chessington, Surrey, is a 65 acre theme park-cum-zoo with the same sort of white-knuckle rides as at Alton Towers further north. Proximity to London guarantees long queues for the rides on sunny summer days, so try and get there early – which also ensures you make the most of the admission fee!

In later October and early November Chessington stays open until 9 pm for special Fright Nights, with lots of lasers and other special effects.

It's open from late March to October from 10 am to 5 or 6 pm, although last admission is at 3 pm. In July and August it stays open until 9.30 pm (last admission 7 pm). Admission costs £17/13.75 (£15/11 if bought in combination with your bus ticket; £14.50/10.75 if bought with your train ticket).

Getting There & Away

Eight or nine Green Line buses a day leave Victoria Coach Station for Chessington. The journey takes 1¼ hours and tickets cost £5/2.50 for a day return. Alternatively take a train from Waterloo to Chessington South, a half-hour ride. A cheap day return costs £3.70/1.85.

Index

Map references are in **bold** type.
Map numbers refer to the colour maps at the back of the book.

Boxed Asides

SPOT THE LP TAXI

Until March 1999 the Lonely Planet taxi will be cruising the streets of London. Send us your photos or slides showing the taxi and they could be published in our next London guide!

DOUG McKINLAY

All photos received will be shown in a window display at Stanfords, 12-14 Long Acre, Covent Garden, London, in spring 1999.

The best entries will be judged by Lonely Planet's Tony Wheeler and Stanfords' Douglas Shatz and will be reproduced in the next edition of this book. Winners will receive a free copy of the next edition.

To enter, send your photo before 31st March 1999 with your full name and address to:
Lonely Planet Taxi Competition,
10a Spring Place,
London NW5 3BH
UK

Photos become the property of Lonely Planet and will not be returned.
Entrants grant Lonely Planet the right to use these photographs in any form throughout the world.

LONELY PLANET PHRASEBOOKS

Building bridges,
Breaking barriers,
Beyond babble-on

- handy pocket-sized books
- easy to understand Pronunciation chapter
- clear and comprehensive Grammar chapter
- romanisation alongside script to allow ease of pronunciation
- script throughout so users can point to phrases
- extensive vocabulary sections, words and phrases for every situation
- full of cultural information and tips for the traveller

***'...vital for a real DIY spirit and attitude in language learning'* – Backpacker**

***'the phrasebooks have good cultural backgrounders and offer solid advice for challenging situations in remote locations'* – San Francisco Examiner**

'...they are unbeatable for their coverage of the world's more obscure languages' – The Geographical Magazine

---

Arabic (Egyptian)
Arabic (Moroccan)
Australia
Australian English, Aboriginal and Torres Strait languages
Baltic States
Estonian, Latvian, Lithuanian
Bengali
Burmese
Brazilian
Cantonese
Central Asia
Central Europe
Czech, French, German, Hungarian, Italian and Slovak
Eastern Europe
Bulgarian, Czech, Hungarian, Polish, Romanian and Slovak
Egyptian Arabic
Ethiopian (Amharic)
Fijian
French
German
Greek
Hindi/Urdu
Indonesian
Italian
Japanese
Korean
Lao
Latin American Spanish
Malay
Mandarin
Mediterranean Europe
Albanian, Croatian, Greek, Italian, Macedonian, Maltese, Serbian, Slovene
Mongolian
Moroccan Arabic
Nepali
Papua New Guinea
Pilipino (Tagalog)
Quechua
Russian
Scandinavian Europe
Danish, Finnish, Icelandic, Norwegian and Swedish
South-East Asia
Burmese, Indonesian, Khmer, Lao, Malay, Tagalog (Pilipino), Thai and Vietnamese
Spanish
Sri Lanka
Swahili
Thai
Thai Hill Tribes
Tibetan
Turkish
Ukrainian
USA
US English, Vernacular Talk, Native American languages and Hawaiian
Vietnamese
Western Europe
Basque, Catalan, Dutch, French, German, Irish, Italian, Portuguese, Scottish Gaelic, Spanish (Castilian) and Welsh

LONELY PLANET JOURNEYS

JOURNEYS is a unique collection of travel writing – published by the company that understands travel better than anyone else. It is a series for anyone who has ever experienced – or dreamed of – the magical moment when they encountered a strange culture or saw a place for the first time. They are tales to read while you're planning a trip, while you're on the road or while you're in an armchair, in front of a fire.

JOURNEYS books catch the spirit of a place, illuminate a culture, recount a crazy adventure, or introduce a fascinating way of life. They always entertain, and always enrich the experience of travel.

THE GATES OF DAMASCUS

Lieve Joris

Translated by Sam Garrett

This best-selling book is a beautifully drawn portrait of day-to-day life in modern Syria. Through her intimate contact with local people, Lieve Joris draws us into the fascinating world that lies behind the gates of Damascus. Hala's husband is a political prisoner, jailed for his opposition to the Assad regime; through the author's friendship with Hala we see how Syrian politics impacts on the lives of ordinary people.

Lieve Joris, who was born in Belgium, is one of Europe's leading travel writers. In addition to an award-winning book on Hungary, she has published widely acclaimed accounts of her journeys to the Middle East and Africa. *The Gates of Damascus* is her fifth book.

'Expands the boundaries of travel writing' **– Times Literary Supplement**

KINGDOM OF THE FILM STARS

Journey into Jordan

Annie Caulfield

Kingdom of the Film Stars is a travel book and a love story. With honesty and humour, Annie Caulfield writes of travelling in Jordan and falling in love with a Bedouin. Her book offers fascinating insights into the country – from the traditional tent life of nomadic tribes to the first woman MP's battle with fundamentalist colleagues. *Kingdom of the Film Stars* unpicks some of the tight-woven Western myths about the Arab world, presenting cultural and political issues within the intimate framework of a compelling love story.

Annie Caulfield, who was born in Ireland and currently lives in London, is an award-winning playwright and journalist. She has travelled widely in the Middle East.

'Annie Caulfield is a remarkable traveller. Her story is fresh, courageous, moving, witty and sexy!' **– Dawn French**

LONELY PLANET TRAVEL ATLASES

Lonely Planet has long been famous for the number and quality of its guidebook maps. Now we've gone one step further and in conjunction with Steinhart Katzir Publishers produced a handy companion series: Lonely Planet travel atlases – maps of a country produced in book form.

Unlike other maps, which look good but lead travellers astray, our travel atlases have been researched on the road by Lonely Planet's experienced team of writers. All details are carefully checked to ensure the atlas corresponds with the equivalent Lonely Planet guidebook.

The handy atlas format means no holes, wrinkles, torn sections or constant folding and unfolding. These atlases can survive long periods on the road, unlike cumbersome fold-out maps. The comprehensive index ensures easy reference.

- full-colour throughout
- maps researched and checked by Lonely Planet authors
- place names correspond with Lonely Planet guidebooks – no confusing spelling differences
- legend and travelling information in English, French, German, Japanese and Spanish
- size: 230 x 160 mm

Available now:
Chile & Easter Island • Egypt • India & Bangladesh • Israel & the Palestinian Territories •Jordan, Syria & Lebanon • Kenya • Laos • Portugal • South Africa, Lesotho & Swaziland • Thailand • Turkey • Vietnam • Zimbabwe, Botswana & Namibia

---

LONELY PLANET TV SERIES & VIDEOS

Lonely Planet travel guides have been brought to life on television screens around the world. Like our guides, the programmes are based on the joy of independent travel, and look honestly at some of the most exciting, picturesque and frustrating places in the world. Each show is presented by one of three travellers from Australia, England or the USA and combines an innovative mixture of video, Super-8 film, atmospheric soundscapes and original music.

Videos of each episode – containing additional footage not shown on television – are available from good book and video shops, but the availability of individual videos varies with regional screening schedules.

Video destinations include: Alaska • American Rockies • Australia – The South-East • Baja California & the Copper Canyon • Brazil • Central Asia • Chile & Easter Island • Corsica, Sicily & Sardinia – The Mediterranean Islands • East Africa (Tanzania & Zanzibar) • Ecuador & the Galapagos Islands • Greenland & Iceland • Indonesia • Israel & the Sinai Desert • Jamaica • Japan • La Ruta Maya • Morocco • New York • North India • Pacific Islands (Fiji, Solomon Islands & Vanuatu) • South India • South West China • Turkey • Vietnam • West Africa • Zimbabwe, Botswana & Namibia

The Lonely Planet TV series is produced by:
Pilot Productions
The Old Studio
18 Middle Row
London W10 5AT UK

For video availability and ordering information contact your nearest Lonely Planet office.

Music from the TV series is available on CD & cassette.

PLANET TALK

Lonely Planet's FREE quarterly newsletter

We love hearing from you and think you'd like to hear from us.

PLANET TALK

Slovenia:
River Deep, Mountain High

When...is the right time to see reindeer in Finland?
Where...can you hear the best palm-wine music in Ghana?
How...do you get from Asunción to Areguá by steam train?
What...is the best way to see India?

For the answer to these and many other questions read PLANET TALK.

Every issue is packed with up-to-date travel news and advice including:

- a letter from Lonely Planet co-founders Tony and Maureen Wheeler
- go behind the scenes on the road with a Lonely Planet author
- feature article on an important and topical travel issue
- a selection of recent letters from travellers
- details on forthcoming Lonely Planet promotions
- complete list of Lonely Planet products

To join our mailing list contact any Lonely Planet office.

Also available: Lonely Planet T-shirts. 100% heavyweight cotton.

LONELY PLANET ONLINE

Get the latest travel information before you leave or while you're on the road

Whether you've just begun planning your next trip, or you're chasing down specific info on currency regulations or visa requirements, check out Lonely Planet Online for up-to-the minute travel information.

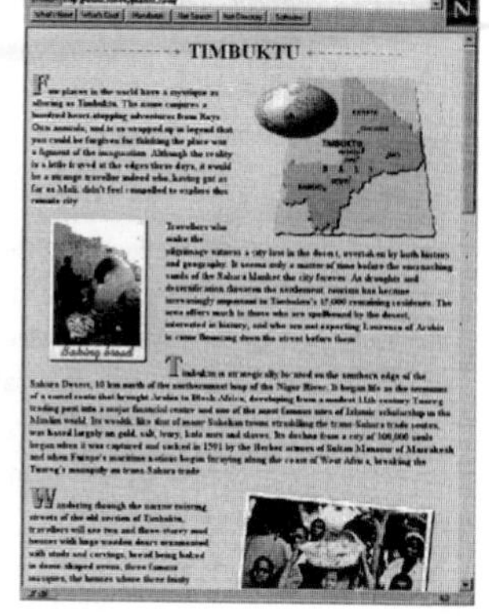

As well as travel profiles of your favourite destinations (including maps and photos), you'll find current reports from our researchers and other travellers, updates on health and visas, travel advisories, and discussion of the ecological and political issues you need to be aware of as you travel.

There's also an online travellers' forum where you can share your experience of life on the road, meet travel companions and ask other travellers for their recommendations and advice. We also have plenty of links to other online sites useful to independent travellers.

And of course we have a complete and up-to-date list of all Lonely Planet travel products including guides, phrasebooks, atlases, Journeys and videos and a simple online ordering facility if you can't find the book you want elsewhere.

www.lonelyplanet.com
or
AOL keyword: lp

LONELY PLANET PRODUCTS

Lonely Planet is known worldwide for publishing practical, reliable and no-nonsense travel information in our guides and on our web site. The Lonely Planet list covers just about every accessible part of the world. Currently there are eight series: *travel guides*, *shoestring guides*, *walking guides*, *city guides*, *phrasebooks*, *audio packs*, *travel atlases* and *Journeys* – a unique collection of travel writing.

EUROPE

Amsterdam • Austria • Baltic States phrasebook • Britain • Central Europe on a shoestring • Central Europe phrasebook • Czech & Slovak Republics • Denmark • Dublin • Eastern Europe on a shoestring • Eastern Europe phrasebook • Estonia, Latvia & Lithuania • Finland • France • French phrasebook • German phrasebook • Greece • Greek phrasebook • Hungary • Iceland, Greenland & the Faroe Islands • Ireland • Italian phrasebook • Italy • Mediterranean Europe on a shoestring • Mediterranean Europe phrasebook • Paris • Poland • Portugal • Portugal travel atlas • Prague • Russia, Ukraine & Belarus • Russian phrasebook • Scandinavian & Baltic Europe on a shoestring • Scandinavian Europe phrasebook • Slovenia • Spain • Spanish phrasebook • St Petersburg • Switzerland • Trekking in Spain • Ukrainian phrasebook • Vienna • Walking in Britain • Walking in Switzerland • Western Europe on a shoestring • Western Europe phrasebook

Travel Literature: The Olive Grove: Travels in Greece

NORTH AMERICA

Alaska • Backpacking in Alaska • Baja California • California & Nevada • Canada • Florida • Hawaii • Honolulu • Los Angeles • Mexico • Miami • New England • New Orleans • New York City • New York, New Jersey & Pennsylvania • Pacific Northwest USA • Rocky Mountain States • San Francisco • Southwest USA • USA phrasebook • Washington, DC & the Capital Region

CENTRAL AMERICA & THE CARIBBEAN

Bermuda • Central America on a shoestring • Costa Rica • Cuba •Eastern Caribbean •Guatemala, Belize & Yucatán: La Ruta Maya • Jamaica

SOUTH AMERICA

Argentina, Uruguay & Paraguay • Bolivia • Brazil • Brazilian phrasebook • Buenos Aires • Chile & Easter Island • Chile & Easter Island travel atlas • Colombia • Ecuador & the Galápagos Islands • Latin American Spanish phrasebook • Peru • Quechua phrasebook • Rio de Janeiro • South America on a shoestring • Trekking in the Patagonian Andes • Venezuela

Travel Literature: Full Circle: A South American Journey

ANTARCTICA

Antarctica

ISLANDS OF THE INDIAN OCEAN

Madagascar & Comoros • Maldives• Mauritius, Réunion & Seychelles

AFRICA

Africa - the South • Africa on a shoestring • Arabic (Moroccan) phrasebook • Cape Town • Central Africa • East Africa • Egypt • Egypt travel atlas• Ethiopian (Amharic) phrasebook • Kenya • Kenya travel atlas • Malawi, Mozambique & Zambia • Morocco • North Africa • South Africa, Lesotho & Swaziland • South Africa, Lesotho & Swaziland travel atlas • Swahili phrasebook • Trekking in East Africa • West Africa • Zimbabwe, Botswana & Namibia • Zimbabwe, Botswana & Namibia travel atlas

Travel Literature: The Rainbird: A Central African Journey • Songs to an African Sunset: A Zimbabwean Story

MAIL ORDER

Lonely Planet products are distributed worldwide. They are also available by mail order from Lonely Planet, so if you have difficulty finding a title please write to us. North American and South American residents should write to Embarcadero West, 155 Filbert St, Suite 251, Oakland CA 94607, USA; European and African residents should write to 10a Spring Place, London NW5 3BH; and residents of other countries to PO Box 617, Hawthorn, Victoria 3122, Australia.

NORTH-EAST ASIA

Beijing • Cantonese phrasebook • China • Hong Kong • Hong Kong, Macau & Guangzhou • Japan • Japanese phrasebook • Japanese audio pack • Korea • Korean phrasebook • Mandarin phrasebook • Mongolia • Mongolian phrasebook • North-East Asia on a shoestring • Seoul • Taiwan • Tibet • Tibet phrasebook • Tokyo

Travel Literature: Lost Japan

MIDDLE EAST & CENTRAL ASIA

Arab Gulf States • Arabic (Egyptian) phrasebook • Central Asia • Central Asia phrasebook • Iran • Israel & the Palestinian Territories • Israel & the Palestinian Territories travel atlas • Istanbul • Jerusalem • Jordan & Syria • Jordan, Syria & Lebanon travel atlas • Lebanon • Middle East • Turkey • Turkish phrasebook • Turkey travel atlas • Yemen

Travel Literature: The Gates of Damascus • Kingdom of the Film Stars: Journey into Jordan

ALSO AVAILABLE:

Travel with Children • Traveller's Tales

INDIAN SUBCONTINENT

Bangladesh • Bengali phrasebook • Delhi • Hindi/Urdu phrasebook • India • India & Bangladesh travel atlas • Indian Himalaya • Karakoram Highway • Nepal • Nepali phrasebook • Pakistan • Rajasthan • Sri Lanka • Sri Lanka phrasebook • Trekking in the Indian Himalaya • Trekking in the Karakoram & Hindukush • Trekking in the Nepal Himalaya

Travel Literature: In Rajasthan • Shopping for Buddhas

SOUTH-EAST ASIA

Bali & Lombok • Bangkok • Burmese phrasebook • Cambodia • Ho Chi Minh City • Indonesia • Indonesian phrasebook • Indonesian audio pack • Jakarta • Java • Laos • Lao phrasebook • Laos travel atlas • Malay phrasebook • Malaysia, Singapore & Brunei • Myanmar (Burma) • Philippines • Pilipino phrasebook • Singapore • South-East Asia on a shoestring • South-East Asia phrasebook • Thailand • Thailand's Islands & Beaches • Thailand travel atlas • Thai phrasebook • Thai audio pack • Thai Hill Tribes phrasebook • Vietnam • Vietnamese phrasebook • Vietnam travel atlas

AUSTRALIA & THE PACIFIC

Australia • Australian phrasebook • Bushwalking in Australia • Bushwalking in Papua New Guinea • Fiji • Fijian phrasebook • Islands of Australia's Great Barrier Reef • Melbourne • Micronesia • New Caledonia • New South Wales • New Zealand • Northern Territory • Outback Australia • Papua New Guinea • Papua New Guinea phrasebook • Queensland • Rarotonga & the Cook Islands • Samoa • Solomon Islands • South Australia • Sydney • Tahiti & French Polynesia • Tasmania • Tonga • Tramping in New Zealand • Vanuatu • Victoria • Western Australia

Travel Literature: Islands in the Clouds • Sean & David's Long Drive

THE LONELY PLANET STORY

Lonely Planet published its first book in 1973 in response to the numerous 'How did you do it?' questions Maureen and Tony Wheeler were asked after driving, bussing, hitching, sailing and railing their way from England to Australia.

Written at a kitchen table and hand collated, trimmed and stapled, *Across Asia on the Cheap* became an instant local bestseller, inspiring thoughts of another book.

Eighteen months in South-East Asia resulted in their second guide, *South-East Asia on a shoestring*, which they put together in a backstreet Chinese hotel in Singapore in 1975. The 'yellow bible', as it quickly became known to backpackers around the world, soon became *the* guide to the region. It has sold well over half a million copies and is now in its 9th edition, still retaining its familiar yellow cover.

Today there are over 240 titles, including travel guides, walking guides, language kits & phrasebooks, travel atlases and travel literature. The company is the largest independent travel publisher in the world. Although Lonely Planet initially specialised in guides to Asia, today there are few corners of the globe that have not been covered.

The emphasis continues to be on travel for independent travellers. Tony and Maureen still travel for several months of each year and play an active part in the writing, updating and quality control of Lonely Planet's guides.

They have been joined by over 70 authors and 170 staff at our offices in Melbourne (Australia), Oakland (USA), London (UK) and Paris (France). Travellers themselves also make a valuable contribution to the guides through the feedback we receive in thousands of letters each year and on our web site.

The people at Lonely Planet strongly believe that travellers can make a positive contribution to the countries they visit, both through their appreciation of the countries' culture, wildlife and natural features, and through the money they spend. In addition, the company makes a direct contribution to the countries and regions it covers. Since 1986 a percentage of the income from each book has been donated to ventures such as famine relief in Africa; aid projects in India; agricultural projects in Central America; Greenpeace's efforts to halt French nuclear testing in the Pacific; and Amnesty International.

'I hope we send people out with the right attitude about travel. You realise when you travel that there are so many different perspectives about the world, so we hope these books will make people more interested in what they see. Guidebooks can't really guide people. All you can do is point them in the right direction.'

– Tony Wheeler

LONELY PLANET PUBLICATIONS

Australia
PO Box 617, Hawthorn 3122, Victoria
tel: (03) 9819 1877 fax: (03) 9819 6459
e-mail: talk2us@lonelyplanet.com.au

USA
Embarcadero West, 155 Filbert St, Suite 251,
Oakland, CA 94607
tel: (510) 893 8555 TOLL FREE: 800 275-8555
fax: (510) 893 8563
e-mail: info@lonelyplanet.com

UK
10a Spring Place,
London NW5 3BH
tel: (0181) 742 3161 fax: (0181) 742 2772
e-mail: lonelyplanetuk@compuserve.com

France:
71 bis rue du Cardinal Lemoine, 75005 Paris
tel: 1 44 32 06 20 fax: 1 46 34 72 55
e-mail: 100560.415@compuserve.com

World Wide Web: http://www.lonelyplanet.com
or *AOL keyword: lp*

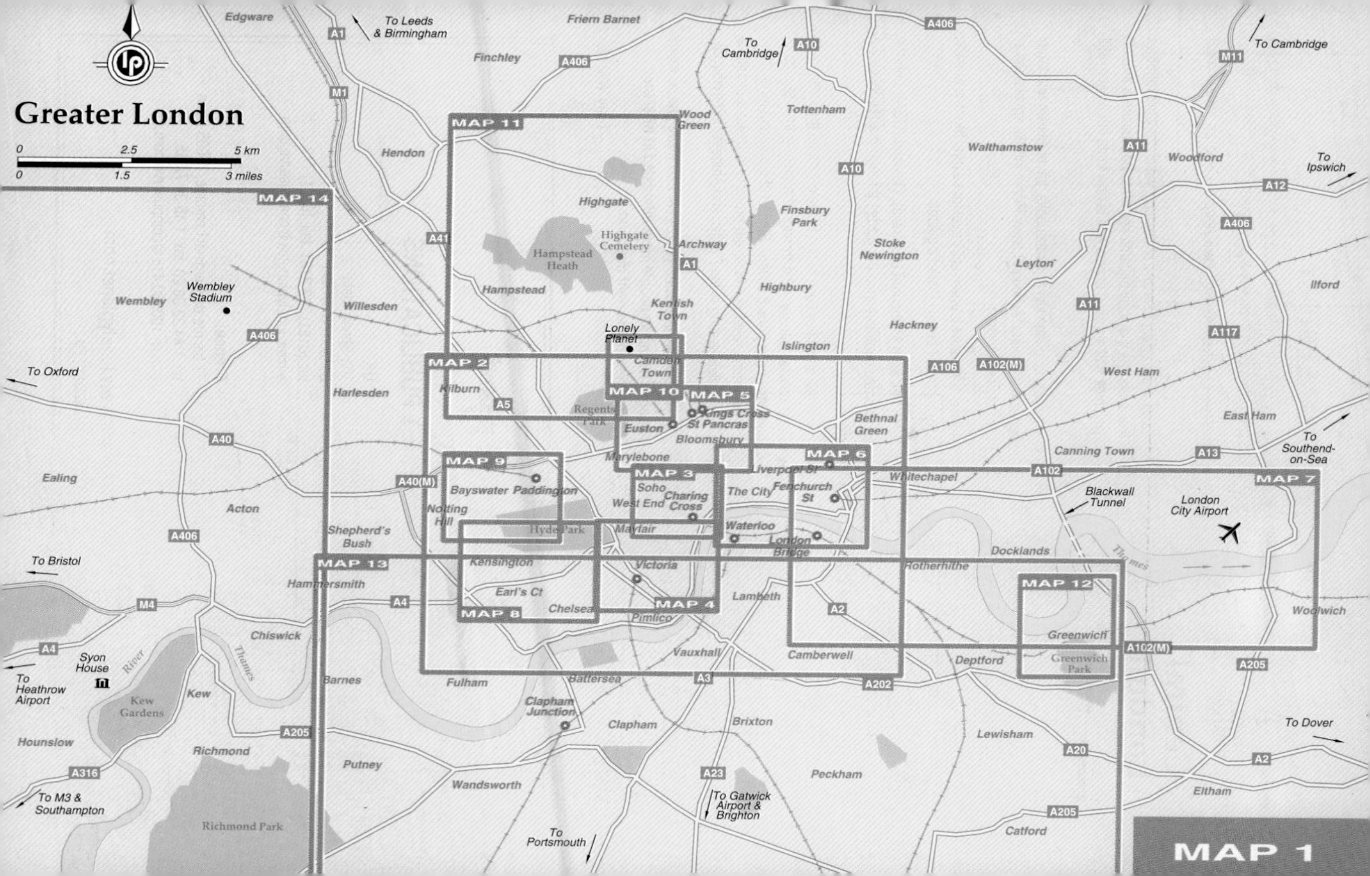

Greater London
0 2.5 5 km
0 1.5 3 miles
MAP 1
MAP 2
MAP 3
MAP 4
MAP 5
MAP 6
MAP 7
MAP 8
MAP 9
MAP 10
MAP 11
MAP 12
MAP 13
MAP 14
Edgware
To Leeds & Birmingham
Friern Barnet
Finchley
To Cambridge
Tottenham
Walthamstow
Woodford
To Ipswich
Hendon
Wood Green
Highgate
Highgate Cemetery
Hampstead Heath
Hampstead
Archway
Finsbury Park
Stoke Newington
Leyton
Ilford
Wembley
Wembley Stadium
Willesden
Kentish Town
Highbury
Lonely Planet
Camden Town
Islington
Hackney
West Ham
To Oxford
Harlesden
Kilburn
Regents Park
Euston
Kings Cross
St Pancras
Bloomsbury
Bethnal Green
East Ham
Canning Town
To Southend-on-Sea
Marylebone
Liverpool St
Whitechapel
Ealing
Bayswater
Paddington
Soho
Charing Cross
West End
The City
Fenchurch St
Blackwall Tunnel
London City Airport
Acton
Notting Hill
Hyde Park
Mayfair
Waterloo
London Bridge
Shepherd's Bush
Docklands
Thames
To Bristol
Kensington
Victoria
Rotherhithe
Hammersmith
Earl's Ct
Chelsea
Lambeth
Pimlico
Woolwich
Chiswick
Vauxhall
Camberwell
Greenwich
Greenwich Park
Syon House
River
To Heathrow Airport
Kew Gardens
Kew
Barnes
Fulham
Battersea
Deptford
Clapham Junction
Clapham
Brixton
Lewisham
To Dover
Hounslow
Richmond
Putney
Peckham
To M3 & Southampton
Wandsworth
To Gatwick Airport & Brighton
Eltham
Richmond Park
To Portsmouth
Catford
A1
M1
A406
A10
A406
M11
A11
A10
A12
A41
A1
A406
A11
A406
A117
A106
A102(M)
A5
A40
A13
A40(M)
A102
A406
A4
M4
A4
A2
A3
A202
A102(M)
A205
A205
A23
A20
A2
A316
A205

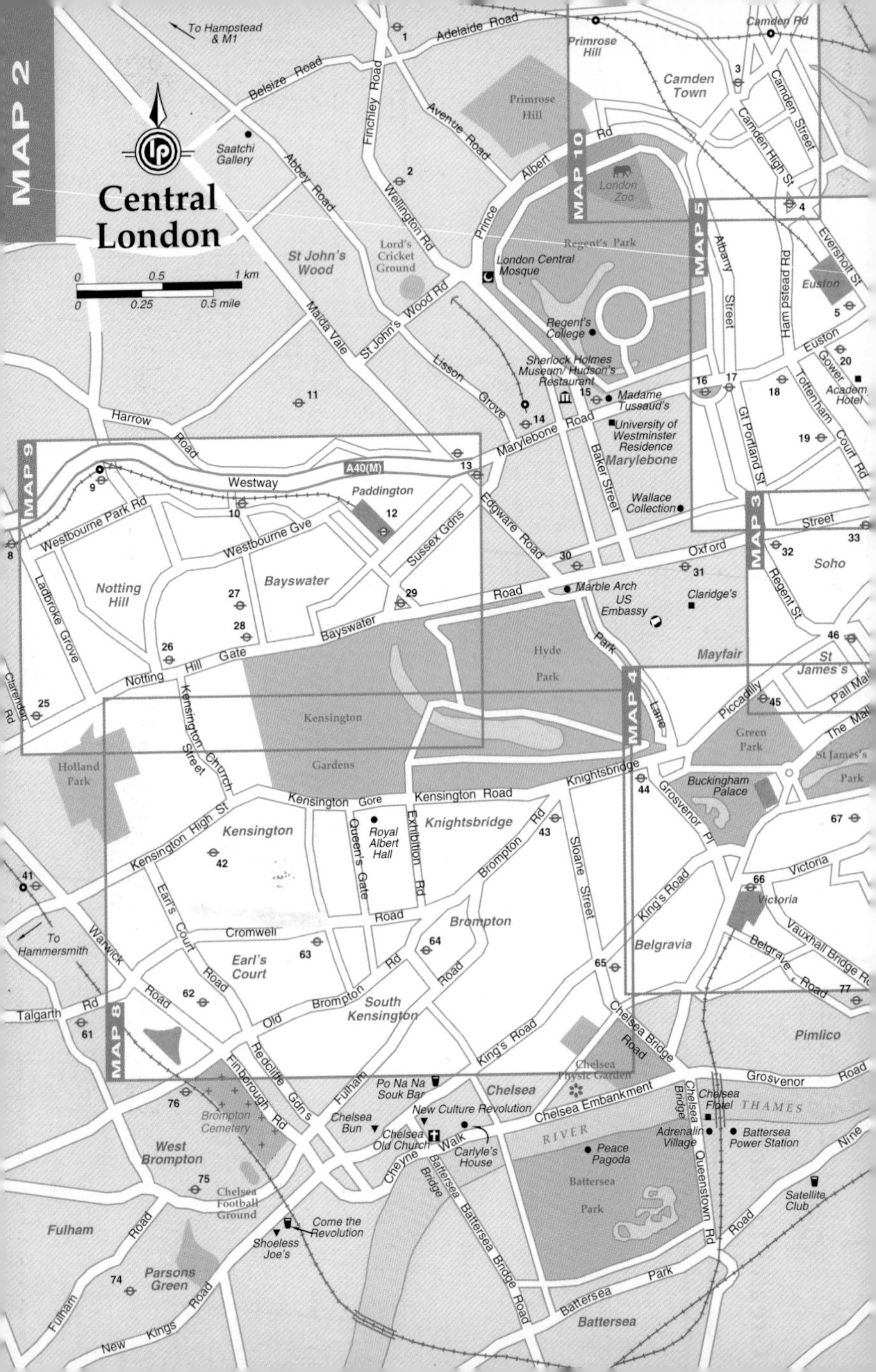

MAP 2

Central London

0 0.5 1 km
0 0.25 0.5 mile

To Hampstead & M1
Adelaide Road
Belsize Road
Finchley Road
Avenue Road
Primrose Hill
Camden Rd
Camden Town
Camden Street
Camden High St
Saatchi Gallery
Abbey Road
Wellington Rd
Albert Rd
Prince Albert Rd
London Zoo
MAP 10
MAP 5
Regent's Park
Albany Street
Hampstead Rd
Eversholt St
Euston
St John's Wood
Lord's Cricket Ground
London Central Mosque
St John's Wood Rd
Maida Vale
Lisson Grove
Regent's College
Sherlock Holmes Museum/ Hudson's Restaurant
Madame Tussaud's
University of Westminster Residence
Marylebone
Marylebone Road
Euston Road
Gower St
Tottenham Court Rd
Academy Hotel
Gt Portland St
Baker Street
Harrow Road
MAP 9
A40(M)
Westway
Paddington
Wallace Collection
Westbourne Park Rd
Westbourne Gve
Sussex Gdns
Edgware Road
Oxford Street
MAP 3
Regent St
Soho
Notting Hill
Bayswater
Bayswater Road
Marble Arch
US Embassy
Claridge's
Ladbroke Grove
Notting Hill Gate
Park Lane
Mayfair
St James's
Hyde Park
MAP 4
Piccadilly
Pall Mall
The Mall
Green Park
Clarendon Rd
Kensington Church Street
Kensington Gardens
Holland Park
Knightsbridge
Grosvenor Pl
Buckingham Palace
St James's Park
Kensington Gore
Kensington Road
Kensington High St
Kensington
Royal Albert Hall
Queen's Gate
Exhibition Rd
Knightsbridge
Brompton Rd
Sloane Street
King's Road
Victoria
Victoria St
Vauxhall Bridge Rd
Belgrave Road
To Hammersmith
Warwick Road
Earl's Court Road
Cromwell Road
Earl's Court
Brompton
Belgravia
South Kensington
Old Brompton Rd
Talgarth Rd
MAP 8
Redcliffe Gdns
Finborough Rd
Fulham Rd
Chelsea Bridge Road
Pimlico
Chelsea Physic Garden
Chelsea
Grosvenor Road
Po Na Na Souk Bar
New Culture Revolution
Chelsea Embankment
Chelsea Bridge
Chelsea Flotel
Thames
River
Brompton Cemetery
Chelsea Bun
Chelsea Old Church
Carlyle's House
Cheyne Walk
Adrenalin Village
Battersea Power Station
Peace Pagoda
West Brompton
Battersea Bridge
Battersea Bridge Road
Battersea Park
Queenstown Rd
Nine Elms Road
Satellite Club
Chelsea Football Ground
Fulham
Fulham Road
Come the Revolution
Shoeless Joe's
Parsons Green
Battersea Park Road
Battersea
New Kings Road

1 2 3 4 5 8 9 10 11 12 13 14 15 16 17 18 19 20 25 26 27 28 29 30 31 32 33 41 42 43 44 45 46 61 62 63 64 65 66 67 74 75 76 77

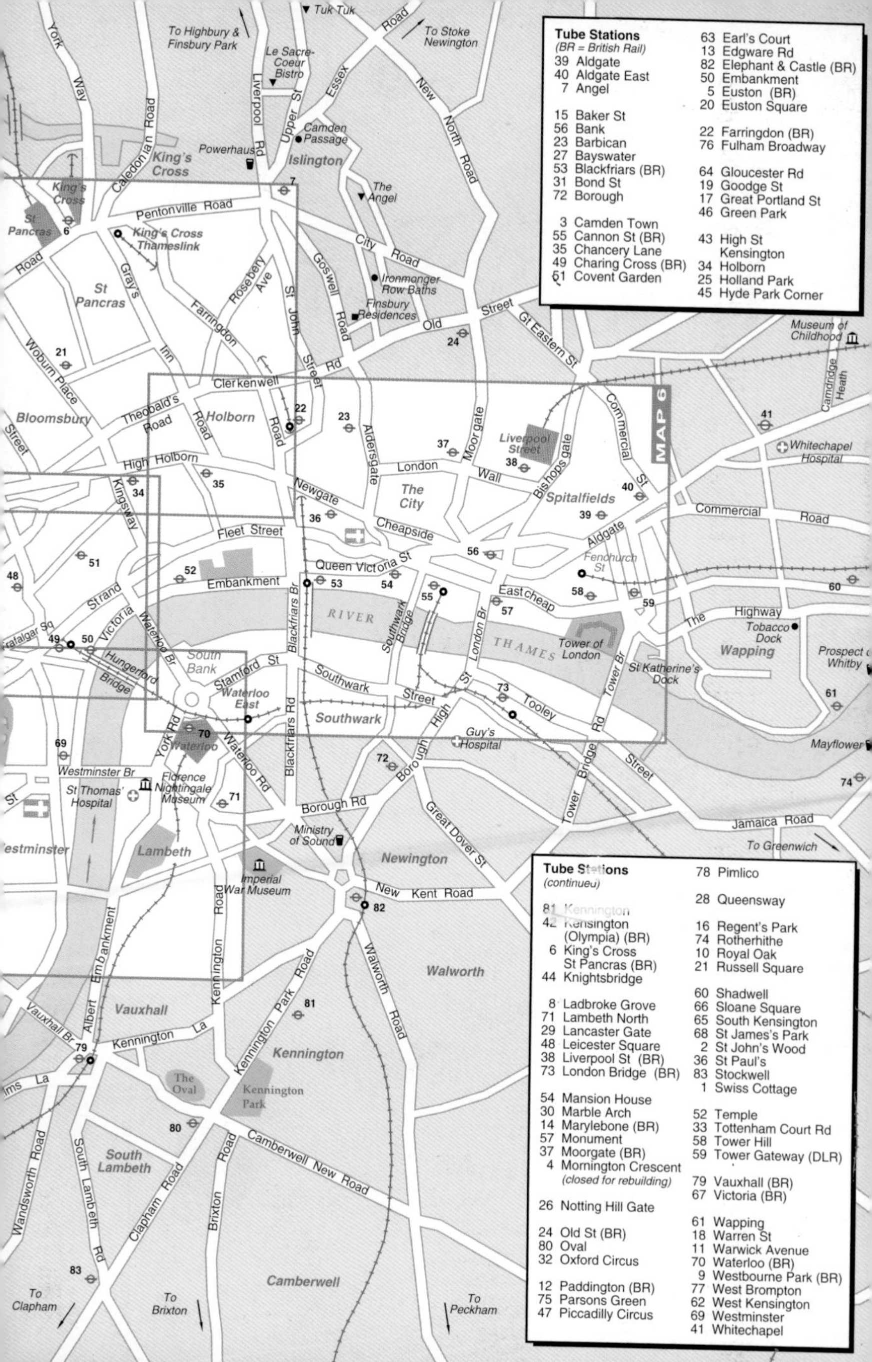

Tube Stations
(BR = British Rail)
39 Aldgate
40 Aldgate East
7 Angel
15 Baker St
56 Bank
23 Barbican
27 Bayswater
53 Blackfriars (BR)
31 Bond St
72 Borough
3 Camden Town
55 Cannon St (BR)
35 Chancery Lane
49 Charing Cross (BR)
51 Covent Garden
63 Earl's Court
13 Edgware Rd
82 Elephant & Castle (BR)
50 Embankment
5 Euston (BR)
20 Euston Square
22 Farringdon (BR)
76 Fulham Broadway
64 Gloucester Rd
19 Goodge St
17 Great Portland St
46 Green Park
43 High St Kensington
34 Holborn
25 Holland Park
45 Hyde Park Corner
MAP 6
Tube Stations
(continued)
81 Kennington
42 Kensington (Olympia) (BR)
6 King's Cross St Pancras (BR)
44 Knightsbridge
8 Ladbroke Grove
71 Lambeth North
29 Lancaster Gate
48 Leicester Square
38 Liverpool St (BR)
73 London Bridge (BR)
54 Mansion House
30 Marble Arch
14 Marylebone (BR)
57 Monument
37 Moorgate (BR)
4 Mornington Crescent
(closed for rebuilding)
26 Notting Hill Gate
24 Old St (BR)
80 Oval
32 Oxford Circus
12 Paddington (BR)
75 Parsons Green
47 Piccadilly Circus
78 Pimlico
28 Queensway
16 Regent's Park
74 Rotherhithe
10 Royal Oak
21 Russell Square
60 Shadwell
66 Sloane Square
65 South Kensington
68 St James's Park
2 St John's Wood
36 St Paul's
83 Stockwell
1 Swiss Cottage
52 Temple
33 Tottenham Court Rd
58 Tower Hill
59 Tower Gateway (DLR)
79 Vauxhall (BR)
67 Victoria (BR)
61 Wapping
18 Warren St
11 Warwick Avenue
70 Waterloo (BR)
9 Westbourne Park (BR)
77 West Brompton
62 West Kensington
69 Westminster
41 Whitechapel
To Highbury & Finsbury Park
Tuk Tuk
To Stoke Newington
Le Sacre-Coeur Bistro
Camden Passage
Powerhaus
Islington
King's Cross
St Pancras
King's Cross Thameslink
The Angel
Ironmonger Row Baths
Finsbury Residences
Museum of Childhood
Bloomsbury
Holborn
The City
Liverpool Street
Spitalfields
Whitechapel Hospital
Fenchurch St
River Thames
Tower of London
St Katherine's Dock
Wapping
Tobacco Dock
Prospect of Whitby
Mayflower
South Bank
Waterloo East
Waterloo
Southwark
Guy's Hospital
St Thomas' Hospital
Florence Nightingale Museum
Westminster
Lambeth
Imperial War Museum
Ministry of Sound
Newington
Walworth
Vauxhall
Kennington
The Oval
Kennington Park
South Lambeth
Camberwell
To Greenwich
To Clapham
To Brixton
To Peckham

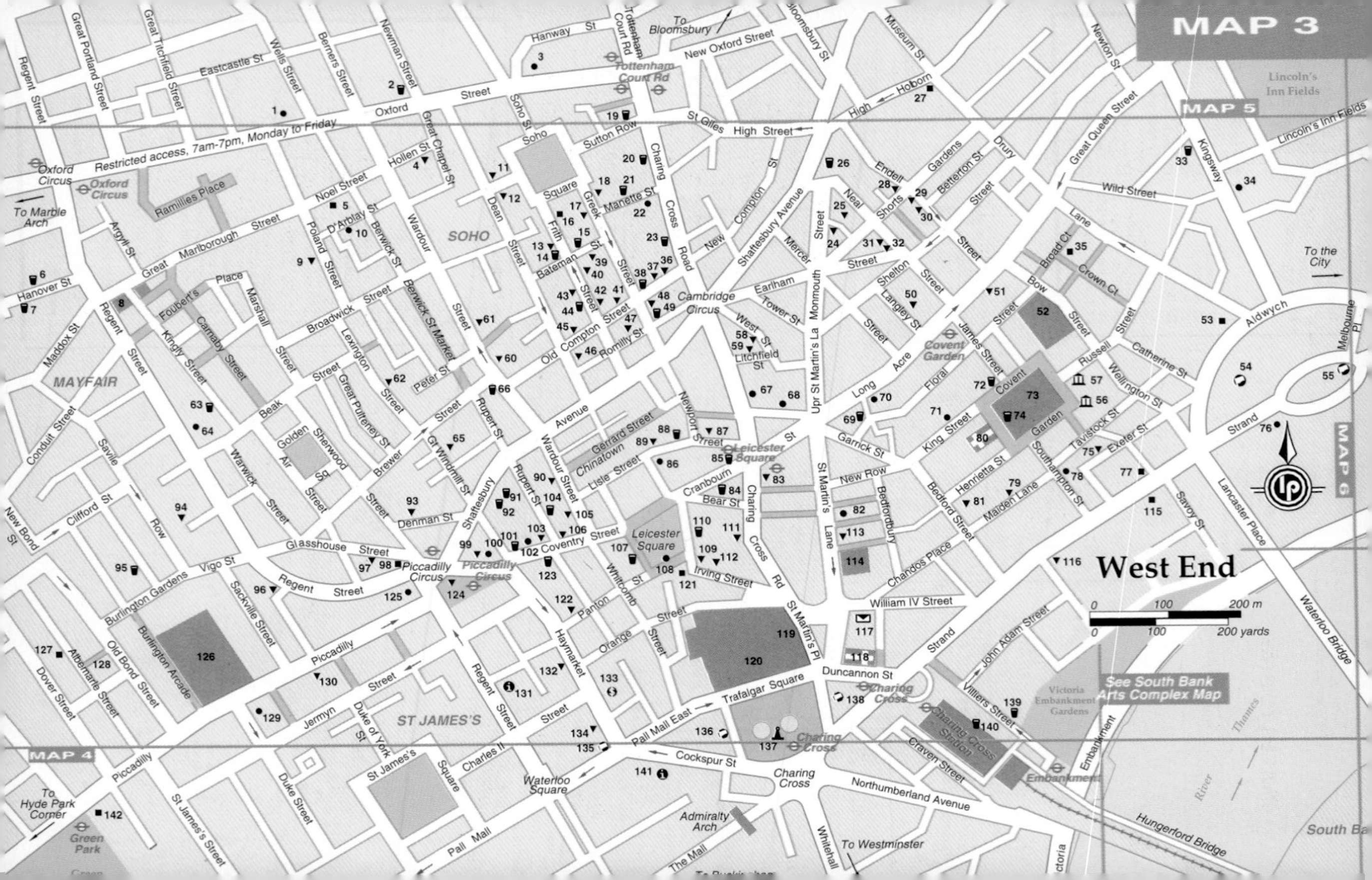

MAP 3
West End
MAP 4
MAP 5
MAP 6
SOHO
MAYFAIR
ST JAMES'S
Oxford Street
Restricted access, 7am-7pm, Monday to Friday
Oxford Circus
Tottenham Court Rd
Leicester Square
Piccadilly Circus
Covent Garden
Charing Cross
Embankment
Green Park
To Marble Arch
To Bloomsbury
To the City
To Westminster
To Hyde Park Corner
Lincoln's Inn Fields
Victoria Embankment Gardens
See South Bank Arts Complex Map
River Thames
Charing Cross Station
Chinatown
Trafalgar Square
Cambridge Circus
Waterloo Square
Admiralty Arch
Berwick St Market
0 100 200 m
0 100 200 yards

PLACES TO STAY

5 Oxford St Youth Hostel
16 Hazlitt's
27 High Holborn
35 Fielding Hotel
53 Waldorf Hotel
77 Strand Palace Hotel
98 Regent Palace Hotel
115 Savoy Hotel
121 The Hampshire Hotel
127 Brown's
142 The Ritz

PLACES TO EAT

4 Star Café
9 Yo Sushi
11 Pizza Express
12 Nusa Dua
13 Dell'ugo
17 Mildred's
18 Gay Hussar
24 Monmouth Coffee Company
25 Neal's Yard Salad Bar
28 Rock & Sole Plaice
29 Diana's Diner
30 Designer Sandwiches
31 Food for Thought
32 Belgo Centraal
36 Stockpot
37 Pollo
39 Living Room & Gopal's of Soho
40 Garlic & Shots
41 Compton St Café
42 Bar Italia
43 Chiang Mai
45 Pâtisserie Valerie
46 French House Pub & Dining Room
47 Kettners
48 Maison Bertaux
50 Café Pacifico
51 Café des Amis du Vin
58 The Ivy
59 Bunjies
60 Freedom Café
61 Mezzo
62 Wagamama
65 Melati
75 Joe Allen
79 Rules
81 Porters
83 Gaby's Continental
87 Tokyo Diner
89 Poons
90 Wong Kei
93 New Piccadilly
94 Momo
96 L'Odéon
97 Atlantic Bar & Grill
99 Rock Island Diner
103 Planet Hollywood
105 Cheun Chen Ku; Jade Garden
106 Fashion Café
109 Capital Radio Café
111 Sofra
112 Mr Wu
113 Café Pelican
116 Simpson's -in-the-Strand
122 Stockpot
124 The Criterion
130 The Wren at St James
132 Football Football
134 Sports Café

PUBS & CLUBS

2 100 Club
6 Hanover Grand
7 Flamingo Bar
14 Dog & Duck
15 Riki Tik
19 Astoria
20 Velvet Underground
21 Borderline
23 Moon Under Water
26 Freud
33 Browns
38 Three Greyhounds
44 Ronnie Scott's
49 Coach & Horses
63 Emporium
66 Village Soho & The 'O' Bar
69 Lamb & Flag
72 Rock Garden; Gardening Club
74 Punch & Judy
84 Cork & Bottle
85 Hippodrome
88 Polar Bear
91 Bar Rumba
92 Thunder Drive
95 Legends
101 Café de Paris
104 Waxy O' Connors
107 All Bar One
110 Moon Under Water
123 Comedy Store
139 Gordon's
140 Heaven

OTHER

1 HMV Records
3 Virgin Megastore
8 Liberty
10 Black Market Records
22 Foyle's Bookshop
34 Peacock Theatre
52 Royal Opera House
54 India House
55 Australia House
56 London Transport Museum
57 Theatre Museum
64 Hamley's
67 Silver Moon (Bookshop)
68 Photographers' Gallery
70 Stanfords
71 The Africa Centre; Calabash Restaurant
73 Covent Garden Market
76 Courtauld Gallery; Somerset House
78 YHA Adventure Shop; Campus Travel
80 St Paul's Church
82 Globetrotters Club
86 Prince Charles Cinema
100 Rock Circus
102 Pepsi Trocadero
108 Half-Price Ticket Booth
114 Coliseum/English National Opera
117 Trafalgar Square Post Office
118 St Martin's in the Fields; Café in Crypt
119 National Portrait Gallery
120 National Gallery
125 Tower Records
126 Royal Academy of Arts
128 Royal Arcade
129 Fortnum & Mason
131 British Travel Centre
133 American Express
135 New Zealand House
136 Canada House
137 Nelson's Column
138 South Africa House
141 Scottish Tourist Board

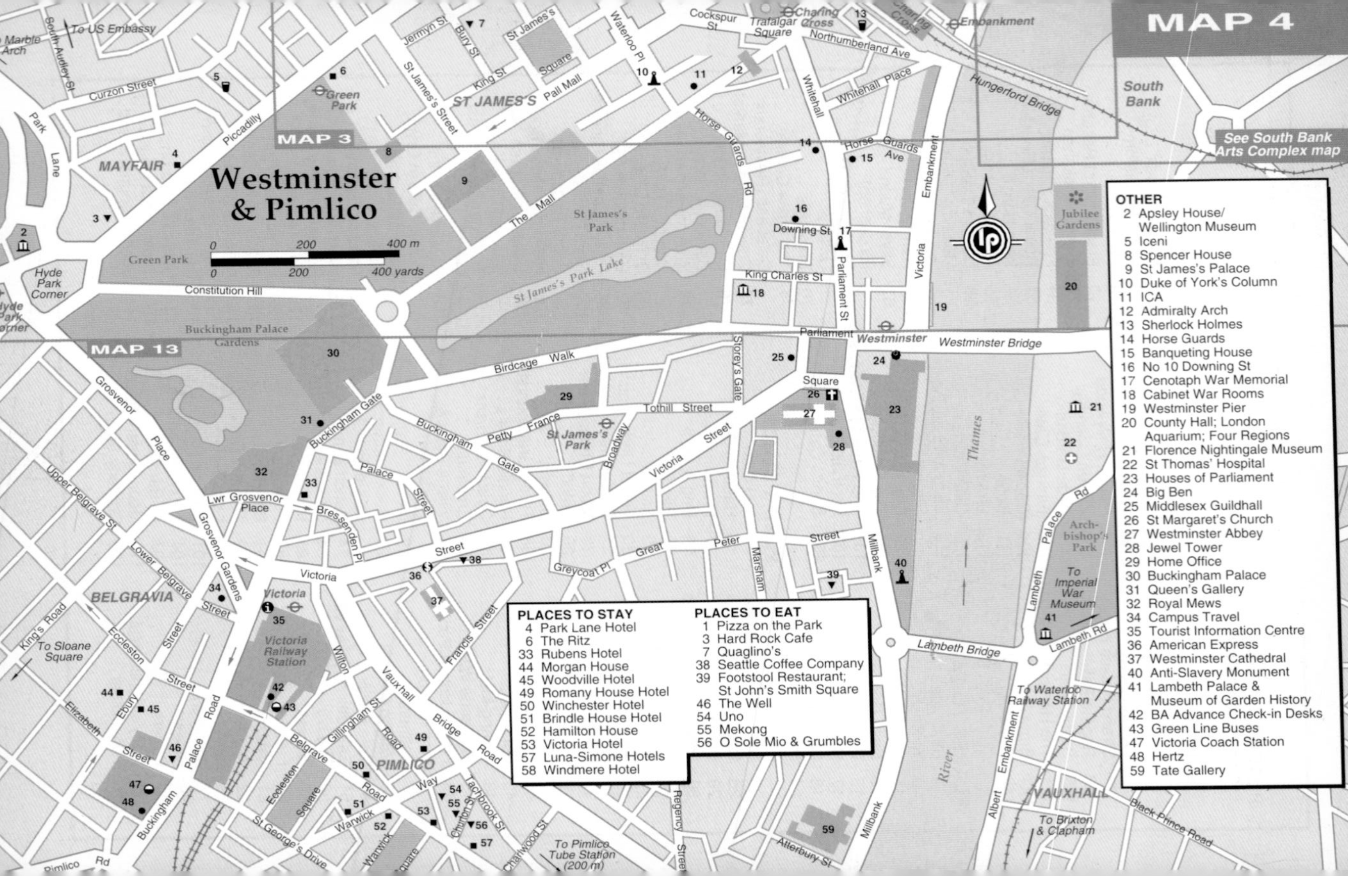

MAP 4
Westminster & Pimlico
0 200 400 m
0 200 400 yards
MAP 3
MAP 13
See South Bank Arts Complex map
PLACES TO STAY
4 Park Lane Hotel
6 The Ritz
33 Rubens Hotel
44 Morgan House
45 Woodville Hotel
49 Romany House Hotel
50 Winchester Hotel
51 Brindle House Hotel
52 Hamilton House
53 Victoria Hotel
57 Luna-Simone Hotels
58 Windmere Hotel
PLACES TO EAT
1 Pizza on the Park
3 Hard Rock Cafe
7 Quaglino's
38 Seattle Coffee Company
39 Footstool Restaurant; St John's Smith Square
46 The Well
54 Uno
55 Mekong
56 O Sole Mio & Grumbles
OTHER
2 Apsley House/ Wellington Museum
5 Iceni
8 Spencer House
9 St James's Palace
10 Duke of York's Column
11 ICA
12 Admiralty Arch
13 Sherlock Holmes
14 Horse Guards
15 Banqueting House
16 No 10 Downing St
17 Cenotaph War Memorial
18 Cabinet War Rooms
19 Westminster Pier
20 County Hall; London Aquarium; Four Regions
21 Florence Nightingale Museum
22 St Thomas' Hospital
23 Houses of Parliament
24 Big Ben
25 Middlesex Guildhall
26 St Margaret's Church
27 Westminster Abbey
28 Jewel Tower
29 Home Office
30 Buckingham Palace
31 Queen's Gallery
32 Royal Mews
34 Campus Travel
35 Tourist Information Centre
36 American Express
37 Westminster Cathedral
40 Anti-Slavery Monument
41 Lambeth Palace & Museum of Garden History
42 BA Advance Check-in Desks
43 Green Line Buses
47 Victoria Coach Station
48 Hertz
59 Tate Gallery
MAYFAIR
ST JAMES'S
BELGRAVIA
PIMLICO
VAUXHALL
South Bank
Green Park
St James's Park
St James's Park Lake
Buckingham Palace Gardens
Jubilee Gardens
Archbishop's Park
Thames
River
To Marble Arch
To US Embassy
To Sloane Square
To Pimlico Tube Station (200 m)
To Waterloo Railway Station
To Imperial War Museum
To Brixton & Clapham
Hyde Park Corner
Victoria Railway Station
Westminster Bridge
Lambeth Bridge
Hungerford Bridge
Piccadilly
Constitution Hill
The Mall
Birdcage Walk
Victoria Street
Whitehall
Parliament St
Millbank
Victoria Embankment
Albert Embankment

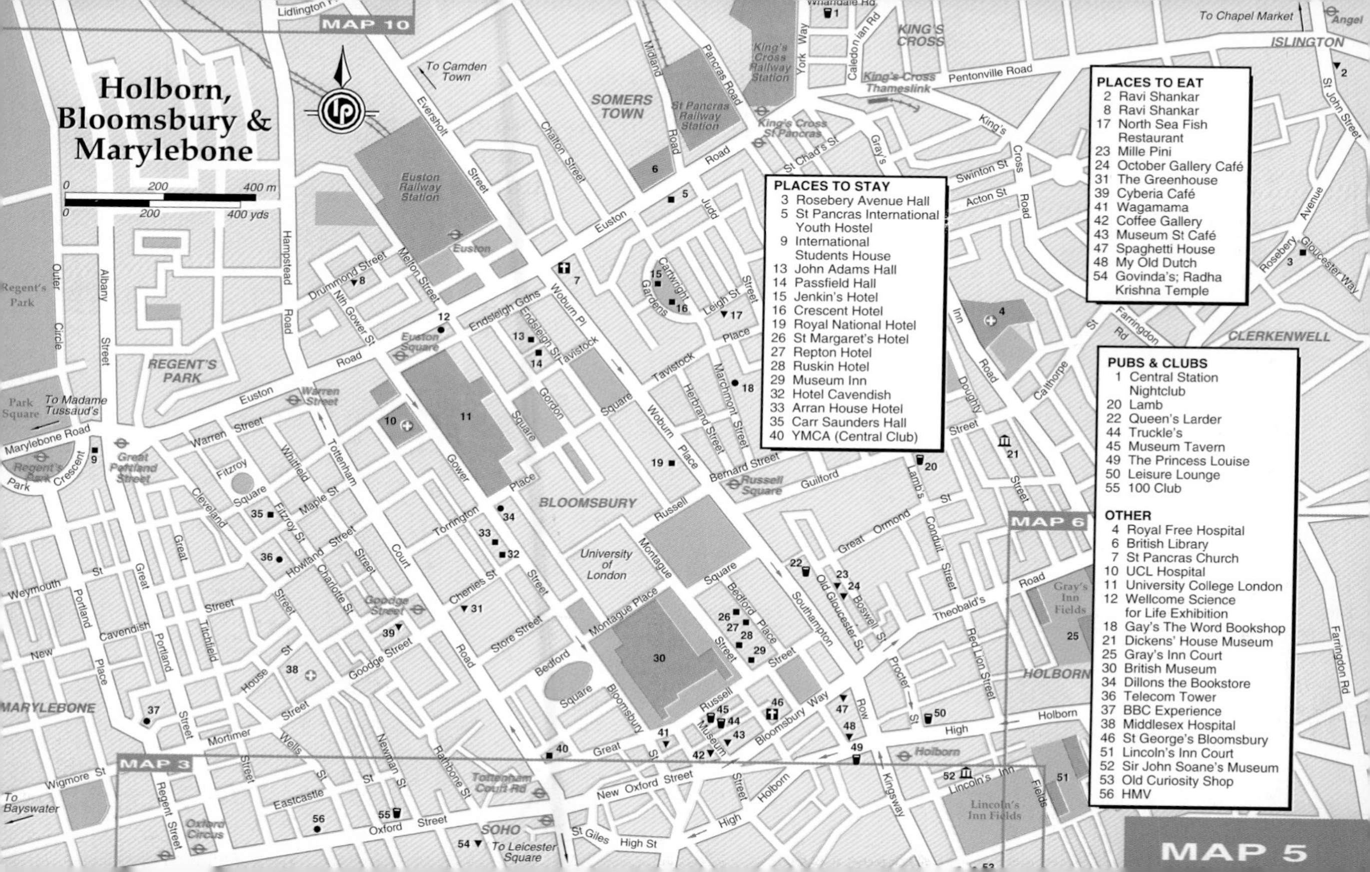

Holborn, Bloomsbury & Marylebone
MAP 5
PLACES TO STAY
3 Rosebery Avenue Hall
5 St Pancras International Youth Hostel
9 International Students House
13 John Adams Hall
14 Passfield Hall
15 Jenkin's Hotel
16 Crescent Hotel
19 Royal National Hotel
26 St Margaret's Hotel
27 Repton Hotel
28 Ruskin Hotel
29 Museum Inn
32 Hotel Cavendish
33 Arran House Hotel
35 Carr Saunders Hall
40 YMCA (Central Club)
PLACES TO EAT
2 Ravi Shankar
8 Ravi Shankar
17 North Sea Fish Restaurant
23 Mille Pini
24 October Gallery Café
31 The Greenhouse
39 Cyberia Café
41 Wagamama
42 Coffee Gallery
43 Museum St Café
47 Spaghetti House
48 My Old Dutch
54 Govinda's; Radha Krishna Temple
PUBS & CLUBS
1 Central Station Nightclub
20 Lamb
22 Queen's Larder
44 Truckle's
45 Museum Tavern
49 The Princess Louise
50 Leisure Lounge
55 100 Club
OTHER
4 Royal Free Hospital
6 British Library
7 St Pancras Church
10 UCL Hospital
11 University College London
12 Wellcome Science for Life Exhibition
18 Gay's The Word Bookshop
21 Dickens' House Museum
25 Gray's Inn Court
30 British Museum
34 Dillons the Bookstore
36 Telecom Tower
37 BBC Experience
38 Middlesex Hospital
46 St George's Bloomsbury
51 Lincoln's Inn Court
52 Sir John Soane's Museum
53 Old Curiosity Shop
56 HMV
MAP 10
MAP 6
MAP 3
0 200 400 m
0 200 400 yds

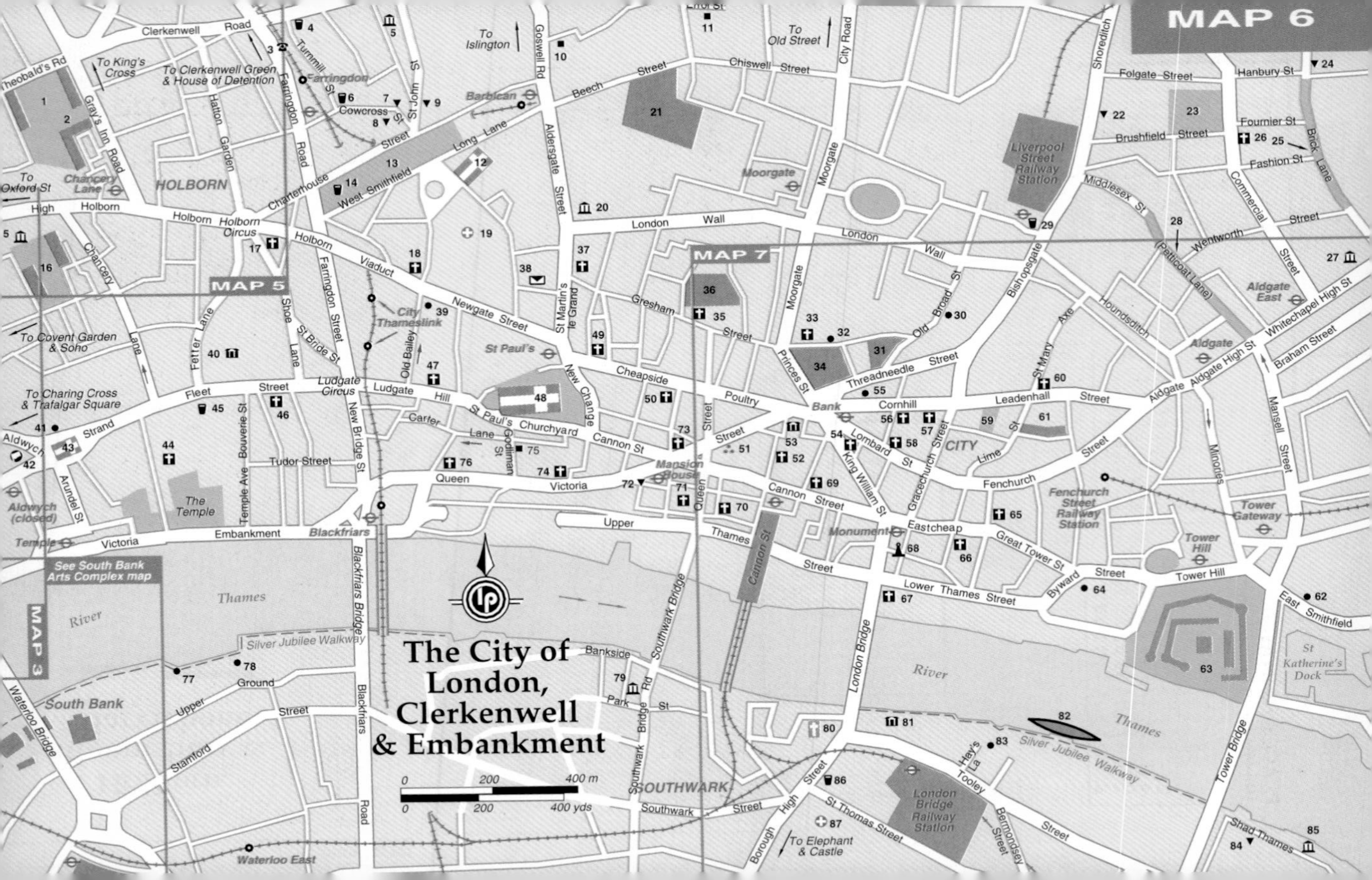
MAP 6
The City of London, Clerkenwell & Embankment
0 200 400 m
0 200 400 yds
MAP 5
MAP 7
MAP 3
See South Bank Arts Complex map
To King's Cross
To Clerkenwell Green & House of Detention
To Islington
To Old Street
To Oxford St
To Covent Garden & Soho
To Charing Cross & Trafalgar Square
To Elephant & Castle
HOLBORN
CITY
SOUTHWARK
South Bank
Liverpool Street Railway Station
Fenchurch Street Railway Station
London Bridge Railway Station
St Katherine's Dock
The Temple
River Thames
Silver Jubilee Walkway
Farringdon
Barbican
Moorgate
Chancery Lane
St Paul's
City Thameslink
Blackfriars
Mansion House
Bank
Monument
Aldgate
Aldgate East
Tower Hill
Tower Gateway
Temple
Aldwych (closed)
Waterloo East
Cannon St
Clerkenwell Road
Theobald's Rd
Gray's Inn Road
Hatton Garden
Farringdon Road
Turnmill St
Cowcross St
St John St
Goswell Rd
Aldersgate Street
Beech Street
Chiswell Street
City Road
Shoreditch
Folgate Street
Hanbury St
Brushfield Street
Fournier St
Fashion St
Brick Lane
Commercial Street
Wentworth St
Middlesex St (Petticoat Lane)
Long Lane
Charterhouse Street
West Smithfield
High Holborn
Holborn Circus
Holborn Viaduct
Farringdon Street
London Wall
Moorgate
Bishopsgate
Houndsditch
Whitechapel High St
Braham Street
Aldgate High St
Mansell Street
Minories
St Mary Axe
Old Broad St
Threadneedle Street
Princes St
Gresham Street
St Martin's le Grand
Newgate Street
Old Bailey
Cheapside
New Change
Poultry
Cornhill
Leadenhall Street
Lime St
Fenchurch Street
Gracechurch Street
Lombard St
King William St
Cannon Street
Queen Street
Queen Victoria Street
Godliman St
Carter Lane
St Paul's Churchyard
Ludgate Hill
Ludgate Circus
New Bridge St
St Bride St
Shoe Lane
Fetter Lane
Chancery Lane
Fleet Street
Strand
Aldwych
Arundel St
Bouverie St
Temple Ave
Tudor Street
Victoria Embankment
Upper Thames Street
Lower Thames Street
Eastcheap
Great Tower St
Byward Street
Tower Hill
East Smithfield
Tower Bridge
London Bridge
Southwark Bridge
Blackfriars Bridge
Waterloo Bridge
Bankside
Park St
Southwark Bridge Rd
Southwark Street
Borough High Street
St Thomas Street
Tooley Street
Hay's La
Bermondsey Street
Shad Thames
Upper Ground
Stamford Street
Blackfriars Road
1 2 3 4 5 6 7 8 9 10 11 12 13 14 16 17 18 19 20 21 22 23 24 25 26 27 28 29 30 31 32 33 34 35 36 37 38 39 40 41 42 43 44 45 46 47 48 49 50 51 52 53 54 55 56 57 58 59 60 61 62 63 64 65 66 67 68 69 70 71 72 73 74 75 76 77 78 79 80 81 82 83 84 85 86 87

PLACES TO STAY

10 Barbican YMCA
11 London City YMCA
75 City of London Youth Hostel

PLACES TO EAT

7 The Greenery
8 Mange-2
9 St John
22 Fatboy's Diner
24 Aladin & Nazrul
72 Sweeting's
84 The Apprentice

PUBS & CLUBS

4 Turnmill's & Café Gaudi
6 The Castle
14 The Cock Tavern
29 Hamilton Hall
45 El Vino's
86 George Inn

WREN CHURCHES

17 St Andrew Holborn
18 St Sepulchre Holborn
33 St Margaret Lothbury
35 St Lawrence Jewry
37 St Anne & St Agnes
43 St Clement Danes
46 St Bride's
47 St Martin Ludgate
49 St Vedast Foster Lane
50 St Mary-le-Bow & Place Below Café
52 St Stephen Walbrook
56 St Michael Cornhill
57 St Peter Cornhill
58 St Edmund King & Martyr
60 St Clement Eastcheap
65 St Margaret Pattens
66 St Mary-at-Hill
67 St Magnus the Martyr
69 St Mary Abchurch
70 St Michael Paternoster Royal
71 St James Garlickhythe
73 St Mary Aldermary
74 St Nicholas Cole Abbey
76 St Andrew-by-the-Wardrobe

OTHER

1 Gray's Inn Fields
2 Gray's Inn
3 CallShop etc
5 St John's Gate
12 St Bartholomew-the-Great
13 Smithfield Market
15 Sir John Soane's Museum
16 Lincoln's Inn
19 St Bartholomew's Hospital
20 Museum of London
21 Barbican Centre & Searcy's Brasserie
23 Spitafields Market & Spitz Café
25 Brick Lane Market
26 Christ Church Spitalfields
27 Whitechapel Art Gallery
28 Petticoat Lane Market
30 NatWest Tower
31 Stock Exchange
32 Lothbury Gallery
34 Bank of England
36 Guildhall
38 GPO
39 Central Criminal Court/Old Bailey
40 Dr Johnson's House
41 Royal Courts of Justice
42 Australia House
44 Temple Church
48 St Paul's Cathedral
51 Temple of Mithras
53 Mansion House
54 St Mary Woolnoth Church
55 Royal Exchange
59 Leadenhall Market
61 Lloyd's of London
62 World Trade Centre
63 Tower of London
64 All Hallows by the Tower; Brass Rubbing Centre
68 The Monument
77 Gabriel's Wharf
78 Oxo Tower
79 Shakespeare Globe Centre & Theatre
80 Southwark Cathedral
81 St Olave's House
82 HMS *Belfast*
83 Hay's Galleria
85 Design Museum & Blue Print Café
87 Guy's Hospital

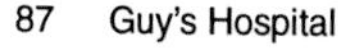

TONY WHEELER

Dutch Flowery

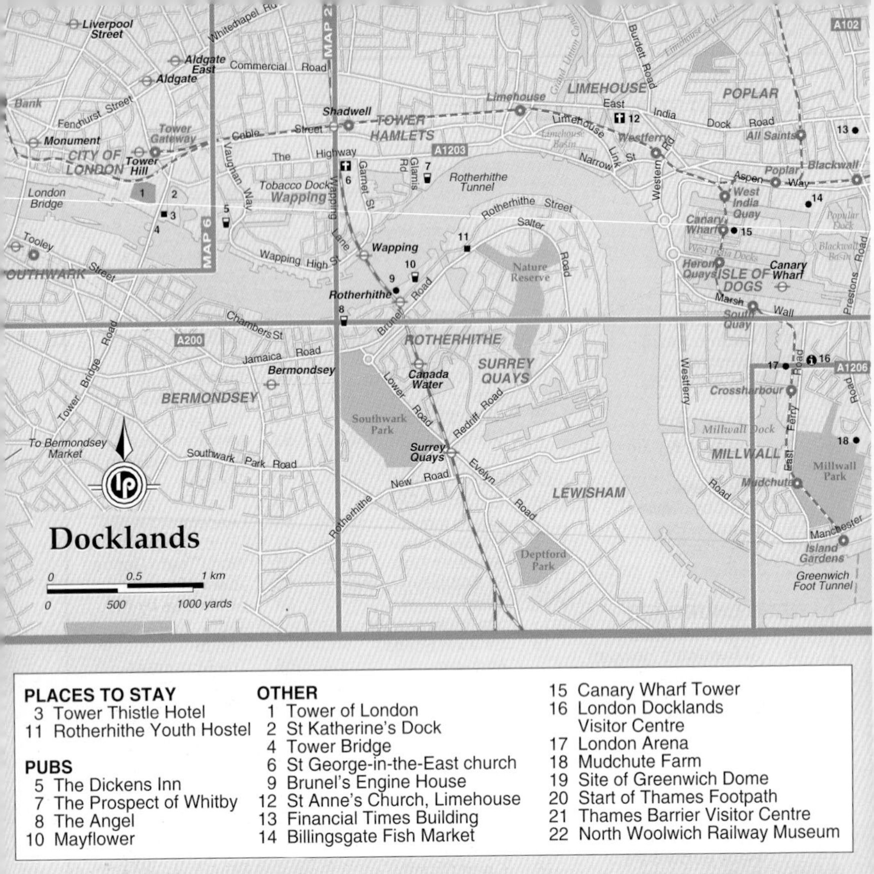

Docklands

0 0.5 1 km

0 500 1000 yards

PLACES TO STAY	OTHER	
3 Tower Thistle Hotel	1 Tower of London	15 Canary Wharf Tower
11 Rotherhithe Youth Hostel	2 St Katherine's Dock	16 London Docklands Visitor Centre
	4 Tower Bridge	17 London Arena
PUBS	6 St George-in-the-East church	18 Mudchute Farm
5 The Dickens Inn	9 Brunel's Engine House	19 Site of Greenwich Dome
7 The Prospect of Whitby	12 St Anne's Church, Limehouse	20 Start of Thames Footpath
8 The Angel	13 Financial Times Building	21 Thames Barrier Visitor Centre
10 Mayflower	14 Billingsgate Fish Market	22 North Woolwich Railway Museum

PAT YALE

The Docklands starred in the movie *'A Fish Called Wanda'*

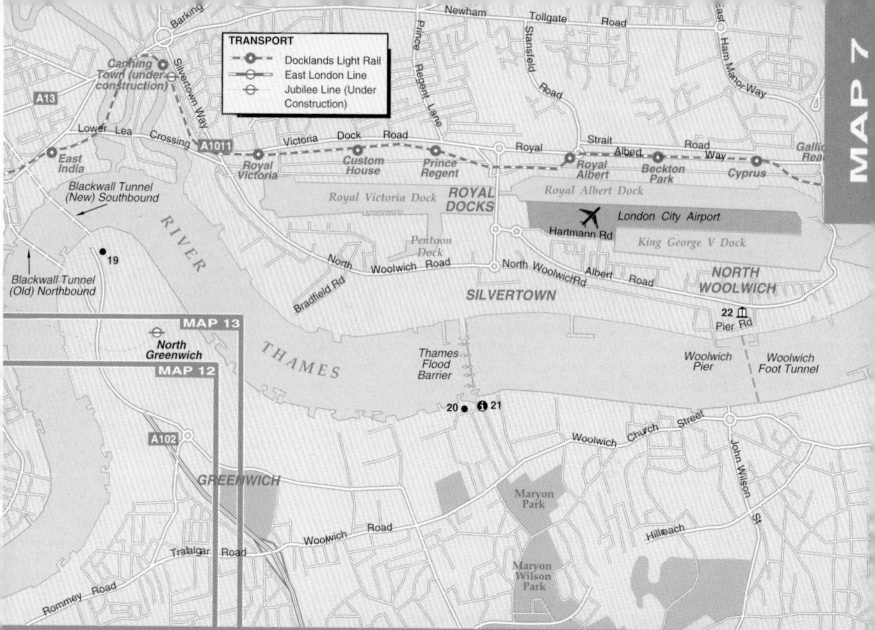

TRANSPORT
Docklands Light Rail
East London Line
Jubilee Line (Under Construction)

Barking
Newham
Tollgate
Road
Prince Regent Lane
Stansfeld Road
East Ham Manor Way
Canning Town (under construction)
Silvertown Way
A13
Lower Lea Crossing
A1011
Victoria Dock Road
Royal
Strait
Road
Albert Way
Gallions Reach
East India
Royal Victoria
Custom House
Prince Regent
Royal Albert
Beckton Park
Cyprus
Blackwall Tunnel (New) Southbound
Royal Victoria Dock
ROYAL DOCKS
Royal Albert Dock
London City Airport
Hartmann Rd
King George V Dock
RIVER
19
Pontoon Dock
North Woolwich Road
North Woolwich Rd
Albert Road
NORTH WOOLWICH
Blackwall Tunnel (Old) Northbound
Bradfield Rd
SILVERTOWN
22
Pier Rd
MAP 13
North Greenwich
MAP 12
THAMES
Thames Flood Barrier
Woolwich Pier
Woolwich Foot Tunnel
20
21
Woolwich Church Street
A102
John Wilson St
GREENWICH
Maryon Park
Woolwich Road
Hillreach
Trafalgar Road
Maryon Wilson Park
Rommey Road

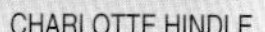
CHARLOTTE HINDLE

St Anne's Church

CHARLOTTE HINDLE

Canary Wharf

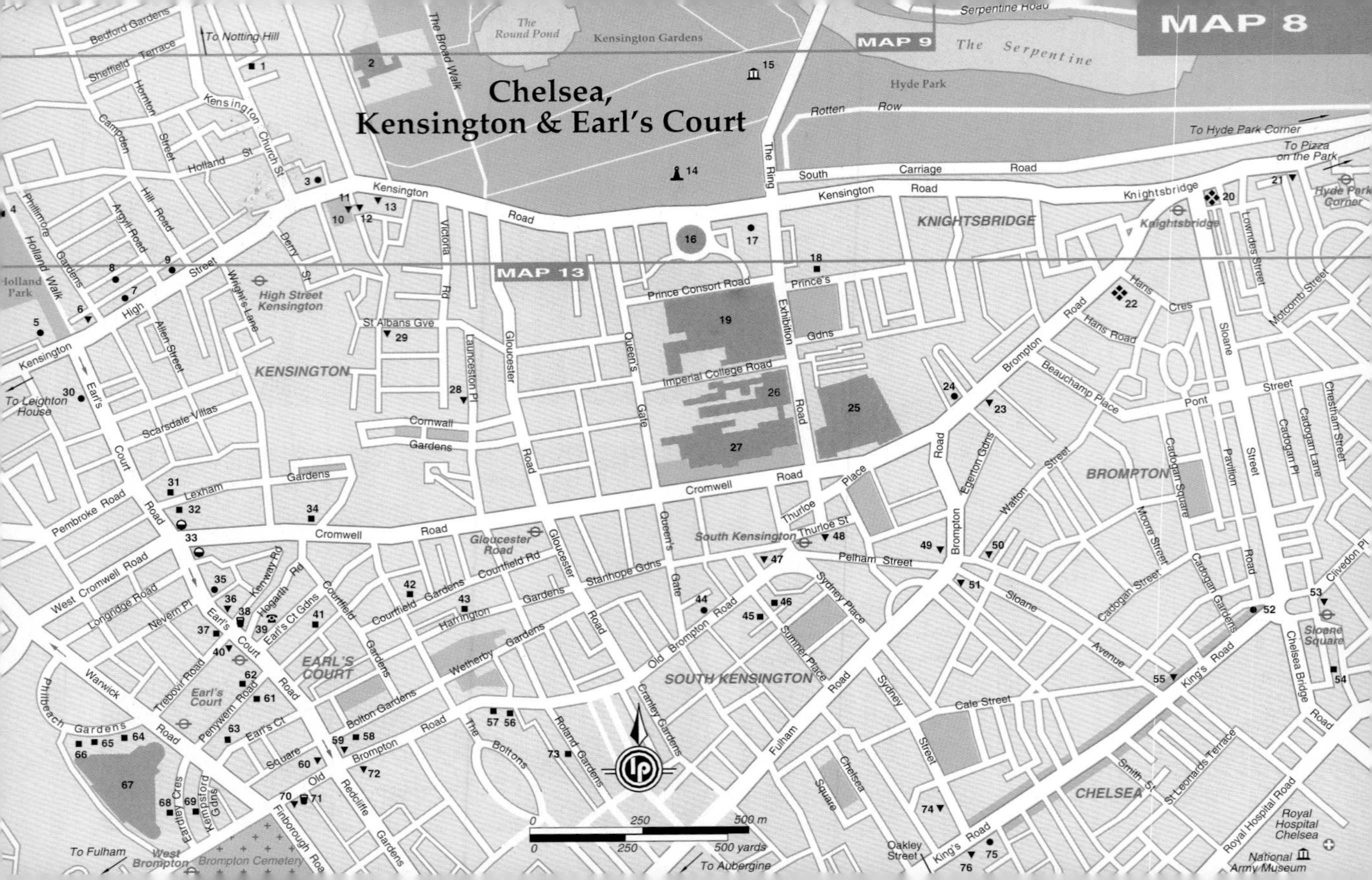
MAP 8
Chelsea, Kensington & Earl's Court
MAP 9
MAP 13
To Notting Hill
To Hyde Park Corner
To Pizza on the Park
To Leighton House
To Fulham
To Aubergine
The Round Pond
Kensington Gardens
The Broad Walk
Serpentine Road
The Serpentine
Hyde Park
Rotten Row
The Ring
South Carriage Road
Kensington Road
Knightsbridge
KNIGHTSBRIDGE
Hyde Park Corner
Lowndes Street
Motcomb Street
Chesham Street
Cadogan Lane
Cadogan Pl
Sloane Street
Pont Street
Pavilion Road
Hans Cres
Hans Road
Brompton Road
Beauchamp Place
BROMPTON
Cadogan Square
Cadogan Gardens
Cadogan Street
Moore Street
Walton Street
Egerton Gdns
Clivedon Pl
Sloane Square
Chelsea Bridge Road
King's Road
Avenue
Sloane Avenue
Royal Hospital Road
Royal Hospital Chelsea
National Army Museum
St Leonards Terrace
Smith St
CHELSEA
Cale Street
Sydney Street
Oakley Street
Chelsea Square
Fulham Road
Sydney Place
Sumner Place
Pelham Street
Thurloe St
Thurloe Place
South Kensington
SOUTH KENSINGTON
Old Brompton Road
Cranley Gardens
Roland Gardens
The Boltons
Queen's Gate
Exhibition Road
Prince's Gdns
Prince Consort Road
Imperial College Road
Cromwell Road
Stanhope Gdns
Gloucester Road
Courtfield Rd
Courtfield Gardens
Harrington Gardens
Wetherby Gardens
Bolton Gardens
Brompton Road
Redcliffe Gardens
Old Brompton Road
Finborough Road
Brompton Cemetery
West Brompton
Eardley Cres
Kempsford Gdns
Philbeach Gardens
Warwick Road
Earl's Ct Square
EARL'S COURT
Earl's Court
Earl's Court Road
Penywern Road
Trebovir Road
Earl's Ct Gdns
Hogarth Rd
Kenway Rd
Nevern Pl
Longridge Road
West Cromwell Road
Pembroke Road
Lexham Gardens
Cornwall Gardens
Launceston Pl
Victoria Rd
St Albans Gve
KENSINGTON
High Street Kensington
Kensington High Street
Wright's Lane
Derry St
Allen Street
Scarsdale Villas
Kensington Church St
Holland St
Hornton Street
Campden Hill Road
Argyll Road
Sheffield Terrace
Bedford Gardens
Phillimore Gardens
Holland Walk
Holland Park
0
250
500 m
0
250
500 yards
1
2
3
4
5
6
7
8
9
10
11
12
13
14
15
16
17
18
19
20
21
22
23
24
25
26
27
28
29
30
31
32
33
34
35
36
37
38
39
40
41
42
43
44
45
46
47
48
49
50
51
52
53
54
55
56
57
58
59
60
61
62
63
64
65
66
67
68
69
70
71
72
73
74
75
76

PLACES TO STAY

1 Vicarage Private Hotel
4 Holland House Youth Hostel
18 Imperial College of Science & Technology Residence
31 London Lodge Hotel
32 Amber Hotel
34 Shellbourne Hotel
37 Court Hotels
41 Merlyn Court Hotel
42 Curzon House Hotel
43 St Simeon
45 Five Sumner Place
46 Hotel Number Sixteen
54 Annandale House Hotel
56 Hotel 167
57 Swiss House Hotel
58 Earl's Court Youth Hostel
61 London Town Hotel
62 Regency Court Hotel & Windsor House
63 Chelsea Hotel
64 York House Hotel
65 Philbeach Hotel & Wilde About Oscar Restaurant
66 New York Hotel
68 Boka Hotel
69 Court Hotels
73 Blakes Hotel
77 Magnolia Hotel

PLACES TO EAT

6 Sticky Fingers
11 Arcadia
12 Dôme
13 Cuba
21 Vong
23 Pâtisserie Valerie
28 Launceston Place
29 Wodka
36 Benjy's
40 Nando's
47 Spago
48 Daquise
49 The Collection
50 Daphne's
51 Bibendum & Michelin Building
53 Oriel
55 Chelsea Kitchen
59 Mr Wing
60 Blanco's
70 Troubadour
72 Krungtap
74 Chelsea Farmers' Market
76 Henry J Bean's

PUBS & CLUBS

38 Prince of Teck
71 Coleherne

OTHER

2 Kensington Palace
3 Hyper-Hyper
5 Commonwealth Institute
7 Trailfinders (Main Office)
8 Linley Sambourne House
9 YHA Shop & Campus Travel
10 Kensington Market
14 Albert Memorial
15 Serpentine Art Gallery
16 Royal Albert Hall
17 Royal Geographical Society
19 Imperial College of Science & Technology
20 Harvey Nichols & Fifth Floor Café
22 Harrods
24 Brompton Oratory
25 Victoria & Albert Museum
26 Science Museum
27 Natural History Museum
30 Trailfinders
33 Airbus, Route A1, Stop 6
35 Top Deck Travel
39 CallShop etc
44 STA Travel
52 Peter Jones
67 Earl's Court Exhibition Centre
75 Chelsea Old Town Hall

DOUG McKINLAY

Three taxis outside Harrods

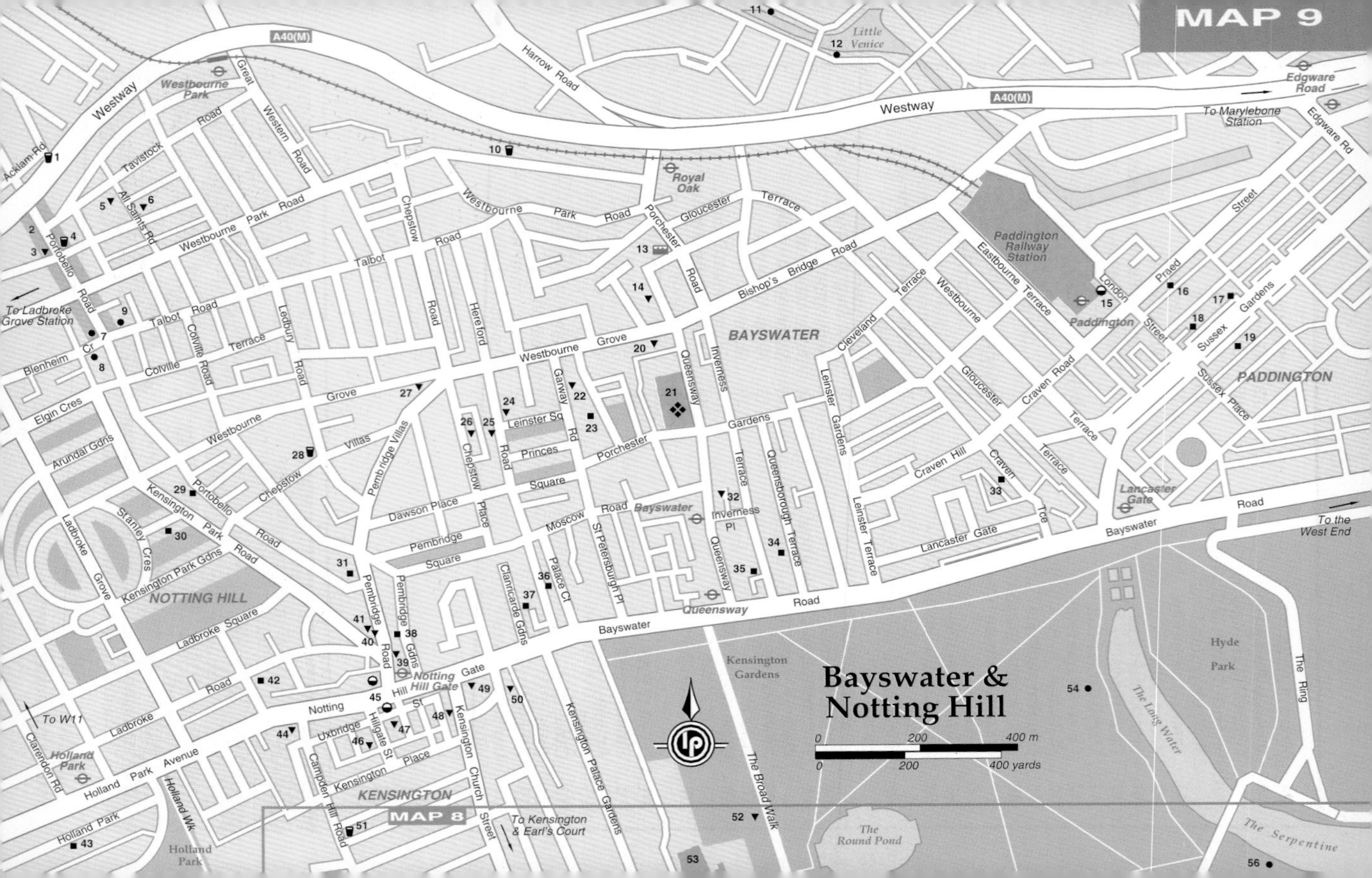
MAP 9
Bayswater &
Notting Hill
0
200
400 m
0
200
400 yards
BAYSWATER
PADDINGTON
NOTTING HILL
KENSINGTON
MAP 8
Westway
A40(M)
Little Venice
Edgware Road
Edgware Rd
To Marylebone Station
Harrow Road
Westbourne Park
Royal Oak
Paddington Railway Station
Paddington
London
Praed Street
Sussex Gardens
Sussex Place
Eastbourne Terrace
Westbourne Terrace
Gloucester Terrace
Craven Road
Craven Hill
Craven Terrace
Craven Tce
Lancaster Gate
Leinster Gardens
Leinster Terrace
Cleveland Terrace
Queensborough Terrace
Inverness Terrace
Inverness Pl
Queensway
Bayswater
Bayswater Road
To the West End
Porchester Road
Porchester Terrace
Gloucester Terrace
Bishop's Bridge Road
Westbourne Grove
Westbourne Park Road
Great Western Road
Tavistock Road
All Saints Rd
Acklam Rd
Portobello Road
Talbot Road
Ledbury Road
Chepstow Road
Hereford Road
Garway Rd
Leinster Sq
Princes Square
Chepstow Place
Chepstow Villas
Pembridge Villas
Pembridge Square
Pembridge Road
Pembridge Gdns
Dawson Place
Moscow Road
St Petersburgh Pl
Palace Ct
Clanricarde Gdns
Notting Hill Gate
Kensington Church Street
Kensington Place
Hillgate St
Uxbridge St
Campden Hill Road
Kensington Palace Gardens
To Kensington & Earl's Court
Colville Terrace
Colville Road
Blenheim Cr
Elgin Cres
Arundel Gdns
Westbourne Villas
Kensington Park Road
Kensington Park Gdns
Stanley Cres
Ladbroke Grove
Ladbroke Square
Ladbroke Road
Holland Park Avenue
Holland Park
Holland Wk
Clarendon Rd
To W11
To Ladbroke Grove Station
Kensington Gardens
Hyde Park
The Ring
The Long Water
The Serpentine
The Broad Walk
The Round Pond
1
2
3
4
5
6
7
8
9
10
11
12
13
14
15
16
17
18
19
20
21
22
23
24
25
26
27
28
29
30
31
32
33
34
35
36
37
38
39
40
41
42
43
44
45
46
47
48
49
50
51
52
53
54
56

PLACES TO STAY

16 Norfolk Court & St David's Hotel
17 Gresham Hotel
18 Balmoral House Hotel
19 Europa House Hotel
23 Garden Court Hotel
29 Portobello Gold Hotel
30 Portobello Hotel
31 The Gate Hotel
33 Oxford Hotel & Sass House
34 Quest Hotel & Royal Hotel
35 Inverness Court Hotel
36 Palace Hotel
37 Manor Court Hotel
38 Hillgate Hotel
42 Holland Park Hotel
43 London Independent Hostel

PLACES TO EAT

3 Café Grove
5 Sugar Club
6 All Saints
14 Churreria Espanola
20 Khan's
22 L'accento
24 Inaho
25 Veronica's
26 Assagi at The Chepstow
27 The Mandola
32 Kalamaras Taverna
39 Seattle Coffee Company
40 Modhubon
41 Prost
44 Nachos
46 Costa's Grill
47 Geales
48 Kensington Palace
49 Pierre Victoire
50 Novelli W8
52 The Orangery

PUBS & CLUBS

1 Subterania
4 Market Bar
10 The Westbourne
28 Beach Blanket Babylon
51 Windsor Castle

OTHER

2 Portobello Rd Market
7 Books for Cooks
8 Travel Bookshop
9 Rough Trade Records
11 Jason's Boats;Jason's Restaurant
12 Waterbus/Waterside Café
13 Porchester Spa
15 Stationlink Bus Stop
21 Whiteley's Shopping Centre
45 Airbus, Route A2, Stop 14
53 Kensington Palace
54 Statue of Peter Pan
55 Serpentine Art Gallery
56 Lido

DOUG McKINLAY

Portobello Rd Market

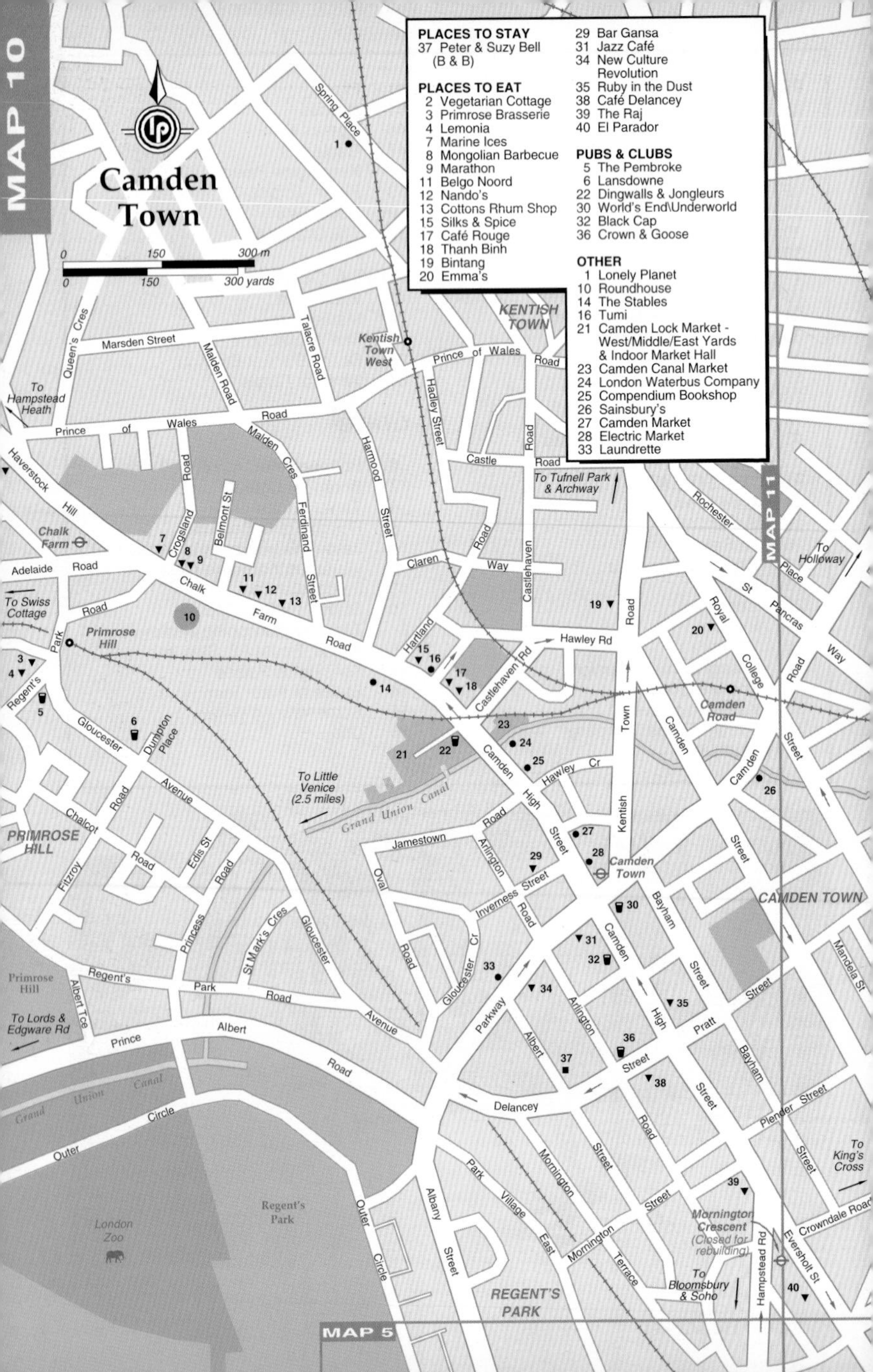
MAP 10
Camden Town
0 150 300 m
0 150 300 yards
PLACES TO STAY
37 Peter & Suzy Bell (B & B)
PLACES TO EAT
2 Vegetarian Cottage
3 Primrose Brasserie
4 Lemonia
7 Marine Ices
8 Mongolian Barbecue
9 Marathon
11 Belgo Noord
12 Nando's
13 Cottons Rhum Shop
15 Silks & Spice
17 Café Rouge
18 Thanh Binh
19 Bintang
20 Emma's
29 Bar Gansa
31 Jazz Café
34 New Culture Revolution
35 Ruby in the Dust
38 Café Delancey
39 The Raj
40 El Parador
PUBS & CLUBS
5 The Pembroke
6 Lansdowne
22 Dingwalls & Jongleurs
30 World's End\Underworld
32 Black Cap
36 Crown & Goose
OTHER
1 Lonely Planet
10 Roundhouse
14 The Stables
16 Tumi
21 Camden Lock Market - West/Middle/East Yards & Indoor Market Hall
23 Camden Canal Market
24 London Waterbus Company
25 Compendium Bookshop
26 Sainsbury's
27 Camden Market
28 Electric Market
33 Laundrette
Spring Place
Kentish Town West
KENTISH TOWN
Prince of Wales Road
To Hampstead Heath
Queen's Cres
Marsden Street
Malden Road
Talacre Road
Hadley Street
Castle Road
To Tufnell Park & Archway
Malden Cres
Harmood Street
Ferdinand Street
Crogsland Road
Belmont St
Haverstock Hill
Chalk Farm
Adelaide Road
Chalk Farm Road
To Swiss Cottage
Primrose Hill
Regent's Park Road
Claren Way
Castlehaven Road
Hartland Road
Hawley Rd
Kentish Town Road
Royal College Street
St Pancras Way
To Holloway
Rochester Place
MAP 11
Camden Road
Camden Street
Gloucester Avenue
Dumpton Place
Chalcot Road
Fitzroy Road
Edis St
Princess Road
St Mark's Cres
To Little Venice (2.5 miles)
Grand Union Canal
Camden High Street
Hawley Cr
Jamestown Road
Arlington Road
Inverness Street
Oval Road
Gloucester Cr
Camden Town
Bayham Street
CAMDEN TOWN
Mandela St
Parkway
Albert Street
Pratt Street
Primrose Hill
Albert Tce
To Lords & Edgware Rd
Prince Albert Road
Delancey Street
Plender Street
Outer Circle
London Zoo
Regent's Park
Park Village East
Albany Street
Mornington Street
Mornington Terrace
Mornington Crescent (Closed for rebuilding)
To King's Cross
Crowndale Road
Eversholt St
Hampstead Rd
To Bloomsbury & Soho
REGENT'S PARK
MAP 5

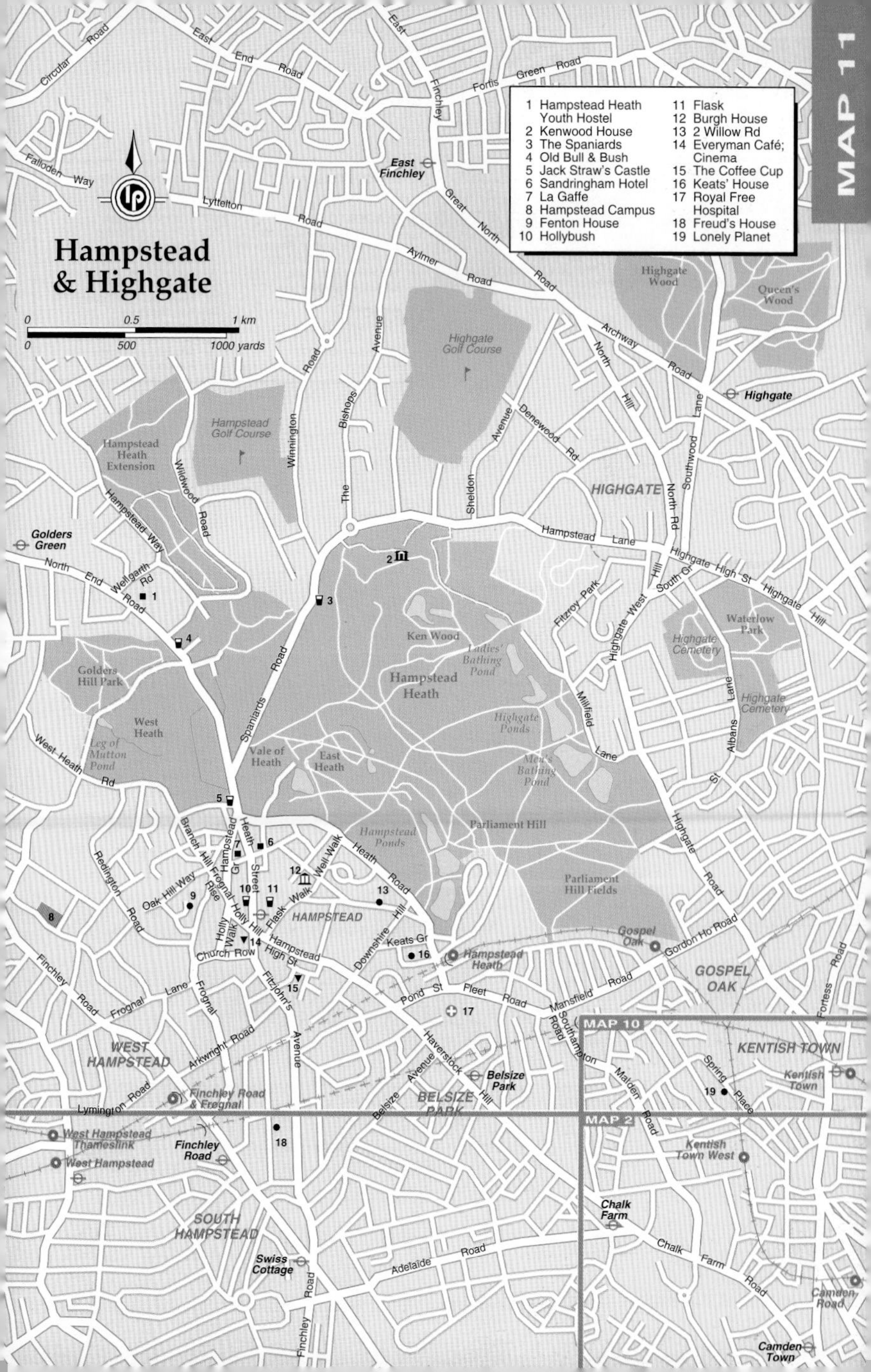

Hampstead & Highgate
0 0.5 1 km
0 500 1000 yards
1 Hampstead Heath Youth Hostel
2 Kenwood House
3 The Spaniards
4 Old Bull & Bush
5 Jack Straw's Castle
6 Sandringham Hotel
7 La Gaffe
8 Hampstead Campus
9 Fenton House
10 Hollybush
11 Flask
12 Burgh House
13 2 Willow Rd
14 Everyman Café; Cinema
15 The Coffee Cup
16 Keats' House
17 Royal Free Hospital
18 Freud's House
19 Lonely Planet
Circular Road
East End Road
East Finchley
Fortis Green Road
Falloden Way
Lyttelton Road
Aylmer Road
Great North Road
Archway Road
Highgate Wood
Queen's Wood
Highgate Golf Course
Highgate
Hampstead Golf Course
Hampstead Heath Extension
Winnington Road
The Bishops Avenue
Sheldon Avenue
Denewood Rd
North Hill
Southwood Lane
HIGHGATE
North Rd
Hampstead Lane
Highgate High St
Highgate Hill
Golders Green
North End Road
Wellgarth Rd
Hampstead Way
Wildwood Road
Spaniards Road
Ken Wood
Ladies' Bathing Pond
Hampstead Heath
Highgate Ponds
Men's Bathing Pond
Waterlow Park
Highgate Cemetery
Highgate West Hill
Fitzroy Park
South Gr
Millfield Lane
Swains Lane
Golders Hill Park
West Heath
Leg of Mutton Pond
West Heath Rd
Vale of Heath
East Heath
Hampstead Ponds
Parliament Hill
Parliament Hill Fields
Highgate Road
Gospel Oak
GOSPEL OAK
Gordon Ho Road
Branch Hill
Hampstead Gr
Heath Street
Well Walk
Heath Road
Redington Road
Oak Hill Way
Frognal Rise
Holly Hill
Flask Walk
HAMPSTEAD
Downshire Hill
Keats Gr
Holly Walk
Church Row
Hampstead High St
Hampstead Heath
Pond St
Fleet Road
Mansfield Road
Southampton Road
Finchley Road
Frognal Lane
Frognal
Fitzjohn's Avenue
Haverstock Hill
Arkwright Road
WEST HAMPSTEAD
Belsize Park
BELSIZE PARK
Belsize Avenue
Lymington Road
Finchley Road & Frognal
West Hampstead Thameslink
West Hampstead
Finchley Road
MAP 10
MAP 2
KENTISH TOWN
Spring Place
Kentish Town
Malden Road
Kentish Town West
Fortess Road
Chalk Farm
Chalk Farm Road
SOUTH HAMPSTEAD
Swiss Cottage
Adelaide Road
Camden Road
Camden Town

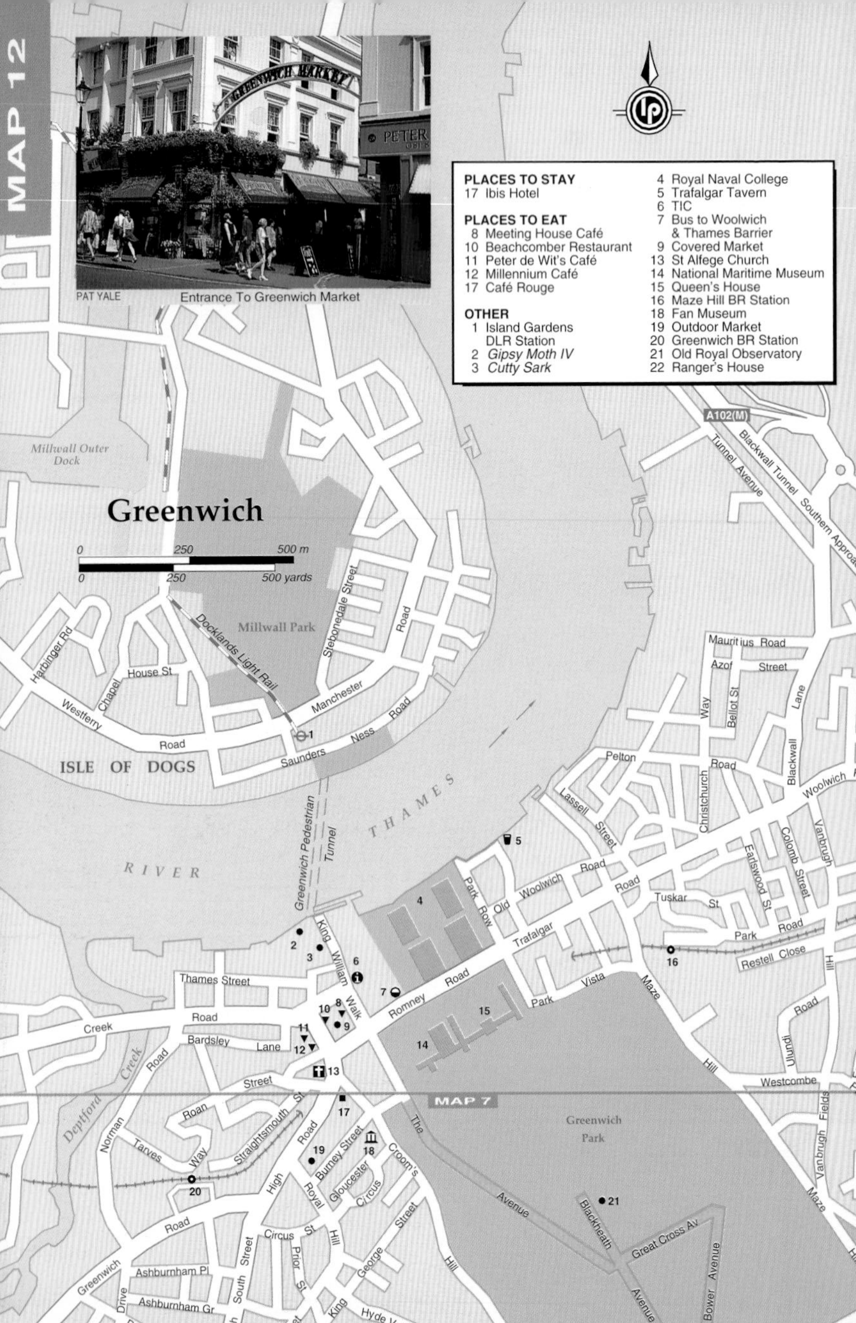

PAT YALE
Entrance To Greenwich Market

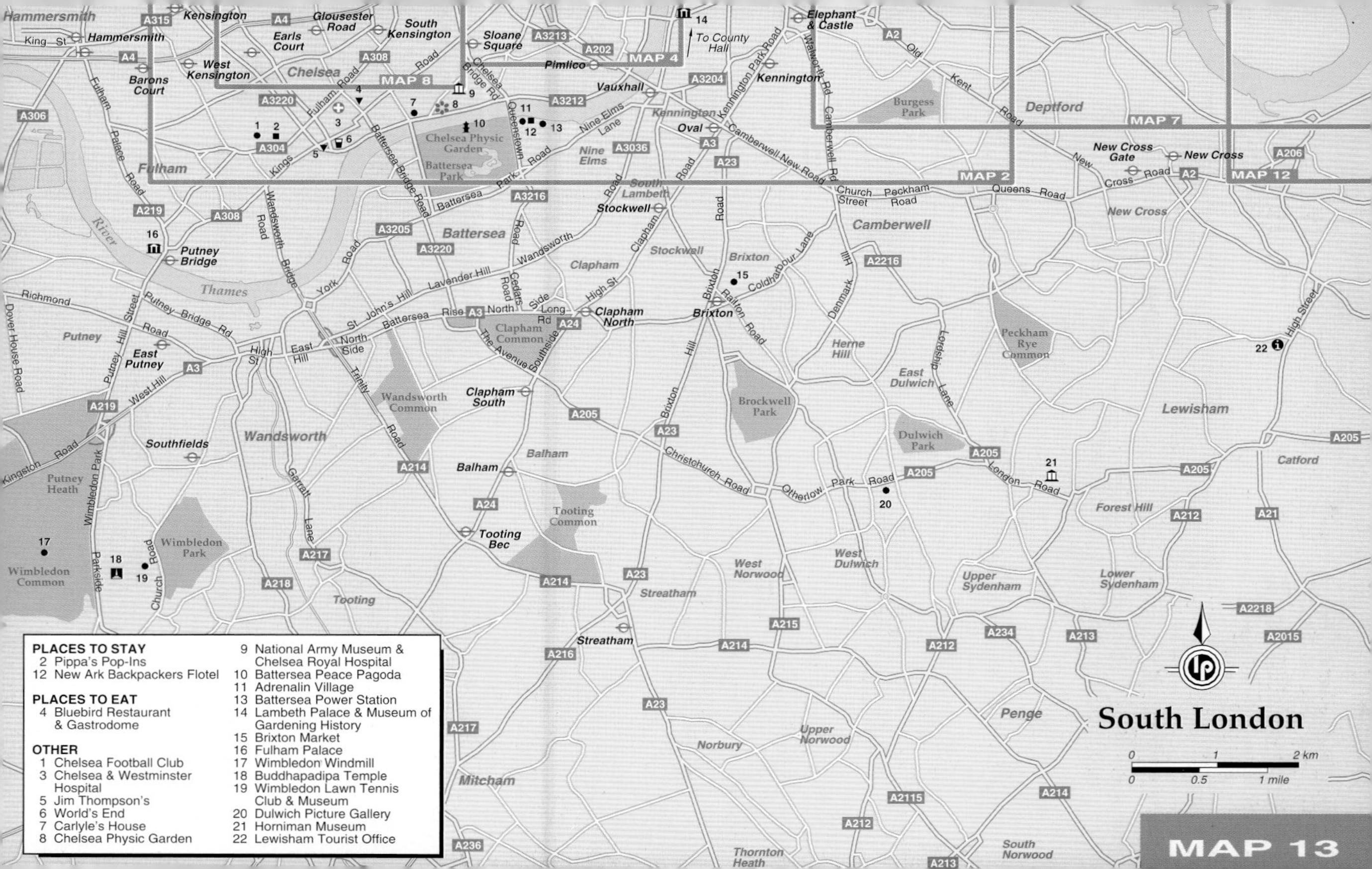
MAP 13
South London
0 1 2 km
0 0.5 1 mile
PLACES TO STAY
2 Pippa's Pop-Ins
12 New Ark Backpackers Flotel
PLACES TO EAT
4 Bluebird Restaurant & Gastrodome
OTHER
1 Chelsea Football Club
3 Chelsea & Westminster Hospital
5 Jim Thompson's
6 World's End
7 Carlyle's House
8 Chelsea Physic Garden
9 National Army Museum & Chelsea Royal Hospital
10 Battersea Peace Pagoda
11 Adrenalin Village
13 Battersea Power Station
14 Lambeth Palace & Museum of Gardening History
15 Brixton Market
16 Fulham Palace
17 Wimbledon Windmill
18 Buddhapadipa Temple
19 Wimbledon Lawn Tennis Club & Museum
20 Dulwich Picture Gallery
21 Horniman Museum
22 Lewisham Tourist Office

West London

To Wembley Stadium & Wembley
Grand Union Canal
Perivale
Western Avenue
Ruislip Road
B455
Hanger Lane
A40
Park Royal
The Parkway
A4127
A312
Greenford Road
Brent
Castlebar Rd
North Ealing
West Acton
Ealing Broadway
Southall
Canal
Uxbridge Road
Pitshanger Manor
Ealing Common
Ealing
Acton Town
Winmill Lane
Tentelow Lane
Osterley Park
Boston Manor
Flyover
Northfields
South Ealing
Gunnersbury Park
Brentford
Turnham Green
Chiswick
To Heathrow Airport
M4 Motorway
M4
Gunnersbury
Musical Museum
Hogarth's House
Osterley House
Syon Lane
Chiswick Park
Chiswick House
Kew Palace
Kew
Osterley
A4
Great West Road
Osterley
Kew Gardens
Syon House
Kew Gardens
Bath Road
Hounslow West
Sutton Lane
Hounslow East
Hounslow Central
Isleworth
River Thames
Old Deer Park
Kew Road
Mortlake
Hounslow
Richmond Palace
Richmond Theatre
London Road
Wellington Road
Hounslow Heath
St Margarets
Twickenham Rugby Football Ground
Richmond
Richmond
Hanworth Road
Twickenham
Star & Garter Home
Roehampton Gate
Marble Hill House
Richmond Gate
Chertsey Road
Orleans Gallery
Ferry
Richmond Park
Strawberry Hill
Uxbridge Road
Hampton Rd West
Ham House
White Lodge
Eel Pie Island
Petersham
Pembroke Lodge
Robin Hood Gate
Hampton Rd
Staines Road
Country Way
Hounslow Road
Wellington Rd
To Wimbledon Common & Wimbledon Windmill
Fulwell Golf Course
Ham
Ham Common
Teddington Lock
Kingston Vale
Park Road
Teddington
Uxbridge Road
High Street
Hampton Road
Richmond Road
Hampton Wick
Kingston Upon Thames
Coombe Hill Golf Course
Hampton
Bushy Park
A307
Kingston Hill
Coombe Lane
Hampton Court Palace
Coombe Road
Hampton Court Road
Cambridge Road
East Molesey
Hampton Court Park
Home Park
Kingston Road
Thames Ditton
Portsmouth Road

0 1 2 km
0 0.5 1 mile

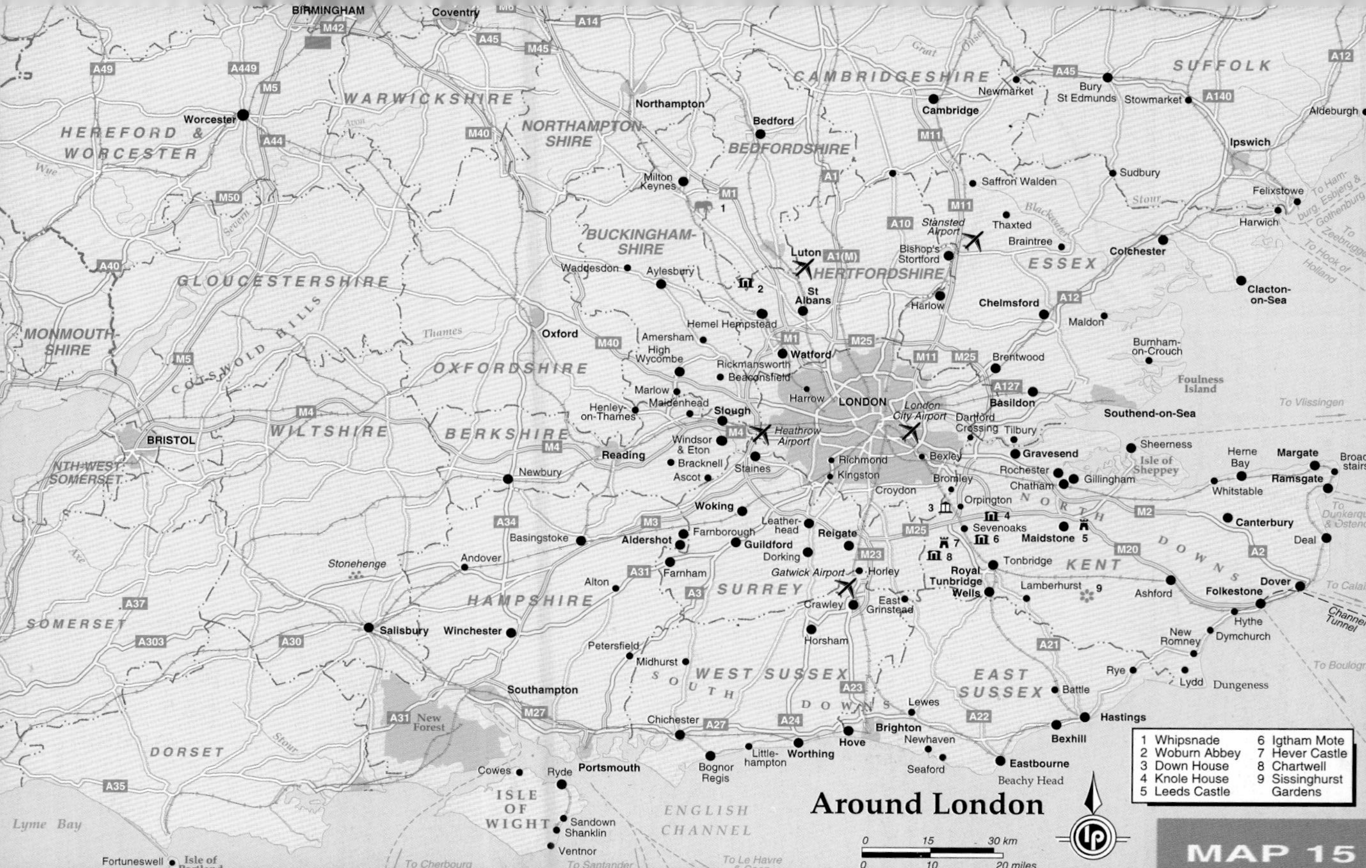
MAP 15
Around London
1 Whipsnade
2 Woburn Abbey
3 Down House
4 Knole House
5 Leeds Castle
6 Igtham Mote
7 Hever Castle
8 Chartwell
9 Sissinghurst Gardens
0 15 30 km
0 10 20 miles
LONDON
London City Airport
Heathrow Airport
Gatwick Airport
Stansted Airport
Luton
BIRMINGHAM
Coventry
Worcester
Northampton
Bedford
Cambridge
Newmarket
Bury St Edmunds
Stowmarket
Ipswich
Aldeburgh
Felixstowe
Harwich
Colchester
Clacton-on-Sea
Sudbury
Saffron Walden
Thaxted
Braintree
Bishop's Stortford
Harlow
Chelmsford
Maldon
Burnham-on-Crouch
Foulness Island
Southend-on-Sea
Basildon
Brentwood
Milton Keynes
Aylesbury
Waddesdon
St Albans
Hemel Hempstead
Watford
Amersham
High Wycombe
Rickmansworth
Beaconsfield
Marlow
Maidenhead
Henley-on-Thames
Slough
Windsor & Eton
Bracknell
Ascot
Staines
Harrow
Richmond
Kingston
Croydon
Bexley
Bromley
Orpington
Dartford Crossing
Tilbury
Gravesend
Rochester
Chatham
Gillingham
Sheerness
Isle of Sheppey
Herne Bay
Whitstable
Margate
Ramsgate
Broadstairs
Canterbury
Deal
Dover
Folkestone
Hythe
Dymchurch
New Romney
Lydd
Dungeness
Rye
Ashford
Maidstone
Sevenoaks
Tonbridge
Royal Tunbridge Wells
Lamberhurst
Battle
Hastings
Bexhill
Eastbourne
Beachy Head
Seaford
Newhaven
Lewes
Brighton
Hove
Worthing
Little-hampton
Bognor Regis
Chichester
Portsmouth
Southampton
Winchester
Salisbury
Stonehenge
Andover
Basingstoke
Newbury
Reading
Oxford
BRISTOL
Woking
Farnborough
Aldershot
Farnham
Guildford
Leatherhead
Reigate
Dorking
Horley
Crawley
East Grinstead
Horsham
Alton
Petersfield
Midhurst
Cowes
Ryde
Sandown
Shanklin
Ventnor
Fortuneswell
Isle of Portland
Lyme Bay
New Forest
ISLE OF WIGHT
ENGLISH CHANNEL
To Cherbourg
To Santander
To Le Havre & Caen
To Vlissingen
To Calais
To Boulogne
To Dunkerque & Ostende
Channel Tunnel
To Hamburg, Esbjerg & Gothenburg
To Zeebrugge
To Hook of Holland
SUFFOLK
CAMBRIDGESHIRE
WARWICKSHIRE
NORTHAMPTON-SHIRE
BEDFORDSHIRE
HERTFORDSHIRE
ESSEX
BUCKINGHAM-SHIRE
HEREFORD & WORCESTER
GLOUCESTERSHIRE
MONMOUTH-SHIRE
OXFORDSHIRE
BERKSHIRE
WILTSHIRE
NTH-WEST SOMERSET
SOMERSET
DORSET
HAMPSHIRE
SURREY
WEST SUSSEX
EAST SUSSEX
KENT
NORTH DOWNS
SOUTH DOWNS
COTSWOLD HILLS
Thames
Severn
Avon
Wye
Axe
Stour
Ouse
Granta
Blackwater

MAP 16
London Underground-Geographical
0 0.5 1 km
0 0.25 0.5 mile
Bakerloo
Central
Circle
District
Hammersmith & City
Jubilee
Metropolitan
Northern
Piccadilly
Victoria
Docklands Light Rail
British Rail
To West Hampstead & Wembley Park
To Hampstead
To Highgate
To Finsbury Park
To Highbury & Islington
To Stratford
To Barking
To Docklands
To Willesden Junction
To Wembley Stadium
To Hammersmith
To Ealing
To Hammersmith, Richmond, Ealing & Heathrow
To Fulham & Wimbledon
To Brixton
To Balham & Morden
St John's Wood
Camden Town
Mornington Crescent (closed for renovation)
Euston
St Pancras
King's Cross
King's Cross Thameslink
Angel
Old Street
Shoreditch
Liverpool Street
Aldgate East
Aldgate
Fenchurch St
Tower Hill
Tower Gateway
Moorgate
Barbican
Farringdon
Russell Square
Euston Square
Warren St
Great Portland St
Regent's Park
Baker St
Marylebone
Edgware Rd
Paddington
Warwick Avenue
Royal Oak
Westbourne Park
Ladbroke Grove
Goodge St
Tottenham Ct Rd
Holborn
Chancery Lane
St Paul's
City Thameslink
Bank
Monument
Cannon St
Mansion House
Blackfriars
Temple
Aldwych
Covent Garden
Leicester Square
Oxford Circus
Bond St
Marble Arch
Lancaster Gate
Queensway
Bayswater
Notting Hill Gate
Holland Park
Piccadilly Circus
Charing Cross
Embankment
Waterloo
Waterloo East
London Bridge
Borough
Lambeth North
Elephant & Castle
Kennington
Oval
Vauxhall
Pimlico
Victoria
Westminster
St James's Park
Green Park
Hyde Park Corner
Knightsbridge
Sloane Square
South Kensington
Gloucester Road
High St Kensington
Kensington (Olympia)
Earl's Court
West Kensington
West Brompton
Primrose Hill
London Zoo
Regent's Park
Lord's Cricket Ground
Hyde Park
Kensington Gardens
Holland Park
RIVER THAMES
Belsize Road
Finchley Road
Avenue Road
Albert Rd
Prince Albert
Abbey Road
Wellington Rd
Maida Vale
St John's Wood Rd
Lisson Gve
Harrow Road
Westway
Westbourne Gve
Sussex Gdns
Edgware Road
Baker Street
Albany Street
Camden Street
Camden High St
Hampstead Rd
Euston Road
Gt Portland St
Gower Street
Woburn Place
York Way
Pentonville Rd
Gray's Inn Road
Theobald's Road
Clerkenwell Rd
Farringdon Rd
Rosebery Ave
St John St
Goswell Road
City Road
Old Street
Gt Eastern St
Commercial St
Bishopsgate
Moorgate
Cheapside
Fleet Street
Strand
Kingsway
Oxford Street
Regent St
Trafalgar Sq
Piccadilly
The Mall
Park Lane
Bayswater Road
Kensington Church Street
Kensington High St
Kensington Road
Knightsbridge
Grosvenor Pl
Brompton Rd
Exhibition Rd
Queen's Gate
Cromwell Road
Sloane Street
Earl's Court Rd
Warwick Road
Old Brompton Road
Redcliffe Gdn's
Finborough Rd
Fulham Road
King's Road
Chelsea Bridge Road
Chelsea Embankment
Grosvenor Road
Belgrave Road
Vauxhall Bridge Road
Victoria St
Albert Embankment
Nine Elms La
Kennington La
Kennington Road
Kennington Park Rd
Walworth Road
Borough Rd
Blackfriars Rd
Waterloo Rd
Tooley St
Tower Bridge Rd
Ladbroke Gve
Upper St
Essex Rd
Liverpool Rd